IRISH LAW TEXTS

ADMINISTRATIVE LAW

by

DAVID GWYNN MORGAN,
LL.M. (LOND.)

of the Middle Temple, Barrister,
Lecturer in Law, University College, Cork

and

GERARD HOGAN, B.C.L., LL.M.
(N.U.I.), LL.M. (PENN.), M.A.,

of King's Inns, Barrister,
Lecturer in Law, Trinity College, Dublin

LONDON
SWEET & MAXWELL
1986

Published in 1986 by
Sweet & Maxwell Limited of
11, New Fetter Lane, London.
Computerset by Burgess & Son (Abingdon) Limited.
Printed in Great Britain by
Hazell Watson & Viney Limited,
Member of the BPCC Group,
Aylesbury, Bucks.

British Library Cataloguing in Publication Data

Hogan, G.
    Administrative law.—(Irish law texts)
    1. Administrative law—Ireland
    I. Title II. Morgan, D. III Series
    344.1702's KDK 1380

    ISBN 0–421–33060–0

©
Sweet & Maxwell
1986

To my parents
(G.H.)

To Deirdre, Declan, Gwendolen, Daniel and
Gareth
(D.G.M.)

Introduction

Irish Law Texts aims to provide reasonably priced works on the main fields of Irish law to meet the needs of the broadest range of interested readers in Ireland and abroad.

Contrary to the situation in existence some years ago, whilst gaps remain, there is now a healthy stream of books being published on legal topics in both the Republic and Northern Ireland. *Irish Law Texts* has played its part and the sucess of the series is shown in the appearance of second editions such as Robert Clark's expanded book on *Contract* as well as in the continued publication of new titles.

Books in the series are concerned primarily with the law of the Republic of Ireland, which is the larger Irish jurisdiction and the one which has lately seen the great changes in legal principles and statute law. However, wherever possible, reference is made to the law of Northern Ireland, particularly the decisions of the courts. *Irish Law Texts* thereby continues to make a contribution to the needs of students of legal subjects and the professions in both parts of the island.

Kevin Boyle
University College Galway

Preface

It is impossible to doubt the large and growing need for Administrative Law in this jurisdiction. The prevalence of Leviathan in all our lives can be demonstrated, for instance, by the large sums of money of which he disposes: at two-thirds of gross national product Irish public expenditure is higher than in practically any country outside the Communist world. Moreover, state authority in its multi-various forms looms especially large in any small country like Ireland, which lacks any significant private institutions (like, say, an equivalent of the City of London) which would act as a counter-weight. Yet pulling in the opposite direction is a strong national preference for the individualistic rights such as private property, political freedom and privacy: a preference which is conveniently implemented via a written Constitution containing an entrenched Bill of Rights, administered by an activist judiciary.

In spite of this rich raw material, lawyers have been slow (for reasons examined briefly in Chapter 1) to admit Administrative Law to the charmed circle of blocs of law which are officially regarded as discrete legal subjects. Even in Britain, the sounds of self-congratulation celebrating the coming of age of Administrative Law have only recently died down. In this jurisdiction although the last 20 years have witnessed many important developments the law in this area remains rather immature. While the majority of recent developments certainly represent an improvement on what went before (*e.g.* the removal of State immunity in *Byrne* v. *Ireland*) some of their implications have not always been fully worked out. Notable examples of judicial inconsistency and confusing statements of principles are not wanting. The Supreme Court, for example, has had several recent opportunities to deal with the fundamental question of jurisdictional review. Yet the authorities are in a state of disarray and firm criteria on the issue of what errors of law are jurisdictional and which are not have yet to emerge. Confusion also reigns in other important areas: can a plaintiff with no merits complain of a breach of natural justice? Do the rules of constitutional justice apply to mere employees, as opposed to office-holders, and if not, is there any convincing statement of principle which can justify this differing treatment? Does the Supreme Court's ruling on *locus standi* in constitutional cases apply to ordinary administrative law cases, and, again, if not, why not? Divergent attitudes have also been adopted to the emerging tort of negligent exercise of a discretionary power. It would appear that following a period of rapid reform, a period of reflection and consolidation is now needed.

Not all of the developments have come through the judiciary. The position of the ombudsman created by the Ombudsman Act 1980 has now been filled, and two interesting reports have been published. There has also been the 1985 White Paper on reform of the civil service, and legislative action to implement at least some of the proposals contained therein is in the offing. Finally, the new Rules of the Superior Courts will in substance introduce the judicial review procedure recommended by the Law Reform Commission in their 8th Working Paper in 1979.

Traditionally among lawyers, in the common law world, the lion's share of whatever attention was given to Administrative Law was lavished upon that segment known as "judicial review of administrative action." More recently a reaction against this tendency has developed, in part on account of the artificial, technical nature of judicial review. In Britain, its relevance has been questioned on the ground that compared to the vast number of administrative decisions taken each day, very few give rise to applications for judicial review. However, such figures as are available seem to show that there is vastly more litigation *per capita* here than in Britain. The growing importance of Administrative Law is evidenced by the fact that in recent years, more than 50 per cent. of the written judgments emanating from the Supreme Court are concerned with public law issues. At a more political level it has also been suggested that over-emphasis upon the constraints on administration, militated against good administration and pushed the balance between the needs of the community and individual rights too far in favour of the individual. This debate which has been characterised as a controversy between "red" and "green-light" theorists (see generally Davis, "English Administrative Law—an American View" (1962) Public Law 139 and Harlow and Rawlings, *Law and Administration* (1984) is also relevant here). For the imbalance between the present individualistic temper of the Irish judiciary ("*fiat justitia, ruat coelum*") and, on the other side, the rather conservative public service (time well what effect the currently-mooted reforms will have) may be in danger of creating a lop-sidedness at some points in our system of Administrative Law (see, *e.g.* aspects of constitutional justice (pp. 235–296), executive privilege (pp. 401–406); principle against policy rules (see pp. 316–319) and the judicial hostility to ouster clauses (pp. 200–202).

It would, however, be an affectation to claim that this brief pioneering work is dedicated either to thesis or antithesis. Rather it attempts to steer a middle course, dealing first with certain of the instruments of government, namely, ministers, departments and the civil service; state-sponsored bodies and local government. Bearing in mind the exigencies of the economics of legal publishing in a small jurisdiction we have dealt very briefly with local government (and, in particular, with planning law) because the needs of the reader in these areas have been met elsewhere. For the same reason, we have kept our account of the constitutional law background to a minimum. After the instruments of government, we describe the instruments of control, namely tribunals and inquiries, the Ombudsman, judicial review (in Chapters 8–11) and the modifications in ordinary litigation when public authorities are involved (in Chapters 12–13).

The emphasis is very much on the law and practice of the Republic, although we have endeavoured to cite the relevant Northern Irish authorities where appropriate. We have attempted to cover developments up to early March 1986, (including the new Rules of Court which come into effect on October 1 1986), whilst, in some instances, referring to later material. As regards the readership: we have tried to cater both for the needs of practitioners and students by providing a detailed analysis of recent developments and fairly comprehensive footnote references for the former, while at the same time taking care to outline fundamental principles and to describing certain concepts whose artificiality requires some explanation.

It is a pleasure to record our thanks to the many people who have given so freely of their time and wisdom to add to, or improve, the contents of this book: Mr. Michael Byrne; Ms. Marcella Doyle; Mr. Liam Drain; Chief Justice Finlay; Mr. Colm Gallagher; Mr. Dermot Gleeson S.C.; Ms. Lee Guckian; Mr. David Hegarty; Mr. Felix McEnroy; Ms. Mary McNamara; Mr. Registrar Mongey; Mr. Michael Murphy; Mr. Maurice O'Connell; Ms. Valerie O'Connell; Mr. Declan Quigley; Ms. Karen Quirk; Dr. Yvonne Scannell and Mr. Gerry Whyte. Part of the chapter on the Ombudsman is taken from an article by one of the authors which appeared in the 17th volume of the Irish Jurist in 1982 and we are grateful to Professor W.N. Osborough for allowing us to reproduce this material. Part of the material contained in Chapters 12 and 13 is taken from the Irish submission to the U.K. National Committee of Comparative Law Colloquium on Governmental Liability, Compensation and the Law of Civil Wrongs which was held in Birmingham in September 1985. The Irish submission was prepared jointly by Mr. Tony Kerr and one of the authors. The authors are grateful to Mr. Kerr and Professor A. W.

Bradley for allowing us to make use of this material. We should like to pay a special tribute to Mr. Brendan Dineen and Ms. Hilary Coonan who read much of the book in proof form and made many helpful suggestions and also to Ms. Deidre Morgan for her constant encouragement.

Gerard Hogan
David Gwynn Morgan
May 1986

Addendum

The following is a brief account of some of the more important developments which came to hand after March 1986.

Joint Oireachtas Committee on Legislation (pp. 26–29)
The Committee's (first) "*Report on 18 Statutory Instruments*" (P1.4006) which was published in June 1986 states at para. 27:
"In the course of examination by the Sub-Committee of the statutory instruments laid or laid in draft before either House in the first two years since the appointment of the Joint Committee explanations were sought from the relevant Government Departments regarding a number of instruments or particular provisions thereof. These explanations were required where it appeared that the instruments took a form or contained particular provisions which may not have been in the contemplation of Members when the Bills for the parent Statutes were being considered by the Houses or where the purport of particular provisions or the implications of the instrument were unclear."
Whilst the guidelines suggested in the second sentence of this extract are not identical with those contained in the former Senate Committee's terms of reference (quoted at p. 26) it is perhaps of greater significance that the grounds quoted are certainly wide enough to cover all the defects enumerated in the Senate Committee's catalogue and, in any case, the Committee is not as concerned as a court would be with textual niceties. Accordingly, the work of the Senate Committee appears to be of continuing relevance and this suggestion is borne out by the nature of the defects in the 18 statutory instruments to which the sub-committee drew the Houses' attention.

The Legal Nature of Powers
(pp. 190–196) In *The State (Keegan* v. *Stardust Victims Compensation Tribunal.* High Court, July 31, 1986 Blayney J. held that if the Tribunal erred in refusing to make an award to the applicant, "the error was within jurisdiction and so certiorari does not lie." Blayney J. quoted with approval the passage from the judgment of Henchy J. in *Abenglen Properties* (see p. 194).

Control of Discretionary Powers
(p. 326)   In *The State (Sheehan)* v. *Government of Ireland.* High
Court, July 29, 1986 Costello J. held that the Government's failure
to bring section 60 of the Civil Liability Act 1961 (see pp.
366–367) into effect was subject to review by the court. He
rejected the argument that the discretion was an "open-ended"
one: "If parliament intended . . . that the law should be reformed,
it did not intend to confer a discretion which would permit that
discretion to be frustrated." In the present case the Government's
delay was inexcusable. He did not think that arguments relating to
the separation of powers were well founded and he thought that
there was "no constitutional impropriety" involved if the courts
"require the Government to obey the requirements of an Act of
the Oireachtas."

The Supreme Court has now accepted that decisions of the
D.P.P. are subject to review where, *per* Finlay C. J., "it can be
demonstrated that he reaches a decision *mala fide* or influenced by
an improper motive or improper policy": *The State (McCormack)* v.
Curran, July 31, 1986. Nevertheless, the Court refused to
interfere with the D.P.P.'s decision not to prosecute in this case as
there was no evidence that he had abdicated his functions or that
he had been improperly motivated. Both *McCormack* and *Sheehan*
push back even further the boundaries of judicial review, and the
former decision tends to cast doubt on earlier authorities such as
Killian, Savage and *Judge* (see pp. 328–330).

Remedies
(p. 356)   In *The State (Sheehan)* v. *Government of Ireland*, Costello J.
held that an applicant who, allegedly, had suffered personal
injuries as a result of the non-feasance of a local authority in
failing to repair a footpath had sufficient standing to seek an order
of mandamus compelling the Government to make an order
bringing section 60 of the Civil Liability Act 1961 (see p. 367) into
operation, even though it was conceded that such an order could
not have retrospective effect. Costello J. rejected the argument
that the applicant's interest was merely "academic" as he was "an
aggrieved citizen who may have suffered the loss of a substantial
amount of money due to the Government's failure to carry out its
duty." Although the judge recognised that the *locus standi* test in
ordinary administrative law cases (such as the instant one), "should
be formulated somewhat differently" from that in constitutional
cases he nevertheless held that the test in *Cahill* v. *Sutton* (see p.
357) was applicable and that the applicant had a "sufficient
interest" in the proceedings to maintain the action. Costello J. also
referred with approval to the decision in the *Self-Employed* case
(see p. 360) and observed that our courts "should now look with

caution on earlier authorities which have now been discarded by the House of Lords" and which "may have formed the basis of earlier decisions in this country." Costello J.'s attitude to *locus standi* is a decidedly liberal one. In this respect, *Sheehan* is in line with the *actio popularis* approach espoused by him in *Martin* v. *Dublin Corporation* rather than the more traditional and orthodox approach of Keane J. in *Irish Permanent Building Society* v. *Caldwell (No. 1)* (see p. 357).

State Liability

(p. 367) In *The State (Sheehan)* v.*Government of Ireland* Costello J. granted an order of mandamus requiring the Government to make an order by January 29, 1987 bringing section 60 of the Civil Liability Act 1961 into operation. Costello J. also suggested that the applicant might have an action for damages against the Government in respect of its failure to carry out its statutory duty.

(Pp. 367–368) In *Kelly* v. *Dublin C.C.*, High Court, February 21, 1986 the defendants had made use of a vacant site beside the plaintiff's cottage for the purpose of storing vehicles and materials used in an extensive road construction project. The plaintiffs sued in nuisance, and the defendants argued that they enjoyed statutory protection under the Local Government Act 1925. O'Hanlon J. held that the defendants had caused an actionable nuisance which was not authorised by the terms of the 1925 Act. While the 1925 Act afforded protection for the defendant's road construction work, this did not extend to the provision and use of a depot for vehicles and materials. Even if he was wrong on this point, O'Hanlon J. ruled that, in any event, the nuisance not an inevitable result of the exercise of statutory powers. There was no evidence to show that the Council had no alternative, or no reasonable alternative, but to use this particular site for these purposes.

(Pp. 382–384) The State's liability for damages for infringment of constitutional rights has been discussed in three recent cases: *Moyne* v. *Londonderry Harbour Commissioners*, High Court, June 6, 1986; *McHugh* v. *Garda Commissioner*, Supreme Court, July 8, 1986 and *Pine Valley Developments Ltd.* v. *Ireland*, Supreme Court, July 29, 1986. In *Moyne*, Costello J. held that the defendants had acted *ultra vires* and in breach of statutory duty in restricting the use of a pier. The judge accepted that as the Londonderry Port and Harbour Acts 1854–1882 imposed the duty to maintain the pier for the benefit of a definable class of persons (namely, those living near the pier) and not for the benefit of the general public, the plaintiffs (as members of that definable class) had standing to sue for breach of statutory duty. Nevertheless, Costello J. concluded that this *ultra vires* action did not infringe the plaintiff's constitutional rights, as the "infliction of a pecuniary loss does not in itself establish that an infringement of the constitutionally protected right to earn a livelihood has taken place." However, in *McHugh* the Supreme Court appeared to take a different attitude to this question. In that case the plaintiff had suffered financial loss arising from the costs of defending himself before a Garda disciplinary inquiry which was subsequently adjudged to be *ultra vires*. Despite the fact that the relevant regulations did not provide for the payment of legal costs, Finlay C. J. held that the State owed the plaintiff an obligation arising from Article 40.3 to protect his property rights and thereby "not to initiate an inquiry which might result in being a nullity and put him to entirely unnecessary expense." The plaintiff was thus entitled to recover of such an invalid inquiry. But if *McHugh* implied that *ultra vires* administrative action which caused pecuniary loss was a *per se* actionable breach of constitutional rights, the judgments in *Pine Valley* (see p. 381) struck a different note. Finlay C. J. (with whom Griffin, Hederman and Lardner JJ. agreed) held that the Minister had not acted negligently as he had acted on the basis of competent legal advice, so therefore the claims based on negligence and misfeasance of public office failed. As regards the alternative line of action—for breach of constitutional rights—in Finlay C. J.'s view a *persona designata* (such as the Minister was when hearing planning appeals, see p. 229) enjoyed protection when he took an administrative decision in good faith and this was a sufficient defence to any action for breach of constitutional rights.

Yet both *Pine Valley* and *McHugh* involved quasi-judicial decisions and given that the characterisation of the Minister as a *persona designata* is such an artificial one, it is difficult to see why a different result should have been reached in one case rather than the other unless it can be said that *McHugh* involved negligence, whereas *Pine Valley* did not. In *Pine Valley*, Henchy J. took a different approach: he emphasised that it had not been shown that the State had failed in its constitutional duty under Article 40.3.2 to vindicate, in the case of injustice done, the plaintiff's property rights. The State by its laws had provided the plaintiff with other adequate remedies, *e.g.* an action against the vendor for brach of the implied covenants as to title under section 7 of the Conveyancing Act 1882 or for unjust enrichment. It is questionable whether the rather restricted scope of these implied covenants embrace planning permission: see *David* v. *Sabin* [1893] 1 Ch. 523.

The State in Litigation
(Pp. 387–389) In *Webb* v. *Ireland*, High Court, July 29, 1986, Blayney J. said that the reasoning on which *Byrne* v. *Ireland* was

based "was that none of the prerogatives had survived under the 1922 Constitution." He therefore concluded that the prerogative of treasure trove had not survived the enactment of the Constitution.

Table of Contents

Table of Cases

Table of Cases

Table of Statutes

xli

Table of Statutory Instruments

Table of Constitutional Provisions

Constitution of the Irish Free State 1922

Constitution of Ireland 1937

Rules Of The Superior Courts 1986 (S.I. No. 15 of 1986)

Part 1

Introduction

1 Introduction

1. Flavour of administrative law

Administrative law is conventionally defined as the law regulating the organisation, composition, functions and procedures of public authorities[1]; their impact on the citizen; and the restraints to which they are subject. By public authorities, we mean (to list the examples principally covered in this book): the Government in the sense, which is the one employed in Article 28, of the Constitution of the fifteen ministers who are the central directorate of the executive; a Minister in his Department[2]; state sponsored bodies[3] like CIE or RTE; local authorities[4]. There are other public bodies, such as the Universities; the Gardai Siochana; and the Defence Forces, which there is no space to cover specifically here, apart from noticing that the general ideas and rules of administrative law apply to them. It ought also to be noted that there are certain private bodies which discharge public (or "quasi-public") functions, for example, the trade unions or professional associations, like the Incorporated Law Society or the Medical Council. Such bodies have been characterised as "domestic governments" and it has accordingly seemed appropriate, to the courts and legislature, to extend to them, certain of the characteristic principles of administrative law, for example, the rules of constitutional justice.

Administrative law is clearly a public law subject, that is to say, that its focus are relations between the individual and the state in contrast with private law, for example, the law of contract or tort,

---

[1] Of course large public companies may be as much in need of control by the law as public authorities. Companies are, in fact, controlled by company law and labour law and an interesting book remains to be written comparing these controls with those imposed by administrative law.

[2] See pp. 35–42.

[3] See Chapter 4.

[4] See Chapter 5.

which regulates relations between private individuals. Classification of administrative law as public law raises the difficult question of the boundary with constitutional law. One point of distinction stems from the fact that administrative law focuses on the executive and the other two major organs (legislature and judicature) are important only so far as they impact on the executive—by contrast, constitutional law covers all three organs equally. The second point of distinction is that, generally speaking, matters of principle are fixed by constitutional law; whereas administrative law looks more to questions of detail and to matters of function more than structure. Thirdly, constitutional law includes the law of fundamental rights—those legal rights which are regarded as so essential to decent, dignified life as a human being that they are established by the Constitution and judicial exegesis and prevail over all other types of law. And very often, it is in cases involving administrative actions of the executive that the fundamental rights have to be invoked. Thus there is a substantial, if adventitious, connection between administrative and constitutional law and at various points[5] we shall notice the fundamental rights, as part of the controls upon administrative actions.

In the mid-nineteenth century, following the Industrial Revolution, and with the rise of political democracy, there was a vast increase in the activity of the executive and its intervention in the affairs of the citizen. This has taken various forms, including the regulation of land use and commercial transactions; the provision of social welfare benefits and free or subsidised health and education services; the management of the economy by such measures as the control of prices and incomes, tax actions, subsidies, etc.[6] Since administrative law is the law regulating the administration of the executive arm of government one might have expected such trends to be reflected in the development of administrative law as a coherent subject.

Yet the reality is that in the common law world, administrative law has only recently come to be acknowledged and studied, as a

---

[5] See pp. 240–242, 313–316 and 324–325.

[6] See Holdsworth, *History of English Law*, vol. xiv pp. 90–204.

[7] The first lectures on Administrative Law in Irish Universities were given as indicated: T.C.D. (1946, F. C. King); U.C.D. (early 1950s, P. McGilligan); U.C.G. (1975, J. M. G. Sweeney); U.C.C. (1978, D. Gwynn Morgan); Q.U.B. (1953). For recent works on Irish Administrative Law, see—Stout, *Administrative Law in Ireland* (Dublin, 1985); Casey, "Ireland" (written in English) in *Geschicte der Vewaltungsrecht wissenschaft in Europa* (ed. Hegen) (Frankfurt am Main, 1982), Koekkoek, "Ierland" (written in Dutch) in *Het bestuursrecht van de landen der Europese Gemeenschappen* (ed. Prakke and Kortmann) (Kluwer, 1986).

unified discipline.[7] There are at least three reasons for this, the first of which is historical and is common to Ireland and Britain. The Parliamentary victory in the English Civil War in the seventeenth century led to the eradication of the central, executive machinery built around the Privy Council. The organs which evolved to fill these gaps did so in a cramped, *ad hoc* way. It is to this historical factor that is owed such features of our system of administrative law as the absence of the specialised administrative courts which exist on the Continent; the distorting fiction that public law is simply a special case of private law; the crab-like growth of our system of judicial review, proceeding from the baseline of the *ultra vires* doctrine[8]; the formal significance of the legislature in the control of governmental administration[9]; and the late development of professionalism in the public service. At the local level too, the institutions of government were not tailor-made for their tasks. Before the nineteenth century, the principal institution was the amphibious justices of the peace, who also acted as local courts of law. When, following the Civil War, the justices were released from the control of the Privy Council, they could only be called to account by the Court of King's Bench. It seemed natural simply to apply to the justices in their administrative role the same remedies as those which controlled them in their judicial duties. By another apparently natural development, the courts extended these remedies and, with them, the substantive law for the control of the justices' administrative action to cover all the other public authorities as these grew up.

The second factor was the enormous, ideological influence of the turn-of-the-century scholar, Dicey. His principal tenet was that ministers and other state organs ought to be subject to the same law, administered by the same courts, as a private individual and that this ideal was achieved in the British system of law. Contrasted with this was the French institution of the *droit administratif* in which specialised tribunals applied special law to the acts of the executive and, it was implied, gave the executive an easy ride. From such an outlook, it was a short step to the conclusion that a system of administrative law which acknowledged the unique position of the state and systematically granted it special powers and subjected it to special controls was anathema. It followed that to embark on a study of such elements of administrative law as there happened to be in British Law was to court disaster.

The third reason why administrative law was so slow to develop as a coherent, unified whole is that the territory which it covers is so voluminous and diverse. The subject really consists of general

[8] See pp. 183–188.
[9] See pp. 36–39.

principles, with the substantive details being contained in such subjects as land-use planning law; housing and public health law; social welfare law; licensing law; and economic law. Throughout this work, we shall be examining material which could be re-located in one or other of these categories. This is a feature which distinguishes administrative law from discrete subject-blocs, like tort or criminal law, where a single book can cover more or less the whole area and where the overlap with neighbouring subjects is less significant. The result of this feature is that the most fruitful approach in explaining administrative law is to describe the leading principles and to observe their operation in certain specimen areas.

Administrative law may be regarded as made up of two components: the instruments of government and the instruments of control. The instruments of government—ministers and departments, state-sponsored bodies, local authorities, etc.—are, or should be, designed to enable administrators, working under the control, direct or indirect, of elected politicians, to take decisions and provides services, which are in the best interests of the community. But the powers of these agencies are delineated by the law—albeit it is a law which allows them a great deal of latitude. The law is administered by the instruments of control: the tribunals[10]; the Ombudsman[11]; and, most important of all, the courts, enforcing a bloc of law known as judicial review.

2. Two distinctions

The major difficulty inherent in administrative law is the sheer diversity of the decisions, powers, function etc. (there words mean more or less the same) which it comprehends. Here are some examples of typical governmental decisions: the expulsion of an undesirable alien; a local authority's decision to build a concert hall or theatre under the Local Government Act 1960; the award of a public works contract to contractor A rather than contractor B; the making of a statutory instrument regulating the procedure of An Bord Pleanala; the making of a development plan by a local planning authority; a decision whether to grant planning permission in respect of a particular building; assessment of capital gains following the sale of a piece of land; award of a social welfare benefit; allocation of a corporation house. In ordering these disparate functions and in understanding the controls which administrative law imposes on them, we shall be assisted by two sets of distinctions: first, policy and administration; and secondly, legislative and individual decisions.

[10] See Chapter 6.
[11] See Chapter 7.

Policy-Administration

Put briefly, administration[12] assumes that there is already in existence a principle and that all the administrator has to do is to establish the facts and circumstances and then to apply the principle. It is of the essence of good administration that the principle must be fairly clear and precise so that, in any given situation, the result should be the same, whether it is administrator A or administrator B who has taken the decision. For, in its purest form, administration requires only a knowledge of the pre-existing principle and an appreciation of the facts to which it is being applied: it is an intellectual process involving little discretion. By contrast, policy-making is largely discretionary: the policy-maker must decide, as between two alternatives, the one which he considers best in the interest of the community. He must take into account all the relevant factors and which factors are relevant is, to a considerable extent, left to him. In doing this, the policy-maker will have to draw on his own values and, in the light of this, it is no coincidence that the words policy and politics come from the same Greek root (*polis*). Each word relates to choice in the affairs of the community and it is natural, in a democracy, that major policy questions should be taken by politicians (often on the advice of senior public servants) whether ministers or, at local government level, elected councillors. As Mèndes-France observed: "To govern is to choose." According to the democratic ideal, one elected politician is chosen in preference to another politician just because it is his policy which finds favour with the electorate.

Applying the policy-administration dichotomy to the list of governmental functions given earlier, we can say that; expulsion of an alien; building of a concert hall; making of procedural regulations; making of a development plan; even the awards at a large public works contract—are policy matters, whereas the grant of planning permission; assessment of capital gains; award of a welfare benefit; and allocation of a corporation house are acts of administration. Indeed the planning functions afford particularly neat illustrations in that the development plan is the pre-existing standard on which the administrator bases his decision whether to grant permission for a specific development. It must of course be admitted that such classification over-estimates the neatness of reality: policy and administration really represent the opposite poles of a scale and, most decisions fall at

---

[12] Administration is one of these awkward words which takes its meaning from the word to which it is opposed—*i.e.* in this Part, to "policy." Unfortunately for clarity, it can also be used in other senses as when it is opposed to legislation or when an administrative decision is contrasted with a quasi-judicial decision (on which, see pp. 285–286).

some intermediate point on the scale. It would, for instance, be plainly wrong to suppose that a manager or planning officer deciding whether to grant planning permission for a small bungalow in an area zoned as "primarily agricultural" would not have to use some of his own discretion.

Clearly the question of whether a decision is one of policy or of administration will depend in part on the wording of the statute or other instrument creating the decision. For instance, the Aliens Act 1935, s.5(1) provides that the Minister for Justice may "if and whenever he thinks proper" expel an alien.[13] Plainly, this is a policy decision. However, the legislature might have provided that the alien could only be expelled on (say) "health grounds" or in the case of "criminal activity." Such a test would be closer to the administrative end of the scale, but would still leave considerable discretion to the Minister. The decision could have been rendered entirely administrative by providing that an alien could only be expelled if (say) he were suffering from one of a list of specified diseases or if he had been convicted of any indictable offence.

Legislative—Individual decisions

The second major distinction in the field of governmental decision-making lies between legislative and individual decisions. A legislative decision affects a potentially unlimited category of persons or situations which share the specified common characteristics; whereas an individual decision is directed to, and affects only, some particular individual(s). The reader with a background in constitutional law will immediately see that an Act of the Oireachtas is an example of a legislative decision. This is true but the Act is not the only example for the meaning of "legislation" invoked here is wider than the artificially-restricted meaning which has been imposed upon "law-making" in the context of Article 15.2.1[14] which provides that only the Oireachtas may "mak[e] laws for the State." The definition used here is intended to comprehend any rule: for instance, a statutory instrument or by-law.

Before a legislative decision has any effect in a particular instance, an individual decision[15] is necessary, to apply the rule to the particular situation to which it is relevant. One way in which this may be done is by the application of a law by a court. But it often happens that law, especially public law, is applied not by a court but by an administrative agency and, of the list of examples

---

[13] For control of a discretionary (policy) decision, see Chapter 10.

[14] See further pp. 13–15.

[15] As used here, "individual decision" comprehends an "administration of justice" (Art. 34.1. See pp. 145–147 as well as a quasi-judicial or administrative decision (see pp. 285–286).

given earlier, the grant of planning permission (local planning authority: county or city manager); the assessment of capital gains (the Revenue Commissioners); the award of a social welfare benefit (deciding officer in the Department of Social Welfare) are all instances of individual decisions taken by the administrative agency indicated in brackets.

We can summarise the relationship between the two sets of distinctions by saying that a legislative decision is inevitably a policy decision. On the other hand, an individual decision will usually be nearer the administrative end of the spectrum in that it is the product of the application of some (more or less) precise standard—and three examples of this were listed in the previous paragraph. However in some cases an individual decision will be the direct result of the decision maker's discretion and such individual policy decisions include, for example, the expulsion of an alien or the building of a concert hall.

Application of the two classifications

The significance of these two types of classification lies in the part they have played in influencing the design of the organs and procedures of government administration and of the controls which are exercised over this administration. Much of the remainder of the book consists of illustrations of this observation. Thus, here we can only advert to a few examples of it and direct the reader to the place where they are amplified. For example, consider the design of governmental structures at the local government level: broadly speaking, the reserved functions, which are the preserve of the elected councillors, deal with policy matters; whereas the executive functions, which are vested in the top official, the county or city manager, consist of administrative acts[16]. For historical reasons, the picture is not so clear when one examines the central government ministers and departments though here too there is an approximate observation of the distinction[17].

Necessarily where there are pre-existing rules, the control exercised over the decision will be stricter. In the first place, the legislature is more likely to have established a tribunal to take the decision[18] and/or to have created an appeal to a court in respect of the decision. Secondly, even where this has not been done, a court may intervene on the ground of error of law[19]. Policy decisions may, it is true, be reviewed by a court—but it is only in a very clear

---

[16] See pp. 104–107.
[17] See pp. 35–42 but see also 228–233.
[18] See pp. 135–137.
[19] See pp. 196–200.

case, that they will be struck down and at an earlier stage in the development of administrative law, courts have even been heard to say that they must leave policy questions to be dealt with through the agency of ministerial responsibility to the legislature.[20] These results flow from the idea that elected persons or bodies take policy decisions, whilst courts customarily take decisions on the basis of pre-existing principles.

Reinforcing the trend noted in the previous paragraph is the fact that administrative decisions are always individual decisions. It is because individual decisions have a direct effect of individual rights that they are more stringently controlled than legislative decisions: for example certain types of decision must be taken by a Minister personally rather than through his civil servants.[21] Again, where the significant procedural safeguard of constitutional justice is concerned, we find that these rules are less likely to apply to policy than to administrative decisions and usually do not apply to legislation.[22] The law of remedies also formerly observed the two distinctions we have described.[23] Finally, the Ombudsman's jurisdiction is confined to "action[s] taken in the performance of administrative functions"[24] thereby excluding legislative, though not other types of policy, decision.

[20] See p. 39.
[21] See pp. 228–233.
[22] See pp. 286–288.
[23] See p. 24.
[24] Ombudsman Act 1980, s.4(2). See further pp. 166–172.

2 Sources of Administrative Law

1. Fundamental constitutional principles: rule of law

The twin concepts of the rule of law[1] and the separation of powers[2] are among the most fundamental principles of Irish administrative law. Both the structure of our system of government and the basis of judicial review of administrative action are founded on these principles. While a thorough analysis of these constitutional principles more properly belongs to a textbook on constitutional law, some of the major aspects of these principles may be sketched out here.

At the heart of the rule of law there are four inter-related notions.[3] The first is the principle of legality. Every executive or administrative act which affects legal rights, interests or legitimate expectations must have legal justification. Where no such authority exists, the aggrieved party may have recourse to the courts where this decision will be invalidated. This is no more than an application of the principle of *ultra vires*. And it is not enough for the administrative authority concerned to show that it possessed ostensible legal authority, for the courts will review the exercise of discretionary power according to settled principles of reasonableness, proper motives and compliance with natural justice.[4] The second principle is that everyone, including the Government and its servants, is subject to the law. This principle received graphic affirmation in cases such as *Macauley* v. *Minister for Posts and*

---

[1] Gwynn Morgan, *Constitutional Law of Ireland* (Dublin, 1985) at pp. 42–45; Wade, *Administrative Law* (Oxford, 1982) at pp. 22–24.

[2] Gwynn Morgan, *op. cit.*, at pp. 36–41; Kelly, *The Irish Constitution* (Dublin, 1984) at pp. 28–32.

[3] There are other aspects of the rule of law which pertain to the administration of criminal justice, and thus are not our present concern. For example, the prohibition of retroactive penal legislation contained in Article 15.5 of the Constitution may be said to a feature of the rule of law.

[4] See pp. 297–330.

Telegraphs,[5] (where a statutory provision requiring the prior
permission, or *fiat*, of the Attorney-General before an action could
be taken against a Minister of State was found to be unconstitutional) and *Byrne* v. *Ireland*[6] (holding that the former Crown
immunity from suit had not survived the enactment of the
Constitution). The third meaning of the rule of law is that the
legality of executive or administrative acts is to be determined by
judges who are independent of the Government. The principle of
judicial independence is enshrined in Article 34.1 of the Constitution,[7] and the courts have always jealously safeguarded their
powers to review administrative action. Thus, legislative attempts
to curb—or even altogether to prevent—review of administrative
action have been viewed with disfavour by the judiciary.[8]

The final aspect of the rule of law is that the law must be public
and precise: the law should be ascertainable and its operation
predictable. This principle underlies a number of important rules
of statutory construction such as the presumption against retro-
spectivity[9] and the principle that taxing statutes must be strictly
construed.[10] This allows the citizen to arrange his behaviour to
conform with the law.

---

[5] [1966] I.R. 345.
[6] [1972] I.R. 241. See pp. 391–393.
[7] Kelly, *op. cit.*, pp. 232–255. See generally, *Buckley* v. *Att.-Gen.* [1950]
I.R. 67; *Re Haughey* [1971] I.R. 217 and *The State (McEldowney)* v.
Kelleher [1983] I.R. 289.
[8] In *The State (Pine Valley Developments Ltd.)* v. *Dublin C.C.* [1984] I.R.
407, 426 Henchy J. commented that the courts "should be reluctant to
surrender their inherent right to enter on a question of the validity of
what are prima facie justiciable matters," and see further at
pp. 200–202 on the issue of ouster and preclusive clauses. See also the
comments of O'Higgins C.J. in *Condon* v. *Minister for Labour* [1981] I.R.
62 at p. 69: "A strong, healthy and concerned public opinion may, in
the words of Edmund Burke, 'snuff the approach of tyranny in every
tainted breeze,' but effective resistance to unwarranted encroachment
on constitutional guarantees and rights, depends, in the ultimate
analysis on the courts. If access to the courts is denied or prevented or
obstructed, then such encroachment, being unchallenged, may become
habitual, and, therefore, unacceptable."
[9] *Hamilton* v. *Hamilton* [1982] I.R. 466; *Doyle* v. *An Taoiseach*, Supreme
Court, March 28, 1985.
[10] For a general exposition of this principle, see *e.g. Inspector of Taxes* v.
Kiernan [1981] I.R. 117. See also *Att.-Gen.* v. *Wilts United Dairies Ltd.*
(1921) 39 T.L.R. 781 (administrative body had no power to levy charges
for public purposes, save where this is expressly authorised by statute).

2. Fundamental constitutional principles: separation of powers

Article 6 provides for a tripartite division of the powers of government: legislative, executive and judicial. Article 6 does not in terms prescribe a separation of powers, but the effect of other constitutional provisions—most notably, Articles 15, 28 and 34—is to "entrench the different arms of government in varying degrees and prescribe their sovereignty in their own areas, without, however, hermetically insulating the different powers from one another in all respects."[11] The constitutional distribution of powers, is, however, an imperfect one, and this is recognised by the very terms of the Constitution itself. For example, Article 13.6 allows the Executive to commute or remit penalties imposed by the judiciary. The principle is also much modified in practice, for such is the strength of the party whip system, that the Oireachtas is almost completely under the control of the Government of the day. It is only the judiciary who enjoy a secure position *vis-à-vis* the other branches of government.[12] Four aspects of the separation of powers are of particular importance for administrative law: executive privilege; ouster and preclusive clauses; Article 15.2.1 (which vests the Oireachtas with sole and exclusive legislative power) and Article 37 (which allows the Oireachtas to confer judicial functions of a limited nature on persons or bodies who are not judges appointed under the Constitution).

As executive privilege; ouster clauses and Article 37 are examined elsewhere,[13] it remains to consider the provisions of Article 15.2. While Article 15.2 vests the Oireachtas with exclusive power of legislation, it is nevertheless permissible for the Oireachtas to delegate power to make regulations which will give effect to the principles and policies contained in the parent Act. The question therefore is whether the parent Act has actually sanctioned the delegation of a power which goes beyond the mere giving effect to its principles and policies. In *Pigs Marketing Board v. Donnelly*[14] Hanna J. rejected the argument that the price-fixing powers given to the defendant Board by the Pigs and Bacon Acts 1935–1937 amounted to an unconstitutional delegation of legislative power. The Board in exercising these powers was not making

[11] Kelly, *op. cit.*, at p. 29.
[12] Kelly, *op. cit.*, at pp. 232–255.
[13] At pp. 401–406 (executive privilege); at pp. 200–202 (ouster clauses) and pp. 145–147 (Art. 37).
[14] [1939] I.R. 413. See also *National Union of Railwaymen* v. *Sullivan* [1947] I.R. 77; *de Burca* v. *Att.-Gen.* [1976] I.R. 38; *The State (Devine)* v. *Larkin* [1977] I.R. 24; *The State (Gilliland)* v. *Governor of Mountjoy Prison (No. 2)* [1986] I.L.R.M. 381 and Kelly, *op. cit.*, at pp. 74–79.

new law, but were merely giving effect to the statutory provisions
as to how they should determine that price.

The Supreme Court has given authoritative rulings as to the
effect of Article 15.2 in *City View Press Ltd.* v. *An Comhairle
Oiliuna*[15] and *Cooke* v. *Walsh.*[16] In the former case the provisions of
the Industrial Training Act 1967 had been challenged as granting
an unconstitutional delegation of legislative power. The defendants were empowered to fix the amount of a levy to be collected
from industrial enterprises which was then used to train apprentices in that industry. O'Higgins C.J. observed that in this instance
the Oireachtas had reserved unto itself the right to annul
regulations made under the Act, and that this power of annulment
was a common feature of many items of legislation. While this was
a safeguard, the ultimate responsibility of ensuring that there had
not been an unconstitutional delegation of power rested with the
courts. The relevant test was whether the impugned legislation was
more than:

> "[A] mere giving effect to principles and policies contained in
> the statute itself. If it be, then it is not authorised, for such
> would constitute a purported exercise of legislative power by
> an authority which is not entitled to do so under the
> Constitution. On the other hand, if it be within the permitted
> limits—if the law is laid down in the statute and details only
> filled in or completed by the designated Minister or subordi-
> nate body—there is no unauthorised delegation of legislative
> power."[17]

Judged by these standards there had not been any unconstitutional delegation of legislative power, as the 1967 Act contained
clear statements of policies and objectives, and the only task left to
the defendants was to calculate the size of the levy for any
particular industry by reference to these principles.

In *Cooke* v. *Walsh* the validity of certain ministerial regulations
purportedly made pursuant to the Health Act 1970 was at issue.
This Act conferred full eligibility to receive free health services on
certain classes of individuals (of which the infant plaintiff was one).
But another section of the Act, s.72, enabled the Minister for
Health to make regulations providing for any service "being made
available only to a particular class of the person" who had
eligibility or that service. Ministerial regulations made pursuant to
this latter provision purported to exclude persons otherwise

[15] [1980] I.R. 381.
[16] [1984] I.L.R.M. 208. See also *The State (Gallagher, Shatter and Co.)* v. *de
Valera* [1986] I.L.R.M. 3.
[17] [1980] I.R. at p. 399.

entitled under the Act to free medical services from such entitlements where their injuries were sustained as a result of a road accident and where they were entitled to receive compensation in respect of their injuries. Read at its full width, section 72 would probably have permitted the Minister to alter the eligibility provisions contained in the Act itself. But such a construction would render section 72 invalid having regard to Article 15.2, as the Minister would have been authorised to change or alter the Act by executive decree. However, section 72 was given a more limited construction in the light of the presumption of constitutionality. While the validity of section 72 was thus saved, it rendered the impugned regulations *ultra vires*, as the section as interpreted did not permit the Minister to alter the eligibility requirements when making regulations thereunder.[18] *City View Press* and *Cooke* v. *Walsh* both severely limit and mark off the boundaries of delegated legislation, and it is probable that the significance of these decisions has yet to be realised. Two important statutes are particularly vulnerable to challenge in the wake of these developments. Section 1 of the Imposition of Duties Act 1957[19] gives the Government power by order to impose, vary or terminate any excise, customs or stamp duty. The only check on this raising of taxation by executive decree is contained in section 2(1) of the Act: any such order will expire at the end of the year following that in which it is made unless confirmed by the Act of the Oireachtas.[20] Such is the comprehensiveness of the statutory language that it is almost impossible to contend that orders made thereunder are *ultra vires*.[21] It is difficult herefore to see how section 1 can withstand challenge in view of the test articulated in *City View Press*. The Government has been given power to amend earlier legislation and to raise taxes by executive decree, thus going far beyond the mere giving effect to "principles and

---

[18] O'Higgins C.J. thought that s.72 might enable the Minister to regulate the provision of certain services provided by the Health Boards. See now Health (Amendment) Act 1986, which reverses the decision of the Supreme Court as far as hospital charges are concerned.

[19] As amended by s.22 of the Finance Act 1962. See generally Hogan, "Note on the Imposition of Duties Act 1957" (1985) 7 D.U.L.J. (n.s.) 180.

[20] In *Doyle* v. *An Taoiseach* (1982–83) J.I.S.E.L. 83 (H.C.) Barrington J. suggested that the confirmation procedure provided for by s.2(1) of the Act might not apply to orders which were void *ab initio*.

[21] But the Act does not give the power to the Government to create new duties; it simply allows the Government to vary or amend *existing* duties: see Barrington J. in *Doyle's* case. Such an order may also be void for unreasonableness: *Doyle* v. *An Taoiseach*, Supreme Court, March 28, 1985.

policies" contained in the legislation which has been amended.[22] It is true that such orders must be confirmed by legislation by the end of the following year, but even where the order lapses for want of statutory confirmation, this is without prejudice to all acts done under cover of the order. In any event, given the clear infringement of Article 15.2, this feature of the Act cannot save it from constitutional challenge.

Similar difficulties exist in the case of the European Communities Act 1972 and the European Communities (Amendment) Act 1973. The 1972 Act provides, *inter alia*, that future acts adopted by the institutions of the Communities shall be binding on the State and "shall be part of the domestic law thereof under the conditions laid down in those treaties". In the case of directives issued by Community institutions, Article 189(3) of the EEC Treaty provides that: "A directive shall be binding, as to the result but shall leave to the national authorities the choice of the form and methods."

In nearly all cases implementing measures will be necessary on the part of the Member State in order to give the directive full force and effect.[23] One of the principal methods of implementing directives in this jurisdiction is contained in section 3 of European Communities Act 1972, which enables a Minister of State to implement such directives by statutory order. Section 3(2) states:

> "Regulations made under this section may contain such incidental, supplementary and consequential provisions as appear to the Minister . . . to be necessary for the purposes of the regulations (including provisions repealing, amending or applying with or without modification, other law, exclusive of this Act)."[24]

Section 4 of the 1972 Act had originally provided that such Ministerial regulations required legislative confirmation, but it was later felt that this method was too cumbersome.[25] Section 4 was amended by section 1 of the European Communities (Amend-

---

[22] Thus, the Imposition of Duties (No. 278) (Stamp Duty on Letter of Renunciation) Order 1985 (S.I. 1985 No. 152) purports to amend s.23 of the Finance Act 1964. This change has now been confirmed by the Finance Act 1986, s.97.

[23] Community directives, unlike Community regulations, are not directly applicable, *i.e.* they do not immediately become part of the domestic law of each Member State.

[24] However, such regulations may not create an indictable offence: s.3(4).

[25] In fact one such confirming measure was enacted: see European Communities (Confirmation of Regulations) Act 1973.

ment) Act 1973, and it now provides that ministerial regulations made under the Act shall have statutory effect.[26]

This method of implementing directives would appear to be in conflict with Article 15.2, as section 4 permits a Minister of State to make regulations which do more than give effect to the principles and policies contained in the 1972 Act. A regulation of this nature could effect a far-reaching change in the existing law. It is true that Article 29.4.3 gives constitutional cover to "measures adopted by the State necessitated by the obligations of membership of the Communities" and that the State is obliged by Article 189 of the Treaty to implement such directives. But as we have seen, Article 189 deliberately leaves the *method of implementation* of directives to the Member States, and does not require or prescribe that these directives be implemented by ministerial order. Article 29.4.3 cannot therefore be called in aid to justify what would otherwise be a breach of Article 15.2.[27] Of course, no such difficulties arise where the directive is implemented by an Act of the Oireachtas.

[26] The amended s.4 provides for an elaborate system of parliamentary scrutiny by the Joint Committee on the Secondary Legislation of the European Communities (now vested in the Joint Oireachtas Committee on Legislation) and also includes procedures whereby regulations made under the Act may be annulled by either House of the Oireachtas. For an account of the work of the Joint Committee, see Robinson, "Irish Parliamentary Scrutiny of European Community Legislation" (1979) 16 C.M.L.R. 9.

[27] However, the Joint Committee on Secondary Legislation of the European Communities have consistently taken a contrary view on this question. In their Twenty-Second Report (Prl. 5141) (1975), the Committee commenting (at pp. 17–18) on European Communities (Road Traffic) (Compulsory Insurance) Regulations 1975 (S.I. 1975 No. 178) which amended the Road Traffic Act 1961, observe as follows:
"The Joint Committee accepts that Ministerial Regulations made under section 3 of the European Communities Act 1972 may lawfully amend Acts of the Oireachtas or other statutes in force if such is required by the Community secondary legislation which the Regulations are to implement. However, the fact that the power exists ought not, in the Joint Committee's opinion, to mean that it is appropriate to use it in every case. Regard should be had to the relative importance of the statute to be amended and to the range of its application to determine whether the amendment should be effected by a statutory instrument or amending statute. In the case of a statute such as the Road Traffic Act 1961 which is of such importance in the everyday life of citizens the Joint Committee considers that any proposals for its amendment should be initiated by a Bill introduced in the Dail or Seanad. It recommends that when opportunity offers Regulation S.I. No. 178 of 1975 should be repealed and its terms incorporated in an amending statute."

One other feature of Article 15.2 which may be mentioned here is that sub-Article in conjunction with other constitutional principles[28] prevents the statutory exclusion of judicial review of delegated legislation. In *Institute of Patent Agents* v. *Lockwood*[29] the House of Lords held that rules which "were to have the same effect as if they were contained in [the parent statute]" ("Henry VIII clauses") could not be examined by the courts. The Irish courts—even prior to independence—have never been willing to assent to this proposition, and *Lockwood* has been distinguished —rather unconvincingly—in a series of subsequent Irish cases.[30] However *Lockwood* is now simply of historical interest only as this decision and the principle which it embodies cannot have survived the enactment of the Constitution. Any statutory provision which purported to confer such an immunity on delegated legislation would be the equivalent of a delegation of legislative power, and this would be contrary to Article 15.2 for the reasons given in *City View Press*.

3. Delegated legislation

Delegated legislation is legislation which has been made by some person or body other than the Oireachtas to whom the Oireachtas had delegated its legislative functions for strictly limited purposes. While delegated legislation is now an established feature of our law, it could scarcely be otherwise given the growth of the modern state. There are several practical reasons which justify the existence of delegated legislation. Parliamentary time is scarce and the Oireachtas could not reasonably be expected to legislate for every administrative detail. It is, therefore, content to state the general principles in legislation and to allow the details to be regulated by ministerial order. There is also a need for flexibility and the law must be capable of rapid adjustment to meet changing circumstances.[31] In some cases regulations giving effect to the

---

[28] Art. 34.3.1 (High Court's original jurisdiction) and Art. 40.3 (guarantee of fair procedures). See *Tormey* v. *Att.-Gen.* [1985] I.L.R.M. 375 and Pye, "The s.104 Certificate of Registration—The Impenetrable Shield No More?" (1985) 3 I.L.T. (n.s.) 213 and Hogan, "Reflections on Tormey v. Attorney-General" (1985) 7 D.U.L.J. (n.s.).

[29] [1894] A.C. 347.

[30] *R. (Conyngham)* v. *Pharmaceutical Society of Ireland* [1894] 2 I.R. 132; *Commissioners of Public Works* v. *Monaghan* [1909] 2 I.R. 718; *Mackey* v. *Monks* [1916] 2 I.R. 200 (reversed) on other grounds by the House of Lords: [1918] A.C. 59 and *Waterford Corporation* v. *Murphy* [1920] 2 I.R. 165. See Donaldson, *Some Comparative Aspects of Irish Law* (Duke, 1957) at pp. 200–203.

[31] *Craies on Statute Law* (7th ed., Edgar) at pp. 290–292.

principles enshrined in the parent Act are drawn by a specialist body possessing particular expertise.[32]

Statutory Instruments Act 1947

The Statutory Instruments Act 1947 is designed to ensure the publication of all items of delegated legislation, thus rendering academic any doubts as to whether the Rules Publication Act 1893 applied to Ireland.[33] The term "statutory instrument" is defined by section 1(1) as meaning every "order, regulation, rule, scheme or by-law" made in the exercise of a statutory power. However, the Act then goes on to make the quite unnecessary distinction between statutory instruments to which the Act primarily applies, and other statutory instruments to which the Act's provisions may apply. The Act "primarily applies"[34] to statutory instruments made after January 1, 1948 by either the President; Government; Minister; Minister of State; an authority having for the time being power to make rules of court or

> "[A]ny person or body, whether corporate or unincorporate, exercising throughout the State any functions of government or discharging throughout the State any public duties in relation to public administration."[35]

In fact, the phrase "primarily applies" is something of a misnomer, for the Act does not apply in a secondary sense to other delegated legislation. In other words, if the Act does not primarily apply to certain instruments, then they fall outside the scope of the Act.

[32] *E.g.*, orders made by Joint Labour Committee under the Industrial Relations Act 1946 fixing minimum wages for certain industries.

[33] In *The State (Quinlan)* v. *Kavanagh* [1935] I.R. 249 Kennedy C.J. had assumed that the Rules Publications Act 1893 applied to Ireland, but in *Re McGrath and Harte* [1941] I.R. 69 Sullivan C.J. pointed out that this Act had not been adapted for application in this jurisdiction. In fact, the 1893 Act was repealed by s.7 of the 1947 Act.

[34] The certificate of the Attorney-General to the effect that in his opinion a particular instrument is one to which to the Act primarily applies is conclusive: s.2(2). Section 4(1) of the Documentary Evidence Act 1925 provides that prima facie evidence of the making of any delegated legislation by the Government, a Minister, or any statutory body, corporate or unincorporate exercising any function of government or discharge throughout the State "any public duties in relation to public administration" may be given by production of a copy of *Iris Oifigiuil* purporting to contain such regulations.

[35] The instrument must also be one which is required by statute to be laid before both or either Houses of the Oireachtas or is of such character as effects the public generally or any particular class or classes of the public (s.2(2)) and must not be a statutory instrument which is required by statute to be published in Iris Oifigiuil, (s.2(1)).

The matter is further complicated by the fact that the Attorney-General is given power to exempt from the provisions of the Act a particular instrument of a type or class on the grounds that it is only of local or personal or temporary application or for "any other reason."[36] Section 1 of the Statutory Instruments (Amendment) Act 1955 requires that a copy of each statutory instrument must be sent to ten listed libraries within ten days of its being made and that each instrument must also be published by the Stationery Office. Section 3(2) of the 1947 Act provides that in civil cases the validity or effect or coming into operation of any statutory instrument shall not be affected by non-compliance with these publication requirements. As far as criminal cases are concerned, section 3(3) provides that where a person has been charged with the offence of a contravening a provision in a statutory instrument to which the Act applies, the prosecution must prove that notice of the making of the order had been published at the date of the alleged offence unless the prosecutor can satisfy the court that reasonable steps have been taken to bring the purport of the statutory instrument to the attention of the public.[37]

The requirements as to publication in the case of statutory instruments to which the Act does not primarily apply are governed by the common law. In *The People* v. *Kennedy*[38] the Court of Criminal Appeal held that orders made under the Emergency Powers Act 1939 were not in the same position as a statute (*i.e.* not in the public domain), and must, therefore, upon a prosecution for a contravention of the order, be proved in evidence. This decision was later distinguished in *The State (Taylor)* v. *Wicklow Circuit Judge*,[39] where it was sought to quash a conviction under the provisions of the Road Traffic Act 1933 on the grounds that the existence of a ministerial order bringing into force the relevant portions of the Act had not been formally proved in evidence. Davitt J. observed that the relevant order in *Kennedy's* case was:

> "[S]ubstantive legislation made by exercise of delegated authority; that it was continuous in its effect and that from day to day it affected personal rights and liabilities; whereas the order in question here was but momentary in its

---

[36] s.2(3)(4). Notice of exemption must be published in Iris Oifigiuil. The compatibility of this exemption procedure with the equality guarantee contained in Article 40.1 of the Constitution seems doubtful. For a more extensive discussion of the 1947 Act, see Jackson, "Delegated Legislation in Ireland" [1962] *Public Law* 417.

[37] Section 3(3) thus preserves the common law principles recognised in cases such as *Lim Chin Aik* v. *R.* [1963] A.C. 160.

[38] [1946] I.R. 517. See also *People* v. *Griffin* [1974] I.R. 416.

[39] [1951] I.R. 311.

operation, bringing into force a piece of legislation enacted by the Oireachtas."[40]

In this case Davitt J. held that the Circuit Court judge who had been administering the Road Traffic Act 1933 for many years was entitled to take judicial notice of the ministerial order without the need for formal proof of its making. Another restriction on the general principle was laid down in *D.P.P.* v. *Collins*[41] concerning the need to prove in evidence the existence of regulations implementing the Road Traffic Act 1978. While Henchy J. conceded that formal proof of the legislative provisions may be necessary where the precise ingredients of the offence are uncertain, it was otherwise where (as here):

> "[A] course of judicial conduct is so inveterate and unques-tioned and of such a nature that it necessarily postulates the existence and validity of a statutory instrument. In such circumstances the court is entitled to take judicial notice of the statutory instrument."[42]

Given that in *Collins* the regulations were ones to which the 1947 Act primarily applied,[43] the court could have arrived at the same result by reference to section 3(3) of that Act. The necessity for the prosecution to prove that the order had been published could have been thereby dispensed with, as it seems clear that "reason-able steps" had been taken for the purpose of bringing the regulations to the attention of the public.

Section 11 of the Interpretation Act 1937 permits a Minister to make regulations and orders in advance of the Act coming into force, where this is necessary to enable the Act to have "full force and effect on the coming into force of the Act." It was on this basis that in *The State (McColgan)* v. *Clifford*[44] the Supreme Court upheld the validity of advance regulations made by the Minister for the Environment prior to the coming into force of the Road Traffic Act 1978. Henchy J. declared that the court could take judicial notice of the fact that the earlier legislation had broken down, and that fresh legislation was imperative. Given these circumstances, advance regulations were necessary in order to give the Act "full force and effect" once it became operational.

While there is some English authority for the proposition that delegated legislation does not come into force until it is

[40] [1951] I.R. at 319.
[41] [1981] I.L.R.M. 447. See Stevenson (1983) 19 Ir.Jur. (n.s.) 95.
[42] [1981] I.L.R.M. at 450.
[43] *I.e.* regulations made by a Minister of State after January 1, 1948 which were not of a purely "local or personal" application.
[44] [1980] I.L.R.M. 75.

published,[45] this point is dealt with by section 9(2) of the Interpretation Act 1937 which provides:

> "Every instrument made wholly or partly under an Act of the Oireachtas shall, unless the contrary intention is expressed in such instrument, be deemed to be in operation as from the end of the day before the day on which such instrument is made."

However, the idea that delegated legislation should have the force of law in advance of its publication would seem to be inimical to constitutional values such as fair procedures.

In most cases the parent statute will require that the statutory instrument be "laid" before the Houses of the Oireachtas within a specified period—generally, twenty-one sitting days.[46] Such authority as there is suggests that failure to comply with this "laying" requirement does not invalidate the statutory instrument.[47]

Judicial control

Even where the delegation of power is not in breach of Article 15.2, the courts may nevertheless examine the validity of any delegated legislation according to the standard criteria of *vires* or reasonableness. As executive or administrative bodies do not possess an inherent legislative power, the validity of delegated legislation falls to be tested against the background of what is authorised by the parent statute either expressly or by necessary implication. While the question of whether an individual statutory instrument is *ultra vires* the parent statute is essentially one of statutory interpretation, there are a number of standard presumptions which are employed by the courts. Thus, the Oireachtas is presumed not to have delegated the power to raise taxes[48]; or to

---

[45] *Johnson* v. *Sargant* [1918] 1 K.B. 101. See Lanham, "Delegated Legislation and Publication" (1974) 37 M.L.R. 510.

[46] The "laying procedure" is regulated by statute: see Houses of the Oireachtas (Laying of Documents) Act 1966.

[47] *Premier Meat Packers Ltd.* v. *Minister for Agriculture*, High Court, July 28, 1971. See also *R.* v. *Sheer Metalcraft Ltd.* [1951] 1 Q.B. 586. But given that the object of the 1966 Act is to enable the Houses of the Oireachtas to examine a statutory instrument with a view to its possible annulment, it could be argued that the "laying requirement" is mandatory, and not merely directory. On mandatory/directory requirements, see pp. 205–212.

[48] *Att.-Gen.* v. *Wilts United Dairies Ltd.* (1921) 39 T.L.R. 781. For a discussion of whether the Oireachtas may validly delegate the power to raise taxes in view of the provisions of Arts. 17 and 22 of the Constitution, see Hogan, "A Note on the Imposition of Duties Act 1957" (1985) 7 D.U.L.J. (n.s.).

oust the jurisdiction of the courts[49]; or encroach upon the liberty of the citizen[50] or give retrospective effect to delegated legislation[51]; or to infringe any provisions of the Constitution.[52] Subject to these presumptions the task of the courts is to ascertain the true intent of the enabling Act.

The courts exercise control over delegated legislation in the same manner as other administrative action and thus delegated legislation may be condemned as invalid on the grounds that it is unreasonable[53] or has been made in bad faith[54] or in breach of natural justice.[55] These issues are considered elsewhere.[56]

---

[49] *Newcastle Breweries Ltd.* v. *The King* [1920] 1 K.B. 854; *Commissioners of Customs and Excise* v. *Cure and Deeley Ltd.* [1962] 1 Q.B. 340 and see generally *Tormey* v. *Att.-Gen.* [1985] I.L.R.M. 357.

[50] *The State (O'Flaherty)* v. *O'Floinn* [1954] I.R. 295; *Murphy* v. *P.M.P.A. Insurance Co. Ltd.*, High Court, February 21, 1978 (presumption against interference with right to privacy).

[51] This is a general presumption of statutory interpretation: *Hamilton* v. *Hamilton* [1982] I.R. 466; *Doyle* v. *An Taoiseach*, Supreme Court, March 28, 1985. But *cf. Re McGrath and Harte* [1941] I.R. 68 and *Minister for Agriculture* v. *O'Connell* [1942] I.R. 600.

[52] There is a presumption that statutory powers (including power to make delegated legislation) by an Act of the Oireachtas do not authorise the donee of such powers to infringe the Constitution: *East Donegal Co-Operatives Ltd.* v. *Att.-Gen.* [1970] I.R. 317. An extradition treaty which was promulgated by means of statutory instrument pursuant to s.8 of the Extradition Act 1965 was declared unconstitutional as it created a charge on public funds without the approval of Dail Eireann contrary to Article 29.5.2: *The State (Gilliland)* v. *Governor of Mountjoy Prison*, [1986] I.L.R.M. 381. Statutory instruments which effected unconstitutional religious discrimination contrary to Art. 44.2.3 were declared invalid in *Quinn's Supermarket Ltd.* v. *Att.-Gen.* [1972] I.R. 1 and *Mulloy* v. *Minister for Education* [1975] I.R. 88. It appears that delegated legislation can qualify as an "enactment" for the purposes of Art. 40.1, thus bringing the "proviso" to that sub-Article into play: *Dillane* v. *Ireland* [1980] I.L.R.M. 167. But *cf.* the views of Walsh J. in *East Donegal Co-Operatives Ltd.* v. *Att.-Gen.* [1970] I.R. 317. See generally, Kelly *op. cit.* at pp. 447–449.

[53] While some English war-time cases (*e.g. Carltona Ltd.* v. *Commissioners of Public Works* [1943] 1 K.B. 111 and *Sparks* v. *Edward Ash Ltd.* [1943] 1 K.B. 223) suggest that the courts may not invalidate ministerial regulations (as opposed to a local by-law) on the grounds of unreasonableness, these cases cannot be regarded as good law in the light of later authorities such as *Commissioners for Customs and Excise Ltd.* v. *Cure and Deeley Ltd.* [1962] 1 Q.B. 340 and *Cassidy* v. *Minister for Industry and Commerce* [1978] I.R. 297.

[54] *Listowel U.D.C.* v. *McDonagh* [1968] I.R. 312. See also a decision of the Australian High Court to the same effect: *Re Toohey* (1981) 38 A.L.R. 439.

One practical problem relates to the methods by which a statutory instrument may be challenged. Invalidity can certainly be raised as a defence to a prosecution[57] or in proceedings for a declaration or an injunction. What is not clear is whether certiorari or prohibition may be used for this purpose. These remedies strictly speaking only apply to judicial as opposed to legislative acts,[58] but in *The State (Lynch)* v. *Cooney*[59] no objection was raised to the use of certiorari in a *direct* challenge to the validity of a statutory instrument.

By-laws

By-laws are another category of delegated legislation. Section 4(1) of the Documentary Evidence Act 1925 provides that prima facie evidence of any by-law may be given by the production of a copy of *Iris Oifigiuil* purporting to contain such a by-law. However, this subsection does *not* apply to by-laws made by local authorities, as individual local authorities cannot be said "to be exercising throughout the State any functions of government or discharging throughout the State any public duties in relation to public administration" within the meaning of section 4(2)(d) of the 1925 Act. For the same reason, local authorities fall outside the scope of the Statutory Instruments Act 1947. Sections 125–127 of the Municipal Corporations (Ireland) Act 1840 enable certain local authorities to make by-laws "for the good rule and government of the borough." County councils were given similar powers by section 16 of the Local Government (Ireland) Act 1898. Other legislation vests local authorities with power to make by-laws

---

[55] *Burke* v. *Minister for Labour* [1979] I.R. 354. However, it is doubtful if there is a duty to consult in every case.

[56] See pp. 297–330.

[57] As in *Listowel U.D.C.* v. *McDonagh* [1968] I.R. 312. But while the District and Circuit Courts may rule on the validity of a statutory instrument, regard must be had to the jurisdictional limits imposed by s.25 of the Courts (Supplemental Provisions) Act 1961: *Greaney* v. *Scully* [1981] I.L.R.M. 340.

[58] For this reason prohibition will not lie to quasi-legislative proceedings: *Re Local Government Board, ex p. Kingstown Commissioners* (1886) 18 L.R.Ir. 509. But these restrictions do not apply to mandamus, which has been used to compel the making of a by-law: *R.* v. *Manchester Corporation* [1911] 1 K.B. 560. On the possible impact of the new rules of court on this matter, see p. 340.

[59] See also the like effect: *The State (Randles)* v. *Minister for Industry and Commerce*, High Court, April 13, 1973. There is, of course, no objection to the use of certiorari to raise an indirect (or collateral) challenge the validity of a statutory instrument: see Hogan, "Challenging the Constitutionality of an Act of the Oireachtas by way of Certiorari" (1982) 4 D.U.L.J. (n.s.) 130.

in relation to specific subjects, especially in relation to environmental and public health matters.[60]

In addition to the specific controls contained in the particular statutory provisions the courts may, as with other forms of delegated legislation, invalidate by-laws on the grounds of lack of *vires*, unreasonableness etc.[61]

Parliamentary control

Many hundreds of statutory instruments are promulgated each year, some of them of a very far-reaching nature. In an attempt to deal with this difficulty the Oireachtas often seeks to retain some measure of parliamentary control. The parent statute typically provides that every regulations made pursuant to that Act must be laid before each House of the Oireachtas. Either House may then pass a resolution within 21 sitting days annulling any such regulation but without prejudice to anything previously done thereunder.[62] While this procedure is of some value in permitting the discussion of a contentious statutory instrument, it ignores the reality of a Government majority in both Houses of the Oireachtas. One might also mention that while this annulment procedure has been described by O'Higgins C.J. as a "valuable safeguard," it cannot authorise that which is not otherwise sanctioned by Article 15.2.[63]

---

[60] See *e.g.* Public Health (Ire.) Act 1878.

[61] See, *e.g. Kruse* v. *Johnson* [1898] 2 Q.B. 91 (by-law prohibiting singing within 50 yards of a dwelling-house not void for unreasonableness); *Dublin Corporation* v. *Irish Church Missions* [1901] 2 I.R. 387; *Enniscorthy U.D.C.* v. *Field* [1904] 2 I.R. 518; *Dun Laoghaire Corporation* v. *Brick* (1952) Ir.Jur.Rep. 37; *Limerick Corporation* v. *Sheridan* (1956) 90 I.L.T.R. 56 *Listowel U.D.C.* v. *McDonagh* [1968] I.R. 312 and see generally pp. 310–313.

[62] On this "laying" procedure, see p. 22. Note that in *Immigration and Naturalisation Service* v. *Chada*, 462 U.S. 919 (1983) a majority of the U.S. Supreme Court held that the "legislative veto" was unconstitutional. This decision was the outcome of a formal, logical application of the separation of powers: if the veto is an executive or judicial function it is not for Congress, alternatively, if it is a legislative function it must be decided by both Houses and signed by the President rather through the resolution of one House acting alone. If *Chada* were applied in this jurisdiction it would probably render unconstitutional the power to annul statutory instruments given to both individual Houses of the Oireachtas. It is unlikely that *Chada* would be followed in this jurisdiction if only because in Ireland the legislature is responsible to the executive. However, this result could also be avoided if the Houses of the Oireachtas are regarded as being merely designated bodies to whom an administrative power (*viz.* the power of annulment) has been given.

[63] *City View Press Ltd.* v. *AnCO* [1980] I.R. 380.

Occasionally a statute may require that confirming legislation be passed within a particular stated period[64]; or that the draft instrument will not come into force unless confirmed by resolution of both Houses[65]; or provide for an appeal by any person aggrieved against the making of the instrument to the High Court.[66]

Parliamentary scrutiny is now vested in the Joint Oireachtas Committee on Legislation. This Committee has taken over the work of the Senate Select Committee on Statutory Instruments. The Joint Committee on the Secondary Legislation of the European Communities reports on statutory instruments made under the European Communities (Amendment) Act 1973.[67]

Joint Oireachtas Committee on Legislation

The Joint Oireachtas Committee is empowered to require any instrument-making authority to submit a memorandum explaining any statutory instrument or to send a representative to appear before the Committee as a witness to explain the instrument. The Committee is bound to give the instrument-making authority an opportunity to be heard before drawing the special attention of the Houses of the Oireachtas to any instrument. The Committee's terms of reference do not specify the grounds on which it may draw the House's attention to a statutory instrument. However, these will presumably follow the same broad lines as the former Senate Committee which was mandated to report an instrument on the following grounds:

"(i) that it imposes a charge on the public revenues or contains provisions requiring payments to be made to the Exchequer or any Government Department or to any local or public authority in consideration of any licence or consent, or of any services to be rendered or prescribes the amount of any such charge or payments;

(ii) that it appears to make some unusual or unexpected use of the powers conferred by the statute under which it is made;

---

[64] *E.g.* Imposition of Duties Act 1957, s.2; Provisional Collection of Taxes Act 1927, s.3.
[65] *E.g.* Electoral Act 1963, s.6(3); Health Act 1970, s.4(5).
[66] *E.g.* Fisheries (Consolidation) Act 1959, s.8 (appeal to High Court). See *Moloney* v. *Minister for Fisheries*, High Court, February 28, 1979; *Dunne* v. *Minister for Fisheries* [1984] I.R. 230.
[67] Gwynn Morgan, *Constitutional Law of Ireland* (1985) at p. 110. For an account of the work of these bodies, see Jackson "Delegated Legislation in Ireland" [1962] *Public Law* 417 and Robinson, "Irish Parliamentary Scrutiny of European Community Legislation" (1979) 16 C.M.L.R. 9.

(iii) that it purports to have retrospective effect where the parent statute confers no express authority so to provide;
(iv) that there appears to have been unjustifiable delay either in the laying of it before either House of the Oireachtas or in its publication;
(v) that for any special reason its form or purport calls for elucidation;
(vi) that its drafting appears to be defective; or on any other ground which does not impinge on its merits or on the policy behind it; . . . "[68]

The high constitutional significance of the first and third heads require no underlining. In fact, the former Senate Committee seldom had to invoke these grounds. The second ground covers a noticeably diverse collection of blemishes. For example, one instrument raised by several million pounds the maximum borrowings of certain body which could be guaranteed by the Minister for Finance.[69] In another case, a statutory instrument which attempted to control the sale of commercial cream was cast so widely that it even caught a householder skimming cream off a bottle of milk with a teaspoon.[70]

The remaining heads may be illustrated by reference to the last Report (1978–1981) of the former Senate Committee[71] which considered 333 instruments. The attention of the Senate was drawn to thirty-six of them. Twenty-one instruments were reported on the grounds of "unjustifiable delay" under head (iv). The criterion set by previous select committees was that a delay of more than seven days was "unjustifiable" and the delays in respect of which the Committee complained averaged eighteen days and ranged from nine days to three months. The significance of these delays lies in the fact as the Committee observed that a member of either the Dail or the Senate may put down a motion for annulment only after the instrument has been laid, yet the instrument comes into force at the date it is made and the annulment is not retrospective.

In the Senate Committee's last report, fourteen statutory

[68] For slightly different approach of Joint Committee, see Addendum.
[69] Second Report of the Select Committee on Statutory Rules, Orders and Regulations (1949) (T. 122) at p. vii. The instrument in question was the Emergency Powers (No. 157) Order 1942 (Seventh Amendment) Order 1948 (S.I. 1948 No. 357).
[70] First Report of The Select Committee on Statutory Rules, Orders and Regulations (1949) (T. 121) at pp. xii–xviii.
[71] First Report of the Select Committee on Statutory Instruments (1978) (Prl. 9747).

instruments succumbed under the miscellaneous head (v)
(" ... for any special reason its form or purport calls for
elucidation"). The two most significant defects were: first, the lack
of a brief explanatory memorandum describing the general
purport of the instrument, in spite of a Department of Finance
instruction to all Departments that this should be provided, and,
secondly, the absence of a precise citation of the parent sections of
the legislation under which the instrument had been made. The
point underlying this defect is the need for persons affected by the
instrument to be able to check whether the instrument is *ultra vires*
the enabling power contained in the parent legislation. In earlier
reports, the Committee had complained that the titles of certain
instruments had failed to identify the subject-matter. The Committee also condemned the practice of expressing regulations as
amendments to existing regulations so that their effect could only
be discovered by reference to the other regulations. Each of these
defects are of importance in the context of the Rule of Law and
are issues on which the Committee has had to return to the attack
on more than one occasion.[72]

An example of head (vi) (" ... drafting appears to be defective ... ") is to be found in the 1978–1981 Report of the former
Senate Committee. This concerned an order made under section
31 of the Broadcasting Authority Act 1960[73] which purported to
ban interviews with a spokesman "for any other or more of the
following organisations. ... " The Committee took the view that
the words which it had underlined rendered the instrument
meaningless. The Department of Posts and Telegraphs had replied
that in the original instrument the underlined phrase read "any
one or more." The Committee reported to the Senate that the
Department had failed in its duty to supply an accurate copy of the
instrument to the House.

The inclusion of the final, unnumbered residual head ("any
other ground ... ") meant that the former Senate Committee's
jurisdiction was very wide and went beyond the grounds of review
exerciseable by a court. On the other hand, the Joint Committee's
only sanction was to report an instrument to the Houses and the
Senate Select Committee's annual reports were seldom debated.
Nevertheless, the Senate Committee received consistent co-
operation from Departments of State .and other instrument-
making bodies and difficulties were often resolved in a satisfactory
manner by an exchange of correspondence. In general, the
Committee's existence be it as a Senate Select Committee

---

[72] See, *e.g.*, Second Report of the Select Committee on Statutory
Instruments (1954) (Pr. 3864) at p. 17.
[73] See also at pp. 323–325.

or as a Joint Oireachtas Committee has improved the quality of the
statutory instruments.

4. Administrative rules and circulars

The legal status of administrative rules is unclear. Administrative codes such as the Judges' Rules or the rules for the operation
of the Criminal Injuries Compensation Tribunal[74] are clearly
capable of having legal effects even though statutory authority for
these rules is wanting. Can such rules be distinguished from mere
statements of policy and practice emanating from government
departments? For example, are the Revenue Commissioners free
to make extra-statutory concessions to one group of taxpayers and
not to another group of similarly situated taxpayers?[75] Even if
these practices are not regarded as delegated legislation or has
having the force of law, constitutional principles of fair procedures and equality before the law might well be invoked to prevent
a public authority from acting in a manner inconsistent with its
administrative rules and practices.

Departmental circulars also pose similar difficulties. Unless the
circular is published as a statutory instrument,[76] its legal effects are
uncertain. Nevertheless, many circulars contain valuable insights
into the manner in which administrative bodies propose to
exercise discretionary powers.[77] There are some English authorities which hold that departmental circulars may have legally
binding consequences.[78] *The State (Melbarien Enterprises Ltd.)* v.
Revenue Commissioners[79] is the furthest that the Irish courts have
gone in this direction. In 1984, the Minister for Finance informed

---

[74] *E.g.* a decision of the Criminal Injuries Compensation Tribunal may be
    quashed for error of law or breach of natural justice.
[75] See, *e.g.*, *Vestey* v. *I.R.C.* [1980] A.C. 1148.
[76] The Minister of the Environment is entitled to make statutory
    instruments containing general statements of policy in planning
    matters: Local Government (Planning and Development) Act 1982, s.7.
    Thus, for example, Local Government (Planning and Development)
    General Policy Directive, 1982 (S.I. 1982 No. 264) gives guidance on
    large scale retail shopping developments.
[77] *E.g.* the exchange control notices published by the Central Bank which
    indicate the manner in which the Bank proposes to exercise its
    discretionary powers under the Central Bank Act 1971 and the
    Exchange Control Acts 1954–1982.
[78] *Blackpool Corporation* v. *Locker* [1948] 1 K.B. 349; *Patchett* v. *Leathem*
    (1949) 65 T.L.R. 69 and *Acton Borough Council* v. *Morris* [1953] 1
    W.L.R. 1228.
[79] High Court, April 19, 1985.

the Dail that all companies tendering for public service contracts would be obliged to produce tax clearance certificates from the Revenue Commissioners. Such a certificate was not forthcoming in the present case, because although the applicant company was not in arrears, another company which had connections with the applicant had gone into liquidation owing arrears of income tax. Hamilton P. held that the applicant company was entitled to have its application considered on its merits, and that in refusing the application the Revenue Commissioners had taken irrelevant considerations into account. However, the judgment does imply that, as the Revenue Commissioners would not have been acting on irrelevant considerations if they had abided by the terms of the circular, even an administrative policy statement is capable of having legal consequences.

Lardner J. adopted a similar approach to the question of a departmental circular in *Staunton* v. *St. Lawrence's Hospital*.[80] In this case, acting on foot of a departmental circular, the defendants appointed the plaintiff as a medical consultant at rates of salary higher than those which had previously been paid to consultant medical staff. Some months later the hospital received a new circular from the Department of Health which directed that any special salary increases above government guidelines should not be paid. As a result, the hospital declined to pay the special rates appropriate to the common contract to the plaintiff.

Lardner J. found that there was a concluded contract between the plaintiff and the hospital, and that the hospital was liable to pay the plaintiff at the special rates applicable to the common contract. However, the hospital had served a third party notice on Ireland and the Attorney-General seeking an indemnity in respect of extra cost of paying the plaintiff at the rates provided by the common contract. It was common case that there was no statutory obligation imposed on the Minister for Health to make the reimbursements claimed by the hospital. Nevertheless, Lardner J. held that the state was bound by the terms of the original circular:

> "[W]hen the hospital acted in accordance with, and in reliance upon its terms, clause 12 [of the circular] gave rise to a contractual obligation which bound the Minister to adjust ... the hospital's financial allocation to the extent that was necessary to cover the additional cost incurred by the hospital in respect of the common contract made with the plaintiff."

Another way in which a circular may indirectly acquire legal force is where it indicates the conditions on which the public

[80] High Court, February 21, 1986.

authority issuing it will exercise a discretion. *Latchford* v. *Minister for Industry and Commerce*[81] is a case in point. This case concerned the payment of subsidies to bakers by the Minister. There was no legislation in force determining who were to be the recipients of the subsidy. However, the Minister had published certain conditions with which the recipients were obliged to comply. The plaintiffs had complied with all the conditions, but the Minister refused to pay the subsidy on the ground that plaintiffs had been convicted of an offence relating to the sale of bread. The published conditions did not, however, disqualify a claimant on this ground. The Supreme Court accordingly made a declaration that the Minister was not entitled to withhold payment of the subsidy. Murnaghan J. commented as follows:

> "After having made and published the conditions on which the payment of subsidy would be made, the Minister can alter these conditions from time to time or withdraw them: but until altered or withdrawn, the conditions apply, and persons who have complied with the conditions are entitled to claim that they have qualified for payment of subsidy."[82]

Latchford may best be classified as a case where the circular is taken to lay down all the relevant considerations according to which the public authority may exercise its discretion.

While the exact legal status of a circular awaits clarification, cases such as *Latchford* and *Staunton* show that the administrative authority may be bound by the terms of its own circular where the private citizen acts on it to his detriment.

[81] [1950] I.R. 33.
[82] [1950] I.R. at 42.

Part II

Institutions of Government

3 Dail, Ministers, Departments and Civil Servants

The object of this chapter is to sketch the constitutional and legal framework within which the administration of central government[1] proceeds, dealing, in Part 1, with the part played by the Dail; in Part 2, with the legal persona of a Minister; and in the remaining parts with the civil service.

1. Formal control by the Dail

Following the British model[2] the members of the Government (Cabinet) are formally responsible to the Dail, though not the Senate,[3] in two ways.

(i) **Collective Government responsibility.** The Constitution makes the Government collectively responsible to the Dail. This means that, after an election, the Dail elects a Government and also that it can remove and, without reference to the people, replace it with a new Government. However, its power to elect a replacement Government is restricted by the provision that even a Taoiseach who has been defeated in the Dail may advise a

---

[1] We do not deal with the process of law-making.
[2] Though at the inception of the State, some efforts were made to modify this model: on this and on the entire subject, see Gwynn Morgan, *Constitutional Law of Ireland* (Dublin, 1985) at pp. 54–87.
[3] The Government is not formally responsible to the Senate in the way that it is to the Dail. Informally, the Senate's position in regard to publicising and criticising the Government's activities and policy decisions is similar to, though less important than, that of the Dail. For instance, the select committees constituted to review a specific area of government activity (*e.g.* the Joint Committee on Developing Countries) are invariably joint committees, but with a minority of members from the Senate. Accordingly in the limited space available the role of the Senate has not been examined.

dissolution followed by a general election and, thus far, no President has seen fit to reject such advice.[4] Moreover, all the Dail's powers over the Government are conditioned by the basic fact of political life which is that a Government can almost always command the support of a majority of deputies, because deputies are elected principally on the basis of the party which they have pledged themselves to support in the Dail. Such is the strength of the whip-system that the legislature cannot be regarded as speaking with a voice independent of the executive and, so, it is realistic to characterise the central element in the Irish governmental system as a fused executive-legislature.

The principal form of responsibility to the Dail is styled as "collective" which means, first, that the Government, as a collective authority, speaks with one voice and, secondly, that if the Taoiseach resigns from office (or is removed), the other members of the Government also leave office.[5] In other words, the Government stands, or falls, as a single, united entity.

(ii) Individual ministerial responsibility. A governmental decision is seldom so grave that an error in relation to it would warrant the bringing down of a Government. Thus, although from the broad constitutional perspective, collective responsibility is the more important element, it is the individual ministerial doctrine which could potentially be of greater significance in checking undesirable governmental action. According to the individual ministerial doctrine, if a Minister commits certain types of error then there is an obligation on him, and on him alone, to resign. In appropriate circumstances, so the theory runs, a Minister is supposed to resign of his own accord; but if he fails to do this, he

---

[4] See generally, Arts. 13.1; 13.2; 28.4.1; and 28.10. Notice, however, this observation of a former Governor of the Central Bank: "It is doubtful if the normal life of a government of four years or so is now adequate for the preparation and implementation of national plans. . . . This 'efficiency argument' points to the advisability of providing, by statute, that parliament should have a fixed, rather than a maximum, life of five years. This would not necessarily mean that governments would have a correspondingly fixed life of five years, but it could be a significant step in that direction": Murray, "Irish Government Further Observed" (1983) 31 *Administration* 284 at p. 287.

[5] Arts. 28.4.2; 28.11.1. There is no reference to this doctrine in the Constitution. However it has been accepted that the rule exists as a convention derived from the relationship of ministers to the Dail: see *e.g.*, Vol. 187, *Dail Debates* cols. 19–59, March 7, 1961 (second stage of the Mental Treatment (Detention in Approved Institutions) Bill 1961), Vol. 256, *Dail Debates* cols. 1473–1501, (November 9, 1970), cols. 1732–66, (November 10, 1970) (motion of no confidence in Minister for Agriculture).

must certainly resign if a vote of no confidence in him is passed by the Dail. The type of error which attracts this duty may be a personal act of dishonour or indiscretion; a failure of policy; or an act of maladministration, within his Department.

As is well known, the individual ministerial doctrine has been more honoured in the breach than in the observance and there have been very few resignations for breach of the doctrine since 1922.[6] The principal reason for the failure of the doctrine is the lack of a non-partisan agency to determine conclusively when a Minister should resign: as with the collective responsibility doctrine, the Dail is prevented from playing this part because of the strict party system. There are other reasons for the failure: the single sanction of resignation affords no gradation of sanctions to deal with the varied offences of widely varying culpability which may arise; again, resignation would not even be available as a sanction where the responsible Minister had left office before the error came to light. Moreover a particular difficulty arises in relation to a type of error which is common in the area of administrative law, namely, abuse of power or an act of maladministration, occurring during the course of routine administration. For in any department of state, there will be hundreds or thousands of civil servants serving under a Minister and such an error may be wholly the fault of a civil servant.[7] Where the Minister is not personally involved in the error, is it not dogmatic to expect his head to roll?[8] This situation was illustrated in 1961 in the context of the involuntary detention of mental patients. According to the relevant statute, the Minister for Health's permission had to be renewed after every six-month period of detention. The junior civil servant whose task it was to pass on the applications for the Minister's permission fell ill and failed to perform this task, with the result that almost 300 patients were illegally detained. Yet the Minister convincingly brushed aside calls for his resignation as unrealistic.[9]

Before going further, it ought to be emphasised that, apart from

---

[6] One definite example involved the resignation of a Parliamentary Secretary in 1946 because of allegations of a conflict of interest between his official duties and a firm in which he had an interest: see *Report of the Tribunal appointed by the Taoiseach on November 7, 1947* (P.No. 8576). It is often difficult, and seldom profitable, to determine whether a resignation is an act of individual or collective responsibility.

[7] See Vol. 187, *Dail Debates*, cols. 19–59 (March 7, 1961).

[8] Murray, "A Working and Changeable Instrument" (1982) 30 *Administration* 43, at p. 52. See also Wheare, *Maladministration and its Remedies* (London, 1973), Chap. 3; and Murray, "Irish Government Further Observed" (1983) 31 *Administration* 284 at pp. 288–298.

[9] See Vol. 187, *Dail Debates*, cols. 19–59 (March 7, 1961).

theoretically controlling the Government and making laws, the
Dail has a third function, namely, acting as the "Grand Inquest of
the Nation." What this rather grandiloquent phrase means is that
the House investigates, appraises, publicises and even dramatises
the Government's decisions and highlights the alternatives. It
provides a continuous critical commentary on the Government's
performance and, thereby, it is hoped, helps to educate the
individual members of the public in casting their vote at the
subsequent election. This is a peculiarly elusive function with the
result that the Dail's performance is difficult to assess, especially as
the effect of the "Grand Inquest" is more likely to be preventative,
rather than curative, *i.e.* to discourage a Government from doing
something which will not bear the light of day. However, it is
reasonable to suppose that in this role, the Dail has some effect in
forestalling the worst excesses. Plainly, the Dail's success in this, as
in its other duties, depends on how well-informed it is and various
reforms have recently been instituted—notably a more extensive
committee system—to try to improve the quality of information
and advice available to it.[10]

Consequences of individual ministerial doctrine
    Although the ministerial responsibility doctrine is such a
broken-backed rule, it bears mentioning because its existence
(real or supposed) has had a formative influence upon the
machinery for the performance and control of Ministers and
Departments in the following ways.
    1. It remains the formal position that a Minister is responsible
to the Dail for all activities going on within his Department. In
part, as a result of this, the Dail attempts to cover too wide an area
and has insufficient time and attention for what should be its
principal concern, namely major matters of policy. Thus, for
instance, one element of ministerial responsibility to the Dail is the
Minister's duty to answer questions on behalf of his Department.
A large proportion of these questions relate to the personal
minutiae of constituents[11] and the discussion of these issues tends
to crowd out the examination of policy issues. Again, the Dail's
supposed power and duty to police all of a Department's activities
may impede the development of other, more effective means of
controlling routine actions, for instance, along the lines proposed

[10] On which see Gwynn Morgan, *op. cit*, at pp. 144–151.
[11] One half of all questions to the Minister for the Environment concern
    individual constituents' problems. This figure is exceeded in the case of
    the questions for the Minister for Social Welfare: see *The Irish Times*,
    January 20, 1984.

in the note on Administrative Law and Procedure appended to the Devlin Report.[12]

2. Another effect of the doctrine is to "politicise" every decision taken in a department by converting every decision—however minor, technical or inherently non-controversial—into a potential bone of contention in a parliamentary dog-fight, which may affect the credit of the entire Government. One consequence of this is that the caution of an already-cautious civil service is increased in order to obey the supreme obligation of "protecting the Minister." Thus, for instance, files are pushed up from one level of the civil service hierarchy to another so that issues have to be resolved at a higher level than would otherwise be considered necessary. Another result is " "the representations' system [which] helps to perpetuate the misconception that everything can be 'fixed'."[13]

3. The personification of the entire activity of the Department in its Minister (politically, by the ministerial responsibility doctrine and, legally, through the Ministers and Secretaries Act 1924) leaves no formal position for anyone else, even senior management. The effect of this arrangement is to militate against personal responsibility and initiative on the part of civil servants. One symbol of this is the practice, now falling into disuse, of civil servants commending routine letters with the formula, "I am directed by the Minister to. . . . "

4. In the past, courts have offered it as a reason (or pretext) to justify a refusal to review some administration actions that "this is a matter for which the Minister is responsible to Parliament." This traditional and unrealistic view—which relies upon a model of Parliament which existed, only, for a brief period in mid-nineteenth century Britain, before the growth of the party system and "big government"—is not part of the thinking of the contemporary Irish judiciary. Nevertheless, it was an influence in shaping the doctrine of judicial review, which exists in Ireland today.[14]

---

[12] Prl. 792, Appendix 1.

[13] *Ibid.* at p. 448.

[14] See *e.g. Liversidge* v. *Anderson* [1942] A.C. 206 (a case involving individual liberty). See also the comments of Shaw L.J. in *Raymond* v. *Att.-Gen.* [1982] Q.B. 839, 847 on political responsibility for decisions of the D.P.P.: "The safeguard against an unnecessary or gratuitous exercise of this power [to enter a *nolle prosequi*] is that . . . the Director's duties are exercised under the superintendence of the Attorney-General. That officer of the Crown is, in his turn, answerable to Parliament, if it should appear that his or the Director's powers have . . . in any case been abused."

We shall return to some of these features in Part 3 which deals
with the reform of the civil service.

2. Legal structure of the ministers and departments

Before independence, the separate executive which was the
great anomaly of the Act of Union which fused the British and
Irish Parliaments, consisted of about fifty units described variously
as "departments," "boards" or "offices." Ireland, it was said, had
as many boards as would make her coffin. The administrative
units, some of which were merely the Irish branches of a mainland
Department, enjoyed a variety of relationships with the Lord
Lieutenant (the formal head of the executive) and the Chief
Secretary (a sort of Minister for Irish Affairs who represented the
Irish administration in the House of Commons).[15]
The objective of the post-Independence Government was to
sweep away this *disjecta membra* and to replace it with a uniform
system in which the central executive power of the state flowed
directly through the members of the Government, so that the Dail
could exercise control over the entire administration—for in
those heady days, it was hoped that the Dail would wield
substantial influence over governments. We have already seen that
these hopes were not realised on the political plane, in the form
anticipated. A complementary change was made on the legal
plane by the Ministers and Secretaries Act 1924 (a code
contemplated at Article 28.12 of the Constitution) which is the
chief organic law determining the framework of the executive arm
of government.[16]
The 1924 Act established the (say) Minister for Justice as a
statutorily created corporation sole,[17] distinct from the temporary
incumbent of the office. Linked with this development was the
practice of vesting almost all central government functions[18] in a

---

[15] McDowell, *The Irish Administration* (London, 1964); McColgan, "Parti-
tion and the Irish Administration 1920–1922" (1980) 28 *Administration*
147.
[16] Minister and Secretaries Act 1924, s.9.
[17] 1924 Act, s.2(1). On the Minister as corporation sole, see further at
pp. 389–396.
[18] There are a few functions which, in order to mark their importance or
to add lustre, are vested in the President or the Government. In
addition, a very few functions are vested in designated civil servants.
The principal example is the deciding officer/appeals officer in the
Department of Social Welfare: see pp. 149–154. Plainly, too, the
generalisation in the text does not refer to the functions vested in a
state-sponsored body.

particular Minister.[19] The 1924 Act provides that "each . . . Department . . . and the powers, duties and functions thereof shall be assigned to and administered by the Minister"[20] but that whenever any power is vested by statute in a Minister, the administration entailed in the exercise of that power is deemed to be allocated to the Department of that Minister.[21] The result of these provisions is that the Minister is not only head of the Department; he also personifies the Department and, as corporation sole, bears responsibility in law for its every action. At the same time, most, at least, of these actions may be performed by departmental civil servants, rather than the Minister himself.

The Ministers and Secretaries Act 1924 "establishe[s] . . . the several Departments of State amongst which the administration and business of the public services in [the State] shall be distributed."[22] The Act also gives a generalised description of the duties of the Departments which it establishes, of which the following may be taken as representative:

> "The Department of Justice shall comprise the administration and business generally of public services in connection with law, justice, public order and police, and all powers, duties and functions connected with the same except such powers . . . as are by law reserved to the Executive Council and such powers . . . as are by the Constitution or by law excepted from the authority of the Executive Council or of an Executive Minister and shall include in particular the business, powers, duties and functions of the branches and officers of the public service specified in the Second Part of the Schedule to this Act [which includes the Courts, the Public Record Office and the Registry of Deeds] and of which

---

[19] Though this is subject to the overriding imperative contained in Art. 28.4 of the Constitution that "The Government . . . shall be collectively responsible for the Departments of State administered by the members of the Government." See also Ministers and Secretaries Act 1924, s.5. It is thus open to the Government to direct a Minister as to how a decision should be taken, although the decision has been statutorily vested in a Minister.

[20] 1924 Act, s.1.

[21] Ministers and Secretaries (Amendment) Act 1939, s.6(3). See, too Article 28.12 of the Constitution and Kiely, "Ministers and Departments" (1986) 7 *Seirbhis Phoibli* 7. But for *delegatus non potest delegare*, see pp. 227–233.

[22] As of early 1986, the full list of departments of state is as follows: Taoiseach; Energy; Foreign Affairs; Industry, Trade, Commerce, and Tourism; Environment; Defence; Public Service; Fisheries and Forestry; Communications; Finance; Health; Social Welfare; Agriculture; Justice; Labour; Education.

Department the head shall be, and shall be styled, an t-Aire Dli agus Cirt or (in English) the Minister for Justice."

Nevertheless, it is to be noted that almost all governmental functions are created by a specific statute, and such a statute would prevail against the description in the 1924 Act even if it involved vesting a function in what would seem, according to that Act, to be an inappropriate Department. However, a Minister is a corporation sole and, as such, he has the capacity to contract, but only for the purpose of his authorised function or purposes incidental thereto. The description in the 1924 Act[23] would be significant in divining what these purposes were and, thus, in determining whether a particular contract was *ultra vires* the Minister's power. In addition the description might be helpful in fixing the scope of a civil servant's employment in the context, for instance, of a tort action against the State.[24] It might also be invoked by the Controller and Auditor General, if he were deciding whether some item fell outside an imprecisely worded vote.

Where a new Minister and Department is established, then fresh legislation has to be enacted. Legislation is necessary because the creation (or dissolution) of a corporation sole requires an Act of the Oireachtas. In addition, the process of enacting the bill affords a convenient opportunity for the Oireachtas to discuss what is, after all, an important change in the structure of Government.

3. Reform in the Civil Service

Until 1973, the personnel and organisation functions for the entire civil service were vested in the Minister for Finance. Because the civil service pay and pensions salary bill accounts for a large and increasing share of public expenditure, this function had been regarded since the foundation of the State as an intrinsic element in the control of Government expenditure. However, with the economic programming of the late 1950s, the civil service was required to play a new and more dynamic part in the economic life of the country. To assist it to adapt to this change, the Minister for Finance constituted the Public Services Organisation Review Group ("the Devlin Report"), which reported in 1969.[25] One of its

---

[23] 1924 Act, s.1. For the supercession of the title Ministry by Department in 1924, see Fanning, *The Irish Department of Finance, 1922–1958* (Dublin, 1978), p. 39.
[24] See pp. 365–380 and 389–396.
[25] Prl. 792.

major proposals was implemented fairly quickly, namely, the creation of a Minister for the Public Service, with a separate Department of State, freed of the shadows cast by preoccupation with the functions of the Department of Finance and the transfer to the new Minister of powers over the civil service.[26] The object of this change, effected by the Ministers and Secretaries (Amendment) Act 1973,[27] was to promote a more positive attitude towards matters of organisation and personnel, as contrasted with the exclusive emphasis on cost-consciousness natural to the Department of Finance. In particular, it was hoped that the new Department would possess sufficient authority and enthusiasm to push through the other reforms proposed by the Devlin Report. In fact, for wider political reasons, very little happened until the mid-1980s.

The Governments of 1981–82 and 1982 were elected on a programme of public service reform, symbolised by the fact that, between 1982 and 1986, for the first time ever, the incumbent of the office of Minister for the Public Service did not hold a second portfolio. The result was a number of specific reforms, including the articulation of major expenditure programmes in each Department so as to pin-point the link between costs and performance; the appointment, with effect from early 1984, of an Ombudsman to hold the office which had remained vacant since it was constituted in 1980; the establishment, in 1984, of the "Top Level Appointments Committee" (consisting of a number of secretaries, plus the chairman of the Public Service Advisory Council) to make recommendations for filling posts at Assistant Secretary level or above, applying the criterion of merit rather than seniority and not confining itself to candidates from particular departments or grades; the opening up of a number of principal and assistant principal posts[28] to selection along similar lines; and the appointment of Secretaries for a maximum period of seven years (it being unclear to what celestial plane they would proceed thereafter). In addition, there is to be a wider and more attractive presentation of information; all civil servants dealing with the public now give their names; and a special unit of the

---

[26] Public Service (Transfer of Departmental Administration and Ministerial Functions) Order (S.I. 1973 No. 294).

[27] 1973 Act, s.2. It was provided by the 1973 Act, that the Minister for the Public Service should always be the same person as the Minister for Finance. This provision was revoked by the Ministers and Secretaries Act 1980, s.7. Section 4 and 5 of the 1973 Act also established the Public Service Advisory Council.

[28] A similar scheme had been in existence for higher executive officers since 1973.

Department of the Public Service has undertaken responsibility to "dejargonise" (*sic*) all Government or departmental forms.[29]

Finally, *Serving the Country Better: A White Paper on the Public Service* was published in 1985.[30] The major constitutional-legal change proposed by the White Paper was a modification of the ministerial responsibility doctrine, along the same lines as the Devlin Report's concept of the *Aireacht*. This change followed from an analysis of a defect in the governmental system which has been explained by Dr Barrington as follows:

> "The basic system established to ensure the democratic accountability of government rested on the idea that the job of a Minister in charge of a Government Department is very like that of a manager of a small business. He should take all the decisions and have his finger in every pie. [But] government is not small business, but very big business indeed."[31]

The White Paper envisages a remedy for this ill according to the following prescription:

> "Where departments have a sufficiently large volume of purely executive work, Ministers will be enabled by legislation to transfer such work to separate offices to be known as executive offices which will have full responsibility for discharging it effectively. The transfer will be effected by Order made by the Minister with the consent of the Ministers for Finance and the Public Service and subject to affirmative resolution of each House of the Oireachtas. The purpose of establishing executive offices is twofold: to free Ministers of involvement in time-consuming day-to-day administration and to enable the officials responsible for the delivery of services to concentrate on good management. This approach will be followed in departments where there is sufficient volume of executive work to make it feasible to set up separate organisations for its performance.
>
> Examples of possible areas where executive offices might be set up are the payment of social insurance benefits and

---

[29] These reforms are summarised in *Serving the Country Better: A White Paper on the Public Service* (1985) (Pl. 3262) ("The White Paper"). For comment, see "A special issue on the White Paper". (1985) 6 *Serbhis Phoibli* No. 4. The full implications of some of the changes described in the text will only be appreciated when the rest of this chapter has been read.

[30] Pl. 3262. The sub-title was a misnomer since the White Paper dealt almost exclusively with the civil service.

[31] *The Irish Administrative System* (Dublin, 1980), p. 32.

social assistance by the Department of Social Welfare; Central Statistics Office; school building work in the Department of Education; and the Air Navigation Services Office and the Meteorological Service, which at present operate in many respects as executive offices of the Department of Communications on a non-statutory basis.

The work transferred will no longer be regarded as part of the business of the department for which the Minister is responsible and, accordingly, the Minister will not be answerable to the Dail for the day-to-day operations of the office. (He will, of course, remain responsible for the policy under which it operates). The following arrangements will generally apply:

Ministers will have power to appoint and, if necessary, replace the chief executives of such offices, subject to normal procedures. The chief executive and other staff will be civil servants who will be graded in accordance with their responsibilities.

Each executive office will have a separate Vote for which the chief executive will be the Accounting Officer, *i.e.*, the official statutorily accountable to the Dail.

The statutory orders setting up the individual executive offices will spell out in more detail the relationship between the offices and their departments and Ministers.[32]

To improve management, the chief executives of the executive offices will be given greater managerial autonomy than is normally possible within the civil service context, including authority in relation to appointment, discipline and dismissal of staff."

4. Civil Service: definitions and context

The widest term used in this area (though not generally in the context of legislation) is the "public sector," a category which embraces not merely civil servants but all those who are employed, directly or indirectly, by some public body. This comprises in all about 300,000 people,[33] compared with a gross figure for national employment (excluding the self-employed) of 900,000. A slightly

---

[32] The White Paper at pp. 27–28. As of May 1986 the legislation to implement the new règime had not been published.

[33] Made up roughly as follows: civil servants (35,000); employees of the health boards (61,000); the state-sponsored bodies (90,000); the local authorities and county committees of agriculture (36,000); security forces (25,000); and educational sector (46,000).

narrower term than the public sector is the public service[34]—those
employees whose salary and pension bill (approx £2,500 million in
1985) is paid for, directly or indirectly, out of public funds—a
term which is obviously very significant in economic and financial
contexts. At the centre of the public service lies the civil service
manning, *inter alia*, the departments of state. The number of civil
servants increased from 28,000 in 1960, to 70,000 in 1983, just
before the establishment of *An Post* and *Bord Telecom Eireann*. By
1986, there were 35,000 civil servants.[35] The numbers and
remuneration of the civil servants in each Department, formerly
shown in the Book of Estimates, have appeared since 1966, in a
separate publication, the *Directory of State Services*.

It is necessary to define the terms "civil servant" and "civil
service" more precisely, if only because these terms are used in
various statutes which provide no definition of the terms. Most
important, the term "civil servant" is used to indicate the scope of
both the Civil Service Commissioners Act 1956 which regulates
the selection of civil servants and the Civil Service Regulation
Act 1956 (which deals with the terms and conditions of Civil
Servants). A useful historical sketch of the terms was given by
Kingsmill Moore J. in *McLoughlin* v. *Minister for Social Welfare*[36]:

> "The words 'civil service' and 'civil servant' . . . are not terms
> of legal art. . . . The phrase seems to have been first used to

---

[34] The public service includes the same groups as the public sector, save
that employees of the commercial state-sponsored bodies are excluded.
For a rare statutory example of the use of "public service," see
Ministers and Secretaries (Amendment) Act 1973, ss.1, 3 and 5 (setting
up the Minister for the Public Service and the Public Service Advisory
Council).

[35] This figure includes 5,000 industrial civil servants, most of whom are
craftsmen or general workers employed in the Department of Fisheries
and Forestry or the Office of Public Works. The rules regarding the
employment of these civil servants differ to a considerable extent from
those affecting the non-industrial civil service, for instance, industrial
civil servants are usually in "scheduled" positions (see pp. 52–54) and
thus not recruited by the Civil Service Commissioners. The closest we can
come to a definition of an industrial civil servant is to say that they are
those grades which have been designated as "workers" by the Minister
for the Public Service for the purposes of the Industrial Relations Act
1946 Part VI (which gives the Labour Court power to investigate trade
disputes). See also Industrial Relations Act, 1969, s.17(1) and Public
Service (Transfer of Departmental Administration and Ministerial
Functions) Order (S.I. 1973 No. 294). The remaining parts of the
chapter will deal principally with non-industrial civil servants.

[36] [1958] I.R. 1.

describe the non-combatant service of the East India Company, and was well established in English political language by the middle of the nineteenth century.... In Britain civil servants were servants of the Crown, that is to say, servants of the King in his politic capacity, but not all servants of the Crown were civil servants. Those who used the strong arm—military, naval and police forces—were excluded from the conception, for the service was civil, not combatant; and so also, by tradition, were judges and holders of political offices. Civil servants were paid out of monies voted by parliament and if permanent, had the benefit of the Superannuation Acts. In theory, as servants of the King, they held their positions at pleasure but in practice they were treated as holding during good behaviour.... The bulk of British civil servants working in Ireland, were taken into the service of Saorstat Eireann and the phrase, with the ideas attached to it, was assimilated into Irish political life. Soon it made its appearance in the Irish statute book, and after the passing of our present Constitution, in statutes of the Republic. Borderline cases have been dealt with by special legislation. Persons have been deemed to be civil servants for one purpose and deemed not to be civil servants for another. But, if we substitute 'State' for 'King' the summary which I have already given corresponds to the present conception of civil servants in Ireland."[37]

Partly in the light of this evolution, we can suggest the following guidelines in defining a civil servant. First, civil servants are paid out of monies provided annually, through the Appropriation Act, by the Oireachtas.[38] Secondly, they serve the various organs of state created by the Constitution, including the President, the Dail and Senate, the Attorney-General, the Comptroller and Auditor General, the Taoiseach and the other Ministers who are in charge of departments of State. To this list must be added other offices, like the Ombudsman, which, although established by Act of Parliament,[39] rather than by the Constitution, are plainly constitutional in nature. As might be expected from the term, "servant" the actual incumbents of these offices themselves—for instance, the Ministers or Comptroller and Auditor General are not usually

[37] [1958] I.R. at pp. 14–15.
[38] Civil Service Regulation Act 1956, s.18
[39] Ombudsman Act 1980, s.2.

created civil servants[40] and other political appointees are also excluded from the category of "civil servants." So, too, are those who help to exercise the military, police or judicial function. Although it involves an element of circularity, it should be noted that civil servants are public officials who are subject to the règime (described in subsequent Parts) which is created by the two 1956 Acts. Finally, the Civil Service Regulations Act 1956, s.20 provides that "for the purposes of this Act," the question of whether a person is a civil servant "shall be decided by the Minister [for the Public Service], whose decision shall be final."

A distinction between the civil service of the State and the civil service of the Government was drawn in *McLoughlin* v. *Minister for Social Welfare*. The plaintiff was a temporary assistant solicitor in the Chief State Solicitor's office, which is one of the services assigned to the Attorney-General by the Ninth Part of the Schedule to the Ministers and Secretaries Act 1924. He argued that he was not to be regarded as being employed in the "civil service of the Government" and hence was not an "employed contributor" for the purposes of the Social Welfare Act 1952. The majority of the Supreme Court[41] founded itself on the following high constitutional principle: a civil servant is a servant of the State and the State has many organs, including not only the Government, but also the President, the Oireachtas, the Comptroller and Auditor General and the Attorney-General. It is necessary for the proper functioning of each organ that it should be free and independent of any other organ of the State. Specifically, it is vital for the Attorney-General to be independent of the Government. It follows that the Attorney's staff should not be subject to the instructions of the Government or any of its Ministers and, thus, that they should be classified as civil servants of the State and not of the Government. Following this line of reasoning, the form is now applied, by statute to the staff of other major organs of state including the President, the Oireachtas and the Ombudsman. Not only the Attorney-General, but also the other organs of state, listed earlier need to be independent of the

---

[40] Modern statutes frequently state explicitly that the posts they create are to be civil servants, *e.g.* Law Reform Commission Act, s.10(6)(*b*); Ombudsman Act, s.10(2). The Ministers and Secretaries Act 1924, s.2(2) does not do this but it is clear that the positions which it contemplates meet the tests for a civil servant given in the text.

[41] The dissenting judge, Maguire C.J., relied on a narrower argument, which is peculiar to the Attorney-General (and does not extend to the President etc.), namely, that by the 1924 Act, s.1 the administration of any public services which are not located in any of the other departments of state is vested in the Department of the Taoiseach: see [1958] I.R. at pp. 11–12, 19–20, 23–24.

Government and its Ministers and so it seems that their staff too must be classed as being in the civil service of the State. The term "civil servant of the State" has been applied not only to those who serve bodies established by the Constitution, but also to the servants of certain bodies constituted by statute—such as the Ombudsman—whose functions require them to be independent.[42]

Yet in face of the fundamental principle enunciated by the Supreme Court at a time just before the Civil Service Commissioners Act 1956 and the Civil Service Regulation Act 1956 were enacted, each of these Acts applies a common régime to the civil service of the State and of the Government. The distinction between these two categories has collapsed in that each statute is made to apply to the "civil service" which is defined in the interpretation sections to include both the civil service of the State and of the Government.[43] But this draftsman's legerdemain cannot dissolve a difference of substance which stems from the special position of independence which (in most cases) the Constitution requires the organs of state to possess. Thus a law which does not take account of the need for independence from the Government—for example, the rule that it is the Government which dismisses established civil servants who are servants of the State (but not of the Government) is probably unconstitutional.

5. Appointment and selection

The framework of rules governing the appointment, selection, dismissal and conditions of employment of civil servants is largely statutory. However, by way of warning, in connection with the description which follows, it must be emphasised that there are extra-statutory rules, often contained in circulars, which in practice often make a greater impact than the statutory rule. Decisions regarding the creation of new posts in the civil service, including their numbers and the grade at which they are located, are taken by the Minister for the Public Service.[44]

---

[42] See, *e.g.*, Presidential Establishment Act 1938, s.6; Staff of the Houses of the Oireachtas Act 1959, s.3; Ombudsman Act 1980, s.9(2). The logic of the derivation of the two terms is such that the term "civil service of the State" ought to include both the "civil service of the Government" and the staff working for the Attorney-General, etc. (*cf. Byrne* v. *Ireland* [1972] I.R. 241, 286). In fact, common usage is to treat the two terms as if they were mutually exclusive: See, *e.g.*, Civil Service Commissioners Act 1956, s.2; Civil Service Regulation Act 1956, s.2.

[43] While the acts define the terms slightly differently see Civil Service Commissioners Act, s.3(1) and Civil Service Regulation Act, s.2(1)), which agree on most points.

[44] Civil Service Regulation Act 1956, s.17(1)(*b*).

With the exception of the Secretary, who is appointed by the Government on the recommendation of the Minister responsible for the Department involved,[45] at present all the civil servants in a Department[46] are appointed by the Minister of that Department, though subject to the power of veto of the Minister for the Public Service[47] (which has been waived in the case of higher executive officers and posts at lower levels).[48]

With any post, the important initial question is whether the post is to be "promotional" in the sense that competition for it is to be confined to existing civil servants, either in the Department in which is arises or throughout the entire civil service. Alternatively, the post may be open to all comers. This question is settled by the Minister for the Department involved, in consultation with the Minister for the Public Service; following negotiations with the civil service unions. Where the post is at a basic recruitment grade, competition for it will necessarily be open and, it is important to note, selection will usually be by the Civil Service Commissioners, and when this is so, appointment becomes merely a formal function.[49] For higher posts, subject to the new régime described in part 3, *supra*, the competition will usually, though not

---

[45] Note that most personnel functions in respect of individual civil servants of the State are vested in a Minister. The reason is, perhaps, a desire to retain responsibility and answerability to the Dail for these functions. In any case, the way in which this result has been achieved is to create the position of "appropriate authority" in whom the 1956 Acts vest the powers, for instance, to discipline or to seek an exclusion order in respect of a civil servant. However, the appropriate authority may delegate his powers (*e.g.* to the Attorney-General in respect of the Attorney-General's staff) and such a delegation has usually been made: see Ministers and Secretaries Act 1924, s.2(2); Civil Service Commissioners Act 1956, s.3; Civil Service Regulation Act 1956, s.2; Ombudsman Act 1980, s.10(3).

[46] Civil Service Regulation Act 1956, s.17(1)(*b*); Public Service (Transfer of Departmental Administration and Ministerial Functions) Order 1973 (S.I. 1973 No. 294), art. 4(4).

[47] Ministers and Secretaries Act 1924, s.2(2); Public Service (Transfer of Departmental Administration and Ministerial Functions) Order 1973 (S.I. 1973 No. 294), art. 4(4).

[48] The White Paper proposes (at para. 7.12) that the law should be changed so that Secretaries and other designated officials will have power to appoint staff up to levels prescribed by the Minister in charge of the Department, but, in any case, not above Higher Executive Officer level. However, the White Paper envisages that staff will continue to be selected through normal procedures.

[49] Civil Servants of the State are usually appointed by a Minister: see *e.g.* Civil Service Regulation Act 1956, s.19; Ombudsman Act 1980, s.10(1)(*b*). But *cf.* Staff of the Houses of the Oireachtas Act 1959, s.8.

invariably, be confined either to the particular department or to the entire civil service. In this case, the *modus operandi* for selection is not fixed by statute, but is determined by the Minister in whose Department the vacancy exists, in consultation with his senior officials.[50] He may hold a formal competition of the interview-board type, possibly operated by the Civil Service Commissioners on an agency basis; or he may observe the "seniority rule."[51] Where the outcome of the selection process is a promotion which is not "in the customary course of promotion or transfer," as that course has been decided by the Commissioners, for instance from Assistant Principal to Assistant Secretary (jumping a grade) or Engineer to Assistant Principal (crossing class barriers) the Civil Service Commissioners must be involved because the appointment is subject to the Commissioners certifying that the person selected is qualified as regards knowledge, ability and health for the post.[52]

As already stated, appointment[53] to most basic recruitment posts is a formality since the selection for most of these posts is made by the independent Civil Service Commissioners,[54] first set up in 1923,[55] but presently constituted under the Civil Service Commissioners Act 1956. The object of this system is to prevent jobbery and nepotism. Although the Act purports to state that the Commissioners are dismissible at "the will and pleasure of the Government,"[56] their independence has been consistently respected since the foundation of the state. They have carried their independence to the lengths of (for example) giving the Department involved the name of only the candidate placed first in the competition for a particular post and refusing to disclose whether any other candidates were regarded as qualified for the post (thereby, incidentally, weakening the position of the Department if it comes to any bargaining with the successful candidate over

---

[50] Ministers and Secretaries Act 1924, s.2(2).

[51] Civil Service Commissioners Act 1956, ss.13(1), 14(1).

[52] For an account of a dispute arising from the Minister for the Public Service's decision to appoint a candidate who was fifteenth in order of seniority, see *The Irish Press*, November 10, 1983.

[53] Civil Service Commissioners Act 1956, ss.13(2), 19. Sometimes, even in these circumstances, the Minister for the Public Service may prefer to ask the Commissioners to hold a competition under the Civil Service Commissioners Act 1956, s.29(1)(*b*). Such competitions are often held on a service wide basis for promotion from executive officer to higher executive officer.

[54] Civil Service Commissioners Act 1956, ss.13(2), 14(2), 18, 19 and 20.

[55] Civil Service Regulation Act 1923; Civil Service Regulation Act 1924. See also Fanning, *The Irish Department of Finance 1922–1958* (Dublin, 1978) at pp. 63–72.

[56] Civil Service Commissioners Act 1956, s.10(1).

salary). According to the Act, the Commissioners are appointed by
the Government, but the convention is for the Ceann Comhairle
to be *ex officio* Chairman of the Commissioners and the other two
members to be the Secretary to the Government and an official
from the Department of the Public Service (usually the Director of
Recruitment in the Department). Their staff, who are appointed
by the Minister for the Public Service[57] and who service both the
Civil Service Commissioners and the Local Appointments Commission, presently number about 200.

Subject to the exceptions to be outlined below, all civil servants
must be selected by the Commissioners,[58] and the person whom
they recommend is invariably appointed. Indeed, in practice the
names of persons selected for appointment to the basic general
service grades are not even submitted to the Minister concerned.
In filling an established or an unestablished post, the Commissioners must hold a competition.[59] The competition is governed by
regulations made by the Commissioners (subject to the consent of
the Minister for the Public Service), dealing with such matters as
for example, the qualifications of candidates (*e.g* Irish citizens
only, or certain specified academic qualifications).[60] The Commissioners must make their selection in accordance with the order of
merit, as determined under the regulations, but only from
amongst candidates whom they regard as qualified for appointment.[61]

There are various exceptional initial appointments in which the
Commissioners are not involved. In addition to the appointment
of Secretaries of Departments and promotions in the
customary course already described, these exceptions include,
first, the posts listed in the Schedule to the Civil Service
Commissioners Act, for instance, porters, messengers and clean-
ers.[62] The method of recruitment to such posts is left to the
individual Departments.

Secondly, the Commissioners may, on the request of the
appropriate authority, and with the consent of the Minister for the
Public Service, (assuming that he is not the appropriate authority)

[57] *Ibid.* ss.13(1), 14(1).
[58] It is clear that this must be the position in the case of the Local
Appointments Commission: see Local Authorities (Officers and Servants) Act 1926, s.6(4) and *The State (Minister for Local Government)* v.
Sligo Corporation (1935) 69 I.L.T.R. 72. See also *Local Appointments
1926–1972* (anniversary booklet) at p. 11.
[59] Civil Service Commissioners Act 1956, s.13(1), 14(1).
[60] *Ibid.*, ss.15, 16 and 30. For an example, see *The State (Cussen)* v. *Brennan*
[1981] I.R. 181, on which see p. 305.
[61] Civil Service Commissioners Act 1956, s.17.
[62] *Ibid.*, ss.4.6(2)(*b*) and First Sched.

declare that posts of a specified grade are an "excluded position." In this case too, recruitment is done by the individual Department and is often a patronage appointment. "Excluded position" orders (which are usually only for a limited period) must be publicised by a notice in *Iris Oifigiuil* and can only be made in respect of unestablished positions.[63] The Commissioners will only give their permission if the appropriate authority can make a good case (*e.g.* need for speed in obtaining staff or need to recruit local staff).

Next, a person may be appointed to a particular post (either established or unestablished), without the intervention of the Commissioners, if the appropriate authority with the consent of the Minister for the Public Service recommends the appointment and the Government decides that it would be "in the public interest."[64] Publicity must be given to such unusual appointments in the form of a notice in *Iris Oifigiuil*.[65] This exemption has been used, for instance, in the appointment of persons formerly employed by public bodies which have become defunct, such as the Hospitals Commission. Personal political advisers to a Minister are usually appointed to an unestablished, temporary post for the life of the Government, by an excluding order (described in the previous paragraph). However, in 1979 there were protests when the Government used the public interest exemption to appoint their political advisers as established civil servants.

Fourthly, women in the civil service, who under the pre-1973 rules had been forced to retire on marriage,[66] may, if their husbands die, be readmitted to their old departments or offices by the appropriate authority without undergoing the usual selection process; but subject to the consent of the Minister for the Public Service and subject to the Commissioners certifying that an applicant is qualified as regards knowledge, ability and health.[67]

---

[63] *Ibid.*, ss.5, 6(2)(c). *Cf. The State (Minister for Local Government)* v. *Ennis U.D.C.* [1939] I.R. 258.

[64] Civil Service Commissioners Act 1956, ss.13(3), 14(3). Discontent with the analogous "exceptional" system of promotion in the Garda Siochana (by Garda Siochana (Promotion) Regulations 1960 (S.I. 1960 No. 203), art. 5(2): "Promotion of Guards who have shown special zeal and ability in the performance of their duties notwithstanding that they may not have passed Class 3 promotion examinations or the Irish proficiency test") and its possible abuse is examined in *Aughey* v. *Ireland* [1986] I.L.R.M. 206.

[65] Civil Service Commissioners Act 1956, s.27(1).

[66] Civil Service Regulation Act 1956, s.10. See now Civil Service (Employment of Married Women) Act 1973.

[67] Civil Service Commissioners Act 1956, s.2.

6. Dismissal and discipline

Dismissal

For certain purposes, the régime for the employment of civil servants distinguishes between established and unestablished positions, according to whether the position is one in respect of which a pension may be granted under the Superannuation Act 1834.[68] One context in which this distinction is important is dismissal. Under the Civil Service Regulation Act 1956, s.5, every established civil servant (a category which now catches the bulk of civil servants) "shall hold office at the will and pleasure of the Government." On its own, this would mean that established civil servants could be dismissed for any or no reason and that the procedure followed would be immaterial. The inspiration behind this remarkable provision is the legally insecure position of the British Crown servant.[69] This owes its origin to the exigencies of British history—frequently in the military and/or colonial context—which were thought to require the power of immediate dismissal of a Crown servant unhampered by any fear of legal consequences.[70]

The power to dismiss at pleasure, as contained in section 5, is probably unconstitutional on two counts.[71] First, it violates the civil servant's right to constitutional justice. Secondly, unless the provision were reinterpreted very drastically in the light of the presumption of constitutionality, it would allow dismissal on

[68] Note that as regards pension rights, the Superannuation Acts of 1936, 1942, 1946, 1947 and 1954 have merely incorporated 19th-century British legislation (see Superannuation Act 1834, s.30; Superannuation Act 1859). By virtue of s.2 of the 1859 Act the decision of the Minister for the Public Service as to any claim for a pension "shall be final." See further Emden, *The Civil Servant in the Law and the Constitution* (London, 1923) at pp. 25–31 and Appendix I. There is now also a non-statutory pension scheme for unestablished civil servants.

[69] For a summary of the legal position of the Crown servants in Britain and the Commonwealth, see Marshall, "The Legal relationship between the State and its Servants in the Commonwealth" (1966) 15 I.C.L.Q. 150, and see also *B.B.C.* v. *Johns* [1965] Ch. 32 and *Council of Civil Service Unions* v. *Minister for the Public Service* [1985] A.C. 385. For the wider rule that the executive cannot fetter its discretionary powers, see pp. 225–227.

[70] *Cf. Garvey* v. *Ireland* [1981] I.R. 75 at pp. 95–97, and see pp. 273–277.

[71] See Casey, "Natural and Constitutional Justice: The Policeman's Lot Improved" (1979–80) 2 D.U.L.J.(n.s.) 95 at pp. 99–100. An unestablished civil servant, or an established civil servant in a probationary capacity who has failed to fulfil his conditions of promotion, may be removed by the appropriate authority: Civil Service Regulation Act, 1956, ss.6 and 7.

unreasonable or unconstitutional grounds, for instance, a dismissal which was motivated by religious discrimination.

In fact, such dismissals as do occur are almost certainly within the Constitution. For dismissals only occur on plainly justifiable grounds, often where a crime of dishonesty has either been proved before a court or, at least, is strongly suspected. And as regards procedure, the practice is to inform the civil servant why his dismissal is being contemplated and to allow him an opportunity to put his side of the case to the Government in written form.

In any case, the percentage of established civil servants who have had to be dismissed has always been unnaturally low, by comparison either with employees in the private sector or even with unestablished civil servants. In part, this a consequence of the cumbersome procedure which requires every dismissal to go before the Government. The White Paper proposed, as part of its policy of giving Secretaries greater legal responsibility for the management of their Departments, that subject to an appropriate right of appeal, they should be empowered to dismiss staff up to clerical level.[72]

At present, non-industrial civil servants and established civil servants are excluded from the protection of the Unfair Dismissals Act 1977[73] and the Minimum Notice and Terms of Employment Act 1973,[74] respectively. Moreover, no period of notice is stipulated in a civil servant's terms and conditions of service; in practice, however an *ex gratia* period of two or three weeks is usually allowed. Most civil servants are excluded from the scope of the Redundancy Payments Act 1967.[75] However, all categories of civil servant come within the Anti-Discrimination (Pay) Act 1974, the Employment Equality Act 1977 and the Maternity Protection of Employees Act 1981.

Discipline

Each civil servant's conditions of service provide that "the grant of increments is subject to the Head of Department being satisfied with the officer's service." Thus, the commonest type of discipline—the deferment or withholding of the annual salary increase—is within the competence of the Minister of the particular department. The Civil Service Regulation Act 1956 creates a number of other disciplinary powers. The "suspending

---

[72] The White Paper at para. 7.12.
[73] 1977 Act, s.2(1)(*h*).
[74] 1973 Act, s.3(1)(*c*). The White Paper proposes at (para. 7.2) that the law be changed to give civil servants the benefit of the Minimum Notice and Terms of Employment Act 1973 and the Unfair Dismissals Act 1977.
[75] 1967 Act, s.4(1).

authority"—almost always the Minister for the Department in which the civil servant works—may suspend a civil servant if, for example, "it appears to the suspending authority that the civil servant has been guilty of grave misconduct."[76] The suspension is without pay though in certain circumstances it may be reimbursed.[77] This power is invariably delegated to higher executive officers.[78] The appropriate authority—usually the responsible Minister—is also authorised to make reductions in the pay or grading of civil servants.[79] Finally, a civil servant will not be paid his remuneration for any period of unauthorised absence.[80] Each of these disciplinary powers is now conditioned by procedural rules[81] which amount largely to a detailed specification of how the *audi alteram partem* precept applies in the particular circumstances. However these procedural rules do not apply where, because of the seriousness of the situation, immediate removal from duty is necessary.

7. Terms and conditions of employment[81]

The basic legal provision in this field is section 17 of the Civil Service Regulation Act 1956,[82] which provides as follows:

"(1)   The Minister shall be responsible for the following matters—
  (a) the regulation and control of the Civil Service,
  (b) the classification, re-classification, numbers and remuneration of civil servants,
  (c) the fixing of—

---

[76] Civil Service Regulation Act 1956, ss.3(1), 13. Disciplinary action taken pursuant to this Act probably has a sufficient "public law" character to bring it within the scope of an application for judicial review: see *R.* v. *Home Secretary, ex p. Benwell* [1985] Q.B. 152 and Hogan, "Public Law Remedies and Judicial Review in the Context of Employment Law" (1985) 4 J.I.S.L.L. 19 and see generally at pp. 337–338.

[77] *Ibid.*, s.14.

[78] *Ibid.*, s.3(2). Although where there has been a loss of money, the decision is vested in the first place in the Minister for the Public Service but is usually delegated to the responsible Minister. The White Paper proposes (at para. 7.12) that Secretaries and other nominating officers should be empowered, subject to appropriate appeals procedures, to take disciplinary measures.

[79] *Ibid.*, s.15.

[80] *Ibid.*, s.15(5).

[81] See Department of the Public Service Circular 9/84, which deals with procedures for dealing with grievance, disciplinary and promotion eligibility problems.

[82] This section replaced the Ministers and Secretaries Act 1924, s.2(3).

> (i) the terms and conditions of service of civil servants, and
> (ii) the conditions governing the promotion of civil servants.
>
> (2) The Minister may, for the purpose of subsection (1) of this section, make such arrangements as he thinks fit and may cancel or vary those arrangements."

It is under this provision that the Minister for the Public Service; fixes a civil servant's conditions of employment including such matters as pay-scale; hours of work and holidays; issues personnel circulars altering these conditions; creates new posts; divides civil servants into classes and grades; agreed the Conciliation and Arbitration Scheme; imposed the 1981 embargo on the refilling of every two vacancies in the civil service; and announced its replacement, in 1986, by a more discriminating embargo which depended on the Minister of the Public Service's determination of the staffing needs of each Department.

In Britain,[83] and elsewhere, there has been much debate as to whether a contract of employment exists between a civil servant and the State.[84] This speculation has been prompted, at least partly, by the fact that a civil servant may be dismissed at will. But as the Privy Council has observed "a power to determine a contract at will is not inconsistent with the existence of a contract until it is so determined."[85] In Ireland, there is some authority— admittedly, not conclusive authority—favouring the existence of a contract. First, in the fairly similar situation of the Defence Forces, the Supreme Court has described the relationship between the State and a member of the Defence Forces as a "statutory contract."[86] Again, in *McMahon* v. *Minister for Finance*,[87] Kenny J., without hesitation, characterised the Conciliation and Arbitration Scheme as a contract, and the terms of employment of an individual civil servant looks even more like a typical contract than does the Scheme itself. This question was also at issue in *Inspector of Taxes Association* v. *Minister for the Public Service*,[88] a case which

---

[83] Logan, "A Civil Servant and his Pay" (1945) 61 L.Q.R. 240.
[84] Thus The White Paper proclaims (at p. 63) that civil servants up to and including Clerical Officers will be given "contracts of employment" but it seems that all this means is that the conditions on which they may be dismissed will be amended, by statute, so that these civil servants are no longer dismissible at pleasure.
[85] *Reilly* v. *R.* [1934] A.C. 176 at pp. 179–180.
[86] *The State (Gleeson)* v. *Minister for Defence* [1976] I.R. 280 at p. 296.
[87] High Court, May 3, 1963.
[88] High Court, March 24, 1983. See further p. 321. See also the interlocutory decision, High Court, November 30, 1981.

arose out of the defendant's refusal to recognise the defendant's association for the purposes of the Civil Service Conciliation and Arbitration Scheme. The aspect of the case which is relevant here is that the plaintiffs were confronted with the difficulty that, even assuming that the Scheme was a contract, the plaintiffs were not parties to it, and, consequently, were incapable of asserting any rights which arose under it. However, Murphy J. was prepared to adopt a roundabout way to reach the same result:

> "In my view the only basis on which the plaintiffs could rely upon the [Conciliation and Arbitration] scheme and the contract which constitutes it is on the basis that the members of the plaintiff association are officers or employees of the State whose terms of employment include by implication a provision that each of them shall have the benefit of the contract and scheme in accordance with its terms and provisions. Whilst the facts which would support such an inference were not canvassed in great detail, I would be satisfied to accept for the purposes of this judgment that the plaintiffs, as representing employees of the State, are entitled in contract to have the terms of the scheme implemented by the Minister. . . . It seems to me the high-water mark of the contractual rights of the plaintiff association derived from its members is to have an application made by a staff association fairly considered by the Minister and that being done this bona fide decision to grant or withhold recognition is conclusive."[89]

This admittedly rather tentative analysis depends on the assumption that there is a contract between a civil servant and the state. which creates legally enforceable rights. A significant *caveat* is that on appeal to the Supreme Court,[90] essentially the same conclusion was reached namely that the Minister's decision in regard to grading (on which recognition on the instant case turned) must be fairly and reasonably taken. But this conclusion was grounded on more orthodox public law principles. As well as judicial authority, the Constitution with its preference for individual rights militates in favour of a civil servant enjoying some sort of legal right in respect of his employment.

However, the standard civil service conditions of employment explicitly (and, perhaps, unnecessarily) preserve the power,

[89] High Court, March 2, 1983. The Supreme Court affirmed the judgment of Murphy J. in the High Court. See note 90.

[90] *Inspector of Taxes Association* v. *Minister for Public Service* [1986] I.L.R.M. 296. See further at pp. 321–322.

bestowed on the Minister by the 1956 Act, s.17(2) namely to "cancel or vary [the terms and conditions of service]." Thus, the terms could be altered unilaterally by the Minister (though presumably, not retrospectively, because of the Constitution's protection of property rights) without violating a civil servant's contract of employment. In view of this and (where it still applies) of the power to dismiss at will, a civil servant's contract would seem to be an unusual one, from which not all the normal legal consequences flow. It would seem though, that if, for instance, the State were refusing to pay a civil servant's salary, his claim would sound in contract, rather than on a *quantum meruit* basis.[91]

Structure of the Civil Service classes and grades

There are three broad (non-statutory) divisions among civil servants: the general services; the departmental; and the professional and technical classes.[92] The general service officers perform the general duties of their department from routine clerical operations to the higher advisory or managerial work. They are subdivided into—in ascending order in the pyramid—sub-clerical, clerical, executive and administrative classes.[93] The other two broad divisions are specialists. The members of the departmental classes are recruited with a general educational qualification, but are assigned to work peculiar to a Department in which they specialise, *e.g.* the Taxes Classes in the Office of the Revenue Commissioners or the Social Welfare Inspectorate in the Department of Social Welfare. In contrast, the members of the professional and technical classes specialise in work which is performed outside, as well as within, government service, for example engineers or electricians.

---

[91] *McMahon* v. *Minister for Finance*, High Court, May 2, 1963. See further pp. 63–64.

[92] Devlin Report, paras. 7.3.1–7.8.5. Dooney, *The Irish Civil Service* (Dublin, 1976) Chap. 3 and pp. 147–152.

[93] The grades within the administrative classes are as follows: Secretary, Deputy Secretary, Assistant Secretary; Principal; Assistant Principal; Administrative Officer (Higher Executive Officer). A.O. and H.E.O. are equivalent grades; the difference is that A.O.s enter straight from university; whereas the H.E.O. is a promotional post.

Within these broad groupings, there are divisions into grades.[94]
The significance of this administrative classification is that
positions in the same grade share the same type of qualification,
work and conditions, including a common pay scale; progress
from one point on the scale to the next is usually automatic. Thus,
grading effects not only pay and the other conditions of work, but
also career prospects. Throughout the civil service there are about
700 different grades[95]: proliferation is assisted by the fact that
equivalent grades in different departments usually bear different
titles.[96] The question of grading was at the centre of *Inspector of
Taxes Association* v. *Minister for the Public Service*[97] which took the
form of a claim by the plaintiff association that the Minister's
refusal to recognise it for the purposes of the Conciliation and
Arbitration Scheme on the sole ground that the Inspectors of
Taxes (Technical) were not a separate grade was invalid. To
appreciate this claim, it is necessary to recall that in 1960, the
PAYE system of income tax collection, which had formerly been
confined to the public sector, was extended to cover all employees.
One consequence of this was the creation of a new post of
Inspector of Taxes, holders of which were recruited from persons
in the tax clerical grades; they possessed no technical qualifica-
tions; were not granted a commission by the Minister; and were
designated "Clerical Inspector" as distinct from the traditional
Inspector of Taxes (which then became known as "Technical
Inspector").

The occasion for the case, in 1983, was that proposals were
being prepared which would fundamentally alter the entire career
structure open to Inspectors of Taxes. Accordingly, the plaintiff
association, which had been formed in 1980 to represent only
Technical Inspectors, wrote to the Minister for the Public Service

[94] And also, less significantly, into classes. In the original conception, as it
operated in the Irish Free State and earlier, a class meant a grouping of
grades engaged on a particular type of work within which an officer
would expect to make his civil service career, entering at the bottom
and working up towards the top. But his final grade was normally
dependent on the grade at which he entered and thus on his
educational qualifications at that time. However, for the past 30 years
or so, this strict concept of class has been modified so that promotion
between classes is fairly common.
[95] " . . . Fewer than 200 grades account for two-thirds of staff. At the
higher levels, there are many single person grades with identical or
similar pay scales. This pattern will be progressively simplified but it is
recognised that this will take some time.": The White Paper at
para. 4.10.
[96] See *e.g.* Prl. 2674 (1972).
[97] [1986] I.L.R.M. 296 (S.C.); High Court, March 24, 1983.

requesting recognition for the purposes of the Conciliation and Arbitration scheme. The Minister rejected the plaintiff's application for recognition because it was established administrative policy (the propriety of which was not challenged) to confine recognition to only one association in respect of each grade and the constitution of the plaintiff association excluded Clerical Inspectors of Taxes from its membership.

Thus the case came down to the issue of whether the Technical Inspectors and the Clerical Inspectors constituted separate grades, even though the Minister had taken a decision not to create separate grades. According to Finlay C.J.:

> "It would be quite inconsistent with the responsibilities thus placed by [the Civil Service Regulation Act 1956, s.17] on the Minister, of his overall power to run and regulate the civil service within the terms of that section were subject to concepts of grading arising from a legal definition of what constituted a grade capable of being imposed upon him by the decision of a Court. In so far, therefore, as the plaintiff's claim in this case consisted of an assertion that a grading of Inspector of Taxes (Technical) had spontaneously occurred as a result of the development of the work of the Revenue Commissioners between 1960 and 1980 and without a decision made by the Minister under section 17, I would affirm the dismissal of that portion of the claim."

The Chief Justice went on to hold, however, that the Minister's decision whether to create a new grade was, like any other administrative action, subject to judicial review. But, on the facts of the case, he found against the plaintiff:

> "It could not be said that the differences established between the work-load, responsibility, qualifications and training of Inspectors of Taxes (Technical) and Inspectors of Taxes (Non-Technical) were such that having regard to other considerations it was not open to the Minister to decide to leave both of these categories of Inspectors of Taxes in the same grade."[98]

Conciliation and Arbitration Schemes

Notwithstanding the wide discretionary powers conferred upon

---

[98] [1986] I.L.R.M. at p. 303. For the decision that there is no rank of detective garda in the Garda Siochana, where the ranks are determined by statutory instrument (Garda Siochana (Promotion) Regulations (S.I. 1960 No. 203)) made by the Government under the Garda Siochana Act 1924, see *Aughey* v. *Ireland* [1986] I.L.R.M. 206, citing Murphy J.'s judgment in the High Court in *Inspector of Taxes* case.

the Minister for the Public Service by the 1956 Act, s.17, these
powers are not usually exercised in regard to conditions of service,
including pay. In the first place, any increases made under any
National Wage Agreement are granted automatically. Secondly, in
the case of the higher civil servants—the 150 or so secretaries,
deputy-secretaries and assistant-secretaries and their equivalent in
the professional classes—the Minister has always accepted the
recommendations of the "Review Body on Higher Remuneration
in the Public Sector." This body was first established in 1972,
under the chairmanship of Mr. Liam St. John Devlin, as a standing
body to advise the Government on the level of pay for civil
servants and local authority officers outside the scope of conciliation and arbitration schemes as well as the chief executives of
state-sponsored bodies and the judiciary.

In the case of the great majority of the civil service, pay
increases are determined by negotiation within the framework of
the Conciliation and Arbitration Schemes. Up until 1983, principals and assistant principals were included among the so-called
"Devlin Grades" but now they have their own Conciliation and
Arbitration Scheme which is modelled on the older-established
scheme which serves all non-industrial civil servants at the level of
higher executive officer or below.[99] This scheme constitutes first, a
General Council which deals with problems which are not peculiar
to any one Department, (often claims from grades which are
common to more than one Department), and, secondly, Departmental Councils to deal with matters which are relevant only to a
particular Department, for example, claims by departmental
classes like the building inspectors in the Department of the
Environment. The official representatives on either type of
council consist of no more than six (on the General Council) or
four (on a departmental council) members nominated by the
Minister for the Public Service, almost always from among his
officers. On the other side are an equal number of staff
representatives, drawn from the various staff associations which
have been recognised by the Minister. In practice, if the official
side agrees with the staff side, at either of the two types of council,
it does so because the terms of the agreement are acceptable to the
Minister. Thus, it will invariably happen that if there is an agreed
recommendation to the Minister for Public Service it will be
accepted. Alternatively, where the two sides disagree, the Minister's response to the report will not be favourable to the staff side

[99] The first scheme was established in 1950. The present Scheme,
established in 1955 and revised in 1976 is an appendix to Department
of the Public Service Circular 6/76; for a summary of it see Dooney, *op.
cit.* App. 7.

and, in this case, the staff representatives have the right to refer the matter to arbitration provided that it is an arbitrable claim, a category which includes for instance pay and allowances, but excludes re-grading or productivity claims[1]: the borderline excludes matters of policy but includes issues such as pay which, it is assumed, can be resolved by reference to comparable terms outside the service.

The Arbitration Board is a standing body with a chairman (usually a lawyer) chosen by the Minister for the Public Service. In addition, each side chooses two members.[2]

There may also be one workers' member and one employers' member, of the Labour Court, nominated by the Chairman of the Court. The Board's report, which does not have to be unanimous, is sent to the Minister. If the Government wishes to reject or modify a recommendation from the Board, then it may only do so by securing the passage of a Dail motion to this effect.[3]

Legal status of the Scheme

The legal status of the Scheme was examined in *McMahon* v. *Minister for Finance*,[4] a case brought by a dissident member of the staff side. It was held that there were three irregularities in connection with a General Council meeting and thus a declaration was granted that the meeting was invalid.[5] As a consequence, there could be no valid report from the meeting and, since a report is an essential preliminary to arbitration, the arbitration could not proceed.

The significant part of Kenny J.'s judgment is his finding that

[1] The Scheme excludes individual cases which are dealt with according to procedures laid down in Department of Public Services Circular 9, 1984 ("Procedures for dealing with grievance, disciplinary and promotion eligibility problems.")

[2] Recognition will not be accorded to any association which is affiliated to any political organisation unless the affiliation subsisted prior to 1949. (This restriction is a device to include the Post Office Workers' Union, which was introduced at a time when William Norton, formerly Secretary General of the P.O.W.U., was a member of the Government).

[3] Such a motion has only been passed once, in 1953. However a motion to this effect was passed, in 1986, under a similar Conciliation and Arbitration Scheme for teachers: see Vol. 363, *Dail Debates*, cols. 1839–2005 (February 6, 1986).

[4] High Court, May 13, 1963.

[5] The Scheme had been violated in that (1) the chairman of the staff panel had been regarded as *ex officio* principal staff representative on the General Council; (ii) one of the staff representatives who was absent from the Council meeting, had been represented by a substitute, (iii) a person had been wrongfully barred from standing for election as a staff representative.

the Scheme amounted to a contract between the Minister for Finance and the staff associations. The judge said:

> "Throughout the case the plaintiffs' counsel have referred to it as a 'statutory scheme' with the implication that it has been confirmed by statute or that it has in some undefined way the force of statute. Section 17 of the Civil Service Regulations Act 1956, seems to me to be intended to give the Minister for the Public Service power to make schemes or contracts for the regulation of civil service pay: it is a section which enables the Minister to make schemes or contracts (I think that this is what 'arrangement' means) but it does not follow that an arrangement made by the Minister is 'a statutory scheme' or 'a statutory arrangement.' The scheme is a contract and nothing more."

Together with this passage, we must bear in mind that the 1956 Act, s.17(2) explicitly authorises the Minister to "cancel or vary those arrangements" which may be taken to mean, *inter alia*, that the Minister may abrogate the Scheme unilaterally.[6] Furthermore, Article 2 of the Scheme itself states (possibly *ex abundante cautela*):

> "The existence of this scheme does not imply that the Government have surrendered or can surrender their liberty of action in the exercise of their constitutional authority and the discharge of their responsibilities in the public interest."

Bearing all this in mind, the following propositions may be tentatively suggested:

(i) The Minister is free to revoke the Scheme,
(ii) He is also free not to use it, though in fact, for political reasons, most "conciliable" matters are negotiated through the Scheme;
(iii) However once a matter has been entrusted to the machinery created by the Scheme, it must be pursued to its conclusion, following the procedure laid down in the Scheme (a point illustrated by the *McMahon* case) and including, if necessary, a Dail vote.

Politics
Finally, two aspects of a civil servant's terms of employment

---

[6] Quoted in full *supra*. The important part for the purposes of this judgment is s.17(2) by which "The Minister may for the purpose of subsection 1 of this section, make such arrangements as he thinks fit and may cancel or vary those arrangements."

which have wider constitutional implications may be mentioned.[7] Essentially, there is a complete embargo on political activity. According to Department of Finance Circular 21/32 which is still in force:

"The Minister is aware that it is the view of the Civil Service itself that the action of an official who identifies himself actively or publicly with political matters is indefensible, and that such conduct is detrimental to the interests of the Service as a whole. The nature and conditions of a Civil Servant's employment should, of themselves, suggest to him that he must maintain a reserve in political matters, and not put himself forward on one side or another and, further, that he should be careful to do nothing that would give colour to any suggestion that his official actions are in any way influenced or capable of being influenced, by party motives. That is the attitude which the Minister, while not wishing in any way to interfere with or influence political views privately held, expects Civil Servants at all times to observe. Should any departures from official impartiality occur it will be followed by disciplinary action. If the Head of Department (after such consultation as he may think fit with his Minister) takes the view that the official has overstepped the bounds of propriety, he should send for him, point out to him the gravity of his fault, and obtain from him an undertaking that there will be no recurrence of similar impropriety in the future. If more severe action is called for, its severity will be related to the time and place, the standing of the official concerned, and the degree of publicity, but the Minister will look to Heads of Departments to ensure that, where punishment is deserved, it will follow.

While the Minister appreciates that it would not be feasible to anticipate every occasion of the kind in question that might arise for consideration, he desires to lay down specific directions on the following points, namely,

(1) An official shall not be a member of an Association or serve on a Committee having for its object the promotion of the interests of a political party or the promotion or prevention of the return of a particular candidate to the Dail.

---

[7] Note also the Prevention of Corruption Acts 1889–1916, as adapted by Adaption Order No. 37 of 1928 which deals with corruption among civil servants; and Department of Finance Circulars 50/1929 and 16/1936 on outside employment and conflict of interest.

(2) An official shall not support or oppose any particular candidate or party either by public statement or writing.

(3) An official shall not make any verbal statements in public (or which are liable to be published), and shall not contribute to newspapers or other publications any letters or articles, conveying information, comment or criticism on any matter of current political interest, or which concerns the political action or position of the Government or of any member or group of members of the Oireachtas.''

Since 1974, this ban has been modified, but only in its application to industrial civil servants and (subject to a proviso that officers engaged in a particular category of work may be excluded from this freedom) clerical workers.[8] Civil servants in these groups may engage in political activity, including standing for election to local authorities, but may not stand as candidates for either House of the Oireachtas.

There are, however, more insidious ways in which the impartiality of the civil service may be eroded and, in 1982, various practices gave rise to protests from, *inter alia*, the Association of Higher Civil Servants.[9] First, there had been an increase in the size of "private offices," *i.e.* offices within a Department, which may be staffed by as many as twenty civil servants under a higher executive officer and which assist the Minister in dealing with a range of constituency and party political activities, including obtaining a health card for one constituent, sending circulars to all of a Minister's constituents; or helping to organise the Minister's local party branch. Sometimes this involves civil servants in working in the constituencies of members of the Government. This development carries obvious dangers that the civil servants involved will become, or will be regarded as being, politicised. Connected with this is the older problem of the extent to which civil servants should prepare material for ministerial speeches to party meetings. The conventional rule is that when civil servants are asked to provide such material, they should ensure that it is balanced and objective. The present Government has met such criticisms by agreeing that this range of functions should be performed by a restricted number of temporary civil servants, appointed on a contract basis, for the life of the Government. This approach,

---

[8] Department of the Public Service Circular No. 22 of 1974: see statement made by the Minister for the Public Service on March 6, 1974 (reproduced by Dooney, *op. cit.* Appendix 8) See also Department of Finance Circulars Nos. 23/1925 and 20/1934.

[9] See Association of Higher Civil Servants, *Discussion Paper on Civil Servants and Politics* (April 1983).

which may be the lesser of two evils, has, however, also been criticised by the Association of Higher Civil Servants, on the grounds that it may injure civil service structures and morale.

Confidentiality

It has been suggested that ministerial confidentiality is one of the causes of our secretive system of government.[10] In any event, for whatever reason of constitutional system or inherited political culture, it is clear from paragraph 3 of the Circular quoted *supra* that civil servants are barred from publishing material on public affairs or appearing on radio or television, without permission "and in practice have found it quite hard to get this permission even for innocuous material."[11] This state of affairs may be inevitable but one consequence of it is to further reduce the sluggish flow of expert information available to the general public and to keep the level of public debate low.

On the plane of criminal law, the most stringent provision is section 4(1) of the Official Secrets Act 1963, which forbids any person to communicate:

> "[A]ny official information to any other person unless he is duly authorised to do so or does so in the course of and in accordance with his duties as the holder of a public office or when it is his duty in the interests of the State to communicate it."[12]

The remarkably wide sweep of this provision arises from the definition of "official information" as, *inter alia*, "any . . . information which is secret or confidential or is expressed to be either. . . . " In the light of the reasoning used in *Maher* v. *Attorney-General*,[13] it is probable that the extension of the definition to catch information which is "expressed to be either . . . " is unconstitutional. The phrase "duly authorised" in section 4(1) is amplified in a later subsection, which provides that a person may

---

[10] P. Cook, "Why we need open government in Ireland" (1984) 5 *Seirbhis Phoibli* 23 at p. 25. "[A] small nation with a written constitution and a neutral standing in international affairs has virtually the same draconic powers of Government Secrecy as [Britain] a front-line NATO state with no written constitution."

[11] Chubb, *The Government and Politics of Ireland* (Stanford, 1982) at p. 326.

[12] There has only been one prosecution for breach of the 1963 Act but that prosecution (which was brought against *The Irish Independent* in 1984) concerned Pt. III, which creates the more serious type of offence involving the safety of the State. The only case involving the precursor Official Secrets Acts 1911–1920 was brought in 1933 and resulted in an acquittal.

[13] *Maher* v. *Att.-General.* [1973] I.R. 140.

be authorised to disclose information by a Minister or State authority. It is also an offence to obtain official information where a person is aware or has reasonable grounds to believe that the communication of the information to him would contravene section 4(1).[14] Each of these offences normally carries a maximum penalty of six months' imprisonment and/or £100 fine, on summary conviction.[15]

[14] 1963 Act, s.4(3).
[15] *Ibid.*, s.13.

4 State-Sponsored Bodies[1]

1. Introduction

The principal objective of the Ministers and Secretaries Act 1924 was, as has been seen, to provide that all the central, executive power of the state should flow through Ministers responsible to the Dail. However, by 1927, the first four state-sponsored bodies had been established. The functions of these four give some idea of the work of the state-sponsored sector: the Electricity Supply Board was set up to provide public financing of a huge investment project which it was believed could not be privately financed; the Agricultural Credit Corporation was constituted to make loans to farmers and to promote the co-operative movement; the Dairy Disposal Co. Ltd. was set up to acquire, and thus prevent a foreign take-over of, Newmarket Creameries; the purpose of the Medical Registration Council—whose functions were passed on to the newly-constituted Medical Council in 1978—was to regulate the practice of medicine in the state.

In 1961, there were over fifty state-sponsored bodies. By 1986, on one count[2] the figure was about 100, the increase being largely

---

[1] See Chubb, *The Government and Politics of Ireland* (London, 1982) Chap. 14; Chubb, *A Source Book of Irish Government* (Dublin, 1963) Chap. 10; Fitzgerald, *State-Sponsored Bodies* (Dublin, 1963).

[2] For the list, see *Dail Debates* Vol. 311, cols. 868–886 (February 8, 1979). Notice, however that the parliamentary question to which this list (together with informative comments) was the answer, defined "state-sponsored body" in fairly expansive terms but the Public Expenditure Division of the Department of Finance, which operates a general over-view of the entire state-sponsored body sector regarded there as being (in 1985) only 65 bodies. The reason for this discrepancy is the

due to the proliferation of non-commercial bodies. The total number employed in the entire sector was just below 90,000 (or 8 per cent. of the total work-force). The sector accounted for 6 per cent. of gross national product and consumed one-half of the state's annual investment programme.

By way of introduction, it ought to be stressed that our concern is with the structure of state bodies and their relationship with the Government, rather than their performance, which is a matter of economics and public administration.

Meaning of "state-sponsored body"

There is no statutory definition of a state-sponsored body[3] for the reason that the term is seldom used in statute law, which almost always directs itself to a specific body as opposed to the entire sector. Yet although there is a variation from one body to another, (so that propositions in this field are inevitably generalisations) the term is useful for descriptive purposes because these bodies do raise common problems of accountability, patronage, staffing, control, organisation and legal status. Broadly speaking, the term "state-sponsored body" denotes an authority which discharges specialised, executive, central functions yet which is set at a distance from the Government and Ministers. This last point is the central feature in the concept of the state-sponsored body. For, on the one hand, these agencies exercising public functions are owned by the state and rely, in the case of non-commercial bodies, substantially on state finance; and are controlled by boards whose members are selected by the Government or a Minister. But, on the other hand, they are subject to a lesser degree of

considerable tolerance in the definition of a state-sponsored body (see pp. 70–71). In particular, the Department requires that to qualify as a state-sponsored body, all or almost all members of the board should be appointed by a Minister and (in the case of a non-commercial body) the bulk of the funds should emanate from the Government; also the Department's definition excludes advisory agencies.

[3] But see Ministers and Secretaries (Amendment) Act 1973, s.1 (which speaks of "such bodies established by or under statute and financed wholly or partly by means of grants or loans made by a Minister of State or the issue of shares taken up by a Minister of State as may stand designated for the time being by regulations made by the Minister [for the Public Service]." By 1986, no such regulations had been made. See also Ryan, "The Role of the State-Sponsored Body in the new Public Service" (1973) 21 *Administration* 387 at p. 397.

control by the responsible Minister and the Dail than would apply to the activities of a department of state. As was said by the Minister when piloting the Bill to constitute the ESB through the Dail:

" ... [T]here are going to be no Parliamentary questions with regard to this Board. There are going to be no complaints from a Deputy that his area is not served at such a rate as some other Deputy ... this Board is not going to be regarded as a machine for wiping off all political obligations of this, that and the other Deputy."[4]

In addition, a state-sponsored body is usually constituted by its own distinctive statute and its staff are not civil servants.[5] Finally as stated already, a state-sponsored body administers a specialised, executive, central function. Thus, local or regional bodies—such as health boards or harbour boards are usually excluded. Again the epithet "executive"—deliberately a rather vague term—alludes to the fact that it is also conventional to exclude quasi-judicial bodies as well as advisory bodies (*e.g.* the Public Service Advisory Council) which are in any case usually staffed by civil servants. What is more significant is that the three traditional specialist services of education,[6] police and defence are not regarded as being part of the state-sponsored body sector.

Commissions

There are, however, other functions in regard to which it is desirable that a settled policy should be followed under the direction of an independent agency, which is free of suspicions of political favour yet which is not a state-sponsored body. Such is the explanation for the existence of the Irish Land Commission (1881); Revenue Commissioners (1923); Civil Service Commission (1924)[7] and the Local Appointments Commission (1926). These

[4] *Dail Debates*, Vol. 18, col. 1919 (March 15, 1927).
[5] Another troublesome term, examined at pp. 46–48.
[6] In the case of the Universities, see also the Ministers and Secretaries Act 1924, s.9(4).
[7] "The fact that the Civil Service Commissioners hold office at the pleasure of the Executive Council would appear ... unsatisfactory in view of the statutory intention that they should exercise a more or less judicial independence in certain matters ... [we] hope that the steady

bodies are not state bodies because their staff are civil servants of the Government; because they are not constituted as independent legal entities ("corporations sole"); and because, historically, apart from the Local Appointments Commission, they were set up before the earliest state-sponsored bodies. However, it is more important that they do enjoy the same kind of arms-length relationship with the responsible Minister. This has been achieved by vesting their functions in statutory commissioners which are free of interference in day-to-day matters, largely as a result of convention, supported by such devices as a separate vote. Since these bodies have so much in common with state-sponsored bodies it may be instructive to examine the structure of one of them briefly.

The Revenue Commissioners were constituted in 1923 to take over the functions of tax-assessment and collection formerly exercised by the British Commissioners of Inland Revenue and the British Commissioners of Customs and Excise. The three Revenue Commissioners are appointed for an indefinite term, at the pleasure of the Taoiseach, from among the existing officials of the Commissioners.[8] Finance Acts traditionally embody a provision to the effect that all taxes or duties imposed or continued by the Act "are hereby placed under the care and management of the Revenue Commissioners." It is true that the Revenue Commissioners Order of 1923 requires the Commissioners to obey any instructions which may be issued to them by the Minister for Finance. However, this provision has been substantially glossed by a convention which has frequently been enunciated by Ministers, for instance in reply to deputies' questions in the Dail. One of its earliest formulations (in 1923) is contained in a letter sent, on the

development of a sound practice over a considerable number of years will eventually prove a better safeguard than might be afforded by some other system of a more logical character" (*Commission of Inquiry into the Civil Service 1932–35*, Vol. 1, p. 82).

[8] Revenue Commissioners Order of 1923 made under Adaptation of Enactments Act 1922, s.7. Read literally the Ministers and Secretaries Act 1924, s.1(ii) (" . . . The Department of Finance which shall comprise . . . the collection . . . of the revenues of [the State] . . . ") and Schedule, First Part could be taken to mean that the Department of Finance had swallowed the Revenue Commissioners, but this result was not intended: see *Re Irish Insurance Association Ltd.* [1955] I.R. 176 at pp. 182–183. Sean Reamon, *History of the Revenue Commissioners* (Dublin, 1981) Chap. 5.

Minister's behalf, to the Commissioners' first chairman from which the following is an extract:

" . . . [W]hile the Revenue Commissioners will be responsible directly to the Minister for Finance for the administration of the Revenue Services, the Commissioners will act independently of Ministerial control in exercising the statutory powers vested in them in regard to the liability to tax of the individual taxpayer."[9]

Plainly, a well understood convention to this effect is helpful to Ministers and deputies in warding off importuning taxpayers.

Inevitably, some taxpayers will be dissatisfied with the decisions of the Commissioners' staff and these disputes are the responsibility of the tribunal known as the Appeal Commissioners appointed by the Minister for Finance, one Commissioner from among the senior staff of the Revenue Commissioners and the other from the Bar. Their jurisdiction covers income taxes but not Customs and Excise.[10]

A note on legal status

State-sponsored bodies are generally subject to the ordinary law, for example, as to torts or tax, save where they enjoy some specific statutory exemption. Yet there are a number of contexts in which the status of a body or, more precisely, its degree of independence of the central executive organ, is significant. The first context stems from the international law precept, followed by most national courts, that "foreign states" are exempt from their jurisdiction. Thus, in *Gibbons* v. *Udaras na Gaeltachta*,[11] the question arose before the New York Courts as to whether the semi-state promotional agency fell within the ambit of this immunity[12], in the context of an action for breach of contract and fraudulent misrepresentation allegedly arising from a joint venture agreement partially concluded in New York. The court rejected the agency's claim for sovereign immunity, emphasising its view of the Udaras operation as being "no different . . . from the promotional activities engaged in by a private public relations firm."

---

[9] The letter is quoted in Reamon, *op. cit.*, at pp. 56–61 where other evidence for the convention is given.

[10] Income Tax Act 1967, s.156(1); Finance (Miscellaneous Provisions) Act 1968, s.1(1).

[11] 549 F. Supp. 1094 (S.D.N.Y. 1982). An identical conclusion as to the agency's immunity was reached in *Gilson* v. *The Republic of Ireland* 682 F. 2 d. 1022 (D.C. Cir 1982).

[12] As facilitated by s.1605 of the U.S. Foreign Sovereign Immunities Act.

Secondly, a state-sponsored body might claim that it fell within the rule that "the State" is not bound by a statute unless the contrary is indicated in the statute.[13] Thirdly, by the Prevention of Corruption Act 1906—which is still law in Ireland—it is an offence for an employee of a "public body" to corruptly accept a gift as an inducement to show favour to persons doing business with the body. In *R. v. Manners*,[14] the House of Lords held that the North Thames Gas Board came within the definition of a "public body" for the purposes of the 1906 Act. A similar question could arise in an Irish court in a case in which the employee of a state-sponsored body was being prosecuted for the same offence.

Such questions, each of which requires a slightly different categorisation, have generated a certain amount of case law, in Britain and elsewhere in the common law world[15] but not in Ireland. However, the principle is not in doubt. As was said by Kingsmill Moore J. in regard to an analagous issue (involving the Commissioners of Public Works, rather than a state-sponsored body):

> "The degree of direction and control which is exercised by the executive over the conduct of the work may afford an indication as to whether the Commissioners in executing the work are acting as servants of the State."[16]

This is, of course, a very imprecise guideline. However, it seems likely, both from the persuasive authority of English case law and from the Irish courts' disapproval of special privileges[17] that a state-sponsored body would be regarded as sufficiently indepen-

[13] See pp. 397–401.
[14] [1978] A.C. 43.
[15] Foulkes, *Administrative Law* (London, 1982) at pp. 12–17; Hogg, *Liability of the Crown* (Melbourne, 1971), Chap. 8.
[16] *Re Irish Employers' Mutual Insurance Association Ltd.* [1955] I.R. 176 the facts were that the Commissioners of Public Works had taken out insurance with a company, which subsequently went into liquidation. The Commissioners claimed that the monies due to them from the company should, as a matter of prerogative right, be paid in priority to the debts due to other creditors. For present purposes, the relevant question was whether assuming that this prerogative existed, the Commissioners would be characterised as sufficiently part of the State to be able to invoke it. It was held that, in general, the Commissioners were to be regarded as servants of the State. However, where the Commissioners were performing work on behalf of local authorities, then they were not acting as servants of the State. See also *Re Maloney* [1926] I.R. 202 at p. 206, *Irish Land Commission* v. *Ruane* [1938] I.R. 148 at pp. 152–157, 161 (Irish Land Commission characterised as a servant of the State).
[17] See, *e.g.* pp. 391–392.

dent of "the State" to be bound by statutes.[18] On the other hand, it may well be that the term "public body" used in the Prevention of Corruption Act 1906, is ample enough to catch a state-sponsored body.

Other state involvement in the economy

State-sponsored agencies are comparatively straightforward in that they are bodies which, subject to some exceptions, are under the exclusive and visible control and ownership, of the state. If we range even further away from the traditional arrangement of public functions being discharged by a department of state with a Minister at the head, we encounter manifold and subtle (even subterranean) forms of state interference in the economy. One significant example is the state's capacity to make contracts, a phenomenon which was sketched briefly by the then Minister for the Public Service in the following passage:

> "Where in the past a civil service of limited size carried out the administrative functions of the state, today the range of instruments required by government for the achievement of its objectives goes well beyond the traditional concept of the organs of the state. At its extreme, this tendency has gone farthest in the United States where the phenomenon is common of the large private sector corporation almost entirely dependent on public contracts and producing almost exclusively for government. The development of bodies of this type side by side with the more familiar agencies of government has led to questioning in some countries of the traditional institutional arrangements of the performance of the executive functions of government. It has produced the concept of the 'contract state' where executive functions are performed by a range of bodies included in the broad category of 'quasi non-governmental institutions' with an emphasis on the contractual rather than the structural relationships between government and these bodies.
>
> It would be interesting to analyse the instruments through which the purposes of government are achieved in this country and to ascertain the extent, if any, to which there has been a move towards performance by contract rather than by traditional agencies. . . . I don't think there has been any large scale move in this direction, but I think that the idea of a

---

[18] Note that "State authority" is defined for the purposes of the Postal and Telecommunications Services Act 1983, s.1 (10(1)) to include only Ministers of the Government, Commissioners of Public Works and the Irish Land Commission.

contractual relationship between government and its traditional agencies is emerging behind some of the thinking
here in recent years. What is valuable about this thinking is
that it concentrates attention on the problem of what
government can and should do directly and what it can and
should have undertaken for it by other means."[19]

Other examples of the state spreading its tentacles through the
economy by means other than complete ownership include: wage-
control through the (extra-statutory) annual National Wage
Agreements[20]; statutory control over prices for various goods and
services under the Prices Acts 1958–1972[21]; informal attempts by
the Minister for the Environment to influence building society
interest rates; a complex of industrial grants and subsidies to set
beside the system of taxes[22]; joint ventures between state bodies
and other (often foreign) business organisations; and state
shareholding in private companies, either directly through the
Minister for Finance or by way of a state-sponsored body, like the
Industrial Development Association or Foir Teo.[23]

---

[19] Ryan: "The Role of the State-Sponsored Body in the New Public
Service" (1973) 21 *Administration* 387–388. At present, so far as state
contracts are centrally regulated at all, it is by way of the Government
Contracts Committee which is chaired by an assistant secretary from the
Public Expenditure Division of the Department of Finance. The other
members include civil servants, usually at principal officer level, from
the Departments of Defence and of Industry, Transport, Commerce
and Tourism and from the Office of the Board of Works and the
Stationery Office. The Committee administers a non-statutory code of
rules, first established in the 1920s and deriving their authority from
the Minister for Finance's statutory duties in regard to "the supervision
and control of all purchases made for or on behalf of, and all supplies
of commodities and goods held by any Department of State and the
disposal thereof . . . " (Ministers and Secretaries Act 1924, s.1(ii)). The
rules require the Committee's permission for any purchase above a
certain value if a department wishes to buy from a purchaser other than
the lowest tenderer. In the case of contracts worth more than £20,000
the supplier must also be able to provide a certificate that he is up to
date with his tax payments. In addition, the rules lay down detailed
instructions regarding tendering, including time-limits, advertisements,
opening the tenders, etc.
[20] For a case arising from statutory wage control, see *Burke* v. *Minister for
Labour* [1979] I.R. 354.
[21] See, *e.g.*, *Cassidy* v. *Minister for Industry* [1978] I.R. 197.
[22] See McMahon, *Economic Law in Ireland* (Brussels, 1977) at Chap. 3 and
generally.
[23] Notice also that in 1925 the Abbey Theatre became the first state-
subsidised theatre in the English speaking world: Drabble, *The Oxford
Companion to English Literature* (Oxford, 1984) at p. 1.

It would be beyond our brief to do more than allude to the novel questions of control, responsibility, consistency and adequate public debate raised by arrangements like these.

2. Functional classification

Commercial and non-commercial state-sponsored bodies
Commercial state-sponsored bodies, known in other countries as "public enterprises," are under a theoretical duty to make sufficient profit to cover capital expenditure and, in practice, they receive at least a substantial portion of their revenue from the sale of their products or services. By contrast, non-commercial bodies are agencies for the disbursement of state funds, which are given to them as grants-in-aid which appear as sub-heads of their parent Department's Estimates. These funds may only be released with the permission of the Minister for Finance and the responsible Minister. Stemming from this difference, the Government has a much closer control over the salaries, and numbers, of persons employed in the case of a non-commercial, agency. For example, non-commercial state-sponsored bodies must make quarterly returns to the parent department supplying this information. In addition, they were subject to the one-in-three embargo on the filling of vacancies within the public service, introduced in 1981.

With commercial state-sponsored bodies, control is slightly less tight. There is no direct control over numbers of staff. However, as part of the policy that there should be a co-ordinated approach to pay in the entire public sector, all state-sponsored bodies are subject to central control over wages, including National Wage Agreements. There is, however, no statutory basis for this particular control save in some of the statutes enacted since the late sixties. Accordingly the White Paper on the Public Service proposes to extend this statutory control to all commercial bodies.[24]

Commercial state-sponsored bodies
Although there are only twenty-odd commercial bodies (about a quarter of the total), they employ approximately 80,000 people (as against nearly 10,000 in the non-commercial sector). Their birth-rate has fluctuated, being particularly high at times of economic change. Thus, most of the commercial bodies were established

---

[24] *Serving the Country Better* (1985) (Pl. 3262) ("The White Paper"), para. 8.14. Though note that even without statutory control, in 1978 the Minister for Finance instructed a state-sponsored company to cut the salary of its chief executive by 25 per cent. and this instruction was obeyed.

during one of the following three periods; the drive for self-sufficiency in 1932–39; the post-war recovery period; or the years of economic expansion immediately after 1958. Professor Bristow has given the following historical sketch of the growth of this sector:

"The 1930s saw the nearest thing Ireland has experienced to the use of public enterprise in pursuit of an ideology—that is, economic self-sufficiency (which was an ideology rather than merely a development strategy in that it was the reflection of a political philosophy). The Irish Sugar Company was set up in 1933 and the decade saw the beginnings of governmental involvement in peat production (which led to the eventual establishment of Bord na Mona in 1946) and in air transport with the foundation of Aer Rianta in 1937. Import substitution continued to be important in the 1940s with the nationalisation of Irish Steel in 1947 and even after self-sufficiency had ceased to occupy a central position in development policy (Nitrigin Eireann and the British and Irish Steam Packet Company were set up as late as 1961 and 1965 respectively). A variant of it—security of supply of imports in times of international trouble—is still alive today. Not only did this idea provide the rationale for the foundation of Irish Shipping in 1941 but, in 1979, it was the stated justification for the establishment of the Irish National Petroleum Corporation (INPC) and the taking over by that company of the Whitegate refinery in 1982. . . .

"The Industrial Credit Company was created in 1933 to remedy a lack of underwriting facilities and to provide a channel of industrial finance. Ceimici Teoranta was established in 1938 to use surplus potatoes to produce industrial alcohol (no such surplus ever materialised and this operation has always had to rely on imported molasses), and Coras Iompair Eireann was set up in its present form in 1950 because the market mechanism was in danger of eliminating the railways."[25]

The most natural question to ask is why a particular commercial enterprise is not in the private sector rather than why it is not vested in some Minister for execution by the civil service. Often, the reason why the work is not done by private enterprise is that it is not profitable. Why then does the state do it? In the first place,

[25] Bristow, "State-Sponsored Bodies" (1982) 30 *Administration* 165 at p. 166.

the activity may form part of the infrastructure for the entire economy, frequently in sectors in which, irrespective of profit, the amount of capital required would be too great for the Irish private sector.[26] Secondly, the objective may be to develop natural resources.[27] Thirdly, the state-sponsored body may originate as a rescue operation designed to maintain employment after the demise of some private company.[28] The postal and telecommunication services were special cases in that until 1983 their functions were vested in the Department of Posts and Telegraphs. They were transferred to state-sponsored bodies in the anticipation that this change would promote a more flexible response to the challenges of the technological and commercial world.[29]

It should be emphasised that commercial state bodies have been set up as *ad hoc* responses to various needs and not as a device to supplant private enterprise for ideological reasons. Indeed the Directive Principles of State Policy contained in Article 45.3.1 of the Constitution enjoin the State "[to] favour and where necessary, supplement private initiative in industry and commerce."

Nevertheless, a number of state-sponsored bodies have been granted monopolies by their constituent statute, so as to allow them to provide a comprehensive range of service even in areas where this is not profitable, free of the danger that some private business will "cream-off" the profitable areas. The constitutionality of such monopolies was upheld in *Attorney-General and Minister for Posts and Telegraphs* v. *Paperlink Ltd.*[30] The defendants, who operated a substantial courier service, were breaching a monopoly, granted by the precursor of the Postal and Telecommunications Services Act 1983, s.63. They defended

[26] *e.g.* ESB; Aer Lingus; British and Irish Steam Packet Co. Ltd.; Irish Shipping Ltd. (now defunct); An Post; Bord Telecom Eireann.
[27] *e.g.* Bord na Mona; Ceimici Teo., CSET; National Stud Co. Ltd.
[28] *e.g.* Irish Life Assurance Co. Ltd.; Irish Steel Holdings Ltd.; Coras Iompair Eireann.
[29] See *Report of the Posts and Telegraph Review Group 1978–79* (Prl. 7883) ("the Dargan Report"), Chap. 9; see also *Reorganisation of Postal and Telecommunication Services* (Prl. 8809) Chaps. II and III.
[30] [1984] I.L.R.M. 373. See also *Nova Media Services Ltd.* v. *Minister for Posts and Telegraphs* [1984] I.L.R.M. 161 at p. 167; *Ulster Transport Authority* v. *Brown* [1953] N.I. 70; McCormack, "Monopoly Power in the High Court" (1984) 6 D.U.L.J.(n.s.) 152. For the suggestion that RTE's *de facto* monopoly broadcasting power is unconstitutional on the ground of infringement of the constitutional right to free speech, see Kelly, "The Constitutional Position of R.T.E." (1967) 15 *Administration* 205; Kelly, (1978) *Irish Broadcasting Review* 5; McRedmond, (1978) *Irish Broadcasting Review* 62.

themselves unsuccessfully against the plaintiffs' claim for an
injunction to restrain them by attacking the monopoly. Their
major argument was that the monopoly violated their right to earn
a livelihood and carry on a business which is one of the unspecified
rights bestowed by Article 40.3.1. Costello J. accepted this
argument, but he held that the monopoly could be justified as
enhancing "the common good." He also accepted that he could
utilise Article 45.3.1 for the purpose of determining what
limitations were legitimate and in the interests of the common
good. The judge, however, rejected the defendants' interpretation
of this provision. It admittedly demonstrated a preference for
private enterprise, albeit with an explicit recognition of the State's
role *faux de mieux*, yet it did not follow from this very general
guideline that there was an onus of proof upon the State to justify
the existence of a State monopoly in legal proceedings. The
defendants' second argument was that the postal monopoly did
not promote "the common good," first because it was being
operated inefficiently and, secondly,—a related point—because it
would be possible to gain the advantages claimed for the
monopoly by a system, which was less restrictive of the defendants'
rights. To support these claims, the defendants wished to call
economists and accountants to give evidence that, for instance, the
Department was paying wages which were above the market rate;
that the accounting system was a bad one; and that "overnight"
money was not properly invested. Costello J. refused to hear such
evidence because he held that to determine the legal arguments
founded on it—in other words to determine whether a particular
postal service serves the common good—was the prerogative of
the legislature rather than a court. This attitude of course, harks
back to an earlier era of constitutional jurisprudence.[31] Nevertheless, considering the multifarious controversial issues which such a
quest would present for decision, it is submitted that the judge
adopted the wiser course.

   A second type of accusation which surfaces periodically is that
the Government is abusing its powers in order to give a state-
sponsored body some unjustified immunity[32] or some unfair
advantage over trade competitors as, for instance, when £13
million of taxes owed by Ostann Eireann in respect of Great
Southern Hotels was waived by the Revenue Commissioners; or
when the Government promoted the Air Transport Act 1986,

[31] Principally in the interpretation of Arts. 40.3.2 and 43, on which see
   Kelly, *The Irish Constitution* (Dublin, 1984) at pp. 644–661.
[32] See *e.g.* Postal and Telecommunication Services Act 1983, ss.64 and 88
   discussed at pp. 365–366.

which would have inflicted severe penalties on tour operators cutting their prices below Aer Lingus rates.[33]

Non-commercial state-sponsored bodies

Non-commercial bodies are even more difficult to schematise. On one classification, they can be grouped into four types. First, there are those promotional bodies, which operate as a stimulus and back-up to private enterprise.[34] Secondly, there are research bodies.[35] Thirdly, there are bodies which regulate a particular profession or business, dealing with education and entry, maintaining proper standards and sanctions for breach of these standards. These bodies are at the fringe furthest away from the civil service and closest to the private sector in that some of their funds are provided by the profession itself; and a minority of their controlling boards are usually appointed by the Minister, whilst the majority are elected by members of the profession. For instance, on the Dental Board, one member is nominated by the Government and three by the Medical Council, whilst the remaining five are elected by dentists. This characteristic is present, though in a weaker form, outside the professions. Thus, the members of Bord na gCon, which regulates the greyhound racing industry, are all appointed by the Minister for Agriculture, but three out of the seven members must be members of the Standing Committee of the Irish Coursing Club.[36] Another example of shared control is the Foyle Fisheries Commission where control is divided between the Governments of the Republic and the United Kingdom.[37] Fourthly there is a large group, embracing half the non-commercial bodies, which provide miscellaneous services frequently in the health field.[38]

Because the non-commercial state body group spans such a

---

[33] *Dail Debates*, Vol. 352, cols. 853–910, (June 27, 1984). See also Lemass, "The Role of the State-Sponsored Body in the Economy" (1958) 6 *Administration* 277 at p. 278.

[34] *e.g.* Industrial Development Authority; Irish Export Board (Coras Trachtala); Bord Failte Eireann.

[35] *e.g.* An Foras Forbartha Teo. National Board for Science and Technology.

[36] See Greyhound Industry Act 1958, s.9.

[37] See Foyle Fisheries Act 1952 and Foyle Fisheries (Northern Ireland) Act 1952.

[38] *e.g.* Blood Transfusion Service Board, Medical Bureau of Road Safety, and the Agency for Personal Service Overseas. Following EEC entry, agricultural marketing bodies concerned with the disposal of agricultural products surplus to commercial requirements which were formerly state-sponsored bodies were converted into co-operatives; see *e.g.* An Bord Bainne Co-operative Ltd.

diverse range, it follows that there are various reasons why the
functions they perform have not been vested in departments of
state. In the case of the promotional bodies, the same sort of
reasons apply as in the case of commercial groups, namely that
their duties require "exceptional initiative and innovation"[39]
qualities which are not always to be found in the civil service.
Again, the civil service culture may be regarded as an inappropriate milieu for research. It is plain too that, given the attitude of
uncritical trust adopted by successive Governments towards the
professions, their domestic arrangements will always be placed at
arms length from the Government. In addition, the state body
form is useful in that it can accommodate the election or selection
of some members of a state body's controlling agency by persons
other than the Minister. However, many of the non-commercial
state bodies—including several in the miscellaneous category are
discharging functions which could equally well have been assigned
to executive branches of departments of state. Why, for instance,
should the Department of Social Welfare administer unemployment benefit while AnCO (the Industrial Training Authority)
is responsible for industrial training and the Department of
Labour, through the National Manpower Service, looks after
placement and occupational guidance? In an area where *ad hocery*
abounds and fashions change, this type of anomaly is common. It
led the Devlin Report to propose that while the commercial state
bodies should be allowed to operate with the maximum permissible freedom, the activities of non-commercial bodies and executive branches of departments dealing with similar subject-matter
should be pooled and re-allocated to a common executive
unit which would be subject to the control of a central
Aireacht.[40]

3. Legal form

A state-sponsored body must have a legal existence, which is
independent not only of the Government but also of its members
and staff. The reason for this is the need for it to be a continuing
entity, which can own property, make contracts, employ servants,
sue and be sued, etc. This distinct legal existence, may be achieved
in either of two ways. First, a state-sponsored body may be

[39] Lemass, "The Organisation behind the Economic Programme" (1961)
9 *Administration* 3 at pp. 4–6.
[40] Gaffney, "The Central Administration" (1982) 30 *Administration* 115 at
p. 122.

constituted as a statutory corporation (or board) by its own separate statute[41] which typically provides that:

> "(1) As soon as may be after the passing of this Act a board to be styled and known as [*e.g.*] the Electricity Supply Board . . . shall be established in accordance with this Act to fulfil the functions assigned to it by this Act.
>
> (2) The Board shall be a body corporate having perpetual succession and may sue and be sued under its said style and name.[42]

Alternatively, it may be a statutory company, *i.e.* an ordinary company (usually registered under the Companies Acts 1963), in which almost all the shares are held by a Minister. In this case, the corporate nature of the body arises from the companies legislation and not from its own tailor-made statute, which only provides—typically—that "the Minister shall take steps to procure that a limited company conforming to the conditions laid down in the schedule to the Act shall be registered under the Companies Act."[43] As a matter of law, a special statute is unnecessary since, provided that any necessary expenditure is authorised by the Appropriation Act, a Minister, as a corporation sole, under the Ministers and Secretaries Act, is free, like any natural person, to set up a company either by drawing up a memorandum and articles of association or by taking over all the shares in an existing company, as occurred in 1946 when the state purchased the Irish Steel Holdings Ltd., which was in the hands of the receiver. The reason why it is usual for the creation of a state-sponsored body, even as a company, to be preceded by an enabling statute is a political one, namely to afford the Oireachtas some opportunity to discuss its objectives and structure. Consonant with this, the enabling statute usually contains a broad description of the functions, duties and powers of the state body in addition to the more detailed statement which is contained in the articles of association.[44] These are necessarily stated broadly (*inter alia*, so as not to be enforceable in a court) for example:

> "The principal objects of [An Post] shall be stated in its

[41] Or statutory instrument: see Blood Transfusion Service Board (Establishment) Order (S.I. 1965 No. 78) made under Health (Corporate Bodies) Act 1961, s.3 by which the Blood Transfusion Board was set up.

[42] Electricity Supply Act 1927, s.2.

[43] Sugar Manufacturing Act 1933, s.4 constituting Comhlucht Suicre Eireann Teo.

[44] Which Deputy Cooney suggested should be laid before the Oireachtas: see, *Dail Debates*, Vol. 256, col. 2215 (November 17, 1971).

memorandum of association to be—(*a*) to provide a national postal service within the State and between the State and places outside the State. . . . "[45]

Because of the *ultra vires* doctrine restricting statutory corporations to powers expressly mentioned in their constituent statute or powers necessarily incidental thereto (an uncertain support), it is necessary for their constituent statutes to expressly bestow the powers, for instance: to contract; to employ officers and servants; to hold land. In the case of statutory companies, general company law applies and renders this wearisome particularisation unnecessary.

The obvious question which arises is: on what criterion is it determined whether a state-sponsored body should be poured into the vessel of a statutory corporation rather than a statutory company? There is no firm rule. As has been said of the variety of organisational forms for public bodies in Britain: "Like the flowers in spring, they have grown as variously and as profusely and with as little regard for conventional patterns."[46] So far as there is any guide, it is that more than two-thirds of commercial bodies are statutory companies; whereas non-commercial bodies are almost all cast as boards (or even "councils"). One significant factor is that it is easier to change the memorandum and articles of a company than it is to pass the necessary legislation to alter a board and such flexibility may be important to a commercial body. Moreover, the division of a company's assets is facilitated by the existence of shares and, in the first decade of the state-sponsored sector's existence, the public was usually invited—though without success—to subscribe for shares in the companies (hence the original name—"semi-state bodies"). In line with this trend, Comhlucht Siuicre Eireann was set up in 1933 in the form of a (public) company because it was expected that it would be sold off sooner or later; whereas bodies like ESB or Bord na Mona were never expected to go into private hands and so were created as statutory boards. Again, if an activity is being carried on as a private company which becomes the subject of a take-over then it will naturally remain as a company.

It was decided to cast An Post and Bord Telecom Eireann as registered companies. The reasons given by the Post and Tele-

---

[45] Postal and Telecommunications Services Act 1983, s.12(1). In some cases the lack of enforceability in a court is express, *e.g.* 1983 Act, ss.13(2), 15(2); Transport Act 1958, s.7(3).

[46] Street, "Quasi-Governmental Bodies since 1918" in *British Government since 1918* (ed., Campion) (London, 1948).

graphs Review Group Report was that a company may be altered more easily and can take quicker decisions.[47]

In principle, general company law applies to statutory companies, though it may not be well-adapted to the artificial circumstances involved.[48] The position of an state-sponsored body which wears the guise of a statutory corporation is even more cloudy. It has been suggested:

> " . . . [T]hat the general common law of corporations will govern [statutory corporations] except in so far as this is expressly or impliedly modified and that many of the judge-made principles of company law will be equally applicable to this more recent growth. But in applying common law principles recognition must be given to the consequences flowing from their dual role as commercial enterprises and public authorities. . . . [In addition] the absence of shares and shareholders automatically renders large and important branches of company law totally inapplicable. . . . "[49]

This guideline means, *inter alia*, that the *ultra vires* principle, in its pristine common law form,[50] would apply to statutory corporations.

4. Control by the Minister[51]

In most cases, the Minister who controls and is ultimately responsible for a state-sponsored body is the Minister whose departmental duties fall closest to the work of the body.[52] Thus,

---

[47] *Report of (Dargan) Posts and Telegraphs Review Group 1978–79* (Prl. 7883) at p. 63. However, because of union pressure to protect conditions of employment, 1983 Act, s.22(2) provides that the Minister may not transfer shares: see *Dail Debates* Vol. 337, cols. 1573–1577 (July 1982). (The earlier stages of the Bill were promoted by a Fianna Fail Government, the later stages by a Coalition Government). See *Dail Debates* Vol. 343, col. 1526 (June 15, 1983)

[48] Golding, "The Juristic Basis of the Irish State Enterprise" (1978) 13 Ir.Jur.(n.s.) 302 at pp. 310–312.

[49] Gower, *Modern Company Law* (London, 1979) at pp. 287–288.

[50] *i.e.* unaffected by Companies Act 1963, s.8; and European Communities (Companies) Regulations 1973 (S.I. 1973 No. 163).

[51] For a study of independence control in relation to the Central Bank of Ireland (a somewhat untypical state body) in a comparative setting, by its former Governor, see Murray, "The Independence of Central Banks: An Irish Perspective" (1982) 30 *Administration* 33.

[52] Note, however, that the Minister for Finance is responsible for C.S.E.T. and has some limited statutory functions (*e.g.* appointment of directors, approval of borrowing, in relation to Ceimici Teo and the now defunct Irish Shipping).

Agricultural Credit Corporation (Finance); Irish Steel Holdings Ltd. (Industry, Trade, Commerce and Tourism); E.S.B. (Energy); Aer Lingus Teo (Communications); National Rehabilitation Board Ltd. (Health). Vested in the responsible Minister (or, very occasionally, in the Government) are five statutory powers which may be used to control a state-sponsored body. Whilst some are seldom, if ever, used, their very existence helps to shape the relationship between a Minister and the body for which he is responsible and to ensure that his merest "suggestion" commands respect. After these legal powers have been described, the factors which determine the use which the minister actually makes of his formal ascendancy will be examined.

Appointment etc.

In the case of statutory corporations, members of the board are usually selected by the responsible Minister but with the consent of or, after consulting in certain cases, the Minister for Finance. The chairman is usually chosen from among the directors, either by the responsible Minister or by the Board, subject to the Minister's approval. The term of office is typically three to five years, after which a director may be re-appointed (or disappointed!). The terms and conditions of employment are usually fixed by the responsible Minister with the consent of the Minister for the Public Service. There will usually be four to nine directors. However, in bodies to which the Worker Participation (State Enterprises) Act, 1977[53] applies the size of the board has been increased to accommodate the workers' directors. Large boards are also a feature of those non-commercial bodies which include the (usually elected) representatives of different interests, *e.g.* the Nursing Board or the Medical Council (29- and 25-member boards, respectively).

The position is similar for statutory companies save that their boards are usually smaller and that, in accordance with general company law, board members retire by rotation, two at each Annual General Meeting.

Dismissal

In the case of a statutory corporation the power of dismissal is vested usually in the responsible minister, in some cases subject to the consent of the Minister for Finance or the Minister for the

---

[53] Aer Lingus, Bord na Mona, British and Irish Steampacket Co. Ltd.; CIE; ESB; NET; CSET An Post and Bord Telecom Eireann also have employee directors: Postal and Telecommunications Services Act 1983, s.34. See generally, Worker Participation (State Enterprises) (General) Regulations 1978 (S.I. 1978 No. 47).

Public Service. Occasionally, the power is vested in the Government. However, dismissal is an extreme step and, whatever the statutory provision may say, this is a decision which would only be taken following anxious deliberation by the entire Government.[54] Frequently, the power of removal is conditioned on broad and subjectively-worded grounds, for instance, ill-health, stated misbehaviour or failure to perform duties effectively.[55] Where a state-sponsored body is a company, removal is usually not dealt with in the body's own statute, but in the articles of association which list specific grounds on which the shareholder, *i.e.* the Minister, may dismiss a director. A *cause célébre* in this field occurred in 1972 and involved the members of the RTE Authority (for whom the appointing and dismissing agency is now, and was then, the Government). The episode arose out of the Minister for Posts and Telegraph's use of his power under the Broadcasting Authority Act 1960, s.31 to issue an order which forbade RTE from broadcasting any matter calculated to promote the aims of "any organisation which engages in, promotes, encourages or advocates the attaining of any political objectives by violent means." The Authority protested against the vagueness of this wording and a month after the order had been made RTE broadcast an interview with the IRA Chief of Staff. The Government gave the Authority the option of dismissing the interviewer,[56] or being removed from office and the Authority took the second option. The sequel came in the Broadcasting Authority (Amendment) Act 1976 which, first, narrowed the scope of section 31[57] and, secondly, provided some additional protection for the members of the Authority. Thenceforth, a member could only be removed "by the Government from office, for stated reasons if, and only if, resolutions are passed by both Houses of the Oireachtas calling for his removal."[58]

Dissolution

The most draconian power of all, the (presumed) power to dissolve a state body,[59] has never been used.

---

[54] But for the resignation of Dr. Joseph Brennan from the Central Bank in 1953, see Murray, *op. cit.*, "The Role of the State-Sponsored Body in the Economy" (1958) and *Administration* 277, 289. Pp. 41–42; see also Lemass "The Role of the State-Sponsored Body in the Economy" (1958) 6 *Administration* 277.

[55] *e.g.* Gas Act 1976, Sched. 1, art. 4(7); Transport Act 1950, s.7.

[56] This interview also led to *Re Kevin O'Kelly* (1974) 108 I.L.T.R. 97.

[57] On which, see pp. 322–325.

[58] Broadcasting Authority (Amendment) Act 1976, s.2.

[59] Ministers and Secretaries Act 1924, s.9; see Central Bank Act 1942, s.5(*b*) excluding the Bank from the sweep of the 1924 Act.

Finance[60]

The control of finance affords the Government a range of convenient levers over most spheres of activity. In the case of non-commercial bodies, funds are delivered in the form of grants-in-aid which can only be released with the permission of the responsible Minister and the Minister for Finance.

With commercial bodies, the position is more complicated. Investment capital may be raised by borrowing (either from the Exchequer or private sources) or, in the case of companies, by the issue of shares to a Minister, almost always to the Minister for Finance. Among the key provisions in the constituent statute of a state-sponsored body are those which fix the maximum amounts which it is empowered to raise, by borrowing or issuing shares. These limits take the form of legislation and thus their alteration provides an opportunity for the Oireachtas to review the policy and performance of the body involved. It is customary to fix the limits at such a level that if the organisation is expanding fairly rapidly, amending legislation is necessary every four to six years. As well as the Oireachtas' authorisation, the consents of the responsible Ministers, and the Minister for Finance are necessary where shares are issued or money is borrowed from the Exchequer.

Where funds are borrowed from a private source, (in some cases, by issuing stock) the Minister for Finance, after consultation with the responsible Minister may guarantee repayment and such a guarantee constitutes a charge on the central fund. Until 1984,[61] these guarantees were given very readily. However, the Minister for Finance has now made it clear that such guarantees will only be given for good cause and that the State will not undertake responsibility for loans which are not guaranteed.

The expectation, which is sometimes expressed in the parent statute,[62] is that taking account of the need to make an adequate return on capital, a commercial body should break even taking one year with another. In fact, in recent years, only two of the bodies (Irish Life and Arramara Teo.) have paid any dividend.

Where loss on current expenditure is involved or pre-existing

---

[60] For the law on central government finance, see generally, Gwynn Morgan, *op. cit.*, at pp. 112–132.

[61] The occasion for the change of policy (announced by the Minister for Finance in a speech made to the Institute of Bankers on November 16, 1984) was the Irish Shipping liquidation. Irish Shipping Ltd. had liabilities estimated at £114 million of which only some were state guaranteed and the (substantial) remainder went unpaid: see *Business and Finance* November 22 and 29, 1984.

[62] *e.g.* Electricity (Supply) Act 1927, s.21(2); Gas Act, 1976, s.10, *cf.* Transport Act 1958, s.7(2).

debts have to be written off, constituent statutes or amendments may provide for the making of a subsidy by the Minister for Finance.

There may also be indirect assistance. For example, the Minister for Finance's guarantee, just mentioned, means that it is the taxpayer rather than the creditor who bears the risk of the debt not being repaid and, accordingly, the interest rate is lower than would otherwise be the case.[63] Subsidisation also exists between, and within, state-sponsored bodies. For instance, ESB has been directed to purchase peat from Bord na Mona though it might be possible for it to purchase cheaper raw material abroad. NET receives gas from Bord Gais on favourable terms.[64] Again, ESB has been instructed to charge urban and rural consumers at the same rates and thus one group of electricity users subsidises another.

Information

All state bodies are under duties—stated, variously, in the parent statute or articles of association—to give their Minister important information as to, for instance, profit and loss account, capital account, revenue account, etc. Frequently, the Minister has power to settle the form of annual reports and accounts and also to be given whatever specific information he requests.[65] There is often a statutory obligation, failing which there is a practice, that the annual report and accounts should then be laid before each House of the Oireachtas. (In practice, it often happens that these annual reports and accounts are not published until two or more years after the year to which they relate.)

[63] Joint Oireachtas Committee on State-Sponsored Bodies: *Second Report: Irish Shipping Ltd.* (1985) (Pl. 3091) at para. 35.
[64] Comment of the Joint Committee on Commercial State-Sponsored Bodies in their Report on Irish Shipping on the fact that ESB had awarded only a half of the contract to carry coal from USA to Moneypoint to Irish Shipping, with the other half going to a Japanese company. The Joint Committee said that "appropriate Government guidelines should be developed which, on the one hand, would not impinge on the competitiveness of open market quotations but, on the other hand, would provide for due consideration of the Exchequer's involvement in both bodies."
[65] The Joint Oireachtas Committee on State-Sponsored Bodies discovered that in spite of these extensive powers, the Department of Communications was not sufficiently aware of the crisis into which Irish Shipping was sailing during the period 1979–84: see *Second Report: Irish Shipping Ltd.* (1985) (Pl. 3091) at paras. 1, 23, and 24.

Balance of authority between minister and state-sponsored body

The division of jurisdiction is usually taken to be that "day-to-day" decisions are for the state body itself whereas strategic and policy issues have to be resolved, if possible, by agreement between the board and the Minister, but with the Minister having the last word. Thus, for instance, whilst capital investment by ESB would involve the Minister for Energy, decisions as to staff allocation or electricity load management would not.[66] It is a striking feature of the constituent statutes of state-sponsored bodies that, with a few exceptions, they do not deal directly with the overall relationship between the Minister and the body. The principal exception[67] is the Postal and Telecommunications Services Act 1983, s.110(1) but what is laid down there, in regard to An Post and Bord Telecom Eireann may also be taken as an accurate guide to the convention determining relations between the responsible Minister and other state-sponsored bodies. According to the 1983 Act:

> "The Minister [for Communications] may issue directions in writing to either company [*sc*. An Post or Bord Telecom Eireann] requiring the company:–
>
> (*a*) to comply with policy decisions of a general kind made by the Government concerning the development of the postal or telecommunications services ...   ·
>
> (*b*) to do (or refrain from doing) anything which he may specify from time to time as necessary in the national interest. ...
>
> (*c*) to perform such work or provide such work or provide or maintain such services for a state authority as may be specified in the direction. ... "

In fact, the lack of written statement of the relationship makes little difference in practice. Take, as an example, the intervention by the Minister for Industry and Commerce in the CIE bus strike in 1963. The Minister had written a letter encouraging CIE to reach a settlement and the letter used the phrases "strongly request" and "direct" pretty well interchangeably. Questioned in the Dail on the source of his power to intervene, the Minister said:

> "I have no statutory power to issue directions to CIE in relation to trade disputes between the company and its employees. In view of the functions assigned to me under the Ministers and Secretaries Act, I do not need to have special

---

[66] See *Dail Debates* Vol. 311, col. 868 (February 8, 1979).
[67] For partial exceptions, see Gas Act 1976 s.11; Central Bank Act 1971, s.43.

powers to enable me to make a strong request to the company. . . . When I issued a request to the company in the first place, the company knew well that I was making an attempt to solve the strike and they agreed to accept my direction in the matter."[68]

Indeed, it often suits a Minister to intervene without appearing to do so, as in another CIE labour dispute at a time when Todd Andrews was then (full-time) chairman of CIE. Mr Andrews wrote in his autobiography:

"Finally the Taoiseach, Sean Lemass, decided that the lock-out should be lifted and the bus services restored. Jack Lynch phoned me to say that 'the boss' (*i.e.* Lemass) wanted me to take the men back. I told him I would refuse to do so unless I got a directive either from the Taoiseach or from himself as Minister for Industry and Commerce to end the lock-out and that the terms of the directive be published. . . .

Later [Mr. Lynch] phoned to say that he had read over the directive to 'the Boss' who agreed with the wording but did not think it was necessary to publish it. I replied that unless it was published the lock-out would not be lifted by me. He phoned me back again in due course to say that publication had been arranged."[69]

Three glosses

To obtain some idea of how the Minister/state-sponsored body relationship operates in practice, one needs to add three glosses or exceptions to the conventional policy/operational matter demarcation outlined above.

(1) A Minister must ensure—said Sean Lemass—that state-sponsored body is "kept in line . . . with the overall development plans of the Government."[70] This means that the Government will often use its convenient hold over a large sector of industry and

---

[68] *Dail Debates*, Vol. 202, col. 34 (April 23, 1963). The Minister's reference to the Ministers and Secretaries Act might be a reference to his general job description (see pp. 41–42) powers under the Ministers and Secretaries Act 1924, s.1(vii).

[69] Andrews, *Man of No Property* (Cork, 1982) at p. 257. Note also the episodes in which: the Minister for Agriculture "instructed" RTE not to carry a report of a National Farmer Association's criticism of him see: *Dail Debates*, Vol. 227, cols. 1661–1664 (April 13, 1967); and the Taoiseach informed the chairman of RTE that in the opinion of the Government "the best interests of the nation would not be served by sending an RTE team to Vietnam": *Dail Debates, loc. cit.*

[70] Lemass, "The Role of the State-Sponsored Body in the Economy" (1959) 6 *Administration* 278 at p. 288.

commerce to impose its line on economic, social or other issues. One example is the Worker Participation (State Enterprises) Act 1977 which provided for worker-directors in the case of the larger commercial state-sponsored bodies listed *supra*, although the Oireachtas has not sought to apply this policy anywhere in the private sector. In other cases, Ministers have intervened to require a decision to be taken in order to maintain employment, even though this is not in line with commercial consideration. Take, for instance, the following Dail question:

> "Mr. Hegarty asked the Minister for Tourism and Transport [who was then responsible for British and Irish Steampacket Co. Ltd.] in view of the likelihood of redundancies at Verolme Cork Dockyard, will he consider giving the green light to have the new B. and I. roll-on roll-off car ferry built at the yard immediately."[71]

There is no concession in this question to the notion that B. & I. is a separate entity from the Department of Tourism and Transport, responsible for taking its own decisions along commercial lines and it is normal political practice that there should have been no such concession. The protest of state-sponsored bodies at this type of behaviour by Ministers, has taken the limited form of suggesting that in the interests of presenting a fair picture of the agency's performance, allowance should be made in its accounts —or even a grant paid—to allow for the value of the social benefits.[72]

Another motive for intervention is the fact that many of the commercial state bodies have recently made enormous losses for which the state is ultimately responsible. Up to the early 1960s almost all the commercial bodies at least broke even and hence the main danger, identified by Sean Lemass, in an article published in 1959, was that politicians might endanger the system by interfering too much in the activities of state bodies.[73] However, by the mid-1980s, the Government was grappling desperately with an economic crisis—a major element which was massive expenditure—both on capital investment and the financing of a current deficit by state-sponsored bodies. With the responsibility of the Government for the economy as a whole, the natural reaction has been for the Ministers to exercise a closer control over state

---

[71] *Dail Debates*, Vol. 307, cols. 2429–2430 (June 29, 1978).

[72] NESC Report; Bristow *op. cit.* p. 180. See also Postal and Telecommunications Services Act 1983, ss.51, 75. For history of these sections see Byrnes, "Profitability *vis-á-vis* the Public Interest" (1984) 31 *Administration* 372.

[73] Lemass, "The Role of the State-Sponsored Body in the Economy" (1958) 6 *Administration* 278 at p. 291.

bodies. One element of this control is the Department of Finance's recently imposed requirement that a five-year corporate plan, including a statement of objectives, pricing policies and annual forecasts should be agreed between the Government and each state-sponsored body.[74]

The commercial body sector's response to this change of attitude by the Government has been to stand on the original *raison d'être* of the bodies and to complain that too much centralisation discourages initiative and is inappropriate for a heterogeneous group.[75]

(2) Closely related to the impact which a state body can make on the Government's general policies is the question of party-political advantage. This is the very factor which the state-sponsored body form of organisation was designed to exclude. But, in a highly-politicised environment, this is a counsel of perfection. The average voter may know little about the constitutional position of an state body but he knows that it is in the public domain and accordingly (he may think) under the Government's control. To a considerable extent, the state sponsored body sector's deeds, whether good or bad, will tend to rub off on the Government and so here is another motive for intervention, in some cases even in day-to-day activities. For instance, the Minister for Agriculture is asked annually in the Dail how much sugar beet Comhlucht Siuicre Eireann will require for the coming year; he always answers the question rather than turning the matter aside as an operational decision. Again, state bodies may sometimes delay impending price rises where these rises would have coincided with an election.

(3) Government's power of control is much greater over a non-commercial, than a commercial, body. The reasons are, first, that the commercial bodies are already subject to the discipline of the market-place (of which there is no equivalent for the non-commercial bodies which are usually little more than executive agencies) and, secondly, that the Government control over the provision of grants is even more significant where this is a state-sponsored body's only source of funds. As has been said earlier, non-commercial bodies often amount to little more than an agency of the responsible department.

Special statutory controls

Broadly speaking, state-sponsored bodies are subject to the same law as other persons. In some cases there are modifications

[74] See further, O'Neil "Corporate Planning and State Bodies" (1984) 6 *Seirbhís Phoibli* 3 at p. 31.
[75] See, 49th Report of the National Economic and Social Council, *Enterprise in the Public Sector* (1979) (Prl. 8499).

and of these, RTE affords the most striking examples. However, as
they constitute an attempt to control the enormous and pervasive
influence which the broadcasting medium commands, they may be
mentioned briefly as characteristic of the general field of public
law rather than as typical of the constitutional form of the state-
sponsored body. The best known of these controls is the
Broadcasting Authority Act 1960, s.31 (as amended).[76] There is
another analagous but broader provision which prohibits the
authority from broadcasting "anything which may reasonably be
regarded as being likely to promote, or incite to, crime or as
tending to undermine the authority of the State."[77] On a broader
front, the Authority is under a duty to broadcast news and current
affairs "in an objective and impartial manner" without giving its
own views (save on broadcasting policy) and to ensure that its
programmes do not "unreasonably encroach on the privacy of an
individual." The Authority is under positive, though necessarily
imprecise, duties: to uphold "rightful liberty of expression"; to
pay regard to the values and traditions of foreign states,
particularly EEC Member States; and

> "[T]o be responsive to the interests and concerns of the
> whole community, be mindful of the need for understanding
> and peace within the whole island of Ireland, ensure that the
> programmes reflect the varied elements which make up the
> culture of the people of the whole island of Ireland, and have
> special regard for the elements which distinguish that culture
> and in particular for the Irish language."[78]

In addition, the total number of hours broadcast each year must
fall within a range whose extremities are fixed by the Authority
with approval of the Minister for Communications.[79] Again, the
total daily time for advertising and the maximum hourly period is
subject to the Minister's approval. Advertisements on certain
subjects—those directed towards any religious or political end or

[76] For s.31, (as amended by the Broadcasting Authority (Amendment) Act
1976, s.16), see pp. 322–325.
[77] Broadcasting Authority (Amendment) Act 1976, s.3. The relationship of
this provision with s.3 (as amended) has not been judicially explored. In
1984, when a Noraid spokesman was banned from the air-waves by the
Minister for Communications, Noraid not being on the list of
proscribed organisations authorised by s.31, the Minister relied upon
his power under s.3 of the 1976 Act.
[78] 1976 Act, s.3. The duty of impartiality does not affect the Authority's
right to transmit "political party broadcasts" (a phrase which is not
defined) 1960 Act, s.18(2).
[79] 1976 Act, s.13.

related to any industrial dispute—may not be accepted.[80] Finally, it should be noted that the Minister retains the power of fixing the amount of the broadcasting licence fee, RTE's major source of income.[81]

There is a Broadcasting Complaints Commission to consider such complaints as that any of the obligations outlined in the previous paragraph have been broken or that the Authority's advertising code has been violated. To assist the Commission, the Authority must record and retain for at least 180 days, a copy of every broadcast. The Commission has no power to award damages, but it may require the Authority to publish its decision on a complaint and it must make a report to the Minister which is laid before the Houses of the Oireachtas. If the Authority does not accept any decision, it must give its reasons so that they can be published in the annual report.[82]

In addition the RTE Authority may, with the consent of the Minister for Communications, appoint advisory committees.[83] This power has been exercised, to appoint the Radio 2 Advisory Committee which has now lapsed and the Council for Radio na Gaeltachta which exerts a significant influence upon Radio na Gaeltachta.

5. Control by the Oireachtas

One of the points which emerges from a survey of the Government's controls over a state body is that the occasions at which the most effective controls are exercisable are usually points at which the Oireachtas is not consulted. The Oireachtas is, of course, involved in the legislation designing a state body and any amending legislation which may be necessary, for instance to authorise an increase in share capital. But this operates spasmodically and not necessarily at the time of greatest significance, for instance: when a new board is being appointed; when a decision whether to withdraw or to go into a certain area of activity is taken; or when a guarantee is given by the Minister for Finance to a private lender. Where administration going on within a department of state is concerned, these lacunae do not exist because the

---

[80] 1960 Act, s.20. See generally, Hall and McGovern, "Regulation of the Media: Irish and European Community Dimensions" (1985) 7 D.U.L.J.(n.s.).

[81] 1976 Act, ss.1, 8; 1960 Act, ss.1(b), 22; Wireless Telegraphy Act 1926, s.5.

[82] 1976 Act, s.4. See also Hall and McGovern, *loc. cit.*

[83] 1976 Act, s.5; *cf.* Postal and Telecommunications Services Act 1983, ss.48, 49 ("Minister shall establish [for each company a . . . Users 'Council')."

Government is responsible, to the Dail, for all administrative acts even if these do not require a change of law. This means that such activity may be debated and Ministers may be questioned in the Dail about them. By contrast, where any question is raised as to the activity of a state-sponsored body, it is likely to be met by the imprecise rule which excludes responsibility for day-to-day matters. And where a state body is operating in the commercial world there is obviously an additional reason for confidentiality.

Nevertheless, the performance of state-sponsored bodies is sometimes discussed in the Oireachtas. For instance, where money is given (whether in exchange for shares or simply as a grant) or lent to commercial state bodies, this is usually done on the authority of the constituent Act or an amendment thereof, rather than during the Estimates or by way of an Appropriation Act. However, in spite of this, during the Estimates debate, deputies are permitted to discuss the performance of a state-sponsored body which comes under the wing of a Department whose vote is under examination and a Minister does sometimes take the opportunity to give an account of the past record and prospects of a state body which comes within his jurisdiction. However, the reality is, first, that many estimates go undebated for lack of time and, secondly, even where there is a debate, discussion ranges over the entire of a Department's activities. Thus it is inappropriate as a vehicle for the kind of detailed, technical debate necessary to a state-sponsored body. The present Government has suggested as part of its package of parliamentary procedural reform that there should be an annual debate, in November or December, upon the State's entire capital investment programme for the coming year. One of the major preoccupations of such a debate would have to be very broad. Again, although annual reports from each body have to be laid before each House, they have seldom, if ever, been made the occasion for a "take note" debate. Certain state bodies (chiefly non-commercial bodies) allow their accounts to be audited by the Comptroller and Auditor General and his report may be discussed in the Dail Public Accounts Committee—but this form of control is very limited and *ex post facto*. The conclusion must be that debate in the Oireachtas is spasmodic and often superficial.

It is true that it was precisely to achieve substantial exclusion of the Oireachtas that the state body form was invented. Nevertheless it came to be felt, especially in the light of the recent huge expenditure of public funds by the state body sector and of greater control over this sector, by the Government, that this process had gone too far. To meet such criticisms the Joint Oireachtas Committee on State-Sponsored Bodies was established. It was anticipated, correctly, that the technique of a small select committee would create the kind of non-partisan, technical milieu which is appropriate for discussion of this area. Following suggestions down the years that such a committee be established, it was eventually constituted in 1976.[84] Its jurisdiction is confined to all the commercial bodies plus Gaeltarra Eireann. The reasons given[85] for the exclusion of the non-commercial bodies were, first, that with the commercial bodies, profit and loss provides an objective yard-stick for evaluating their success—which is lacking in the case of the non-commercial sector; and secondly, that the performance of non-commercial bodies could be examined in isolation from the policy, including allocation of resources, of their parent department. In any event, this gap has now been filled by the Joint Committee on Public Expenditure whose remit includes both the departments of state and the non-commercial state-sponsored bodies associated with each of them.

6. Board and Chief Executive

In theory, the rights, duties and identity of a state-sponsored body are concentrated in the board. The board is the body corporate, the legal personality of the body: everyone else is merely a creature, whether an officer or servant, of the board. In practice, the position is radically different. The Devlin Report offered the following list of the usual duties discharged by a board:

> "(a) Implement government policy; (b) Appoint top management; (c) exercise financial control; (d) stimulate development; (e) maintain liaison with the minister; (f) supervise personnel policy; (g) measure management performance."[86]

[84] See *Dail Debates*, Vol. 293, col. 1403 (November 10, 1976). It has been reconstituted in subsequent Houses (apart from the 1981–82 Houses). The Joint Oireachtas Committee on State-Sponsored Bodies has issued reports on the following bodies: National Stud (1979, Prl. 7869); B. & I. (1979, Prl. 8063); Min Fheir (1979, Prl. 8242); CIE/OIE (1979, Prl. 8438); Ceimici Teo (1979, Prl. 8475); Aer Rianta (1979, Prl. 8582); Arramara (1980, Prl. 8686); Bord na Mona (1980, Prl. 8808); VHI (1980, Prl. 8899); ACC (1980, Prl. 8944); ICC (1980, Prl. 9261); NBA 1980, (Prl. 9480); CSET (1980, Prl. 9555); Aer Lingus/Aer Linte (1980, Prl. 9584); Irish Shipping Ltd. (1981, Prl. 9663); NET (1981, Prl. 9752); Foir Teo (1981, Prl. 9944); RTE (1981, Prl. 9945). First Report: Ostann Iompair Eireann (1984) (Pl. 2); Second Report: Irish Shipping Ltd. (1985) (Pl. 3091); Third Report: Bord Gais Eireann (1985) (Pl. 3638); Fourth Report: Udaras na Gaeltachta (1986) (Pl. 3747).

[85] *Dail Debates*, Vol. 319, cols. 169–199, (March 19, 1980) (unsuccessful motion to extend the Committee's bailiwick to the non-commercial sector).

[86] Devlin Report, para. 5.2.21.

Dr Barrington is less expansive: according to him, the principal task of the board is to integrate two major influences, first, the overall policy of the responsible minister; secondly, the stream of advice from management based on operational experience. Both these contributions are "discussed and weighed by board members of broad general experience from many walks of life. The development of policy, therefore, is a broadly participate affair in which the board plays a central role."[87]

However even these accounts, it seems to the writer, exaggerate the usual influence of the board. The central facts are that there are no statutory qualifications for membership (other than not being a deputy or senator) and members are often chosen as a reward for their political loyalties. The duties of membership, for which the remuneration was £800 per annum in 1985,[88] usually take up a few hours at once-monthly meetings.[89] On the other hand, a state-sponsored body's senior officials will be full-time experts who are in frequent, informal contact with the civil servants in the responsible Department.[90] The board's effective authority is, thus, curtailed from above by the Minister and Department as seen in Part 4 but also from below, by the officials. In reality, the average board member's contribution is likely to be small and may amount merely to confirming proposals brought before it by the management. This poses a classic danger, namely that there may be divorce between responsibility and effective power. Something of the sort materialised in the events leading up to the liquidation of Irish Shipping in 1984. One significant factor in the company's losses arose from imprudent long-term charter-ing agreements entered into by the company. Another source of loss was a joint pool of shipping together as Celtic Bulk Carriers. In each case the Board was not properly informed and, thus, was not properly in control.[91]

The constituent statutes scarcely ever mention the chief executive and never provide a description of his functions. Nevertheless—and regardless of whether the chief executive has or has not been made a member of the board—there is no doubt

---

[87] Barrington, *The Irish Administrative System* (Dublin, 1980) at p. 59.

[88] For the prerequisites, see *Magill*, September 1980.

[89] There are rare exceptions: the chairman of the boards of ESB and CIE were employed full-time and four days per week, respectively, (in 1985).

[90] It often happens that a Minister will appoint one or two of his departmental civil servants as board members, a practice which has been justified as aiding smooth communication and attacked as subverting the independence of state-sponsored bodies. Apart from five years in the 1950s, the Secretary of the Department of Finance has always been a "service director" of the Central Bank of Ireland.

[91] Pl. 3091, paras. 17, 23.

of his position as effectively the "managing director."[92]

In view of all these restrictions upon the board, it has been suggested by one experienced observer[93] that the only role which the board can play is to use the advantage of "distance" to monitor the state body's performance and to provide a forum in which the chief executive and his senior executives can meet. An episode involving tension between a board and the Government of the day occurred in 1985, when the Minister for Communications, relying upon an unusual provision[94] by which his approval is necessary for an appointment to the position of Director General of RTE withheld his approval from the RTE Authority's choice for the post.

---

[92] The title used is usually "chief executive," save that certain state bodies, (*e.g.* I.C.C. and Comhlucht Siuicre Eireann Teo.) have a "managing director."

[93] Kenny, "Boards of Directors in Ireland" (1978) 26 *Administration* 107.

[94] Broadcasting Authority Act 1960, s.13(4).

5 Aspects of Local Government Law

1. Historical introduction

It has been stated that the "basic structure of [Irish] local government remained that enacted by the British parliament in 1898."[1] In that year the Local Government (Ireland) Act 1898 was passed, and this legislation effected a major reorganisation of the system of local government which had operated prior to that date. Until 1898 the functions of local government had been discharged by a number of bodies. The construction, repair and maintenance of roads and bridges lay in the hands of the grand jury, who also had a supervisory function in relation to other public works.[2] The grand jury was appointed by the assize judge, who was required to approve the grand jury's "presentments," *i.e.* expenditure proposals. The grand jury raised revenue by means of taxes on local landowners, and these taxes were known as the "grand jury cess." The corrupt[3] and undemocratic nature of this system led to demands for reform, but this was not to come until the grand juries were abolished by the Local Government (Ireland) Act 1898.

The poor law and sanitary services were administered by boards of guardians. In Ireland, the poor law union was an area ten miles in radius around each of the 130 market towns,[4] and the guardians

---

[1] Alexander, "Local Government in Ireland" (1979) 27 *Administration* 3 at p. 7. What follows is necessarily a brief and very much compressed account of the principal features of local government law. Readers who desire a fuller treatment of this complicated subject are referred to Keane, *The Law of Local Government in the Republic of Ireland* (Dublin, 1982), and Street, *The Law of Local Government* (Dublin, 1955).

[2] The grand jury system had been established by the Grand Jury (Ireland) Act 1836.

[3] See generally Roche, *op. cit.*, at pp. 29–43.

[4] See Alexander, *loc. cit.*, at p. 6.

were elected by the local poor law ratepayers. Local ratepayers also sat, *ex officio*, on the board of guardians. Because the guardians—unlike the grand juries—were permanent bodies holding regular meetings, their functions were extended by legislation throughout the nineteenth century.[5] By 1840 there were a number of borough corporations to certain of which some or all of the powers of grand juries had been transferred. Section 12 of the Municipal Corporations (Ireland) Act 1840 confirmed the corporate status of these boroughs. Further reform came with the passage of the Local Government Board Act 1871, which gave a centralised body—the Local Government Board—control over the activities of local boards. By the end of the nineteenth century the local guardians enjoyed wide powers and "not only relieved destitution and furnished public and personal health services, but, from 1883, provided rural housing as well."[6] Town commissioners were elected in the towns which had adopted the Towns Improvement (Ireland) Act 1854, or which were appointed under the Lighting of Towns (Ireland) Act 1828, or other local Acts.[7] The town commissioners had functions in relation to lighting, draining, paving, water supplies, land acquisitions, railways, and in some cases, policing.[8]

Major reform of this system was not to come until the Local Government (Ireland) Act 1898. This Act set up a two-tier system of local government, organised along county lines. Each county was to have a county council, but the six largest cities were made county boroughs, in which the Corporations were to have the functions of a county council, together with those functions which as borough councils they previously enjoyed. Each county was divided into local districts, with an urban or rural district council. The grand jury system was abolished, and its functions in relation to roads and other public works were transferred to urban district councils. In rural areas the public health functions of the boards of guardians were transferred to the rural district councils. The power to levy the poor law rates was assigned to the county councils, but the boards of guardians were still responsible for the administration of the poor law system, including the provision of medical relief. Finally, and perhaps most importantly, the fran-

[5] Thus, *e.g.* the Births and Deaths Registration Act 1863 (requiring the compilation of mortality statistics) and Sanitary Services Act 1863 (designating the guardians as sewer authorities in rural areas).
[6] Chubb, *The Government and Politics of Ireland* (Stanford, 1982) at p. 292.
[7] Some towns had elected representatives by virtue of local Acts: see Vanston's *Law of Municipal Towns*, pp. 6 and 358.
[8] See generally, Roche, *op. cit.*, pp. 32–36.

chise was extended to all adult, male, ratepayers.[9] This extension
of the franchise not only ensured that local government was to be
more representative in nature, but also created a form of local
politics in Ireland which, in the following twenty years or so, was to
be the backbone of the nationalist struggle for Irish independence.

Post-1922 developments

The first major piece of local government legislation following
the establishment of the Irish Free State in 1922 was the Local
Government Act 1925. This provided[10] that rural district councils
were to be abolished and that their functions were to be assigned
to the county councils. The duties of county councils as sanitary
authorities were to be performed by boards of health,[11] a situation
which was to prevail until the Health Act 1970. Central control
was also strengthened, inasmuch as the Minister for Local
Government was given power to order the dissolution of a local
authority where he was satisfied following the holding of a local
authority meeting that, *inter alia*, the authority was not "duly and
effectually" discharging its duties,[12] and the Minister was empowered to transfer the powers and duties of such local authority
"to any body or persons" he thought fit.

The Local Authority (Officers and Employees) Act 1926 (as
amended by the Local Authority (Officers and Employees)
(Amendment) Act 1940 and the Local Government Act 1955) now

[9] The franchise was extended to women aged 30 years and upwards by
the Representation of the People Act 1918. This 30-year age limit was
removed by the Local Government (Extension of Franchise) Act 1935,
which also granted the vote to all Irish citizens aged 21 and upwards
who were not subject to legal incapacity. The citizenship requirement
was deleted by the Local Elections Act 1972, and the franchise was
granted to all persons aged 18 years and upwards resident in the locality
who have duly complied with the registration requirements: see
Electoral (Amendment) Act 1973, s.2. The Local Government (Ireland)
Act 1918 introduced proportional representation for local elections.

[10] By s.3 of the 1925 Act.

[11] s.11.

[12] Similar provisions are now contained in the Local Government Acts
1941–1946, save that under this later legislation the Minister for the
Environment is not entitled to dissolve local authorities as such, but he
is empowered to direct the removal of the elected representatives. This
power was frequently exercised in the early days of the Irish Free State:
see Roche, *op. cit.*, at pp. 53–54. A dispute between the Minister and
one of the dissolved councils forms the background to *The State (Kerry
County Council)* v. *Minister for Local Government* [1933] I.R. 513. See also
pp. 126–127.

provides that the appointment of most local authority officers and
employees cannot be filled save on the recommendation of the
Local Appointments Commissioners.[13] This process of selection by
an independent body was a desirable reform, and guards against
the political and other forms of patronage which are an all too
common feature of Irish life. Another major step in the same
direction was the introduction of the management system by the
County Management Act 1940[14]. This constitutes the most far-
reaching change in the local government system since the passing
of the Local Government (Ireland) Act 1898, and is described
below.

The Health Act 1970 represented the next major change in the
local government system. This legislation established eight regional health boards composed of representatives of local authorities, the medical and other professions and ministerial nominees.
The Act removed the administration of the health services from
the local authorities, a stark reminder of the stringent control of
local authorities by centralised government. This reforming trend
was continued by the Local Government (Financial Provisions) Act
1978 which abolished domestic rates. Finally, the Supreme
Court's decision in *Brennan* v. *Attorney-General*[15]—which held that
the method of collecting rates on agricultural land was unconstitutional[16]—rendered urgent reform of the local government system
imperative. The critical financial position of local authorities was
alleviated to an extent by the passage of the Local Government
(Financial Provisions) (No. 2) Act 1983 which enabled the local
authority to charge for certain essential services (*e.g.* water supply
and refuse collection), but this was recognised as a stop-gap
measure, and was not intended to be a substitute for a radical
overhaul of the entire local government system.[17]

---

[13] There are some exceptions to this general rule including the
posts of part-time professional staff, nurses, midwives and technical
posts.
[14] The management system had earlier been imposed by a series of local
Acts on Cork, Dublin, Limerick and Waterford. See Roche, *op. cit*, at
pp. 100–104.
[15] [1984] I.L.R.M. 355.
[16] The Supreme Court observed that an anomalous, or even unjust
method of valuing property was not of itself unconstitutional.
However, once the anomalous method of valuing agricultural land
contained in the Valuation (Ireland) Act 1852 was used as the basis for
assessing rates, then the method of collecting such rates (s.11 of the
Local Government Act 1946) infringed the plaintiff's property rights as
guaranteed by Art. 40.3, and was unconstitutional.
[17] See O'Hagan, McBride, Sanfey, "Local Government Finance: The Irish
Experience" [1985] B.T.R. 235.

2. The management system

The essence of the management system is that certain functions (known as "reserved functions") may be exercised by the elected representatives, while all other executive functions are discharged by a salaried officer, known as "the City Manager" or "the County Manager," as the case may be. In addition, the elected members are entitled to give the manager binding directions as to the manner in which certain executive functions shall be discharged.[18] Although under this formal separation of powers the Manager is consigned to a purely administrative role, in practice, the Council will rely on the manager's expertise for advice and guidance, and the manager's "contribution to the development of local policy is considerable."[19] The Manager will, for example, draw up the estimates of expenditure for the year which must then be approved or rejected by the elected representatives. The manager's stature *vis-á-vis* the local authority is further enhanced by the fact that he is appointed, not by the local authority, but by the Local Appointments Commission, and that he can only be removed from office with the sanction of the Minister for the Environment.[20]

The reserved functions of the local authority are set out in the Second Schedule to the County Management Act 1940. Section 16(3) of that Act provides that the Minister for the Environment might by order direct that certain functions or powers should also be reserved functions. The number of reserved functions have been increased by subsequent legislation.[21] Section 17 of the 1940 Act states that every power, function or duty of a local authority or

[18] City and County Management (Amendment) Act 1955, s.4.
[19] Report of the Public Services Organisation Review Group ("the Devlin Report") (1969) (Prl. 792) at para. 25.2.12. The Manager will, for example, draw up the estimates of expenditure. For a less sanguine view as to the effect of the County Management Act 1940, see the comments of John Kelly T.D. at the second stage of the Local Government (Reorganisation) Bill 1985: "[E]arly local government representatives in this country were not infrequently corrupt and very frequently incompetent. So incompetent were they, in fact, that in 1940 Mr. DeValera, who was no Fascist, stripped them of nearly all of their powers. He left them their tricorn hats, their chains, their gowns and their coaches, but vested nearly all their powers in managers" (*Dail Debates*, Vol. 357, col. 313) (March 21, 1985).
[20] County Management Act 1940, s.6.
[21] A full list of the reserved functions is to be found in Keane, *op. cit.*, at pp. 20–30, and see also County Management (Reserved Functions) Order 1985 (S.I. 1985 No. 341) (making of service charges under ss.2 and 8 of Local Government (Financial Provisions) (No. 2) Act 1983 to be a reserved function).

elected body which is not a reserved function shall be an "executive function" of such council or body and exercisable by the manager. An executive function must be performed by the Manager by way of a signed order in writing. A register must be kept of all such orders made by him for inspection by the elected members at a council meeting.[22] There is no comprehensive method of distinguishing reserved from executive functions, nevertheless, it is generally true to say that the latter are of an administrative nature. Reserved functions tend to deal with political and policy-making matters, or involve quasi-legislative or financial powers. Section 13 of the Local Government (Financial Provisions) Act 1978 provides a good example of this distinction. The section provides that "the making of a rate" (*i.e.* the individual assessment of a multitude of rateable properties) shall not be a reserved function, but section 13(2) stipulates that this shall not be taken to affect the local authorities' power to strike a rate in the pound.[23] Accordingly, the power of the elected local representatives to levy finance is not affected,[24] but the execution of that policy decision—essentially an administrative function—is assigned to the manager.

One further aspect of the separation of powers between the elected members and the manager must now be mentioned. Section 4 of the City and County Management (Amendment) Act 1955 enables the elected members to give the Manager directions as to how certain of his executive functions shall be performed. Section 4(1) of the 1955 Act provides:

> "[A] local authority may by resolution require any particular act, matter or thing specifically mentioned in the resolution and which the local authority or the manager can lawfully do or effect to be done or effected in performance of the executive functions of the local authority."

But the power of the local authority to pass such a resolution is subject to a number of important qualifications. Special notice must be given[25] and not only must there be a majority of members

---

[22] s.19 of the 1940 Act.

[23] This power is contained in s.10(4) of the City and County Management (Amendment) Act 1955.

[24] However, from a practical point of view, the abolition of domestic rates has diminished the power of the elected representatives. The local authorities are now increasingly dependent on central government as a source of revenue.

[25] s.4 of the 1955 Act requires that the notice of the resolution must specify a day not later than seven days after the receipt of the notice by the manager for the holding of the meeting at which the resolution is to be considered.

in favour of the resolution, but that majority must exceed at least one-third of the total number of the members of the local authority. A resolution of this nature can only require the performance of an executive function in a lawful manner, and it seems clear that a resolution which required the manager to act in an unreasonable or arbitrary manner, or in a manner contrary to the requirements of constitutional justice, would be *ultra vires*.[26] Furthermore, section 4(9)(*a*) states that a resolution may not "apply or extend" to:

> "[T]he performance of any function or duty of a local authority generally [or] to every case or occasion of the performance of any such function or to a number or class of such cases or occasions so extended as to be substantially or in effect every case or occasion on which any such function is performed in that area. . . . "

The purpose of this subsection is to ensure that the manager is not stripped of an entire executive function by means of a general resolution. So, for example, while a section 4 resolution may validly direct that a particular planning permission, should be granted, it may *not* require that all applications of that should be acceded to.[27] In addition, it would seem that this procedure cannot be used to compel the manager not to do any particular act, matter or thing, *i.e.* it can only be used to direct the manager to take some positive step.[28]

The manager may decline to put a section 4 resolution before the elected members for their consideration where it is clear that the resolution requires the performance of an illegal act.[29] In

---

[26] *McDonald* v. *Feeley*, Supreme Court, July 23, 1980. See also Keane, *op. cit.*, at p. 33.

[27] Such resolutions do not apply to the exercise or performance of the manager's executive functions in relation to the control, remuneration etc. of the council's officers or servants.

[28] See Keane, *op. cit.*, at pp. 35–36.

[29] The assistant city manager advised members of the Dublin City Council in August 1979 that it would be illegal for him to order a halt to the construction of the civic offices at Wood Quay. A motion had been placed before the Council directing such action pending the completion of further archaeological excavation of a site which had earlier been declared by the High Court to be a national monument. The deputy Lord Mayor followed the advice of the assistant manager, and ruled the motion out of order. See *The Irish Times*, August 14, 1979.

If the chairman of a meeting refused to put such a resolution to a vote, he could be compelled to by an order of mandamus. However, an order of mandamus will not be granted where this would further the commission of an illegal act: see *The State (Pine Valley Developments Ltd.)* v. *Dublin County Council* [1984] I.R. 417.

addition, section 16 provides that if such a proposed resolution would involve an illegal payment, or would likely result in a deficiency or loss of the authority's funds, then the names of the persons voting for such a proposal must be recorded, and those persons voting in favour of the resolution are liable to be surcharged.

3. The doctrine of ultra vires

Local authorities do not possess any inherent powers. To put it another way, statutory authority must exist before the actions of a local authority—even those which inhere in a natural person—can be deemed to be valid, and any action which does not come within the scope of these powers is *ultra vires* the authority. It should be noted that *express* statutory authorisation is not necessary, for it will be enough if the powers in question may be necessarily inferred from the terms of the enabling statute:

> "Whatever may be fairly regarded as incidental to, or consequential upon, those things which the legislature has authorised, ought not (unless expressly prohibited) to be held by judicial construction to be *ultra vires.* . . . "[30]

Many of the reported cases turn on the question of whether the actions of the local authority may be said to be reasonably incidental to the powers expressly conferred. Thus, for example, in *Hendron* v. *Dublin Corporation*[31] it was held that because of the Housing (Miscellaneous Provisions) Act 1931 simply conferred on the local authority the right to acquire land compulsorily where such land was required immediately for housing purposes, no such

[30] *Att.-Gen.* v. *Great Eastern Ry. Co.* (1880) 5 App.Cas. 473 at p. 478, *per* Lord Selbourne L.C.
[31] [1943] I.R. 566. For other recent examples of cases raising the question of *ultra vires*, see *Frank Dunne Ltd.* v. *Dublin C.C.* [1974] I.R. 566; *Murphy* v. *Dublin Corporation* [1976] I.R. 143; *Dublin Corporation* v. *Raso*, High Court, June 1, 1976; *Killiney and Ballybrack Residents Assoc. Ltd.* v. *Minister for Local Government (No. 2)*, Supreme Court, April 24, 1978; *The State (Finglas Industrial Estates Ltd.)* v. *Dublin County Council*, Supreme Court, February 17, 1983; *The State (F.P.H. Properties S.A.)* v. *An Bord Pleanala*, High Court, February 14, 1986. *Cf.* the comments of the Devlin Report at para. 25.3.8 "The current application of the doctrine of *ultra vires*, together with the specific terms in which local government statutes tend to be drawn, encourage rigid control over local authority activities by the Department and deter local authority initiative. In a number of other countries, local authorities operate successfully within a general competence to act for the good of the community. Similar powers could be extended to local authorities, subject to such specific limitations as were considered necessary."

power of compulsory acquisition existed where the land was to be used for future housing purposes, or where (as in the instant case) the authority had yet to reach a final decision on the matter.

An even stricter attitude is taken towards the question of *ultra vires* where the authority's action involves the imposition of financial charges or the creation of criminal sanctions. If a local authority is vested with a discretionary power, it may not lawfully impose a charge as a condition of exercising that power unless this is clearly authorised by statute.[32]

Even though the local authority may have the legal capacity to do certain acts, its decision may well be flawed by some procedural irregularity or abuse of discretionary power. These general principles of administrative law which apply to all public bodies are explained elsewhere.[33] Thus, a local authority may not surrender or contract out of its statutory powers[34] and it must exercise its discretionary powers in good faith[35] and in a reasonable manner.[36]

The audit system

A local authority owes a fiduciary duty to its ratepayers,[37] and it seems that a ratepayer may take appropriate action to restrain proposed expenditure which is *ultra vires* the local authority.[38] But the audit system which exposes financial irregularities and surcharges those responsible[39] is an even more effective means of ensuring that local authority finances are strictly controlled.[40] An auditor, known as the local government auditor, is appointed by

---

[32] *City Brick and Terra Cota Co. Ltd.* v. *Belfast Corporation* [1958] N.I. 44. See also *Commissioners of Customs and Excise* v. *Cure and Deeley Ltd.* [1962] 1 Q.B. 340 (charge imposed without statutory authority by customs officials held to be invalid) and *The State (Finglas Industrial Estates Ltd.)* v. *Dublin Corporation*, Supreme Court, February 17, 1983.

[33] At pp. 297–330.

[34] *Ayr Harbour Trustees* v. *Oswald* (1883) 8 App.Cas. 623.

[35] *The State (O'Mahony)* v. *Cork Board of Health* (1941) Ir.Jur.Rep. 79; *Limerick Corporation* v. *Sheridan* (1956) 90 I.L.T.R. 59 and *The State (Divito)* v. *Arklow U.D.C.* [1986] I.L.R.M. 123.

[36] *Limerick Corporation* v. *Sheridan* (1956) 90 I.L.T.R. 59.

[37] *Prescott* v. *Birmingham Corporation* [1955] Ch. 210; *Bromley L.B.C.* v. *Greater London Council* [1983] 1 A.C. 789.

[38] *R. (Bridgeman)* v. *Drury* [1894] 2 I.R. 489; *Arsenal F.C.* v. *Ende* [1977] A.C. 1. But see *Weir* v. *Fermanagh County Council* [1913] 1 I.R. 193.

[39] County Management Act 1940, s.10.

[40] But see the comments of the Devlin Report (at para. 25.3.10): "The practice of surcharge should be abolished. Surcharges are rarely upheld on appeal and adequate alternative sanctions exist with which to discipline inefficient local authority officers."

the Minister for the Environment[41] and the Minister may also decide to hold an extraordinary audit.[42] By virtue of section 12 of the Local Government (Ireland) Act 1871 a person aggrieved by an auditor's decision has two distinct remedies. He may appeal to the Minister for the Environment, or apply to the High Court for an order of *certiorari*. The High Court's jurisdiction to hear a *certiorari* application under section 12 of the 1871 Act is plenary in nature, and is not confined to issues of law, but can also deal with issues of fact.[43] Only the person authorising the making of an illegal payment may be surcharged under the provisions of section 12, but section 16 of the City and County Management (Amendment) Act 1955 provides that councillors who vote in favour of a section 4 resolution involving the making of an illegal payment are also liable to be surcharged.[44]

Although in some respects a local government auditor may be compared to a company auditor, his functions are altogether more onerous. Although not bound by any rules of procedure, he must act in an independent manner[45] and he is obliged to give all interested parties a fair hearing, and to give them an opportunity to show why they should not be surcharged.[46] The auditor is entitled to take evidence on oath, and he can also compel the attendance of any person at an extraordinary audit and issue the equivalent of a *subpoena duces tecum* to that person.[47] Nevertheless, the auditor cannot be compelled to turn the audit into a judicial inquiry. In *The State (Deane and Walsh)* v. *Moran*[48] the applicants objected to the auditor's allowance of certain expenditure on what were claimed to be private roads. They contended that the only way in which the matter could have been satisfactorily resolved was if a sworn inquiry had been conducted, with legal representation

---

[41] Local Government Act 1941, s.68.

[42] Local Government (Ireland) Act 1902, s.21. For an instance of where an extraordinary audit was held to be warranted, see *Asher* v. *Environment Secretary* [1974] Ch. 208.

[43] *R. (King-Kerr)* v. *Newell* [1903] 2 I.R. 335; *R. (Ferguson)* v. *Moore O'Ferrall* [1903] 2 I.R. 141; *Walsh* v. *Minister for Local Government* [1929] I.R. 377 (Murnaghan J. (*dubitante*)); *The State (Raftis)* v. *Leonard* [1960] I.R. 381. An appeal also lies (by virtue of s.12) to the Minister for the Environment against the making of a surcharge.

[44] The City Manager is obliged to inform the members that if they vote in favour of such a resolution that they will be surcharged; and the names of those voting in favour of the resolution is recorded in the minutes.

[45] *R. (Local Government Board)* v. *McLoughlin* [1917] 2 I.R. 174; *The State (Deane & Walsh)* v. *Moran* (1954) 88 I.L.T.R. 37.

[46] *The State (Dowling)* v. *Leonard* [1960] I.R. 421; *R. (Butler)* v. *Browne* [1909] 2 I.R. 333; *R. (Kennedy)* v. *Browne* [1907] 2 I.R. 505.

[47] Local Government Act 1941, s.86.

[48] (1954) 88 I.L.T.R. 37.

and an opportunity to cross-examine witnesses. Davitt P. rejected this suggestion. He agreed that the auditor was obliged to act fairly and to give the parties concerned a fair opportunity of making their case, but he stressed that an audit:

> "[W]as primarily and essentially an examination of accounts which was usually conducted by a person whose qualifications were those of an auditor and accountant and not those of a judge.... A close examination of the enactments ... left the impression that it was never intended that such an audit could be turned into something essentially different such as a sworn inquiry or a judicial trial at the mere wish of some interested person, no matter how well intentioned."[49]

Power to surcharge

Section 12 of the 1871 Act entitles the auditor to raise a surcharge in respect of payments which are "contrary to law, or which he deems unfounded." The phrase "contrary to law" clearly deals with *ultra vires* payments,[50] but the phrase "one which he deems unfounded" has given rise to some difficulty. Is the phrase "unfounded" simply a synonym for *ultra vires*, or does it extend to expenditure on the part of the local authority which in the circumstances is "unnecessary and extravagant?" The weight of authority now supports the latter construction, and indeed, the matter can now be regarded as settled.

Some doubts have been created by the observations of Palles C.B. in *R. (Duckett)* v. *Calvert*[51] to the effect that while the auditor might surcharge councillors for a breach of trust, this must be established in substantive proceedings. In other words, it was only where a court had ruled that the payments were unnecessary and extravagant that the auditor could surcharge on the grounds that such expenditure had been "unfounded." The other pre-independence authorities disputed this view, and it was stated that the auditor was entitled to surcharge not only in the case of *ultra vires* expenditure, but also where the authority had entered into contracts which imposed an unnecessary burden on the ratepayers.

Not surprisingly, given the unsatisfactory nature of these

---

[49] (1954) 88 I.L.T.R. 43.

[50] *R. (Bridgeman)* v. *Drury* [1894] 2 I.R. 489; *R. (Ferguson)* v. *Moore O'Ferrall* [1903] 2 I.R. 141.

[51] [1898] 2 I.R. 511. Palles C.B. adhered to this view in *R. (King-Kerr)* v. *Newell* [1903] 2 I.R. 335. A Divisional Court had earlier reached the contrary conclusion in *R. (Inglis)* v. *Drury* [1898] 2 I.R. 528; and this was affirmed in *R. (Kennedy)* v. *Browne* [1907] 2 I.R. 505.

authorities, Davitt P. in *The State (Raftis)* v. *Leonard*[52] felt he was justified in taking a fresh approach to the interpretation of the section. In his view the purpose of the section was to prevent the ratepayer "from being burdened with expenses for which there was no proper justification." Accordingly, the auditor was entitled to surcharge, not only in respect of *ultra vires* payments, but also payments which are *intra vires*, and which are, in the opinion of the auditor, unfounded, and the judge instanced a payment under an enforceable contract which was wholly unnecessary as an example of expenditure of the latter variety. He conceded that the court might be bound to follow *Calvert* as an authority for the proposition that the payment of a judgment debt cannot be deemed by the auditor to be unfounded,[53] but he did not think that the principle of that case should be further extended.

Section 20 of the Local Government (Ireland) Act 1902 also enables the auditor to impose a surcharge on any member or officer of a local authority in respect of "any deficiency or loss incurred by his negligence or misconduct." Although the matter is not entirely free from doubt, it would seem that the negligence referred to in the section is the ordinary standard of negligence applied in civil cases.[54]

4. The rating system

Up to quite recently the rating system was the principal source of revenue for local authority expenditure. With the passage of the Local Government (Financial Provisions) Act 1978 rates on domestic dwellings were abolished, and local authorities came to depend heavily on grants in aid from the Exchequer for financial support. Another severe—and, perhaps, fatal—blow to the viability of the present rating system came with the decision of the Supreme Court in *Brennan* v. *Attorney-General*[55] where it held that the system of collecting rates on agricultural land was unconstitutional. The Court observed that the method of collecting rates contained in section 11 of the Local Government Act 1941 was based on the anomalous Griffiths poor law valuation of agricultural land in 1852, and the use of such an outdated system combined

---

[52] [1960] I.R. 381.
[53] In *Calvert*, a Divisional Court quashed a surcharge which had been imposed in respect of a street lighting contract. Judgment had been entered against the Council, and although the Court's reasoning was not unanimous, all were agreed that payment of a sum due on a judgment could not be regarded as unnecessary or unfounded.
[54] See Keane, *op. cit.*, at pp. 313–314. But *cf.* the comments of Lord O'Brien C.J. in *R. (Kennedy)* v. *Browne* [1907] 2 I.R. 505.
[55] [1984] I.L.R.M. 355.

with the absence of any effective review mechanism constituted, in the circumstances, an unjust attack on the plaintiff's property rights.[56] Although the anomalies do not exist to the same extent in the case of non-agricultural land,[57] there nevertheless would seem to be some doubt as to whether the continued use of the poor law valuation system in other areas of rating law is constitutionally justified.

As far as urban houses and buildings are concerned, the valuation is based upon "an estimate of the net annual value thereof."[58] These valuations are also based on the Griffiths valuation survey, and they bear scant relation to present letting values. Unlike the position which formerly existed in relation to agricultural land, the valuations can be revised in various ways. First, there is the possibility of a general revision.[59] Secondly, each clerk of a local authority may send to the Commissioner of Valuation a list of specific items of property for revision.[60] Finally, an aggrieved ratepayer may appeal to the Commissioner of Valuation against the decision of the Valuation Office following the annual valuation revision.[61] As the Commissioner has no power of initiative in selecting the items of property for revision, the annual revisions have, not surprisingly, failed to keep the majority of valuations up to date. Since about 1947 a practice evolved in the Valuation Office of fixing the valuation at about one-third of the current net rental value, and of giving revised valuations

---

[56] O'Higgins C.J. was of opinion that a valuation system—even one which was anomalous or unjust—was in and of itself neutral as far as constitutional rights were concerned. It was only when the valuation system was used as the basis of assessing rates that the method of collecting these rates could be attacked as unconstitutional.

[57] But *cf.* the comments contained in the White Paper, *Local Finance and Taxation* (Prl. 2745) (1972) at para. 51.2: "The defects in the system have given rise to inequities which have become more pronounced with the passage of time and have been aggravated by the constant and substantial increases in rate poundages." See de Buitleir, *Problems of Irish Local Finance* (Dublin, 1974) at pp. 9–16.

[58] Valuation (Ireland) Act 1852, s.11.

[59] Under s.34 of the Valuation (Ireland) Act 1852 a county council may apply to the Minister for the Environment for a general revision of lands in the county, but no such valuation has ever been carried out. By virtue of s.65 of the Local Government (Ireland) Act 1898 the corporations of the cities of Dublin, Cork, Limerick and Waterford may apply for a general revision of 14 years. Dublin City was revalued in 1908–15 and Waterford in 1924–26. See de Buitleir, *op. cit.*, at pp. 11–12.

[60] Valuation (Ireland) Amendment Act 1854, s.4 and art. 37(d) of Local Government (Adaptation of Irish Enactments) Order 1899.

[61] Valuation (Ireland) Act 1852, s.20.

broadly in line with the general run of figures for similar properties in the areas involved.[62] In *Schofield v. Commissioner of Valuation*,[63] O'Keeffe P. held that there was no statutory authority for this practice, and he held that the proper valuation of the hereditament corresponded to its current letting value. The Valuation Act 1986 is designed, *inter alia*, to deal with the problems caused by *Schofield's* case. Section 5(1) of the Act now provides that the amount of a valuation may be reduced by such amount as is necessary to ensure, in so far as it is reasonably practicable, that:

> "[T]he amount of the valuation bears the same relationship to the valuations of other tenements and rateable hereditaments as the net annual value of the tenement or rateable hereditament bears to the net annual values of the other tenements or rateable hereditaments."

There appears to be a general recognition that the present rating system is unsatisfactory, and that some new method of local taxation expenditure must be devised.[64] For this reason, and given that the topic has been dealt with adequately elsewhere,[65] what follows is simply an outline of the current rating system.

The principal method of valuing units of property (upon which the assessment of rates is then based) is contained in the Valuation Acts 1852–1986. The Valuation (Ireland) Act 1852 requires every tenement or rateable hereditament to be separately valued. The method of rate collection is now contained in the Local Government Act 1946, and this Act also effected some minor changes to the Valuation Acts themselves. The Local Government (Financial Provisions) Act 1978 abolished domestic rates, and also provided that the making of the rates (*i.e.* the individual assessment of ratepayers) was no longer to be a reserved function. However, the elected representatives retained the right (subject to ministerial control) to fix the rate in the pound.

Rates are levied on the "occupier of rateable hereditaments."[66] But the word "occupier" has been given a special extended meaning by virtue of sections 14 and 23 of the Local Government Act 1946, and the term now includes the owner of the building

---

[62] de Buitleir, *op. cit.*, at pp. 12–13.
[63] High Court, July 24, 1972.
[64] See the recommendations of the Commission on Taxation, *Fourth Report: Special Taxation* (Prl. 2917, 1985) at paras. 5.43 to 5.45.
[65] See Keane, *op. cit.*, at pp. 280–306.
[66] Poor Relief (Ireland) Act 1838, s.24.

where it is unoccupied.[67] These sections also provide for rebates where the building is unoccupied because of the execution of repairs, alterations or additions[68] or where the owner is *bona fide* unable to find a tenant at a reasonable rent. The occupation of the hereditament must be permanent and not merely transitory in nature[69]

Hereditaments, which would otherwise be rateable are exempt if they are used for purely charitable or public purposes. The principal statutory basis[70] for the exemption is contained in the proviso to section 63 of the Poor Law (Ireland) Act 1838, which exempts buildings used exclusively for religious worship, or for education of the poor, cemeteries, burial grounds and hospitals or other buildings used exclusively for charitable or public purpose. It had been held that the term "charitable" in the proviso to section 63 excludes any charitable purpose which is not mentioned therein.[71] Accordingly, it was thought up to quite recently that buildings used for educational purposes must be confined to the education of the poor.[72] But in its most recent pronouncement on this vexed question, *Governors of Wesley College* v. *Commissioner for Valuation*,[73] the Supreme Court has struck a slightly different note. In that case an exemption had been claimed on behalf of a private fee-paying school which was geared towards making a profit. It was this fact, rather than that the education provided was not exclusively for the benefit of the poor, which meant that the plaintiffs could not obtain the benefit of the exemption. The *Wesley College* decision may well extend the grounds for exemption, for the test now appears to be whether the buildings are used exclusively for charitable or public purposes (*i.e.* in the sense of no private gain), and a building is not precluded from being considered charitable simply because its benefits are not confined to the poor.

---

[67] The test as regards occupancy is the *de facto* position, and, accordingly, mere licensees or even trespassers may be liable for rates if they have the unrestricted use and enjoyment of the hereditament: see *Carroll* v. *Mayo County Council* [1967] I.R. 364.

[68] The term includes demolition of the premises: see *Carlisle Trust Ltd.* v. *Dublin Corporation* [1965] I.R. 456.

[69] Keane, *op. cit.*, at 185–186.

[70] Certain relief against rates is provided in the case of secondary schools and community halls by s.2 of the Local Government (Finance Provisions) Act 1978.

[71] *Barrington's Hospital* v. *Commissioner of Valuation* [1957] I.R. 299.

[72] *O'Neill* v. *Commissioner of Valuation* [1914] 2 I.R. 447; *McGahan and Ryan* v. *Commissioner of Valuation* [1934] I.R. 736.

[73] [1984] I.L.R.M. 117. Neither *O'Neill* nor *McGahan and Ryan* are referred to in Henchy J.'s judgment for the Supreme Court.

The decision in *Wesley College* may well have other implications in this area, for in *Maynooth College* v. *Commissioners for Valuation*,[74] it was held that a Catholic seminary was a rateable hereditament. The building was not "exclusively dedicated to religious worship" (to use the language of the proviso to section 63 of the 1838 Act), and as the word "charitable" excluded any charitable purpose expressly mentioned earlier in the proviso, the seminary could not be said to be used for charitable purposes, merely because it was for the advancement of religion.[75] In the light of the *Wesley College* decision, it may be that an institution of this nature could now claim to be charitable *if it was non-profit* making in nature, and which would otherwise be regarded as charitable for tax purposes.

The same difficulties do not arise in the case of the final ground of exemption in favour of "infirmaries, hospitals ... or other buildings used exclusively for charitable purposes" because such charitable purposes have not already been expressly mentioned in the proviso. Thus, in *Barrington's Hospital* v. *Commissioner for Valuation*,[76] a public voluntary hospital was held to be charitable in its purpose, despite the fact that some of its patients were fee-paying, as these fees were not used for private profit. It may well be argued that in the *Wesley College* decision the Supreme Court effectively applied this test to *all* charitable or public institutions, despite the fact that in the case of educational and religious institutions the scope for exemption would appear to have been severely limited by the terms of the proviso.

A person aggrieved by a valuation contained in the annual revised list may appeal to the Commissioner for Valuation. A further appeal may be taken to the Circuit Court within 21 days of the publication of the Commissioner's decision. The decision of the Circuit Court is final, save that the Circuit Court may state a case on a point of law to the High Court,[77] from which there is a further appeal (also confined to the point of law) to the Supreme Court.

An appeal also lies against the "making of the rate"[78] and thus it is open to him to allege that any persons have been wrongly included or excluded from the rate, or that the rate itself is illegal.

---

[74] [1958] I.R. 189.

[75] Even though the building would be regarded as charitable for ordinary tax purposes under the test laid down by the House of Lords in *Income Tax Special Purposes Commissioners* v. *Pemsel* [1891] A.C. 531. See also *Brendan* v. *Commissioner of Valuation* [1969] I.R. 202.

[76] [1957] I.R. 299. See also *Dublin Corporation* v. *Dublin Cemeteries Committee*, Supreme Court, November 12, 1975.

[77] Courts of Justice Act 1936, s.31(3).

[78] Poor Relief (Ireland) Act 1838, ss.106–12, as amended by Valuation (Ireland) Act 1852, s.28 and ss.22, 23, 29 and 30 of the Poor Relief (Ireland) Act 1849.

An appeal lies to the Circuit Court, and from there to the High Court with the possibility of a further appeal to the Supreme Court.

A rate may be quashed on certiorari,[79] but a ratepayer who fails to avail of the statutory procedure to correct the determination of the Commissioner, will be later estopped from doing so.[80] A local authority is empowered to amend the rates "so as to make them conform with the enactments relating thereto."[81]

In an effort to restore some fiscal autonomy to local authorities, the Local Government (Financial Provisions) (No. 2) Act 1983 allows the authorities to charge for the provision of certain services (water, domestic refuse collection etc.). This Act evoked considerable political opposition, and, following the 1985 local elections, it is no longer utilised by the vast majority of local authorities.[82]

5. Specimen functions

Local authorities have been vested with a variety of important functions and statutory powers. Thus, local authorities have responsibility for such matters as the maintenance and improvement of roads[83]; the protection of the environment[84]; vocational education[85]; street trading[86]; the compilation of electoral registers[87]; and miscellaneous functions relating to the administration of justice, such as the appointment of coroners and the provision of courthouses.[88] While a detailed consideration of the exercise of

[79] *R. (McEvoy)* v. *Dublin Corporation* (1878) 2 L.R.Ir. 371.
[80] *Whaley* v. *Great Northern Ry. Co.* [1913] 2 I.R. 142; *Stevenson* v. *Orr* [1916] 2 I.R. 619. But this estoppel does not apply to entries which are *ultra vires*: see *Dublin Corporation* v. *Dublin Cemeteries Committee*, Supreme Court, November 12, 1975.
[81] Local Government Act 1941, s.60. Dublin and Dun Laoghaire Corporations derive similar powers from the Local Government (Dublin) Act 1930, ss.73 and 94.
[82] By virtue of the County Management (Reserved Functions) Order 1985 (S.I. 1985 No. 341) the power to make charges for services provided in respect of domestic services (including water supplies) provided by ss.2 and 8 of the 1983 Act is now a reserved function and most local councils have voted not to impose such charges.
[83] See generally Roche, *op. cit.*, at pp. 244–256.
[84] Scannell, *The Law and Practice relating to Pollution Control in Ireland* (London, 1982).
[85] Roche, *op. cit.*, pp. 273–275.
[86] Local authorities are designated as licensing authorities under the Casual Trading Act 1980.
[87] Electoral Act 1963, ss.6 and 7.
[88] Courthouses (Provisions and Maintenance) Act 1935, s.3.

these functions lies well outside the scope of this book, we must examine briefly the two most important local authority functions, planning control and housing.

Planning control[89]

Although planning control legislation has been in existence in Ireland since 1934,[90] it was not until the coming into force of the Local Government (Planning and Development) Act 1963 that a truly comprehensive scheme of planning control was established. Local authorities were designated by this Act to be planning authorities for their functional area,[91] and were now obliged to produce, and regularly to update, a development plan. Furthermore, enforcement powers and the power to restrain unauthorised developments were greatly increased.

But even this legislation proved to be defective in a number of important respects. An appeal lay to the Minister for Local Government, who in practice was susceptible to local political pressures[92] and who often granted permissions which materially contravened the development plan.[93] Moreover, the enforcement powers proved to be wholly ineffective to deal with the growing problem of unauthorised developments. The Local Government (Planning and Development) Act 1976 sought to deal with these problems. It transferred the Minister's appellate functions to an

---

[89] See generally, Walsh, *Planning and Development Law*, (2nd ed.); O'Sullivan and Sheppard, *A Sourcebook on Planning Law in Ireland* (Abingdon, 1984); Scannell, *Planning Control: Twenty Years On* (1982) 4 D.U.L.J.(n.s.) 41 (Part 1); (1983) 5 D.U.L.J.(n.s.) 225 (Part 2).

[90] Town and Regional Planning Act 1934; Town and Regional Planning Act (Amendment) Act 1939. For an account of this legislation (which was repealed in its entirety in 1963) see Miley and King, *Town and Regional Planning in Ireland* (Dublin, 1951).

[91] Local Government (Planning and Development) Act 1963 ("the 1963 Act") s.2(2). An exception arises in the case of town commissioners, who, although they are local authorities, are not designated as planning authorities. These functions are discharged in the case of a town with commissioners by the county council of the county in which the town is situated.

[92] *Cf.* the comments of Henchy J. in *The State (Pine Valley Developments Ltd.) v. Dublin County Council* [1984] I.R. 417, 425 and see p. 136.

[93] This was held to be *ultra vires* by the Supreme Court in *The State (Pine Valley Developments Ltd.) v. Dublin County Council* [1984] I.R. 417. This decision was reversed by the Local Government (Planning and Development) Act 1982, s.6. An Bord Pleanala is expressly vested with a jurisdiction to depart from the terms of the development plan: Local Government (Planning and Development) Act 1976, s.14(8).

impartial body, which was to be known as An Bord Pleanala.[94] In addition, the enforcement controls were strengthened, and the Act envisaged a greater role for third party objectors. Section 27 of the 1976 Act created a new summary jurisdiction, whereby any citizen—regardless of whether he satisfied traditional *locus standi* requirements or otherwise[95]—could seek a court order restraining unauthorised development. This section has proved to be an invaluable method of enforcing the planning code.[96]

While undoubtedly the most important function of a planning authority—the granting and attaching of conditions to a planning permission—is an executive function, and vested in the city or country manager, nevertheless the elected representatives do have an important say in the planning process. It is the task of the local councillors to draw up a development plan,[97] and they may also revoke or modify a planning permission.[98] In addition, the councillors may declare any particular area to be one of special amenity.[99]

A local authority must have regard to certain objectives[1] when drawing up a development plan. A local authority is required to keep a draft of the development plan on public display for at least three months, and to take into consideration any objections or representations made with regard to the draft plan. The authority

---

[94] The Local Government (Planning and Development) Act 1983 sets out the procedure governing the appointment of the chairman and members of An Bord Pleanala. This Act represents yet another legislative attempt to augment the impartiality of the Board and to reduce political interference with its operations. For a fuller account of this legislation, see Walsh, *op. cit.*, at pp. 79–83; Stevenson, "Planning Appeals in the Republic of Ireland" (1985) 7 *Urban Law and Policy* 170, and see at p. 148.

[95] In *Buckley* v. *Holland Clyde Ltd.*, High Court 1974, Kenny J. held that a third party had no *locus standi* to complain that a developer had not kept within the terms of his planning permission. Section 27 is designed to rectify the consequences of decisions such as this.

[96] See generally Scannell, "Planning Control: Twenty Years On" (1983) 5 D.U.L.J.(n.s.) at pp. 241–247.

[97] s.19(7) of the 1963 Act.

[98] s.30 of the 1963 Act.

[99] s.42 of the 1963 Act, as amended by s.40 of the 1976 Act.

[1] s.19(2)(a) of the 1963 Act. In the case of urban areas, a local authority is required to have regard to the following objectives: (a) indicating the zoning of particular areas for particular purposes; (b) improving road safety by the provision of parking places or road improvements; (c) the development and renewal of obsolete areas; (d) the preservation, improvement and extension of amenities. In rural areas, the objectives include (c) and (d), but also the improvement and extension of water and sewage supplies.

is entitled to make non-material alterations to the draft plan without going through the statutory notification and exhibition procedure again.[2]

Subject to one qualification, the planning authority is bound by the terms of the development plan, and the manager is not entitled to grant a permission which materially contravenes the terms of the development plan.[3] However, the elected members are entitled to grant such a permission following a passing of a special resolution to that effect.[4] It would also seem that a manager can be required to grant planning permission by virtue of a resolution passed under section 4 of the City and County Management (Amendment) Act 1955, where the proposed development would not materially contravene the development plan.

The manager is entitled by virtue of section 26(1) of the 1963 Act to attach conditions to a grant of permission, but all such conditions imposed must be in furtherance of the proper planning and development of the area. Section 26(2) states that, without prejudice to the generality of section 26(1), the conditions attached may include "any and all" of a list of specified conditions.[5] The planning authority is required to give reasons in respect of each condition imposed.[6] The discretionary power to attach conditions is, of course, governed by ordinary principles of administrative law. The conditions imposed must fairly and reasonably relate to the proposed development, and the reasons given in support of the condition must be capable of justifying the imposition of the condition.[7] Not only that, but the courts will quash the decision to attach conditions—even where the conditions are valid on their face—where it has been shown that the

[2] s.37 of the 1963 Act.
[3] Generally speaking only An Bord Pleanala is entitled to grant a permission which materially contravenes the terms of the development plan. Section 39(g) of the 1976 Act also permits the planning authority to contravene materially the development plan in certain circumstances, and once the elaborate procedure specified in the subsection had been followed.
[4] See n. 15 *supra.*
[5] Among the conditions specifically authorised are included conditions requiring the carrying out of works (including the provision of car parks) which the authority consider are required for the purposes of the development authorised by the permission: conditions abating noise or vibration levels and conditions requiring contributions in respect of local authority expenditure.
[6] Local Government (Planning and Development) Act 1963, s.26(8), as inserted by Local Government (Planning and Development) Act 1976, s.39(9).
[7] *Killiney and Ballybrack Residents Assoc. Ltd.* v. *Minister for Local Government (No. 2)*, Supreme Court, April 24, 1978.

decision has been actuated by improper motives, or that the planning authority has rejected legitimate considerations, or has introduced irrelevant considerations, or has otherwise manifested unreasonableness in arriving at its decision.[8]

An applicant may also obtain planning permission in default, for section 26(4) of the 1963 Act provides that where an application has been made to a planning authority in accordance with the regulations for the time being in force,[9] then if notice has not been given to the applicant within the appropriate period (which is generally two months[10]), a decision by the planning authority to grant permission shall be regarded as having been granted on the last day of the period. The purpose of these default provisions is to compel the planning authority to direct its mind to the planning application and to adjudicate upon such application within the appropriate period.

It is now clear that a decision which, even if *ultra vires* (and thus liable to be set aside as a nullity), is still a "decision" for the purposes of section 26(4), and thus the applicant cannot claim that "no decision" has been given in such a case and that he is consequently entitled to permission in default.[11]

An Bord Pleanala

An interested party (including a third party objector) may appeal[12] against the decision of the planning authority to An Bord

---

[8] *The State (Fitzgerald)* v. *An Bord Pleanala* [1985] I.L.R.M. 117 and pp. 305–306.

[9] The following are the principal regulations currently in force: Local Government (Planning and Development) Regulations 1977 (S.I. 1977 No. 65); Local Government (Planning and Development) Regulations 1982 (S.I. 1982 No. 342); Local Government (Planning and Development) (Exempted Development and Amendment) Regulations 1984 (S.I. 1984 No. 348) and Local Government (Planning and Development) (Exempted Development) Regulations 1985 (S.I. 1985 No. 130). For a recent example of a case where the applicant was held to have failed to comply with these regulations, (and was, thus, disentitled to default permission) see *Crodaun Homes Ltd.* v. *Kildare C.C.* [1983] I.L.R.M. 1.

[10] Although the time period is extended where the local authority makes a bona fide request for further information: see s.26(4)(*b*) of the 1963 Act.

[11] *The State (Abenglen Properties Ltd.)* v. *Dublin Corporation* [1984] I.R. 384: *Creedon* v. *Dublin Corporation* [1984] I.R. 428 (reaching similar conclusions in respect of the analogous default provisions contained in s.10 of the (now lapsed) Housing Act 1969).

[12] One may simply appeal against a condition imposed by a planning authority: see Local Government (Planning and Development) Act 1983, s.19.

Pleanala. An Bord Pleanala is required to act judicially and there have been several cases where decisions have been quashed because the Board breached the rules of natural justice, or where it acted on irrelevant considerations.[13] Save in unusual cases, a litigant must first exhaust his appellate remedies by appealing to An Bord Pleanala, as otherwise he will be precluded from seeking an order of certiorari quashing the adjudication upon his planning application.[14] The Board is alone entitled to determine whether development has taken place, and, if so, whether it is exempted development[15] for the purpose of the planning code. The Board is also entitled to refer any point of law to the High Court for determination.[16]

Enforcement

The planning code may be enforced by way of criminal sanctions, enforcement or warning notices or by the granting of injunctive relief. By virtue of section 24 of the 1963 Act a person who carries out any development in respect of which permission is required without or in contravention of such permission is guilty of an offence. The prosection may proceed summarily or by way of an indictment.[17] On the other hand, the planning authority may choose to take the less drastic step of issuing an enforcement notice or a warning notice, if of the opinion that a development is being carried out in an unauthorised manner, or contrary to the requirements of conditions attached to the permission. The enforcement notice,[18] must specify the nature of the unauthorised development, or the development constituting non-compliance with a condition, and require the developer to take such steps as are necessary to restore the land to its original condition. Alternatively, a warning notice may be issued by a planning authority where it appears that the land is being, or is likely to be, developed in an unauthorised manner,[19] or where unauthorised *use* is being made of the land, or where any structural or natural

---

[13] See, *e.g. The State (Genport Ltd.)* v. *An Bord Pleanala* [1983] I.L.R.M. 12; *The State (Fitzgerald)* v. *An Bord Pleanala* [1985] I.L.R.M. 117.

[14] *The State (Abenglen Properties Ltd.)* v. *An Bord Pleanala* [1984] I.R. 384.

[15] s.14(2) of the 1976 Act.

[16] s.42 of the 1976 Act.

[17] s.24 of the 1963 Act, as amended by s.8 of the Local Government (Planning and Development) Act 1982.

[18] The differing types of enforcement notices which may be issued are discussed by Walsh, *op. cit.*, at pp. 145–154. Failure to comply with an enforcement notice is an offence: Local Government (Planning and Development) Act 1963, s.37(7).

[19] s.26 of the 1976 Act. This matter is discussed by Walsh. *op. cit.*, at pp. 154–155.

feature of the land, the preservation of which is required by a condition subject to which a permission for the development of any land was granted, may be removed or damaged.

The planning injunction is undoubtedly the most effective method of ensuring compliance with the planning code. Section 27(1) of the 1963 Act authorises the High Court to restrain unauthorised development or use of land. The High Court is empowered by section 27(2) to require any specified person to do or not to do or to cease to do anything which the court considers necessary to ensure that the development is carried out in conformity with the planning permission.[20] Section 27 expressly provides that an applicant need not satisfy ordinary *locus standi* requirements:

> "We are all, as users and enjoyers of the environment in which we live, given a standing to go to the Court and to seek an order compelling those who have been given a development permission to carry out the development in accordance with the terms of that permission. And the Court is given a discretion sufficiently wide to make whatever order is necessary to achieve that objective."[21]

The effectiveness of the section 27 remedy has been strengthened by a series of decisions which make it plain that it would require exceptional circumstances for the court to refrain from exercising its powers under this section in the case of unauthorised development or use of land.[22]

The planning authority is also entitled in certain limited situations to revoke or modify a permission granted.[23] This is a reserved function, and is exercisable only by the elected representatives. The power to modify or revoke such a permission may itself only be used where (if the permission relates to the carrying out of works) such works have been commenced or (if the permission relates to a change of use of land) at any time prior to a change of use. A person affected by a revocation notice may appeal to An Bord Pleanala. This power of revocation was granted to planning authorities to deal with the problem of unimplemented permissions. Passage of time, or changes in the development plan may make it desirable that a particular permission should not be implemented. Accordingly, the revocation power

---

[20] However, the Court will not make a mandatory order in s.27(2) proceedings: see *Dublin C.C.* v. *Kirby* [1985] I.L.R.M. 325.

[21] *Morris* v. *Garvey* [1983] I.R. 319, 323 *per* Henchy J.

[22] *Morris* v. *Garvey* [1983] I.R. 319; *Stafford and Bates* v. *Roadstone Ltd* [1980] I.L.R.M. 1 and see generally Scannell, "*Planning Control—Twenty Years On II*" (1983) 5 D.U.L.J.(n.s.) 225 at 241–7.

[23] s.30 of the 1963 Act. See Walsh, *op. cit.*, at pp. 99–102.

must be exercised with these objectives in mind, and it would not seem that this power may be validly exercised for no better reason than that a particular permission has been granted on appeal,[24] or because the applicant has succeeded in obtaining permission in default.

Housing

Numerous pieces of legislation dating from the mid-nineteenth century have sought to deal with the problem of poor and overcrowded housing, and to provide suitable accommodation for persons of modest means. The principal legislation on this topic is now contained in the Housing Act 1966, although this reforming and consolidating Act has been amended on a number of occasions, most notably by the Housing (Miscellaneous Provisions) Act 1979, and the Housing Act 1984.[25]

The local authority is vested with the powers of a housing authority for its functional area.[26] It is the duty of the housing authority from time to time (but at least once every five years) to inspect and assess the adequacy of the supply and the condition of housing within its functional area. It is also required to draw up a building programme designed, among other things, to relieve overcrowding and to provide adequate and suitable accommodation for persons in need of housing and who are unable to provide accommodation from their own resources.[27] Section 60 of the Housing Act 1966 requires the local authority to draw up a scheme of priorities for the letting of housing accommodation, and again, the Act lays emphasis on the requirements of persons in need of housing, but who have insufficient means to provide their own accommodation.

The purpose and effect of section 60 was examined by the Supreme Court in *McDonald* v. *Feeley*.[28] In this case itinerants residing within the county council's functional area had trespassed

---

[24] *The State (Cogley)* v. *Dublin Corporation* [1970] I.R. 244.

[25] See Keane, *op. cit.*, at pp. 128–147: Roche, *op. cit*, at pp. 220–243.

[26] Housing Act 1966, s.2. In *McNamee* v. *Buncrana U.D.C.* [1983] I.R. 213, the Supreme Court held that the 1966 Act did not entitle a local authority to house someone resident outside the functional area. This decision was felt to be an undesireable restriction on the powers of local authorities, and it has been reversed by statute: see Housing Act 1984, s.4.

[27] Section 53 of the 1966 Act. The Supreme Court made reference to the section in *Siney* v. *Dublin Corporation* [1980] I.R. 400 in order to demonstrate that it was an implied term of every letting made by a housing authority under the Housing Act 1960 that the dwelling was fit for human habitation.

[28] Supreme Court, July 23, 1980.

on lands belonging to the council. The council members resolved, pursuant to section 4 of the City and County Management (Amendment) Act 1955 that the county manager should take action to evict the itinerants. Initially, no alternative accommodation had been offered to the itinerants. The Supreme Court noted that a city manager could only be required to perform a lawful act by lawful means, and hinted that action of this nature would not have been lawful had not alternative accommodation been offered at the eleventh hour by the county council. Such action would not have been lawful because the housing authority would have acted without having regard to the housing needs of persons resident within their functional area. A housing authority is now entitled to house persons not normally resident within their functional area.[29] In drawing up their scheme of priorities, a housing authority may provide that priority is to be given to certain categories of persons, but a report of a medical officer of the appropriate health board must be considered before drawing up such a scheme.[30] Lettings made by a housing authority under the provisions of the Housing Acts are subject to an implied warranty that the premises are fit for human habitation.[31]

In regard to private accommodation, a local authority is also entitled to send the equivalent of warning notices where it is satisfied that a particular house is overcrowded,[32] or is unfit for human habitation. Section 65 of the 1966 Act entitles the authority to serve a notice on the owner of a premises requiring him to desist from causing or permitting the overcrowding. Failure to comply with such a notice is an offence.[33] In the case of unfit houses, the authority may serve a notice on the owner of such premises requiring him within twenty eight days to carry out

---

[29] Housing Act 1984, s.4.

[30] s.60 of the 1966 Act, as amended by s.16 of the Housing (Miscellaneous Provisions) Act 1979.

[31] *Siney* v. *Dublin Corporation* [1980] I.R. 400. For an excellent account of this case, see Kerr and Clarke, "Council Housing, Implied Terms and Negligence—A Critique of *Siney* v. *Dublin Corporation*" (1980) 15 Ir.Jur.(n.s.) 32. See also *Coleman* v. *Dundalk U.D.C.*, Supreme Court, July 17, 1985.

[32] By virtue of s.63 of the 1966 Act, a house is deemed to be overcrowded when the number of persons ordinarily sleeping in the house and the number of rooms therein either: (i) are such that any two of those persons, being persons of ten years of age or more of opposite sexes and not being persons living together as husband and wife must sleep in the same room, or (ii) are such that the free air space in any room used as a sleeping apartment for any person is less than 400 cubic feet.

[33] s.65(4) of the 1966 Act. The maximum penalty which may be imposed is a fine of £100 and one month's imprisonment.

specified works. If the house is unfit for human habitation, but is not capable of being rendered habitable at a reasonable expense, then the owner must be afforded the opportunity of carrying out such specified works, or using the house in a particular manner. If this is not possible, the authority may make a closing order (which prohibits the use of the house or any part thereof for any purpose specified by the housing authority) or a demolition order. A person aggrieved by a closing order or a demolition order may generally appeal to the Circuit Court.[34]

Now that the Housing Act 1969[35] has lapsed, the demolition of habitable houses is dealt with by the Local Government (Planning and Development) (Exempted Development and Amendment) Regulations 1984.[36] These regulations have amended the classes of development which are exempted from the requirement of obtaining planning permission contained in the Third Schedule to the Local Government (Planning and Development) Regulations 1977.[37] The demolition of a habitable house is no longer regarded as an exempted development and consequently planning permission is required.

6. Central government controls

Local authorities are subject to extensive controls from central government. These controls commonly take the form of requiring the consent of the Minister for the Environment before a certain act may lawfully be done,[38] or where the Minister is authorised by statute to make regulations which concern local government matters. But central control penetrates to the very heart of local administration, for the Minister is entitled to take the ultimate step of removing the elected members where a ministerial directive has not been complied with. The abolition of domestic rates has had the result of greatly increasing central control at the expense of the local authorities, for local authorities are now virtually dependent on central funds for financial survival. Not only do local authorities operate under severe budgetary constraints, but

[34] ss.72 and 73 of the 1966 Act.
[35] The Act required permission from a housing authority for the demolition of a habitable house, or the use "otherwise than for human habitation" of any habitable house. The Act lapsed on December 31, 1984.
[36] S.I. 1984 No. 348.
[37] S.I. 1977 No. 65.
[38] For example, s.26(1) of the Local Government Act 1941 provides that the consent of the Minister for the Environment is necessary before an officer of any local authority may lawfully be removed from his post. See *O'Mahony* v. *Arklow U.D.C.* [1965] I.R. 710.

the striking of the rate in the pound and expenditure proposals
are subject to ministerial control.[39] It is true that the Local
Government (Financial Provisions) (No. 2) Act 1983—which
authorises local authorities to charge for certain services—constitutes a step in the direction of greater local fiscal authority, but
until an adequate substitute for the rating system is found, the
situation is bound to remain unsatisfactory.[40]

The power of the Minister to remove elected members is now
contained in the Local Government Acts 1941–1946. The
Minister may exercise this power for any of the following reasons:

(i)   where he is satisfied following a local inquiry that the
      authority is not effectively performing its duties;
(ii) where the local authority refuses to obey any court order;
(iii) where the authority refuses to permit its accounts to be duly
      audited;
(iv) where the number of members is not sufficient to permit a
      quorum to be formed for meetings[41];
(v)   where the authority refuses to strike an adequate rate[42];
(vi) where the authority refuses or wilfully neglects to comply
      with an express requirement which is imposed upon them
      by any enactment or order.[43]

It should be noted that ground (vi) would authorise the Minister to
dismiss the elected members if, for example, they refused to
comply with his directive that the rate struck in the pound should
not exceed a specific amount. These powers were employed to
dismiss the members of Dublin County Council where the Council
had deliberately struck a rate less than the full amount required to

[39] Local Government (Financial Provisions) Act 1978, s.10(2). The
exercise of powers by local authorities in non-financial areas may also
be subject to strict ministerial control, *e.g.* the making of by-laws:
Municipal Corporations (Ireland) Act 1840, s.125; Housing Act 1966,
s.70. The Minister is often empowered to make delegated legislation to
fill in the details of local government statutes (see *e.g.* Local
Government (Water Pollution) Act 1977, ss.26, 27 and 30) and in some
situations the Minister may give instructions to local authorities as to
how to discharge their functions (see, *e.g.* Local Government (Roads
and Motorways) Act 1974, s.6; Local Government (Financial Provisions) Act 1978 s.15).
[40] Following the local elections in June 1985—at which the issue of local
authority service charges became politically contentious—most local
authorities are no longer making such charges.
[41] Grounds (i)–(iv) are contained in the Local Government Act 1941, s.44.
[42] Local Government Act 1946, s.30(4).
[43] Local Government Act 1941, s.44 as inserted by s.64 of the Local
Government Act 1946.

meet the demand for health services.[44] Where the elected
members are dismissed, the Minister may appoint one or more
persons to act as commissioners for the local authority.[45] The
commissioner discharges the reserved functions of the elected
members in the interim period pending the next elections.[46]

---

[44] Roche, *op. cit.*, p. 123. The members of Naas U.D.C. were dismissed in
similar circumstances in 1985; see *The Irish Times*, August 3, 1985.
[45] Local Government Act 1941, s.48.
[46] s.49 of the 1941 Act. Local authorities now come within the
Ombudsman's remit: see Ombudsman Act, 1980 (Second Schedule)
(Amendment) Order 1985 (S.I. 1985 No. 69).

Part III

Institutions of Control

6 Tribunals and Inquiries[1]

1. Introduction

One may begin an explanation of the nature of tribunals by listing a few examples (most of which are considered *infra*). In the fields of taxation and compulsory acquisition, there are: Special Commissioners[2]; the Commissioners of Valuation[3]; Employment Appeals Tribunal[4]; the Farm Tax Tribunal[5]; the Mining Board,[6] together with arbitrators appointed by the Land Values Reference Committee under various statutes to fix compensation for land compulsorily acquired.[7] Tribunals which resolve disputes arising from the running of the welfare state include the deciding officers and the appeals officers in the Department of Social Welfare[8], and the General Medical Services Payments Board. In related fields there are the Criminal Injuries Compensation

[1] See generally, Grogan, *Administrative Tribunals* in F. G. King (ed.) *Public Administration in Ireland* III (Dublin, 1954) 32, Donaldson, *Some Comparative Aspects of Irish Law* (Duke, 1957) at pp. 192–198 and Grogan, *Administrative Tribunals in the Public Service* (Dublin, 1961).

[2] Income Tax Act 1967, Pt. XXVI.

[3] Valuation (Ireland) Act 1852.

[4] Redundancy Payments Act 1967, s.39, as amended by s.1 of the Unfair Dismissals Act 1977. The Employment Appeals Tribunal has replaced the former Redundancy Payments Tribunals which had been established under the 1967 Act. For an account of the work of this tribunal, see Redmond, *Dismissal Law in the Republic of Ireland* (Dublin, 1982) at pp. 120–128.

[5] Farm Tax Act 1985, s.8.

[6] Minerals Development Act 1940, s.33.

[7] Acquisition of Land (Assessment of Compensation) Act 1919, as amended by Acquisition of Land (Reference Committee) Act 1925.

[8] See pp. 149–154.

Tribunal[9] and the Legal Aid Board.[10] Several tribunals have been set up to operate the various types of control and regulation in the public interest, often by way of a licensing system. These include the Censorship of Films Board[11]; the Censorship of Publications Board[12]; An Bord Pleanala[13]; the Registrar of Friendly Societies[14] and the Controller of Patents, Designs and Trade Marks.[15] A number of tribunals exist to discipline members within the public service, for instance in the police and defence forces and in the prison service.[16]

As can be seen, the majority of the tribunals operate in the field of public law, assisting in the dirigiste and welfare aspects of the State's responsibilities. However, when creating a statutory innovation in the private law area, the Oireachtas sometimes vests responsibility for implementing the new scheme in a tribunal, rather than a court. Examples include An Bord Uchtala[17]; the Labour Court[18]; the Employment Appeals Tribunal[19] and the Rent Tribunal.[20]

A further anomaly is that while most tribunals have been established by statute, in some cases—for instance, the Criminal

---

[9] *Scheme of Compensation for Personal Injuries Criminally Inflicted* (1974) (Prl. 3658). See Osborough, "The Work of the Criminal Injuries Compensation Tribunal" (1978) 13 Ir.Jur.(n.s.) 320.

[10] *Scheme of Legal Aid and Advice* (1979) (Prl. 8534) at pp. 7–11. See Whyte, "And Justice for Some" (1984) 6 D.U.L.J.(n.s.) 88.

[11] Censorship of Films Act 1923, s.1.

[12] Censorship of Publications Act 1946, s.2. Nowadays, the Censorship Board is rarely used.

[13] Local Government (Planning and Development) Act 1976, ss.3–13 and Schedule to the Act. See Stevenson, "Planning Appeals in the Republic of Ireland" (1985) 7 *Urban Law and Policy* 170.

[14] For an account of the miscellaneous work of the Registrar, see Kerr and Whyte, *Irish Trade Union Law* (Abingdon, 1985) at pp. 41–48.

[15] Patents Act 1964, ss.77 and 78.

[16] See, *e.g.* the disciplinary mechanism established by the Garda Siochana (Discipline) Regulations 1971 (S.I. 1971 No. 316) and the proposed Garda Siochana Complaints Board (from which an appeal will lie to the Garda Siochana Complaints Appeal Board): see Garda Siochana (Complaints) Bill 1985, ss.3 and 10.

[17] Adoption Act 1952, s.8.

[18] Industrial Relations Act 1946, Pt. II. See Mortished, "The Industrial Relations Act 1946" in King (Ed.), *Public Administration in Ireland* II, (Dublin, 1949).

[19] See n. 4 *supra*.

[20] Housing (Private Rented Dwellings) (Amendment) Act 1983, ss.2–4. For an account of the procedure before the Rent Tribunal, see de Blacam, *The Control of Private Rented Dwellings* (Dublin, 1984) at pp. 55–62.

Injuries Compensation Tribunal, Legal Aid Board Motor Insurance Bureau and the Stardust Compensation Scheme—they are established merely by administrative scheme. The extra-statutory character of these tribunals does not, however, preclude judicial review of their decisions. This question was raised in *R.* v. *Criminal Injuries Compensation Board, ex p. Lain,*[21] where the applicant sought to quash a decision of the Board on the grounds of error on the face of the record. Although the Board was an extra-statutory tribunal, a Divisional Court of the English Queen's Bench held that it sufficed for the purposes of judicial review that the Board was a body with a public character, set up by executive act to administer moneys voted by Parliament, according to a published scheme while following a quasi-judicial procedure. On the point that the Board's payments were merely *ex gratia,* rather than enforceable legal rights, the court was equally expansive. Indeed, speaking in the context of the grant of certiorari, Ashworth J. said that where a duty to act judicially was entailed, Atkin L.J.'s oft-quoted phrase "affecting the rights of subjects"[22] meant no more than "affecting subjects" and, hence, certiorari would lie in a suitable case. It is symptomatic of the activist temper of Irish law and its lack of sympathy with technical doctrine that these points were actually conceded (correctly, said Finlay P.) in the *The State (Hayes)* v. *Criminal Injuries Compensation Tribunal,*[23] which is the Irish equivalent of *Lain.* In *Hayes,* Finlay P. said that the High Court would review a decision of the Tribunal in appropriate cases, such as where the principles of constitutional justice had been violated, or where the scheme of compensation had been misinterpreted.

Another extension to the basic category of tribunals embraces those bodies through which a profession, association or trade union regulates its own internal affairs. Although these bodies are not formally part of the public sector, many of them were erected upon statute.[24] Others—notably the trade unions—derive their authority from contract.[25] In either case the High Court has been prepared to review the proceedings of these tribunals.[26] The

[21] [1967] 2 Q.B. 864.
[22] *R.* v. *Electricity Commissioners, ex p. London Electricity Joint Committee Co. (1920) Ltd.* [1924] 1 K.B. 171, 205. See further at pp. 338–339.
[23] [1982] I.L.R.M. 210.
[24] See, *e.g.* Solicitors (Amendment) Act 1960, Pt. II; Medical Practitioners Act 1978, Pt. V; Dentists Act 1985, Pt. II.
[25] See Kerr and Whyte, *Irish Trade Union Law* (Abingdon, 1985) at pp. 100–102.
[26] See, *e.g.* O'Donoghue v. *Veterinary Council* [1975] I.R. 398 and *Re M., a Doctor* [1984] I.R. 479 (review of statutory tribunals) and *McGrath and*

rationale for this intervention is doubtless that while these bodies
may not be formally or completely "public" in nature, they make
such a crucial impact on their members on the rest of the
community that their affairs warrant the attention of the court. In
Abbott v. *Sullivan*[27] Denning L.J. said of trade union committees:

> "These bodies, which exercise a monopoly in an important
> sphere of human activity, with the power of depriving a man
> of his livelihood, must act in accordance with the elementary
> rules of justice. They must not condemn a man without giving
> him an opportunity to be heard in his own defence: and any
> agreement or practice to the contrary would be invalid."[28]

Although Denning L.J. was in dissent, it is these views which
represent the modern law.[29] However, in certain cases a court may
be reluctant to interfere with the internal affairs of a tribunal
whose authority derives from contract. Thus, in *McGrath and
O'Ruairc* v. *Trustees of Maynooth College*[30] Henchy J. observed that a
civil court was not the ideal forum in which to decide what was a
"grave delinquency against clerical obligations" within the meaning of the college's own internal statutes. The court could only
reject the conclusion of a domestic tribunal when it was one "that
could not reasonably have been come to in the circumstances," or
where the decisions had been arrived at in breach of natural
justice or other internal procedural pre-requisites.

As the final item in this catalogue, it should be noted that even
ministers are sometimes required to act in ways rather analagous
to tribunals inasmuch as they must take decisions personally, and
not through civil servants; and they must also observe the rules of
constitutional justice. This development is decribed in Chapters 9
and 16.

As with Cleopatra, so with tribunals: "Age cannot wither them
not custom stale their infinite variety." This lack of uniformity
extends even to the nomenclature. Not only do the names of
tribunals differ—board; commission; tribunal; officer; registrar;
controller; referee; umpire—but different authorities use differ-

---

O'Ruairc v. *Trustees of Maynooth College*, Supreme Court, November 1,
1979 and *Connolly* v. *McConnell* [1983] I.R. 172 (domestic bodies).
[27] [1952] 1 K.B. 189.
[28] [1952] 1 K.B. 189 at p. 198.
[29] See *e.g. Edwards* v. *SOGAT* [1971] Ch. 354; *Enderby Town F.C.* v. *Football
Association* [1971] Ch. 591; *N.E.E.T.U.* v. *McConnell* (1983) 2 J.I.S.L.L.
97 and *Connolly* v. *McConnell* [1983] I.R. 172.
[30] Supreme Court, November 1, 1979.

ent titles. Thus one finds tribunals described as administrative tribunals; special tribunals; statutory tribunals, or even, quasi-judicial tribunals. Modern usage, adopted here, prefers—simply—"tribunals."

2. Why a tribunal?

Not only is consistency lacking from tribunal to tribunal, there is also a lack of consistency as to whether a tribunal should be created at all. If one leaves aside local authorities, semi-state bodies and other specialist institutions, it may be said that an individual decision may be vested in any one of three different types of body: a Minister and his Department; a court, or a tribunal.

Tribunal or Minister?
It would certainly make for consistency if the following demarcation line for functions between a Minister and a tribunal were consistently observed by the Oireachtas: matters should be allocated to a tribunal where they require a decision to be taken independently of the executive by the determination of facts according to a fairly formalised procedure, and the application to the facts, of a fairly precise set of rules. In short, a tribunal would take all quasi-judicial decisions. This would leave to the Minister and his Department decisions containing a high policy content, which are not susceptible to regulation by a code of law.[31]

In fact, this separation of powers as between a tribunal and a Minister fails as an adequate description of reality at two points. First, by no means all of the decisions of a type suitable for resolution by a tribunal are actually vested in a tribunal. Dealing with the question of allocation of functions in Britain, the Council of Tribunals remarked frankly:

> "[T]he choice is influenced by the interplay of various factors—the nature of decisions, accidents of history, departmental preferences and political considerations—rather than by the application of a set of coherent principles."[32]

This is at least as true in Ireland as it is in Britain. Occasionally, functions which one would expect to be located in a tribunal are, for historical or other reasons, vested in a court, or, more often, in a Minister. The lack of correlation between a particular type of decision and a particular forum can be illustrated by the fact that

---

[31] This allocation of functions would be in line with the proposals contained in the Devlin Report: see Prl. 792, Appx. 1.
[32] *The Functions of the Council on Tribunals* (1980) (Cmd. 7805) at para. 1.7.

in regard to three important functions, a decision is taken in the
first instance by a quasi-tribunal, thence an appeal may be taken to
a tribunal, with a further right of appeal (in two cases, on a point
of law only) to the High Court. One can see this pattern in the
areas of planning, tax and social welfare law. Moreover, the
transfer of planning appeals from the Minister for Local
Government to An Bord Pleanala in 1977 does not appear to have
radically altered the decisions emerging from the planning appeals
process.[33]

As compared with a Minister, tribunals possess various advantages. The first of these was adverted to by Henchy J. in *The State
(Pine Valley Developments Ltd.)* v. *Dublin C.C.*.[34] Speaking in the
context of an "aberrant" and *ultra vires* grant of outline planning
permission by the Minister for Local Government, Henchy J. said
that the Minister had:

> "[I]gnored the rights of the respondent planning authority
> and of those who were entitled to get notices and to be heard
> before such a material contravention could take place. It is no
> wonder that Parliament, in its wisdom, by the [Local
> Government (Planning and Development) Act 1976] trans-
> ferred to an independent appeal board the appellate power
> which had been vested by the [Local Government (Planning
> and Development) Act 1963] in an individual who might be
> influenced in his decisions by political pressures or other
> extraneous or unworthy considerations."[35]

Secondly, a tribunal is less affected by changes of Government and
thus there may be some gain in consistency. Finally, the amorphous quality of a Department of State with its various activities
and interests may mean that an individual would be more
confident that his arguments had been fully taken into account by
a tribunal. In short, tribunals are regarded as more likely to be fair
and to provide greater safeguards for the individual than would be
the case with a Minister. It follows that a tribunal is more often
created where the area of government administration involved
requires interference with valuable private property rights.

There is a further qualification which must be made to the
principle that decisions for which the Oireachtas has fairly
stringent guidelines are vested in tribunals. This is pin-pointed in
the distinction which has been drawn by British writers between

---

[33] But for the advantages of An Bord Pleanala over the Minister for Local
Government, see Stevenson, "Planning Appeals in the Republic of
Ireland" (1985) 7 *Journal of Urban Law and Policy* 170.

[34] [1984] I.R. 407.

[35] [1984] I.R. 407 at p. 425.

"court-substitute tribunals" which conform more or less to this criterion, and "policy-orientated tribunals," which do not.[36] The purpose of a policy-orientated tribunal is to allow policy, in a narrow field, to be worked out case by case by a specialist body, free of day-to-day interference by party politics and party politicians. The essential feature of such a tribunal is the width of the guiding principle—an example being the criterion of "proper planning and development" administered by An Bord Pleanala.[37] The Labour Court, which is vested, *inter alia*, with the function of making recommendations in order to resolve trade disputes, provides another example of a "policy-orientated tribunal" at work.[38]

Tribunal or court?

The other general perspective from which to survey tribunals is by a comparison with the courts. Since most Irish tribunals are of the court-substitute type, could their functions not simply have been vested in a court of the appropriate level?[39] The short answer is that the growth of tribunals is largely due to the failure of the legal system to respond in a flexible manner to new challenges. Indeed, the creation of one of the first modern tribunals—the court of referees system, established under the National Insurance Act 1911 to hear national insurance claims—occurred because of the dissatisfaction with the handling of workman's compensation cases by the county court.[40]

It is usually agreed that, by comparison with courts, tribunals carry certain practical advantages. In the first place, the procedure before a tribunal is simpler and more flexible than that of a

[36] Farmer, *Tribunals and Government* (London, 1984), Chap. 8.
[37] Local Government (Planning and Development) Act 1963, s.26(1). Note that s.7 of the Local Government (Planning and Development) Act 1976 allows the Minister for the Environment to issue general policy directives to local authorities. This power was exercised once in 1982: see Local Government (Planning and Development) General Policy Directive, 1982 (S.I. 1982 No. 264).
[38] Industrial Relations Act 1946 s.68(1), as inserted by s.19 of the Industrial Relations Act 1969. See Von Prondzynski and McCarthy, *Employment Law* (London, 1984) at p. 21: "This new criterion [*sc.* of the 1969 Act] was intended to reflect a belief, current in the [Labour] Court itself, that it should approach its task in a wholly pragmatic and flexible way."
[39] Indeed, because tribunals are so similar to courts, the question has arisen in Britain as to whether they are to be treated as courts for particular purposes such as contempt of court (*Att.-Gen.* v. *British Broadcasting Corporation* [1981] A.C. 303) and immunity from defamation proceedings for witnesses (*Trapp* v. *Mackie* [1979] 1 W.L.R. 377).
[40] Abel Smith and Stevens, *Lawyers and the Courts* (London, 1967) at pp. 111–118.

court.[39] Although a tribunal may not adopt procedures which are
unfair or which imperil a just result, it is nonetheless master of its
own procedures, and enjoys a considerable discretion as to
whether to depart from the strict rules of evidence or permit legal
representation or cross-examination of witnesses.[41] These features
together with the general absence of the adversarial contest[42]: the
fact that the proceedings are often held in private[43]; and the less
formal atmosphere of a tribunal combine to make an appearance
before a tribunal a less daunting experience than the "day in
court." Often, especially to people from a humbler background,
the very image of a court—with its criminal connotations—is
unwelcome. For example, the Housing (Private Rented Dwellings)
Act 1982—which provides for a new system of rent assessment
following the invalidation of the former Rent Restrictions Act
1960[44]—originally vested this jurisdiction in the District Court.
This jurisdiction was subsequently transferred to a Rent Tribunal
by the Housing (Private Rented Dwellings) (Amendment) Act
1983 because of the concern aroused among the tenants by the
prospect of the courtroom.[45]

Secondly, many tribunals possess a particular expertise. This
would be true, for example, in the case of bodies such as An Bord
Pleanala, the Appeal Commissioners for Income Tax and the
Employment Appeals Tribunal. The courts take cognisance of this
fact, for they are more reluctant to interfere with the workings of
specialist tribunals.

Thirdly, tribunals are quicker and cheaper for all the parties
concerned. Their simpler procedure means that it is usually
unnecessary for a lawyer to appear.

Fourthly, tribunals can be incorporated within a variety of
institutional frameworks, and they are often vested with diverse
non-judicial functions. A leading example is the Labour Court,
which combines general arbitration functions in the field of
industrial relations with quasi-judicial (or, indeed, possibly judicial) functions under the Redundancy Act 1967, and the Anti-

---

[41] See the comments of *Report of the Public Services Organisation Review
Group* ("the Devlin Report") (1969) (Prl. 792), App. I at pp. 448–449,
on this aspect of tribunals.

[42] For tribunal procedure, see pp. 142–144.

[43] Contrast Art. 34.1 which requires that the administration of justice by
courts shall be in public, save in "such limited and special cases as may
be prescribed by law."

[44] *Blake* v. *Att.-Gen.* [1982] I.R. 117. For an account of this decision, and
the flurry of legislative activity which followed in its wake, see
McCormack, "Blake-Madigan and its Aftermath" (1983) 5
D.U.L.J.(n.s.) 205.

[45] See generally *Dail Debates*, Vol. 344, cols. 2514–2544 (July 7, 1983).

Discrimination (Pay) Act 1974[46]. Were a court involved in such a combination of roles it is possible that the arrangement might contravene Article 34.1,[47] and it would certainly be regarded as undesirable and unconventional.

Finally, tribunals tend to take a less rigid attitude to questions of statutory interpretation and to precedent. Indeed, it is possible that a tribunal which adhered rigidity to a doctrine of precedent would run foul of the rule against inflexible policies.[48] However, in the very interests of consistency, tribunals do follow precedent to some extent and also employ the standard principles of statutory interpretation.

As against these advantages, the wisdom of allocating certain judicial functions to tribunals rather than courts may be questioned. Speaking in the context of the work of An Bord Uchtala, Walsh J. has written extracurially that:

> "[C]ertain aspects of family law are of such fundamental importance, such as those cases which can alter the legal status of a person, that they should be decided in the High Court. . . . This prompts one to question the wisdom or desirability of permitting the legal adoptions to take effect without judicial intervention or confirmation. . . . [The powers of the An Bord Uchtala] are limited. It cannot decide questions concerning the validity of the marriage of couples who seek to adopt. Yet if adoption is approved for a couple whose marriage is not a valid subsisting marriage in the eyes of the law of the State the resulting invalidity of the adoption may not . be discovered until it is too late to avoid . . . the inevitable legal consequences."[49]

---

[46] *Cf. Employment Appeals Tribunal Sixteenth Annual Report* (1983) (Pl. 2733): "While the procedures of the Tribunal were intended to be informal, speedy and inexpensive, the increasing involvement by the legal profession, particularly in claims under the Unfair Dismissals Act 1977, has tended to make the hearings more formal, prolonged and costly, with an over-emphasis on legal procedures and technicalities" (at p. 4). According to the 1983 Report, 19.7 per cent of employees and 23.9 per cent of employers opted for legal representation in all claims coming before the Tribunal.

[47] Legislation which vested a court with non-judicial arbitral functions in the area of industrial relations was held to be contrary to s.71 of the Commonwealth Constitution in *Att.-Gen. of Australia* v. *R. and the Boilermakers' Society of Australia* [1957] A.C. 288.

[48] *R.* v. *Greater Birmingham Appeal Tribunal, ex p. Simper* [1974] Q.B. 543 (tribunal cannot consider itself bound by its own "rules of thumb").

[49] In foreword to Binchy, *A Casebook on Irish Family Law* (Abingdon, 1984) at p. vii.

Webster J. made similar observations about the functions of prison disciplinary tribunals in *R.* v. *Home Secretary, ex p. Tarrant*[50] when listing a number of considerations which the prison authorities should take into account before deciding whether to permit the prisoner to be legally represented. These factors included: the seriousness and gravity of the charge; whether any points of law are likely to arise; the capacity of a particular prisoner to present his own case; the need for reasonable speed in making the adjudication and the need for fairness as between prisoners, and as between prisoners and prison officers. If the result of this decision was that serious disciplinary offences were more frequently referred to the criminal courts, Webster J. did not regard such a result "as a matter of regret,"[51] and it seems fair to infer that he considered that prison tribunals were inherently unsuited to the task of adjudication in cases involving serious disciplinary charges.

3. Common features

Something must now be said about the four qualities some or all of which each tribunal possesses to some extent.

Rule bound

As far as one can generalise about tribunals it can be said that they take decisions in regard to which the range of options is sufficiently narrow and predictable for it to be crystalised in the form of a reasonably precise set of rules. This is in contrast with the wide discretionary power which, for instance, permits a Minister to exercise a particular power if he deems it "necessary in the public interest."[52] To take some examples: first, An Bord Uchtala must not make an adoption order unless it is satisfied "that the applicant is of good moral character, has sufficient means to support the child, and is a suitable person to have parental rights and duties in respect of the child."[53] Again, the Rent Tribunal is required to fix the rent in respect of formerly rent-controlled tenancies by having regard to the:

"[N]ature, character and location of the dwelling, the other

---

[50] [1985] Q.B. 251.
[51] [1985] Q.B. at p. 287.
[52] For controls of discretionary powers, see Chapter 10.
[53] Adoption Act 1952, s.13(1).

terms of the tenancy; the means of the landlord and the
tenant; the date of purchase of the dwelling by the landlord
and the amount paid by him therefor; the length of the
tenant's occupancy of the dwelling and the number and ages
of the tenant's family residing in the dwelling."[54]

Law administered by a tribunal is more likely than law administered by a court to include standards as opposed to rules.[55] In
contrast to rules, standards—such as "good moral character"—
call for the exercise of some discretion. It is, however, a discretion
which must be exercised reasonably, objectively and judicially.
This means that even where the wording of the statutory test
administered by the tribunal is vague, the effect of the open,
formal procedure, together with an accumulation of informal
precedents will have the effect of restricting its discretion. This is
especially so when the tribunal maintains a public register of its
decisions, as does the Employment Appeal Tribunal. However it
must be said that these developments have not taken place in the
case of some tribunals. For example, the reports submitted by
planning inspector—who chairs an oral inquiry—to An Bord
Pleanala are not published at all. This effectively means that no
system of precedent is established whereby the members of the
public can assess the likelihood of a successful appeal.[56]

Appeals

Since decisions taken by tribunals are, first, bound by fairly
precise rules and, secondly, involve questions of individual rights,
it might be predicted on the basis of earlier discussion[57] that a
statutory appeal would be created from a tribunal to a court. In
fact, provision is generally made for an appeal to the High Court

---

[54] Housing (Private Rented Dwellings) Act 1982, s.13(2).

[55] But this is not always the case: see *e.g.* Succession Act 1965, s.117
(which allows the court to make provision for the child out of a
deceased parent's estate where it is of opinion "that the testator has
failed to make proper provision for the child in accordance with its
means").

[56] Clark, "Social Welfare Insurance Appeals" (1978) 13 Ir.Jur.(n.s.) 265 at
p. 282 makes the same point about the non-publication of decisions of
social welfare appeals officers' decisions: "If decisions are at present
poorly recorded, this will hinder even the most primitive and informal
system of *stare decisis*. Appeals officers may then run the risk of
operating within an appeals system in which uniformity of decision
making is singularly absent."

[57] See pp. 9–10.

but this is usually confined to points of law.[58] In some cases an appeal will lie to a specialised appellate tribunal. For instance, a party aggrieved by a prohibition order made by the Censorship of Publications Board—nowadays, happily, a comparatively rare event—may appeal *de novo* to the Censorship of Publications Appeal Board.[59] A further example is provided by the Seanad Electoral (Panel Members) Act 1947, whereby an appeal lies to a Judicial Referee from a decision of the returning officer on the eligibility of a candidate for a particular electoral panel.[60] In other cases, an appeal will lie to a Minister.[61] However, occasionally the decision of the tribunal will be declared to be final, and no appeal will lie.[62]

The High Court retains an inherent right of review of decisions of tribunals, irrespective of any appeal mechanism.[63] However, the modern rule appears to be that the applicant must exhaust all other rights of appeal before he can seek judicial review of a tribunal's decision.[64]

Procedure

Procedure is laid down, in the first instance, by the constituent statute, and is generally supplemented by procedural regulations made pursuant to statutory instrument. These provisions typically

[58] See *e.g.* Adoption Act 1952, s.30(1); Local Government (Planning and Development) Act 1976, s.42(a); Social Welfare (Consolidation) Act 1981, s.299; Housing (Private Rented Dwellings) (Amendment) Act 1983, ss.12 and 13. In the case of the Appeals Commissioners for Income Tax, the tax-payer may appeal *de novo* to the Circuit Court. Either party may ask for a case stated on a point of law from the decisions of the Appeal Commissioners or the Circuit Court: Income Taxes Act 1967, ss.428–431. For the difficult distinction between law and fact, see *Rahill* v. *Brady* [1971] I.R. 69 and p. 215.

[59] Censorship of Publications Act 1946, ss.2 and 3.

[60] Sections 36–38 of the 1947 Act. In *Ormonde and Dolan* v. *MacGabhann*, High Court, July 9, 1969, Pringle J. held that the plaintiffs were entitled to by-pass this judicial referee procedure in order to seek a declaration from the High Court that they had the proper and appropriate qualifications for nomination on the Labour Panel.

[61] See *e.g.* Local Government (Water Pollution) Act 1977, s.8 (appeal to Minister for the Environment against local authority decision to refuse, or to attach conditions to, grant of trade and/or sewage effluent licence).

[62] Social Welfare (Consolidation) Act 1981, s.299. But *cf. Kingham* v. *Minister for Social Welfare*, High Court, November 25, 1985 and pp. 152–154.

[63] *Tormey* v. *Att.-Gen.* [1985] I.R. 289 and p. 196.

[64] *The State (Abenglen Properties Ltd.)* v. *Dublin Corporation* [1984] I.R. 381; *Creedon* v. *Dublin Corporation* [1984] I.R. 427 and see pp. 354–355.

deal with matters such as the following: how many members constitute a quorum and a majority; the circumstances in which an oral hearing is required; and whether the tribunal has the power to subpoena witnesses and to administer oaths. The provisions may also specify whether certain types of hearings are to be in public or in private. The tribunal may also be authorised to delegate its powers to a smaller group of members. These issues aside, the tribunal is generally authorised to regulate its own procedure.[65]

But irrespective of what the constituent statute may say or what administrative practice may develop, a tribunal is always subject to constitutional justice in its more stringent form and it is the courts, which have the last word on such questions as whether an oral hearing should have been held.[66] The impact of constitutional justice is demonstrated by a British parallel: out of the three examples, cited by Professor Wade, of amendments to draft procedural regulations secured by the British Council on Tribunals, two of these changes (disclosure to both sides of information given to the tribunal; unrestricted rights of representation) have been effected in Ireland through the courts.[67]

Accusatorial v. inquisitorial style

There are two factors which it might be expected would draw many tribunals towards the inquisitorial model. First, as regards subject-matter, the accusatorial model is appropriate in ordinary

---

[65] See *e.g.* Adoption Act 1952, First Sched.; Social Welfare (Insurance Appeals) Regulations 1952 (S.I. 1952 No. 376), Art. 54–11 (appeals officers); Local Government (Planning and Development) Regulations 1977 (S.I. 1977 No. 65), Art. 45 (An Bord Pleanala). In *The State (Casey)* v. *Labour Court* (1984) 3 J.I.S.L.L. 135 at p. 138 O'Hanlon J. observed that the Labour Court was given a discretion by s.21 of the Industrial Relations Act 1946 to regulate its own procedures in relation to the taking of evidence on oath. Accordingly, neither the parties nor the High Court could dictate to the Labour Court the manner in which it conducts its own procedures "once it exercises its powers in accordance with the statute from which it derives its authority to act."

[66] "Tribunals exercising quasi-judicial functions are frequently allowed to act informally—to receive unsworn evidence, to act on hearsay, to depart from the rules of evidence, to ignore courtroom procedures and the like—but they may not act in such a way as to imperil a fair hearing or a fair result" *per* Henchy J. in *Kiely* v. *Minister for Social Welfare* [1977] I.R. 267 at p. 281. See generally at pp. 263–265.

[67] *Geraghty* v. *Minister for Local Government* [1976] I.R. 153; *Nolan* v. *Irish Land Commission* [1981] I.R. 23; *The State (Williams)* v. *Army Pensions Board* [1983] I.R. 308; (disclosure of information); *McGrath & O'Ruairc* v. *Trustees of Maynooth College*, Supreme Court, November 1, 1979 (legal representation). Professor Wade's third example is the right to reasons on which see pp. 239–240.

civil proceedings where the court is usually deciding a *lis inter partes* involving two identifiable private parties, each with diametrically opposing interests. By contrast there is often only one individual interest at a hearing before a tribunal, as, *e.g.* in an application for a grant or a licence.

There is, secondly, a practical factor militating in favour of the inquisitorial system, namely, that the accusatorial system works best when the two adversaries are equally experienced and informed. This requirement will often not be met in the case of tribunals where the private individuals involved are often not legally represented.

However, there are two other factors which work in favour of the accusatorial system. First, the rules of constitutional justice—which are administered by judges with the court system in mind—apply to hearings before tribunals. Secondly, in certain tribunals it has been thought necessary to establish a *legitimus contradictor* and this tends to give a hearing an adversarial flavour. Thus, the responsible Inspector of Taxes appears in front of the Appeal Commissioners to argue in support of his earlier decision.

Independence

Tribunals exercising public law powers are required to strike an even balance between the individual on the one hand and the administrative authorities who represent the public interest on the other: they should be guided only by the law and their own non-partisan discretion. At times, queries have been raised—either in regard to tribunals as a whole or in regard to specified tribunals—as to whether they measure up to these standards. In the first place, tribunals lack the tradition, status and institutional arrangements necessary to promote the independence which the courts have long enjoyed. Moreover, the fact that all the cases before a particular tribunal often involve the same administrative agency may breed a certain cosiness.

Particular doubt has arisen about the independence of the deciding officer/appeals officer system for determining social welfare claims because it is manned by serving civil servants operating within a department of state. Deciding officers are selected by the Minister for Social Welfare at executive or staff officer level and they hold this position at the pleasure of the Minister. Deciding officers appear to regard themselves as subject to departmental directions and policy considerations, although it seems likely that it was the intention of the Oireachtas to give the deciding officer a similar status to that of the appeals officer. After some years as a deciding officer a civil servant will generally return to service within the Department. Later he may be appointed, usually at assistant principal grade, as an appeals officer by the Minister and again holds his position at pleasure.[68]

Suspicion of the appeal officer's independence—and, by implication, that of the deciding officer—had been fuelled by decisions such as *McLoughlin* v. *Minister for Social Welfare*.[69] In this case the question arose as to whether the plaintiff was employed "in the civil service of the Government" for social insurance purposes. The appeals officer considered that he was bound to adhere to the terms of a minute from the Minister for Finance which, in effect, directed the officer to find that the plaintiff was so employed. This decision was reversed by the Supreme Court, with O'Daly J. stating that the appeals officer had abdicated his duty to act in an impartial and independent fashion:

> "The Appeals Officer said that he was bound to adhere to a direction, purported to have been given to him by the Minister for Finance, an observation which disclosed not a concern for the niceties of the probative value, but the belief that a public servant in his position had no option but to act on the direction of a Minister of State. Such a belief on his part was an abdication by him from his duty as an Appeals Officer. That duty is laid upon him by the Oireachtas and he is required to perform it as between the parties that appear before him freely and fairly as becomes anyone who is called upon to decide on matters of right or obligation."[70]

Further recognition of the anomalous position of the social welfare appeals system is provided by the fact that decisions of both the deciding officer and the appeals officer come within the scope of the Ombudsman's jurisdiction.[71]

Doubts about the independence of the tribunals were probably part of the inspiration for the constitutional rule (Article 34.1) which provide that—subject to certain limited exceptions—justice must be administered by courts and not by tribunals. Article 37 is an exception to the pure separation of powers principle in that it permits the Oireachtas to vest judicial powers of a limited nature in non-criminal matters in persons or bodies who are not judges.[72] The wording of Article 34.1 and Article 37 is unsatisfactory in that it does not appear to provide any clear criteria which would enable the courts to determine (i) the distinction between judicial and

[68] See generally Clark, "Social Welfare Insurance Appeals" (1978) 13 Ir.Jur.(n.s.) 165.

[69] [1958] I.R. 1.

[70] [1958] I.R. 1 at p. 27.

[71] Ombudsman Act 1980, s.5(1)(*a*)(iii).

[72] See Kelly, *The Irish Constitution* (Dublin, 1984) at pp. 363–368; Gwynn Morgan, *Constitutional Law of Ireland* (Dublin, 1985) at pp. 36–40.

non-judicial powers; and (ii) what is a "limited" judicial function. This in turn tends to cast doubt on the constitutionality of the operations of certain tribunals,[73] though it must be said that there are many tribunals which do not administer justice.

The leading case is *Re Solicitors' Act 1954*,[74] in which the power of the Disciplinary Committee of the Incorporated Law Society to strike off solicitors who had been found guilty of serious disciplinary offences was held to be an administration of justice. The statutory provisions in question were also found to be unconstitutional, in that the judicial powers vested in the Committee were not "limited" in nature. As Kingsmill Moore J. observed:

> "It is the 'powers and functions' which must be 'limited,' not the ambit of their exercise. Nor is the test of limitation to be sought in the number of powers and functions which are exercised. The Constitution does not say 'powers and functions limited in number'.... A tribunal having few powers and functions but those of far-reaching effect and importance could not properly be regarded as exercising 'limited' powers and functions.... The test as to whether a power is or is not 'limited' in the opinion of the Court, lies in the effect of the assigned power when exercised. If the exercise of the assigned powers and functions is calculated ordinarily to affect in the most profound and far-reaching way the lives, liberties, fortunes or reputations of those against whom they are exercised, they cannot properly be described as 'limited'."[75]

The effect of this decision is that it has now been deemed necessary to constitute the High Court as the body which will take the final step to strike off solicitors, doctors etc. in cases of professional misconduct.[76] Doubt was also cast on the validity of the activities of An Bord Uchtala, and a constitutional amendment was necessary to order to safeguard the validity of adoption

---

[73] In 1979 it was thought necessary to pass a constitutional amendment to safeguard An Bord Uchtala against constitutional attack on the grounds that by making adoption orders it was exercising judicial powers of a non-limited nature.

[74] [1960] I.R. 239.

[75] [1960] I.R. 239 at p. 263.

[76] See *Re M., a Doctor* [1984] I.R. 479 and *M.* v. *Medical Council* [1984] I.R. 485. As to the High Court's power in these disciplinary matters, see for example, Medical Practitioners Act 1978, ss.45–48; Dentists Act 1985, ss.39–42 and Nurses Act 1985, ss.39–42.

orders.[77] A slightly more flexible approach may be discerned in the judgment of McMahon J. in *Madden* v. *Ireland*.[78] At issue in this case was the power of the Land Commission's lay commissioners and appeal tribunal to fix the price of land in cases of compulsory acquisition. McMahon J. first accepted that this was not merely the exercise of an administrative function, but involved the administration of justice, as there was no room "for policy concepts, and what is being decided is solely a question of legal right." But the judge went on to hold that this was a power of a limited nature and he adverted to the role which Article 37 had obviously been intended to play:

> "Experience has shown that modern government cannot be carried on without many regulatory bodies and those bodies cannot function effectively under a rigid separation of powers. Article 37 had no counterpart in the Constitution of Saorstat Eireann and in my view introduction of it to the Constitution is to be attributed to a realisation of the needs of modern Government. The ascertainment of the market value of a holding of lands by an administrative body with special experience appears to me to be the kind of limited judicial power contemplated by Article 37."[79]

The Supreme Court has now ruled in *Tormey* v. *Attorney-General*[80] that the Oireachtas may confer exclusive jurisdiction in certain justiciable matters on lower courts or on tribunals operating under cover of Article 37. As far as the application of the principle of *nemo iudex in causa sua* is concerned, it is now settled that an administrative authority is not debarred from adjudicating on an issue merely because it has an institutional interest in the outcome of the proceedings.[81] However, the *nemo iudex* principle will apply with the same strictness as in the case of a court where the administrative body is exercising judicial powers.[82]

Appointment and removal of members of tribunals
The type of institutional arrangements designed to create

---

[77] Art. 37.2 was enacted in 1979 in the light of the doubts raised by the Supreme Court's decision in *M.* v. *An Bord Uchtala* [1977] I.R. 287.

[78] High Court, May 22, 1980.

[79] At p. 9 of his judgment. For another example of where the exercise of judicial powers was found to be "limited in nature," see *Central Dublin Development Association Ltd.* v. *Att.-Gen.* (1975) 109 I.L.T.R. 9.

[80] [1985] I.R. 289, see Hogan, "Reflections on the Supreme Court's decision in *Tormey* v. *Attorney-General*" (1985) 7 D.U.L.J.(n.s.).

[81] *Collins* v. *County Cork Vocational Educational Committee*, High Court, May 27, 1982.

[82] *O'Brien* v. *Bord na Mona* [1983] I.R. 255, and see pp. 250–254.

independent pedestals for judges[83] are largely absent in the case of tribunals. Thus, in the case of a typical tribunal, the chairman and other members will be selected by the Minister. The term of office is usually fixed at a maximum of three to five years. Members are generally eligible for reappointment.[84] However, in certain other cases, the appointment is intended as a full-time career post.[85]

Frequently no statutory qualifications are laid down for appointment. In some cases the chairman must be a lawyer. The two ordinary members of the Mining Board[86] must be property arbitrators, and it is assumed that some members of the Rent Tribunal[87] must have knowledge or experience of the valuation of property. There are also some examples of "balanced" or representative tribunals. This principle is adopted in the composition of the Labour Court[88] and the Employment Appeals Tribunal[89] where the employers and employees are represented equally. By convention one of the Appeals Commissioners is chosen from among the senior officials of the Revenue Commissioners while the other is a member of the Bar. The most sophisticated attempt in this direction involves An Bord Pleanala. Section 7 of the Local Government (Planning and Development) Act 1983 allows the Minister for the Environment to prescribe certain organisations[90] which are representative of particular interest groups: professions or occupations relating to physical planning; protection and preservation of the environment; the construction industry and community groups. The Minister is then required to choose four of the five members of the Board from among the names nominated by these organisations. The fifth ordinary member is chosen from among the Minister for the Environment's own civil servants.[91]

[83] See Kelly, *op. cit.*, at pp. 354–358.
[84] See, *e.g.* Minerals Development Act 1940, s.33; Adoption Act 1952, s.8 and First Sched. (art. 2); Housing (Private Rented Dwellings) (Amendment) Act 1983, ss.2 and 3; Local Government (Planning and Development) Act 1983, ss.5 and 7.
[85] See, *e.g.* Controller of Patents, Designs and Trade Marks: see Patents Act 1964, s.78.
[86] Minerals Development Act 1979, s.41.
[87] Housing (Private Rented Dwellings) Regulations 1983 (S.I. 1983 No. 222), art. 6(6).
[88] Industrial Relations Act 1969, s.2.
[89] Redundancy Payments Act 1967, s.39(4).
[90] The list of prescribed organisations is to be found in Local Government (Planning and Development) (An Bord Pleanala) Regulations 1983 (S.I. 1983 No. 285).
[91] s.7(2)(*e*) of the 1983 Act. Appointment of the Chairman of An Bord Pleanala is by way of a similar, if not quite identical, process: see s.5 of the Act.

Removal of members of tribunals is generally a matter for the responsible Minister. The power to remove members is generally confined to specific grounds, such as ill-health, stated misbehaviour or where the removal appears to the Minister to be necessary for the effective performance of the Board's functions.[92] In fact, dismissals are rare, and the most spectacular dismissals in recent times—that of the members of An Bord Pleanala in 1983—were brought about directly by an Act of the Oireachtas.[93]

4. The social welfare appeals system[94]

A study of the detailed substantive operation of a tribunal is excluded from most administrative law textbooks because it is conventionally regarded as part of some other legal subject. An attempt is now made to meet this difficulty by giving an account of the social welfare appeals system.

Each year over 1 million claims are made on the Minister for Social Welfare[95] in respect of such social welfare payments as disability benefit; unemployment benefit and assistance; occupational injuries benefit and old-age pensions. The statutory basis for these vast administrative schemes is now consolidated in the Social Welfare (Consolidation) Act 1981, under which entitlement to payment turns on the interpretation of such phrases as "not incapable of work and available for work" (unemployment benefit)[96]; "accident arising out of and in the course of employment" (occupational injury benefits)[97]; or whether a claimant has submitted to the necessary medical examinations (maternity allowance).[98]

The system by which these schemes are implemented involves a

[92] See, *e.g.* Mineral Developments Act 1940, s.33(3) (Mining Board); Adoption Act 1952, s.3(1) (An Bord Uchtala); Local Government (Planning and Development) Act 1983, ss.4 and 7 (An Bord Pleanala).
[93] Local Government (Planning and Development) Act 1983, s.10.
[94] The principal statutory provisions and regulations include the following: Social Welfare (Consolidation) Act 1981, Pt. VIII; Social Welfare (Insurance Appeals) Regulations 1952 (S.I. 1952 No. 376); Social Welfare (Assistance Decisions and Appeals) Regulations (S.I. No. 9) of 1953. These statutory instruments are continued in force by s.312 of the 1981 Act. See generally, Clark, "Social Welfare Insurance Appeals" (1978) 13 Ir.Jur.(n.s.) 265.
[95] According to the Department of Social Welfare's Annual Report, *Statistical Information on Social Welfare Services 1984* (Pl. 2950), there were 1,150,105 claims in the period from July 1, 1983 to June 30, 1984.
[96] Social Welfare (Consolidation) Act 1981, s.29(4).
[97] 1981 Act, ss.42 and 43.
[98] *Ibid.*, s.27.

dichotomy between on the one hand, social insurance schemes (where the benefits are in part financed out of contributions already made by the claimant) and, on the other hand, social assistance allowances (in respect of which no direct contributions have been paid). The administration of social insurance schemes and most social assistance schemes fall within the jurisdiction of the deciding officer, from which an appeal lies to the appeals officer.[99] Each of these officers are designated officers in the Department of Social Welfare.[1]

In practice most applicants will be advised by Department of Social Welfare officials as to their entitlement to the benefit which has been claimed. If the advice is in the negative, then the applicant can insist that a deciding officer adjudicate upon the claim. This officer may make various inquiries (*e.g.* to former employers of the applicant) but there is no oral hearing and no attempt is made to observe the rules of natural justice. If the claim is refused the applicant is informed in general terms of the reasons for the decision.

An appeal against a refusal must be filed within twenty-one days. The appeal is initiated by a "notice of appeal" (which states the relevant facts and arguments on which the applicant proposes to rely) and accompanied by any relevant documentary evidence.[2] The deciding officer will file a replying statement, which is not disclosed to the applicant. The appeals officer hears the appeal *de novo*.[3]

---

[99] There are a number of other schemes which are administered by the Health Boards. These include: supplementary welfare allowances (Social Welfare (Consolidation) Act 1981, s.119); domiciliary care allowance (Health Act 1970, s.61); infectious diseases maintenance allowance (Health Act 1947, s.41). The payment of unemployment benefit or unemployment assistance to employees on strike is now a matter for the Social Welfare Tribunal: see Social Welfare (Consolidation) Act 1981, s.301B, as inserted by Social Welfare (No. 2) Act 1982, s.1 and Social Welfare (Social Welfare Tribunal) Regulations 1982 (S.I. 1982 No. 308). See generally Kerr and Whyte, *Irish Trade Union Law* (Abingdon, 1985) at pp. 371–376; Clark, "Towards the 'Just' Strike? Social Welfare Payments for Persons Affected by a Trade Dispute in the Republic of Ireland" (1985) 48 M.L.R. 569. The effect of this Act is to interpose a tribunal between the two existing appellate tiers, *viz.* the appeals officer and the High Court.

[1] The deciding officer has a seldom used power to refrain from deciding the case himself, but to seek the assistance of an appeals officer: Social Welfare (Consolidation) Act 1981; s.298(3).

[2] Social Welfare (Insurance Appeals) Regulations 1952 (S.I. 1952 No. 376), arts. 6 and 7.

[3] 1981 Act, s.298(5); Social Welfare (Assistance Decisions and Appeals) Regulations 1953 (S.I. 1953 No. 9), art. 9(4).

Procedure before the appeals officer

The appeals officer is given a broad discretion to decide whether to grant an oral hearing.[4] In fact, oral hearings are held in over half of all appeals.[5] Each appeals officer decides an average of about 2,000 cases each year, and many oral hearings are disposed of in less than fifteen minutes.

The decision as to whether to grant legal representation is at the discretion of the appeals officer.[6] In practice, legal representation is unusual but solicitors and counsel are awarded costs in accordance with the scale rate. While constitutional justice does not require legal representation in all cases, the failure on the part of the appeals officer to permit representation in an appropriate case would probably amount to an unreasonable exercise of his discretion.[7]

The appeals officer has power to subpoena witnesses and to take evidence on oath.[8] Written evidence may also be admitted if the appeals officer thinks it "just and proper" to do so; however, this evidence ceases to have effect if "oral evidence of probative value is adduced which contraverts the written statement so admitted."[9] The decision of the appeals officer is then sent to the Minister for Social Welfare. The applicant will then receive a memorandum of the Minister's decision. The memorandum is in standard form, and, in the case of unsuccessful appeals, sets forth a list of alternative reasons for the decision. The reasons which are inapplicable are deleted. The fact that appeals officers' decisions are not published means that there is no system of *stare decisis*, and

---

[4] Social Welfare (Insurance Appeals) Regulations 1952 (S.I. 1952 No. 376) art. 3. In *Kiely* v. *Minister for Social Welfare (No. 2)* [1977] I.R. 267 at p. 278 Henchy J. stated that if there were "[U]nresolved conflicts in the documentary evidence, as to any matter essential to a ruling of the claim, the intention of these Regulations is that those conflicts shall be resolved by an oral hearing." But this approach tends to overlook the fact that in practice "[m]ost, if not all, of the documentary evidence will be adduced by the deciding officer who may fail to set out clearly the appellant's view of the appeal": Clark, "Social Welfare Insurance Appeals" (1978) 13 Ir.Jur.(n.s.) 265 at p. 274.

[5] Clark, *loc. cit.,* at pp. 273–277.

[6] Social Welfare (Insurance Appeals) Regulations 1952 (S.I. 1952 No. 376), art. 11(1).

[7] *R.* v. *Home Secretary, ex p. Tarrant* [1985] Q.B. 251 and see p. 265.

[8] Social Welfare (Consolidation) Act 1981, s.298(7)–(10).

[9] *Kiely* v. *Minister for Social Welfare* [1977] I.R. 267 at p. 279. See Social Welfare (Insurance Appeals) Regulations 1952 (S.I. 1952 No. 376), art. 11(5) which gives a discretion to the appeals officer to admit evidence in writing.

this in turn leads to the operation of an appeals system "in which uniformity of decision-making is singularly absent."[10]

The Minister is empowered to appoint an assessor to sit with an appeals officer in an appropriate case. Two assessors—one drawn from an employees' panel and the other from an employers' panel—sit on unemployment benefit appeals.[11] The role of the assessors is to assist the appeals officer with their knowledge of prevailing local employment conditions. This information is, of course, relevant in considering, for example, whether an applicant is making himself available for work. The role of the medical assessors under the Social Welfare (Occupational Injuries) Act 1966 was examined by the Supreme Court in *Kiely* v. *Minister for Social Welfare.*[12] In the view of Henchy J. the regulations envisaged that the medical assessors' role should be a strictly limited one. The assessor should not take any active part in the proceedings: their task was simply to give information on medical matters when requested to do so by the appeals officer.

Given the institutional bias of the appeals system, it may be questioned whether the procedures adopted are compatible with constitutional justice. If, as seems likely, the appeals officers are discharging judicial functions of a limited nature under cover of Article 37, then a judicial standard of impartiality is required.[13] This standard is scarcely met where the system is administered by civil servants working in the Department of Social Welfare whose independence is not guaranteed by law, who incline to follow Departmental directions and who, perhaps, are unduly influenced by Departmental policy considerations.[14]

Review of appeals officers' decisions

Section 299 of the Social Welfare (Consolidation) Act 1981

[10] Clark, *loc. cit.*, at p. 382.

[11] Social Welfare (Consolidation) Act 1981, s.298(12); Social Welfare (Insurance Appeals) Regulations 1952 (S.I. 1952 No. 376), art. 10(1).

[12] [1977] I.R. 276. See Clark, *loc. cit.*, at pp. 278–279.

[13] *O'Brien* v. *Bord na Mona* [1983] I.R. 265 and see pp. 250–254.

[14] Clark, "Towards a 'Just' Strike? Social Welfare Payments for Persons Affected by a Trade Dispute in the Republic of Ireland" (1985) 48 M.L.R. 659 comments as follows (at p. 666): "Appeals officers provide an efficient method of internal administrative *review* but, given the status of the appeals officer—at the time of such appointment such a person is, and remains, employed within the Department of Social Welfare and holds officer 'during the pleasure of the Minister'—it is unrealistic to regard this form of adjudication as an independent appeals mechanism." See also the Private Members Bill designed to establish an independent appeals tribunal: Social Welfare (Appeals) Tribunal) Bill 1986 (No. 16 of 1986).

creates an appeal on a point of law[15] from a decision of an appeals officer to the High Court. However, read literally, the scope of this appeal would seem to be extraordinarily narrow in that every "question arising in relation to a claim for benefit" would be excluded, and the decision of the appeals officer rendered "final and conclusive."[16] As Lynch J. observed in *Kingham* v. *Minister For Social Welfare*,[17] such a literal interpretation would have the effect of excluding appeals in:

> "[T]he vast majority of questions that might arise under the provisions of the 1981 Act, leaving only a minority of cases where persons claim not to be within the Act and therefore not liable to pay contributions under the Act nor entitled to benefits thereunder."

In addition the Act purports to exclude from judicial review virtually all decisions of an appeals officer. It is significant that the scope of the decisions so excluded is defined to be co-terminous with the extent of the decisions from which no appeal is allowed. In sum, apart from the negligible area identified in the passage quoted from *Kingham*, there is neither appeal nor review. This demarcation line would appear to be based on the rather quaint view there should be an appeal in all cases where the citizen was required to make payments to the State, but not where the appellant was a mere recipient of the State's largesse. In *Kingham's* case, Lynch J. reacted against such a construction of section 299, saying that the matter excluded should be construed narrowly so as not to oust the jurisdiction of the High Court "save where such ouster is clear." The apparent effect of *Kingham* is that an appeal now lies to the High Court by virtue of section 299 of the 1981 Act in respect of *all* decisions of an appeals officer, the provisions of section 298(6) notwithstanding.

In *The State (Power)* v. *Moran*[18] Gannon J. ruled that an absence of probative evidence to support a decision of an appeals officer was not an error affecting jurisdiction, and the decision could not be impeached in certiorari proceedings. This restrictive interpretation of the scope of jurisdictional error is out of line with the modern authorities, and it is doubtful whether this decision

---

[15] The Minister for Social Welfare is entitled to refer "any question" arising from a decision of the appeals officer to the High Court (*i.e.* the Minister is not confined to points of law): 1981 Act, s.299(*a*).

[16] s.299 states that the decision of the appeals officer on any question to which s.298(6) applies shall be "final and conclusive." s.111(*a*) is the principal provision to which s.298(6) applies, and s.111(*a*) refers to "every question arising in relation to a claim for benefit."

[17] High Court, November 25, 1985.

[18] High Court, February 2, 1976.

represents good law.[19] Nevertheless, there is some evidence that the courts are reluctant to interfere with the decisions of specialists such as appeals officers,[20] especially if this means interfering with a long-standing interpretation of the relevant regulations.[21]

5. Statutory inquiries

There are, generally speaking, two types of statutory inquiry. The first type of inquiry (and the one which is the more frequently availed of) is the "standard device for giving a fair hearing to objectors before the final decision is made on some question of government policy affecting citizens' rights or interests."[22]

This type of statutory inquiry may be regarded as having many of the characteristics of a tribunal. In particular, the procedures adopted before statutory inquiries and tribunals are similar in that each of them approximates to that of a court. However, the essential difference between an administrative tribunal and a statutory inquiry is that the latter's conclusions do not bind the Minister or other responsible decision-making authority. In practice, of course, it would be rare for the Minister to depart from the conclusions of an inquiry. The circumstances in which the first type of statutory inquiry may be held include: the siting of a new burial ground[23]; the removal or suspension of persons holding office under the Vocational Education Acts[24]; the removal of members of a local authority for failure to perform their duties[25]; the making of a compulsory purchase order by a

---

[19] *R.* v. *Deputy Industrial Injuries Commissioner, ex p. Moore* [1965] 1 Q.B. 456; *M.* v. *M.*, Supreme Court, October 8, 1979 and see pp. 191, 196.

[20] "Where a real error of law is shown then this court will interfere, but it would in my opinion be wrong to set up this Court as in effect a court of appeal of fact from decisions of these specialised tribunals," *per* May J. in *R.* v. *National Insurance Commissioner, ex p. Michael* [1976] I.C.R. 90 at p. 94 (D.C.), affirmed [1977] 1 W.L.R. 109 (C.A.). See also *R.* v. *Industrial Injuries Commissioner, ex p. Amalgamated Engineering Union* [1966] 2 Q.B. 31; *R.* v. *Preston Supplementary Benefits Appeal Tribunal, ex p. Moore* [1975] 1 W.L.R. 624.

[21] *R.* v. *National Insurance Commissioner, ex p. Stratton* [1979] Q.B. 361 at p. 369 (Lord Denning).

[22] Wade, *Administrative Law* (Oxford, 1982) at p. 829.

[23] Public Health (Ireland) Act 1878, s.163.

[24] Vocational Education Act 1930, s.27(2).

[25] Local Government Act 1941, s.44. See also Harbours Act 1946, s.164 (local inquiry into performance by harbour authority of their "powers, duties and functions" and other related matters).

local authority[26] and the determination of certain planning appeals.[27]

The second type of inquiry is in effect a post mortem: the inquiry is given the task of investigating the causes of accidents, natural disasters and other matters of general public concern. The terms of reference of this type of inquiry—which usually involves fact-finding as to the causes of, say, a major accident and recommendations as to improvements for the future—will usually be "at large," simply because the conclusions of the inquiry cannot be anticipated in advance. The most dignified and high-powered example of this latter type of inquiry is a tribunal of inquiry constituted under the Tribunals of Inquiry (Evidence) Acts 1921–1979.[28] Other examples include inquiries which investigate accidents involving railways,[29] shipping[30] and aeroplanes.[31]

Procedure before an inquiry

As regards the procedure adopted at a statutory inquiry of either type, much will be left to the chairman of the tribunal, but

[26] See *e.g.* Housing Act 1966, s.76 and Third Schedule (Compulsory Purchase Order) Procedure.

[27] Local Government (Planning and Development) Act 1963, s.82 and Local Government (Planning and Development) Regulations 1977 (S.I. 1977 No. 65).

[28] Tribunals of Inquiry have been appointed to investigate such diverse matters as allegations against members of the Oireachtas (*Report of the Tribunal appointed by the Taoiseach on November 7, 1947* (P. No. 8576) (sale of Locke's distillery); *Report of the Tribunal appointed by the Taoiseach on 4 July 1975* (Prl. 4745) (allegations against Minister for Local Government)); Garda practices (*Coghlan shooting inquiry: Tribunal Report* (1928) J.34; *Death of Liam O'Mahony: Report of the Tribunal appointed by the Minister* (1967) (Pr. 9790); *Report of the Tribunal of Inquiry: The "Kerry Babies" case* (1985) (Pl. 3514) and natural disasters (*Report of the Tribunal of Inquiry: Disaster at Whiddy Island, Bantry, Co. Cork* (1980) (Pl. 8911); *Report of the Tribunal of Inquiry: Fire at the Stardust, Artane, Dublin* (Pl. 853). The only other Tribunal of Inquiry appointed since 1922 concerned an investigation into the making of an RTE programme on moneylending: *Report of the Tribunal appointed by the Taoiseach on 22 December, 1969* (Prl. 1363).

[29] Regulation of Railways Act 1871, s.9. For a recent example of an inquiry held under the terms of this section, see *Report of the Investigation into the Accident on the CIE Railway at Buttevant, Co. Cork on 1 August, 1980,* (Prl. 9698) (1981).

[30] Merchant Shipping Act 1894, s.465.

[31] Air Navigation and Transport Act 1936, s.60 and Air Navigation (Investigation of Accidents) Regulations 1957 (S.I. 1957 No. 19). For a recent example of an inquiry held pursuant to these provisions, see *Accident to Reims Cessna F.182 Q in the Blackstairs Mountains, Co. Wexford on 7 September, 1983* (Department of Communications, 1984).

he must act subject to the procedural requirements imposed by
the particular statute and the overriding requirements of constitutional justice. Normally, statutory inquiries take the form of public
hearings where the witnesses give evidence under oath and are
subject to cross-examination by the opposing parties.[32]

Accusatorial v. inquisitorial procedure. It is sometimes argued
that the principles of constitutional justice should not apply in the
case of persons conducting preliminary statutory inquiries (*e.g.*
such as where the report of an inspector requires confirmation by
the decision-making authority). This argument has been rejected
by the Irish courts. In *The State (Shannon Atlantic Fisheries Ltd.)* v.
McPolin[33] an inspector had been appointed to investigate the
causes of the wrecking of the applicant's fishing vessel. The
inspector took depositions from members of the ship's crew, but
he did not interview the owners of the vessel or give them an
opportunity of refuting the allegations against them. The inspector's findings of fact impugned the good name and reputation of
the shipowners and Finlay P. ruled that the inspector's report
should be quashed for breach of the *audi alteram partem* rule.
Finlay P. continued:

> "The fact that it is not the investigating officer but the
> Minister for Transport and Power who must decide, having
> regard to the content of the report, whether any further
> action should be taken by him in relation to prosecutions
> under the Act seems to me not to affect the true decision-
> making role of the person carrying out the preliminary
> inquiry."[34]

In the unusual case of *Re Haughey*[35] the Supreme Court had
emphasised that the duty to observe fair procedures could arise
despite the fact that the report of an inquiry did not of itself
apportion liability or impose penalties. In *Haughey*, the plaintiff
had sought leave to cross-examine either witnesses appearing
before the Dail Committee of Public Accounts, and to have
counsel appear on his behalf. O'Dalaigh C.J. rejected the
argument that Haughey was a mere witness before the Committee—he was in effect a party. His conduct was the very subject-
matter of the investigation. In that situation he had the same rights

---

[32] See, *e.g.* Local Government Act 1941, s.86.
[33] [1976] I.R. 93. The inquiry was held pursuant to s.465 of the Merchant
Shipping Act 1894.
[34] [1976] I.R. 93 at p. 98.
[35] [1971] I.R. 217. See also *Mahon* v. *Air New Zealand Ltd.* [1984] A.C.
808.

as those guaranteed by Article 38.1 to accused persons facing trial, and basic fairness of procedures demanded that he be afforded the right to cross-examine (by counsel, if he wished); to call rebutting evidence; and to make closing submissions. Without those rights no person in the plaintiff's position could hope to defend his good name.

One might contrast this decision with that of the House of Lords in *Bushell* v. *Environment Secretary*.[36] *Bushell's* case concerned a statutory inquiry into whether a particular motorway should be constructed or not. The planning inspector who was chairman of the inquiry refused to allow the objectors to cross-examine witnesses as to the reliability of the Department of the Environment's predictions as to future traffic flow, or to query witnesses as to the need for such a motorway. The House of Lords ruled that the inspector had not acted contrary to natural justice as the objectors had been allowed to voice their opinions on these matters. Lord Diplock cautioned against the "over-judicialisation" of such inquiries, and he observed that it was fallacious to assume the cross-examination was the only procedure of ascertaining matters of fact and opinion. Perhaps these comments should be read in light of the fact that the proposed cross-examination concerned issues of policy. It may be surmised that Lord Diplock would have taken a different approach had the witnesses impugned the good name or reputation of the witnesses, or if there had been a conflict of evidence as to the essential facts at issue.

These cases recall the earlier discussion in the context of tribunals of the choice between the accusatorial and inquisitorial approaches.[37] It could be argued that in relation to the non-post-mortem type of inquiry (*i.e.* inquiries taken as a prelude to certain policy decisions) the inquisitorial approach with its higher regard for seeking the whole truth and its reduced emphasis on individual rights in regard to a narrow issue, is the more appropriate model.

The difficult question of whether the deciding authority is free to act on the basis of extrinsic evidence which was not before the parties at the inquiry is considered elsewhere.[38]

Attendance of witnesses etc. In the case of inquiries held at the instance of the Minister for the Environment (whether under the provisions of section 83 of the Local Government Act 1941 or any other Act), the inspector conducting the inquiry enjoys a statutory power to subpoena witnesses and to take evidence on oath.[39]

[36] [1981] A.C. 75.
[37] See pp. 143–144.
[38] See pp. 260–263.

Similar provisions exist in respect of other statutory inquiries.[40]

In the case of Tribunals of Inquiry, section 4 of the Tribunals of Inquiry (Evidence) (Amendment) Act 1979 provides that the Tribunal "may make such orders as it considers necessary for the purposes of its functions," and it is invested with all such "powers, rights and privileges of the High Court" in that regard.

Immunity from defamation proceedings. There is no general statutory provision which provides that statements made during the course of a statutory inquiry are privileged. Although the issue is not free from doubt, it would seem that the common law rule that statements during the course of judicial proceedings are absolutely privileged extends to statutory inquiries which follow a quasi-judicial procedure.[41] Since a tribunal of inquiry is invested with the status of the High Court by virtue of section 4 of the Tribunals of Inquiry (Evidence) (Amendment) Act 1979, it would seem that statements made during the course of proceedings before the tribunal are absolutely privileged.[42]

Appointment of assessors. Statutory provision has been made for the appointment of assessors to assist in certain types of inquiries.[43] An assessor will generally be appointed to assist in the evaluation of complex scientific and technical evidence.[44]

Costs. Costs may be awarded against a local authority or other body in the case of inquiries held at the instance of the Minister for the Environment under the provisions of section 83 of the Local Government Act 1941 or any other Act.[45] The Minister may certify for the payment of a contribution by the local authority or

---

[39] Local Government Act 1941, s.86.

[40] See *e.g.* Regulation of Railways Act 1871, s.7(3); Air Navigation and Transport Act 1936, s.60.

[41] McMahon and Binchy, *The Irish Law of Torts* (Abingdon, 1981) at p. 359. See also *Trapp* v. *Mackie* [1979] 1 W.L.R. 377.

[42] By virtue of s.5 of the 1979 Act, statements made during the course of a hearing before a Tribunal of Inquiry are inadmissible in all subsequent criminal prosecutions (with the exception of perjury).

[43] Regulation of Railways Act 1871, s.7(i); Air Navigation (Investigation of Accidents) Regulations 1957 (S.I. No. 19 of 1957), art. 7(2); Tribunal of Inquiry (Evidence) (Amendment) Act 1979, s.2.

[44] Assessors were appointed in the two recent Tribunals of Inquiry concerning natural disasters, *Whiddy Island* and *Stardust*. See n. 28 *supra*.

[45] Local Government Act 1941, s.83(2). A similar provision exists in relation to inquiries held pursuant to the Public Health (Ireland) Act 1878: see s.210 of the 1878 Act.

other body towards the costs and expenses reasonably incurred by any person (other than the local authority or other body) in relation to the inquiry. These provisions would appear to be broad enough to cover most statutory inquiries.

In the case of Tribunals of Inquiry, the Tribunals of Inquiry (Evidence) (Amendment) Act 1979, s.6, enables the chairman of the tribunal to certify that the whole or part of the costs of any person appearing before the tribunal shall be borne by another party (generally the State).[46]

In some cases, however, there is no statutory authority to award costs to or against any person appearing before the inquiry. In *Condon* v. *C.I.E.*[47] Barrington J. ruled that a statutory inquiry constituted under the provisions of section 7 of the Railway Regulation Act 1871 did not have power to award costs. Section 7 provided that the persons conducting the formal investigation were to have all the powers of a court of summary jurisdiction and certain other additional powers. These additional powers did not include the power to award costs, and, as Barrington J. noted, the power of courts of summary jurisdiction to award costs has always been strictly circumscribed.

In *Condon's* case itself, the plaintiff was an employee of C.I.E. and he claimed that he had been "singled out" as the person principally responsible for a serious train crash at Buttevant Station, Co. Cork, in 1980. Since his good name and his livelihood were at stake, the plaintiff engaged solicitor and counsel to represent him at the inquiry. It was argued that if the inquiry had no jurisdiction to award him costs, a constitutional duty was imposed on the State by the terms of Article 40.3 to defray the cost of such representation. Barrington J. rejected this argument, saying that while the guarantee of fair procedures contained in Article 40.3 required that the plaintiff be allowed to defend himself, "it was quite another thing to say that the State must pay the costs of his defence."[48] However, as C.I.E. had been negligent

---

[46] The general tendency so far has been for the chairman to award costs in favour of the private parties (but not institutions such as local authorities or major companies) who were properly represented before the Tribunal: see the comments of Costello J. at Chap. 24 of the Whiddy Island Report, and those of Lynch J. at Chap. 36 of the "Kerry Babies" Report.

[47] High Court, November 1984. For the background to this case, see *Report of the Investigation into the Accident on the CIE Railway at Buttevant, Co. Cork* on August 1, 1980 (Prl. 9698) (1981).

[48] Barrington J. followed the earlier decision of *K. Security Ltd.* v. *Ireland* High Court, July 15, 1977 in this regard. In *K. Security*, Gannon J. held that the State was not under any constitutional duty to discharge the costs of the plaintiff company which had been legally represented at a

and responsible for the accident, Barrington J. found (i) that it was almost unthinkable that the Minister for Transport would not establish a statutory inquiry into the disaster and (ii) that the plaintiff, as a person immediately involved in the events leading up to the disaster, would seek to be legally represented before the inquiry. The judge concluded that as the plaintiff "was placed in the position of needing such representation as a consequence of the negligence of C.I.E.," this was a reasonably foreseeable consequence of such negligence. Under these circumstances he was entitled to recover the reasonable costs of being legally represented before the inquiry. Taken at its full width *Condon* would lead to the rather extreme proposition that the person responsible for a particular accident will be liable to pay the legal costs of the other parties appearing before the inquiry, as this will generally be a reasonably foreseeable consequence of their negligence.

tribunal of inquiry. (This was before the enactment of the Tribunal of Inquiry (Evidence) (Amendment) Act 1979, s.5 of which makes provision for the payment of the parties costs by the State or other part appearing before the Tribunal).

7 The Ombudsman[1]

1. Introduction

The task of the Ombudsman is to secure redress when a person suffers harm or loss, through some act of governmental maladministration. It might be expected that the courts would fulfil this role. In fact, as we shall see in Chapters 7–13, the structure of our law on the judicial review of administrative action is—perhaps inevitably—so designed as to exclude from its scope many cases of injustice arising from maladministration. Moreover, the High Court—and it usually is only the High Court which has jurisdiction—is an expensive and inaccessible place. The result is that relatively few instances of maladministration surface as court cases. Traditionally, public representatives have seen it as their principal duty to use their moral authority, behind the scenes, to remedy the grievances of individual constituents against governmental services, a fact reflected in the title of Basil Chubb's classic study of public representatives, "Going about persecuting civil servants . . . "[2] as well as in the very high number of representatives per head of population. There are, indeed, twice as many deputies per person in Ireland compared with any other EEC State, apart from Greece. Yet this is not a desirable approach, either from the view-point of the effective and economic settlement of grievances or from the wider perspective of the health of the body politic.

[1] This chapter draws, to some extent, on Gwynn Morgan, "The Ombudsman Act" (1982) 17 Ir.Jur.(n.s.) 105.
[2] "Going about Persecuting Civil Servants: The Role of the Irish Parliamentary Representative" (1963) 11 *Political Studies* 272. *Cf.* the views of the Minister for Finance reported in *The Irish Times*, November 12, 1966 (and quoted by Kelly, "Administrative Discretion and the Courts" (1966) 1 Ir.Jur.(n.s.) 209 at p. 211): "There is hardly anyone without a direct personal link with someone, be he a Minister, T.D., clergyman, county or borough councillor who will interest himself in helping a citizen to have a grievance examined and, if possible, remedied. . . . The reason that we do not need an Ombudsman is that we already have many unofficial efficient Ombudsmen."

There are also, it is true, tribunals to oversee government administration; but these only exist in a few areas. The gaps and defects in these traditional institutions for remedying grievances suffered at the hands of officialdom means that there remained a need for the sort of comprehensive, flexible, informal, free service which is offered by the Ombudsman. This need has been acknowledged outside Ireland too and there are now about 100 Ombudsmen in existence, in states and provinces, throughout the world.

The idea of an Irish Ombudsman was first suggested, authoritatively, as part of the package of reforms proposed by the Devlin Report.[3] Later, a debate was held in the Dail,[4] which resulted in the constitution of an All-Party Informal Committee on Administrative Justice. This committee produced a report (the All-Party Report) in 1977, favouring the introduction of an Ombudsman.[5] Eventually, goaded by a Private Member's Bill put forward by the Opposition in 1979, the Government published its own Bill,[6] which was modelled fairly closely on the All-Party Report. This Bill became law, as the Ombudsman Act 1980, following an unusually constructive debate in the Oireachtas. However, the first and current (1986) incumbent of the office (Mr. Michael Mills) did not take up office until January 3, 1984.[7]

Constitutional setting
The Ombudsman must be, and be seen to be, independent of

[3] *Report of Public Services Organisation Review Group 1966–69,* (Prl. 792) App. I (pp. 447–458). The Devlin Committee's working paper on Administrative Law and Procedure proposed a "Commissioner for Administrative Justice," whose secondary role would be to act as an Ombudsman. His primary task would have been to watch over the extensive system of tribunals required by Devlin's chief proposal which was to remove routine executive functions from control by ministers and the Dail, and vest them in executive units overseen by the tribunals.

[4] The motion was: "That Dail Eireann favours the appointment of an Ombudsman." See *Dail Debates,* Vol. 280, cols. 1199–1206, 1257–1284, May 6 and 7, 1975.

[5] The committee held ten meetings in 1976 and 1977. It received three submissions including one (dated October 29, 1976) from a well-qualified group convened by the Institute of Public Administration and chaired by Mr. Justice Hamilton.

[6] Bill No. 20 of 1979.

[7] Following resolutions passed in the Dail (October 25, 1983) and Senate (November 2, 1984). His warrant of appointment is dated November 8, 1983. The 1980 Act was brought into force as from July 7, 1983: Ombudsman Act 1980 (Commencement Day) Order 1983 (S.I. 1983 No. 424). See further *Dail Debates,* Vol. 345, col. 605 (October 25, 1983).

the Government or any other body or person. Thus he has been provided with a similar, though not identical, institutional pedestal to that occupied by the higher judiciary. The Act contains a declaration that: "[t]he Ombudsman shall be independent in the performance of his functions." He is to be appointed by the President, acting on a recommendation contained in a resolution passed by both Houses. No qualifications are laid down for the incumbent save that he must be not more than 61 years of age (at the time of first appointment), and cannot be a public representative, or a member of the Reserve Defence Force, or hold any other paid office or employment apart from that of Ombudsman. The Ombudsman may only be removed from office "for stated misbehaviour, incapacity or bankruptcy," and then only on resolutions passed by each House of the Oireachtas. The term of office is six years and a holder is eligible for a second or subsequent term. The Ombudsman is to be paid the same salary and expenses as a High Court judge.[8]

Finally, since the Ombudsman's resources affect his performance, it may be worth noting that the size of his staff which in late 1985, included four senior investigators and sixteen investigators, is to be set by the Minister for the Public Service.[9] However, the Ombudsman derives some support for his independence from the fact that his civil servants are to be civil servants of the State[10] and that, he has his own separate vote in the Estimates.

In view of the expansionist policy adopted by the present Ombudsman, it is worth stating that like any other public authority, the Ombudsman is subject to judicial review, to ensure that he remains within his jurisdiction. It may be suggested, though, that in view both of the Ombudsman's function as an overseer of the executive and of his lofty constitutional position, it is likely that his action would receive the benefit of any doubt from the courts.

2. Jurisdiction

The type of complaint which the Ombudsman is empowered to scrutinise may be examined under four heads. First, the public bodies whose actions may be investigated must be considered. Secondly, the action must have "adversely affected" some person.

---

[8] 1980 Act, ss.2, 3.

[9] *Ibid.*, s.10(1)(a).

[10] The Minister for the Public Service is the "appropriate authority" for the purpose of the Civil Service Regulation Act 1956 but this power has been delegated to the Ombudsman: 1980 Act, s.10(4); Annual Report for 1985 (Pl. 3748) (hereafter "the 1985 Report") Chap. 10.

Thirdly, the action must have been taken in the performance of administrative functions. Finally, the action must bear one of the (seven) types of defect specified.[11] These questions will now be examined *seriatim*.

Public bodies within field of investigation

The bodies against whom a complaint may be heard include all the departments of state but not the Government itself or, with two exceptions, any state-sponsored bodies.[12] Since April 1, 1985, the Ombudsman's bailiwick has been extended to include Bord Telecom Eireann, An Post, local authorities (excluding the "reserved functions" exercised by elected representatives) and health boards excluding

> "[p]ersons when acting on behalf of health boards and (in the opinion of the Ombudsman) solely in the exercise of clinical judgment in connection with the diagnosis of illness or the care or treatment of a patient, whether formed by the person taking the action or by any other person."[13]

These are significant additions: the 5,500 complaints made to the Ombudsman in 1985 break down as follows: departments of state (44 per cent); local authorities (10 per cent); health boards (7 per cent); outside jurisdiction (14 per cent). The remaining 25 per

---

[11] Even where all four conditions are satisfied, the Ombudsman still has a discretion whether to exercise his jurisdiction: see 1980 Act, s.4(2) and (8) and Foulkes, "The Discretionary Provisions of the Parliamentary Commissioner Act 1967" (1971) 43 M.L.R. 377 at pp. 391–393.

[12] 1980 Act, s.4(2) and First Sched. See also Ombudsman Act 1980 (First Schedule) (Amendment) Order 1984 (S.I. 1984 No. 332); Ombudsman Act 1980 (First Schedule) (Amendment) Order 1985 (S.I. 1985 No. 66). However, the Ombudsman may not investigate decisions of a Department of State "as respects functions in relation to [bodies which fall outside his jurisdiction because of inclusion in the Second Schedule]": s.1(3)(b). This emerged when the Ombudsman accepted the Department of Education's legal argument that he was not competent to investigate the Department's refusal to sanction the appointment of a lecturer by a V.E.C.: 1984 Report, p. 11 and 1985 Report, p. 45.

[13] Ombudsman Act 1980 (First Schedule) (Amendment) Order 1984 (S.I. 1984 No. 332) 356 *Dail Debates*, col. 852ff. Bord Telecom Eireann, the local authorities and health boards have always co-operated with the Ombudsman though they were not formally within his jurisdiction until 1985. The Ombudsman was, of course, able to investigate complaints about phone accounts for the period between July 1983, his base-date for taking complaints, and December 31, 1983 when Telecom Eireann was officially established as of right because during this period telephones were the responsibility of the Department of Posts and Telegraphs.

cent were complaints about Telecom Eireann of which the great majority alleged excessive phone bills.[14] Of the complaints about the departments of state, most related to the Department of Social Welfare (50 per cent in 1984; 58 per cent in 1985) and the Revenue Commissioners (20 per cent in each year).[15]

The Government may extend (or restrict) the Ombudsman's jurisdiction by making an order amending the First Schedule to the 1980 Act. Such an order requires the approval of each House.[16]

Complainant

It must appear to the Ombudsman that the action has or may have "adversely affected" (which wide phrase is not defined) some person and if the investigation is initiated by way of complaint (rather than by the Ombudsman of his own motion) the complainant must have, in the Ombudsman's opinion, "a . . . sufficient interest in the matter."[17]

The All-Party Committee realistically recommended that there should be no requirement that a complaint should be made by the victim himself.[18] It seems that the wide provision used in the Act has left the Ombudsman sufficient discretion to enable him to take

[14] A typical complaint out of a large group which presents a few features of wider interest is the following: "A subscriber complained about the charges on an account in respect of a period in which he alleged the telephone had been locked away. He complained that the usage recorded could not be consistent with a private telephone. Telecom Éireann said that increased usage was first recorded on the line immediately following the conversion of the telephone from manual to automatic working. They also claimed that the telephone was used for business purposes. In the course of my examination of the case, I confirmed that the telephone was, in fact, used for business purposes. In the circumstances, I found no reason to make a recommendation in the complainant's favour." As can be seen from this example, until Bord Telecom Eireann, as it proposes to do, introduces an itemised billing system, there is no incontrovertible method of establishing how many phone calls have been made. However, the Board had by late 1985, agreed on methods to streamline their investigation of complaints.
[15] Figures taken from 1984 Report (Pl. 2909) and 1985 Report.
[16] 1980 Act, s.4(10), as amended by Ombudsman (Amendment) Act 1984, s.1. See *Dail Debates*, Vol. 356, cols. 1300 *et seq.*, November 7, 1984.
[17] 1980 Act, s.4(2)(*a*), (3), 9.
[18] Section VIII: " . . . since a significant proportion of those affected by administrative action may lack of skills or confidence to approach the Ombudsman themselves, they may feel more secure if the matters can be taken up on their behalf. . . . " See 1984 Report, p. 54 (where a social worker made a report on behalf of a deserted wife).

this position and to entertain complaints submitted by, for instance, social workers, deputies, professional advisers, etc. In addition, the person affected or the complainant must not be a department or other body specified in the First or Second Schedule.[19] Indeed the chief, though not the only (see *infra*) purpose of the Second Schedule which consists of a number of public bodies, including state-sponsored bodies, is to extend the category of public authorities which may not make a complaint and, thus, to remove the possibility that the Ombudsman might be used as a forum for internecine warfare by public bodies (as has happened in Britain).

"Taken in the performance of administrative functions"

The requirement, that the "action" be "taken in the perform-ance of administrative functions,"[20] is designed to exclude judicial or legislative decisions. Since, as already mentioned, the only bodies against whom the Ombudsman can hear complaints are departments or other executive agencies, this requirement has been inserted largely *ex abundanti cautela*, but not entirely so. It does at least have the effect of excluding actions taken by the executive which are incidental to the judicial function, *e.g.* a department deciding whether to institute extradition proceedings or whether to prosecute for breach of some specialist legislation, for which it is responsible. It seems clear, however, that quasi-judicial decisions—broadly, those which have a low policy content and which directly affect a single individual—are regarded as falling within the Ombudsman's jurisdiction, for instance, de-cisions in regard to housing grants or certain actions taken by the Revenue Commissioners (*infra*).

A more difficult question arises where the adverse consequences of an administrative action can be traced back, not to any error by the administrator, but to the content of a statute, statutory instrument or extra-legal rule (contained in, for example, a circular), which determined the way the administrative decision had to be taken. If it is the rule which is the source of say unfairness, has the Ombudsman jurisdiction? In the first place, where the maladministration is dictated by an Act of the Oireachtas or a common law rule, the Ombudsman has no authority to deal with the case: all he can do is to state his opinion that the law is in need of reform and this will presumably be of some weight with a Government deciding whether to bring

[19] 1980 Act, s.4(2)(*a*), 3(*a*), (9). See also Ombudsman Act 1980 (Second Schedule) (Amendment) Order 1985 (S.I. 1985 No. 69) extending this Schedule.

[20] For definition of "action" and "function" see s.1.

forward amending legislation. Indeed, large parts of the Ombudsman's Annual Reports are taken up with criticism of various laws,
for instance the rule that workers who do not gain from a strike by
fellow workers which causes them loss of employment can still be
prevented from obtaining unemployment benefits, if they are
members of the same grade as those on strike.[21] Another example,
involving the common law, was the Ombudsman's failure to obtain
deserted wife's allowance for a woman whose "husband" had
deserted her, gone abroad and obtained a divorce. The fact that
the husband had gone abroad meant, according to the law of
dependent domicile, (until it was abolished by the Domicile and
Recognition of Foreign Divorces Act 1986, s.1), that the wife was
also deemed to be domiciled abroad. Accordingly, her divorce was
recognised by Irish law and she was entitled to no financial
assistance from the State. The Ombudsman added his voice to
others criticising the law of dependent domicile as—in Lord
Denning's words—"the last barbarous relic of a wife's servi-
tude."[22]

The impact of this restriction on the Ombudsman's jurisdiction
is exacerbated, where a payment of compensation (as opposed to
an entitlement) is involved, by the fact that the constitutional rules
requiring the Oireachtas' consent, usually in the form of an
Appropriation Act, to the expenditure of state moneys leave so
little lee-way. For example, there is no provision in social welfare
legislation for the payment of interest on delayed payments and
the Minister for Finance is most reluctant to authorise extra-
statutory payments. Accordingly the Ombudsman was unable to
assist, for instance, a man who was not paid his disability payment
in respect of 1981 until 1984 and claimed interest on the unpaid
money.[23]

On the other hand, the Ombudsman has succeeded in getting a
department to alter a statutory instrument.[24] This arose from his

---

[21] 1984 Report, pp. 14, 48; 1985 Report, p. 7. This is a result of the Social
Welfare (Consolidation) Act 1981, ss.35(1) and 142(3). Persons
disqualified from unemployment benefit or assistance because of the
"grade or class" rule following a ruling of an Appeals Officer may now
apply for benefit to the Social Welfare Tribunal on the grounds that he
has been "unreasonably deprived of his employment" as a result of the
work stoppage: see 1981 Act, s.301A, as inserted by the Social Welfare
Act 1982 (No. 2), s.1. See generally Kerr and Whyte, *Irish Trade Union
Law* (Abingdon, 1985) at pp. 362–376.

[22] *Gray* v. *Formosa* [1963] P. 259, 267; 1984 Report, p. 13; 1985 Report,
p. 46.

[23] 1984 Report, p. 42. 1985 Report, p. 8. For the position in the context
of a court, rather than the Ombudsman, see pp. 409–410.

[24] 1984 Report, pp. 41–42.

criticisms of the procedure for the revision of rateable valuations
by the Commissioners of Valuation. One defect was that the date
for the publication of revised rating valuation lists was December 1
so that, given the Christmas holiday period, the statutory period of
twenty-eight days within which an appeal to the Circuit Court had
to be lodged was substantially reduced. The Minister for Finance
acceded to the Ombudsman's request to change the date for
publication of lists from December 1 to November 1 and this
change necessitated a statutory instrument. Since this was done
amicably the question was not squarely raised, whether statutory
instruments[25] should be regarded as legislation (as opposed to
administration), and, thus, strictly speaking, as falling outside the
Ombudsman's bailiwick. It may be that in future cases, some
demarcation line will be drawn within the category of statutory
instruments excluding certain types from his jurisdiction.

The Ombudsman has also succeeded in getting departments to
issue or amend circulars.[26] The second defect in the rateable
valuations revision system, described in the last paragraph,
concerned the function (which is vested in local authorities) of
informing a person that the valuation of his premises has been
increased so that he can decide whether he wishes to appeal.
Certain local authorities did not inform the persons affected
directly but simply placed a notice in a newspaper. The Ombudsman could not address himself directly to the local authorities
concerned because this case occurred before local authorities
were brought within his terms of reference. Instead, the Department of the Environment issued a circular suggesting to local
authorities that they should notify ratepayers affected, personally
by letter.

Types of defect

The British Parliamentary Commissioner Act 1967 relies heavily
on a term, "maladministration" which it does not define. In
contrast, the Irish legislation does not use this term, but section
4(2)(*b*) of the 1980 Act does contain a list of defects which may
attract the Ombudsman's attention.

> "... the Ombudsman may investigate any action ... where
> ... it appears to the Ombudsman
>
> (*b*)   that the action was or may have been:
>
>> (i)   taken without proper authority;
>> (ii) taken on irrelevant grounds;

[25] For the different types, see pp. 18–31 and Gwynn Morgan *loc. cit.* at
pp. 108–109.
[26] For examples, see 1984 Report, pp. 46–48; 1985 Report, pp. 27–28.

(iii) the result of negligence or carelessness;
(iv) based on erroneous or incomplete information;
(v) improperly discriminatory;
(vi) based on an undesirable administrative practice; or
(vii) otherwise contrary to sound or fair administration."

In view of the vagueness of some of these categories, the discretion in their application which is vested in the Ombudsman and the informal attitude adopted by the Ombudsman, there seems to be little point in a comprehensive scrutiny of each type of defect. However, the following tentative observations may be made. First, whilst in Britain a tension has been built into the 1967 Act by a ban on investigation of the merits of a complaint by the Parliamentary Commission or Administration,[27] there is no such ban in Ireland, and it seems clear enough, from headings (ii)–(v), that the Ombudsman is entitled at least, to approach the question of merits. Secondly, head (v) "improperly discriminatory" is similar to Article 40.1[28] of the Constitution which would be available to a court reviewing an administrative action. Again, heads (i) ("taken without proper authority") and (ii) ("taken on irrelevant grounds") establish grounds which would also be available in a court reviewing an administrative action. Take, for instance, a complaint arising from the health boards' refusal to pay Disabled Persons' Maintenance Allowance to persons attending secondary school because this meant that they were not available for employment. The Ombudsman upheld the complaint because the statute created an entitlement to payment provided that three factors—which related to the applicant's age, means and level of disability—were satisfied. In conventional legal parlance, the health boards had taken irrelevant considerations into account.[29] However, the remaining heads create wider powers than their judicial equivalents. Thus, in head (iii) ("the result of negligence or carelessness"), since negligence is mentioned, "carelessness" must mean something other than, or more than, negligence. It may be

---

[27] s.12(3). For discussion of this tension see, *e.g.* Marshall, *op. cit.,* pp. 32–39.
[28] "All citizens shall, as human persons, be held equal before the law. This shall not be held to mean that the State shall not in its enactment have due regard to differences of capacity, physical and moral, and of social function."
[29] 1985 Report, p. 32. For taking into account irrelevant considerations see pp. 304–308 and for a close parallel to the facts in the text, in the context of judicial review, see *The State (Keller)* v. *Galway Co. Co.* [1958] I.R. 142.

that the "duty of care" or "remoteness of damage" elements do not have to be established or, at least, not to the same standard as for negligence. In any case, given the under-developed state of the law on public authority torts,[30] it is useful to have a flexible alternative to negligence *stricto sensu*. And head (iv) ("based on erroneous or incomplete information") is clearly wider than the embryonic and limited "no-evidence" rule in the field of judicial review of administrative acts.[31] Likewise, as we shall see, head (vii) ("otherwise contrary to fair or sound administration") goes beyond constitutional justice.

The Ombudsman has been able to use this statutory catalogue to review complaints which a reasonable, informed person would regard as "maladministration," without legalism yet without abusing his powers. The Annual Reports (which do not refer to individual statutory heads) disclose that the Ombudsman has been prepared to intervene on such broad bases as consistency, equity and flexibility, as for instance: where the Department of Agriculture refused to deal with an accountant as a professional representative of a farmer on the ground that it was departmental policy only to deal with solicitors[32]; where a local authority's method for valuing a house for a Housing Finance Agency loan was based only on site cost plus building cost per square metre, with the result that small houses in urban areas were under-valued[33]; where welfare payments had been made as from the date of certification of eligibility by the health board rather than the date of application[34]; or because there is an absolute entitlement under the Urban Fuel Scheme which operates in seventeen urban districts, whereas the National Fuel Scheme, which applies elsewhere, is discretionary.[35]

It is also clear from the evidence, presently available, that the Ombudsman is more prepared, than a court would be, to review questions of merit or judgment. Thus, under the rubric of "fairness," the Ombudsman was prepared to intervene when a mother complained that the Department of Education bus route for taking children to school was so drawn that her five-year-old child had to walk one-a-half miles to the bus, whilst certain older children were being picked up much closer to their homes. The Ombudsman put forward a proposal which, without extra overall cost, enabled the bus to collect the five-year-old closer to his home

[30] See pp. 369–384.
[31] See pp. 191, 196.
[32] 1985 Report, p. 65.
[33] *Ibid.*, p. 53.
[34] *Ibid.*, p. 52, 31.
[35] *Ibid.*, p. 33.

whilst requiring some older children to walk somewhat further. And the Department of Social Welfare accepted this proposal.[36] The Ombudsman also condemned as a case of "Catch 22" a situation in which the Department of Social Welfare had refused to allow a complainant to register retrospectively as unemployed in respect of the five-week period during which the Department was hearing his appeal against the termination of his disability benefit. The complainant was naturally unwilling to register prospectively as unemployed during this period for to do so would be to imply that he was capable of work and thus, possibly, to jeopardise his appeal on the disability benefit claim. The result was that he had been unable to claim either benefit in respect of this period.[37]

On the other hand, the Ombudsman must not usurp the position of the body in which the decision in question has been vested. Thus, for instance, a dispute had arisen as to whether planning permission should be allowed for an access between two housing estates so as to shorten the children's journey to school, even though this access would disturb the privacy of the complainant who lived in one of the estates. The Ombudsman concluded that whatever decision was reached was bound to be unacceptable to one of the parties and that the local authority had "acted reasonably and with common sense." Accordingly, he did not recommend any change.[38]

In another case, he rejected a complaint that the Revenue Commissioners, in refusing a cartographer a tax exemption under the Finance Act 1969 for producing work which is "original and creative" and displays "cultural or artistic merit," had taken no account evidence of his work's artistic merit. The Ombudsman's view was that:

> "Having studied and consulted on the case at length I came to the conclusion that no fault could be found with the efforts of the Revenue Commissioners to arrive at a decision in a fair and reasonable way. I might not agree with the decision but I have no authority to set up an alternative source of assessment to challenge the advice given to the Commissioners."[39]

In another case involving the artist's/writer's tax exemption, the Ombudsman reached the same conclusion but suggested that an

[36] 1984 Report, p. 37.
[37] *Ibid.*, p. 33.
[38] 1985 Report, p. 54.
[39] 1984 Report, p. 46.

independent appeals system should be established, a suggestion which he has also made in other contexts.[40]

In a number of cases, investigation by a member of the Ombudsman's staff led to the discovery of new information or cast a fresh light on the existing information and this led to a change of heart in the responsible authority. For example, the Department of Social Welfare had decided that the complainant was not available for employment except as an actor and that this constituted "unreasonable limitations on his availability for work" which was a statutory ground for terminating his unemployment benefit. The Ombudsman suggested various new factors to the appeals officer—including the fact that the complainant had previously worked as a car-park attendant and that this showed that he was willing to take any kind of work. Accordingly, the appeals officer reversed the original decision.[41] In another case, the Department of Health had refused to grant financial assistance in respect of medical treatment which he had received in London on the ground that the treatment had been available in Ireland free of charge. The Ombudsman was able to establish that at *the relevant time* the treatment had not been available. The Department reversed its decision and also reviewed its administrative arrangements for obtaining the relevant information (requirement of hospital consultant's certificate).[42]

Another category of case (which could go under the head of "negligence or carelessness") included the "administrative bungling"[43] by which a wedding dress and two bridesmaid's dresses, which had been sent by registered post, were mislaid—though eventually recovered—a few days before the wedding. Following the intervention of the Ombudsman, An Post made an *ex gratia* payment of £80 to compensate for expenses (travelling and phone calls) incurred in searching for the dresses. In a more typical case, the Department of Social Welfare said that the complainant had a record of insufficient contributions for the payment of a contributory widow's pension. Following a request from the Ombudsman, the Department re-checked and discovered a second contribution record which brought her total of contributions up to the necessary level.[44]

As might be expected a great number of complaints to the Ombudsman fall into a category which might broadly be called "procedure." Procedural defects include not only breach of the

[40] 1985 Report, p. 30.
[41] 1984 Report, pp. 49–50.
[42] 1985 Report, p. 47.
[43] 1984 Report, pp. 39–40.
[44] 1985 Report, pp. 56–57.

rules of constitutional justice or the particular procedural regulations but also delay[45]; and bureaucratic bad manners shading into "the insolence of office." As regards insensitivity, speaking generally about the performance of the Revenue Commissioners, the Ombudsman made the following observation[46]:

> "Coping with the harsh economic realities of the eighties is a traumatic experience particularly for widows and pensioners. Both are extremely vulnerable and dependent. When sharp cryptic demands for payments are issued from the computer system no account is taken of the age or circumstances of the recipient. The elderly are easily frightened and upset by authoritative demands for payment. It may be that such categories are difficult to identify but some thought should be given as to how the problem might be overcome in order to avoid unnecessary distress to the weak and elderly in our community."

A concrete case which is relevant in the present context involved an American citizen (there is, of course, no requirement that a complainant should be Irish) who arrived at Dublin Airport, on holiday with his golf clubs. Because he attempted to carry the clubs through the green channel, a customs officer decided that he was attempting to smuggle them into the country and accordingly that they were liable for forfeiture. As a compromise, they were returned to the complainant on payment of £100 (import tax plus penalty). The Ombudsman recommended that as there was a reasonable doubt about the complainant's intentions the penalty should be refunded and that, if he subsequently removed the clubs from the country, the taxes should also be refunded. The Ombudsman also disapproved of two other features of the Customs authorities' treatment of the visitor: first, he had not been given a receipt for his golf club until he had asked for one; secondly, the customs officers had seized a private letter of the visitor's, explaining this action on the ground that it might contain evidence. The Ombudsman's judgment was that there was insufficient justification for opening the letter and, further, that the (non-statutory) instructions governing the opening of such letters, issued by the Revenue Commissioners had not been followed. The Ombudsman recommended that the instructions for opening personal letters be conveyed clearly to all customs staff.

---

[45] In 1984, 10 per cent of all complaints to the Ombudsman involved delay. (See chap. 7 of his Report). By s.1(1) of the 1980 Act, his jurisdiction includes "failure to act."
[46] 1984 Report, p. 18.

Finally, in a number of complaints, the Ombudsman appears to have drawn upon a broad, though unspecified, principle that the State is under a positive duty to supply the citizen with relevant information about his rights. For instance, he censured the Departments of State involved, for their failure, over a period of five years, to reply to letters from a public servant, inquiring what her pension rights would be.[47] Another complaint arose because a welfare officer informed an undertaker that he would recommend to the health board that they should pay the costs of a funeral, which they then failed to do. Following the Ombudsman's intervention, the health board approved a funeral grant.[48] Another problem stemmed from section 37 of the Road Traffic Act 1961, under which a person can apply for the removal of driving licence endorsement after he has had a clean licence for a *continuous* period of five years, *i.e.* if a new licence is necessary, there must be no gap between the two licences. The Department of the Environment agreed to the Ombudsman's suggestion that the explanatory leaflet, provided by the Department, should be amended to make it clear that, if a person in this situation has to obtain a new licence, he should ensure that the two licences are absolutely continuous.[49]

3. Exemptions from jurisdiction

Even within the subject area thus staked out, six categories of case are exempted from the Ombudsman's jurisdiction.

(1) The Ombudsman is excluded where there is a right of appeal in respect of the decision of a court.[50] It is striking that, in contrast with the position in Britain, there is no provision preventing a potential complainant from going to the Ombudsman merely because he could have instituted legal proceedings in a court in

---

[47] 1985 Report, p. 63. *Cf.* Civil Service Executive Union Annual Report 1985–86 App. 2, para. 4.6 and 4.7. ("If an application [for a housing grant] is refused and the citizen disputes the refusal on certain grounds, the Department of the Environment will arrange for the matter to be investigated again by an Officer of higher rank than the officer who carried out the first investigation. However, the citizen is not told that such a facility exists. Again, in instances such as this, the necessity for intervention by the Ombudsman's office would be reduced if the appeals system were formalised and the public made aware of their rights.")

[48] 1985 Report, p. 55.

[49] *Ibid.* p. 28.

[50] s.5(1)(*a*)(ii). But though a person is entitled to apply to the High Court for habeas corpus, he may still refer his grievance to the Ombudsman: see Gwynn Morgan *loc. cit.* at p. 110.

respect of the complaint. In view of the doubt and fluidity in administrative law, and the ignorance of it among lawyers, this is a sensible omission. The Ombudsman is, naturally, prevented from hearing a case where the person aggrieved has actually initiated "civil legal proceedings."[51] Even then, the Ombudsman will not be excluded if "the proceedings have . . . been dismissed for failure to disclose a cause of action or a complaint justiciable by that court."[51] This limitation upon the matters over which the Ombudsman has no jurisdiction evidently arises because (as noted *supra*), the grounds on which complaints may be made to the Ombudsman are wider than those which apply to a court, and it is thought to be harsh to prevent a case going to the Ombudsman on the basis that the case has been before a court, if the grounds of complaint anyway fall outside the court's jurisdiction. Pursuing a similar line of reasoning, it might be asked whether a complainant ought to lose his chance of going to the Ombudsman if his court case had failed because it was out of time, or because he had adopted the wrong procedure, or for any other reason unrelated to the merits. If the provision is read strictly, such a person would not be within the Ombudsman's jurisdiction. There is, however, an equitable proviso which permits the investigation of actions which would otherwise be excluded, under the present, or the following, head "if it appears to the Ombudsman that special circumstances make it proper to do so."[52] This proviso would probably enable the Ombudsman to investigate in a case in which the court had turned the complainant away for some reason other than the merits of his claim.

(2) The Ombudsman has no jurisdiction over a decision from which an appeal lies to "a person other than a Department of State or other person specified in Part I of the First Schedule . . . ," irrespective of whether any appeal has actually been taken.[53] The effect of the phrase quoted is that, following the recommendation of the All-Party Report,[54] the Ombudsman retains jurisdiction over decisions if the appeal lies to a Minister or civil servant[55] in a department, but where the appeal is to an external body, the Ombudsman has no jurisdiction over the initial decision or the appeal. Thus subject to the local remedies' rule (see para. 5 *infra*), the Ombudsman has jurisdiction over claims for social welfare benefit which are heard by deciding officers in the Department of

[51] s.5(1)(*a*)(ii). "Civil legal proceedings" is evidently (if only from its context) intended to include both civil actions and applications for judicial review.
[52] Proviso to s.5(1).
[53] s.5(1)(*a*)(ii), (iii).
[54] All Party Report, s.VII, para. 12.
[55] See s.1(2).

Social Welfare or appeals from deciding officers which are heard by appeals officers, again within the Department.[56] However, on the other side of the line, the exclusion of cases where there is an appeal to someone other than a Department means, for instance, that the Ombudsman is excluded from planning cases because of the appeal to An Bord Pleanala. Similarly, he may not review decisions of the Revenue Commissioners where there is an appeal to the Appeals Commissioners. Nevertheless the Ombudsman has investigated a large number of complaints against the Revenue Commissioners in respect of other matters, for instance: delay in sending out tax rebates or statements of allowance; excessive zeal in investigating suspected evasion; or the Customs and Excise area in respect of which there is no appeal.

(3) The Ombudsman does not have jurisdiction over actions relating to "national security or military activity or (in the opinion of the Ombudsman) arrangements regarding participation in organisations of states or governments"; "the administration of the law relating to aliens or naturalisation"; the exercise of the power of pardon and the administration of prisons or other similar institutions.[57] In addition, the Ombudsman is forbidden to investigate recruitment or appointment to any of the bodies listed in the First Schedule[58] or any matter relating to the terms or conditions upon which a person holds any office or employment in any of the bodies listed in the First or Second Schedule.[59] However, there is no ban on investigating the dismissal of a servant or officer nor (as there is in Britain) the making or terms of a commercial contract between a department and a private person.

(4) A Minister of the Government may prevent or restrain the Ombudsman from investigating any action of that Minister's Department (or of a person "whose business and functions are comprised" in that Department) simply by making a written request to that effect, setting out in full the reasons for the request.[60] The justification for this provision, offered by the Minister of State at the Department of the Public Service piloting the Bill through the Dail, is the need to exclude from the

---

[56] In spite of the plain words of the statute, appeals officers argued at first that the Ombudsman had no authority to investigate their decisions but eventually withdrew this contention: 1985 Report, p. 47. For other examples of appeals to Ministers (from local authorities), see p. 231.

[57] s.5(1)(*b*), (*e*).

[58] s.5(1)(*c*).

[59] s.5(1)(*d*)(i). (In 1984 and 1985, 13 per cent and 3 per cent, respectively of all complaints made to the Ombudsman had to be excluded on the grounds that they involved the civil service (personnel matters, etc.).

[60] s.5(3).

Ombudsman's jurisdiction points of judgment for which a Minister should be answerable only to the Dail.[61] The safeguard, which is designed to prevent ministers from drawing too freely on this blank cheque, is publicity: not only must the communication to the Ombudsman be in writing, but it must be passed on by the Ombudsman to the complainant and must also be recorded in the reports which the Ombudsman has to lay before the Oireachtas.[62]

(5) The Ombudsman has a jurisdiction not to hear a complaint if he considers that it is "trivial or vexatious"; that the complainant has not exhausted his local remedies; or that the subject-matter of the complaint has been, is being, or will be, sufficiently investigated in another investigation by the Ombudsman.[63]

(6) The complaint must be made within twelve months of the time of the action or—and this could be a significant extension—the time when the complainant became aware of the complaint, whichever is the later. However, an exception to this rule may be allowed where "it appears to the Ombudsman that special circumstances make it proper to do so."[64] In addition, the action must not have been taken before the commencement of the Act.[65]

4. Procedure

An investigation (which must be "conducted otherwise than in public") may be initiated either by way of complaint or by the Ombudsman acting of his own motion if it appears to him that an investigation would be warranted.[66]

First, the Ombudsman carries out a preliminary examination[67] at which a number of complaints are weeded out, for instance,

[61] *Dail Debates*, Vol. 321, col. 867–869, (May 28, 1980). See too, All Party Report, ss.VII, II.
[62] s.4(5), (6).
[63] s.5(1), proviso.
[64] s.5(1)(*g*). The Act was brought into force on July 7, 1983, by statutory order, made under s.12(2). s.5(2) provides that notwithstanding the time limits in the text, the Ombudsman may investigate insurability and entitlement to benefit under the Social Welfare Acts 1952–79. Even apart from specific provision the Ombudsman observes a general "continuing effect" doctrine by which he is prepared to investigate circumstances or facts occurring before his time limit if these are relevant to decisions taken after the time limits.
[65] s.8(1). This phrase may have been used in preference to "in private" so as to indicate that the Ombudsman retains a power to allow selected persons to attend.
[66] s.4(3)(*b*).
[67] s.4(2). See also s.4(5).

because they involve social welfare claims by persons who clearly have not paid sufficient contributions; or because they seek to inveigle the Ombudsman to intervene in the merits of income tax disputes which are the preserve of the Appeals Commissioners.[68] Where the Ombudsman decides not to proceed with a complaint, then he must write to the complainant stating his reasons.[69]

The 1980 Act, s.8(3) provides that: "[s]ubject to the provisions of this Act, the procedure for conducting an investigation shall be such as the Ombudsman considers appropriate. . . . " And in fact the majority of the Ombudsman's case are handled by a "review procedure," which is not mentioned in the Act. This method is applied to straightforward cases in which the Ombudsman's staff notice some new fact or failure of mutual comprehension between the public authority and the person involved and on the basis of the fresh light which this sheds, the public authority[70] agrees (it may be over the telephone) to provide an acceptable remedy. Explaining this review procedure, the Ombudsman also revealed a hint of steel

> "If in the course of seeking to bring about a solution to a problem, I ask a Department to review a case, *I am not making representations*. I am indicating a formula for resolving the problem. . . . I am giving senior civil servants in the particular Department an opportunity to revise a decision on their own initiative rather than await a recommendation to carry out the change."[71] (Italics added).

However, the Ombudsman may decide to follow the formal investigation procedure which is outlined in his constituent statute. First, the Ombudsman sends a summary of the complaint to the head of the public authority concerned who replies with a counter-statement and comments. Thereafter, the Ombudsman

---

[68] *Cf.* Civil Service Executive Union Report for 1985–86, App. 2, para. 3.3, complaining that provided a matter falls within his jurisdiction, "the Ombudsman's enquiries are becoming akin to representations by public representatives—*i.e.* almost all cases taken up without discrimination."

[69] s.6(1).

[70] The Department of the Public Service has issued DPS Circular 30/83 specifying procedures for communication between the Ombudsman and public authorities and asking each authority to designate a liaison officer (at about Principal Officer level in the civil service and the equivalent elsewhere).

[71] 1985 Report, p. 19.

almost always investigates by way of interviews.[72] He must send a written statement of his investigation to specified persons, including: the department or other government body in which the action under investigation was taken; the public servant who actually took the action; and the complainant (if there be one).[73] If, as a result of the investigation, it does appear to the Ombudsman that the action had an adverse affect and that it otherwise fell within his jurisdiction, then the Ombudsman may choose between three specified types of recommendation to the department which took the decision, *viz.* that the action be reconsidered; that the reasons for it be given to the Ombudsman; or, finally, that measures or specified measures be taken to remedy, mitigate or alter the adverse effect of the action.[74] In some cases, there might have to be further sets of responses and recommendations in the dialogue.

If the response to any recommendation is not "satisfactory," then the Ombudsman's only sanction is to make a "special report" on the case to the Houses the Oireachtas.[75] This report could either be included as part of the annual report "on the performance of the Ombudsman's functions under the Act," which must be laid before each House of the Oireachtas, or, as seems more likely in these circumstances, it could be laid forthwith as a separate report.[76]

The 1980 Act also contains a fairly elaborate formulation of the *audi alteram partem* rule as it must be observed in order to protect the interests of both the Department of State (or other agency) and the actual official who took the action under investigation.[77]

In addition, the Act gives the Ombudsman virtually full access to all relevant files for the purposes of a preliminary investigation or an examination. Considering the extent to which Departments record information, it is one of the Ombudsman's most potent weapons that he may require any person who, in his opinion, possesses relevant information, or a relevant document or "thing," either to send the information, document or thing to the

---

[72] His wide discretion in regard to procedure would allow him to hold oral hearings (s.8(3), (4)) but not a single hearing has yet (October, 1985) been held.

[73] s.6(2), (4).

[74] s.6(3).

[75] s.6(5).

[76] s.6(7). The Ombudsman's functions under s.6(5), (7) (together with those in the personnel field are the only ones which he is not empowered to delegate to his officers: s.10(3).

[77] See ss.6(6), 8; Gwynn Morgan *loc. cit.* at pp. 115–116.

Ombudsman or, where appropriate, to attend before the Ombudsman to furnish the information, document or thing.[78]

There are only two curbs on the Ombudsman's access to information. The first is that the Ombudsman may not ask for information or a document which "relates to decisions and proceedings of the Government or of any of its committees."[79] And, for the purposes of determining whether information or a document does fall within this category, a certificate given by the Secretary to the Government is to be conclusive.[79] The second exception is only partial: it does not prevent information or a document from being given to the Ombudsman, but only from being disclosed by the Ombudsman to anyone else, even those involved in the complaint. It applies where any Minister of the Government has given notice, in writing, to the Ombudsman, that the disclosure of any document or information or class thereof would in his opinion and for the reasons stated in the notice, "be prejudicial to the public interest."[80]

5. Appraisal

It is worth emphasising some of the new institution's more novel features. The first of these is the lack of any formal sanction by which the Ombudsman can enforce his decisions. For while the Ombudsman is not on a par with a deputy or local councillor making "representations"[81]—the Act indeed uses the term "fin-

---

[78] s.7(1)(*a*). Failure to comply is not made an offence by the Act (whatever the common law position). It is assumed that public servants would not wish to jeopardise their careers by a refusal to comply. The basic principle that the Ombudsman may call for whatever evidence is relevant is buttressed by other rules: witnesses are entitled to the same privileges as High Court witnesses (s.7(1)); their evidence may not be used against them in criminal proceedings (s.7(6)); expenses of witnesses or complainant may be paid (s.7(5)); the Official Secrets Act 1963 is suspended in respect of examinations or investigations (s.7(4)); executive privilege is restricted to the rules stated in the next paragraph of the text (s.7(4)); the same protection created for a court by the contempt of court rules is extended to the Ombudsman, though no power is given to commit for contempt (s.7(3)); and information obtained by the Ombudsman can be disclosed only for the purpose of the Act or for proceedings under the Official Secrets Act and not for any other proceedings (s.9(1)).

[79] s.7(1)(*b*). This is the first statutory acknowledgement of the existence of Government committees.

[80] s.9(2)(*a*)(*c*). See also s.9(2)(*b*), (*c*).

[81] 1985 Report, p. 16 (" . . . some County Managers saw my role as making representations").

ding"[82]—yet if a recalcitrant department or other public agency fails to heed a "recommendation" from the Ombudsman, then his sole recourse is a report laid before the Oireachtas.[83] The effect of such a report would be to attract adverse publicity to the Government, the extent of which would depend upon how far the Ombudsman retains the same respect of the public, politicians and media that he enjoys at the moment.

It is, thus, significant that the Oireachtas has taken considerable interest in the Ombudsman's work, formally, through debates, and informally in that many complaints are referred on to the Ombudsman by way of Deputies or Senators (although there is no requirement that complaints must proceed by way of a Deputy, as there is in Britain). The office of Ombudsman has been deliberately designed to promote maximum usage. It is flexible, allowing the Ombudsman ample scope to vary the procedure to suit the circumstances of the case. He can, for instance, initiate his own investigations, without waiting for a complainant. Again, the interplay of recommendation from the Ombudsman and response, from the governmental agency complained against, is more likely to yield a result satisfactory to all parties than would the polarised concepts administered in a court. And on the substantive side, the statutory grounds on which the Ombudsman may intervene allow for a good deal of discretion.

The Ombudsman himself has taken steps which are likely to increase the use of his office. These include: regional visits by his staff to facilitate access by complainants; a prompt response to complaints; and the publication of attractively set out reports within three months of the year to which they relate.

The result has been that the number of complaints, 5,496 received in 1985, the second year of operation, was more than double the figure for 1984 and also very high by international standards.[84] Moreover, the public service has co-operated, by and large, with the Ombudsman. In terms of the results of cases, the Ombudsman appears to have made an impact. In 1985 [1984], out of the 3,411 [1,013] cases finalised, a successful outcome for the complainant was achieved in 30 per cent [40 per cent] of the cases, help or advice was given in a further 34 per cent [15 per cent] of cases in that the Ombudsman was able to suggest other courses of action that were open to the complainant; and in 19 per cent [30 per cent] of cases, it was decided that, given the state of

[82] 1980 Act, *e.g.*, s.6(6).
[83] *Ibid.* s.6(7).
[84] See 1985 Report, Chap. 6; Civil Service Executive Union Report, App. 2 ("Memorandum on Relations Between The Ombudsman's Office And Government Departments").

the relevant legislation, there had been no maladministration. The remaining complaints were withdrawn or discontinued, in some cases because the complainant had obtained satisfaction in the meantime.[85]

Many of the Ombudsman's cases come from poor, uneducated people, lacking professional advisers, (who may be heavily dependent on social welfare benefits). And the high percentage, given in the previous paragraph, for those cases in which the Ombudsman was able to give help or advice suggests that he has a part to play in regard, not just to maladministration, but also to a frequent failure of communication at the interface at which the citizen meets his government. Thus the Ombudsman has described his duty as "giving the citizen a role in government administration."[86]

The Ombudsman has a further task: his status, experience and the lack of restriction on his office give him the opportunity of stimulating improvements in administration or even legislative reform: in other words, in prevention as opposed to cure. In these first two reports, there are a number of examples of this, some of which have been cited *supra*.[87] It may be that the Ombudsman's most significant service will, in the long term, be to stimulate improvements which raise the level of public administration (quicker decisions; more flexibility; better explanations) and so reduce the amount of clientelism embedded in the Irish political system.

---

[85] Figures from 1984 Report, Chap. 2 and 1985 Report, Chap. 3.

[86] See *e.g. Senate Debates* Vol. 94; col. 1593, (July 2, 1980). For debates on 1984 Annual Report, see *Dail Debates*, Vol. 364, cols. 483 *et seq.*, February 26, 1986; *Senate Debates*, Vol. 109, cols. 478 *et seq.* (October 17 and November 7, 1985). The Irish version of the Ombudsman is Fear a 'Phobal (literally, "the man of the People") although the office translation in the 1980 Act is simply "Ombudsman."

[87] See pp. 166–167.

8   The Legal Nature of Powers

1. Introduction

Judicial review of administrative action is founded on the doctrine of *ultra vires*. Although the High Court possesses an inherent jurisdiction to supervise the activities of inferior courts,[1] tribunals and other public authorities, it is a cardinal principle (which is considered below) that this power of review may only be exercised in circumstances where the inferior court or tribunal has exceeded its jurisdiction. The High Court, when exercising its powers of judicial review, is not concerned with the *merits*, but rather with the *legality* of the decision under review. In short, a finding of *ultra vires* is a pre-requisite to judicial intervention by means of judicial review. To this there is one recognised exception: the court may quash a decision, otherwise within jurisdiction, which is flawed by the presence of an error "on the face of the record," *i.e.* where an error of law is patent.[2] The power to quash for error of law on the record is an historical anomaly which is now probably too well established to be disregarded. Where a decision exhibited a patent error of law, this irregularity is regarded "as an affront to the law which cannot be overlooked" and more than judicial flesh and blood could resist."[3]

A decision which is vitiated by jurisdictional error is void, and will, save in exceptional cases, be declared to be void *ab initio* in the appropriate proceedings. Nevertheless such a decision—unless flagrantly illegal—remains valid for all purposes unless and until it

---

[1] The inferior courts are the District Court, the Circuit Court and the Special Criminal Court. The High Court, Court of Criminal Appeal and the Supreme Court are all superior courts of record and are not subject to judicial review.

[2] See pp. 196–200.

[3] Wade, *Administrative Law* (Oxford, 1982) at p. 272. Professor Wade's account of the historical development of error on the face of the record (pp. 272–276) is excellent.

is set aside by the courts.[4] The public law remedies are discretionary in nature, and a quashing order will only be granted to a proper plaintiff with the requisite *locus standi* who can persuade the court to exercise its discretion in his favour. No comprehensive account can be given of what errors will destroy the jurisdiction of a lower court or tribunal, thus rendering its decisions liable to be quashed. It is clear that an error committed in the course of an adjudication may go to jurisdiction,[5] but having said that, the leading authorities do not disclose a governing principle which facilitates the classification of errors as "jurisdictional" as opposed to those which are merely errors committed within jurisdiction and which—unless they appear on the face of the record—stand immune from correction upon an application for judicial review. In truth, the common law doctrine of *ultra vires* is based on the artifice of statutory interpretation. The courts presume that Parliament did not intend that the donee of a statutory power should exercise that power in an unfair or arbitrary fashion. Thus the courts will intervene not only to restrain administrative action which contravenes some express statutory provision, but also where some implied condition of the Act—adherence to the rules of natural justice, or the doctrine of reasonableness—has been infringed. The common law principles of judicial review of administrative action are based upon this edifice of parliamentary intent and statutory interpretation.

In recent times, Irish courts have elevated these common law doctrines unto the constitutional plane. Legislation authorising administrative action which was arbitrary, unfair, or contrary to principles of fair procedures would plainly be unconstitutional.[6] The presumption of constitutionality requires that a constitutional interpretation be given to the impugned statutory provisions if this is at all possible, and the presumption extends to proceedings, procedures, discretions and adjudications which are permitted, provided for or prescribed by an Act of the Oireachtas. Thus, a statutory provision is entitled to the presumption:

"[T]hat what is required, is allowed to be done, for the

---

[4] *The State (Llewellyn)* v. *UaDonnachada* [1973] I.R. 151; *Campus Oil* v. *Minister for Industry and Energy* [1983] I.R. 88; *The State (Abenglen Properties Ltd.)* v. *Dublin Corporation* [1984] I.R. 381 and *Hoffman-La Roche* v. *Trade Secretary* [1975] A.C. 295. But *cf.* the comments of Lord Denning in *R.* v. *Paddington Valuation Officer, ex p. Peachy Properties Ltd.* [1966] 1 Q.B. 380 and those of Lord Diplock in *Dunlop* v. *Woolahra M.C.* [1982] A.C. 158.

[5] *The State (Holland)* v. *Kennedy* [1977] I.R. 193.

[6] See, *e.g. Loftus* v. *Att.-Gen.* [1979] I.R. 221; *O'Brien* v. *Bord na Mona* [1983] I.R. 265.

purpose of its implementation, will take place without breaching any of the requirements, express or implied of the Constitution. . . . If [the donee of the statutory power] exercised his discretion or his powers capriciously, partially or in a manifestly unfair manner it would be assumed that this could not have been contemplated or intended by the Oireachtas and his action would be restrained and corrected by the Courts.''[7]

The courts have used this principle to hold that the exercise of administrative discretion in an improper fashion,[8] or in a manner contrary to natural justice[9] is *ultra vires* the principal Act, while at the same time upholding the constitutionality of the parent legislation.

The modern tendency has been to increase the range of errors which affect the jurisdiction of administrative bodies and lower courts, almost to the point where all errors of law are assumed to destroy that jurisdiction. But this tendency—which is doubtless prompted by a judicial desire to protect the citizen against legally unjustifiable administrative actions—is often at odds with the legislative policy of allocating tasks to a specialised public body.[10] In view of this fact, and given the inherent difficulty in distinguishing satisfactorily between matters bearing on the merits and those relating to *vires* (or jurisdiction), the entire doctrine of jurisdictional review has become increasingly artificial and complex. It may be useful, therefore, to sketch out, by way of introduction, the six heads of judicial review.

Correct authority

The power may only be exercised by the administrative authority in whom it was vested by the Oireachtas. One aspect of this is the *delegatus non potest delegare* principle: a power may only be delegated to a body or person other than that designated by the Oireachtas if this is authorised, expressly or by implication by the

---

[7] *Loftus* v. *Att.-Gen.* [1979] I.R. 221 at pp. 238, 241, *per* O'Higgins C.J.
[8] *Irish Family Planning Assoc. Ltd.* v. *Ryan* [1979] I.R. 295.
[9] *O'Brien* v. *Bord na Mona* [1983] I.R. 255.
[10] *R.* v. *Preston Supplementary Benefits Appeal Tribunal, ex p. Shine* [1975] 1 W.L.R. 624; *R.* v. *National Insurance Commissioner, ex p. Stratton* [1979] Q.B. 361. There are traces of this attitude in *Irish Permanent Building Society* v. *Caldwell* [1981] I.L.R.M. 242; *The State (Casey)* v. *Labour Court* (1984) 3 J.I.S.L.L. 135 and in the judgment of Henchy J. in *The State (Abenglen Properties Ltd.)* v. *Dublin Corporation* [1984] I.R. 381.

legislation in question. The authority must also be properly appointed, properly constituted and, where relevant, properly qualified.[11]

Conditions precedent to jurisdiction

An administrative authority can only exercise its powers over subject-matter which falls within the description, as to facts and circumstances, specified in the authority's field of competence. In other words, some errors of fact made by an administrative authority can affect its jurisdiction, where that jurisdiction depends upon certain objective facts whose existence must be established before the authority has power to act.

In *The State (Ferris)* v. *Employment Appeals Tribunal*[12] the respondent body declined to rule on the merits of an unfair dismissal case. The Tribunal had erroneously concluded that wrongful dismissal proceedings arising out of the case were pending in the High Court, and that, as a result, it was precluded that section 15(3) of the Unfair Dismissals Act 1977 from ruling on the case. The Tribunal's decision was quashed by the Supreme Court, for, as Henchy J. pointed out, the initiation of "a claim [for wrongful dismissal] as an objective fact must be proved before the Tribunal can exercise the jurisdiction given to it by section 15(3)." As the Tribunal had made an order dismissing the case under that subsection when, in point of fact, such common law claim for damages had not been initiated, that order was invalid as being in excess of jurisdiction. But there does not appear to be any satisfactory method of determining which facts are to be regarded as "collateral" to jurisdiction, and this would appear to be a flexible doctrine which can be invoked to control, where necessary, an abuse or excess of power.[13]

Within the power conferred by the statute

The administrative action must fall within the power conferred—whether expressly or by implication—by the statute. In many of the reported cases on this topic, the real issue has been whether impugned administrative action is reasonably incidental

---

[11] *The State (Walshe)* v. *Murphy* [1981] I.R. 275 (conviction imposed by improperly qualified district justice quashed). As far as the *delegatus* principle is concerned, see pp. 227–233.

[12] (1985) 4 J.I.S.S.L. 100.

[13] See further at pp. 189–190.

and thus falls within these implied powers.[14] In some cases—such as where the liberty or property of the citizen is at stake—clear statutory language is required. In a recent case, *Hussey v. Irish Land Commission*,[15] the Supreme Court ruled that the Land Commission had acted *ultra vires* when acquiring land which was not needed for immediate re-sale. The relevant legislation authorised the Commission to acquire lands for the purposes of re-sale, and it was argued that this empowered the Commission to create a stockpile of acquired lands, from which resales may take place from time to time. Rejecting this argument, Henchy J. noted that in compulsory purchase cases, the power will be held not to have been validly exercised "unless the exercise relied on has been strictly in accordance with the limitations laid down by statute."[16]

Discretionary powers

One of the corollaries of the presumption of constitutionality is that the courts assume (unless the contrary is clearly established) that the Oireachtas did not intend to confer a discretionary power on public authorities which would enable them to act in an unreasonable or arbitrary fashion.[17] Consequently discretionary powers must be exercised reasonably and bona fide; relevant considerations taken into account and irrelevant considerations ignored. These matters are considered elsewhere.[18]

Procedural controls

Where an administrative authority violates the principles of natural justice or constitutional justice, its decisions will generally be quashed as an application of an aggrieved party. The position in the case of disregard of other procedural and formal requirements is not as clear-cut. In some cases procedural requirements have been found to be directory only, breach of

---

[14] See *e.g. Irish Benefit Building Society* v. *Registrar of Friendly Societies* [1981] I.L.R.M. 73 (registrar given statutory power to ensure the "orderly and proper regulations of building society business"; held this power relates only to matters of honesty, legality, administration and propriety and does not cover matters of business judgment such as the interest rate paid to shareholders); *McMeel* v. *Minister for Health* [1985] I.L.R.M. 616 (ministerial power to give directions concerning "arrangements for providing services" in hospitals contemplates positive action, and not the discontinuance of hospital services).

[15] Supreme Court, December 13, 1984.

[16] See also *Meaney* v. *Cashel U.D.C.* [1937] I.R. 56; *Hendron* v. *Dublin Corporation* [1943] I.R. 566.

[17] *East Donegal Co-Operatives Ltd.* v. *Att.-Gen.* [1970] I.R. 317; *Loftus* v. *Att.-Gen.* [1979] I.R. 221.

[18] See pp. 297–322.

which will not lead to the nullification of the administrative decision under challenge. These matters are considered elsewhere.[19]

Unconstitutionality

Any administrative authority which acts in an unconstitutional fashion will thereby exceed jurisdiction.[20]

2. Jurisdictional review

Not every error committed by an administrative authority[21] will affect the jurisdiction of that body so as to invalidate the resulting decision. But the question of jurisdictional error is an intractable one, and is intrinsically linked to questions of statutory interpretation and judicial policy. At the end of the day, the matter is not one of abstract logic, but judicial pragmatism, for the court will decide what degree of supervision they wish to exercise over decision of administrative authorities.

Something must be said at this stage about the various theories of jurisdiction.

The original jurisdiction doctrine

This theory held sway from the first half of the nineteenth century until very recently.[22] The crucial feature of this theory is that jurisdiction is determined at the "commencement, and not at the conclusion of, the inquiry."[23] If an administrative authority has "subject-matter" or "original" jurisdiction, it does not lose such jurisdiction even if there is no evidence to support its findings of fact.[24]

There are numerous Irish cases which attest to the vitality of this

[19] See pp. 207–212.
[20] See the comments of Henchy J. in *The State (Holland)* v. *Kennedy* [1977] I.R. 193, 201 and *The State (Byrne)* v. *Frawley* [1978] I.R. 326, 345. This appears to be such a self-evident proposition that there do not appear to be any cases where any argument to the contrary has been advanced.
[21] "Administrative body" in this context not only includes decisions of individuals vested with public powers (such as Ministers) but also covers decisions of the "inferior" or lower courts.
[22] For an historical account of these developments, see Rubinstein, *Jurisdiction and Illegality* (Oxford, 1965), Chap. 4; Jaffe and Henderson, "Judicial Review and the Rule of Law: Historical Origins" (1956) 72 L.Q.R. 345 and Jaffe, "Constitutional and Jurisdictional Fact" (1957) 70 Harv.L.Rev. 953 and de Smith's *Judicial Review of Administrative Action* (4th ed.) at pp. 108–119.
[23] *R.* v. *Bolton* (1841) 1 Q.B. 66, 74 *per* Lord Denman C.J.
[24] *R. (Martin)* v. *Mahoney* [1910] 2 I.R. 695.

theory. In *The State (Batchelor & Co.)* v. *O'Floinn*[25] the applicants sought to quash a search warrant issued under section 12 of the Merchandise Marks Act 1887. It was said that there was insufficient evidence before the respondent District Justice to justify his order. But O'Daly J. for the Supreme Court disposed of this argument by stating that it was well settled that providing the error did not appear on the face of the record, questions as to the sufficiency of error amounted to errors within jurisdiction. The District Justice clearly had jurisdiction to make an order under the Act, and he did not lose jurisdiction by making an error of this nature. In the view of O'Daly J. questions as to the sufficiency of evidence were the very matters committed to the jurisdiction of the District Justice. The result of these decisions were that the scope of review was rather narrow, and this could often lead to injustice, particularly in criminal cases.[26]

One method of escaping the confines of this doctrine was to classify certain findings of fact as "collateral" or as "conditions precedent to jurisdiction."[27] Administrative authorities do not possess an inherent jurisdiction; their jurisdiction depends upon facts which must have an objective existence before the authority has power to act. Hence, any decision of the authority as to the boundaries of its jurisdiction could not be conclusive, as otherwise it would usurp power never conferred on it by the Oireachtas. If, for example, the Circuit Court has jurisdiction to hear ejectment cases where the rateable valuation of the premises does not exceed £60, that court cannot acquire jurisdiction by reason of an erroneous conclusion as to the rateable valuation of the premises.[28] In other words, an administrative authority cannot give itself a jurisdiction which it cannot have, and the High Court will enforce the *ultra vires* doctrine by insisting on the objective existence of certain facts upon which some jurisdiction depends.

---

[25] [1958] I.R. 155. See also *R. (Limerick Corporation)* v. *Local Government Board* [1922] 2 I.R. 76.

[26] See *e.g. The State (Lee-Kiddier)* v. *Dunleavy*, High Court, August 17, 1976 where McWilliam J. held that the question of whether there was sufficient evidence to support a conviction was not reviewable in certiorari proceedings, absent error on the face of the record. Contrast this with the observations of Kenny J. in *The State (Holland)* v. *Kennedy* [1977] I.R. 193 where he doubted whether the rule in *Mahoney* was compatible with Art. 38.1 of the Constitution which prescribes trial "in due course of law."

[27] Thus, in *The State (O'Neill)* v. *Shannon* [1931] I.R. 691 it was held that the principle of *Martin's* case only applied to decisions arrived at on the merits and was not relevant in the case of preliminary objections to jurisdiction.

[28] *The State (Att.-Gen.)* v. *Durcan* [1964] I.R. 279.

The difficulty with this, of course, is that there does not appear to be any clear-cut method of determining which facts are "jurisdictional," and which are not.[29] In *The State (Davidson)* v. *Farrell*[30] Kingsmill Moore J. sought to answer this question by referring to the jurisdiction conferred—whether expressly or by necessary intendment—by statute or the authority concerned. In this case the applicant, a tenant in a controlled dwelling, sought to quash decisions of the district and circuit courts awarding her landlord certain sums as allowances in respect of the repair of the premises. She claimed that these decisions were flawed by jurisdictional error as a result of the misconstruction of the phrase "premises," as defined by the Rent Restrictions Act 1946. A majority of the Supreme Court concluded, following an examination of the 1946 Act, that the Oireachtas had intended to vest the District Court with jurisdiction to determine the basic rent and allowances. It was not a pre-condition to jurisdiction that the word "premises" be correctly construed, and as Kingsmill Moore J. explained:

> "The [District] Court may make an error in law in interpreting the word 'premises,' or an error in fact in determining that money has been expended when it has not, but these are errors within the jurisdiction conferred."[31]

But difficulties nevertheless remain. The concept of "collateral fact" is a malleable one—virtually any fact may be classified as "collateral" to jurisdiction. Moreover, this jurisdiction is not solely one of statutory interpretation. The essential legal policy behind the *ultra vires* doctrine is that it is vital that administrative authorities respect the principle of legality and have due regard to constitutional precepts of fairness. For these reasons the courts have recently tended to turn away from this theory of jurisdiction in order to increase the scope of review.

The modern doctrine of jurisdictional error
The modern trend is to treat all errors of law committed by lower courts or administrative tribunals as jurisdictional in character. There have also been suggestions that the courts may

---

[29] See *e.g.* the divison of judicial opinion in the "orchard" cases: *R. (De Vesci)* v. *Queen's Co. JJ.* [1908] 2 I.R. 365; *R. (D'Arcy)* v. *Carlow JJ.* [1916] 2 I.R. 313 and *R. (Greenaway)* v. *Armagh JJ.* [1924] 2 I.R. 55.

[30] [1960] I.R. 438. See also *The State (Att.-Gen.)* v. *Durcan* [1964] I.R. 279 for a useful judicial discussion of this question.

[31] [1960] I.R. 438 at p. 455.

intervene to quash findings based on inadequate evidence.[32] But
the law in this area is far from settled. Contradictory opinions have
been expressed by eminent judges and the Supreme Court has yet
to give an authoritative exposition on the subject of jurisdictional
error. Earlier authorities such as *Farrell's* case have never been
formally overruled, and are still on occasion relied on as good
law.[33]

The leading Irish authority is *The State (Holland)* v. *Kennedy*.[34]
The Children's Act 1908 forbids the imposition of a prison
sentence on a young person between the ages of 15 and 17 unless
it is shown that he is of such an "unruly character" that he cannot
be detained in an approved place of detention. The prosecutor
had been convicted of a particularly serious assault. He was
certified as of unruly character by the respondent District Justice,
and she sentenced him to a period of imprisonment.

The Supreme Court held that the bare facts of this assault,
unrelated to any previous evidence of a behavioural pattern, could
not justify a conclusion that this young person would not be
amenable to detention in a suitable institute. Turning to the
question of whether an error of this nature was reviewable on
certiorari, Henchy J. observed:

> "Having considered the authorities, I am satisfied that this
> error was not within jurisdiction. [I]t does not necessarily
> follow that a court or tribunal . . . which commences a hearing
> within jurisdiction will be treated as continuing to act within
> jurisdiction. For any number of reasons it may exceed
> jurisdiction and thereby make its decisions liable to be
> quashed on certiorari. For instance, it may fall into an
> unconstitutionality, or it may breach the requirements of
> natural justice, or it may fail to stay within the bounds of the
> jurisdiction conferred on it by statute. It is an error of the
> latter kind that prevents the impugned order in this case from

---

[32] *Kiely* v. *Minister for Social Welfare* [1971] I.R. 21. *The State (Holland)* v.
Kennedy [1977] I.R. 193; *The State (Cork C.C.)* v. *Fawsitt (No. 2)*,
Supreme Court, July 28, 1983; *The State (Casey)* v. *Labour Court* (1984) 3
J.I.S.S.L. 135; *M.* v. *M.*, Supreme Court, October 8, 1979; *The State
(Burke)* v. *Garvey*, Supreme Court, November 11, 1979 and *The State
(McKeown)* v. *Scully* [1986] I.L.R.M. 133. But there are also modern
authorities which point in the opposite direction: *The State (Power)* v.
Moran, High Court, February 2, 1976 (decision based on evidence of
little probative value not reviewable by certiorari); *The State (Shinkaruk)*
v. *Carroll*, High Court, December 15, 1976 (wrongful exclusion of
evidence not reviewable by certiorari).

[33] *The State (Lee-Kiddier)* v. *Dunleavy*, High Court, August 17, 1976; *The
State (Cole)* v. *Labour Court* (1984) 3 J.I.S.S.L. 128.

[34] [1977] I.R. 193.

being held to have been made within jurisdiction. It was necessarily the statutory intention that a legally supportable certificate to that effect is to be a condition precedent to the exercise of jurisdiction to impose a sentence of imprisonment. Otherwise the sentencing limitation could be nullified by disregarding what the law regards as essential for the making of the certificate. In the present case, the certificate, having been made without evidence, was as devoid of legal validity as if it had been made in disregard of uncontroverted evidence showing that the young person was not what he had been certified to be."[35]

An order of certiorari quashing the conviction and sentence was granted.

The precise significance of *Holland* is difficult to assess. The above passage from the judgment of Henchy J. suggests that errors of law committed by a lower court or tribunal in the course of a hearing will be deemed—almost as of course—to go to jurisdiction. Yet other passages in the judgments of Henchy and Kenny JJ. give the impression that the existence of a legally supportable certificate was a collateral fact—a condition precedent to jurisdiction which the District Justice had failed to satisfy. If the latter interpretation is correct, *Holland* represents no more than an application of principles approved in earlier decisions such as *The State (Davidson)* v. *Farrell*, and the case can hardly be said to have broken new ground.

The judgments in the two *Fawsitt* cases point towards wider scope for review. Both cases concerned an application by the local authority to enter upon certain lands in order to ascertain whether the lands were suitable for the setting up of a waste disposal site. The Circuit Court judge initially refused the application because he was not satisfied that the lands were not manifestly unsuitable. The relevant statutory provisions[36] only authorised the judge to refuse the request if he were satisfied that the lands were manifestly unsuitable. In *The State (Cork C.C.)* v. *Fawsitt*,[37] McMahon J. held that the Circuit Court judge had made an error of law in so holding, and that he thereby had stepped outside his jurisdiction. McMahon J. referred approvingly to the epoch-making decision of the House of Lords in *Anisminic Ltd.* v. *Foreign Compensation Commission*[38] ("an extreme example of an error of

---

[35] [1977] I.R. 193 at p. 201.
[36] Public Health (Ireland) Act 1878, s.271.
[37] High Court, March 13, 1981. For a recent example of where "asking the wrong question" was held to be a jurisdictional defect, see *The State (McMahon)* v. *Minister for Education*, High Court, December 21, 1985.
[38] [1969] 2 A.C. 147.

law . . . being held to be jurisdictional")[39] and *The State (Holland)* v. *Kennedy* (which McMahon J. cited as an example of a case where an order of the District Court made without evidence was quashed). The tenor of McMahon J.'s judgment suggests that *every* error of law is to be deemed to affect jurisdiction.

The case was remitted to the Circuit Court judge following the quashing of the first order. On this occasion the Circuit Court found as a fact that the lands were "manifestly unsuitable" within the meaning of the statutory provisions, and the application to enter upon the lands was refused. Once again, the local authority sought to impeach this order in *certiorari* proceedings. On this occasion the case reached the Supreme Court.[40]

The Supreme Court upheld the validity of the impugned order. Henchy J. noted that in the first case, the Circuit Court judge had stepped outside his jurisdiction because he had "answered the wrong question"—a question which the statutory provisions gave him no jurisdiction to answer. If he had decided that it was not necessary for the county council to enter upon the lands to carry out the preliminary tests

"[h]is orders would have been unassailable, because there was evidence to support such a finding so it could not be said that he acted without or in excess of jurisdiction."

In the present case, he had found as a fact that the lands were manifestly unsuitable for the purposes of a waste disposal site. The judge acted *intra vires*: he approached the evidence from a different standpoint, and he reached the same conclusion for a valid reason.

The first *Fawsitt* judgment (which now, of course, has the approval of the Supreme Court) is an example of an error of law which, up to relatively recently, would almost certainly have been treated as an error within jurisdiction.[41] Yet such errors are now condemned as *ultra vires*. In the light of the *Fawsitt* litigation, one may reasonably ask whether the time-honoured distinction between errors which go to jurisdiction and those which do not has been effectively abolished. Certainly, the Supreme Court has failed to establish criteria whereby the distinction (if any) between the two types of error may be established. With such judicial guidance absent, it is fair to assume that all major errors of law will be regarded as affecting jurisdiction. In addition, the *obiter* remarks of Henchy J. in *Fawsitt (No. 2)* imply that insufficiency of evidence to support a finding is itself an error of law going to

[39] Wade, *Administrative Law* (Oxford, 1982) at p. 264.
[40] *The State (Cork C.C.)* v. *Fawsitt (No. 2)*, July 26, 1983.
[41] See *e.g. The State (Davidson)* v. *Farrell* [1960] I.R. 439.

jurisdiction, thus rendering the impugned order liable to be quashed.[42]

Yet the recent pronouncements by the Supreme Court on this question have not always been in favour of widening the scope of judicial review. The judgment of Henchy J. in *The State (Abenglen Properties Ltd.)* v. *Dublin Corporation*[43] demonstrates that the distinction between errors of law going to jurisdiction and those which do not retains a surprising vibrancy in our law. In *Abenglen Properties*, the Supreme Court had been invited to quash an allegedly *ultra vires* planning permission. It was said that the respondents had acted *ultra vires* in attaching restrictive conditions to the grant of permission, and that the entire permission rested on an erroneous identification of the relevant development plan. To this submission Henchy J. replied by stating:

> "The alleged errors arose in the course of identifying and construing the Dublin City Development Plan. There is no doubt but that on a true reading of the relevant Acts and Regulations, the Corporation . . . had jurisdiction to identify and construe the relevant Dublin City Development Plan in its relation to Abenglen's application. If, therefore, they erred in either respect, they erred within jurisdiction, and any error they may have made does not appear on the face of the record."[44]

In these circumstances certiorari would only lie if the respondents had disregarded the principles of natural justice, and the alleged error of law was one within jurisdiction.

Henchy J.'s reasoning is similar to that employed by the former Supreme Court in *The State (Davidson)* v. *Farrell*: if a court or tribunal has "subject-matter" jurisdiction then it does not lose that jurisdiction by erring in the course of its adjudication, unless that error relates to a collateral fact, or where the rules of natural justice have been breached. It is difficult to reconcile this aspect of *Abenglen Properties* with other recent decisions such as *Holland*, *Fawsitt (No. 1)* and *Fawsitt (No. 2)*.

Barrington J. employed a more sophisticated approach to this question in *Irish Permanent Building Society* v. *Caldwell*.[45] In this

---

[42] Contrast this with the observations of O'Daly J. in *The State (Batchelor & Co.)* v. *O'Floinn* [1958] I.R. 155 and those of Lord Sumner in *R.* v. *Nat Bell Liquors Ltd.* [1922] 2 A.C. 125 at p. 151.

[43] [1984] I.R. 381. Hederman J. joined in the judgment of Henchy J. The other three members of the Court reserved their position on this question.

[44] [1984] I.R. 381 at pp. 399–400.

[45] [1981] I.L.R.M. 242. See also the judgment of Finlay P. in *Re Riordan* [1981] I.L.R.M. 2 for a similar approach.

case the Registrar of Building Societies had misconstrued the relevant sections of the Building Societies Act 1976 when he came to register the Irish Life Building Society, and Barrington J. was satisfied that the Registrar had "asked himself the wrong question," and had erred in law in registering the Society's rules under the 1976 Act. But the judge did not think that the case turned on that point:

> "The real issue in the present case is whether, because of the Registrar's mistake of law, the incorporation of the building society is a nullity. It seems to me that the answer to this question is not to be found in abstract questions of law, but in ascertaining the intentions of the legislature in this particular statute.[46]

Barrington J. pointed out that the scheme of the Act was such that had the Registrar failed to reach a decision within the prescribed time, the Society would have been entitled to have been incorporated under the Acts, the defect in its rules notwithstanding. Furthermore, it was no longer required that the Registrar should be a person with legal qualification. He concluded that it would have been surprising

> "[I]f the incorporation of a society could be invalidated by an honest mistake such as was made by . . . the Registrar in the present case. If the law were otherwise people might in good faith deal with a society for many years only to find that because of some defect in the rules the society did not exist as a corporate body. . . . To hold that the society was not validly incorporated would clearly cause great damage to many innocent people, and I cannot accept that the Oireachtas intended that such a catastrophic result should ensue."[47]

It is instructive to compare *Caldwell* with *The State (Costello)* v. *Bofin*,[48] where a coroner's decision to adjourn an inquest *sine die* was quashed. The Supreme Court ruled that the Coroner's Act 1962 simply permitted the coroner to adjourn for a definite period of time, and that as a result of this mere error of statutory construction, the coroner thereby exceeded his jurisdiction. The Court appeared to assume that a mere error of construction automatically destroyed the coroner's jurisdiction. But was this not a case of an administrative authority making an 'honest mistake,' just as was the case with *Abenglen Properties* and *Caldwell*? All three cases involved errors of statutory construction, but why

[46] [1981] I.L.R.M. 248 at p. 268.
[47] *Ibid.* at pp. 269–270.
[48] [1980] I.L.R.M. 223.

should such an error be deemed to be jurisdictional in one of those cases, but not in the others[49]? No satisfactory interpretation to these questions can be given pending an authoritative review of the recent cases by the Supreme Court.

Some indications of possible future developments in this area of the law are provided by *Tormey* v. *Attorney-General*.[50] In this case, speaking of a situation in which *exclusive* jurisdiction has been committed to a lower court or administrative authority exercising judicial powers under cover of Article 37, Henchy J. observed that the High Court's full jurisdiction under Article 34.3.1 might be invoked so as to ensure that "the hearing and determination will be in accordance *with law*" (italics supplied). In its context— a contrast with the wider powers exercisably by the High Court where there has *not* been a devolution of *exclusive jurisdiction*—this remark can be taken to mean that the High Court's power of review must be broad enough to allow it to quash at least for major errors of law committed by a lower court or administrative authority exercising exclusive jurisdiction. It may also be that the High Court may review decisions of lower courts or administrative authorities which have been based on insufficient evidence. Similar results might well be achieved through an extension of the constitutional principles of fair procedures and the right of access to the courts.[51] In any event, our courts will probably find the trend towards increasing the scope of jurisdictional review to be well nigh irresistable.

3. Error on the face of the record

The jurisdiction to review for error on the face of the record is an anomalous one since the power to review is not based on

[49] English law has now developed to the point where the courts presume that Parliament did not intend to confer administrative authorities with power to determine the limits of their own jurisdiction. As a result, any error of law committed by such a body is deemed to have been outside their jurisdiction. But no similar presumption applies in respect of lower courts, and every error of law committed by a lower court does not of itself destroy that court's jurisdiction: *Re Racal Communications Ltd.* [1981] A.C. 374; *O'Reilly* v. *Mackman* [1983] 2 A.C. 237. It is not easy to see how such a principle of statutory interpretation could be properly adapted for use in this jurisdiction in view of the provisions of Art. 37 (which allows the Oireachtas to confer limited judicial functions of a civil nature on administrative bodies) and the reasoning of the Supreme Court in *Tormey* v. *Att.-Gen.* [1985] I.R. 289.

[50] [1985] I.R. at pp. 296–297.

[51] For example, it could be argued that the constitutional guarantee of fair procedure requires that a decision be based on adequate, probative evidence, and Henchy J. has already argued along these lines in *M.* v. *M.*, Supreme Court, October 8, 1979. See pp. 191, 239.

jurisdiction or *ultra vires*.[52] This power of review enables the High Court to quash a decision, otherwise within jurisdiction, if that decision contains an error of law,[53] provided that error appears on the face of the record.

What is the record? Denning L.J. has provided us with a comprehensive answer:

> "[T]he record must contain at least the document which initiates the proceedings; the pleadings, if any; and the adjudication; but not the evidence, nor the reasons, unless the tribunal chooses to incorporate them. If the tribunal does state the reasons, and the reasons are wrong in law, certiorari lies to quash the decision.[54]

To this it may be objected that a court or tribunal could avoid review by the High Court by the simple expedient of refusing to make a judgment part of the final order or refusing to give any reason for a decision at all. But it is clear that English law, at any rate, has now progressed to the point whereby the reasons given orally for a decision are now regarded as forming part of the record, *i.e.* what is sometimes known as a "speaking order." It has been recently suggested that the High Court may have the power

---

[52] This anomaly has sometimes led judges to hold that error on the face of the record must be a form of jurisdictional error: see the comments of Palles C.B. in *R. (Martin)* v. *Mahoney* [1910] 2 I.R. 695 at p. 721. By the turn of the century the jurisdiction to quash for error of law on the face of the record had fallen into decline, and in England, the very existence of this jurisdiction was denied by the Court of Appeal in *Racecourse Betting Control Board* v. *Secretary of State for Air* [1944] Ch. 114. This jurisdiction was revived following the decision of the Court of Appeal in *R.* v. *Northumberland Compensation Appeal Tribunal, ex p. Shaw* [1952] 1 K.B. 338.

[53] But this jurisdiction does not extend to errors of fact: see *per* Carroll J. in *The State (C.I.E.)* v. *An Bord Pleanala*, High Court, February 12, 1984.

[54] *R.* v. *Northumberland Appeal Compensation Tribunal, ex p. Shaw* [1952] 1 K.B. 338 at p. 352. The record is not uniform in all cases, and the courts are prepared to regard other documents as part of the record if this is necessary to do justice. Thus, in criminal cases, the record includes the warrant, the formal records and the transcript of the trial: *Re Tynan*, Supreme Court, December 20, 1963. See also *R.* v. *Medical Appeal Tribunal, ex p. Gilmore* [1957] 1 Q.B. 574 (medical report referred to in tribunal's judgment regarded as part of the record) and *Re Stevenson's Application*, N.I. High Court, December 21, 1984 (respondent's affidavit part of the record). In some cases the record may be defined by statute: see *e.g.* Courts Act 1971, s.14 (record of District Court proceedings in cases of summary jurisdiction confined to formal court order signed by District Justice).

to compel a lower court to give reasons for its decision.[55] Thus, English courts will now quash for error of law, otherwise within jurisdiction, regardless of whether it is the former written record, or just a speaking order, which discloses the error.

The scope of certiorari for error on the face of the record does not appear to be quite as broad in Ireland. Yet again, the authorities are not easily reconcilable. In *Walsh* v. *Minister for Local Government*,[56] the former Supreme Court agreed that if the Minister had set out his reasons in arriving at a decision, these reasons would form part of the record, thus rendering the impugned decision liable to be quashed if the Minister had erred in law. In this case the prosecutor sought to quash a surcharge imposed by the local government auditor. The auditor's certificate was said to contain an error of law. The prosecutor exercised his statutory right of appeal to the respondent Minister, who issued a sealed order upholding the auditor's decision. The ministerial order mentioned—but it did not set out—the reasons given by the auditor. Murnaghan J. observed:

> "We do not see how this [ministerial] order can in any sense be said to be a speaking order, stating the views of the Minister upon some point of law, so as to make an erroneous view of the law apparent on the record."[57]

The court went on to hold that the Minister's order had not incorporated the reasons of the auditor so as to make these reasons the view of the law taken by the Minister.

In *The State (Attorney-General)* v. *Binchy*,[58] the former Supreme Court implied that the record in a criminal trial on indictment was confined to the formal record of the trial (*i.e.* only the official court documents, the verdict and record of conviction, if any). Yet, some three years later, the Supreme Court held in *Re Tynan*[59] that the record in such a case included the court orders and the

---

[55] *R.* v. *Medical Appeal Tribunal, ex p. Gilmore* [1957] 1 Q.B. 574 ("The Court has always had power to order an inferior tribunal to complete the record," *per* Denning L.J.); *R.* v. *Knightsbridge Crown Court, ex p. International Sporting Club Ltd.* [1982] Q.B. 304. On the question of "speaking" orders forming part of the record, see the *Knightsbridge* case; *Tangney* v. *Kerry D.J.* [1928] I.R. 358 and *R.* v. *Leeds Crown Court, ex p. Bradford Chief Constable* [1975] Q.B. 314. But *cf.* Courts Act 1971, s.14 which confines the record in District Court summary proceedings to formal court orders.

[56] [1929] I.R. 377.

[57] [1929] I.R. 377 at p. 404.

[58] [1964] I.R. 395.

[59] Supreme Court, December 20, 1963.

transcript (thus, rendering a conviction or (*quaere*) an acquittal[60] liable to be quashed if, for example, the judge erred in law in his summing-up). More recently, in *The State (Abenglen Properties Ltd.)* v. *Dublin Corporation*,[61] Henchy J. adopted a more restrictive attitude to this question. The judge implied that the record in planning cases is confined to the formal decision of the local authority or An Bord Pleanala, *i.e.* whether or not to grant planning permission.[62] An authoritative decision of our courts delineating the scope of review for error on the face of the record is clearly required.

It should be noted that traditionally certiorari was the only remedy which could correct an error of law on the face of the record.[63] The combined effect of Ord. 84, rr. 18 and 19 of the new Rules of the Superior Courts is to remove this procedural anomaly.[64] Ord. 84, r. 18 provides that all applications for certiorari, mandamus, prohibition or *quo warranto* shall be by way of an application for judicial review, and that this procedure may be invoked upon an application for a declaration or an injunction. Ord. 84, r. 19 states that on an application for judicial review any relief mentioned in rule 18 may be claimed "as an alternative or in addition to any other relief so mentioned" and, in any event, the court may grant any relief mentioned in rule 18 "which it considers appropriate notwithstanding that it has not been specifically claimed." In other words, the High Court would be empowered upon an application by way of judicial review for a declaration invalidating an administrative decision to grant an order of certiorari quashing that decision on the grounds that it exhibited an error of law on the face of the record. But given the

---

[60] See the comments of Walsh J. in *People* v. *O'Shea* [1982] I.R. 384 casting doubt on *The State (Att.-Gen.)* v. *Binchy* [1964] I.R. 395.

[61] [1984] I.R. 381.

[62] The judge appears to have overlooked the provisions of s.26(8) of the Local Government (Planning and Development) Act 1963 which provides that the conditions attached to the grant of a planning permission, together with the reasons given for the imposition of such conditions, form part of the record. See further Hogan, "Remoulding Certiorari" (1982) 17 Ir.Jur.(n.s.) 32 at pp. 37–39.

[63] *Punton* v. *Ministry for Pensions (No. 2)* [1964] 1 W.L.R. 226. But *cf. King* v. *Att.-Gen.* [1981] I.R. 233, where a declaration was granted invalidating a conviction for error on the face of the record. The conviction had failed to show jurisdiction on its face, and this is a well recognised ground for quashing for error of law on the face of the record: *The State (Carr)* v. *Youghal D.J.* [1945] I.R. 43; *The State (Leahy)* v. *Cork D.J.* [1945] I.R. 426 and *The State (Browne)* v. *Feran* [1967] I.R. 147.

[64] See further at pp. 347–348.

expansion in the scope of jurisdictional error the entire issue may be rather academic.

4. Ouster and preclusive clauses

Even at common law the courts have never looked favourably on legislative attempts to curb the High Court's supervisory jurisdiction over decisions of lower courts and administrative bodies.[65] Even in the case of widely-drafted ouster clauses both the High Court[66] and the Supreme Court[67] have affirmed on many occasions that such clauses will not protect a decision which is *ultra vires*. But it seems that an ouster clause does prevent the High Court from granting certiorari where the alleged defect is a non-jurisdictional error of law only.[68]

Furthermore, the constitutionality of legislative attempts to oust the High Court's power of review must be doubtful in light of the decision of the Supreme Court in *Tormey* v. *Attorney-General*.[69] In that case Henchy J. observed that Article 34.3.1[70] when read in

---

[65] "[T]he courts should be reluctant to surrender their inherent right to enter on a question of what are prima facie justiciable matters" *per* Henchy J. in *The State (Pine Valley Developments Ltd.)* v. *Dublin C.C.* [1984] I.R. 417 at p. 426. And see the strict manner in which the Supreme Court has construed such clauses in cases such as *Pine Valley* and *The State (Finglas Industrial Estates Ltd.)* v. *Dublin C.C.*, February 17, 1983.

[66] *The State (O'Duffy)* v. *Bennett* [1935] I.R. 70; *The State (Hughes)* v. *Lennon* [1935] I.R. 128; *Murren* v. *Brennan* [1942] I.R. 466 and *The State (Horgan)* v. *Exported Livestock Board Ltd.* [1943] I.R. 581. See also *R. (Conyngham)* v. *Pharmaceutical Society of Ireland* [1899] 2 I.R. 132; *Commissioners of Public Works* v. *Monaghan* [1909] 2 I.R. 718; *R. (Sinnott)* v. *Wexford Corporation* [1910] 2 I.R. 403 and *Waterford Corporation* v. *Murphy* [1920] 2 I.R. 165.

[67] *The State (McCarthy)* v. *O'Donnell* [1945] I.R. 126; *Brannigan* v. *Keady* [1959] I.R. 283 (*semble*). This was also the attitude of the House of Lords: see *Ansminic Ltd.* v. *Foreign Compensation Commission* [1969] 2 A.C. 147. But a different attitude prevails in the case of clauses imposing brief limitation periods: *R.* v. *Environment Secretary, ex p. Ostler* [1977] Q.B. 122.

[68] *R.* v. *Medical Appeal Tribunal, ex p. Gilmore* [1957] 1 Q.B. 574. But in *Gilmore* it was decided that the court may still intervene to quash for error of law on the face of the record where the tribunal's decision is expressed to be "final."

[69] [1985] I.R. 289.

[70] Art. 34.3.1 vests the High Court with "full original jurisdiction" in respect of all matters and questions "whether of fact or law, civil or criminal." Art. 34.3.4 permits the Oireachtas to establish by law courts of "local and limited jurisdiction" and Art. 37 enables tribunals to exercise judicial functions of a limited nature in non-criminal matters.

conjunction with Article 34.3.4 and Article 37 permitted the Oireachtas to vest lower courts or administrative tribunals with exclusive jurisdiction in respect of certain justiciable controversies, but where this had been done:

> "[The] full jurisdiction [of the High Court] is there to be invoked—in proceedings such as habeas corpus, certiorari, prohibition, quo warranto, injunction or declaratory action—so as to ensure that the hearing and determination will be in accordance with law. Save to the extent required by the terms of the Constitution itself, no justiciable matter may be excluded from the range of the original jurisdiction of the High Court."[71]

This is a clear indication that legislative ouster clauses are unconstitutional, at least where the lower court or tribunal has been vested with exclusive jurisdiction to determine particular justiciable controversies.[72]

Legislative provisions which, instead of attempting to effect a complete ouster of the High Court's supervisory jurisdiction, purport to impose brief limitation periods on the right to seek judicial review probably stand on a different footing. While the constitutionality of such clauses has been doubted,[73] it seems probable that the right to challenge the validity of an administrative decision is protected by Article 40.3. Such rights are not absolute, however, and it has been surmised that given the overwhelming need for a swift determination and finality in the case of many administrative decisions—especially in matters relating to land and housing development—the courts may be reluctant to upset the balance struck by the legislators.[74] While there is authority to the contrary[75] grave constitutional difficulties will certainly arise if such clauses are construed as barring *all* challenges to the validity of the impugned administrative decisions, even in cases where bad faith or breach of constitutional justice has been established or where the applicant did not know, and could not reasonably have been expected to know, of the

---

[71] [1985] I.R. at pp. 296–297.
[72] See also *Re Loftus Bryan's Estate* [1942] I.R. 185 and *O'Doherty* v. *Att.-Gen.* [1941] I.R. 569.
[73] Casey, "The Constitution and the Legal System" (1979) Ir.Jur.(n.s.) 14 at pp. 20–21.
[74] See Hogan, (1982) Ir.Jur.(n.s.) 397 at pp. 399–401.
[75] *The State (Finglas Industrial Estates Ltd.)* v. *Dublin C.C.*, High Court, July 10, 1981.

salient facts giving rise to the cause of action until after the
relevant limitation period had expired.[76]

5. Consequences of invalidity

As a general rule *ultra vires* decisions are null and void and have
no legal consequences. But this principle is subject to considerable
qualifications, for invalidity can only be established in legal
proceedings.[77] If the court sets aside the impugned decision this
will have retrospective effect, but until this is done it will enjoy a
presumption of validity and the decision will be regarded as
binding.[78] Even where invalidity has been established in the
appropriate proceedings, the court may refuse to grant relief on
discretionary grounds.[79] Moreover there may be statutory provisions which govern the consequences of invalidation,[80] or which
prescribe a limitation period which serves to preclude judicial
review once that time limit has expired.[81] In short invalidity is a
relative concept and the courts have refrained from pushing that
concept to extremes. Perhaps it is because the Irish courts have
taken such a pragmatic approach that the void/voidable controversy which has plagued English administrative law has not given
rise to the same difficulties in this jurisdiction.[82] *Irish Permanent*

[76] Keane, *The Law of Local Government in the Republic of Ireland* (Dublin, 1982) at pp. 242–244.

[77] *Smith* v. *East Elloe R.D.C.* [1956] A.C. 736; *The State (Abenglen Properties Ltd.)* v. *Dublin Corporation* [1984] I.R. 381.

[78] *Hoffman-La Roche & Co.* v. *Secretary for Trade and Industry* [1975] A.C. 295; *Abenglen Properties, supra*; *Campus Oil* v. *Minister for Industry and Energy (No. 2)* [1983] I.R. 88 at p. 107 (O'Higgins C.J.), and, in the special context of constitutional law, *The State (Llewellyn)* v. *UaDonnachada* [1973] I.R. 151; *Pesca Valentia Ltd.* v. *Ireland* [1985] I.R. 193.

[79] See *e.g. The State (Cussen)* v. *Brennan* [1981] I.R. 181; *Murphy* v. *Att.-Gen.* [1982] I.R. 341.

[80] See *e.g.* Electoral Act 1923, s.9 (no election to be declared invalid where non-compliance with rules concerning secrecy and integrity of the ballot did not affect the result); Adoption Act 1976, s.6 (no child to be removed from custody of its adoptive parents solely on the grounds that adoption order was invalid).

[81] Housing Act 1966, s.78(2) (three-week time limit in respect of challenges to validity of a compulsory purchase order); Local Government (Planning and Development) Act 1963, s.42(3A) (two-month time limit in respect of challenges to the validity of a planning permission).

[82] See *e.g. D.P.P.* v. *Head* [1959] A.C. 83; *R.* v. *Paddington Valuation Officer, ex p. Peachey Property Corporation Ltd.* [1966] 1 Q.B. 380; *Hoffman-La Roche & Co.* v. *Secretary of State for Trade and Industry* [1975] A.C. 295; *R.* v. *Environment Secretary, ex p. Ostler* [1977] Q.B. 122. But the English courts no longer view nullity as an absolute concept: *Calvin* v. *Carr*

Building Society v. *Caldwell*[83] provides an interesting example of
this pragmatic judicial attitude. Here Barrington J. refused to
accept that the incorporation of a building society could be
nullified as the result would be "catastrophic," and the judge
could not believe that the Oireachtas intended that "an honest
mistake" could have such consequences. The one recent case
where there was an extended discussion of the nature of invalidity,
Murphy v. *Attorney-General*,[84] arose in the special context of
constitutional law, but a majority of the Supreme Court had little
difficulty in holding that legislation (and, by implication, other
ultra vires administrative action) which was to be unconstitutional
was void *ab initio*. Henchy J. described this principle as one which
was "inherent in the nature of such limited powers."[85]

This, however, does not mean that one is free to ignore or
disregard administrative action which is *ultra vires*. Save, perhaps,
in the case of a flagrantly invalid decision, an administrative act
enjoys a presumption of validity and will have legal consequences
until it is set aside. This fact has been recognised either expressly
or by implication by recent Irish decisions. For example, in *The
State (Abenglen Properties Ltd.)* v. *Dublin Corporation*[86] Henchy J. said
of an allegedly invalid planning permission which was good on its
face that it remained a "decision" for the purposes of the planning
code until it was set aside in the appropriate proceedings. A similar
principle underlies the decision of the Supreme Court in *Pesca
Valentia Ltd.* v. *Ireland*[87] to grant an interlocutory injunction
suspending the operation of section 222(*b*) of the Fisheries
(Consolidation) Act 1959 until the trial of the action. The plaintiff
company had been granted fishing licences, but subject to onerous
conditions which it claimed were unconstitutional and *ultra vires*.
In view of the judicial duty to protect citizens against unconstitutional actions, Finlay C.J. said that it followed that the courts had

---

[1980] A.C. 574 and *London & Clydeside Estates Ltd.* v. *Aberdeen D.C.*
[1980] 1 W.L.R. 182. See generally, Cane, "A Fresh Look at Punton's
Case" (1980) 43 M.L.R. 264.
[83] [1981] I.L.R.M. 242. See also *Re Riordan* [1981] I.L.R.M. 2 for a
similar approach.
[84] [1982] I.R. 241. See also p. 386.
[85] *Ibid.* at pp. 309–310. But *cf.* the observations of Lord Denning in *R.* v.
Paddington Valuation Officer, ex p. Peachey Property Corporation Ltd.
[1966] 1 Q.B. 380 and those of Lord Diplock in *Dunlop* v. *Woolahra
M.C.* [1982] A.C. 158.
[86] [1984] I.R. 381. See also *Campus Oil Ltd.* v. *Minister for Industry and
Energy* [1983] I.R. 88.
[87] [1985] I.R. 193.

power, in an appropriate case, to grant an interlocutory injunction restraining the implementation of administrative action which derived its authority from statutory provisions "which might eventually be held to be invalid having regard to the provisions of the Constitution." From this it may be inferred that the court recognised that administrative action which is not patently illegal will be presumed to be valid. As a result, it will have legal consequences for the individual pending a decision as to its invalidity unless interlocutory relief is granted by the High Court pursuant to Ord. 84, r. 20(7) of the new Rules of Court.[88]

However, if an administrative act which is not flagrantly invalid enjoys a presumption of validity and has the force of law until quashed, how is it possible to assert, once that presumption has been displaced, and the decision quashed as *ultra vires*, that it was a legal nullity? Cane has provided a convincing answer to this apparent paradox by suggesting that *ultra vires* decisions, although void, are not nullities which never had any legal existence or force. In his view, when administrative decisions are invalidated by the courts, this invalidation has retrospective effect:

> "[o]n this view acts done in pursuance of *ultra vires* decisions would be treated as lawful until made unlawful by the quashing of the decision which supported them."[89]

Indeed, one of the most difficult problems facing the courts is that of the *de facto* consequences of *ultra vires* administrative action. Various solutions have been judicially suggested. In *The State (Cussen)* v. *Brennan*[90] a delay of four months was deemed to be sufficient to prevent an applicant from obtaining an order of certiorari quashing an *ultra vires* university appointment. The Supreme Court found that the appointment was now "an accomplished fact," and that it would now be unfair to grant certiorari. Similar public policy considerations loom especially large, where disastrous results might be produced were the courts to undo every act which had been done on foot of an unconstitutional statute. The doctrine of laches was invoked by the Supreme Court in *Murphy* v. *Attorney-General*[91] to permit only very limited recovery of monies paid pursuant to an unconstitutional taxing statute. Although the decision affected thousands of married

---

[88] See p. 335.
[89] Cane, "A Fresh Look at Punton's Case" (1980) 43 M.L.R. 264, 272.
[90] [1981] I.R. 181.
[91] [1982] I.R. 241. See also *Reid* v. *Limerick Corporation* [1984] I.L.R.M. 366 and Kelly, *The Irish Constitution* (Dublin, 1984) at pp. 322–327.

couples, the vast majority of them were unable to recover monies collected in this unconstitutional fashion. Henchy J. explained that the courts had only a limited power to undo what had been done:

> "[T]he law has to recognise that there may be transcendent considerations which make such a course [of legal redress] undesirable, impractical or impossible. Over the centuries the law has come to recognise . . . that factors such as prescription . . . waiver, estoppel, laches, a statute of limitations, *res judicata*, or other matters (most of which may be grouped under the heading of public policy) may debar a person from obtaining redress in the courts for injury . . . which would be justiciable and redressible if such considerations had not intervened."[92]

As Barrington J. has subsequently observed, while Article 40 obliges the State to defend and vindicate the personal rights of the citizen as far as it was practicable to do so, in the *Murphy* case:

> "[I]t was found to be impractical to vindicate the personal rights of the married couples who paid an invalid tax because directing the State to refund taxes unconstitutionally collected would have caused financial and administrative chaos."[93]

Barrington J.'s justification in constitutional terms of the public policy considerations employed by Henchy J. seems eminently sensible, and will probably be used in future cases where the courts are wrestling with the consequences of invalidity.

6. Severance

In some cases, the condemned legislation or administrative act may only be partially invalid. The question arises as to whether the excision of the offending sections of the Act, provision or order is possible. This is a task which the courts will only undertake where the bad can be cleanly severed from the good. For example, in *The State (Sheehan)* v. *McMahon*[94] a Garda challenged the validity of certain disciplinary penalties imposed on him. The Supreme Court found that the Appeal Board acted *ultra vires* in declining to hear his appeal. But as the first tier of the procedure laid down by the

---

[92] [1982] I.R. at p. 314.
[93] *Muckley* v. *Ireland* [1986] I.L.R.M. 364, 370.
[94] Supreme Court, October 25, 1977.

regulations was correctly observed, it did not follow that the error of the Appeal Board in thinking that they had no jurisdiction to review should be held to invalidate what had gone before. The court accordingly remitted the matter back to the Appeal Board who could then hear the appeal. Similarly, in *The State (McKeown)* v. *Scully*[95] that part of the record which recorded a verdict of suicide was quashed as *ultra vires*, leaving untouched the other aspects of the verdict.

This question has also assumed relevance in planning cases where an invalid condition had been attached to the grant of a planning permission. In these cases, the court will quash the entire permission if what remains when shorn of the invalid condition is such that the planning authority would not have been willing to grant it in the first instance. As Keane J. observed in *Bord na Mona* v. *Galway County Council*:

> "[W]here the condition relates to planning considerations and is an essential feature of the permission granted, it would seem . . . wrong that the permission should be treated as still effective, although shorn of an essential planning condition."[96]

In the *Bord na Mona* case a condition requiring the contribution of a large sum of money towards the cost of restructuring a public road was held to be invalid. Keane J. was of the opinion that severance was not possible, and that the entire permission must fall. The offending condition could not be regarded as inessential or peripheral to the grant of the permission, and it would have been unjust to the defendants to enforce a permission stripped of such a vital condition.

Many of the cases on this topic have arisen in the context of partially invalid delegated legislation. In *Pigs and Bacon Commis-*

---

[95] [1986] I.L.R.M. 133. See also *The State (Moloney)* v. *Minister for Industry and Commerce* [1954] I.R. 253 (severance of Ministerial order). But severance is not possible in the case of a criminal conviction: *The State (Kiernan)* v. *deBurca* [1963] I.R. 348.

[96] [1985] I.R. 205, 211. See also to like effect, *Killiney & Ballybrack Development Assoc.* v. *Minister for Local Government (No. 2)*, High Court, April 1, 1977 and, generally, *Potato Marketing Board* v. *Merricks* [1958] 2 Q.B. 316; *Kent C.C.* v. *Kingsway Investments (Kent) Ltd.* [1971] A.C. 72; *Dunkley* v. *Evans* [1981] 1 W.L.R. 1522; *Thames Water Authority* v. *Elmbridge B.C.* [1983] Q.B. 570; *R.* v. *Transport Secretary, ex p. G.L.C.* [1985] 3 All E.R. 300; *R.* v. *North Hertfordshire D.C., ex p. Cobbold* [1985] 3 All E.R. 486; *The State (Irish Pharmaceutical Union)* v. *Employment Appeals Tribunal*, Supreme Court, March 25, 1986.

sioners v. *McCarren & Co.*[97] the plaintiffs were empowered by the
Pigs and Bacon Acts 1935–1941 to fix the rate of an appropriate
levy which pig producers were required to pay, but the prior
consent of the Minister for Agriculture was required for this
purpose. Following a reference by the High Court under Article
177 of the Treaty of Rome, the European Court of Justice held
that inasmuch as the statutory scheme permitted the Commission
to pay export bonuses and to engage in direct selling activities
outside the State it was contrary to Community law. The Supreme
Court rejected the argument that it could now declare the rate of
levy which would have been appropriate to finance those purposes
and activities which would not offend against Community law.
O'Higgins C.J. pointed out that the rate fixed:

> "[Could] not be broken up, and the portion attributable to
> lawful purposes salvaged by severance. To do this would
> involve the Court, and not the plaintiff Commission in
> declaring a rate of levy. This, however, is not what the
> legislature authorises or permits, nor would a rate so declared
> [be compatible with the statutory scheme]."[98]

In that case it was impossible to effect a severance, with the result
that the impugned orders were condemned as wholly *ultra vires*.

In come cases the courts will permit what is known as "horizontal
severance," meaning that the invalid portion may be retained but
ruled inoperative only in so far as their application would run into
an area of *ultra vires*. This happened in *Cassidy* v. *Minister for Industry
and Commerce*[99] where the Supreme Court held that a maximum
prices order was unreasonable and *ultra vires* in so far as it applied
to lounge bars. By virtue of a "horizontal severance" the actual
orders themselves were upheld but the court limited their
operation to public bars, an area which was *intra vires*.

7. Mandatory and directory provisions

Nearly every question pertaining to jurisdiction turns on a
question of statutory interpretation. This is especially true in the
case of disregard of procedural and formal requirements laid
down by statute. When the Oireachtas stipulates that certain
formal and procedural requirements must be observed before a

[97] [1981] I.R. 451. See also *McCrumlish* v. *Pigs and Bacon Commission*, High
Court, May 28, 1975.
[98] [1981] I.R. 451 at p. 469.
[99] [1978] I.R. 297. See also *MacLeod* v. *Att.-Gen. for N.S. Wales* [1891]
A.C. 455; *Ulster Transport Authority* v. *James Brown & Sons Ltd.* [1953]
N.I. 79 and *Belfast Corporation* v. *O.D. Cars Ltd.* [1960] A.C. 490.

power of duty may properly be exercised, it rarely states what consequences follow non-compliance with these statutory requirements. Of course, to this general rule there are exceptions: section 5 of the Adoption Act 1976, for example, states that an adoption order shall not be declared invalid solely on the ground that certain statutory pre-requisites have not been complied with. Nevertheless, it is true to say that the courts are for the most part left to their own devices as far as the non-compliance with procedural requirements is concerned. Whether a statutory provision which on the face appears to be obligatory is to be regarded as truly mandatory or is merely to be regarded as directory in nature depends on the statutory intent and whether compliance with the provision can fairly be said to be essential to the general object intended to be secured by the Act.[1] The relevant test has been stated in the following terms:

> "If the requirement which has not been observed may fairly be said to be an integral and indispensable part of the statutory intendment, the courts will hold it to be truly mandatory, and will not excuse a departure from it. But if, on the other hand, what is apparently a requirement is in essence merely a direction which is not of the substance of the aim and scheme of the statute, non-compliance may be excused.[2]

But even in the case of directory provisions, the courts will not readily sanction a radical departure from what the legislature has ordained. Thus, even provisions which are directory as to *precise* compliance are generally mandatory as to *substantial* compliance.[3] On the other hand, courts are rarely impressed by defects of form, and will often excuse an irregularity where the "requirements of justice and the substance of the procedure have been observed."[4] In addition, in view of the fact that in nearly all cases the remedy sought will lie in the discretion of the court, there is increasing evidence that the crucial factor is probably now whether the irregularities have caused real prejudice. If the party aggrieved cannot show that he has been "wrong-footed or damnified" or

---

[1] *Monaghan U.D.C.* v. *Alf-A-Bet Promotions Ltd.* [1980] I.L.R.M. 64. See also *The State (McCarthy)* v. *O'Donnell* [1945] I.R. 126.

[2] *The State (Elm Developments)* v. *An Bord Pleanala* [1981] I.L.R.M. 108 at p. 110 *per* Henchy J. For a dubious application of similar principles see *Re Philip Clarke* [1950] I.R. 235.

[3] *The State (Doyle)* v. *Carr* [1970] I.R. 87.

[4] *O'Mahony* v. *Arklow U.D.C.* [1965] I.R. 710 at p. 735 (Lavery J.); *The State (Toft)* v. *Galway Corporation* [1981] I.L.R.M. 439; *The State (Elm Developments Ltd.)* v. *An Bord Pleanala* [1981] I.L.R.M. 108; *The State (Coveney)* v. *Special Criminal Court* [1982] I.L.R.M. 284.

that the "spirit and purpose" of the regulations have not been breached then relief may be withheld on discretionary grounds.[5]

There are, however, no universal rules which can be used to determine whether a statutory provision is mandatory or directory—each will turn on the proper construction of the legislation in question, and the citation of authorities is not always especially helpful. Nevertheless, difficult issues of principle have been thrown up in recent Irish cases.

O'Mahony v. *Arklow U.D.C.*[6] is one such case. The plaintiff, who was town clerk of Arklow, was suspended for certain irregularities in the performance of his duties. He was subsequently removed from office with the consent of the Minister for Local Government pursuant to section 26 of the Local Government Act 1941. That application provided that a written application to the Minister for his consent for such dismissal was necessary. No such letter was sent, though the Minister was generally kept informed of the situation and was aware of the dissatisfaction of the council with the plaintiff's performance as town clerk. Although the misconduct of the plaintiff was admitted to be such as would have justified dismissal, the validity of his dismissal was put at issue by the plaintiff.

The dismissal was upheld by a bare majority of the Supreme Court. Lavery J. was of the opinion that as the Minister was fully aware of the situation, and as the plaintiff was given every opportunity to explain his conduct, the irregularities complained of were "defects of form and not of substance." He did not think that the court should:

> "[P]arse and construe rules of procedure in a narrow and unreal way, looking for some flaw in procedure to invalidate a transaction where the requirements of justice and the substance of procedure have been observed."[7]

Kingsmill Moore J. in dissent considered that as the procedural requirements of the Act had not been adhered to, this represented a fundamental procedural defect which invalidated the dismissal. This approach seems unduly narrow and rigid; the majority view that the dismissal should not be invalidated as there was substantial compliance with the statutory requirements seems preferable, given that the plaintiff was given every opportunity to prepare his case—which was the very object of this procedural safeguard.

The conventional distinction between mandatory and directory

---

[5] *The State (Elm Developments Ltd.)* v. *An Bord Pleanala* [1981] I.L.R.M. 108; *The State (Coveney)* v. *Special Criminal Court* [1982] I.L.R.M. 284.
[6] [1965] I.R. 710.
[7] *Ibid.* at p. 735.

regulations has been blurred, however, by two recent Supreme Court decisions. In *Monaghan U.D.C.* v. *Alf-A-Bet Promotions Ltd.*[8] the respondent developer sought planning permission which would enable him to convert a drapery store into a betting office and an amusement arcade. The relevant regulations required the developer to publish a notice in a newspaper stating the "nature and extent of the development." The developer's notice referred only to "alterations and improvements." The Supreme Court held that the notice did not convey the nature and extent of the proposed development. Inclusion in the notice of information as the nature and extent of the proposed development was vital as to the proper orientation of the statutory scheme for the grant of planning permission. The misleading notice that was published was held to be non-compliance with a mandatory provision, and such compliance was held to be fatal to the developer's case. In view of the fact that planning permission could radically affect the rights and amenities of others, and substantially benefit or enrich the grantee of the permission, Henchy J. considered that the courts should not countenance deviation from that which had been deemed obligatory by the Oireachtas save on an application of the *de minimis* rule:

"What the legislature has prescribed in such circumstances as necessary should be treated as nothing short of necessary and deviations from the requirements must, before it can be overlooked, be shown, by the person seeking to have it excused, to be so trivial or so technical, or so peripheral, or otherwise so insubstantial that on the principle that it is the spirit rather than the letter of the law that matters, the prescribed obligation has been substantially, and therefore adequately, complied with."[9]

This matter was further considered by the Supreme Court in *The State (Elm Developments Ltd.)* v. *An Bord Pleanala.*[10] A developer sought and obtained a grant of planning permission from a local authority. An appeal was lodged by local residents against the grant of such permission. The developer claimed that failure by the residents to state the grounds of appeal in writing at the actual time of filing a notice of appeal rendered such appeal a nullity in law. The court concluded that the requirement that the grounds

---

[8] [1980] I.L.R.M. 64. See Cooney (1982) 17 Ir.Jur.(n.s.) 346 and Scannell, "Planning Control: Twenty Years On" (1982) 4 D.U.L.J.(n.s.) 41. See also *Dunne Ltd.* v. *Dublin C.C.* [1974] I.R. 45; *McCabe* v. *Harding Investments Ltd.* [1984] I.L.R.M. 105 and *The State (Multi-Print Labels Ltd.)* v. *Employment Appeals Tribunal* [1984] I.L.R.M. 545.
[9] [1980] I.L.R.M. 64 at p. 69.
[10] [1981] I.L.R.M. 108.

of appeal be stated contemporaneously with the notice of appeal was directory rather than mandatory in nature. The purpose of the regulations was informative in nature: the Board was quite entitled to listen to points other than those mentioned in the grounds of appeal. Furthermore, in the instant case grounds of appeal had been furnished to the satisfaction of the Board within a few weeks of the appeal, and Henchy J. concluded that the developer could not say that he had been in any way "wrong-footed or damnified" or that the "spirit or purpose" of the Planning Acts and regulations had been breached.

As stated, these cases tend to blur distinctions between mandatory and directory regulations. The purpose of the mandatory/directory distinction is to ensure that one party may not rely on minor or technical irregularities in order to invalidate administrative action. In practice this distinction has proved difficult to draw and the *Alf-A-Bet* case shows that it is only very trivial deviations from mandatory requirements which will be overlooked. Perhaps the best way of dealing with this problem is to examine all the circumstances of the case in order to ascertain whether the disregard of procedural requirements has caused real prejudice. If an applicant cannot show that he has been "wrong-footed or damnified" by the breach of prescribed procedure, then relief may be refused on discretionary grounds.[11]

However, *Dublin County Council* v. *Marren*[12] shows that the "absence of real prejudice" test is inoperable where there is a possibility that some member of the public might have been genuinely affected. At issue in this case was whether an applicant for planning permission had complied adequately with the relevant regulations which require the submission of such plans, drawings and other particulars as are necessary "to identify the land and to describe the work or structure to which the application relates." The applicant had previously applied unsuccessfully for planning permission in respect of certain premises. He made a fresh application some years later, but on this occasion he omitted to include details of plans and drawings. The reasons for this omission were, however, contained in the application itself, where he stated that the house plans were to be the same as in the previous application. While Barrington J. took the view that the planning officials were not in any way incommoded or prejudiced by this failure to comply precisely with the terms of the regulations, he observed that this was not simply a matter of *inter partes*. If it had been, he would have ruled that there had been

[11] See *Elm Developments* and *The State (Coveney)* v. *Special Criminal Court* [1982] I.L.R.M. 284.
[12] [1985] I.L.R.M. 593.

substantial compliance and that any non-compliance was covered
by the *de minimis* principle. But it was not simply an *inter partes*
matter, as the relevant regulations contemplated that the application, together with the plans, drawings *etc.* would be made
available to the public. As it was possible that a member of the
public might have been misled or incommoded by the failure to
include the relevant drawings and plans, Barrington J. ruled that
there had not been adequate compliance with the regulations.[13]

Where property rights or fundamental interests are at stake the
court is more likely to insist on a stricter approach in matters of
procedure, as is illustrated by *Healy* v. *Cork Corporation*.[14] By virtue
of section 79 of the Housing Act 1966 where a compulsory
purchase order has become operative the local authority must
serve a notice to treat requiring the owner:

> "[t]o state within a specified period (not being less than *one
> month from the date* of service of the notice to treat) the nature
> of the interest in respect of which compensation is claimed
> and the details of the compensation claimed" (italics sup-
> plied).

In *Healy* the date before which the plaintiff owner had to reply
(which was specified in the notice to treat), was exactly one month
after the date of the notice to treat. In other words it violated the
1966 Act in that less than adequate notice was given. Although the
plaintiff's reply was received within the time specified in the notice
to treat, this infraction was held to render the entire process
invalid because of the presumption that where property rights are
concerned, the wording of a statute should be construed strictly
against the public authority concerned.

8. Appeal from administrative decisions

In some contexts the Oireachtas provides for an appeal from a
decision of an administrative body. The right of appeal is usually
confined to an appeal on a point of law, although this need not
necessarily be the case.[15] The appeal will generally lie to the High

---

[13] For an example of a purely *inter partes* matter in this context, see *The
State (I.B.M. (Ireland) Ltd.)* v. *Employment Appeals Tribunal* [1984]
I.L.R.M. 31.

[14] High Court, February 2, 1981 (*ex tempore*). But *cf.* the indulgent attitude
taken to breaches of the Prison Rules in *Cahill* v. *Governor of Military
Detention Barracks, Curragh Camp* [1980] I.L.R.M. 191.

[15] For example, some administrative bodies have power to state a case for
the High Court: see Adoption Act 1952, s.20 (An Bord Uchtala); Local
Government (Planning and Development) Act 1976, s.42 (An Bord
Pleanala).

Court.[16] If, however, a right of appeal to the lower courts is granted by statute, the decision of the lower court on appeal may itself be quashed upon an application to the High Court for judicial review.[17]

The nature and scope of the court's jurisdiction on a statutory appeal is in all cases a matter of statutory construction. Nevertheless, it would be surprising that if the Oireachtas, having created a statutory right of appeal, did not intend to vest the High Court with powers in addition to those which it enjoyed at common law. As Costello J. explained in *Dunne* v. *Minister for Fisheries*:

> "[It does not follow] that in every case the Court's jurisdiction on a statutory appeal is the same; in every case the statute itself must be construed. In construing a statute it does not seem to me helpful to apply by analogy the rules of judicial review, since, by granting a statutory appeal, the legislature must have intended that the Court would have powers in addition to those already enjoyed at common law."[18]

But in practice there may not be a great deal of difference between the reach of the High Court's jurisdiction to hear appeals on a point of law and its supervisory jurisdiction over administrative bodies and the lower courts now that the reach of jurisdictional error has been so greatly expanded.[19] In particular, one would be hard pressed to draw a satisfactory distinction between the scope of appellate review for errors of law and that of certiorari to quash for errors of law on the face of the record. But other important difficulties remain. In the first place, the remedies available on an application for judicial review are discretionary in nature.[20] Secondly, the High Court's power of judicial review is an inherent jurisdiction derived from Article 34.3.1, and it is doubtful whether this supervisory jurisdiction may be removed by statute.[21] In contrast, any appellate jurisdiction is entirely the creation of statute and there are no constitutional impediments to the abolition of such a jurisdiction. Thirdly, on an appeal the High Court is concerned with the merits of an administrative decision, whereas the Court rules on its legality in judicial review proceedings. This means that when the High Court is exercising an appellate jurisdiction it has, generally speaking, the power to alter or vary an administrative decision, or, if needs be, to remit the case

---

[16] But is not always the case: see *e.g.* Income Tax Act 1967, s.429 (appeal on a point of law to the Circuit Court).
[17] *The State (McEldowney)* v. *Kelliher* [1983] I.R. 289.
[18] [1984] I.R. 230 at p. 237.
[19] See pp. 190–196.
[20] See pp. 348–355.
[21] *Tormey* v. *Att.-Gen.* [1985] I.L.R.M. 375, and see further pp. 200–202.

to the administrative body concerned. However, in judicial review proceedings, the Court is faced with a starker choice: to quash (save where the order is severable) or not to quash.[22] Fourthly, a finding of invalidity will in practice have *erga omnes* effect. In other words, there may be a large category of persons who, being similarly affected by the impugned legislation or administrative act, will be permitted to rely on this finding of invalidity.[23] In contrast, because of the nature of the circumstances in which an appeal has been created, a decision of the High Court on appeal is, in practice, a ruling on what is effectively an *inter partes* matter between the appellant and the administrative body concerned. Such a decision will only rarely have general significance. And even if the courts rule against the administrative body concerned, this will only have prospective effect, and will not call into question the legality of many earlier administrative decisions.[24]

Dunne v. *Minister for Fisheries* concerned section 11 of the Fisheries (Consolidation) Act 1959 which provides that on appeal by a "person aggrieved" the High Court may "confirm or annul" a by-law made by the respondent Minister under the 1959 Act. Costello J. rejected the submission that the court could only interfere where the Minister had erred in law, and held that the court could consider the merits of the case.[25] In contrast, section 428 of the Income Tax Act 1967 allows an appeal on a point of law from the Appeal Commissioners to the High Court. The effect of this section was extensively discussed in *Mara* v. *Hummingbird Ltd.*[26] The Appeal Commissioners had found as a fact that

---

[22] For a more extended discussion of the difference between appeal on the merits and judicial review, see Hogan, "Remoulding Certiorari" (1982) 17 Ir.Jur.(n.s.) 32 at pp. 48–54.

[23] *Blake* v. *Att.-Gen.* [1982] I.R. 117 is, perhaps, the classic example of this. The plaintiff's successful challenge to the validity of the Rent Restrictions Act 1960 had the result that many thousands of properties were no longer subject to the rent control regime. New legislation was necessary to give protection to the tenants who had formerly enjoyed the protection given by the 1960 Act. See Housing (Private Rented Dwellings) Act 1982.

[24] Costello J. did accept, however, that the court should be slow to substitute its opinion for that of the Minister "in cases in which his department's experience and knowledge of the matter in issue would be an important element in reaching its formulation": [1984] I.R. at p. 241.

[25] [1982] I.L.R.M. 421. Kenny J., delivering the Supreme Court judgment, referred with approval to the speech of Lord Radcliffe in *Edwards* v. *Bairstow* [1956] A.C. 14. See also *Rahill* v. *Brady* [1971] I.R. 69.

[26] The test enunciated in *Hummingbird* has been followed in a series of subsequent decisions. See *e.g. O'hArgain* v. *Beechpark Estates Ltd.*, High

Hummingbird's purchase and sale of development property was for investment purposes, and, accordingly, could not be regarded as a sale "in the course of trade."

In the Supreme Court, Kenny J. drew the distinction between findings of primary fact, and the inferences to be drawn from those facts. Findings of primary fact—in this case, for example, Hummingbird's intentions when purchasing the premises—should not be disturbed "unless there was no evidence whatever to support them." In the case of inferences or conclusions based on these primary facts, a different approach was called for. If these conclusions were based on the interpretation of documents, the Court should reverse them, for it was in as good a position as the Appeal Commissioners to determine the meaning of these documents. The court should only reverse other conclusions based on primary facts if these conclusions are ones which could not reasonably have been drawn, or which are based on a mistaken view of the law. Kenny J. urged a cautious approach, noting that the Appeal Commissioners will often have evidence

> "[S]ome of which supports the conclusion that the transaction under investigation was an adventure in the nature of trade and he will have some which points to the opposite conclusion. These are essentially matters of degree and his conclusions should not be disturbed (even if the court does not agree with them, for we are not retrying the case) unless they are such that a reasonable commissioner could not draw them, or they are based on a mistaken view of the law."[27]

The effect of this test is to allow effective control over unreasonable decisions, or decisions based on "no evidence" or a mistaken view of the law, while at the same time allowing the administrative authority a tolerable margin of error. While the extent of the court's appellate jurisdiction is always a matter of statutory construction, the principle enunciated in *Mara* can be readily adopted for other administrative appeals "on a point of law," *e.g.* under section 299(*b*) of the Social Welfare (Consolidation) Act 1981.

Court, March 27, 1979; *Re McElligott* [1985] I.L.R.M. 210; *MacCarthaigh* v. *Daly* [1986] I.L.R.M. 116. For an application of these principles in the non-revenue context, see *Brewster* v. *Burke and the Minister for Labour* (1985) 4 J.I.S.L.L. 98.
[27] [1982] I.L.R.M. 421 at p. 426.

9. Estoppel and res judicata

The related doctrines of estoppel, waiver and *res judicata* apply
(with important modifications) in the realm of public law just as
much as in private law. But a rigid application of these doctrines
would result in conflict with the fundamental principle of *ultra
vires*. A public authority cannot give itself a jurisdiction it does not
possess. It cannot do this by a mistaken conclusion as to the extent
of its own powers and neither can it do so by creating an estoppel.

The leading Irish authority on the question of estoppel and
public bodies is *Re Green Dale Building Co.*[28] Under the Housing
Act 1966, a notice to treat in relation to land purchases may only
be served after the compulsory purchase order has become
operative but such an order does not take effect pending the
determination of proceedings which challenge its validity.[29] In this
case, a notice to treat was served by a local authority in 1972 but
this notice was invalid as proceedings had been commenced by a
third party challenging the validity of the compulsory purchase
order. That order only took effect from 1975, when the third
party proceedings were dismissed. The housing authority immediately served a second notice to treat. The value of Green Dale's
land was less in 1975 than it had been in 1972. The company
contended that, the non-compliance with the requirements of the
Housing Act notwithstanding, the authority should be estopped
from relying on the invalidity of the first notice to treat as (i) the
authority had represented that the first notice to treat had been
validly served and (ii) the company had, relying on the validity of
that representation, acted to their detriment by treating the lands
as sterile from 1972, and by submitting to an abortive arbitration
to assess the compensation payable.

The Supreme Court rejected the submission that the doctrine of
promisory estoppel could have any application in cases of this
nature. Henchy J. reasoned that it would entirely destroy the
doctrine of *ultra vires* if the donee of a statutory power could
extend his power by creating an estoppel. The judge conceded
that there were exceptions to the general rule such as to debar a
public authority from relying on a mere irregularity which it ought
in fairness to have overlooked, but any such exceptions have been
confined to technicalities.[30]

Henchy J. noted that the company was seeking to estop the local
authority from asserting that it had acted in breach of an express

---

[28] [1977] I.R. 256.

[29] Housing Act 1966, s.79(1).

[30] *e.g. Wells* v. *Minister for Housing and Local Government* [1967] 1 W.L.R.
1000; *Lever Finance Ltd.* v. *Westminster L.B.C.* [1971] 1 Q.B. 222.

or implied prohibition or restriction of function in a statute. To permit an estoppel in these circumstances would require the court acting to defy the will of the Oireachtas as set out in the statute.[31]

Henchy J. did not explain why technicalities represented an exception to the rule. It might be an example of the application of the *de minimis* principle. But perhaps the exception represents a wider principle which would allow an estoppel in respect of *ultra vires* action where the injustice to the plaintiff was not outweighed by any tangible public benefit. Such a balancing of interests would surely be acceptable given that the object of the *ultra vires* rule is to protect the public interest.[32] It could also be said that the mere fact that the public authority has acted *ultra vires* should not of itself be decisive, and that regard must be had to other considerations.[33]

There is no doubt but that if the rule is strictly applied it is capable of causing considerable injustice. It has been suggested that a public body should be bound by *ultra vires* representations by its authorised agents when that body is acting in a proprietary rather than in a governmental or administrative capacity.[34] This proposition has a certain superficial attractiveness, but it is difficult to justify in terms of principle, and, moreover, the distinction between what is a governmental and what is a proprietary function is not easy to draw. At another level the doctrine of estoppel might be allowed to apply to representations which were beyond the powers of the official who gave the assurance, but which were not actually *ultra vires* the public body itself. Such an approach has obvious affinities with the "internal management rule" in company law.[35] Nevertheless, it would be of

---

[31] *Green Dale* was followed in *Dublin Corporation* v. *McGrath*, High Court, November 17, 1978. In *Morris* v. *Garvey* [1983] I.R. 319 the Supreme Court ordered the demolition of an unauthorised development in proceedings taken pursuant to s.27 of the Local Government (Planning and Development) Act 1976, despite the fact that the respondent had been assured by a planning official that the planning permission was not necessary in respect of the development. Henchy J. commented thus: "If he wishes to retain the unpermitted walls, the respondent should have applied for a fresh development permission—thus enabling the applicant, or any member of the public to raise such objection as might be thought warranted. In such circumstances the opinion of a planning official—no matter how genuinely given—cannot be allowed to defeat the rights of the public . . . " ([1983] I.R. at pp. 324–325).

[32] Craig, *Administrative Law* (London, 1983) at pp. 567–582.

[33] The courts regularly engage in such reasoning when considering whether to invalidate administrative decisions: see *e.g. The State (Cussen)* v. *Brennan* [1981] I.R. 181.

[34] Craig, *op. cit.,* at p. 517.

[35] See Ussher, *Irish Company Law* (London, 1986) at pp. 152–153.

assistance only in a limited class of cases. In *Dublin Corporation* v. *McGrath*,[36] for example, the defendant submitted that the planning authority was estopped from denying the existence of planning permission in respect of an unauthorised structure. It appeared that an agent of the authority had given verbal permission for the construction of a garage which was subsequently erected by the defendant. The plea of estoppel failed, for, as McMahon J. observed, not only did the agent not have power to make such a representation, but such a representation was also *ultra vires* the planning authority itself.

If the courts propose to adhere rigidly to this "jurisdictional principle," then there is much to be said for compensating individuals who have relied to their detriment on an *ultra vires* representation.[37] Indeed, such cases would seem to come within the ambit of the Ombudsman's powers.[38] However, at the end of the day, it may be that the solution which the courts will adopt is to find the public authority liable under the principle of *Hedley Byrne & Co. Ltd.* v. *Heller & Partners Ltd.*,[39] *i.e.* liability in negligence for careless misrepresentations resulting in pure financial loss to the misrepresentee, even though no contractual or recognised fiduciary relationship between the parties exists.

10. Waiver and consent

The fundamental rule is that waiver and consent cannot confer jurisdiction. Closely related to this is the principle that public bodies may not waive observance of the law by exercising a dispensing power.[40] Accordingly, a planning authority is not at liberty to waive statutory requirements which are clearly imposed

---

[36] High Court, November 17, 1978.
[37] Gould, (1971) 85 L.Q.R. 15 at p. 18.
[38] The Ombudsman Act 1980, s.4(2) provides, *inter alia*, that the Ombudsman may investigate any action where it appears to him that the action was, or may have been, taken "without proper authority" or as "the result of negligence or carelessness."
[39] [1964] A.C. 465.
[40] This raises the question of the legality of the extra-statutory concessions operated by the Revenue Commissioners. There is no Irish authority on the point, but one must doubt whether the Oireachtas could constitutionally delegate such a dispensing power to an administrative body of this nature. As for the position in England, see the comments of Lord Upjohn, in *I.R.C.* v. *Bates* [1968] A.C. 483 and those of Walton J. in *I.R.C.* v. *Vestey* [1960] A.C. 1148. In *Norris* v. *Att.-Gen.* [1984] I.R. 36 McCarthy J. stated that a positive decision on the part of the authorities not to prosecute in respect of certain offences would be unlawful.

for the public benefit.[41] Nevertheless, the principle that waiver or consent cannot validate or modify *ultra vires* action must be treated with some reserve, for it is clear that waiver or consent may operate as a discretionary bar to relief.[42] The doctrines of waiver, acquiescence[43] and estoppel by conduct represent in varying degrees the idea that a plaintiff cannot approbate and reprobate. It has been stated that it would be inconsistent with the due administration of justice if a plaintiff "were allowed to reserve unto himself the right to argue later a point touching on the validity of a decision," should that decision prove adverse to his interests.[44]

The traditional rule has been put in the following terms by Lord Reid:

"[I]t is a fundamental principle that no consent can confer on a court or tribunal with limited statutory jurisdiction any power to act beyond that jurisdiction, or can estop the consenting party from subsequently maintaining that such court or tribunal."[45]

Irish courts have been reluctant, however, to commit themselves unequivocally to such a position. In the leading case, *Corrigan* v.

---

[41] *Dublin Corporation* v. *McGrath*, High Court, November 17, 1978; *Morris* v. *Garvey* [1983] I.R. 319.

[42] *The State (Byrne)* v. *Frawley* [1978] I.R. 326, *Corrigan* v. *Irish Land Commission* [1977] I.R. 317 and *The State (Cronin)* v. *Circuit Judge for the Western Court* [1937] I.R. 34.

[43] Acquiescence means "participation in proceedings without taking objection to the jurisdiction of the tribunal once the facts giving ground for raising the objection are fully known"; de Smith's *Judicial Review of Administrative Action* (London, 1980) at p. 423.

[44] *Corrigan* v. *Irish Land Commission* [1977] I.R. 317 at p. 325 *per* Henchy J. But see *The State (Gallagher, Shatter & Co.)* v. *de Valera* [1986] I.L.R.M. 3 where a solicitor's firm permitted a taxation of costs to proceed while maintaining an objection as to jurisdiction. The Supreme Court, *per* McCarthy J., held that there had been no waiver of jurisdictional objection: "[I]t does not appear to me that justice is served by determining a case of this kind against a solicitor because, whilst maintaining his objection, he thought it more practicable to allow the taxation to proceed, in the hope that the result would, in any event, be satisfactory. When, far from being short of satisfactory it held him guilty of making a gross overcharge, in my view he is not to be defeated by a plea of waiver" ([1986] I.L.R.M. at 9).

[45] *Essex Incorporated Church Union* v. *Essex C.C.* [1963] A.C. 808. See also *The State (Byrne)* v. *Frawley* [1978] I.R. 326 at p. 342 *per* O'Higgins C.J.

Irish Land Commission,[46] Henchy J. acknowledged that a totally new jurisdiction[47] could not be created by means of an estoppel. The crucial test was whether the court or tribunal had initiated jurisdiction to enter upon the inquiry. Once such jurisdiction was present, any errors committed in the course of the inquiry could be waived. In *Corrigan* itself it was clear that the Appeals Tribunal of the Land Commission plainly had jurisdiction to hear the plaintiff's appeal. The question was whether two particular lay commissioners were debarred from exercising that jurisdiction by reason of their prior dealing with the case. Henchy J. found that that point could be, and indeed had been, waived by the plaintiff when he accepted the tribunal as he found it composed on the day of the hearing.

In other cases, waiver and estoppel have been regarded as a bar to discretionary relief. In *R. (Kildare C.C.)* v. *Commissioner for Valuation*[48] the applicants sought to quash a revised valuation order made by a county court. They allowed the appeal to proceed on the basis that there was jurisdiction in the county court to revise the valuation: it was only when the decision of the court did not prove as favourable to their interests as they had expected that they sought to question the jurisdiction of the tribunal. The former Irish Court of Appeal agreed that the adjudication of the county court was *ultra vires*, but held nevertheless that the applicants were precluded by their conduct from obtaining the relief sought. A similar conclusion was reached in *The State (Byrne)* v. *Frawley*[49] where the Supreme Court held that the applicant by his conduct had approbated a jury selected in an unconstitutional fashion. He could not now be heard to say that the jury lacked competence to try him.

---

[46] [1977] I.R. 317. See also *Re Creighton's Estate*, High Court, March 5, 1982; *The State (Grahame)* v. *Racing Board*, High Court, November 22, 1983.

[47] The word "jurisdiction" is used by Henchy J. in the restrictive sense of "jurisdiction to enter upon an inquiry." Contrast this with his judgment in *The State (Holland)* v. *Kennedy* [1977] I.R. 193 where the judge stated that for any number of reasons a tribunal which had jurisdiction at the start of an inquiry could lose that jurisdiction.

[48] [1901] 2 I.R. 215. See also *The State (McKay)* v. *Cork Circuit Judge* [1937] I.R. 650; *The State (Cronin)* v. *Circuit Judge for Western Circuit* [1937] I.R. 34; *R. (Dorris)* v. *Ministry of Health* [1954] N.I. 79.

[49] *The State (Byrne)* v. *Frawley* [1978] I.R. 326. See also *Whelan* v. *R.* [1921] 1 I.R. 310. For cases where the plea of waiver was disallowed, see *The State (Redmond)* v. *Wexford Corporation* [1946] I.R. 409; *The State (Cole)* v. *Labour Court* (1984) 3 J.I.S.L.L. 128 and *The State (Gallagher, Shatter & Co.)* v. *de Valera* [1986] I.L.R.M. 3.

11. Procedural irregularities

A litigant will generally be deemed to have waived objections based on the composition of a tribunal[50] or the procedure adopted if the jurisdictional question is not raised at the appropriate time in the proceedings. Persons who attend court hearings are deemed to have waived any possible irregularities which might exist.[51] In one case,[52] the applicant attended petty sessions and participated in the case to the extent of asking for an adjournment on a number of occasions. It was decided that he was deemed to have waived any possible irregularity, and that he had estopped himself by his conduct from obtaining certiorari. The Supreme Court ruled to like effect in *Re Tynan*[53] where the applicant had sought an order of prohibition restraining the District Court from dealing with an allegedly irregular summons. In the opinion of Walsh J. the conduct of the applicant in appearing at the District Court, his giving of evidence, and his failure to raise prompt objection were all consistent with the inference that he had waived the point.

12. Res judicata

One species of estoppel is *res judicata*. The doctrine of *res judicata* has been defined in the following manner by Holmes L.J.:

> "A judgment not appealed from binds the parties and privies for all time by what appears on its face; and if it can be shown that, in the course of the action that resulted in the judgment a certain definite material issue not set forth in the judgment itself was raised by the parties and determined judicially or by consent, it would be contrary to public policy to allow the same parties to re-agitate the same matter in subsequent legal proceedings."[54]

The two aspects of *res judicata* are contained in this passage. A "cause of action" estoppel precludes the same parties from re-litigating an action which has been finally determined by a court of competent jurisdiction—this is *res judicata* "in its most essential form."[55] An "issue estoppel" (or "constructive *res judicata*")

[50] *Corrigan* v. *Irish Land Commission* [1977] I.R. 317.
[51] *Whelan* v. *R.* [1921] 1 I.R. 310; *The State (Grahame)* v. *Racing Board*, High Court, November 22, 1983.
[52] *R. (Sherlock)* v. *Cork JJ.* (1909) 42 I.L.T.R. 247.
[53] [1969] I.R. 1. See also *Moore* v. *Gamgee* (1890) 25 Q.B.D. 244.
[54] *Irish Land Commission* v. *Ryan* [1900] 2 I.R. 565 at p. 584. For a general discussion of this topic see Spencer Bower, Turner *Res Judicata* (London, 1969).
[55] Spencer Bower, Turner, *op. cit.*, at p. 149.

prevents the parties to the earlier proceedings litigating an essential feature—"a certain definite material issue"—of the earlier decision.[56]

The doctrine of *res judicata* has a limited application in administrative law.[57] Administrative decisions rarely fulfil the required *probanda* for *res judicata*: such determinations do not deal with matters of status[58] and generally do not involve a *lis* between private individuals.[59] More fundamentally, a rigid application of the doctrine would be in conflict with two essential principles of administrative law: that jurisdiction cannot be created by estoppel, and that statutory powers and duties may not be fettered.[60] Subject to this, the doctrine of *res judicata* is not confined to courts of law but may also apply to tribunals and administrative authorities with powers to make binding determinations.[61] In addition the doctrine must not be confused with the situation where the decision taker has become *functus officio*. If a public authority has statutory power to determine some question its decision will generally be final and irrevocable. This is not because of the operation of *res judicata*, but rather because the authority lacks jurisdiction to alter its original decision and has become *functus officio*.[62]

That *res judicata* can only have a limited application in administrative law is well illustrated by a series of important decisions concerning rating and taxation. In *Society of Medical Officers of Health* v. *Hope*[63] a medical society successfully claimed before a Lands Tribunal that it was entitled to an exemption from rates. Some years later, a fresh valuation list was drawn up. Upon a further attempt being made to assess the Society *res judicata* was

[56] *D.* v. *C.* [1984] I.L.R.M. 173; *Hoystead* v. *Federal Taxation Commissioner* [1926] A.C. 155.

[57] Ganz, "Estoppel and Res Judicata in Administrative Law" [1965] *Public Law* 237.

[58] *McMahon* v. *Leahy* [1985] I.L.R.M. 422 (prior extradition order).

[59] *R.* v. *Fulham Rent Tribunal, ex p. Zerek* [1951] 2 K.B. 1 at p. 11 *per* Devlin J.

[60] *Bradshaw* v. *M'Mullan* [1920] 2 I.R. 412 (prior court settlement contrary to Local Government (Ireland) Act 1898; plea of *res judicata* failed as one cannot give "judicial effect to a transaction which the statute expressly forbids" (Lord Shaw)), and see also the comments of Walsh J. in *Kildare C.C.* v. *Keogh* [1971] I.R. 330 at p. 343; "It would be contrary to public policy that an erroneous construction of a statute should be perpetuated so as to decide successive claims between the same parties."

[61] *Athlone Woollen Mills Ltd.* v. *Athlone U.D.C.* [1950] I.R. 1.

[62] *Re 56 Denton Road* [1952] 2 All E.R. 799. See also *Re Lynham's Estate* [1928] I.R. 127.

[63] [1960] A.C. 551.

pleaded before the Lands Tribunal. Although it was conceded that there had been no material change of circumstances, the House of Lords ruled that no such estoppel arose. Emphasis was placed on the limited nature of the tribunal's jurisdiction, and Lord Radcliffe observed that the tribunal's jurisdiction was to decide the liability of a person "for a defined and terminable period." Put another way, the tribunal had a public duty to make a correct assessment on the ratepayer on each occasion, and no estoppel could be raised to prevent the tribunal from carrying out its duties under the statute. A similar conclusion was reached by a majority of the Supreme Court in *Kildare C.C.* v. *Keogh*.[64] Walsh J. pointed out that the doctrine of *res judicata* was inapplicable to rating cases, as the question of liability for rates for one year was always to be treated as inherently a different question to that of liability for another year, even though "there might be an identity on the question of law involved."

It is sometimes sought to explain away the above decisions by saying that "administrative" as opposed to "judicial" decisions were involved.[65] But such technical arguments are unconvincing, for *res judicata* may operate once a tribunal has power to determine an issue. The true principle is, as Lord Keith pointed out in *Hope's* case, that no estoppel can prevent a public body from carrying out its public duty. This principle was recognised by O'Hanlon J. in *Aprile* v. *Naas U.D.C.*[66] where he declined to apply the doctrine of *res judicata* to a decision of a planning authority. The applicant applied for retention permission in respect of an amusement centre. This application was refused by the respondent planning authority on the grounds that the proposed amusement centre would constitute a traffic hazard, and as such would be contrary to the proper planning and development of the area. The applicant took steps to deal with these objections, and he made a further application for permission. Once again the

---

[64] [1971] I.R. 330, following the Privy Council decision in *Caffoor* v. *Colombo Income Tax Commissioner* [1961] A.C. 584 where it was held that a tribunal's determination that a certain trust was charitable was conclusive only for the relevant *year of assessment*. The doctrine of *res judicata* did not prevent the tribunal from re-opening this question in any subsequent years.

[65] Ganz, *loc. cit.*, deals with these arguments, and rebuts them in a convincing fashion.

[66] High Court, November 22, 1983. But *cf. Dublin C.C.* v. *Tallaght Blocks Co. Ltd.*, Supreme Court, May 17, 1983 where Hederman J. stated that where a developer applied for planning permission in respect of an unauthorised structure and was refused, he could not later be heard to argue that permission for the development was not required.

application was refused, but on this occasion the planning
authority gave new grounds for the refusal.

O'Hanlon J. held that the doctrine of *res judicata* was inapplicable in the circumstances of the case. He observed that no estoppel
could work to prevent the authority from carrying out its statutory
duty:

> "[I]f a fresh application is later made in relation to the
> development of the same lands, there is an obligation on the
> planning authority, whenever it is called upon to deal with the
> new application to consider it *de novo* and to have regard to all
> aspects of the proper planning and development of the area
> as of that time, in granting or refusing the application."

But even if the doctrine of *res judicata* has only a limited
application in administrative cases,[67] it may be that a public
authority which issued contradictory decisions would be behaving
in an unreasonable fashion or in a manner which contravened the
constitutional guarantees of equality or fair procedures.[68]

13. Jurisdictional review and res judicata

The doctrine of *res judicata* cannot prevail against the fundamental principle of administrative law that jurisdiction cannot be
conferred by consent.[69] The corollary of this is that the litigant
relying on the decision of an inferior court or administrative body
must show that it was *intra vires*. As Professor Wade notes, since
"such a wide range of questions are held to go to jurisdiction," the
scope of *res judicata* in this area is limited.[70]

It would seem that, up to recently at any rate, *res judicata* was
inapplicable in cases where the public law remedies of certiorari,
prohibition and mandamus had been refused. These remedies
were primarily regarded as being concerned with the maintenance
of order in the legal system. It was argued that they did not

---

[67] It is only in very exceptional circumstances (such as that disclosed in the
Athlone Woollen Mills case) that the doctrine of *res judicata* has been
applied to decisions of planning authorities. However, in *The State
(Kenny and Hussey) v. An Bord Pleanala*, Supreme Court, December 20,
1984, McCarthy J. observed that while he did not have to determine
whether *res judicata* applied to planning decisions, he found it difficult
to see how a planning authority could be permitted "to come to a
different view when circumstances do not change." For a similar
approach, see *O'Dea v. Minister for Local Government* (1957) 91 I.L.T.R.
169.

[68] *McMahon v. Leahy* [1984] I.R. 525.

[69] *R. v. Pugh, ex p. Graham* [1951] 2 K.B. 623.

[70] *Administrative Law* (Oxford, 1982) at p. 244.

purport finally to determine the *private* rights of the parties *inter se*, and it was said that the court was merely required to decide "whether there had been a plain excess of jurisdiction or not."[71] Therefore, where the court has, for example, refused to quash a decision of the Rent Tribunal it would have been always open to the landlord to argue in subsequent civil proceedings that in fact no tenancy had existed and that the rent tribunal lacked jurisdiction. This issue would then be tried *de novo* on oral evidence before the court which was seized of the landlord's application for (say) possession.

The basis for this principle was that the High Court could not readily assess the conflicting evidence on the basis of the affidavits tendered in State side proceedings. (It is for this reason also that *res judicata* does apply where relief was refused following a plenary hearing in the case of an application for a declaration, injunction or damages). But it may be that this rationale had been undermined by the new Ord. 84, r. 25(1), which allows the court to conduct an oral hearing (including cross-examination of deponents on their affidavits) in an application for judicial review. If the court can thus inquire and determine *de novo* on oral evidence whether the facts giving rise to the tribunal's jurisdiction exist, can there be any sound reason why the refusal of certiorari, prohibition or mandamus should not attract the rule of *res judicata*?

14. Fettering a public purpose by contractual or other undertaking

The principle under discussion would appear to lead to the conclusion that no contract may be enforced if it involves an interference with the exercise of "powers for public purposes," an expression which is intended to cover not only discretionary powers but also quasi-judicial functions. Such a rule would run straight into another fundamental legal doctrine, namely that contracts must be honoured, even those made by the State. Before attempting to reconcile these opposing tensions, let us consider examples of cases in which the rule that no contract may impose a restriction upon a public power has been applied.

A most spectacular example occurred in *Rederei Amphitrite* v. *R.*[72] where the public power concerned was the power to refuse clearance to neutral ships in British ports during the First World War and the fetter was an express undertaking by the Crown to grant clearance to the ship in question because it was carrying an

---

[71] *R.* v. *Fulham Rent Tribunal, ex p. Zerek* [1952] 2 K.B. 11.
[72] [1921] 3 K.B. 500 ("the High Court's contribution to the war effort.")

approved cargo. Rowlatt J. took the view that the undertaking was invalid. He said:

" . . . [I]t is not competent for the Government to fetter its future executive actions, which must necessarily be determined by the needs of the community when the question arises. It cannot by contract hamper its freedom of action in matters which concern the welfare of the State."[73]

This passage was quoted with approval by the Supreme Court in *Kenny* v. *Cosgrave*.[74] In this case the President of the Executive Council had told an employer whose workers were on strike that it was essential that the employer resist their demands, and had promised that the Executive Council would indemnify him against any financial loss which ensued from this resistance. The promise was not honoured, but in line with *Amphitrite*, the plaintiff's claim for damages was rejected.

Each of these cases involves rather extreme—and not dissimilar—situations. Accordingly, the principle of unlimited application, enunciated in *Amphitrite* is now regarded, in foreign jurisdictions anyway, as needing to be reformulated in more precise terms.[75] Under the present law, no contract or undertaking will be binding if it purports to disable a public authority from exercising any statutory power of primary importance, for example, implementing an emergency function as in *Amphitrite*; making a by-law, refusing or granting planning permission; or if it purports to bind the public authority to exercise the power in a particular way. However, the test is not whether the contract could hypothetically affect the public body's powers; but, rather, whether it is reasonably foreseeable, at the time of making the contract, that a conflict will arise between the contract and the free exercise of the statutory power.

There appear to be no recent Irish authorities on this point. However, considering both the value set by the judiciary on justice to the individual, and the fact that contractual rights have been judicially regarded as an aspect of the property right,[76] it would seem likely that the restrictive attitude to the doctrine that statutory powers may not be fettered by contract, which is now adopted abroad, would be followed in Ireland.

As regards the context in which this doctrine would apply, it is

[73] [1921] 3 K.B. at 503.
[74] [1926] I.R. 517; See also pp. 407–408.
[75] For the foreign law, see P. W. Hogg, *Liability of the Crown in Australia, New Zealand and the UK* (Melbourne, 1971), Chap. 5; [1971] *Public Law* 288; de Smith, *op. cit.*, pp. 317–320; Craig, *op. cit.*, pp. 597–606.
[76] See, for example, *Condon* v. *Minister for Labour* [1981] I.R. 62 and *Hamilton* v. *Hamilton* [1982] I.R. 462.

clear that it could apply in either of two broad situations: first, as a defence to a breach of contract action brought against a public authority; secondly, to invalidate some administrative action which has been influenced by the supposed existence of a contract.

15. Delegatus non potest delegare

The general principle here is that a power must be exercised by the authority (*delegatus*) in which it has been vested by the legislature. It cannot be transferred (*delegare*) to any other person or body. In principle, the maxim applies to all types of decision, whether judicial, quasi-judicial, administrative, policy (discretionary) or even a court. However these propositions are subject to qualifications, first, in regard to Ministers (see *infra*) and, secondly, in that the courts may allow some latitude in the case of routine administrative matters.[77] Most significantly of all, the maxim is merely a rule of statutory construction, rather than a rule of law, and it has been said that:

> "Whether a person other than that named in the empowering statute is empowered to act will be dependent upon the entire statutory context, taking into account the nature of the subject matter, the degree of control retained by the person delegating and the types of person or body to whom the power is delegated."[78]

As a rule of statutory interpretation, the *delegatus* principle gives way before any express or implied indication to the contrary in the statute. A case in point occurred in *Ingle* v. *O'Brien*[79] which arose out of the revocation of the plaintiff's licence to drive taxis by a Garda Superintendent. The power of revocation is vested, by the relevant statutory regulations, in the Commissioner of the Garda

---

[77] *The State (Keller)* v. *Galway County Council* [1958] I.R. 142 at p. 148 (chief medical officer can delegate physical examination of applicant for a grant, but not duty of forming the necessary opinion as to whether the applicant was substantially handicapped). See also *Bridge* v. *R.* [1953] 1 D.L.R. 305; *Hookings* v. *Director of Civil Aviation* [1957] N.Z.L.R. 929. In the case of routine tasks taken by servants of the statutory authorities, foreign courts have sometimes achieved this result by characterising the situation as involving the creation of an agency and so evading the *delegatus* principle: see de Smith, *op. cit.*, pp. 301–303.

[78] Craig, *Administrative Law* (London, 1983) at p. 373.

[79] (1975) 109 I.L.T.R. 9. For a further example, see *The State (Fagan)* v. *Governor of Mountjoy Prison*, High Court, March 6, 1978 (delegation by Prison Governor to Deputy Governor held to be authorised under Rules for the Government of Prisons 1947).

Siochana. Pringle J. held that the function had been validly
delegated under a regulation which provided that "The functions
of the Commissioner . . . may be performed by an officer of the
Garda Siochane authorised by the Commissioner to perform such
functions." A second most important statutory exception enables
a Government order to be made on the request of a Government
Minister, delegating to his Minister of State all the Minister's
powers and duties under a particular act or, more narrowly, any
particular statutory power.[80]

Thirdly, at local government level, a county (or city) manager is
empowered to delegate any of his functions to an assistant county
(or city) manager, county secretary, town clerk, or officer
approved by the Minister for the Environment, as an approved
officer for the purposes of the delegation.[81]

16. Minister and civil servants

It would plainly be an impossible state of affairs if the law
required a Minister, even with the assistance of his Minister for
State, to keep in personal contact with each of the hundreds of
decisions taken in his Department each day. In most cases, the
delegatus doctrine can be side-stepped by regarding each civil
servant as the *alter ego* of the Minister at the head of the
Department, a fiction which is known as the "*Carltona* doctrine."[82]
(This arrangement is buttressed, in form anyway, by the notion
that the Minister bears political responsibility to the Dail and legal
responsibility, under the Ministers and Secretaries Act 1924, for
all actions going on within his department.[83])

However, recent Irish cases have developed a substantial

---

[80] Ministers and Secretaries (Amendment) Act 1977, s.2. See *e.g.* Public
Service (Delegation of Ministerial Functions) Order S.I. (1978
No. 117). See also *Geraghty* v. *Minister for Local Government* [1976] I.R.
153 at pp. 154, 160.
[81] County Management Act 1940, s.13; City and County Management
(Amendment) Act 1955, s.17; *Cassels* v. *Dublin Corporation* [1963] I.R.
193.
[82] *Carltona Ltd.* v. *Commissioners of Works* [1943] 2 All E.R. 560 at p. 563;
See also *Point of Ayr Colleries Ltd.* v. *Lloyd-George* [1943] 2 All E.R. 546;
Re Golden Chemical Products Ltd. [1976] Ch. 300 and *McKernan* v.
Governor of H.M. Prison [1983] N.I. 83.
[83] Even in Britain, there is said to be a narrow exception to the *Carltona*
doctrine in that in cases involving personal liberty, the responsible
minister must truly bring his mind to bear on the issue: Wade, *op. cit.*,
pp. 328–329; de Smith, *op. cit.*, pp. 307–309. But *cf.* the comments of
Hutton J. in *McKernan* v. *Governor of H.M. Prison* [1983] N.I. 83.

exception to the *Carltona* doctrine, which applies when the Minister is exercising a quasi-judicial function.

The leading case is *Geraghty* v. *Minister for Local Government (No. 2)*[84] which arose out of a planning appeal heard by the Minister (in the period before the creation of An Bord Pleanala). An oral inquiry was held by an inspector who was an official in the Department of Local Government. He made a report on the hearing, recommending that the appeal be rejected for reasons which he stated. This report was channelled through the routes normally followed by internal departmental documents and, as it went, gathered accretions of suggestions, comments and additional information from various civil servants. These included information which had been gained in another appeal from the same locality and suggested alternative reasons which might be given for rejecting the appeal. Eventually, the file reached the Parliamentary Secretary to whom the Minister's powers had been (properly) delegated and he rejected the appeal. According to both the High Court and the Supreme Court, there were two principal defects in this procedure. First, the *audi alteram partem* rule had been broken in that the plaintiff had no opportunity to know about or comment upon the additional material added to the report after the oral inquiry. Secondly, the fact that the inspector and other civil servants had given their views and that the Parliamentary Secretary appeared to have been influenced by them violated the *delegatus non potest delegare* principle. (Although there is no inevitable connection between the *delegatus* and constitutional justice principles, circumstances often arise in which both of them are engaged together.)

Before returning to enlarge on this second point, it ought to be noted that a significant "special case" occurs when the civil servant, whose participation in the decision has gone so far as to compromise the principle that the Minister himself must decide, is an inspector who is reporting back to the Minister after chairing an oral inquiry.[85] Such an inquiry may be part of the compulsory order procedure, under the Housing Act 1966; or in a planning appeal, before the establishment in 1977 of An Bord Pleanala). The reasons why this situation is significant are first, that it has often arisen in the case law in this general area, and secondly, that through his visits to the site, observation of witnesses' demeanour etc., an inspector, much more so than an ordinary departmental civil servant, has access to information and experience which could

---

[84] [1976] I.R. 153. *Geraghty* v. *Minister for Local Government (No. 1)* [1975] I.R. 300 dealt with state immunity from discovery: see pp. 401–406.

[85] Though *cf.* the comments of Henchy and Gannon JJ. in *Geraghty* v. *Minister for Local Government* [1976] I.R. at pp. 168 and 173.

not be made available to his Minister. In spite of this, Walsh J.
speaking *obiter*, for the Supreme Court, in the earliest case on this
topic, the interlocutory decision in *Murphy* v. *Dublin Corporation
(No. 1)*,[86] stated:

> " . . . [T]he inspector's function is to convey to the Minister, if
> not a verbatim account of the entire of the proceedings
> before him, at least a fair and accurate account of what
> transpired. . . . The inspector has no advisory function nor
> has he any function to arrive at *a preliminary judgment which
> may or may not be confirmed or varied by the Minister. . . . If the
> Minister is influenced in his decision by the opinions of the
> inspector, . . . the Minister's decision will be open to review*" (italics
> supplied).[87]

This passage was glossed by O'Keeffe P. in *Murphy* v. *Dublin
Corporation (No. 2)*[88] who said:

> "I do not think for one moment that [Mr. Justice Walsh]
> intended to indicate that the Minister should not receive in
> the report of an inspector holding an inquiry of this kind
> views of the inspector derived from the consideration of the
> evidence—views which the Minister might or might not
> accept."

There would certainly seem to be a difference between Walsh J.'s
view that where a minister's decision is influenced by an
inspector's opinion, it is open to review, and O'Keeffe P.'s
statement that a Minister "might or might not accept" an
inspector's opinion.

As stated already, *Geraghty* involved principally the participation
of departmental civil servants, rather than the inspector. However,

---

[86] [1972] I.R. 215.
[87] [1971] I.R. at p. 239. Murphy involved the Minister for Local
Government's decision on whether to confirm a compulsory purchase
order. However, it is accepted (see *e.g. Geraghty* v. *Minister for Local
Government* [1976] I.R. at p. 168 (Walsh J.)) that the inspector had the
same relation to the Minister in this situation as in a planning appeal.
Cf. Local Government (Planning and Development) Act 1976, s.23 of
which requires an inspector conducting an oral inquiry for the Minister
(or Bord Pleanala) to include a recommendation which must be
considered by the Minister (or Bord Pleanala).
[88] [1976] I.R. 144n. See the comments of O'Higgins J. on this point in
Geraghty v. *Minister for Local Government* [1976] I.R. 153 at p. 162. See
also *per* Henchy J. in *Murphy* v. *Dublin Corporation* [1976] I.R. 143 at
p. 150: "[I]t was for the Minister to reach his own decision, unfettered
by any conclusion the inspector may have reached but on the basis of
the same evidential material as was before the inspector."

the same broad issue is involved in either case, namely, where a decision is vested in a Minister, the extent to which he can be assisted by other persons. Different views on this were expressed in *Geraghty* (although these differences were of no significance, on the facts of the case). Walsh J. said that a Minister could not regard himself as bound even by the findings of fact, made by an inspector holding an oral inquiry. Henchy and Gannon JJ. each disagreed with this and also stated that the inspector could make (non-binding) recommendations as to the outcome which the Minister could take into account. In addition, they said that the Minister, as a lay-person, could obtain expert advice on technical (*e.g.* legal or planning) matters from his departmental civil servants or elsewhere.[89]

These differences are of considerable practical significance for upon their resolution turns the question of how much scope is to be allowed to a civil servant and how much time and attention a Minister may actually give to a case himself. The second practical question is what range of decisions attract the rule that it is the Minister himself who must decide. It seems probable from some discussion in the cases that the rule is confined to what are loosely called "quasi-judicial" decisions. This expression means conventionally, first, that the decision is governed by some fairly precise rules and secondly, that it affects some important individual right or interest. It is suggested that, in addition to compulsory purchase order confirmation and residual planning matters, the following types of decisions (some of which yield very few actual cases) fall within this category: decisions as to the superannuation rights of various categories of public servants (Minister for the Public Service)[90]; questions arising under any scheme of administering higher education grants (Minister for Education)[91]; appeals against refusal by a health board of registration as a food premises (Minister for Health)[92]; appeals against refusal by a local authority, of registration as a person who may carry on dairying (Minister for Agriculture).[93]

Finally, two fundamental criticisms of the *Murphy-Geraghty* line of authority may be suggested. First, the earliest judgment in

---

[89] [1976] I.R. at pp. 174–175 (Henchy J.) and 181–182 (Gannon J.).
[90] Superannuation and Pensions Act 1923, s.9. As with some of the other decisions mentioned in this catalogue, the Minister's decision is said to be "final." But at least where the Minister is exercising judicial functions under cover of Art. 37 this cannot preclude judicial review of his decision: *Tormey* v. *Att.-Gen.* [1985] I.L.R.M. 375 and see pp. 200–202.
[91] Local Authorities (Higher Education Grants) Act 1968, s.7.
[92] Health Act 1970, s.6(2).
[93] Milk and Dairies Act 1935, ss.21–23.

regard to the entire question of a minister's dual-personality, the interlocutory decision in *Murphy* v. *Dublin Corporation (No. 1)* involved the issue of executive privilege against the disclosure of documents. It was against this background that Walsh J. made a distinction, which was critical to his reasoning, between a Minister exercising an executive power, and, on the other hand, a Minister, as *"persona designata"* undertaking a quasi-judicial function with a duty to observe constitutional justice and confined executive privilege narrowly to the former function. In the context of the *delegatus* principle, different considerations apply; yet in *Murphy (No. 2)* and *Geraghty, Murphy (No. 1)* appears to have been treated as an authority, without regard to this significant shift in context.

Secondly, one ought to consider the policy underlying the decision in *Geraghty*. This can best be done by contrasting the views contained in the following quotations. In *Murphy*, Walsh J. stated:

> "[The Minister] is *persona designata* in that the holder of the office of the Minister for Local Government is the person designated for that function. If the Oireachtas had so enacted, the Act could just as easily have assigned the functions to the chairman of Coras Iompair Eireann or to the chairman of the Electricity Supply Board.[94]

He made similar comments in *Geraghty (No. 2)*:

> "The function of considering appeals which is conferred on the Minister as a designated person does not necessarily involve the planning, or any other section, of the Department of Local Government."[95]

By contrast, in *Bushell* v. *Secretary of State for the Environment* Lord Diplock said:

> "To treat the Minister in his decision-making capacity as someone separate and distinct from the department of government of which he is the political head and for whose actions he alone in constitutional theory is accountable to Parliament is to ignore not only practical realities but Parliament's intention. Ministers come and go; departments, though their names may change from time to time, remain. Discretion in making administrative decisions is conferred on a Minister not as an individual but as the holder of an office in which he will have available to him in arriving at his decision

---

[94] [1972] I.R. at p. 238. This passage was quoted with approval by O'Higgins J. in the High Court in *Geraghty*: see [1976] I.R. at pp. 160–161.

[95] [1976] I.R. at p. 189.

the collective knowledge, experience and expertise of all those who serve the Crown in the department of which, for the time being, he is the political head. The collective knowledge, technical as well as factual, of the civil servants in the department and their collective expertise are to be treated as the Minister's own knowledge, his own expertise. It is they who in reality will have prepared the draft scheme for his approval; it is they who in the first instance will consider the objections to the scheme and the report of the inspector by whom any local inquiry has been held and it is they who will give to the Minister the benefits of their combined experience, technical knowledge and expert opinion on all matters raised in the objections and the report. This is an integral part of the decision-making process itself; it is not to be equiparated with the Minister receiving evidence himself, expert opinion or advice from sources outside the department after the local inquiry has been closed."[96]

It may be that at some future date the Supreme Court will come to prefer the policy underlying the last quotation and to regard the present law as being unrealistic in that it imposes too much work on a single, non-expert human being.

17. Acting under dictation by another body

In the field next to the delegation of a decision by an authorised body to another body is a case in which the authorised body does take the decision in form, but in substance is merely rubber-stamping an instruction from another body.[97] A straightforward example of this occurred in *McLoughlin* v. *Minister for Social*

---

[96] [1981] A.C. 75 at p. 95. See also *McKernan* v. *Governor of H.M. Prison* [1983] N.I. 83, a case where an order authorising the solitary confinement of a prisoner was signed by a Minister of State. The relevant prison regulations required that the order be signed by either a member of the prison board of visitors, or the Secretary of State for Northern Ireland. Hutton J. (and affirmed by the Court of Appeal) rejected the argument that this was a matter which was peculiarly committed to the Secretary of State, saying that it was most unlikely that Parliament intended that a member of the board of visitors could sign an authority under the regulations, but that a Minister of State could not.

[97] The two classes plainly overlap. For instance, *Geraghty* v. *Minister for Local Government* [1976] I.R. 300 could have been classified under the present heading, but, as against this, it is usual for the "dictation" to emanate from an internal source. As it happened, the "advice" in *Geraghty* was from civil servants to their Minister. In any event, nothing turns on the distinction.

Welfare.[98] Here the substantive point which has already been discussed was whether the appellant solicitor, employed in the Chief State Solicitor's Office was to be classified as being in the employment of the State or of the civil service of the Government. The context in which this issue arose was that the appellant had claimed that he was not employed in the civil service of the State and accordingly was not an employed contributor for the purpose of making payments under the Social Welfare Act 1952. In deciding against the appellant, the appeals officer in the Department of Social Welfare said that he had received a minute from the Minister for Finance directing that the appellant was in the employment of the civil service of the government and that he believed that he was bound to adhere to the Minister's direction.[99] That belief was characterised by O'Daly J. (as he then was) in the Supreme Court as:

> " . . . [A]n abdication by him from his duty as an appeals officer. That duty is laid upon him by the Oireachtas and he is required to perform it as between the parties that appear before him freely and freely as becomes anyone who is called upon to decide on matters of right and obligation."[1]

[98] [1958] I.R. 1. Another aspect of the case is discussed at pp. 48–49. See also *H. Lavender & Co. Ltd.* v. *Minister of Housing* [1975] 1 W.L.R. 1231.

[99] See also *The State (Meade)* v. *Cork C.C.*, High Court, May 27, 1971 (local authority wrongly considering themselves bound by ministerial circular).

[1] [1958] I.R. at p. 12. The phrase "natural justice" is also used by O'Daly J., but it is submitted that the more appropriate analysis is that adopted in the text. *The State (Kershaw)* v. *Eastern Health Board* [1985] I.L.R.M. 235 would also appear at first sight to engage the principle against acting under dictation. But Finlay P. made it plain that such was not the case: "The Minister has, of course, in addition a general administrative function with regard to the administration of the scheme for supplementary benefits which he himself has prescribed in the Regulations of 1977. In so far, therefore, as the circulars issued on his behalf on 22 June 1983 form advice and guidance to health boards carrying out the National Fuel Scheme it is clearly a proper and valid administrative act" ([1985] I.L.R.M. at p. 239).

9 Constitutional Justice

Constitutional justice is an aspect of procedural law and procedural law looms especially large in the field of administrative law. The reason for this importance is that administrative law is directed to public authorities. One of the cardinal features distinguishing public authorities from the private person—so the theory runs—is that public authorities are taken to be non-partisan and open to persuasion provided that all the relevant facts and arguments are placed before them. With a fair procedure, all the relevant matters are more likely to emerge and to be properly weighted by the decision-maker. Accordingly there is a causative link between proper procedure and the quality of the decision. In short, "[t]he whole theory of 'natural justice' is that ministers, though free to decide as they like, will in practice decide properly and responsibly once the facts have been fairly laid before them."[1] There are other reasons too for the importance of procedure and we shall return to this question in part 6, *post*.

As a second preliminary, it should be emphasised that constitutional justice does not comprehend the whole of procedural law in the field of public administration. For, in addition, each decision may have its own particular procedural rules. Some examples of such rules have already been given in Chapter 7 (under the heading of Mandatory and Directory Provisions for procedural rules provide some graphic examples of this dichotomy). The special feature of constitutional justice is that it applies over such a wide field of public decision-making.

1. Constitutional justice and natural justice

Natural justice
The best way of explaining constitutional justice is to begin with natural justice, which consists of two fundamental procedural

---

[1] Wade, "Quasi-Judicial and its Background" (1949) 10 Camb. L.J. 216 at p. 117.

rules, namely: that the decision-maker must not be biased; and, secondly, that anyone who may be adversely affected by a decision should not be condemned unheard; rather he should have the best possible chance to put his side of the case.

The title, in particular the epithet "natural," has attracted a certain amount of attention. According to Costello J. in *Nolan* v. *Irish Land Commission*:

> " ... [T]he adjective 'natural' before justice was not used to describe justice by reference to man in a state of nature or in primitive society. Rather it has been employed as part of a phrase which developed from a philosophical view of man's nature as that of a being endowed with reason and capable of ascertaining objective moral values. As pointed out by de Smith (Judicial Review of Administrative Action) [now 4th Ed. at p. 157]: 'The term expresses the close relationship between the common law and moral principles and it has an impressive ancestry'."[2]

This quotation draws attention to the universality of natural justice which can also be illustrated by the inclusion of the two principles in the European Convention of Human Rights, which provides that: "In the determination of his civil rights and obligations or of any criminal charges against him, everyone is entitled to a fair and public *hearing* within a reasonable time by an *independent and impartial* tribunal established by law."[3] In similar vein to the quotation from *Nolan*, O'Higgins C.J. has remarked:

> "The application of [the principles of natural justice] to the different situations which competing interests in society create has never been capable of precise definition. For that reason they have been criticised and even rejected by those who believe precise definition to be the *sine qua non* of true law. They came to be recognised, however, at a time when society was emerging from the rule of might and force and when men looked for the protection of their rights in the oral sphere of justice and fairness. Natural justice, imprecise though the term may be, was something which came to be regarded as each man's protection against the arbitrary use of power."[4]

---

[2] [1981] I.R. 23 at p. 34. Costello J. was countering criticism of the term contained in *Green* v. *Blake* [1948] I.R. 242.

[3] Art. 6(1). See *Campbell* v. *United Kingdom* (1985) 7 E.H.H.R. 165 (guarantee of Art. 6(1) extends to adjudications of Prison Boards, at least in serious disciplinary cases).

[4] *Garvey* v. *Ireland* [1981] I.R. 75 at p. 91.

Constitutional justice: "... more than the two well-established principles ... "

In 1965, natural justice in Ireland was reincarnated as constitutional justice, in a seminal *obiter dictum*:

> "In the context of the Constitution, natural justice might be more appropriately termed constitutional justice and must be understood to import more than the two well-established principles that no man shall be judge in his own cause, and *audi alteram partem*."[5]

There has been a striking lack of progress in divining what these additional factors comprise and the courts have sometimes appeared reluctant explicitly to recognise this reservoir of due process (possibly because of the width of natural justice *simpliciter*). Take, for instance, *O'Domhnaill* v. *Merrick*[6] a personal injuries claim which arose from an accident occurring when the plaintiff was three, although the proceedings were not instituted until some sixteen years later. Although the action remained within the limits fixed in the Statute of Limitations 1957, the Supreme Court struck out the action. Speaking for the majority, Henchy J. said:

> "After due regard to all relevant factors, I am driven to the conclusion that not only was the delay in this case inordinate and inexcusable, but that there are no countervailing circumstances which would justify a disregard of that delay. I consider that it would be contrary to natural justice and an abuse of the process of the courts if the defendant had to face a trial in which she would have to try to defeat an allegation of negligence on her part in an accident that would have taken place 24 years before the trial and a claim for damages of which she first learned 16 years after the accident. Apart from the personal unfairness that such a trial would thrust on the defendant, I consider that a trial after such a remove in time from the cause of action would be essentially unfair for being incompatible with the contingencies which insurers of motor vehicles could reasonably be expected to provide against. While justice delayed may not always be justice denied, it usually means justice diminished. ... For a variety of reasons, a trial in 1985 of a claim for damages for personal injuries

[5] *Per* Walsh J. in *McDonald* v. *Bord na gCon* [1965] I.R. 217 at p. 242. For a discussion of the significance of these remarks, see Casey, "Natural and Constitutional Justice—The Policeman's Lot Improved" (1979–80) 2 D.U.L.J. (n.s.) 95 and Hogan, "Natural and Constitutional Justice: *Adieu* to *Laissez-Faire*" (1984) 19 Ir.Jur.(n.s.) 309.

[6] [1984] I.R. 151.

sustained in a road accident in 1961 would be apt to give an unjust or wrong result. . . . "[7]

Although the judge was not completely explicit and did not mention "constitutional justice', *eo nomine*, one may probably take the factors which influenced him as being wider than merely the defendant's difficulty in preparing his case after so many years of delay and thus as ranging beyond the traditional scope of the *audi alteram partem* rule and drawing on the additional element in constitutional justice.

The same judge appears to have applied similar principles in *O'Keefe* v. *Commissioners of Public Works*.[8] In this case, the plaintiff sought to bring an action for damages in respect of an industrial accident which had occurred some twenty-four years earlier. Although a plenary summons had been issued within the three-year limitation period, the plaintiff took no steps to proceed with the action until some seventeen years later. During that period he had accepted a lump sum compensation from the defendants in discharge of all liability under the Workmen's Compensation Acts. Henchy J. took the view that the plaintiff should be estopped from proceeding with his claim, as a hearing in these circumstances would be contrary to natural justice:

"Natural justice requires that both parties to an action be heard before the decision can be said to have legal validity. Where one party, by his words or conduct . . . has put it beyond the capacity of that other party to be effectively heard, in the sense of presenting the potentially successful case which his opponent's conduct has put beyond his reach, the court will hold the party thus in default to be estopped from bringing the matter to a hearing. The reason is that a hearing in those circumstances would lack the mutality and fairness which are necessary for the due administration of justice."

The plaintiff's conduct here would not amount to a breach of *audi alteram partem* in the accepted common law sense of that term. Once again, Henchy J. appears to have drawn on constitutional principles of fair procedures in order to defeat the plaintiff's claim.

There are also a number of other procedural safeguards which are candidates for inclusion under the umbrella of constitutional justice. For example, in *M.* v. *M.*,[9] Henchy J. stated a trial judge was not entitled to disregard "the corroborated and unquestioned

[7] *Ibid.* at pp. 157–158.
[8] Supreme Court, March 24, 1980.
[9] Supreme Court, October 8, 1979.

evidence of witnesses." To do so was not in accordance with the proper administration of justice. The same judge expressed doubt in *N. v. K.*[10] as to whether the court had jurisdiction to grant a decree of nullity in cases where the child of the marriage was not separately represented:

> "[I]f a decree of nullity is to be granted, the automatic and inexorable consequence will be that this child will lose her status of legitimacy and be condemned, unheard, to illegitimacy, with all the legal disability and social stigma attached to that state. The point has not been argued ... but I must confess to an uncertainty whether, having regard to the requirements of basic fairness or natural justice, and other dictates of constitutional propriety, it is within the judicial competence to issue a decree of nullity in the circumstances of this case."[11]

Other aspects of constitutional justice which may achieve judicial recognition include a right to a reasonably prompt decision; a right to have an administrative decision based on adequate probative evidence[12]; or that the burden of proving facts which, if established, would lead to a person being deprived of his livelihood, should be beyond reasonable doubt.[13] It would also seem that an infringement of the constitutional right to fair procedures is actionable where this causes loss and damage.[14] At common law, a breach of natural justice was not of itself tortious.[15] Rather surprisingly, however, in view of the position in other jurisdictions, it has been held that constitutional justice does not require—in the absence of a statutory requirement[16] that an

[10] [1986] I.L.R.M. 75.

[11] *Ibid.* at p. 88.

[12] *M.* v. *M.*, Supreme Court, October, 8 1979; *R.* v. *Deputy Industrial Injuries Commissioner, ex p. Moore* [1965] 1 Q.B. 456; *Mahon* v. *Air New Zealand Ltd.* [1985] A.C. 808. But *cf. The State (Power)* v. *Moran*, High Court, February 2, 1976; *The State (Shinkaruk)* v. *Carroll*, High Court, December 15, 1976 and see further at pp. 191, 196.

[13] *O'Donoghue* v. *Veterinary Council* [1975] I.R. 398 at p. 404.

[14] *Meskell* v. *C.I.E.* [1973] I.R. 121; *Kearney* v. *Ireland*, High Court, March 13, 1986. The wrong need only amount to an unjustified infringement of a constitutional right; it need not rank as a recognised tort.

[15] *Dunlop* v. *Woollahra M.C.* [1982] A.C. 158.

[16] *e.g.* Local Government (Planning and Development) Act. 1963, s.26(8). See *Killiney & Ballybrack Residents Assoc.* v. *Minister for Local Government*, Supreme Court, April 24, 1978.

administrative body give reasons for its *final*[17] decisions.[18] In any event, it is suggested that it would be better to confine constitutional justice to procedural safeguards, and not to stretch it so that it encompasses substantive rights, lest it become too imprecise a concept.[19]

Foundation in the Constitution

There is another point of contrast between constitutional and natural justice, namely that natural justice remains a mere common law (and therefore rebuttable) presumption to be applied, in appropriate contexts, in the interpretation of statutes. By contrast, constitutional justice is judicially regarded as implicit in Article 40.3 of the Constitution.[20] The reasoning seems to be that words like "respect" and "protect" . . . from unjust attack in Article 40.3 refer not only to substantive protection but also mean that even where substantive interference is permitted, it must be accompanied by a fair procedure. This difference in the sources of constitutional and natural justice is important. A British statute can if it uses clear enough words, exclude the rules of natural justice because of the absence of a written constitution.[21] By

---

[17] As contrasted with the duty to give reasons for a provisional decision which may arise as part of the *audi alteram partem* rule: see pp. 258–260.

[18] *Kiely* v. *Minister for Social Welfare (No. 2)* 1977 I.R. 267 at p. 274; *The State (Cole)* v. *Labour Court* (1984) 3 J.I.S.L.L. 128; *The State (Kenny & Hussey)* v. *An Bord Pleanala*, Supreme Court, December 20, 1984.

[19] In *The State (Gleeson)* v. *Minister for Defence* [1976] I.R. 280 at p. 295 Henchy J. defined constitutional justice very widely to include a number of constitutional guarantees some of which are peculiar to criminal courts (*e.g.* the right to jury trial) and some of which are substantive (*e.g.* that unconstitutional laws should not be applied). He then commented: "Because of the wide scope of such constitutional guarantees . . . a plea of denial of constitutional justice lacks the correctness and particularity necessary to identify and bring into focus the precise constitutional issue which is being raised." However, this restrictive view of constitutional justice has largely fallen into disfavour: see Hogan, "Natural and Constitutional Justice: *Adieu to Laissez-Faire*" (1984) 19 Ir.Jur.(n.s.) 309.

[20] *Re Haughey* [1971] I.R. 217; *Kiely* v. *Minister for Social Welfare (No. 2)* [1977] I.R. 267; *Garvey* v. *Ireland* [1981] I.R. 75.

[21] See *e.g.* *O'Brien* v. *Bord na Mona* [1983] I.R. 255 at pp. 270–271 where Keane J. held that an enactment which created a situation where the decision maker was a judge in his own cause would conflict with the constitutional guarantee of fair procedures, unless a different form of procedure was not practicable. By contrast in *Bushell* v. *Environment Secretary* [1981] A.C. 75 the fact that the Minister was the person to consider objections to a provisional motorway route he himself had

contrast, an Irish statute attempting to exclude the rules of constitutional justice in a situation where they would be appropriate would be unconstitutional. Moreover, even where no such clear-cut question has been involved the Irish judges have given constitutional/natural justice a keener cutting edge than have their British counterparts.[22] They have been prepared not only to strike down decisions for breach of constitutional justice but also, on the positive side, to suggest improvements in procedure which would meet the requirements of constitutional justice. For example, in *Nolan* v. *Irish Land Commission*, the Supreme Court upholding the High Court, granted an injunction restraining the hearing of objections by the Land Commission to the compulsory acquisition of the plaintiff's land unless discovery and inspection of the Commission's documents were allowed. Costello J. in the High Court gave an explanation as to how the procedure should operate in this novel setting and this advice was approved in the Supreme Court. The same trend was manifest in the following extract, which has frequently been adopted in later cases, from Walsh J.'s judgment in *East Donegal Co-Operative Ltd.* v. *Attorney-General*:

> "The presumption of constitutionality carries with it not only the presumption that the constitutional construction is the one intended by the Oireachtas but also that the Oireachtas intended that proceedings, procedures, discretions and adjudications which are permitted, provided for, or prescribed by an Act of the Oireachtas are to be conducted in accordance with the principles of constitutional justice."[23]

Walsh J. went on to hold that constitutional justice would apply to

prepared was beyond challenge because *it had been clearly established by statute.* Keane J., commenting on *Bushell's* case, said ([1983] I.R. at p. 270) that it was "a reasonable inference" that the difference between the different approaches in the two jurisdications was to be explained "by the absence in England of a written constitution containing express guarantees of fundamental rights and fair procedures in the protection of those rights." See also *S.* v. *S.* [1983] I.R. 68.

[22] [1981] I.R. 23. For other examples, see *M.* v. *The Medical Council* [1984] I.R. 485; *O'Donoghue* v. *Veterinary Council*[1975] I.R. 398.

[23] [1970] I.R. 317 at p. 341. For a similar approach, see, *e.g. Hogan* v. *Minister for Justice*, High Court, September 8, 1976; *Loftus* v. *Att.-Gen.* [1979] I.R. 221; *O'Brien* v. *Bord na Mona* [1983] I.R. 255 and *McCann* v. *Racing Board* [1983] I.L.R.M. 67.

an application to the Minister for Agriculture for a mart licence,
under the Livestock Marts Act 1967, even though the wording of
the Act would seem on the *expressio unius exclusio altero* principle
of statutory interpretation, to militate against this result.

A number of cases involving court procedure further illustrate
the potency of constitutional justice. The first is *S.* v. *S.*,[24] in which
the High Court, in the name of "constitutional entitlement to fair
procedures," uprooted the long-established common law rule in
Russell v. *Russell*.[25] This rule, whose policy was to maintain the
unity of the family, excluded any evidence from a wife which
would tend to prove that a child born to her during wedlock was
not the child of her husband. Again, in *O'Domhnaill* v. *Merrick*[26] the
Supreme Court held, in effect, that notwithstanding the existence
of the Statute of Limitations fixing precise time limits, the court
retained an inherent power to stay proceedings, where the passage
of time could be taken to work an injustice. Finally, in *The State
(McKeown)* v. *Scully*,[27] a recent case on the powers of a coroner,
O'Hanlon J. said:

> "If this construction of [the Coroners Act 1962, s.30] is
> permissible for a coroner's jury to bring in a verdict of
> suicide, then I would hold that there was a departure from the
> rules of natural and constitutional justice in the present case
> in failing to give the widow and deceased of the next of kin
> any opportunity to be heard before this very grave and
> damaging finding which was made against the deceased
> husband of the prosecutor. Had such opportunity been given
> they could reasonably have sought leave to be represented at
> the inquest, to have the witnesses cross-examined on their
> depositions, to address the jury; and to offer to make available
> to the coroner further evidence which might be of assistance
> at the inquest."

Although constitutional justice has been grounded in Article
40.3 of the Constitution which confers rights explicitly on
"citizen[s]" nevertheless it has been held by Barrington J. in *The*

---

[24] [1983] I.R. 68. This case is an example of where a rule of law (albeit a
rule of law deriving from the common law rather than statute law)
which violated the principles of natural justice was held to be
unconstitutional.
[25] [1924] A.C. 687.
[26] [1984] I.R. 151.
[27] [1986] I.L.R.M. 133 at p. 135.

State (McFadden) v. *The Governor of Mountjoy Prison* [No. 1],[28] (a case arising out of extradition proceedings) that the duty to observe "basic fairness of procedures" applies even where aliens are involved. The reason according to Barrington J. is that:

> " . . . [W]hen the Constitution prescribes basic fairness of procedures in the administration of the law, it does so not only because citizens have rights, but also because the courts in the administration of justice are expected to observe certain forms of due process enshrined in the Constitution. Once the courts have seisin of a dispute, it is difficult to see how the standards they should apply in investigating it should, in fairness, be any different in the case of an alien than those to be applied in the case of a citizen."[29]

Applies to all three arms of government

Whilst it is true that most constitutional justice cases emanate from the executive branch of government, it is an aspect of the rules' universality that they can apply, in appropriate circumstances, to each of the three arms of government: legislature; judicature; or executive.

The rules of constitutional justice regulate decisions affecting individuals directly and these are just the sort of decisions which are usually not taken by the Oireachtas. However, in appropriate circumstances constitutional justice has been extended even to the Oireachtas, as was demonstrated in the multi-faceted case of *Re Haughey*.[30] The aspect of the case which is relevant here is that it applied the *audi alteram partem* rule to an investigation by a committee of the legislature (specifically, the Dail Public Accounts Committee).

At the opposite pole from the legislative function is the judicial function, which deals almost exclusively with individual decisions. But here procedure is regulated by a minute, specialised code of procedural and evidential law. In addition, fair procedure in the courts is underpinned by such specialised constitutional provisions as Articles 38.1, 34.1, as well as 40.3.[31] This law is inspired by the same policy which underlies constitutional justice and for this reason, constitutional justice in the executive field often draws on

---

[28] [1981] I.L.R.M. 113.
[29] *Ibid.* at p. 122.
[30] [1971] I.R. 217.
[31] Art. 38.1 provides that "No person shall be tried on any criminal charge save in due course of law." Art. 34.1 states that "Justice shall be administered in courts established by law. . . . "

the concepts from the judicial field, as unspoken major premises. However, it is not usual to classify procedural law or the law of evidence as part of constitutional justice. Nevertheless, constitutional or natural justice has occasionally been invoked *eo nomine*, to augment procedural law. Examples which have been mentioned already, include *O'Domhnaill*, *O'Keefe* and *McKeown*.[32] In addition, it is likely that in suitable cases, constitutional justice could be used as a device with which to extirpate some of the less justifiable results of the rule excluding hearsay evidence or to supply the omission of the Rules of Court which provide no system of discovery of documents before the District Court.[33] Such examples draw attention to the connection which exists between the principles of constitutional justice and the right of access to the courts, a continium which was acknowledged in the following passage from *S. v. S.*:

> "The combined effect of Articles 34.1, 38.1 and 40.3 of the Constitution] appears to me to guarantee (*inter alia*) something equivalent to the concept of 'due process' under the American Constitution in relation to causes and controversies litigated before the Court. . . . Just as the parties have a right of access to the courts when this is necessary to defend or vindicate life, person, good name or property rights, so they have *a constitutional right to fair procedures* when they get to court. . . . Because the rule in *Russell* v. *Russell* ran counter to [the] paramount public policy [of ascertaining truth and doing justice] and was calculated to defeat the due and proper administration of justice, I would hold that it ceased to have legal effect in the State after the enactment of the Constitution in 1937."[34]

Nomenclature

At least two, and possibly three, different judicial attitudes to the relationship between constitutional and natural justice have

---

[32] See also *The State (Buchan)* v. *Coyne* [1936] I.R. 485; *The State (Killian)* v. *Minister for Justice* [1954] I.R. 207; *The State (Walshe)* v. *Murphy* [1981] I.R. 275 and *The State (O'Regan)* v. *Plunkett* [1984] I.L.R.M. 347. See further at pp. 238, 242–243.

[33] The practical effect of *Nolan* v. *Irish Land Commission* [1981] I.R. 23 has been to provide for a system of discovery of documents before administrative tribunals. And see the comments of Henchy J. in *N.* v. *K.* [1986] I.L.R.M. 75 to the effect that constitutional justice may require separate representation for children in appropriate cases where their welfare is at stake.

[34] [1983] I.R. 75 at p. 80 (O'Hanlon J.).

emerged. The first takes the view that constitutional justice only applies where a possible breach of some constitutionally-protected interest, for example, a property right, is involved, whereas natural justice continues to exist to protect other, rights or privileges created by statute, common law or contract.[35] A further refinement on this attitude has it that whilst constitutional and natural justice should be distinguished as indicated, even natural justice should be read in the light of the Consitution, thereby giving rise to the dual concepts of constitutional justice and constitutionalised natural justice.[36] The other, simpler view is that constitutional justice has succeeded and subsumed natural justice. As McCarthy J. observed: "In my view the two principles of natural justice as they pre-existed the Constitution are now part of the human rights guaranteed by the Constitution."[37]

Both constitutional and natural justice are elastic and vague concepts and the differences between them contemplated in the seminal passage from *McDonald*, quoted *supra* have not developed significantly. Indeed in a number of cases, the phrase "constitutional and/or natural justice" has been used indiscriminately[38] and other judgments have betrayed impatience with the subtle difference between the two concepts.[39] Accordingly, we feel that a split-level procedural system only creates complication without adding anything to the stock of legal ideas or rules. Thus we shall normally speak only of constitutional justice and will take it that such variants as "basic fairness of procedures"[40] are synonymous with constitutional justice. To the extent that ideas peculiar to court procedure, such as "due process" go beyond constitutional justice we shall not be concerned with them in a book whose primary focus is government administration.

---

[35] *The State (Gleeson)* v. *Minister for Defence* [1976] I.R. 280; *Kiely* v. *Minister for Social Welfare* [1977] I.R.287; *The State (Donnelly)* v. *Minister for Defence*, High Court, October 8, 1979; *Ni Bheolain* v. *Dublin V.E.C.*, High Court, January 28, 1983.

[36] See *Gleeson*, *Kiely* and *Nolan* v. *Irish Land Commission* [1981] I.R. 23.

[37] *The State (Furey)* v. *Minister for Defence*, Supreme Court, March 2, 1984. This was the approach taken in *Garvey* v. *Ireland* [1981] I.R. 75 and *The State (Williams)* v. *Army Pensions Board* [1983] I.R. 308.

[38] *e.g. The State (Boyle)* v. *General Medical Services (Payment) Board* [1981] I.L.R.M. 14; *O'Brien* v. *Bord na Mona* [1983] I.R. 255.

[39] See *e.g.* the comments of Costello J. in *Doupe* v. *Limerick Corporation* [1981] I.L.R.M. 456 at 463 and *McHugh* v. *Garda Commissioner* [1985] I.L.R.M. 606.

[40] This was the language used by the Supreme Court in *Re Haughey* [1971] I.R. 217. In *S.* v. *S.* [1983] I.R. 68 at p. 80 O'Hanlon J. spoke of "a constitutional entitlement to fair procedures."

2. Nemo iudex in causa sua

Sources of bias

The principle that no person shall be a judge in his own cause is fundamental[41] and well-established in both public and judicial administration. Possible sources of bias are infinitely varied and the following list is certainly not exhaustive. Moreover, the list is only intended for descriptive purpose since no legal consequences turn on the particular pigeon-hole to which a case is allocated:

(i) **Material interest.** The most obvious source of bias is financial (or material) interest of which *The People (Attorney-General)* v. *Singer*[42] is a straightforward example. In this case, the Court of Criminal Appeal ordered a re-trial on a fraud charge because the foreman of the jury had been an investor in the company which was the vehicle for the alleged fraud and was thus one of the victims. Interest was also found to have been present in *Connolly* v. *McConnell*,[43] a case arising out of the dismissal of a general secretary of a trade union. This dismissal was found to be void, as some of the members of the union's executive council had financial and other interests in the outcome of the disciplinary hearing.

(ii) **Personal attitudes, relationships, beliefs.** Bias may arise from the decision-maker's personal attitudes, relationships, or beliefs in the case. In a number of clear cases personal hostility has been found to be present. For example, in *R. (Donoghue)* v. *Cork County JJ.*[44] a conviction imposed by a magistrate who had remarked shortly after the case that he "would not leave any member of the [accused's] family in the district" was quashed on

---

[41] To impute bias against a judge may amount to a contempt of court: *Att.-Gen.* v. *Connolly* [1947] I.R. 213; *The State (D.P.P.)* v. *Walsh* [1981] I.R. 412; *R.* v. *Editor of New Statesman, ex p. D.P.P.* (1928) 44 T.L.R. 301. See Walker, "Scandalising in the Eighties" (1985) 101 L.Q.R. 359.

[42] [1975] I.R. 408n. (decided in 1963).

[43] [1983] I.R. 172. Griffin J. stated that material interest in the outcome of the case was not confined to pecuniary interests. Interest was found not to exist on the facts in *The State (Divito)* v. *Arklow U.D.C.* [1986] I.L.R.M. 123, where the respondent's refusal of a gaming licence to the applicant company was under challenge. Henchy J. found that there were no "financial or other connections" between the council and a rival company such as "would be likely to deflect the council from fairness or even-handedness in their dealings with the applicant—or such as would be likely to lead a reasonable person to think that the Council would thus act."

[44] [1910] 2 I.R. 271.

this ground. Similarly, in *R. (Kingston) v. Cork County JJ.*[45] an evicted farmer brought charges of assault against the purchaser of the farm. The charges arose out of a boycott which had been imposed on the purchaser by the United Irish League. The purchaser was convicted of assault by a magistrates' bench of four, including two members of the League, who had attended the meeting where the decision to impose the boycott had been taken. The High Court had little difficulty in quashing the conviction. And in more recent times, Carroll J. set aside a dismissal of a fisheries inspector in *Heneghan v. Western Regional Fisheries Board*[46] where she found that the prime mover in the dismissal process had acted as "witness, prosecutor, judge, jury and appeal court."

A case of what, the Supreme Court held, may have appeared to an "unprejudiced onlooker" as personal involvement occurred in *The State (Hegarty) v. Winters.*[47] Here an arbitrator appointed under the Acquisition of Land (Assessment of Compensation) Act 1919 was assessing the amount of compensation to be awarded to the applicant land owner for damage done to his land by a county council. The arbitrator went to inspect the land himself and was accompanied by the county council engineer with nobody to represent the applicant. The court quashed the arbitrator's award. Equally, McMahon J. gave an instance of bias arising from the decision-maker's personal observation in *The State (Fagan) v. Governor of Mountjoy Prison.*[48] Here the validity of certain disciplinary punishments imposed by a deputy prison governor were under challenge:

> "If . . . the Deputy Governor had witnessed some of the events to which the charges related I could understand an objection to his sitting in judgment since it would be difficult for the prisoner to deal with and to be heard in relation to the impression of the facts which may have been formed by the Deputy Governor as distinct from the evidence given by prison officers at the inquiry."

However, McMahon J. ruled that this claim failed on its facts.

Another obvious category of bias would be party political advantage in the context of a Minister (usually the Minister for Environment) taking decisions in regard to elections. The point

---

[45] [1910] 2 I.R. 658. See also *R. (Harrington) v. Clare J.J.* [1918] 2 I.R. 116. For cases on the other side of the line, see *R. (Findlater) v. Dublin JJ.* [1904] 2 I.R. 75 and *R. (Tavener) v. Tyrone JJ.* [1909] 2 I.R. 763.
[46] [1986] I.L.R.M. 225.
[47] [1956] I.R. 320. For a more extreme example than *Hegarty*, see *The State (Horgan) v. Exported Livestock Insurance Board* [1943] I.R. 600.
[48] High Court, March 6, 1978.

was raised obliquely in *Dillon* v. *Minister for Posts and Telegraphs*[49] in which the plaintiff was a Dail candidate yet the Minister would not allow him to circulate his election brochure free of charge to the voters on the ground that some of the material which it contained did not relate to the election. Henchy J. alluded to the possibility of a conflict of interest in the following brief passage:

" ... [T]he expression 'matter relating to the election only' should be liberally construed. This is particularly so when, as in this case, the person seeking to block the free postal circulation of the plaintiff's election brochure is a member of the Dail and whose party leader is seeking re-election to the Dail in the same constituency as the plaintiff has chosen to contest."

Yet there is a presumption that judges and administrators will discharge their function fairly and impartially. Thus, it has been held that a member of a society for the prevention of cruelty to animals may hear a prosecution brought by a member of the society[50] and a tribunal of solicitors may sit in judgment on another solicitor.[51] Persons or bodies not exercising judicial powers are entitled to reach a provisional or tentative conclusion in respect of a dispute, and it will generally suffice if such a tribunal approaches its task with an open mind, and a "will to reach an honest conclusion after hearing what was urged on either side." This statement was made in *McGrath and O'Ruairc* v. *Trustees of Maynooth College*[52] in which two university lecturers were removed from office by the trustees of the seminary at which they taught. The plaintiffs had questioned certain aspects of Church teaching, and although the trustees were bound to have "firm views" on this question, and might very well "have had strong views," this would not have precluded them from giving a fair hearing. Moreover, as the plaintiffs had elected not to attend the hearing, the court would not listen to any complaints concerning the impartiality of the trustees. The outcome was different in *The*

---

[49] Supreme Court, June 3, 1981. The type of point discussed in the text does not appear to have been canvassed in *The State (Lynch)* v. *Cooney* [1982] I.R. 337.

[50] *R.* v. *Deal JJ.* (1881) 45 L.T. 439. See also *Allison* v. *General Medical Council* [1894] 1 Q.B. 750.

[51] *Re Solicitors Act 1954* [1960] I.R. 239. However, in other cases there is a statutory disqualification in cases of personal interest: see *e.g.* s.155 of the Income Tax Act 1967 (special commissioner for income tax disqualified from adjudicating on his own personal tax liability).

[52] Supreme Court, November 1, 1979. See also *R. (Campbell College)* v. *Department of Education* [1982] N.I. 26; *Re Wislang* [1984] N.I. 69.

State (McGeough) v. *Louth C.C.*[53] where the applicant complained of
a county manager's refusal to give his consent to the sale of a
labourer's cottage. This consent was required by the Labourer's
Act 1936. It was clear that the county manager disapproved of the
sale of such cottages; indeed the refusal of the present application
was the twelfth consecutive refusal. The manager's refusal was
struck down on the grounds, of *inter alia*, bias. It may be possible
to reconcile *McGeough* with *McGrath and O'Ruairc* on the grounds
that first, the county manager had gone beyond the stage of
holding "firm views" to the point of no longer having an "open
mind." Secondly, the plaintiffs in *McGrath and O'Ruairc* had
submitted to this contractual jurisdiction, whereas in *McGeough*
the county manager had been invested with statutory powers
which he was bound to exercise fairly.

(iii) Loyalty to the institution. It might be anticipated that the
servants of an institution might be so committed to the objectives
of that institution, that they might be incapable of holding the
balance fairly between these objectives and other interests. Such
an argument has been rejected by Keane J.:

> "It would be manifestly impossible for [public bodies] to
> discharge their particular responsibilities in an efficient and
> sensible manner if every such decision could be successfully
> challenged by a litigant on the ground that the official who
> made it was actuated by a conscientious desire to advance the
> authority's interests rather than a spirit of judicial detach-
> ment. . . . [A] decision is not vitiated simply because the
> official who made it can be said to have a natural bias in
> favour of advancing the interest of the authority whose
> interest he is there to serve; but if, in addition, he exercises an
> administrative discretion 'capriciously, partially or in a mani-
> festly unfair manner' his action would be restrained and
> corrected by the Courts."[54]

The same argument was also rejected by Costello J. in *The State
(McEldowney)* v. *Kelliher*[55] a case in which the applicant had been
refused a permit to collect moneys from the public under the
Street and House to House Collections Act 1962. He had then

---

[53] (1973) 107 I.L.T.R. 13. On the question of a closed mind, see *Franklin*
v. *Minister for Town and Country Planning* [1948] A.C. 87.
[54] *O'Brien* v. *Bord na Mona* [1983] I.R. 255 at p. 269, quoting O'Higgins
C.J. in *Loftus* v. *Att.-Gen.* [1979] I.R. 229. See also *Collins* v. *County Cork
V.E.C.*, High Court, May 26, 1982.
[55] [1983] I.R. 289. See Hogan, "Judicial Independence and Mandatory
Orders" (1983) 5 D.U.L.J.(n.s.) 114. Costello J. was reversed by the
Supreme Court, but nothing was said on this point.

exercised his right to appeal to the District Court. Under the 1962
Act such an appeal must be disallowed if a senior Garda officer
states on oath that the proceeds of an election would be used for
the benefit of an illegal organisation.[56] In this case, the same
Superintendent who had refused the initial application for a
permit had also made such a sworn statement before the District
Court so that the appeal was disallowed. Costello J. rejected the
argument that the Superintendent was a judge in his own cause:

> "By making the statement on oath permitted by the [Act] the
> Chief Superintendent is acting as a public servant to protect
> the public interest as he sees it and he is not acting in a
> manner in which it can be said that he has a direct interest
> within the meaning of the rule [against bias]."[57]

(iv) Prior involvement and pre-judgment of the issues. This
source will often be interwoven with institutional bias, since prior
involvement will often arise because some institution is so
structured that the same person is concerned at two stages of the
decision-making process.

As a matter of principle it seems objectionable that a decision-
maker exercising quasi-judicial functions should sit with an
appellate body to hear an appeal against his own decision. Statutory
recognition of this is to be found in section 24 of the Courts of
Justice Act 1924[57] which prohibits the judge who heard a case from
sitting as a member of the court of appeal when the case at which he
presided is being considered. However, the majority of the judges
have taken a view which entails distinguishing between judicial and
administrative functions and applying a less strict form of the rule
against bias in the case of administrative functions.

This point is illustrated by the leading case of *O'Brien* v. *Bord na
Mona*.[58] The plaintiff challenged the compulsory acquisition of a
large portion of his farm. In the system of compulsory acquisition
created by the Turf Development Act 1946 both the drawing up of
a provisional list of land to be acquired and hearing of objections
to the inclusion of land on that list is vested in the defendant. It
was argued that the fact that the Board had drawn up the
provisional list meant that it might be thought of as prejudiced at
the second stage of the hearing, in that it would be predisposed to
uphold its own earlier decision. Following a review of the

---

[56] However, the section in question was found to be unconstitutional by
the Supreme Court on the grounds that it constituted an improper
invasion of the judicial power.

[57] [1983] I.R. 289 at p. 300.

[58] [1983] I.R. 255. See Coffey, "Procedural Curbs on powers of
Compulsory Acquisition" (1984) 6 D.U.L.J.(n.s.) 152.

provisions of the Act, the Supreme Court concluded that the Board's functions were administrative in nature as they entailed the "balancing of the desirability of the production of turf on the one hand, and the interest of an individual owner of land on the other...." Accordingly, whilst the Board could not act from "an indirect or improper motive or without due fairness of procedure," yet a less stringent standard was required than in the case of persons or bodies exercising judicial functions.

A similar distinction has been drawn by Murphy J. in *Collins* v. *County Cork Vocational Education Committee*.[59] The central point of the case was the plaintiff's claim that the resolution of the defendant body suspending him from his duties as headmaster of a vocational school was void. It was said that the Committee was biased because of the prior involvement by some members of the Committee in the case, and the existence of a conflict of interest. Murphy J. found it necessary to distinguish between:

> "[T]he application of the rules of natural justice where it is sought to set up an independent tribunal and other cases in which a particular function is by the terms of a statute, order or agreement conferred on *a designated body*. In these circumstances the body cannot decline to exercise its function and the most that justice can require, and all that fair play would dictate, would be that a member or members of a tribunal who had a particular interest of which their colleagues might not be aware should declare that interest before participating in any debate."

(By "designated body" Murphy J. appears to have meant a body which had an interest in the outcome of the proceedings.)

The judge observed that were the position otherwise then "the supervision and administration of any organisation involving a number of office holders would be quite impossible." While Murphy J. accepted that there was a likelihood of bias in the case of one member of the committee who had previously made representations about the plaintiff's conduct, and that the other members had been exposed to a relatively one-sided account of events, yet he concluded that:

> "[S]ome real or apparent conflict of interest may arise and must be accepted as inherent in the discharge of the duties of the statutory body.... Certainly there would be no justification or authority for transferring that function to another

---

[59] High Court, May 26, 1982. This decision was affirmed by the Supreme Court on March 18, 1983, but this point was not dealt with. For another authority along the same lines, see *McCann* v. *Racing Board* [1983] I.L.R.M. 67.

body even if it should have the merit of total independence
and a demonstrable freedom from any form of bias."

A point which is explicit in the quotations from *Collins*, and which
clearly must also have been a factor in *O'Brien*, is that, given the
respective statutory structure of the VEC and Bord na Mona some
appearance of posssible bias was inevitable. It is reasonable to
assume that underlying these two decisions was the doctrine of
necessity[60] which states that, in general, the no bias rule will not be
permitted to destroy the only tribunal with authority to decide an
issue.

This point is worth emphasising because the doctrine of
necessity was not always present in a series of cases involving the
Land Commission, in each of which, one of the Commissioners
who originally certified that the lands were suitable for acquisition
had sat as a member of the tribunal which decided whether to
confirm the original decision. There are four Commissioners, two
only of whom are involved at each stage so that, in most
circumstances, it is unnecessary for the same Commissioner to be
involved at both stages. In *Corrigan* v. *Irish Land Commission*[61] a
majority of the Supreme Court, with Kenny J. dissenting, ruled
that an appellant, who with full knowledge of the facts had made
no objection to the membership of an Appeal Tribunal composed
of the two lay Commissioners, who had certified that his land was
required for the relief of congestion, was estopped by his conduct
from raising the issue of bias.

Similar facts arose in *The State (Curran)* v. *Irish Land Commission*[62]
where a provisional list for the acquisition of lands for re-sale was
signed by two lay Commissioners. The appeal was heard by the two
other lay commissioners who had no prior involvement in the case.
These two commissioners could not agree on this matter, and they
felt obliged to reconstitute the appeal with three Commissioners,
one of whom would have to be one of the Commissioners who
originally issued the certificate. At this point, the appellant sought
an order of prohibition restraining the re-constituted panel from
hearing the appeal. Doyle J. adverted to the dissent of Kenny J. in
Corrigan, and noted that the majority of the Supreme Court in
that case did not rule on the question of bias. Nevertheless, he felt
obliged to defer to earlier rulings—which are not extant in written
form—of previous Judicial Commissioners upholding this practice. Similarly, in *Re Creighton's Estate*[63] where the same point was

[60] On this point, see further at pp. 255–257.
[61] [1977] I.R. 317.
[62] High Court, June 12, 1978.
[63] High Court, March 5, 1982.

at issue D'Arcy J. ruled that the matter was not *res integra* and reluctantly followed these earlier rulings.

Corrigan may be justified on the narrow ground of waiver and, on its particular circumstances, *Curran* may be supported by invoking the doctrine of necessity. However it seems, from the tenor of the judgment in these cases and from the decisions in *Re Creighton's Estate* and the other (unnamed) cases, that they were intended to lay down a broader rule, namely, that the no bias principle is not broken when a Land Commissioner is involved at the two stages, even though there are no extenuating circumstances. This line of authority is surprising and is certainly out of step with case law in other jurisdictions. For example, in *R. (Snaith) v. Ulster Polytechnic*[64] the applicant's dismissal was quashed as the members of a special committee who reached this decision sat with the Governors of the University when his appeal was heard.

Whatever about this criticism, the majority of Irish judges appear to have taken the view that to impose the rigorous standard of *nemo iudex in sua causa* which would be appropriate in court proceedings upon an administrative agency staffed almost exclusively by lay people might damage its efficient operation to no advantage. The minority view is represented by Kenny J. in *O'Donoghue v. Veterinary Council* and as the dissenting judge, in *Corrigan* and by Keane J. in *O'Brien* (reversed, on appeal). *O'Donoghue* took the form of an appeal by a veterinary surgeon to the High Court from a finding by the Veterinary Council that he had been guilty of unprofessional conduct. The first stage in the procedure for the investigation of alleged misconduct was an assessment by the Standing and Penal Cases Committee of the Council. Next, the Council convened a special committee of inquiry to investigate the allegations and it reached the unanimous opinion that the appellant was guilty. Finally, the Council considered the transcript of the evidence before the special committee and decided that the facts proved by the special committee had been proved to their satisfaction. The alleged misconduct consisted of duplicating blood tests for brucellosis and the real victim was the person paying for the tests, namely the Minister for Agriculture. However, the Attorney-General had advised the Minister not to act as complainant himself because some members of the Council were veterinarians employed in his Department. In these circumstances N, a member of the council agreed to allow his name to be used as complainant. He took no

[64] [1981] N.I. 28. See also *Cooper v. Wilson* [1937] 2 K.B. 309; *R. v. Kent Police Authority, ex p. Godden* [1971] 2 Q.B. 662; *R. v. Barnsley M.B.C., ex p. Hook* [1976] 1 W.L.R. 1052.

part in the case against the petitioner: the solicitors who nominally acted for him were in fact instructed by the registrar of the Council. However, N was one of the thirteen members of the Council present when the Council met and confirmed the special committee's decision and fixed the petitioner's punishment. In these circumstances, although the judge characterised N as a "nominal complainant" (the real complainant being the Minister) he held that the *nemo iudex* rule was violated and the Council's decision must be cancelled.

The outcome in *O'Donoghue* could be explained on the basis that the Veterinary Council was trying the appellant for a disciplinary offence and was, thus, following the authority of *Re Solicitors Act 1954*[65] administering justice, or at least discharging a quasi-judicial function. Such an analysis would bring *O'Donoghue* within the judicial/administrative functions dichotomy adopted in the *O'Brien-Collins* line of authority and thus reconcile *O'Donoghue* with the view adopted by the majority of judges. However, considering the tenor of the judgment in *O'Donoghue*—the emphasis laid on the need for justice to be seen to be done— coupled with Kenny J.'s dissent in *Corrigan*, it is more realistic to regard *O'Donoghue* as representing the minority view, namely that a more rigorous standard of *nemo iudex* should be adopted.

Test of bias

Two formulations of the text vie with each other in the common law world. The principal test is whether there is a "real likelihood" of bias. It should be noted that bias does not necessarily mean "a corrupt state of mind."[66] Bias may be conscious or unconscious, and the difference does not matter in this context. The alternative test is whether there is a reasonable suspicion of bias, and this stricter test is prompted by a desire on the part of its judicial adherents to maintain public confidence in the administration of justice (a consideration usually expressed as: "justice must not only be done; it must be seen to be done").[67]

From a logical perspective, it is difficult to see the difference between the two tests since the reasonable person would only suspect bias where there was a real likelihood of such occurring.

[65] [1960] I.R. 239.

[66] *R. (de Vesci)* v. *Queen's Co. JJ.* [1908] 2 I.R. 285.

[67] *R.* v. *Sussex JJ., ex p. McCarthy* [1924] 1 K.B. 256 and the dissenting judgment of Kenny J. in *Corrigan* v. *Irish Land Commission* [1977] I.R. 317. *Flynn* v. *D.P.P., cf.* [1986] I.L.R.M. 290 (appointment by D.P.P. of solicitor in full-time employment of Post Office in order to conduct the prosecution on indictment of postman charged with offences under the Postal and Telecommunications Services Act 1983; held, no likelihood that "justice would not be seen to be done.")

In fact, both tests really involve questions of degree, and the difference between them is slight. The reasonable suspicion test is largely concerned with outward appearances whereas the alternative test focuses on the court's own view of the realities of the situation. In most cases, however, it is probably correct to say that the courts have employed the reasonable suspicion test where they wanted to set a higher standard of impartiality. One such case may have been the *The State (Hegarty) v. Winters*[68]—the facts of which have already been recounted. In the High Court, Davitt P. upheld the arbitrator's award, saying that mere suspicion of bias was not enough. However, the award was quashed by the Supreme Court because the actions of the arbitrator in the words of Maguire C.J., might have given rise to the suspicion "that justice was not being done." Another example is provided by Kenny J.'s judgment in *O'Donoghue*[69] and (dissenting) in *Corrigan v. Irish Land Commission*[70] where he employed the test of reasonable suspicion, but, in contrast, one of the majority judges, Griffin J., spoke of the need to establish a real likelihood of bias. It is likely that the outcome of a case would depend less on which formula is used and more on such factors as the type of tribunal or administrative agency involved; the nature of the decision and the source of bias. Indeed, many of the most recent Irish cases have been decided without reference to either test.[71]

Rule of necessity

Throughout the common law world, the no bias rule gives way to necessity in that the disqualification of the adjudicator will not be permitted to destroy the only tribunal with power to decide.

[68] [1956] I.R. 320. For the facts of this case, see p. 247. See also *Killiney & Ballybrack Residents Assoc. v. Minister for Minister for Local Government* (No. 1) (1978) 112 I.L.T.R. 9 and *The State (Cole) v. Labour Court* (1984) 2 J.I.S.L.L. 128.

[69] [1975] I.R. at pp. 405–407, though there is some reference to the other test at p. 405.

[70] [1977] I.R. 317.

[71] See *e.g. The State (Curran) v. Irish Land Commission*, High Court, June 12, 1978; *Collins v. County Cork V.E.C.*, High Court, May 26, 1982; *O'Brien v. Bord na Mona* [1983] I.R. 255 (S.C.). In *The State (Divito) v. Arklow U.D.C.* [1986] I.L.R.M. 123, Henchy J. cited both tests without differentiating between them. The pre-independence cases had all plumped solidly for the "real likelihood" test: *R. (Ellis) v. Dublin JJ.* [1894] 2 I.R. 527; *R. (Findlater) v. Tyrone JJ.* [1909] 2 I.R. 763; *R. (Kingston) v. Cork JJ.* [1910 2 I.R. 658; *R. (de Vesci) v. Queen's Co. JJ.* [1908] 2 I.R. 285; *R. (Donoghue) v. Cork JJ.* [1910] 2 I.R. 272. There is some support for the suspicion test in *R.(Giant's Causeway Tram Co.) v. Antrim JJ.* [1895] 2 I.R. 603. See Sweeney, "Lord O'Brien's Doctrine of Bias" (1972) 7 Ir.Jur.(n.s.) 17.

256 *Constitutional Justice*

Consider, for example, *O'Byrne* v. *Minister for Finance*[72] in which the Supreme Court was obliged to pass judgment on the constitutionality of legislation rendering them (and their judicial brethren) liable to income tax on their salaries. In the High Court Dixon J. had proceeded with the case because there was no other tribunal to which under the law recourse could be had on a matter of this kind. Another example occurred in *Attorney-General (Humphreys)* v. *Governors of Erasmus Smith's Schools*,[73] a relator action involving a charitable trust administered by the defendants. Cherry L.J. commenced his judgment in the Irish Court of Appeal with the following apologia:

> "I am in a rather difficult position in adjudicating upon this case, in as much as I was Attorney-General when the writ was fiated. I would have preferred not to have been a member of the Court which had to decide this appeal, but as all the Judges of the Court except Lord Justice Holmes and myself are Governors of the Schools, a Court could not otherwise have been formed."[74]

Clearly the exemption will be strictly applied. For instance in *The State (Curran)* v. *Irish Land Commission*[75] (already described) in which the two lay Commissioners disagreed as to whether the provisional list should be confirmed so that it was necessary to re-list the case before a tribunal of three Commissioners given that there were only four Commissioners, this would have necessitated enlisting the services of one of the Commissioners who had signed the original acquisition certificate. The resulting decision was held valid. However Doyle J. opined, *obiter*, that the argument of necessity could not have excused the respondents in other circumstances since the Land Act 1950 allowed for the appointment of a temporary replacement where a lay commissioner is temporarily disabled from fulfilling his function on account of illness, absence "or other sufficient reason." Similarly, in *R. (Snaith)* v. *Ulster Polytechnic*[76] the dismissal procedure laid down in

---

[72] [1959] I.R. 1. In *Collins* v. *County Cork V.E.C.*, High Court, May 26, 1982. Murphy J. said that it was the "clear constitutional duty" of the Supreme Court to decide the *O'Byrne* case, "notwithstanding the interest which the members of the Court had in the outcome." See also Kelly, *The Irish Constitution*, (Dublin, 1984) at p. 226 for an explanation of the composition of the Supreme Court in *The State (Killian)* v. *Minister for Justice* [1954] I.R. 207.

[73] [1910] 1 I.R. 325. See also *Dimes* v. *Grand Junction Canal Co.* [1852] 3 W.L.C. 759; *Tolputt (N.) & Co. Ltd.* v. *Mole* [1911] 1 K.B. 836.

[74] [1910] I.R. 325. at p. 332.

[75] High Court, June 12, 1978. See also p. 252.

[76] [1981] N.I. 28.

the University statutes required, first that the initial decision should be taken by a sub-committee of eleven Governors and secondly, that on appeal, this decision must be upheld by a two-thirds majority of the Governors of whom there were forty-two in all. This arrangement plainly breached the "no bias" rule. Given the numbers of Governors involved at each level, it would have been very difficult if not impossible to work this system without some overlap of personnel. However, Hutton J. ruled that the necessity doctrine did not apply because the difficulty arose "from the scheme for termination of appointments which the Governors themselves had provided [in the statutes]" rather than from some externally-imposed instrument.

The rule of necessity is probably compatible with constitutional justice. For, as has been seen, constitutional justice is grounded in Article 40.3 the rights contained in which are not absolute but qualified by such phrases as "far as practicable" and "as best it may." And, as Murphy J. observed in *Collins* v. *County Cork Vocational Education Committee*, the courts cannot conjure up a new tribunal to take the place of a tribunal which has been held unconstitutional. Thus in some cases chaos would result if the *nemo iudex* rule were applied at its full width. On the other hand even, in England, the rule of necessity may not operate to enable an adjudicator to sit where actual bias can be shown and this qualification presumably applies in Ireland.[77]

Waiver

The right to object to a breach of the *nemo iudex* principle may be waived by a party with full knowledge of the facts which entitle him to raise a complaint.[78] The rule has been stated to be as follows:

> "[W]here a decision is challenged on the grounds of bias in the tribunal which gave it, [the] Court will not interfere where it appears that the fact or suspicion of bias was present to the mind of the challenging party at the hearing before the tribunal, and the point as to bias or suspected bias was not made by or on his behalf at the hearing by the tribunal."[79]

Exceptions to the rule exist where the complainant is so taken by surprise that he forgets to make an objection or where the court

---

[77] See de Smith, *op. cit.*, p. 276.
[78] See also at pp. 271–272 and *Corrigan* v. *Irish Land Commission* [1977] I.R. 317; *The State (Cole)* v. *Labour Court* (1984) 3 J.I.S.L.L. 128.
[79] *Per* Sir James Campbell C.J. in *R. (Harrington)* v. *Clare JJ.* [1918] 2 I.R. 116. See also *Corrigan's* case, *supra*, and *The State (Grahame)* v. *Racing Board*, High Court, November 22, 1983.

deems it proper to interfere because of the scandalous state of affairs involved.[80]

Bias is a particularly heinous defect (more so than failure to give a hearing) which may lead to a general erosion of confidence in public or judicial administration. In addition, bias or the possibility of bias, is a matter peculiarly within the knowledge of the deciding authority, giving rise in other contexts, to a duty to declare an interest.[81] Moreover, it is a particularly embarrassing matter for any other person to have to raise. Such factors underlay the dissenting judgment of Kenny J. in *Corrigan* v. *Irish Land Commission.* In his view, the no bias rule itself founded on public policy the desire to maintain and respect for, the administration of justice—and thus it is not competent for the parties to waive this rule. Nevertheless the prevailing consensus seems to be in favour, for practical reasons, of a wide concept of waiver in the context of bias. As Henchy J. remarked in *Corrigan* v. *Irish Land Commission*:

> "It would obviously be inconsistent with the due administration of justice if a litigant were to be allowed to conceal a complaint of that nature in the hope that the tribunal will decide in his favour, while reserving to himself the right, if the tribunal gives an adverse decision, to raise the complaint of disqualification."[82]

3. Audi alteram partem

Introduction

It is trite law that tribunals and administrative agencies are not required to follow the same strict rules of evidence and procedure as a court of law.[83] Thus, for instance, Henchy J. observed in *Kiely* v. *Minister for Social Welfare (No. 2)*:

> "Tribunals exercising quasi-judicial functions are frequently allowed to act informally to receive unsworn evidence, to act on hearsay, to depart from the rules of evidence, to ignore court room procedures, and the like."[84]

---

[80] *R. (Giants Causeway Tram Co.)* v. *Antrim JJ.* [1895] 2 I.R. 603; *R. (Poe)* v. *Close JJ.* (1906) 40 I.L.T.R. 121; *R. (Harrington)* v. *Clare JJ.* [1918] 2 I.R. 116.

[81] *R.(Malone)* v. *Tyrone JJ.* 3 N.I.J.R. 77; *The State (Cole)* v. *Labour Court* (1984) 3 J.I.S.L.L. 128 (*semble*).

[82] [1977] I.R. at p. 326.

[83] *McElroy* v. *Mortished*, High Court, June 17, 1949; *Fitzpatrick* v. *Wymes* [1976] I.R. 301; *The State (Boyle)* v. *General Medical Services (Payment) Board* [1981] I.L.R.M. 14; *Re McNally's Application* (1985) 3 N.I.J.B. 1.

[84] [1977] I.R. 276 at p. 281.

As might be expected from the inexact, pragmatic nature of
constitutional justice, the same standard does not apply in all areas
for "domestic and administrative tribunals take many forms and
determine many different kinds of issues and no hard and fast
rules can be laid down. . . . "[85] Again, there is no particular form in
which the case against a person must be communicated.[86] Whilst
informality is acceptable, there is a limit, as may be illustrated by
the facts which arose in *Nolan* v. *Irish Land Commission*[87] from
compulsory acquisition proceedings brought by the I.L.C. The
landowner claimed successfully that, as a matter of natural justice,
he had a right to inspect, in advance of the hearing by the lay
Commissioners, all the relevant documents in the defendants'
possession. Equally, in *The State (Gleeson)* v. *Minister for Defence*[88] it
was held that the summary dismissal of a member of the defence
forces was invalid. Henchy J. said that:

> "The requirements of natural justice imposed an inescapable
> duty on the army authorities, before discharging the prosecu-
> tion from the army for the misconduct relied on, to give him
> due notice of the intention to discharge him of the statutory
> reason for the proposed discharge, and of the essential facts
> and findings alleged to constitute that reason; and to give him
> a reasonable opportunity of presenting his response to that
> notice. All that was dispensed with in this case."[89]

A public authority's duty to give notice to the person who may be
affected by its decisions is not confined to details of the case
against him but extends to all relevant information. This was
illustrated in *The State (Williams)* v. *Army Pensions Board*,[90] which

[85] *Russell* v. *Duke of Norfolk* [1949] 1 All E.R. 109 at p. 118, quoted with
approval by Henchy J. in *Kiely* v. *Minister for Social Welfare* [1977] I.R.
267.
[86] See *e.g. The State (Curtin)* v. *Minister for Health* [1953] I.R. 93; *Doupe* v.
Limerick Corporation [1981] I.L.R.M. 456; *Ni Bheolain* v. *Dublin V.E.C.*,
High Court, January 28, 1983; *The State (Murphy)* v. *Kielt* [1984] I.R.
458.
[87] [1981] I.R. 23.
[88] [1976] I.R. 281. *Gleeson* was followed by Hamilton J. in *Hogan* v.
Minister for Justice, High Court September 8, 1976 and *The State (Furey)*
v. *Minister for Defence*, Supreme Court, March 2, 1984. *Gleeson*, was
however, distinguished in *The State (Duffy)* v. *Minister for Defence*,
Supreme Court, May 9, 1979 and *The State (Donnelly)* v. *Minister for
Defence*, High Court, October 8, 1979.
[89] *Ibid.* at p. 296. This passage was quoted with approval by Hamilton J. in
Hogan v. *Minister for Justice*, High Court, September 8, 1976.
[90] [1983] I.R. 308. See also *Maunsell* v. *Minister for Education* [1940] I.R.
213; *The State (Hussey)* v. *Irish Land Commission* [1983] I.L.R.M. 407;
The State (Boyd) v. *An Bord Pleanala*, High Court, February 21, 1983.

arose out of a claim by the applicant, who was an army widow, for
a pension. The susbstantive issue for decision by the Board was
whether her husband's death had been caused by service with a
United Nations force. His medical records, which were the most
important evidence in the case were in the custody of the Army
medical authorities. They were made available to, and considered
by, the Board, but the applicant was not allowed to see and
comment upon them. The Supreme Court held that the Board's
procedure was defective in that the applicant was not allowed
access to her husband's medical records. Henchy J. said:

> "Mrs. Williams was unfairly and unjustifiably prevented from
> rebutting, if that was possible, the conclusion reached by the
> Board. There may be cases where, for reasons such as state
> security or other considerations of public policy, the Board
> may be privileged from disclosing . . . the evidence before
> them. But this is not one of them. Counsel for the Board and
> the Minister has frankly and fairly conceded that the only
> reason for non-disclosure is the claim of the Board to be
> entitled to adhere to their settled practice."[91]

Two incidental comments may be made on this passage. First, the
two rules of constitutional justice often march together since the
failure to allow one side to put its case properly looks like bias.[92]
This presumably is the reason for the reference to "one-
sidedness" in the opening sentence of the passage. Secondly, the
last sentence in the passage quoted illustrates once more that the
staff of certain tribunals and administrative agencies have not
taken on board recent developments in the field of judicial review
of administrative actions. The individual affected is entitled to be
given information not only as to facts, but also as to any policy or
principles in the light of which his case is to be decided so as to
have "the opportunity of conforming with or contesting such a
principle or policy."[93]

We turn now to deal with more specific problems in the
operation of the *audi alteram partem* rule.

Information obtained outside the hearing

One form of denial of *audi alteram partem* occurs when although
some type of hearing (whether oral or written) has been allowed,

[91] [1983] I.R. at p. 313.
[92] See *per* O'Higgins C.J. in *Nolan* v. *Irish Land Commission* [1981] I.R. 23
at p. 36: "If one party comes to the hearing with the scales of justice
titled against them because of a procedural defect then the requirements of justice are not satisfied."
[93] *The State (McGeough)* v. *Louth C.C.* (1973) 107 I.L.T.R. 13 at p. 28 *per*
O'Daly J. See also *Mahon* v. *Air New Zealand* [1984] A.C. 808.

the decision-maker relies upon information or argument, which has been obtained outside that hearing and not disclosed to the party adversely affected by it. An illustration of this situation occurred in *Killiney and Ballybrack* v. *Minister for Local Government (No. 1)*[94] which arose from a planning appeal in which one of the factual issues was whether the sewerage disposal facilities in the area of the proposed development were already overloaded. There was a direct conflict of evidence at the oral inquiry as to whether raw sewerage was to be found on the foreshore near the development. After the inquiry had been concluded, the inspector examined the foreshore on his own and included a record of his findings in his report to the Minister who was, at the time of the case, responsible for deciding planning appeals. In the High Court, Finlay P. invalidated the Minister's decision because it was based on evidence which had not been disclosed to the party concerned, who thus had no opportunity to reply to it.

Another authority on the same issue is *Kiely* v. *Minister for Social Welfare (No. 2)*[95] which arose after the appellant's husband had suffered an accident at work which caused severe burns and led eventually to depression. A few months later he died and the appellant, K, claimed a death benefit under the Social Welfare (Occupational Injuries) Act 1966. Her claim was heard by the deciding officer and, on appeal, the appeals officer, in the Department of Social Welfare. Before the appeals officers, the principal issue—on which the medical expert giving evidence for K disagreed with the Minister for Social Welfare's medical adviser—was whether it was possible for a heart attack to have been caused by depression and, thus, to be connected with her husband's employment. This question was settled against K by the appeals officer and her arguments, on appeal to the High and Supreme Courts, all related to the procedure which he had followed. The first of the three grounds on which K succeeded before the Supreme Court involved a defect of this type. During the interval between the hearing of the appeal and the notification of the decision nearly two months later, the medical assessor wrote a letter to the appeals officer giving new evidence as to why depression could not cause a heart attack. This evidence included the bulletin of an international medical symposium and the practice of actuaries in assessing "life mortality in relation to

---

[94] (1978) 112 I.L.T.R. 9. The facts in *The State (Hegarty)* v. *Winters* [1956] I.R. 320 were similar to those of the *Killiney* case, save that in *Hegarty* the successful party had accompanied the decision-maker to the inspection, and, accordingly, The Supreme Court treated the case as an instance of the no-bias rule. See p. 247.

[95] [1977] I.R. 287.

anxiety states." In explaining why this evidence had been obtained
in breach of the rules of constitutional justice, Henchy J. stated
briefly that the assessor's function is "to act as a medical dictionary
and not as a medical report."

A third example of the same broad situation occurred in the
case of *Geraghty* v. *Minister for Local Government (No. 2)*[96] details of
which have already been given in a different context. The relevant
point here is that some of the information on which the decision
regarding the plaintiff's planning appeal had been taken was
material (reports on other appeals from the same area) which the
plaintiff had not seen and had not had the opportunity to
comment upon. This was one of the grounds on which the plaintiff
succeeded in having the decision quashed.

These cases illustrate a difficulty which is likely to loom large in
the future. It arises from a clash of cultures: on the one hand, a
large part of the *raison d'être* of specialised tribunals is that the
tribunal, unlike a court, has the ability and opportunity to
accumulate a wealth of specialised knowledge, information and
expertise. This indeed is said to be one of its advantages over a
court. To some extent, therefore a tribunal's decision is the result
not only of the evidence adduced by the parties at a particular
hearing; it is also the product of the tribunal's own expertise,
which has been brought to bear upon the evidence. However this
attitude collides with a rule which is central to all judicial or quasi-
judicial adjudication, namely that a decision must be made in
accordance only with evidence introduced at the hearing, tested by
the opposing sides and forming part of the record. And thus, the
categories of material of which judicial or official notice may be
taken is severely limited. Outside Ireland, various tests have been
proposed for resolving these two conflicting tensions.[97] First, a
distinction has been made according to whether a tribunal is using
its expertise as a substitute for evidence or only for the purpose of
evaluating the evidence that has already been presented. This test,
which of course involves a difficult question of degree, would seem
to accord with the distinction drawn, in *Kiely (No. 2)* between a
medical dictionary and a medical report. However, it might be
argued that the court misapplied its own test in *Kiely* in that a
medical report is personal to a specific patient, whereas the issue
in that case (whether depression is capable of causing a heart
attack) is a general question appropriately dealt with in a medical
dictionary. Another test, in use elsewhere, distinguishes between
the general accumulated experience of the decision-maker, which

[96] [1976] I.R. 153. See pp. 229–233.
[97] See de Smith's, *Judicial Review of Administrative Action* (London, 1980)
at pp. 203–207; Flick, *Natural Justice*, (Melbourne, 1979) Chap. 4.

need not be shown to an applicant, and material obtained from an identifiable source. Comparing the Irish cases with this test, it seems clear that *Killiney and Ballybrack (No. 1)* is in line with them, but it may be argued that the material relied on by the Minister and his department in *Geraghty (No. 2)* or by the appeals officer in *Kiely (No. 2)* might have been classified as "accumulated experience."

Right to an oral hearing, right to summon witness and right to cross-examine

Plainly whilst these issues may need to be considered independently, there is often a substantial connection between them. In any case with each of them, as with other aspects of the *audi alteram partem*, rule it may be misleading to speak of a "right" since in such an amorphous area, entitlement to the advantage sought will depend on all the circumstances of the case.[98]

However in the case of appeals to an appeals officer of the Department of Social Welfare, it has been held in *Kiely* v. *Minister for Social Welfare (No. 2)*[99] that, as a matter of interpretation of the relevant regulations:

> "[A]n oral hearing is mandatory unless . . . a determination of the claim can be made fairly on a consideration of the documentary evidence. If, however, there are unresolved conflicts in the documentary evidence as to any matter which is essential to a ruling of the claim, the intention of the regulations is that those conflicts shall be resolved by an oral hearing"[1]

---

[98] See *e.g.* the comments of Keane J. in *Williams* v. *Army Pensions Board* [1981] I.L.R.M. 379 at p. 382: "Whether [there must be an oral hearing] in any particular case must depend on the circumstances of that case. . . . The application in the present case was capable of being dealt with fairly . . . in the manner actually adopted by [the Board]." Webster J. made similar comments in relation to prisoner's right to call witness and cross-examine, etc. before a board of prison visitors in *R.* v. *Home Secretary, ex p. Tarrant* [1985] Q.B. 251.

[99] [1977] I.R. 267. On the procedure before a social welfare appeals officer, see pp. 149–154. As far as appeals to An Bord Pleanala are concerned, it is clear that the Board has a discretion as to whether to allow an oral hearing save in the case of appeals specified by regulation: Local Government (Planning and Development) Act 1983, s.15. No such regulations have yet been made.

[1] [1977] I.R. 267 at p. 278.

The case of *Re Haughey*,[2] which arose out of the Dail Committee of Public Accounts investigation into the expenditure of the grant in aid for Northern Ireland relief, is instructive in the context of a right to call witnesses or to cross-examine opposing witnesses. During the course of the Committee's investigations, a senior Garda Officer made a number of serious allegations against Mr. Haughey. These accusations lay at the heart of the Committee's investigation, so much so, that he might be regarded as being in an analogous position to a party in a court case, at any rate, so far as his good name was concerned. Emphasising this factor, O'Dalaigh C.J., writing for the Supreme Court majority, held that the Committee ought to have granted Mr. Haughey the following procedural safeguards:

> "(a) that he should be furnished with a copy of the evidence which reflected on his good name; (b) that he should be allowed to cross-examine, by counsel his accuser or accusers; (c) that he should be allowed to give rebutting evidence; and (d) that he should be permitted to address, again by counsel, the Committee in his own defence."[3]

A case on the other side of the line from *Haughey* was *The State (Boyle)* v. *General Medical Services (Payment) Board*[4] which stemmed from an investigation which had established that the applicant doctor's claims for remuneration, under the "choice of doctor" scheme were excessive. Under the agreement on which the scheme was based, the applicant could, as he did, complain to an appeal committee. His appeal was rejected following an oral hearing. The committee basing its decision on, *inter alia*, statistical data concerning the average number of home visits in the area in which the applicant practiced. The applicant requested that the doctor who had compiled the data should be made available for cross-examination before the committee. This request was refused. Keane J. held that this refusal did not constitute a violation of "natural and constitutional justice" because when the applicant had received a copy of the data he had not raised any specific issue as to its reliability, which required oral evidence in order to be resolved.

---

[2] [1971] I.R. 217. Failure to permit cross-examination was held to be a breach of *audi alteram partem* in *Kiely* v. *Minister for Social Welfare* [1977] I.R. 287 where this right was granted to the other side. As Keane J. observed in *The State (Boyle)* v. *General Medical Services (Payment) Board* [1981] I.L.R.M. 14, *Kiely* turns on the lack of even-handedness displayed by the appeals officer, and it would be wrong to deduce any comprehensive right to cross-examine from the facts of this case.

[3] [1971] I.R. at p. 263.

[4] [1981] I.L.R.M. 14. But *cf. R.* v. *Hull Prison Visitors, ex p. St. Germain (No. 2)* [1979] 1 W.L.R. 1401.

Representation
Where there is an oral hearing, its practical value may depend
on whether the individual is represented by an experienced,
though not necessarily legally qualified, advocate. As against this,
it will often happen that the advocate is a lawyer and it is often said
that the involvement of lawyers has, in the long run, the effect of
protracting and complicating the proceedings, to no advantage.[5]
However, in other jurisdictions the tide appears to be running in
favour of a right to be represented.[6] In Ireland, the position is still
in doubt. In *McGrath and O'Ruairc* v. *Trustees of Maynooth College,*[7]
which involved the dismissal of two University lecturers, the
Supreme Court said that there was a right to be represented by a
lawyer though not as the plaintiffs preferred, by their trade union
representatives. But on the other hand, in two recent disciplinary
cases,[8] a claim for representation was refused. Thus, it may be best
to say only that the deciding authority should always genuinely
consider whether the circumstances are such that representation is
necessary in the interests of justice.[9]

Deciding without hearing
It frequently happens that the decision-making and informa-
tion-gathering functions are divorced from each other, as for
instance where the body in which a decision has been vested by
statutes, either instructs its officials, or constitutes a sub-
committee, to conduct interviews, examine records, etc. The
question arises as to how far this process can go before it is held
that the individuals affected have not been allowed a fair hearing.
One context in which this situation has arisen is the decision as to a
planning appeal or the confirmation of a compulsory purchase
order, which is vested in Bord Pleanala or the Minister for the
Environment respectively. The decision usually requires a hearing
at the site, which is chaired by an inspector and is not attended by
the Board or Minister. Nevertheless, it has been agreed, in the

[5] *Report of the Committee on Civil Legal Aid and Advice* (1978) (Prl. 2574) at
p. 50.
[6] *R.* v. *Home Secretary, ex p. Tarrant* [1985] Q.B. 251, and see de Smith, *op.
cit.* at p. 213 and Jackson, *Natural Justice* (London, 1979) at pp. 73–79.
[7] Supreme Court, November 1, 1979.
[8] *The State (Gallagher)* v. *Governor of Portlaoise Prison*, High Court, May 18,
1977 (prison discipline); *The State (Smullen)* v. *Duffy* [1980] I.L.R.M. 46
(school expulsion).
[9] See *Tarrant, supra*, and *Enderby Town F.C.* v. *Football Association* [1971]
Ch. 598.

Murphy/Geraghty line of cases,[10] that this procedure is valid, provided that the inspector gives the Minister "If not a verbatim account—at least a fair and accurate account of what transpired and one which gives the Minister the evidence and the submissions of each party. . . . "

In *Hession* v. *Irish Land Commission*,[11] the respondent land-owner's objection to the inclusion of his farmland on the ILC's provisional list was heard before two lay Commissioners. However the case was adjourned for two years. At the adjourned hearing, where one of the Commissioners had been replaced by another Commissioner, the respondent's objection was rejected. The Supreme Court held that this result must have been based at least in part upon evidence given at the initial hearing, and accordingly the decision was void. The case is unsatisfactory in that the Court did not find whether there was any record (or if so, what quality of record) of the initial hearing before the reconstituted lay Commissioners or whether there was any other factor to distinguish the case from the *Murphy/Geraghty* line of authority, which was not even mentioned.

However, *Hession* is in line with the principle stated by Gibson L.J. in *Re McNally's Application*[12]:

> "[W]here all or part of the evidence has been given, the participation thereafter in the adjudication or determination by a person, who, though otherwise qualified to sit, did not hear that evidence, will invalidate the decision."

In *McNally*, a Prison Board had sat on an earlier occasion to determine whether a prisoner who faced serious disciplinary charges should be entitled to legal aid, though in order to decide that point it was found necessary to hear evidence from certain prison officers as to the extent of their injuries. At a later stage a differently composed panel heard the substantive case, and the applicant was adjudged guilty of these offences. Gibson L.J. found that these procedures did not amount to a breach of natural justice, as the later proceedings were not simply a continuance of an earlier partly heard case, but were rather "a complete hearing of every aspect of the substantive issue."

---

[10] *Murphy* v. *Dublin Corporation* [1972] I.R. 215, See to like effect, *Murphy* v. *Dublin Corporation (No. 2)* [1976] I.R. 143; *Geraghty* v. *Dublin Corporation* [1976] I.R. 153. There were some differences between the judges, but this was on another point, namely, the operation of the *delegatus* principle. See further at pp. 229–233.

[11] [1978] I.R. 322.

[12] (1985) 3 N.I.J.B. 1. See also *R. (Dobbyn)* v. *Belfast JJ.* [1917] 2 I.R. 297; *R. (Department of Agriculture)* v. *Londonderry JJ.* [1917] 2 I.R. 283.

The final case bearing on this area is *O'Brien* v. *Bord na Mona*[13] which involved the compulsory acquisition of the plaintiff farmer's bogland. The plaintiff had submitted to one of the Board's officials that the Board need only take a leasehold interest, with the land reverting to him after all the turf had been removed. Because of the Board's long established policy of acquiring the fee simple interest, the official did not even bother to transmit this information to the Board. At this point, it ought to be noted that, in the situation under discussion, there is often a close interaction between the *audi alteram partem* rule and the *delegatus non potest delegare* principle.[14] Thus in *O'Brien*, the Supreme Court dealt first with the argument that there had been no breach of the *audi alteram* rule because the decision had been delegated to the official who had received the plaintiff's submission. It held that even had there been a delegation (though there was, on the facts, no sign of one) the decision would still have been invalid because determinations regarding compulsory acquisition are not capable of being delegated to officials. The Court then turned to the alternative issue and held that the *audi alteram* rule had been broken by the official's failure to relay the plaintiff's submission.[15]

O'Brien was distinguished by Carroll J. in the High Court in *ESB* v. *Gormley*[16] which involved the placing of an electric line upon the defendant's land. The defendant relied, *inter alia* upon the fact that her objections had not been relayed to the ESB Board. Carroll J. rejected this argument and distinguished *O'Brien* primarily because the line had already been finally decided by the Board before the defendant acquired the land; and it was permissible for the Board to delegate to its officials negotiations with landowners and decisions, regarding the relatively minor issue of the position of intermediate plyons.

Confirmation of a decision

It has recently come to be accepted, in authorities which will be described, *infra*, that where a "provisional" decision is taken without observing the *audi alteram* rule, this defect can be remedied if the person affected has the chance to put his side of

---

[13] [1983] I.R. 255.

[14] On which, see pp. 229–233.

[15] The court rejected the argument that since the plaintiff's argument would have been so unlikely to sway the Board, this breach did not matter (see further pp. 294–296). The court's decision, at this stage, could also have been put on the ground that the Board's decision [against the plaintiff] would have been founded on an inflexible rule of policy: see pp. 316–319.

[16] [1985] I.R. 129. Carroll J. was reversed, on other grounds by the Supreme Court: see [1985] I.R. at 144.

the case before the decision is made permanent. In short, this two-stage process can be characterised as a single decision, (as opposed to a discrete decision, followed by an appeal) for the purposes of the constitutional justice principles. The significance of this characterisation lies in the rule (the merits of which are discussed in part 5 of this chapter) that an absence of constitutional justice at the initial stage cannot be cured by the provision of an appellate stage, at which the rules are observed.

The first case to be examined is *The State (Duffy)* v. *Minister for Defence*[17] which arose out of the discharge of a petty officer from the Navy. The appellant, who was one of the few people in the history of the Navy to fail to get his engine-room artificer certificate, had been warned by his commanding officer that he was going to be discharged, to which he replied that he was "going to do something about this."[18] His commanding officer told him that he was free to do so and ensured that the decision was not implemented for seven days so that the applicant could make whatever representations he wished. In fact, none were made. Reversing D'Arcy J. in the High Court, Henchy J. for the Supreme Court drew a distinction between "the decision to proceed to discharge" and "the actual discharge" seven days later and held that the fact that the applicant could have made representations during this period of delay, constituted adequate compliance with the *audi alteram partem* rule. Henchy J. thus implicitly rejected the possibility that the commanding officer might, at the final stage, be biased by loyalty to his own previous decision.[19]

---

[17] Supreme Court, May 9, 1979. For a similar case to *Duffy* see *The State (Donnelly)* v. *Minister for Defence*, October 8, 1979. In *The State (McCann)* v. *The Racing Board* [1983] I.L.R.M. 67 which involved the revocation of a course betting permit by the Board, Barron J. distinguished between the Boards "decid[ing] whether matters alleged justified ... revocation" and "the ultimate decision of the Board ... before the ... revocation takes effect." The words italicised confirm the distinction drawn in *Duffy* and in the later case of *Gammell* v. *Dublin County Council* [1983] I.L.R.M. 413 discussed *infra*. Other cases in which the situation under discussion might appear to arise, but was not mentioned by the court are *The State (Boyle)* v. *General Medical Services (Payment) Board* [1981] I.L.R.M. 14 and *The State (Williams)* v. *Army Pensions Board* [1983] I.R. 308.

[18] *Cf.* "I will do such things, What they are yet I know not, but they shall be the terrors of the earth"—*King Lear*, Act II.

[19] It is submitted in regard to both *Duffy* and *Donnelly* that it may be unrealistic to assume that, in a strict military hierarchy, a superior officer who has taken up the definite position that a subordinate ought to be dismissed will resile from that position because of arguments advanced by the subordinate.

Gammell v. *Dublin County Council*[20] involved an order prohibiting the erection of temporary dwellings which had been made under the Local Government (Sanitary Services) Act 1948, in respect of the plaintiff's caravan site, by the defendant council. The plaintiff was not aware of the inspection of her site by the local authority and health board experts on whose certificate the local authority relied in making the order. Following the procedure under the 1948 Act, a notice that the order had been made and that any person aggrieved had fourteen days in which to apply to the Minister for the Environment, asking for the order to be annulled, was published in a newspaper circulating locally. On such an application the order could then be annulled or confirmed by the Minister. Carroll J. held that this opportunity to make representations to the Minister sufficed for compliance with the *audi alteram partem* rule (notwithstanding that the plaintiff had not seen the newspaper notice, a point to which we return in the next section).

Although Carroll J. did adopt a lengthy passage from the judgment in *Duffy* as part of her reasoning, there was an important point at which *Gammell* differed from *Duffy*, namely, that in the former case, the confirmation was to be given by a body other than the body which had taken the initial decision. This made the confirmation look more like an appeal and required the High Court to confront a question not mentioned in *Duffy*, viz. how to distinguish the structure of the administrative process in *Gammell* from the *Ingle/Moran*[21] line of authority. Both *Ingle* and *Moran* had held that a failure to allow a person affected by a decision the right to make his case at the time of the initial decision would not be cured by the provision of an appellate stage at which this right was allowed. Carroll J. drew this distinction in the following important passage:

> "However in this case we are not dealing with an order effective when made and an appeal there from to an appellate body. Under section 31 of the [1948] Act the order has no effect until the person aggrieved has been given an opportunity of stating reasons why it should not come into effect. There is no "appeal' to the Minister from an operative order. There is machinery set up under the section whereby an aggrieved party can make representations why the order should not come into operation. If successful, the order is annulled by the Minister and it never becomes operative. This is very different to the *Ingle* case and the *Moran* case where the revocation of the licence became operative immediately

[20] [1983] I.L.R.M. 413.
[21] *Ingle* v. *O'Brien* (1975) 109 I.L.T.R. 4; *Moran* v. *Att.-Gen.* [1976] I.R. 400.

and of necessity there had to be a time lag between the revocation and the determination of an appeal in the District Court. Is there any real distinction between machinery which provides for an order to be made with delayed effect giving an opportunity to interested parties to make representations of annulment which, if successful, will result in the order survey becoming operative as in the present case, and machinery which gives an opportunity to interested parties to make representations why an order should not be made, which, if successful, will result in the order never being made. . . .

"The fact that the representations are to be made to the Minister and are so the body making the order does not seem to me to be invidious in any respect. In fact, even though the County Council would not appear to be inhibited from acting, it seems preferable that representation should be made to the Minister who can avoid the criticism which might be levelled at the County Council that they are judges in their own cause."[22]

It is submitted that this is a practicable and useful distinction, which can also be applied in other areas.[23] Take, for instance, applications for planning permission: considered, in isolation, the procedure before a local planning authority might appear to violate the *audi alteram partem* rule in that (confining the discussion to the applicant for planning permission and not examining the position of objectors)[24] the applicant is not told of the authority's provisional thinking on his application, much less allowed any opportunity to make representations in regard to it. On the other

[22] [1983] I.L.R.M. 413 at pp. 417–418.
[23] For which some support may be found in *O'Brien* v. *Bord na Mona* [1983] I.R. 268 (See pp. 250–251) in which the plaintiff's case was that the body which had taken a provisional decision as regards a compulsory order would be biased, by the provisional decision, when it came to the stage of confirmation, and, consequently, that there should be an "appeal against the making of a compulsory acquisition order, or . . . conformation by an external authority . . . " ([1983] I.R. at 281). It seems to have been assumed in both the High Court (which upheld the plaintiff's claims) and the Supreme Court (which admittedly, rejected the plaintiff's case) that either confirmation or an appeal to an external authority would cure the defect arising from any bias in the original decision. There is some support here for the idea that an appeal may be treated as being equivalent to a confirmation, for the purposes of the constitutional principles. The same distinction was also drawn, in the context of Art. 34.1, in *Re Solicitors Act 1954 and D. a solicitor* (1961) 95 I.L.T.R. 60.
[24] On which see *The State (Stanford)* v. *Dun Laoghaire Corporation*, Supreme Court, February 20, 1981.

hand, there is ample constitutional justice at the rehearing on appeal to An Bord Pleanala. The crucial question thus is whether the initial application stage is to be examined in isolation or whether it is to be considered together with the proceedings before An Bord Pleanala. In other words, is the structure of the decision-making system analogous to that involved in *Gammell* or does the provision of an appeal fail to cure the initial defect? It is submitted that the two systems are similar and thus that the planning application system does not violate the *audi alteram partem* rule. The key factor is that (as with the prohibition order) a local planning authority decision granting permission does not come into effect until the appeal has been heard or, if no appeal is taken, until the period for appealing has elapsed.[25] Thus to adapt the test laid down in the passage from *Gammell* already quoted: " ... [the planning authority's decision to grant planning of permission] has no effect until the person aggrieved has been given an opportunity of stating reasons why it should not come into effect. There is no appeal to the [Bord] from an *operative* order. ... "

Waiver

The question of waiver, by the individual affected, is an important issue which has received even less attention in the context of the *audi alteram partem* rule than in other contexts.[26] For example, in *Gammell* Carroll J. held that if the statutory machinery permits an aggrieved party to make representations to the Minister before the order prohibiting the erection of any temporary dwelling came into effect, then the procedure conforms to the *audi alteram partem* rule. The only notice of the order before the period for the making of representations expired was a notice in *The Irish Press*, which the plaintiff said (and the defendant accepted) she had never seen. No point was taken in this case as to whether the plaintiff ought to have been individually served with notice; yet it seems plain from the result that the court must have regarded the plaintiff as having waived her right to make representations. By contrast, the *O'Brien* v. *Bord na Mona*,[27] the

---

[25] Local Government (Planning and Development) Act 1963, s.26(9), as amended by s.20 of the Local Government (Planning and Development) Act 1983.

[26] On the issue of waiver and *nemo iudex*, see pp. 257–258.

[27] [1983] I.R. 255 at pp. 276 (Keane J.) and 287 (Finlay P.). See also *Re Mountcharles's Estate* [1935] I.R. 163, where the only notice of Land Commission decisions determining ownership of mining rights was that published in *Iris Oifigiuil*. Finding that these procedures were in breach of *audi alteram partem*, Kennedy C.J. commented ironically ([1935] I.R. at p. 166): "[T]he Land Commission purported to give themselves

High and Supreme Court explicitly left open the possibility that
waiver would only be deemed to have occurred on actual notice or
following the sending of an individual, specific notification. (On
the facts of *O'Brien*, this question did not arise since it was
admitted that the plaintiff had received actual notice by way of the
newspaper advertisement.) Again, in *Glover* v. *B.L.N. Ltd.*[28] a case
involving the removal of an office-holder whose office was
founded on contract, Walsh J. explicitly left open the question,
which did not arise on the facts of the case, of the extent to which
the rules of natural justice could have been excluded by express
provision in the contract. (It should be noted that in this situation
the renunciation of rights would have occurred at the earlier stage
than in *Gammell*). Thus it must be admitted that the standard of
informed consent necessary for a waiver has not yet been
authoritatively determined.

4. Types of decisions which attract the rules of natural justice

It is generally assumed that the rules of natural justice are co-
extensive in their application.[29] This assumption is questionable,
given the differing nature of the rules. Bias is a particularly
heinous defect likely to lead to a general erosion of confidence in
the administrative system, whereas the failure to grant a hearing
does not appear to be such a fundamental flaw. Reflecting this
broader reach, the no-bias limb of constitutional justice shades off
into the rule against exercise of discretionary power in bad faith
with the result that the rule against bias applies in some form to
almost all decisions by public authorities.[30] In contrast, the *audi
alteram partem* rule of its nature applies to a more limited range of
decisions—essentially decisions raising issues of fact or law rather
than matters of policy. Again, it has been stated that the rules of

---

power to determine questions submitted by the Minister behind the
backs of interested parties . . . while the very fact of such "determination" is not brought to their notice unless they happen to be members
of that comparatively small and very select class of persons, the regular
readers of *Iris Oifigiuil*."

[28] [1973] I.R. 388 at p. 425. See further at pp. 274–275. *Cf. The State
(Boyle)* v. *General Medical Services (Payments) Board* [1981] I.L.R.M. 14 at
p. 15.
[29] Clarke, "Natural Justice: Substance or Shadow?" [1975] *Public Law* 27.
[30] See pp. 300–304. For a good example of where the wrongful exercise of
discretionary power was regarded as tantamount to bias: see *The State
(McGeough)* v. *Louth C.C.* (1973) 107 I.L.T.R. 13.

natural justice do not apply where this would defeat the object of the administrative power.[31] Of its nature, this restriction is more likely to apply to *audi alteram partem* than to the no-bias rule. However, these *caveats* notwithstanding, both rules will generally apply to the situations described in this section.

The following classification of the relevant cases, by reference to the type of administrative decision involved, inevitably entails some degree of overlap.

Public and private employment

Historically, there were two distinctions of crucial importance for employment law. Office-holders were distinguished from employees (servants), and, secondly, the category of office-holders was divided into two classes according to whether the holder was dismissible at pleasure or whether he could only be removed for cause. It was only the office-holder removeable for cause who enjoyed the protection of the natural justice principles.

It seems likely that the second distinction, at least, is no longer part of the law. In *Garvey* v. *Ireland*[32] the Commissioner of the Garda Siochana argued successfully that his summary dismissal from office by the Government was contrary to natural justice. Of the four judges who comprised the majority, O'Higgins C.J. (with whom Parke J. agreed) decided that the office was not held merely at pleasure, but concluded that this distinction was no longer significant. Henchy and Griffin JJ. classified the office as one held at pleasure, yet found that the rules of natural justice applied to any decision to dismiss.

It is, however, uncertain whether the distinction between an office-holder and an employee is still significant in the present context.[33] The office is the legal form for a "superior" post (which was, in past centuries, even regarded as a property-right of the holder). An office is a position to which certain important duties are attached, usually of a more or less public character, with its holder likely to be better qualified and freer from day-to-day control than a servant. It thus plays a pivotal part in the administration of government, whether at central or local level, or, sometimes in the administration of a company or other corporation. In addition:

[31] *O'Callaghan* v. *Commissioners of Public Works* [1985] I.L.R.M. 364.
[32] [1981] I.R. 75.
[33] The distinction still appears to have relevance as far as the court's power to order re-instatement in cases of wrongful dismissal is concerned (but *cf. Glover* v. *B.L.N. Ltd.* [1973] I.R. 388 at p. 427) and also for tax purposes: *Edwards* v. *Clinch* [1982] A.C. 845.

"[An office] is created by Act of the National Parliament, charter, statutory regulation, articles of association of a company or of a body corporate formed under the authority of a statute, deed of trust, grant or by prescription."[34]

By contrast, the master-servant relationship is usually founded exclusively upon a contract. It should be stressed, though, that even an office-holder may and usually does have a contract, which fixes a great part of his conditions. Finally, a servant may occupy a temporary, personal post whilst an office:

"[M]ust have a sufficient degree of continuance to admit of its being held by successful incumbents ... it cannot be limited to the tenure of one man, for if it were so, it would lack that independent existence which to my mind the word 'office' imports."[35]

The continuing validity of the distinction between an officer and an employee in the context of the *audi alteram* rule was questioned by the Supreme Court in *Glover* v. *B.L.N. Ltd.*,[36] which arose from the dismissal of a company director for alleged misconduct. The dismissal was invalidated as the plaintiff had not been given a fair hearing by the board of the company. In the High Court, Kenny J. adopted the traditional British view that the rules of natural justice apply to the removal of an office-holder but not a servant, and held that the rules applied in the instant case because the plaintiff was characterised as being an office-holder.

However, Walsh J., writing on behalf of the Supreme Court majority stated:

"[O]nce the matter is governed by the terms of a contract between the parties, it is immaterial whether the employee concerned is deemed to be a servant or an officer ... [because] public policy and the dictates of constitutional justice require that statutes, regulations or agreements setting up machinery for taking decisions which may affect right or impose liabilities should be construed as providing for fair procedures."[37]

[34] *Per* Kenny J. in *Glover* v. *B.L.N. Ltd.* [1973] I.R. 388 at p. 414.
[35] *Per* Lord Wilberforce in *Edwards* v. *Clinch* [1982] A.C 845 at p. 860.
[36] [1973] I.R. 388. See O'Reilly, "The Constitution and the Law of Contract" (1973) 8 Ir.Jur.(n.s.) 197.
[37] [1973] I.R. at pp. 425, 427. See, to like effect, the comments of McWilliam J. in *Garvey* v. *Ireland* [1981] I.R. 75 at p. 82.

However, *Glover* leaves a number of loose ends. In the first place, the contract of service in the case included a clause which expressly stated that a hearing would take place prior to any dismissal for misconduct, thus making it possible for the court to impute a term to the effect that any such hearing or inquiry should be fairly conducted. So that the *excursus* into the broader reaches of constitutional justice was *obiter*. Secondly, Walsh J. explicitly left open the questions of the situation where the relationship between the parties was not grounded in either contract or, statute and the extent to which the rules could be excluded by express agreement. Finally, and most significantly, the passage quoted depends upon the impregnation of contract law by constitutional principles. A number of recent decisions show that there is judicial reluctance—at High Court level at any rate—to follow this innovatory approach.

In *Lupton* v. *Allied Irish Banks Ltd*.[38] it was contended that *Glover* was an authority for the proposition that constitutional justice applies to *all* employees. While Murphy J. was not obliged to decide this point, he doubted whether Walsh J. had equated the position of an employee with that of an officer. He then proceeded to confine the authority of *Glover* to its own facts, *i.e.* a case where the contract of service already envisaged that the office-holder would get natural justice. Murphy J. took the same approach in *Farrell* v. *Minister for Defence*[39] where the summary dismissal of a civilian maintenance man in the employment of the defendant was upheld. Unlike *Glover*, the contract of employment contained no express or implied term compelling the employer to conduct an investigation prior to dismissal. Counsel for the plaintiff was then forced to contend that in virtue of the constitutional guarantee of fair procedures the rules of natural justice should apply. Pending "an authoritative review of the law." Murphy J. was content to apply settled principles: the plaintiff was an employee, not an office-holder, and he was not entitled to natural justice. If, however, the dismissal was in breach of contract then the employee was entitled to recover damages. This reasoning commended itself to Costello J. in *Gunn* v. *National College of Art and Design*,[40] a case arising out of the dismissal of a member of the full-time teaching staff. The judge concluded that the teacher employer relationship was one governed by contract, and not by "the principles of administrative law developed to deal with office-

---

[38] (1983) 2 J.I.S.S.L. 107. For other cases invoking the officer/employee dichotomy, see *N.E.E.T.U.* v. *McConnell* (1983) 2 J.I.S.S.L. 97 and *Connolly* v. *McConnell* [1983] I.R. 172.

[39] (1985) 4 J.I.S.S.L. 105.

[40] High Court, October 29, 1985.

holders in the public service." Thus the defendants were not
bound to apply the rules of natural justice (although they had in
fact done so).

As regards the question of the office-holder/employee distinction, the stance adopted in *Glover* may be preferable to the line of
recent High Court authorities. On policy grounds, the modern
view is that all means of livelihood are so important to the person
to whom they belong (and often more important, in these times, to
the "employee") that dismissal should require a fair procedure.[41]
On the technical plane, the distinction between an office-holder
and a servant is "abstruse and verging on the bizarre".[42]
Moreover, it is usually the case that with an office-holder, the bulk
of the terms of employment are fixed by contract, rather than
statute, deed of trust, etc., a factor which erodes the basis of the
distinction.

Unfair Dismissals Act 1977. In any case, these doubts and
difficulties will often be of only academic interest because of the
1977 Act which brings in the right to sue for unfair dismissal: for it
is now accepted that a fair dismissal requires the observance of the
rules of natural justice.[43] There are, however, two restrictions on
the impact of the 1977 Act. First, the natural justice rules, derived
as a gloss on the statute, may have a different content from that of
common law/constitutional natural justice, in that for instance,
under the Act, it is necessary to balance up procedural and
substantive justice. Secondly, the Act's protection extends among
public sector employees, to all employees of semi-state bodies
(apart from AnCo trainees and apprentices) and to the servants of
local authorities, vocational education committees and health
boards. However about one-fifth of the working population, many
of whom are in public employment, are expressly excluded from
the Act's field of operation.[44] Most, but not all, of those excluded
have some other form of procedural protection against dismissal.
Thus, for instance: officers of local authorities have a special

---

[41] Thus, the justifications given in *Garvey* for the application of the rules of
natural justice (*e.g.* avoiding any injustice caused through acting on an
ex parte view of the facts) are equally applicable in the case of
employees/office holders working in the private sector.

[42] de Smith, *op. cit.*, p. 228.

[43] See *e.g. Warner-Lambert* v. *Tormey* UD 255/1978; *Hynes* v. *Frederick Inns*
UD 172/1978 and the cases cited at p. 245 and in Redmond, *Dismissal
Law in the Republic of Ireland* (Dublin, 1982, at pp. 160–169.

[44] s.2(1). s.2(1)(*h*) actually states "a person employed by or under the State
other than persons designated for the time being under s.17 of the
Industrial Relations Act 1969." The qualification "other than" catches
some 8,000 people, mostly industrial civil servants.

statutory fair dismissal system under the Local Government Act
1941[45]; members of the Defence Forces and of the Garda
Siochana are office-holders and may only be removed in accordance with the principles of constitutional justice[46] and relevant
disciplinary regulations; and it seems likely that civil servants are in
the same position.[47]

Membership of trade unions, professional bodies or clubs

As the relationship between the members and the institutions
concerned is usually grounded ultimately in contract one is again
faced with the question of whether constitutional justice has real
relevance. Can the obligation to grant a fair hearing be ousted by
agreement of the parties? A conceptually satisfactory answer to
this difficult question has yet to be given, but for the moment the
courts are content to construe the contract of membership as
containing an implied term that fair procedures will be observed.[48]
Different considerations, of course, arise in the case of professional bodies exercising *statutory powers,* and there can be no
question but that the rules of natural justice are applicable to the
exercise of such powers. As illustrated in the two preceding parts
of this chapter, the standard and content of the rules of
constitutional justice vary enormously depending on "the circumstances." Thus, for example, it is likely that the classification into
quasi-judicial and administrative functions,[49] in the context of the
nemo iudex rule, would operate so that a less rigorous rule would
apply, at least in regard to trade unions and clubs. It is clear
however that disciplinary action by a trade union,[50] professional
body[51] or club[52] cannot be conducted on a summary, *ex parte* basis

---

[45] ss.24 and 25. See *Dail Debates,* Vol. 294, c. 480 (November 23, 1976).
For an example of the 1941 Act in operation, see *O'Mahony* v. *Arklow
U.D.C.* [1965] I.R. 710.

[46] *The State (Gleeson)* v. *Minister for Defence* [1976] I.R. 280 at p. 294.

[47] The position of civil servants has already been dealt with at
pp. 54–55.

[48] *Fisher* v. *Keane* (1878) 11 Ch.D. 853; *Dawkins* v. *Antrobus* (1881) 17
Ch.D. 615; *Flynn* v. *Grt.N.Ry.Co.* (1955) 89 I.L.T.R. 46.

[49] See pp. 285–286.

[50] *Kilkenny* v. *Irish Engineering and Foundry Worker's Union* (1939)
Ir.Jur.Rep. 52; *N.E.E.T.U.* v. *McConnell* (1983) 2 J.I.S.L.L. 97 *Connolly*
v. *McConnell* [1983] I.R. 172 and see Kerr and Whyte, *Irish Trade Union
Law* (Abingdon, 1985) at pp. 113–121.

[51] *Manning* v. *Incorporated Law Society of Ireland,* High Court, March 8,
1980; *Re M., a doctor* [1984] I.R. 479; *The State (Boyle)* v. *General Medical
Services (Payment) Board* [1981] I.L.R.M. 14; *O'Donoghue* v. *Veterinary
Council* [1975] I.R. 398.

[52] *Forde* v. *Fottrell* (1930) 64 I.L.T.R. 89; *Goggins* v. *Feeney* (1949) 83

and the courts have set aside disciplinary actions which did not observe the rules of natural justice or where the requirements of the association's own constitution relating to notice had not been complied with.[53] Clauses which provide for automatic forfeiture of membership are probably void as contrary to public policy.[54] This has been the conclusion of the English courts, and given that the Constitution may inform notions of public policy, such reasoning would also seem to apply *a fortiori* in this jurisdiction.

A general exception (which is elaborated *infra*) but which is of particular relevance here is that the rules of constitutional justice do not usually apply to suspensions from membership.[55]

Licensing and commercial regulation

The application of the rules of natural justice in this area stems from the desire to protect an individual's livelihood and business interests. Although important interests are at stake, the rules of natural justice will generally be satisfied if the regulatory authority approaches the case with an open mind and gives the applicant an adequate opportunity to deal with the case against him. Should the authority act on evidence which the applicant did not have the opportunity to controvert, then the decision will be set aside.[56]

These principles are well illustrated by the fairly typical recent case of *Doupe* v. *Limerick Corporation*.[57] The plaintiff had been refused permission to operate an abattoir by the defendant body. The gist of their objections was that the scale of the proposed operation posed environmental and health risks. Costello J. observed that the *audi alteram partem* principle did not require that every administrative order which may adversely affect rights "must be preceded by a judicial type hearing involving the examination and cross-examination of witnesses." The plaintiff had been informally told of the nature of the council's objections and Costello J. concluded that he had "ample opportunity" to seek

---

I.L.T.R. 181; *Ahern* v. *Molyneux* [1965] Ir.Jur.Rep. 59; *Cotter* v. *Sullivan*, High Court, April 23, 1980.

[53] *Doyle* v. *Griffin* [1937] I.R. 93.

[54] *Edwards* v. *S.O.G.A.T.* [1971] Ch. 354. But *cf. Moran* v. *Workers Union of Ireland* [1943] I.R. 485.

[55] See pp. 288–290.

[56] *Killiney and Ballybrack Residents Assoc.* v. *Minister for Local Government* (1978) 112 I.L.T.R. 69; *Geraghty* v. *Minister for Local Government* [1976] I.R. 153; *The State (McConnell)* v. *Eastern Health Board*, High Court, June 1, 1983.

[57] [1981] I.L.R.M. 456.

expert advice (if such could be obtained) challenging the council's view that the scale of the proposal posed serious health risks. In the circumstances, the rules of natural justice had been observed. But one could imagine other cases (such as where the revocation of an existing licence would be tantamount to the deprivation of a means of livelihood) where a more exacting procedural standard would be required.[58] The rules of natural justice have also been applied to the revocation or suspension of a taxi driver's licence[59] or a betting permit for a bookmaker[60]; the licensing of agricultural marts[61] and the censorship of publications.[62]

Discipline

Prisons, schools and universities. It was formerly the case that in a disciplined organisation the need for unquestioning obedience to the commands of a superior was regarded as outweighing the advantages of the rules of natural justice.[63] This judicial attitude is no longer in the ascendancy, and there is British authority to the effect that legal representation must be allowed before a prison disciplinary tribunal can impose severe punishments.[64] Nevertheless it remains the case that the procedural standards required of disciplinary bodies are not as strict where fundamental interests are not at stake. In *The State (Gallagher)* v.

---

[58] See *e.g. Ingle* v. *O'Brien* (1975) 109 I.L.T.R. 9; *Moran* v. *Att.-Gen.* [1976] I.R. 400; *The State (Grahame)* v. *Racing Board*, High Court, November 22, 1983.

[59] *Ingle* v. *O'Brien* (1975) 109 I.L.T.R. 7; *Moran* v. *Att.-Gen.* [1976] I.R. 400.

[60] *McDonald* v. *Bord na gCon* [1965] I.R. 217; *The State (Grahame)* v. *Racing Board*, High Court, November 22, 1983.

[61] *East Donegal Co-Operative Ltd.* v. *Attorney General* [1970] I.R. 317. See also *Gammell* v. *Dublin C.C.* [1983] I.L.R..M. 413 (licensing of temporary dwellings.)

[62] *Irish Family Planning Assoc.* v. *Ryan* [1979] I.R. 295.

[63] *R.* v. *Army Council ex p. Ravenscroft* [1917] 2 K.B. 504; *Ex p. Fry* [1954] 1 W.L.R. 730. *Cf.* "Their's not to make reply, Their's not to reason why, Their's but to do and die." (Tennyson, *The Charge of the Light Brigade*.)

[64] *R.* v. *Home Secretary ex p. Tarrant* [1985] Q.B. 251; See further *R.* v. *Governor of Maze Prison ex p. McKiernan* (1985) 6 N.I.J.B. 6. But contrast *R.* v. *Deputy Governor of Camphill Prison ex p. King* [1985] Q.B. 735. In a slightly different context, it may be noted that in *The State (Walsh and McGowan)* v. *Governor of Mountjoy Prison*, Supreme Court, December 12, 1975, the court held that Prison Rules required that remand prisoners should be allowed access to a legal adviser of their own choosing.

Governor of Portlaoise Prison[65] the applicant's privileges (such as associations with other prisoners and the receipt of the letters) had been suspended following a hearing before the Governor when he had been found guilty of relatively minor disciplinary offences. Finlay P. rejected the argument that legal representation was required in this situation: Gallagher had been afforded an opportunity to speak on his own behalf and that sufficed. The judge also referred to the "partly magisterial" nature of the prison governor's functions and seemed to imply that it would be wrong for the courts to impose anything but the most rudimentary procedural standards in the context of prison discipline. This reluctance to exercise a supervisory jurisdiction over disciplinary awards is also to be found in *The State (Smullen)* v. *Duffy*.[66] This case arose following the effective expulsion of the participants in a gang fight at a community school. Although one of the boys involved had not been interviewed prior to his expulsion as he was in hospital, Finlay P. refused to find that this amounted to a breach of natural justice. He said that it was essential to school discipline that the investigation should take place immediately. It may also have been relevant that, on the facts, the applicant appeared to have had no case. All in all, it seems that it is only where there had been a substantial breach of natural justice in such cases that the courts will intervene.

Gardai and the Defence Forces. Two of the leading cases in this area have already been surveyed.[67] In the first *The State (Gleeson)* v. *Minister for Defence*,[68] the applicant had been summarily dismissed from the Defence Forces following an incident involving a group of soldiers of which he was one. This discharge was quashed by the Supreme Court, as the applicant had not been given an

---

[65] High Court, May 18, 1977. See also *The State (Gallagher)* v. *Governor of Portlaoise Prison*, High Court, April 25, 1983 in which, in regard to the withholding, by the Governor, of letters to bank managers, Mr. Tony Gregory T.D., and the Registrars of the High Court and the Supreme Court, McMahon J. said at p. 3 of the transcript: "I am satisfied that in dealing with the prisoner's letters, the Governor was not acting judicially and had no obligation to afford the prisoner a hearing. The Governor's decisions did not involve any disputed questions of fact and were based on his own views as to the requirements of security of the prison."

[66] [1980] I.L.R.M. 82.

[67] See *The State (Gleeson)* v. *Minister for Defence* (at p. 259) and *The State (Duffy)* v. *Minister for Defence* (p. 268).

[68] [1976] I.R. 286. This decision has been applied in *Hogan* v. *Minister for Justice*, High Court, September 8, 1976 and *The State (Furey)* v. *Minister for Defence*, Supreme Court, March 2, 1984.

opportunity to meet the case against him or of dealing with the reason for his discharge.

By contrast, in *The State (Duffy)* v. *Minister for Defence*,[69] the applicant had been dismissed from the Navy on the ground of inefficiency. The applicant's argument founded on breach of constitutional justice was rejected and *Gleeson* distinguished because the applicant had been warned why his position was in danger and allowed an opportunity to reply. A further point of distinction which is of particular relevance in discipline cases is that the procedural standards which must be met in cases involving alleged misconduct are higher than in the case of discharges on the grounds of inefficiency.[70]

In *Garvey* v. *Ireland*, the Supreme Court majority firmly rejected the argument:

> "... [T]hat the confidential and sensitive relationship that must necessarily exist between the Government of the day and the head of the national policy force requires that the statutory right to remove a Commissioner from office at any time should not be interpreted as being shackled by an obligation to give a reason for its exercise. ... [71]

In contrast, there is High Court authority accepting the argument that special considerations apply in relation to the power of the State to dispense with the services of members of the Defence Forces, of the Garda Siochana and of the prison service "because it is of vital concern to the community as a whole that the members of these services should be completely trustworthy."[72] This factor played a part in *The State (Donnelly)* v. *Minister for Defence*[73] and in *The State (Jordan)* v. *Garda Commissioner*.[74] In

---

[69] Supreme Court, May 9, 1979. See also *The State (McGarrity)* v. *Deputy Garda Commissioner* (1978) 112 I.L.T.R. 25 (no obligation to give hearing to recruit Garda who was discharged at the end of his probationary period); *Delaney* v. *Garvey*, High Court, March 14, 1978. *Sed quaere* whether *McGarrity* is applicable in the case of a recruit discharged at end of probationary period on the grounds of misconduct. *Chief Constable of N. Wales Police* v. *Evans* [1982] 1 W.L.R. 1155; *O'Rourke* v. *Miller* (1985) 58 A.L.R. 269.

[70] This point was not mentioned in *Duffy*. In both *Gleeson* and *Collins* v. *County Cork V.E.C.*, High Court, May 26, 1982 it was said that higher procedural standards were required where some specific acts of misconduct or negligence is involved.

[71] [1981] I.R. 75 at p. 102 *per* Henchy J.

[72] *The State (Jordan)* v. *Garda Commissioner*, High Court, October 14, 1985, p. 20 *per* O'Hanlon J.

[73] High Court, October 9, 1979.

[74] High Court, October 14, 1985.

Donnelly the applicant had been discharged from the Defence Forces as he was considered to have been a security risk. Some of the incidents in which the applicant was allegedly involved—such as the theft of a machine gun—were so serious that his commanding officer considered that they would warrant a discharge if no satisfactory explanation was forthcoming. Finlay P. agreed that the fact that the officer had drafted an application for Donnelly's discharge was "suspicious," but he was satisfied that this was simply a recommendation and that the matter would not have been carried any further if the applicant had given a satisfactory explanation of the incidents in question. Accordingly, Finlay P. ruled that there was a no bias or prejudgment of the issue on the part of the commanding officer. The judge also took the view that in the subsequent interviews the applicant had been given an adequate opportunity to make his own case. Nor was Finlay P. impressed by the argument that the applicant had never been convicted of any offences, whether under military law or the ordinary criminal law, since there was a "clear public necessity" that the military authorities should have the discretion to remove persons considered to be a security risk. Similar reasoning prevailed in *Jordan*, where a summary dismissal of a detective Garda was upheld. The applicant had been charged with the assault of a suspect (who was later to die while in policy custody), but was acquitted following a trial in the Circuit Criminal Court. O'Hanlon J. considered that his defence in the criminal proceedings was such as to be tantamount to an admission that he had deceived the members of the Gardai who were investigating this incident by suppressing and concealing vital information. In these circumstances, and in view of the need to maintain public confidence in the members of the Force, it was held that the Garda Commissioner was entitled to dispense with the applicant's services without the need for a formal inquiry.

The cases examined so far could all have been classified under an earlier heading since the sanction was dismissal. It is questionable whether the rules of natural justice apply at all where the punishment involved is the involuntary transfer of personnel. Such transfers are regarded as administrative decisions, and this fact when coupled with the public interest in maintaining the efficiency of the security forces, means that it would probably require something akin to *mala fides* before such an administrative decision could be successfully challenged.[75] Similarly, natural justice does not require a hearing prior to the suspension of a

---

[75] *The State (Boyle)* v. *Governor of the Military Detention Barracks* [1980] I.L.R.M. 242; *The State (Smith & Fox)* v. *Governor of Military Detention Barracks* [1980] I.L.R.M. 208 (prison transfer cases); *Corliss* v. *Ireland*, High Court, July 23, 1984 (transfer of Gardai).

member of the Garda Siochana in the interests of good administration pending a fuller disciplinary hearing, even though financial
loss may be caused as a result.[76]

Property and planning

Even at times and in jurisdictions where the bounds of natural
justice have been narrowly set, there has never been any doubt
that the rules of natural justice apply to state interference with
property rights.[77] Thus, the rules have been applied to compulsory
purchase orders and land acquisition procedures; decisions of
planning authorities and An Bord Pleanala;[78] and the making of a
preservation order by the Commissioners of Public Works.[79]

An interesting and novel application of the principles of natural
justice is to be found in *The State (Philpott)* v. *Registrar of Titles*.[80]
The applicant who was the registered owner of certain freehold
property, was informed that the respondent had entered an
inhibition on the folio, which prevented all dealings with the land
save with the consent of the respondent.[81] The applicant was
engaged in the process of selling the lands in question when this
inhibition had been entered without prior warning or notice. The
Registrar had acted following correspondence with certain third

[76] *McHugh* v. *Garda Commissioner* [1985] I.L.R.M. 606. But *cf. Ni Bheolain*
v. *Dublin V.E.C.* High Court, January 28, 1983 (natural justice applies
to suspension without pay). See further pp. 288–289.
[77] *Re Mountcharles' Estate* [1935] I.R. 754; *Foley* v. *Irish Land Commission*
[1952] I.R. 118; *Re Roscrea Meat Products Estate* [1958] I.R. 47; *The State
(Costello)* v. *Irish Land Commission* [1959] I.R. 353; *Clarke* v. *Irish Land
Commission* [1976] I.R. 375; *Nolan* v. *Irish Land Commission* [1981] I.R.
23; *The State (Hussey)* v. *Irish Land Commission*, [1983] I.L.R.M. 407;
O'Brien v. *Bord na Mona* [1983] I.R. 255. See also *Irish Land Commission*
v. *Hession* [1978] I.R. 322 (decision of Land Commission set aside
where Commissioners acted on the basis of evidence not properly
before them).
[78] *Killiney and Ballybrack Residents Assoc.* v. *Minister for Local Government*
(1978) 112 I.L.T.R. 69. *Geraghty* v. *Minister for Local Government* [1976]
I.R. 153; *The State (Genport Ltd.)* v. *An Bord Pleanala* [1983] I.L.R.M. 12;
The State (Boyd) v. *An Bord Pleanala*, High Court, February 18, 1983; *The
State (C.I.E.)* v. *An Bord Pleanala*, Supreme Court, December 12, 1984;
The State (Hussey & Kenny) v. *An Bord Pleanala*, Supreme Court,
December 20, 1984.
[79] *O'Callaghan* v. *Commissioners of Public Works* [1985] I.L.R.M. 364.
[80] *The State (Philpott)* v. *Registrar of Titles*, High Court, July 29, 1985.
[81] s.120 of the Registration of Title Act 1964 provides that the State will
pay compensation to persons who suffer loss by reason of official errors
in registration or entries obtained by fraud or forgery. S.121 of the Act
enables the Registrar to take action by means of the entry of a caution
to protect the State from possible claims.

parties in which the third parties claimed certain rights over the
lands. Gannon J. ruled that because of the grave nature of the
interference in the land, natural justice required that persons
affected by the entry of an inhibition should be given prior notice
and an opportunity to show cause why it should not be entered.
The judge accepted that in order to protect the common fund, it
would be "imprudent or impractical" to give the owner prior
notice and a hearing in urgent cases. He held, however, that the
instant case did not fall within this category and, accordingly,
quashed the Registrar's decision. It is self evident that this decison
will be of great significance, not only to the Land Registry, but also
for other systems of registration.[82]

Payments of grants, benefits and pensions

Irish courts have largely abandoned the formerly-held notion
that the rules of natural justice did not apply to discretionary
payments to which the applicant had no statutory entitlement. The
modern view is that the rules of natural justice apply to protect the
citizen's "legitimate expectations."[83] A good example of this
modern attitude is to be found in *The State (McConnell)* v. *Eastern
Health Board*.[84] In this case an applicant who was entitled to a
disability allowance had married, and his spouse was also in receipt
of unemployment benefit. Under the relevant regulations, a
person in receipt of a disability allowance was obliged to inform
the Health Board of any material change in their circumstances.
The applicant was unaware of this obligation, and the fact of his
marriage only came to the attention of the Health Board some
eighteen months later, resulting in a substantial overpayment of
the disability allowance to the applicant. Hamilton J. quashed the
respondent's decision to recoup the overpayment by means of
weekly deductions from the applicant's allowance on the ground
that no adequate opportunity had been given to the applicant to
make representations prior to this decision; nor had he been
afforded the opportunity to consider a report from the Department of Social Welfare concerning the case.

[82] *e.g.* the registration of company charges under p. IV of the Companies
Act 1963. See *R.* v. *Registrar of Companies ex p. Easal Commodities Ltd.*
[1986] 2 W.L.R. 117 and Pye, "The s.104 Certificate of Registration—
An Impenetrable Shield No More?" (1985) 3 I.L.T.(n.s.) 213.

[83] *O'Reilly* v. *Mackman* [1983] 2 A.C. 237 at 275 *per* Lord Diplock. For a
similar attitude, see *per* Henchy J. in *Kiely* v. *Minister for Social Welfare*
[1977] I.R. 297 and *per* Finlay P. in *The State (Hayes)* v. *Criminal Injuries
Compensation Tribunal* [1982] I.L.R.M. 210.

[84] High Court, June 1, 1983. See also *McLoughlin* v. *Minister for Social
Welfare* [1958] I.R. 1; *Kiely* v. *Minister for Social Welfare* [1971] I.R. 21
and *Kiely* v. *Minister for Social Welfare* [1977] I.R. 297.

General principle

Thus far, an attempt has been made to pigeon-hole most of the cases in which the constitutional justice principles have been said to apply. The next question is whether there is any general principle which would indicate the common ground shared by these cases and so assist a lawyer advising a client to predict whether the principles apply to new areas. The short answer is that the Irish courts have spent little time in looking for a guiding principle and, in any case such a search would be inherently unlikely to be successful. Traditionally, the English courts invoked the quasi-judicial/administrative distinction to solve this problem. At the root of this classification lay the feeling that it was only decisions which were analogous to those taken by judges in courts which attracted the rules of natural justice. The reason was that these rules are, in essence, similar to the rules of procedure and evidence applied in a court. Thus, the rules of natural justice applied to quasi-judicial, but not administrative, decisions. Straightaway, this raises the difficulty of deciding precisely which decisions of government administration are to be regarded as analogous to decisons by courts, *i.e.* quasi-judicial. In England, various tests have been used (sometimes separately, sometimes in combination). First, does the test to be applied by the deciding body involve reference to require the determination of contested facts and/or the application of some fairly precise standard, as opposed to the exercise of a discretion. Secondly, reliance has been placed on the "trappings of the court" test, for instance; has the body taking the decision the power to summon witnesses and administer oaths? Does it usually sit in public?[85]

The administrative/quasi-judicial function classification has been used in the Irish case law, principally in regard to the first rule of constitutional justice but also, occasionally, in regard to the second rule as, for example, in *The State (Williams) v. Army Pensions Board*.[86] Here the Supreme Court classified the Board's decision as quasi-judicial because it was not exercising a discretion to award a widow's benefit, but was applying a fairly well-defined statutory test namely, whether a person's death was due to disease arising

---

[85] See pp. 137–140.
[86] [1983] I.R. 308. For other examples, see *Re Roscrea Meat Products Estate* [1958] I.R. 47; *The State (Shannon Atlantic Fisheries Ltd.) v. McPolin* [1976] I.R. 98; *Geraghty v. Minister for Local Government* [1976] I.R. 153; *Connolly v. McConnell* [1983] I.R. 172; *The State (Genport Ltd.) v. An Bord Pleanala* [1983] I.L.R.M. 12; *The State (Gallagher) v. Governor of Portlaoise Prison*, High Court, April 25, 1983. In some cases the courts have not used the term quasi-judicial, but have spoken instead of "a duty to act judicially": *McDonald v. Bord na gCon* [1965] I.R. 217; *O'Brien v. Bord na Mona* [1983] I.R. 255. This is only a terminological difference.

during service with the UN. It is significant that, in *Williams*, Keane J. in the High Court differed from the Supreme Court in that he classified the relevant function as "administrative" but then went on to say:

> " . . . [I]t is clear from an abundance of recent authority, that even purely administrative acts of persons such as [the Army Pensions Board and the Minister for Defence] may be affected by the requirements of natural and constitutional justice."[87]

A simpler test as to whether the rules apply is whether any serious individual interest is directly affected by a government action. The noticeable fact which emerges from the case law is that the rules have almost always been held to apply (although, it may be, with a lower standard) even in a case like *East Donegal Co-Operatives Ltd.* v. *Attorney-General*[88] which involved a discretionary decision. Indeed, it is remarkable how seldom the respondent has even bothered to argue that the rules do not apply, confining himself instead to arguments about the content of constitutional justice. For example, the argument that a social welfare benefit is only a privilege is not even mentioned in the judgments in *Kiely (Nos. 1 or 2)*.

However, apart from certain decisions of the D.P.P. and cases of waiver which have been dealt with elsewhere, there are at least four areas which may be exempt from the rules: 1. In the last paragraph, it was said that the rules apply where any individual interest is *directly* affected. However, as was demonstrated in the leading case of *Listowel U.D.C.* v. *McDonagh*,[89] the no-bias rule applies to delegated legislation, albeit in the attenuated form of the rule against *mala fides*. Thus, as the New Zealand courts have made clear, it is sufficient that the donees of the power to make delegated legislation approach the matter with an open mind and genuinely satisfy themselves that the statutory criteria have been complied with.[90] They are not precluded from having a prior opinion. The position is less definite in regard to the *audi alteram partem* rule. Traditionally, legislative decisions were taken as being beyond the reach of the rule.[91] This orthodoxy was confirmed by McMahon J. in the High Court in *Cassidy* v. *Minister for Industry*

---

[87] [1981] I.L.R.M. at 382.
[88] [1975] I.R. 317.
[89] [1968] I.R. 312.
[90] *Creednz Inc.* v. *Governor-General* [1981] 1 N.Z.L.R. 172.
[91] *Bates* v. *Lord Hailsham* [1972] 1 W.L.R. 1373; *Essex C.C.* v. *Minister for Housing* (1967) 66 L.G.R. 23.

and Commerce[92] where he held, without discussion, that the rule did not apply to require consultation with a vintners' association before the making of a statutory instrument fixing maximum prices for the sale of intoxicating liquor in the Dundalk area.

On the other hand, in some cases involving delegated legislation, it has been decided or assumed (although again without any discussion of the difficulties) that the maker was under a duty to consult interested parties. For example, in *Burke* v. *Minister for Labour*[93] a Joint Labour Committee had fixed minimum wages for persons working in the hotel industry by means of an order made under the Industrial Relations Act 1946. Employers were obliged under pain of criminal sanction to respect this order and to comply with its terms. The employers' representatives wished to adduce evidence as to the real cost to the employers of the board and lodging provided for their employees, but the Committee went ahead and fixed minimum wages without regard to this evidence. The Supreme Court was of opinion that the Committee's refusal to admit such evidence rendered the order invalid. In the view of Henchy J.:

> "Where Parliament has delegated functions of this nature, it is to be necessarily inferred as part of the legislative intention that the body which makes the orders will exercise its functions, not only with constitutional propriety and due regard to natural justice, but also within the framework of the terms and objects of the relevant Act and with basic fairness, reasonableness and good faith. The absoluteness of the delegation is susceptible of unjust and tyrannous abuse unless its operation is thus confined; so it is entirely proper to ascribe to the Oireachtas (being the Parliament of a State

[92] [1978] I.R. 297. This point was not dealt with by the Supreme Court who found for the plaintiff on another ground: see pp. 311–312.

[93] [1979] I.R. 354. In *The State (Lynch)* v. *Cooney* [1982] I.R. 337 the Supreme Court appears to have accepted that the Minister could have been under a duty to consult with interested parties prior to the making of a banning order by way of statutory instrument under s.31 of the Broadcasting Authority Act 1960. However, the Minister's failure to do this was excused by the Supreme Court in view of the fact that given the circumstances of the case there was no time to hear the other side. Nor was this point taken in *Crotty* v. *Cobh U.D.C.*, Circuit Court, July 2, 1982, in which local authority had exercised its powers under the Casual Trading Act 1980 to designate land as a casual trading area. The Council was influenced by a petition from local established traders. Judge Fawsitt held that the local authority should also have consulted the casual traders before reaching its conclusion. Both *Crotty* and *Lynch* would appear to be instances of administrative decisions taken under the guise of delegated legislation.

288 Constitutional Justice

> which is constitutionally bound to protect, by its laws, its
> citizens from unjust attack) an intention that the delegated
> functions must be exercised within those limitations."[94]

The rationale usually given for excluding legislative decisions from the scope of the rules is that the *audi alteram partem* rule, at any rate, is more appropriate where a compact range of facts is in issue—for example, in a dismissal case, whether an employee was dishonest—and less appropriate when a broader range of acts and considerations, including it may be, the economy or some other national interest, is concerned. In addition, of course, the fact that the principal type of legislation is an Act of Parliament, where all interests are supposedly represented, has traditionally encouraged courts to avoid this area (although in practice of course, departments of state customarily consult interest groups about the content of draft bills). It may thus be that *Burke* has not laid down any general principle. The order which was invalidated in that case and the other cases cited at footnote 93 only applied to a small narrowly-defined category of situations and may be regarded as involving an administrative decision passed under the guise of delegated legislation. It is, perhaps, only in such unusual cases that the makers of delegated legislation are under a duty to observe the *audi alteram partem* rule.

2. Traditionally it was also the case (for reasons similar to those adduced in the last paragraph) that where a policy question was involved, even though no legislative function was being exercised, it was less likely that natural justice would apply.[95] 3. This is unlikely to be so today. Even in regard to the deportation of a (non-EEC) alien, it has been suggested that the *audi alteram partem* rule might have to be followed.[96] Generally speaking, the rules of constitutional justice do not apply to suspensions. For instance, in *Rochford* v. *Story*,[97] the plaintiffs had been suspended from membership of a trade union sporting club following a dispute over the plaintiff's

[94] [1979] I.R. 354 at pp. 361–362.
[95] de Smith *op. cit.* at pp. 186–187.
[96] *Abdelkefi* v. *Minister for Justice* [1984] I.L.R.M. 138. See also *The State (Kugan)* v. *Station Sergeant, Fitzgibbon St. Garda Station* [1986] I.L.R.M. 95 (refusal of leave to enter; decision quashed as immigration officials had failed to exercise their discretion in reasonable manner). But *cf. Pok Sun Shum* v. *Ireland*, High Court, June 28, 1985 where Costello J. held that because of "the special control of aliens which every State must exercise" natural justice did not require that the Minister for Justice to inform an applicant of the information on the files and give him an opportunity to comment before refusing a certificate of naturalisation under the provisions of the Irish Citizenship and Nationality Act 1956.
[97] High Court, November 4, 1982. See also *McHugh* v. *Garda Commissioner* [1985] I.L.R.M. 606.

eligibility for membership. The suspensions had been imposed when the plaintiffs had failed to attend a meeting which they had been requested to produce evidence of their entitlement to become full members of the club. Even though O'Hanlon J. concluded that natural justice was complied with when the plaintiffs had been put on notice by letter that the validity of their membership was in dispute, he was also of opinion that the decision to suspend did not attract the rules. The judge quoted the following illuminating extract from an English case with approval.

> "[The rules of natural justice] apply, no doubt, to suspensions which are inflicted by way of punishment, as for instance when a member of the Bar is suspended from practice for six months, or where a Solicitor is suspended from practice. But they do not apply to suspensions which are made, as a holding operation, pending enquiries. Very often irregularities are disclosed in a government department or in a business house; and a man may be suspended on full pay pending enquiries. Suspicion may rest on him; and so he is suspended until he is cleared of it. The suspension in such a case is merely by way of good administration. A situation has arisen in which something must be done at once. The work of the department or the office is being affected by rumours and suspicions. The others will not trust the man. In order to get back to proper work, the man is suspended.[98]

However, in line with this passage, it has also been held in Ireland that the rules would apply where the suspension would have the effect of interfering with the affected individual's livelihood as, where he is suspended without pay or where the suspension imputes grave misconduct.[99] In addition, it seems that fair procedure may also require that the final, substantive decision should be taken with as little delay as possible so that the person affected is not kept in suspense longer than is necessary. As is demonstrated at several points in this chapter, the constitutional justice rules allow a considerable margin of appreciation and the courts have held that within these broad limits (and subject, of course, to any particular procedural regulations) it is for the deciding agency itself to exercise "a certain discretion as to the manner in which it conducts the proceedings."[1] However,

[98] *Lewis* v. *Heffer* [1978] 1 W.L.R. 1061 at p. 1073 *per* Lord Denning M.R.
[99] *Ni Bheolain* v. *Dublin V.E.C.*, High Court, January 28, 1983; *Collins* v. *Cork V.E.C.*, Supreme Court, March 18, 1983; *The State (Donegal V.E.C.)* v. *Minister for Education* [1985] I.R. 56.
[1] *The State (Boyle)* v. *General Medical Services (Payments) Board* [1981] I.L.R.M. 14 at p. 16, *per* Keane J. See also *The State (Genport Ltd.)* [1983] I.L.R.M. 12 at p. 16.

following the general principles which govern the exercise of any discretion, substantive or procedural, such a discretion must be genuinely exercised and it must be exercised fairly and reasonably.[2] Another type of exemption which exists in England—but which is probably not part of Irish law—stems from the idea that where a tribunal or other public authority has formulated a comprehensive, detailed code of procedure, the onus on a person who seeks to establish that this code is inconsistent with natural justice is very heavy.[3] By contrast, in Ireland, constitutional justice is not just a general norm of administrative law; it also, as has been seen, enjoys the support of Article 40.3 of the Constitution, and thus the courts will readily inject the rules of constitutional justice into even a comprehensive procedural code.[4]

4. In a number of cases, some of which have already been described, countervailing policies have been said to justify a failure to observe the rules of constitutional justice (or, more correctly, just the *audi alteram partem* limb).[5] Examples of such countervailing policies include the fact that the rule would cause a delay or otherwise defeat the object of the public authority's action[6] or that it was impossible for the public authority to contact the person affected to elicit his representations.[7] A graphic illustration occured in *O'Callaghan* v. *Commissioner of Public Works*.[8] The plaintiff was a farmer who owned a 2,000 year-old promontory fort which had been listed as a "national monument" under the National Monuments Acts 1930–54. Ignoring the order, he instructed an agricultural contractor to plough up the land near the fort. Soon the ploughing had to be temporarily abandoned

---

[2] *Irish Family Planning Assoc.* v. *Ryan* [1979] I.R. 295. Note the significant differences in tone between O'Higgins C.J. (S.C.) and that of Hamilton J. (H.C.) on the other.

[3] Evans, "Some Limits to the Scope of Natural Justice" (1973) 36 M.L.R. 439. (There is some Irish support for this point of view see *e.g. The State (Fagan)* v. *Governor of Mountjoy Prison*, High Court, March 6, 1978) but generally the courts will, if necessary, superimpose constitutional standards on the terms of a statute: see *e.g. O'Domhnaill* v. *Merrick* [1984] I.R. 151.

[4] See *e.g. East Donegal Co-Operatives Ltd.* v. *Att.-Gen.* [1970] I.R. 317; *Kiely* v. *Minister for Social Welfare (No. 2)* [1977] I.R. 267.

[5] *e.g. The State (Donnelly)* v. *Minister for Defence*, High Court, October 9, 1979; *The State (Jordan)* v. *Garda Commissioner*, High Court, October 14, 1985 (need to maintain public confidence in integrity of members of Defence Forces and Gardai). See p. 282.

[6] *The State (Lynch)* v. *Cooney* [1982] I.R. 337. *The State (Philpott)* v. *Registrar of Titles*, High Court, July 28, 1985.

[7] *Irish Family Planning Assoc. Ltd.* v. *Ryan* [1979] I.R. 295, 313–314, *per* O'Higgins C.J.

[8] [1985] I.L.R.M. 364.

because of damage to the plough. However, its imminent resumption led the Commissioners to Public Works to make a preservation order which extended the Commissioners' powers to protect the fort. The Supreme Court rejected the argument that the Commissioners ought to have allowed the plaintiff farmer an opportunity to put forward any objection he might have had to the making of a preservation order. O'Higgins C.J. said:

> "Here an emergency had been created by the plaintiff's own action in defiance of his legal obligations. If the Commissioners had hesitated in acting as they did, the monument which it was their duty to preserve would have been seriously damaged or destroyed. Further, it was not possible to contact the plaintiff, because his address was not then known and did not become known to the Commissioners until sometime later."[9]

Speaking more generally, in *The State (Lynch)* v. *Cooney* O'Higgins C.J. justified his refusal to apply the *audi alteram partem* rule on the ground that "justice [does not] require that those to be affected by action of this kind should receive notice and be heard."[10] This suggests that there is a reservoir of discretionary power to which the principles of constitutional justice do not apply, which is wider than the specific examples mentioned in the previous paragraph. If this reading is correct, it is obviously pregnant with considerable possibilities for the future. It is also noteworthy that the courts have chosen to create a distinct category of exemption rather than simply to exercise their long-established discretion to refuse to grant relief.[11]

5. Concluding comment

It is useful to illustrate the difficulties inherent in constitutional justice by way of the *Kiely* saga. Mrs Kiely's claim for a widow's benefit was rejected by a deciding officer and, on appeal, by the appeals officer, in the Department of Social Welfare; the appeals officer's decision was struck down on review, by the High Court[12]; the case was re-heard again by a second appeals officer and decided against the claimant; this decision was struck down in the Supreme Court[13]; the question was then decided by a third appeals officer, who reached the same decision as his two colleagues, and,

---

[9] [1985] I.L.R.M. at pp. 373–374.
[10] [1982] I.R. 337 at p. 365. See also his comments in *Irish Family Planning Assoc.* v. *Ryan* [1979] I.R. 295 at p. 313.
[11] See pp. 348–351.
[12] *Kiely* v. *Minister for Social Welfare (No. 1)* [1971] I.R. 21.
[13] *Kiely* v. *Minister for Social Welfare (No. 2)* [1977] I.R. 267.

this time there was no review so that the decision was effective. Neither the advantages nor the disadvantages of constitutional justice have not been researched empirically. However, it seems reasonable to make the following assumptions: first, that greater procedural complexity increases delay and expense[14]; secondly, that the rules promote excessive caution among public servants, particularly at the lower levels where the officials cannot reasonably be expected to be familiar with the novel, and sometimes rather artificial, requirements of constitutional justice. To take the example of an official charged with the duty of awarding a licence: he will know that it is more likely that the refusal of a licence will be challenged by a disappointed applicant than that an erroneous award of a licence will be challenged by a competitor or other member of the public. In view of this, there is a pressure, which is contrary to the public interest, upon the administrator to grant the licence. One of the consequences of the constitutional justice rules is to increase this pressure. Often this effect is exacerbated because the duty to give reasons for a public authority's proposed decision (which is included in the *audi alteram partem* rule) imposes something analogous to the procedures of a law court in the very different circumstances of a tribunal or public authority.

As against this, constitutional justice is taken to carry four advantages. In the first place, an impartial decision-maker and an opportunity for the person affected to put forward his comments both help to promote an "appropriate" result. (The decision may be too subjective to speak of the *correct result*). As Megarry J. remarked in a notable passage:

> "As everyone who has anything to do with the law well knows, the path of the law is strewn with examples of open and shut cases which, somehow, were not; of unanswerable charges which, in the event, were completely answered; of inexplicable conduct which was fully explained; of fixed and unalterable determinations that, by discussion, suffered a change."[15]

A hearing means that the risk of injustice caused by acting on an *ex parte* view of the situation will have been obviated. Even if the facts or arguments adduced by the person affected do not cause the decision to be reversed, they may lead to its being varied and thus, for instance, it has been held, in cases involving disciplinary

---

[14] For a rare judicial acknowledgement of these difficulties, see the comments of Megarry J. in *McInnes* v. *Onslow-Fane* [1978] 1 W.L.R. 1520.

[15] *John* v. *Rees* [1970] Ch. 345 at p. 402.

punishments, that there is a right to be heard in mitigation.[16] It has been said that " . . . the holder's office being such a crucial part of his life, basic fairness requires that he should not be sundered from it without first being given a meaningful opportunity of being heard, if only *ad misericordiam*."[17]

Secondly, the duty to give reasons for a public authority's proposed decision (which is included in the *audi alteram partem* rule) might disclose to the person affected that the decision was being taken on grounds, or in circumstances which rendered it substantially invalid. In such a case, the rule would assist the person affected by giving him information which would enable him to launch an action for judicial review on substantive grounds or perhaps, to refer the matter to the Ombudsman or a T.D. or to seek some other sanction. The point was put eloquently in the following passage from Henchy J.'s judgment in *Garvey* v. *Ireland*:

> "If, by maintaining an obscuring silence, a Government could render their act of dismissal impenetrable as to its reasons and unreviewable as to its method, an office-holder such as the plaintiff could have his livelihood snatched from him, his chosen career snuffed out, his pension prospects dashed and his reputation irretrievably tarnished, without any hope of redress, no matter how unjustified or unfair his dismissal might be. I doubt if it would be even contended that the statutory power of removal from office could validly be used to dismiss a person for an unconstitutional reason (for example, because of his race, creed or colour); yet if such were to happen, and suddenness and silence were to be allowed to curtain off the dismissal from judicial scrutiny, the dismissed person, far from getting the constitutionally guaranteed protection from unjust attack, would be abandoned to the consequence of an unjust, unconstitutional and ruinous decision."[18]

Thirdly, it is a matter of satisfaction and dignity to the individual that he should have his say before a decision is taken against him

---

[16] *R. (Hennessy)* v. *Department of Education* [1980] N.I. 109; *The State (Grahame)* v. *Racing Board*, High Court, November 22, 1983.

[17] *Garvey* v. *Ireland* [1981] I.R. 75 at p. 102. Henchy J. pointed out that, in the context of a removal from office, another benefit of the *audi alteram partem* rule is that it requires the ground on which the office-holder was removed to be authoritatively stated, and that this may be less discreditable than the grounds which might otherwise be suspected. For an earlier Supreme Court decision denying that natural justice extends to *ad misericordiam* pleas, see *The State (Costello)* v. *Irish Land Commission* [1959] I.R. 353.

[18] [1981] I.R. 75 at p. 101.

by a governmental agency. (This is the equivalent, in the administrative sphere, of "the day in court"). In *R. (Smyth)* v. *C. Antrim Coroner*[19] it was sought to quash the verdict returned by a coroner's jury on the grounds that, in breach of the relevant regulations, the coroner had failed to sum up the evidence to the jury. Quashing the verdict, Kelly J. conceded that another jury, hearing the same evidence and assisted by a proper and adequate summing up of it by the coroner, might come to exactly the same verdict; but held that the next-of-kin were entitled "to have their unhappiness tempered by the knowledge that such a verdict was reached by a considered and regular inquiry."

Finally, an open consistent procedure in which the state agency taking the decision is seen to be impartial is necessary to maintain the confidence of the general public in the institutions of government. For example, in a case where the failure of a Joint Labour Committee to hear certain relevant evidence was found to be contrary to the principle of *audi alteram partem*, Henchy J. adverted to the dangers of the "no merits" argument:

> "Even if such evidence would have made no difference, the Committee by rejecting it unheard and unconsidered, left themselves open to the imputation of bias, unfairness and prejudice."[20]

The importance which is to be assigned to the disadvantages and to each of the distinct advantages is relevant in considering two policy questions. The first issue, which has divided the judiciary in a number of jurisdictions, and which has arisen mainly in the context of the *audi alteram partem* limb of constitutional justice, is whether a failure to follow the rules is fatal where it is clear that the case was correctly decided.

In Ireland too, diametrically opposing views have been given to this conundrum, though usually without much in the way of discussion. In *Glover* v. *B.L.N. Ltd.*,[21] the majority brushed aside the submission that, if a hearing had been held, there was nothing the plaintiff could have said anyway, with Walsh J. remarking:

> "This proposition only has to be stated to be rejected. The obligation to give a fair hearing to the guilty is just as great as the obligation to give a fair hearing to the innocent."[22]

---

[19] [1980] N.I. 123.

[20] *Burke* v. *Minister for Labour* [1979] I.R. 354 at p. 362. See also the comments of O'Donnell L.J. in *R. (Hennessy)* v. *Department of the Environment* [1980] N.I. 109.

[21] [1973] I.R. 388.

[22] *Ibid.* at p. 429

The dissenting judge in *Glover*, Fitzgerald J., was equally strong and terse in the opposite sense. Again, in *O'Brien* v. *Bord na Mona*,[23] Finlay P. stated on behalf of the Supreme Court that:

> "A necessity for the observance of natural justice in the process of compulsory acquisition of property is too funda-mental and important to be supplied by proof that objections would have been rejected if they had been entertained."[24]

By contrast, in *Corrigan* v. *Irish Land Commission*,[25] another case on compulsory acquisition of land, Henchy J. considered that there was an "overriding reason" why in the circumstances of this case the doctrine of estoppel by conduct should apply: it was inconceivable on the facts "that a fresh hearing could have any result other than a finding adverse to the appellant." Even overlooking the preliminary difficulty of a court being sure that the applicant had an impossible case, this is a difficult question. The most that can be said is that a judge will be more likely to strike down the decision impugned if he assigns importance to the advantages of "the day in court" and confidence in public administration and less likely to do so if he regards these advantages as trivial and outweighed by the disadvantages which were mentioned at the start of this part. In addition, the more serious the consequences for the aggrieved party, the less likely the courts are to refuse relief.[26]

It is of course, always possible for the court to avoid laying down any general principle and, instead, to determine the outcome of

---

[23] [1983] I.R. 266. See Coffey, "Procedural Curbs on Powers of Compulsory Acquisition" 1984) 6 D.U.L.J.(n.s.) 152. For other authorities along the same lines, see *Maunsell* v. *Minister for Education* [1940] I.R. 213; *General Medical Council* v. *Spackman* [1943] A.C. 627; *Ridge* v. *Baldwin* [1964] A.C. 40; *The State (Crothers)* v. *Kelly*, High Court, October 2, 1978, and see generally Clark, "Natural Justice: Substance or Shadow?" [1975] *Public Law* 27.

[24] [1983] I.R. at p. 287.

[25] [1977] I.R. 317 at p. 327. See also, to like effect, *Ward* v. *Bradford Corporation* (1970) 70 L.G.R. 27; *Glynn* v. *Keele University* [1971] 1 W.L.R. 487; *Irish Family Planning Assoc.* v. *Ryan* [1979] I.R. 295 at p. 319; *R. (McPherson)* v. *Ministry of Education* [1980] N.I. 115n; *Cheall* v. *A.P.E.X.* [1983] 2 A.C. 109. Note also the comments of Lord Denning in *R.* v. *Home Secretary, ex p. Mughal* [1974] Q.B. 313 at p. 325. "Only too often the people who have done wrong seek to invoke the rules of natural justice in order to avoid the consequences".

[26] See *e.g. R. (Hennessy)* v. *Department of the Environment* [1980] N.I. 109; *O'Brien* v. *Bord na Mona* [1983] I.R. 255.

the case by refusing relief on discretionary grounds and this approach has often been adopted.[27]

The second policy question arising in this area concerns the effect of an appeal: where a decision is taken in breach of the rules of constitutional justice, is this defect cured where a right of appeal is exercised to a court (or other body) in which the rules are observed. It has been decided that an appeal does not cure the flaw in the original decision.[28] However the significance of this ruling has been reduced by the gloss introduced, in *Gammell* v. *Dublin C.C.*,[29] namely that certain categories of "appeal" can be treated as part of the initial decision.

[27] *Fulbrook* v. *Berkshire Magistrates Courts* (1970) 69 L.G.R. 75; *Ward* v. *Bradford Corporation* (1971) 70 L.G.R. 27; *Glynn* v. *Keele University* [1971] 1 W.L.R. 487; *R. (McPherson)* v. *Department of Education* [1980] N.I. 115n. On the question of the discretionary character of the remedies, see further at pp. 348–351.

[28] *Leary* v. *National Union of Vehicle Builders* [1971] Ch. 34; *Ingle* v. *O'Brien* (1975) 109 I.L.T.R. 9; *Moran* v. *Att.-Gen.* [1976] I.R. 400; *Irish Family Planning Assoc.* v. *Ryan* [1979] I.R. 295. *A contra, The State (Stanbridge)* v. *Mahon* [1979] I.R. 217; *Calvin* v. *Carr* [1980] A.C. 574 and *The State (Collins)* v. *Ruane* [1984] I.R. 105 at p. 124, *per* Henchy J.

[29] [1983] I.L.R.M. 413. See further at pp. 269–271.

10   Control of Discretionary Powers

1. Discretionary power

There is a distinction between decisions involving the resolution of disputed questions of fact coupled with the application of pre-existing law and, on the other hand, those involving the exercise of discretionary power. The first type of decision is quintessentially the domain of a court or tribunal.[1] The second type where a discretionary or policy function is being exercised, may be illustrated by the following examples:

> "On the application of ... a person who proposes to carry on the business of a livestock mart ... in such form ... as the Minister [for Agriculture] may direct, the Minister may, at his discretion, grant or refuse to grant a licence authorising the carrying on of the business of a livestock mart ... "[2]
> "A sanitary authority may by order prohibit the erection ... of temporary dwellings on any land or water in their sanitary district if they are of opinion that such erection ... would be prejudicial to public health ...."[3]

In spite of the apparent *carte blanche* which expressions like " ... may, at his discretion ... " or " ... if they are of opinion ... " appear to bestow, discretionary powers are subject to certain principles regulating their exercise, in addition to the general requirements requiring the decision-maker to observe the *vires* of the parent statute and any other relevant law. These additional controls are conventionally grouped under the headings of: abuse (or excess) of discretionary power, covered in part 2; and

---

[1] See pp. 7–10, 135–141.
[2] Livestock Marts Act 1967, s.3(1) examined in *East Donegal* v. *Att.-Gen.* [1970] I.R. 317 described at pp. 307–308.
[3] Local Government (Sanitary Services) Act 1948, s.31(1) involved in *Listowel U.D.C.* v. *Donagh* [1968] I.R. 312 (see p. 303) and *Corporation of Limerick* v. *Sheridan* (1956) 90 I.L.T.R. 59 (see p. 311).

failure to exercise a discretion described in section 3. By way of
conclusion to this Chapter, section 4 offers some comments on the
broad question of whether there are any unreviewable discretionary powers.

The difficulty of delineating the law in this area is increased by
the fact that:

> "The scope of review may be conditioned by a variety of
> factors: the wording of the discretionary power, the subject-
> matter to which it is related, the character of the authority to
> which it is entrusted, the purpose for which it is conferred,
> the particular circumstances in which it has in fact been
> exercised, the materials available to the court, and in the last
> analysis whether a court is of the opinion that judicial
> intervention would be in the public interest.... Broadly
> speaking, however, one can say that the courts will show
> special restraint in applying tests of legality where (i) a power
> is exercisable in "emergency' conditions...; or (iii) the
> "policy content of the power is large and its exercise affects
> large numbers of people. Their reluctance to intervene is
> likely to diminish the more closely the wording and content of
> the power approximate to those of a discretion typically
> exercised by a tribunal'."[4]

These daunting observations show how wary the reader should be
of generalisations in this field.

2. Abuse of discretionary power

The classic exposition of the principles restraining abuse of
power by public authorities was given by Lord Greene in *Associated
Provincial Picture Houses Ltd.* v. *Wednesbury Corporation*:

> "When an executive discretion is entrusted by Parliament to a
> body such as the local authority in this case, what appears to
> be an exercise of that discretion can only be challenged in the
> courts in a strictly limited class of case. As I have said, it must
> always be remembered that the court is not a court of appeal.
> When discretion of this kind is granted the law recognises
> certain principles upon which that discretion must be
> exercised, but within the four corners of those principles the
> discretion, in my opinion, is an absolute one and cannot be
> questioned in any court of law.... I am not sure myself

---

[4] de Smith, *op. cit.*, at pp. 281, 297. Items (ii) in Professor de Smith's
catalogue refers to immigration, expulsion and deportation cases; it is
omitted because seemingly it does not apply here: see *The State (Kugan)*
v. *Station Sergeant, Fitzgibbon St.* [1986] I.L.R.M. 95.

whether the permissible grounds of attack cannot be defined under a single head. It has been perhaps a little bit confusing to find a series of grounds set out. Bad faith, dishonesty— those of course, stand by themselves—unreasonableness, attention given to extraneous circumstances, disregard of public policy and things like that have all been referred to, according to the facts of individual cases, as being matters which are relevant to the question. If they cannot all be confined under one head, they at any rate, I think, overlap to a very great extent. For instance, we have heard in this case a great deal about the meaning of the word "unreasonable'. . . . It has frequently been used and is frequently used as a general description of the things that must not be done. For instance, a person entrusted with a discretion must, so to speak, direct himself properly in law. He must call his own attention to the matters which he is bound to consider. He must exclude from his consideration matters which are irrelevant to what he has to consider. If he does not obey those rules, he may truly be said, and often is said, to be acting "unreasonably'. Similarly, there may be something so absurd that no sensible person could ever dream that it lay within the powers of the authority. Warrington L.J. in *Short* v. *Poole Corporation*[5] gave the example of the red-haired teacher, dismissed because she had red hair. That is unreasonable in one sense. In another sense it is taking into consideration extraneous matters. It is so unreasonable that it might almost be described as being done in bad faith; and, in fact, all these things run into one another."[6]

One precept which emerges from this passage is that a court reviewing a discretionary action is not to substitute its own view of the merits for that of the public body in which the legislature has vested the decision. An analogy can usefully be drawn between the reviewing court's position and that of an appeal court which is asked to upset a jury verdict; the question is not what the court itself would have done had it been taking the initial decision, but rather whether no reasonable public body could have reached such a decision. Secondly, abuse of power can be sub-divided into different aspects which yet overlap to a considerable degree. It is to an examination of these three aspects—bad faith, taking into account irrelevant considerations or pursuing an improper purpose, unreasonableness—that we shall turn in the following sections. This examination will show that while the principles rehearsed in the passage quoted are well-established, they have to

[5] [1926] Ch. 66 at pp. 90–91.
[6] [1948] 1 K.B. 223 at p. 230.

be so generally stated that their application in concrete situations often gives rise to controversy.

Three other preliminary features must be noticed: first, the source of the law in this field remains the specialised common law rules for the interpretation of statutes together with some auxiliary contributions from the Constitution.[7] Secondly, a substantial practical problem often arises in cases in this area, namely the difficulty of establishing such essential facts as bad faith or, where these have not been divulged, the reasons on which a decision is based. The obvious sources of information include: the minutes of a decision-making meeting; affidavits of participants at such a meeting; or public statements made by the responsible authority. Again, in a characteristic passage in *East Donegal Co-Operatives Ltd.* v. *Attorny-General* Walsh J. noted the existence of such devices as discovery and interrogatories and then issued the following warning: " . . . the resources of the Courts . . . are not so limited that they could facilitate . . . the concealment of an infringement of constitutional rights or the masking of injustice."[8] Finally, if there is an absence of explanation or elucidation, a court is entitled to infer the worst from a discrepancy between the decision taken and the decision which could have been expected, if the proper guidelines had been observed.[9]

Bad Faith (Mala fides)

Bad faith (frequently known as *male fides* or fraud) exists where public body "intends to achieve an object other than that for which he believes the power to have been conferred."[10] Thus bad faith includes, but is wider than, "malice" which should be used only where the repository of the discretionary power is motivated by personal animosity against persons affected by it: the two are not synonymous since bias may have an objective existence[11]; whereas the essence of bad faith is dishonesty. Straightaway, two features emerge: first, cases in which bad faith is established are inevitably rare. Courts naturally shrink from labelling elected representatives and/or public officials as dishonest. Moreover,

---

[7] See pp. 313–316.

[8] [1970] I.R. 317 at p. 349.

[9] *The State (McGeough)* v. *Louth County Council* (1973) 107 I.L.T.R. 13 at p. 25; *Padfield* v. *Minister for Agriculture* [1968] A.C. 1032, 1053 at p. 1061.

[10] de Smith, *op. cit.*, at p. 335.

[11] Thus because of the finding of "pique" in *O'Mahony*, the case is put (at p. 302) under the heading of bad faith; whereas there is no reason to regard the similar case of *McGeough* as involving dishonesty and it is accordingly classified as a case of bias (see p. 249). Little usually turns on this point of characterisation.

public bodies are often made up of groups of people with differing levels of information about the subject-matter and with varying outlooks, motivations and political allegiances. Against this background, it will often be difficult to bring home a charge of bad faith because of the need to prove something akin to the criminal law concept of *mens rea*. Secondly, if a court concludes that a discretionary decision is the product of the consideration of irrelevant factors or is unreasonable, then it will be held invalid, even if there is no element of bad faith. Thus it will usually be otiose to try to establish bad faith. One exception to this observation would occur in an action where a plaintiff is suing for the as yet undeveloped tort of misfeasance of public office as bad faith is a necessary element of this tort.[12] Again, bad faith is regarded as particularly heinous so that the consequences of such a finding are more far-reaching than with other defects and this has an effect, for example, on the exercise of a court's discretion to send a remedy or the interpretation of a statutory clause purporting to exclude judicial review.[13] Another exception involves cases where the subject-matter of the power and other circumstances are such that exercise of the power is beyond the reach of judicial review, for "honest abuse of power," yet the courts would be prepared to intervene if bad faith could be established.

Irish case law tends to bear out these general propositions. It is seldom that bad faith has been alleged, before a court, never mind estabished. Take, for example, the striking case of *The State (Cogley)* v. *Dublin Corporation*.[14] The prosecutor's application for planning permission having been refused by the Corporation, he appealed successfully to the Minister for Local Government. The remaining stage of the planning procedure was to seek the planning authority's approval and this was granted by the assistant city manager. However, subsequently, the elected members of the Corporation, using their power under the Local Government (Planning and Development) Act 1963, s.30,[15] passed a resolution revoking the permission which had been granted by the Minister. The possibility of bad faith was raised, but rejected, with some distaste, by Teevan J., in the following passage:

---

[12] *Roncarelli* v. *Dupleiss* (1959) 16 D.L.R. (2d) 689, 705; *Dunlop* v. *Woollahra M.C.* [1982] A.C. 158; *Bourgoin S.A.* v. *Ministry of Agriculture* [1985] 3 W.L.R. 1027; *Pine Valley Developments Ltd.* v. *Ireland*, High Court, June 28, 1985. See generally at pp. 380–384.

[13] For the court's discretion and exclusion clauses, see further pp. 348–351 and pp. 200–202.

[14] [1970] I.R. 244.

[15] Amended by the Local Government (Planning and Development) Act 1976, s.39(i) which, *inter alia*, reversed the effect of *Cogley*.

"If it could be shown that the resolution was not a bona fide exercise by the Corporation of their authority, and was no more than a colourable device to nullify the Minister's order, then perhaps relief should be granted to the prosecutor. There are some circumstances which excite suspicion of mala fides. The meeting was convened at about the time when grant of approval should have issued, that is to say, as soon as might be after the expiration of one month from notification of the decision to grant approval or from the August 18, 1968; it was carried by the smallest possible majority by means of the casting vote of the Lord Mayor . . . ; and it would seem that the reasons for the revocation quoted in, and grounding, the resolution were such as must have been in mind when the application for outline permission was first made and declined by the Corporation, and on the hearing of the appeal to the Minister. However, these features are no more than suspicions or, I should say, possible suspicious; and it would be very unjust to base any conclusion on them impugning the honour of the members of the Corporation in their approach to the very complex and anxious problems of town planning. . . .
Perhaps I have dwelt to much on this aspect of the case for, while the submission was put forward by the prosecutor's counsel, it was not developed to any appreciable extent—doubtless because he would have felt it unfair to do so in the absence of precise probative facts.[16]"

It is also notable that in what seemed a strong case, the High Court should have taken the unusual course of refusing to grant the applicant even a conditional order and, so, obliging him to appeal to the Supreme Court before the substantive stage of the case could be heard.

In *The State (O'Mahony)* v. *South Cork Board of Public Health*[17] the applicant was a tenant of the Board whose application to purchase the cottage in which she was living (as she was entitled to do under a statutory scheme) had been rejected by the respondent. There

---

[16] [1970] I.R. at pp. 249–250.
[17] [1941] Ir.Jur.Rep. 79. For another case in which what looked like at least a *prima facie* case of bad faith received short shrift, see *The State (Divito)* v. *Arklow U.D.C.* [1986] I.L.R.M. 123 (Respondent local authority passed a resolution under the Gaming and Lotteries Act, 1956, the result of which was that anyone with premises in the relevant area was entitled to apply to the District Court, for a gaming licence. The applicant applied unsuccessfully for a licence, his application being opposed by the local authority. Before he could re-apply, the local authority revoked its resolution under the 1956 Act.)

had been bad blood between the parties for some time. According to Maguire P.:

> "The obligation to repair rested on the landlords. The applicant was active in carrying out repairs to the cottage and had sought to make the respondents responsible for the expense of repairs which she claimed to have done by reason of the default of the respondents. In this she was partially successful. Reading between the lines of the affidavits, it would appear that the Board was annoyed because she had taken on herself to do repairs to her cottage and more annoyed still because she had obtained a decree against them for £18 in respect of these repairs.... Mere pique at an unfavourable judgment in the High Court seems to me to be no justification for attempting to deprive the applicant of her legal rights."[18]

What is notable is that although opining that the authority's decision had been taken through "mere pique", the High Court formally classified the case as one of taking extraneous considerations into account and "failure to consider the tenant's application."

However, about a year before *Cogley* was decided, the Supreme Court had made it clear in *McDonagh* v. *Listowel U.D.C.*[19] that *mala fides* is "a well recognised ground of challenge." By the Local Government (Sanitary Services) Act 1948 a sanitary authority is empowered: "[to] prohibit the erection ... of temporary dwellings ... if they are of opinion that such erection ... would be prejudicial to public health...." Purporting to act under this power, Listowel U.D.C. made an order banning the construction of temporary dwellings on a number of named streets. The defendant was convicted and fined 10 shillings for contravening this order. His principal line of defence was to argue that the order had not been made bona fide in that the sanitary authority did not genuinely hold the necessary opinion. The Supreme Court accepted this legal argument and held that the defendant was free to adduce evidence before the Circuit Court (to which the case had gone on appeal) as to what transpired at the council meeting which considered the passing of the by-law; what views were expressed by members and officials of the Council; and the veracity of the opinion they expressed. In the result, the Circuit

---

[18] (1941) Ir.Jur.Rep. at pp. 81–83.
[19] [1968] I.R. 312 at p. 318.

Court found as a matter of fact, that the order had been made
bona fide.[20]

Improper purposes and irrelevant considerations
  "Improper purpose" in this context refers to the fact that, in
enacting a statute, the legislature is assumed to have had a
defineable purpose(s) or object(s). True to the idea that they are
implementing the mandate of the legislature, the courts seek to
ensure that the power contained in the measure is used only for
the "proper purpose." With knowledge of this purpose (a
difficulty to which we return *infra*) and making certain assumptions[21] it is for the court to deduce the considerations which the
public authority should have in mind when it is exercising a
discretionary power created by the measure. It follows, therefore,
that there is an intimate relationship between the rules that
relevant considerations must be taken into account and irrelevant
considerations excluded and, on the other hand, the rule that the
proper purpose must be observed, when a discretionary power is
being exercised. Accordingly, there seems to be little point in
discussing the cases in separate compartments depending which
label has been used. Instead, our selection of specimen cases is
arranged on the criteria of whether the statute creating the
discretionary power explicitly states its purpose or explicitly
identifies the considerations which must be taken into account in
exercising the discretion.[22] It must be admitted, however, that
even where these guidelines exist, they may be insufficiently
precise to settle specific cases beyond a doubt.
  A simple example of a guideline was given in *Cassidy* v. *Minister
for Industry*.[23] Henchy J. stated that the purpose of price control

[20] The defendant put in evidence a council memorandum entitled "The
   itinerant problem" but, for the prosecution, nine councillors swore
   that they were concerned only with health matters and their evidence
   was accepted.
[21] See pp. 306–310.
[22] See Taylor, "Judicial Review of Improper Purposes and Irrelevant
   Consideration," (1976) Camb.L.J. 272, 77 who argues that "Where the
   reasons [for action, envisaged by the legislature] are enumerated in the
   empowering provision the technique used in most reported cases under
   the rubric 'irrelevant factors' is appropriate. Where there is a discretion
   as to reasons, the 'improper purpose' is the one to be used."
[23] [1978] I.R. 297 at p. 310. See also *Minister for Industry and Commerce* v.
   White, High Court, February 16, 1981. For another example, see
   Corporation of Limerick v. *Sheridan* (1956) 90 I.L.T.R. 59, at pp. 63–64.
   (Local Government (Sanitary Services) Act 1948, s.31 was being used,
   in effect, to constitute the Corporation, as a licensing authority,
   although there were other sections in the 1948 Act which were
   specifically designed to do that.)

orders made under the Prices Act 1958–72 is "to maintain stability of prices generally."[24] The judge hypothesised an order which, by setting the same maximum prices in lounge bars as in public bars, made it uneconomic to run lounge bars and, thus, drove them out of business. He considered that such an order would be invalid because the power conferred by the statute would have been used for an improper purpose.

Another example of a statutory power, the relevant factors in relation to which were fairly plainly indicated, was considered in *The State (Cussen)* v. *Brennan*.[25] This case arose out of the selection, by the Local Appointment Commissioners (of whom Mr. Brennan was one) of a consultant paediatrician. It was established that, as far as paediatrics was concerned, the L.A.C. had judged the applicant to be slightly ahead of his nearest rival but that the rival candidate's knowledge of the Irish language had tipped the balance in his favour. According to the relevant statutory provision (Health Act 1970, s.18), it was for the Minister for Health to lay down the qualifications for the job. The Minister had duly done this and a knowledge of Irish was not among the qualifications which he had specified. Consequently the L.A.C. had taken irrelevant considerations into account.[26]

The most sophisticated formulation of factors which are to guide the exercise of a discretionary (it may be better to style it "a semi-discretionary")[27] power is to be found in the Planning Code. According to the Local Government (Planning and Development) Act 1963, s.26(1), in dealing with a planning application, a local planning authority is:

[24] Prices Act 1958, s.22A inserted by Prices (Amendment) Act 1965, s.1(1).

[25] [1981] I.R. 181. See also *Latchford* v. *Minister for Industry and Commerce* [1950] I.R. 33 and *The State (Keller)* v. *Galway C.C.* [1958] I.R. 142.

[26] Though the court exercised its discretion not to send an order because of delay (see pp. 349–351). The Local Authority (Officers and Employees) Act 1983, s.2 effectively reversed the legal rule established in *Cussen* by providing that the LAC may take into account a knowledge of the Irish language.

[27] On the spectrum running from what appears, on its wording, to be an unlimited discretion to, at the other end, a decision determined by precise rules, there is an infinite variety of gradations. In particular, there is no sharp distinction between a public authority exercising a discretion in respect of which he must be guided by specified factors, as in *Cussen* and, on the other hand, a tribunal applying a standard involving a question of appreciation (see *e.g. Irish Benefit Building Society* v. *Registrar of Building Societies* [1981] I.L.R.M. 73 at p. 75) or even a court exercising certain functions *e.g.* granting a liquor licence (*Re Licensing Acts and Centennial Properties*, High Court, December 20, 1980).

"... [R]estricted to considering the proper planning and development of the area of the authority (including the preservation and improvement of the amenities thereof), regard being
had to the provisions of the development plan, the provisions
of any special amenity area relating to the said area and the
matters referred to in subsection (2) of this section."

Subsection (2) then goes on to empower the planning authority
"without prejudice to the generality" of subsection (1) to impose a
number of conditions which are exemplified *infra*.[28] Following
these guidelines, applications for planning permission have been
refused not only because of contravention of the development
plan but also, for example, because the development would: create
a traffic hazard; put a further strain on water supplies or sewerage
facilities which are already deficient; constitute a traffic hazard;
spoil a worthwhile view; constitute ribbon development; or be out
of character with existing buildings.

On the other hand in *Frank Dunne Ltd.* v. *Dublin County Council*[29]
two conditions attached to planning permission were said to be
invalid as not being related to "proper planning and development." The first of these, which required the developers to inform
all purchasers that aircraft noise would be significant in the area of
the development was plainly a consumer protection device; the
other condition which required extra thick walls and windows was
a matter for building regulations[30]—it improved the amenities of
the development rather than the amenities of the area. Again, in
The State (Fitzgerald) v. *An Bord Pleanala*,[31] the development which
was actually built differed from that for which permission had
been given. However the Board granted retrospective permission,
taking it into account that the degree of injury to the neighbourhood and departure from the plan on the basis of which
permission had been given would not warrant the expense of
removal. The Board's decision was held to be invalid for taking
into consideration a matter which was not relevant according to
the governing statute.

Thus far cases have been examined in which the relevant statute
has provided an explicit statement of the factors which the public
authority must take into account. However it often happens that

---

[28] For planning generally, see pp. 117–123 and 309, the list given in the
following sentence in the text is taken from Walsh, *Planning and
Development Law* (Dublin, 1984) (*2nd ed.* by R. Keane) Chap. VI.

[29] [1974] I.R. 45. See also *Dublin Corporation* v. *Raso*, High Court, June 1,
1976.

[30] But such a condition is now expressly authorised by 1963 Act,
s.26(2)(*bb*) inserted by 1976 Act, s.39(*c*).

[31] [1985] I.L.R.M. 117.

even this limited assistance is not available and the "relevant considerations" have to be deduced by the court from the general tenor of the statute, creating the discretionary power. Something of the difficulties entailed in this process emerges from the *locus classicus, East Donegal Co-Operatives Ltd.* v. *Attorney-General*[32] in which the Supreme Court scrutinised the Livestock Marts Act 1967, in order to decide a claim by a group of agricultural mart owners that the Act was unconstitutional. The Act bestows considerable discretionary power on the Minister for Agriculture enabling him to control marts, through the grant (whether absolutely or subject to conditions) or the revocation, of licences. In spite of the wide discretionary language in which these powers are couched, Walsh J. stated that:

> "The words of the Act, and in particular the general words, cannot be read in isolation and their content is to be derived from their context. Therefore words or phrases which at first sight might appear to be wide and general may be cut down in their construction when examined against the objects of the Act which are to be derived from a study of the Act as a whole including the long title."

Specifically:

> "The provisions of section 6 [of the 1967 Act] throw considerable light upon the purposes, objects and scope of the Act because they refer specifically to the power of the Minister for Agriculture and Fisheries being directed towards the proper conduct of the businesses concerned, the standards in relation to such places and to the provision of adequate and suitable accommodation and facilities for such auctions. Section 6 also provides for the making of regulations dealing with what might be referred to as the mechanics of sale such as book-keeping, accommodation, hygiene, etc. . . . The type of conditions which the Minister may impose [on the grant of a mart licence] would include the site of the mart so as to ensure that, for example, it was not too near a place of worship or a particular road traffic hazard, or conditions aimed at the restriction of the carrying on of business at certain hours or on certain days so as to prevent interference with the activities of persons not connected with the mart, or conditions which indeed might be designed to facilitate the carrying on of business at the particular mart by preventing it being carried on at times which, by reason of particular local conditions or activities, would be detrimental

[32] [1970] I.R. 317. See also *Doupe* v. *Limerick Corporation* [1981] I.L.R.M. 456 at p. 461.

to the business itself and to the persons having stock for sale at the mart or to persons resorting there for the purpose of purchasing livestock."[33]

The learned judge also stated:

"Nowhere in the Act is there anything to indicate that one of the purposes of the Act is to limit or otherwise regulate the number of auction marts as distinct from regulating the way in which business is conducted in auction marts. In the absence of any such indication in the Act, the Minister is not authorised by the Act to limit the number of businesses of the type defined in section 1."[34]

The penultimate sentence in this passage—dealing with control of numbers of marts—may be questioned. Assume that it could be shown that in a particular area, there was a causal connection between the number of marts in a particular area and their profitability and, on the other hand, a matter, such as hygiene which is admittedly within the Act. On that assumption, could it not be said that the Minister was empowered to refuse an application for a mart in order to maintain existing marts in profit and, hence to enable them to maintain the necessary level of hygiene rather than to permit cut-throat competition in which standards of hygiene might fall?[35]

General policy assumptions

So far we have examined cases in which the "relevant considerations" or "proper purposes/objectives" have been deduced by the courts from a study of the particular statute. In addition, there are certain general policy assumptions, which the courts bring to their task and which have become well-established in the case law.

(1) It is said that: "Parliament does not intend to deprive the

[33] [1970] I.R. 317 at pp. 341–343.
[34] *Ibid.* at p. 342.
[35] This comment is relevant in connection with the question of whether the limitation, fixed by the Incorporated Law Society upon the annual number of those who may enter the solicitors final training course, and, hence, the solicitors' profession, is lawful. The reason given for this restriction is the need for solicitors to make an adequate living. It is the Solicitors Act 1954 which authorises the Society to run the course and admit students to it. This Act deals with the enrolling, discipline and education of solicitors and it is questionable whether the prosperity of the profession is within the four corners of the Act. As against this, it may be argued that there is a causative link between a solicitor's income and his standard of ethics and, on this basis, the restriction is within the powers created by the statute.

subject of his common law rights except by express words or necessary implication."[36] Whilst suggestive of the courts' approach, this statement is probably pitched at too high a level of generality to determine the solution to particular problems. For these, specific formulations are more useful. Take, for instance, the following passage (which also happens to be a re-statement of a particular constitutional principle):

" ... [W]here Parliament confers upon a public authority a statutory power which is exerciseable at its discretion ... the authority cannot lawfully impose or levy a money charge on a subject as a condition of exercising that power unless such charge is clearly authorised by statute either in express terms or by necessary implication."[37]

And, thus, it was felt necessary to state explicitly in section 26 of the Local Government (Planning and Development) Act 1963 that a condition could be attached to planning permission: " ... requiring contribution ... towards any expenditure that was incurred by any local authority in respect of works (including the provision of open spaces) which have facilitated the proposed development. ... "[38] An analogous presumption militates against interference with property rights. It may be questioned whether such a presumption is appropriate in the planning field. In any event, (possibly *ex abundante cautela*) the planning code[39] also explicitly authorises conditions requiring the provision of open spaces, trees, roads etc. and conditions regulating the development of other land owned by the developer, provided that it adjoins the proposed development.

(2) Local authorities were originally regarded as being somewhat in the position of "trustees" in relation to their ratepayers and, hence, as owing them a "fiduciary" duty to observe business-like principles in regard to the expenditure of money. This principle severely restricts the discretionary powers of local authorities in relation to discretionary acts of expenditure. It has been relied upon, for example, in cases establishing that, in deciding to which contractor to award a public works contract, a

[36] de Smith, *op. cit.*, p. 99.
[37] *City Brick and Terra Cotta Co. Ltd.* v. *Belfast Corporation* [1958] N.I. 44 at p. 70. The high constitutional principle referred to in the text is that taxation may only be levied with the consent of the Dail: see Gwynn Morgan *op. cit.*, p. 117.
[38] Local Government (Planning and Development) Act 1963, s.26(2)(*g*). See also s.26(2)(*h*).
[39] *Ibid.* s.26(2)(*a*)–(*f*).

local authority is obliged to take at least some account of the prices of the various tenders submitted to it.[40]

The doubt about the present status of this concept arises from the fact that the number of ratepayers and the significance of rates, as part of the income of local authorities, have both been substantially reduced by the elimination of domestic and agricultural rates, so that we are left only with business ratepayers.[41] Even apart from this recent change, the principle is open to criticism on the ground that it raises, but does not help in answering, the question of the balance to be drawn between the interests of ratepayers and of non-ratepayers.

(3) In the field of local government, there is also a presumption that powers may only be exercised by a local authority for the good of its own territorial area. A straightforward example of this principle in action occurred in *Murphy* v. *Dublin Corporation*[42] which involved a compulsory purchase order made by the defendants. The Supreme Court struck down the order because it found that the Corporation had made it, in part at least,[43] in order to meet the needs of another housing authority, namely Dublin County Council.

(4) Recently it has been stated (as a make-weight, rather than a *ratio decidendi*) that it is permissible for a public authority to be influenced by "the declared wishes of responsible members of the community."[44]

Reasonableness

As Lord Greene pointed out in the extract from his judgment in *Wednesbury Corporation*—quoted *infra*—reasonableness can be used, widely, to cover almost all forms of abuse of power. Used more narrowly and, therefore, more usefully, it refers to a

---

[40] See generally, *The State (Raftis)* v. *Leonard* [1960] I.R. 381; *Bromley L.B.C.* v. *G.L.C.* [1983] 1 A.C. 768; H. A. Street, *Law Relating to Local Government* (Dublin, 1954) pp. 1263–1264 and cases cited therein; Kelly, "Local Authority Contracts, Tenders and Mandamus" (1967) 2 Ir.Jur.(n.s.) at p. 7.

[41] See pp. 111–116.

[42] [1976] I.R. 143.

[43] On plurality of purposes see also *Cassidy* v. *Minister for Industry and Commerce* [1978] I.R. 297 at pp. 308–309 and *Hussey* v. *Irish Land Commission* Supreme Court, December 13, 1984.

[44] *The State (Divito)* v. *Arklow U.D.C.* [1986] I.L.R.M. 123; *a contra The State (McGeough)* v. *Louth C.C.* (1973) 107 I.L.T.R. 13 at pp. 17, 18, 26. The cases may be reconcilable on the basis that the council resolution in *McGeough* flew in the place of the statute's policy: see p. 249. For the relationship between this factor and the rule against fettering a discretion, see *Bromley* v. *G.L.C.* [1983] 1 A.C. 768.

decision which departs so radically from the normal standards of cost, convenience, morality, respect for individual rights, etc. that no reasonable public authority could have come to it. In this sense, reaonableness was traditionally seldom used by the courts because it entails deciding questions of judgment in highly political areas, where courts prefer not to tread. An unreasonable decision is usually reached because the responsible public authority took into account irrelevant considerations, failed to take into account relevant considerations; or pursued an improper purpose. Accordingly, it can usually be struck down on one of these grounds, thereby enabling a court to avoid the public controversy which may be stirred up if a court labels the decision of a public and, it may be an elected, body as unreasonable. However these considerable risks notwithstanding,[45] in recent years, Irish courts have been less shy of this head. Consider first, *Limerick Corporation* v. *Sheridan*[46] in which the Corporation used their powers under the Local Government (Sanitary Services) Act 1948 to issue an order, which had the practical effect of banning virtually all such dwellings within the Corporation's geographic area. One of the grounds on which the order was held invalid was unreasonableness. Davitt P. said:

"... [I]f the order were a good one, then it made it illegal for anyone to erect or retain a temporary dwelling anywhere, or, particularly, anywhere in the County Borough without the written consent of the Corporation. Without such consent, nobody could camp out in a tent or a sleeping porch in his own garden. Harvesters could not camp on agricultural land on which they are working... [The] order was manifestly unjust and involved such oppressive gratuitous interference with the common law rights of those affected as could find no justification in the minds of reasonable men.... It was unreasonable, and therefore *ultra vires* ... "[47]

In *Cassidy* v. *Minister for Industry and Commerce*,[48] which arose out

---

[45] See McAuslan, "Administrative Law, Collective Consumption and Judicial Policy" (1983) 45 M.L.R. 1.

[46] (1956) 90 I.L.T.R. 59. For other points in the case see p. 320. For other cases on unreasonableness, see *The State (Kugan)* v. *Station Sergeant, Fitzgibbon St.* [1986] I.L.R.M. 95 (aliens refused entry to Ireland because in the immigration officer's opinion they understood too little English to benefit from course of study in English to be taken in Dublin; Egan J. apparently regarded this decision as perverse); *Greaney* v. *Scully* [1981] I.L.R.M. 340. *Warnock* v. *Revenue Commissioners* [1986] I.L.R.M. 37; *Belfast Corporation* v. *Daly* [1963] N.I. 78.

[47] (1956) 90 I.L.T.R. at p. 64.

[48] [1978] I.R. 297.

of the creation of a maximum prices order in respect of bars in Dundalk, the same maxima were fixed for drinks sold in both public and lounge bars. The chief reason given by the Supreme Court for striking down the order was unreasonableness. Giving the principal judgment, Henchy J. first, adopted the test for unreasonableness enunciated by Diplock L.J. in *Mixnam's Properties* v. *Chertsey U.D.C.*[49] namely that there must be " . . . such manifest arbitrariness, injustice or partiality that a court would say: 'Parliament never intended to give authority to make such rules'." Henchy J. continued:

> "Applied here [this test] produces the conclusion that Parliament could not have intended that licences of lounge bars would be treated so oppressively and unfairly by maximum-price orders. If the Minister had made a maximum-price order which forbade hotel owners to sell drink in their hotels at prices higher than those fixed for public bars, it would be generally accepted that such an order would be oppressive and unfair. The capital outlay and overhead expenses necessarily involved in the residential and other features of hotels are such that to force their drink prices down to those chargeable in a public bar would in many cases be ruinously unfair . . . if the orders are construed as not distinguishing lounge bars in any way, and as forcing their prices down to those of public bars, they fail unreasonably to have regard to the fact that owners of lounge bars, like hoteliers, are entitled because of capital outlay and overhead expenses, to separate treatment in the matter of drink prices . . . "[50]

Another example is provided by the decision of the Supreme Court in *Doyle* v. *An Taoiseach*[51] in which the plaintiffs successfully challenged the validity of a 2 per cent levy on the price of live cattle. While the levy was intended to bring farmers into the tax net, it was the proprietors of slaughterhouses or, in the case of exported animals, exporters, who were made primarily liable for the levy. This anomaly had the result that the primary producer escaped liability for the operation of the levy. Had the levy been payable at the time when an animal was sold for slaughter or for export, this unfairness could have been avoided. As Henchy J. put it:

> "But in the case of exporters, the sale price was not the value

[49] [1964] 1 Q.B. 214 at p. 237.
[50] [1978] I.R. at p. 311.
[51] Supreme Court, March 29, 1985. The judgment of Barrington J. in the High Court is reported at (1982–83) J.I.S.E.L. 83.

of the levy; it was the value of the animal at the pier-head. This value might be, and frequently was, higher than the sale price. The exporter, therefore, became directly liable for a levy of an amount which he could not recover in full from the farmer, because he could not identify the seller of the animal; or, even when he could, because it would not be practicable to seek to recover the full amount of the levy; or because it was not possible for the exporter to assess at the time of purchase what the amount of the levy would be when the animal would arrive at the pier-head."[52]

These anomalies led the Supreme Court to conclude that the relevant statutory instruments were void for unreasonableness. The results produced by these orders were so "untargeted, indiscriminate and unfair" and so removed from their primary policy which, as was admitted by the defendants, was to tax farmers that the delegated legislation must be deemed to have been made in excess "of the impliedly intended scope of the delegation."

Impact of the Constitution
Thus far, we have described the requirements of taking relevant factors into account, excluding irrelevant factors, etc. which are grounded in the long-established common law rules of statutory interpretation. It seems clear that similar but, in certain cases, more far-reaching results can be achieved by invoking the Constitution.[53]

· One example, which occurred in *The State (Lynch)* v. *Cooney*[54] described *infra*, involved Article 40.6.1 (freedom of expression). Other relevant provisions stipulate that laws regulating the right of free expression, assembly and association must "contain no political, religious, or class discrimination." (Article 40.6.1 and 2). Again, there must be no religious discrimination[55] and the State, in providing aid for schools, must not "discriminate" between schools.

A general provision, which is potentially very significant in this field, is Article 40.1 by which: "All citizens shall, as human

[52] At pp. 4–5.
[53] It now appears that constitutional guarantees apply not only to Acts of the Oireachtas, but also to administrative actions and statutory instruments: see *The State (Quinn)* v. *Ryan* [1965] I.R. 70 at p. 130; · *Dillane* v. *Ireland* [1980] I.L.R.M. 167.
[54] [1982] I.R. 337 at pp. 323–325.
[55] See *e.g. Quinn's Supermarket* v. *Att.-Gen.* [1972] I.R. 1; *Mulloy* v. *Minister for Education* [1975] I.R. 88; *M.* v. *An Bord Uchtala* [1975] I.R. 81.

persons, be held equal before the law. . . . "[56] Various passages
from *East Donegal* dealing with what may be called "common law
abuse of power" have already been quoted. It is notable that, in
East Donegal,[57] the Supreme Court (Walsh J.) also deduced similar
law from Article 40.1. The frequent references to the judgment of
the President of the High Court, in the following extract from
Walsh J.'s judgment, arise from the fact that the learned judge was
addressing himself to arguments which had found favour in the
High Court:

> "The learned President of the High Court in his judgment
> considered that the plaintiffs' claim that the power of the
> Minister to attach conditions to licences and to amend or to
> revoke such conditions gave the Minister an uncontrolled
> discretion which, in the words of the President, 'could be so
> exercised within the limits of the legislation as to amount to a
> breach of the guarantee contained in Article 40, s.1, of the
> Constitution.' The President continued as follows: 'It be-
> comes obvious at once that the attachment of conditions to
> licences is subject to no such safe-guards as are provided in
> the case of the refusal or revocation of a licence.' The
> President went on to say later in that portion of his judgment
> that 'The contrast with the provisions of section 3(6), and the
> following subsections is so marked that one is compelled to
> accept the contention of the plaintiffs that it was intended
> that the conditions might be arbitrarily imposed, and that
> such arbitrary imposition of conditions was carefully left free
> from review. In this respect I have concluded that the
> legislation *can* be operated within its lawful limits so as to
> differentiate between citizens in a manner which does not
> reflect differences of capacity, physical or moral or of social
> function and accordingly this provision of the legislation, in
> my view, does offend against the provisions of the Constitu-
> tion.' . . . It is quite true that conditions need not be uniform
> for all licences for the reasons already given in this judgment,
> and that in many cases they are by their nature necessarily
> peculiar to an individual applicant. However, it is not valid to
> infer that the legislation, because it made provision for such a
> scheme of administration or imposition of conditions, author-

---

[56] On which, see Forde, "Equality and the Constitution" (1982) 18
Ir.Jur.(n.s.) 295; Kelly, *op. cit.* pp. 446–466.
[57] Notice also that, in *East Donegal*, the Minister's power to exclude any
particular business from the scope of the licensing system was held
unconstitutional. In an inadequately explained passage, at
pp. 349–351, it is unclear whether this result is founded on Article 40.1
or Article 15.2.1.

ised the exercise of that function in a manner amounting to a breach of a right guaranteed by the Constitution. The conditions must be of the character already indicated in this judgment and they must be related to the objects of the Act in the way already indicated."[58]

The question which arises now is this: given the existence of the well-developed common law rules, how does Article 40.1 strengthen the law in this area? To follow this issue, it must be appreciated that equality cannot exist in the abstract. There must be some yardstick by which to classify individuals, situations, etc. as equal or unequal. There are two ways of approaching this problem.

(i) "Equality" means equal treatment, taking as the standard for what constitutes equal cases, the objects of the statute (*supra*). *East Donegal* itself was an example of this type.[59] As is stated in the passage quoted, the conditions imposed could differ from licence-holder A to licence-holder B, provided that they were justifiable by reference to the object of the Act. Whilst this involves no radical advance on the common law, it does help to give a sharper focus to discrimination as a head of review and thus, for example, to smooth the passage of the doctrine of *proportionalité* into Irish law.[60]

(ii) There must be no arbitrary or unjustifiable discrimination even if this is explicitly authorised by the statute.

The difference between categories (i) and (ii) is that in (i) the standard the court is applying is deduced from the statute; whereas in (ii), the standard is based on what the court itself, independently of the statute, regards as arbitrary. The difficulty in (ii) is thus to decide what constitutes arbitrary discrimination. This is really a question for constitutional, rather than administrative law. All that can be said here is that it would certainly include discrimination on the grounds of political allegiance, race, sex, illegitimacy, or of being an itinerant and that we know, from the wording of Article 40.1 itself that the concept excludes, "enactments [which] have due regard to differences of capacity, physical and moral, and of social function."

The major advance on the common law in Article 40.1 derives from head (ii), specifically from the fact that the provision bans

---

[58] [1970] I.R. at pp. 347–348.

[59] See also *Cassidy* v. *Minister for Industry and Commerce* [1978] I.R. 297, where although Article 40.1 is not mentioned explicitly, Henchy J. refers to "unfair, unequal and arbitrary treatment" and "discrimination."

[60] *Cf. C.C.S.U.* v. *Minister for Civil Service* [1985] A.C. 374 at p. 410 (Lord Diplock).

arbitrary administrative actions even where these are authorised by the parent statute. Attention should be drawn, however, to the restrictive interpretation given to "as human beings" which has restricted the scope of application of Article 40.1.[61]

3. Failure to exercise a discretion

Whereas "abuse of discretion" refers to a wrongly-exercised discretion, failure to exercise a discretion means that a public body vested with a discretionary power has incapacitated itself from being able to exercise its discretion at all. More specifically, there are at least five ways in which this undesirable result may be brought about, *viz.* by delegating the decision to another body; by acting on the dictates of another body; by some previous agreement, representation, etc.; by a general blanket policy in the area; or by taking the decision over such a broad area that all elements of it cannot have been adequately scrutinised. The first three items have already been discussed in Chapter 8, respectively since they apply generally to all types of decision and are not peculiar to discretionary powers. Accordingly here we shall deal only with the remaining two ways in which a body may disable itself from exercising its discretion freely and fully.

Adhering to an inflexible policy rule[62]

Various dangers attend on a discretionary power, for instance, the danger of being, or seeming, arbitrary, partial, inconsistent or unpredictable. One way of avoiding these dangers is to proclaim and follow some precise and rational policy-rule in the exercise of the discretion. Such a solution carries its own difficulty, namely that, to the extent that the rule is rigidly followed, it emphasises a single policy and shuts out consideration of all others and thus neutralises the discretion which it was the intention of the legislature to create. Thus, on some pure plane, one would expect that where a discretionary decision is taken in accordance with a rule, it would therefore be invalid. On the other hand, common sense suggests that, in view of the desirability of avoiding arbitrariness and the other defects mentioned, the law should lean far over to accommodate such rules of practice. The result of these conflicting tensions is that there is a principle banning policy rules, but it is subject to a fairly wide exception.

Straightforward illustrations of the principle occurred in recent

---

[61] The case law is in Kelly, *loc. cit.*
[62] See [1976] *Public Law* 332 (D. J. Galligan).

cases decided by Finlay P. In *Re N a solicitor*,[63] the applicant had
fallen into some difficulties in running his practice, and he
subsequently failed to apply for a practising certificate. The
Incorporated Law Society had a rule that, in such circumstances
an applicant is bound to spend a year as an assistant solicitor in a
solicitor's office before being considered for a full practising
certificate and thus when N did apply for a certificate, he was
refused a full certificate. Finlay P. held that the rule unduly
fettered the discretion of the Society, and prevented full consideration of the merits of the applicant's case. While the Society
was entitled to have a policy, it could not be applied to all cases in
an inflexible manner. Finlay P. accordingly reversed the order
made by the Society, saying that the Society may have paid
insufficient regard "to the likely effect on a prospective employer
of an applicant of the age of this applicant seeking employment
and not carrying a full unqualified certificate."

In the second case, *The State (Kershaw)* v. *Eastern Health Board*,[64]
the applicant was in receipt of unemployment benefit, but was still
experiencing financial difficulties, *inter alia*, because her husband
had deserted her. She applied for a supplementary welfare
allowance in respect of fuel which was operated by the respondents under the terms of the Social Welfare (Consolidation) Act
1981. If the applicant could establish that her means were
insufficient to meet her needs and those of her dependent
children, then she enjoyed a right under the 1981 Act to a
supplementary welfare allowance. However her application was
refused because under the terms of a ministerial circular she was
ineligible for consideration since she was already in receipt of
unemployment benefit. Finlay P. declared the circular invalid and
quashed the decision based on it because the circular "purpor-
t[ed] to exclude absolutely" the health board's discretion to
consider whether .the applicant's means were insufficient for the
her needs.

On the other side of the line was *British Oxygen* v. *Board of
Trade*.[65] The Board had a statutory discretion to make industrial
capital grants: it had adopted a blanket policy of not giving grants
towards expenditure of less than £25 per individual unit. British
Oxygen had invested over £4 million, but the individual unit cost

[63] High Court, June 30, 1980. See also *Rice* v. *Dublin Corporation* [1947]
I.R. 425. *East Donegal* v. *Att.-Gen.* [1970] I.R. 317 at p. 344; *Norris* v.
Att.-Gen. [1984] I.R. 36, at p. 81 (McCarthy J.)
[64] [1985] I.L.R.M. 235. (For the question of why the case did not engage
the principle against "acting under dictation . . . ". See p. 234. See also
Att.-Gen. (ex rel. Tilley) v. *Wandsworth L.B.C.* [1981] 1 W.L.R. 854.
[65] [1971] A.C. 610.

was only £20. The House of Lords held that particularly where a large number of similar decisions is involved, an administrative authority is entitled to evolve a precise policy. The only *caveat* which had been observed by the Board in the instant case, is that the deciding agency must not totally ignore an argument that although a particular case fell outside the policy rule, yet it might be treated as an exception and the discretion exercised in its favour. The same idea has been expressed in the following classic passage from *R.* v. *Port of London, ex p. Kynoch*[66]:

> "There are on the one hand cases where a tribunal in the honest exercise of its discretion has adopted a policy, and without refusing to hear an applicant intimates to him what its policy is, and that after hearing him it will in accordance with its policy decide against him, *unless there is something exceptional in his case.* . . . On the other hand there are cases where the tribunal has passed a rule or come to a determination not to hear any application of a particular character by whomsoever made. There is a wide distinction to be drawn between the two classes."

It can thus be seen that, in England, at least, the exceptions have substantially diluted the principle banning "a policy-rule."

A similar exception probably exists in Ireland. For example where limited resources, like corporation houses, are being distributed, the system often adopted is to give credit to those whose name has been longest on the waiting list. The question arises whether such a waiting list is valid, a question which was relevant, though it was not directly addressed in *McDonald* v. *Dublin Corporation*[67] and *McNamee* v. *Buncrana U.D.C.*.[68]

In *McDonald*, the Supreme Court, *per* O'Higgins C.J. had held that where a person is in need of housing, there is a duty on the relevant housing authority at least to consider whether their needs outweigh those of other applicants even if the other applicants have been waiting longer. However, especially when *McDonald* is read in the light of O'Higgins C.J.'s later comment in *McNamee* on his judgment in *McDonald*, it seems that the idea of the waiting list is not entirely condemned. O'Higgins C.J. said in *McNamee*:

> "It was not intended to suggest [in *McDonald*] that a housing authority need not have regard as a matter of priority

[66] [1919] 1 K.B. 176 at p. 184. See also *Re Findlay* [1985] A.C. 318.
[67] Supreme Court, July 23, 1980. For other issues in *McDonald* and *McNamee*, see pp. 123–124.
[68] [1983] I.R. 213.

to those in its functional area who have been resident or domiciled there for a particular period of time."[69]

What was being said in *McDonald* (which involved rather an extreme case) was only that in a strong enough case—that is, strong in the context of the purposes of the Housing Act 1966—the housing authority must be prepared to override the dictates of the waiting list; and not that the waiting list may always, or even usually, be ignored. On this analysis, there is a good deal in common between *McDonald-McNamee* and the passage quoted *infra* from *Kynoch.*

One can reconcile *N* and *Kershaw* with this line of authority on the basis that these two cases involved situations which were so exceptional that the Incorporated Law Society and the Eastern Health Board, respectively, should have been prepared at least to consider a departure from their usual rule of practice. That said, there is bound to be a margin of appreciation in the word "exceptional" and it seems likely that the House of Lords in *British Oxygen* envisaged a higher standard of exceptional "circumstances" than did the High Court in *N* and *Kershaw.*

There remains a further point: in spite of the substantial relaxation of the principle banning policy rules, it must surely follow from the law explained in part 2 of this chapter, that for a policy rule to be permissible, its content must not fly in the face of the policies envisaged by relevant statute. An example is afforded by the multi-faceted case of *The State (McGeough)* v. *Lough County Council*[70] in which the applicant complained successfully of a county manager's refusal to give his consent, required under the Labourers Act 1936, to the sale of the applicant's labourers cottage. This refusal was motivated, in part, by a general resolution passed by the Council expressing disfavour of any such sale. Leaving aside the fact that the decision was vested not in the council, but in the county manager,[71] one of the grounds on which the applicant succeeded was that the purpose of the 1936 Act was taken to be that the owner of a cottage should be allowed to sell it save in the exceptional cases in which the manager's consent was withheld, whereas the council resolution purported to ban sales in any circumstances whatsoever. The resolution was thus "wholly improper as an attempt on [the Council's] part to amend the statutory conditions on which purchasers hold their cottages."[72]

---

[69] *Ibid.* at p. 220.

[70] (1973) 107 I.L.T.R. 13, 19.

[71] For "acting under the dictation of another body," see *McGeough* (1973) 107 I.L.T.R. 13 at p. 19 and generally see at pp. 233–234.

[72] (1973) 107 I.L.T.R. at pp. 18, 20, 24–26, 28.

320 Control of Discretionary Powers

Failing to address the specific issue[73]

Consider a discretionary power taking the following form: "If it appears to the Minister that [a particular state of affairs is so] then the Minister may exercise [such a power in connection with that state of affairs]." What the present rule means is that the Minister will only be regarded as having properly exercised his discretion if he has genuinely considered whether the requisite state of affairs exists in relation to all the areas which are affected by his exercise of the power.[74] Thus if the power is exercised over a very broad area, a court is liable to say that the Minister cannot be sure that the requisite state of affairs genuinely exists in relation to the entire area caught by the Minister's decision. Two examples of this rule in operation in modern Irish law may be cited[75] of which the first is *Corporation of Limerick* v. *Sheridan,* the facts of which have already been given. To recapitulate, the relevant statutory provision allowed the Corporation to prohibit temporary dwellings on any land where their "erection would be prejudicial to public health." The Corporation made an order affecting almost the entire area of the county borough. One of the grounds, on which the order was struck down was that the area covered was so large that the court thought it unlikely that the Corporation could have formed the requisite opinion with respect to all parts of the land caught by the order.

The second example is the case of *Roche* v. *Minister for Industry*[76] which concerned a mineral acquisition order made by the Minister in respect of "all minerals ... under the land described in the Schedule to this Order ... ". The order was made under the Minerals Development Act 1940, s.14(1) by which:

> "Whenever it appears to the Minister that there are minerals on or under any land and that such minerals are not being worked ... and the Minister is of opinion that it is desirable in the public interest, with a view to the exploitation of such minerals, that the working of such minerals would be controlled by the State, the Minister ... may by order ... compulsorily acquire such minerals."

Dealing with the rule we are illustrating, Henchy J. said, in *Roche*:

> " ... [T]he Minister must make an appraisal of the situation in the light of the particular mineral substances which he

[73] This rubric seems not to be used in the British textbooks.
[74] See further, Craig, *Administrative Law*, p. 383.
[75] For another example, see *The State (Minister for Local Government)* v. *Ennis U.D.C.* [1939] I.R. 258 at p. 260.
[76] [1978] I.R. 149.

invoked ... and must consider whether it is desirable in the
public interest, with a view to their exploitation, that the
working of them should be controlled by the State ... the
acquisition orders in question here [are] bad for they are
blanket orders to cover "all minerals" under the land ... and
thereby show a want of the discrimination and appraisal
necessary on the part of the Minister to comply with
the ... pre-requisites set out in the subsection."[77]

Finally, we should describe a case which whilst not precisely
analogous to *Sheridan* or *Roche* involves a fairly similar illustration
of the notion that a discretionary power must be scrupulously
exercised. It is a case which has already been mentioned in
Chapter 3, namely *Inspector of Taxes' Association* v. *Minister for the
Public Service*.[78] Up to 1960 a staff association known as the
Association of Inspectors of Taxes represented Inspectors of
Taxes (Technical). In 1960 the expansion of the PAYE scheme to
cover all employees necessitated the appointment of extra staff to
the Revenue Commissioners. A number of additional Inspector of
Taxes were appointed, who possessed no technical qualifications;
were not granted a commission by the Minister; and were
designated "Inspectors of Taxes (Clerical)." However the Minister
refused to create a separate grade for these new Inspectors. The
plaintiff association was formed in 1980 to represent the interests
of Inspectors of Taxes (Technical). The association sought
recognition from the Minister for the Public Service in order to be
allowed to participate in the public service Conciliation and
Arbitration Scheme. This claim depended upon the argument that
there should be separate gradings for Technical and Clerical
Inspectors. When this argument was rejected, the association
challenged the decision on the ground that the Minister had not
really examined the possibility of re-grading, but instead had
merely looked back to the refusal by the Minister for Finance (the
predecessor of the Minister for the Public Service) in 1960, of an
earlier request that a distinct grade for clerical Inspectors be
established. Rejecting this argument, Finlay C. J. held that before
taking the 1980 decision:

> "[The Minister had gone] in detail into the existing situation
> in 1980 of the various categories of Inspectors of Taxes; the
> work that they carried out; and the material factors which
> might be appropriate if a re-grading of them had been
> contemplated "

Finlay C.J. concluded that the Minister had come to a considered

[77] *Ibid.* at p. 156.
[78] [1986] I.L.R.M. 296. See also pp. 57–58.

decision on the application to re-grade, and that decision could not be attacked as unreasonable.

4. Are there unreviewable discretionary powers?

Writing in 1966, Professor Kelly stated that:

> " ... provided an authority entrusted with administrative discretion keeps inside its *vires* and (where appropriate) commits no open breach of natural justice it may act as foolishly, unreasonably or even unfairly as it likes and the Courts cannot (or at any rate will not) interfere."[79]

Commenting on this statement only five years later, the same writer made *amende honorable*:

> "In the light of four subsequent Irish decisions, it is clear that this point of view, whatever justification it may have had in 1966, does not now correctly state Irish law on the matter; ... the Courts have, within the last three years, explicitly marked out bridgeheads from which the exercise of statutory discretion can be controlled on more penetrating criteria than mere *vires* (as traditionally understood) or natural justice."[80]

The preceding parts of this chapter consist largely of an account of the break-out from these bridgeheads.

The islands of immunity from judicial review which continue to remain above the waterline are few and each of them has to be justified by cogent reasons. Before going to examine these exceptional areas, it is appropriate to describe some illustrations of the general proposition, namely that the tide of judicial review has been steadily rising. A particularly graphic example is afforded

---

[79] Kelly, "Administrative Discretion and the Courts" (1966) 1 Ir.Jur.(n.s.), 209, 210. But see *The State (McGeough)* v. *Louth C.C.* (1973) 107 I.L.T.R. 13 which was decided in 1956 but not reported until 1973.

[80] Kelly, "Judicial Review of Administrative Action: New Irish Trends" (1971) 6 Ir.Jur.(n.s.) 40. The four subsequent Irish decisions referred to were: *Listowel U.D.C.* v. *McDonagh* [1968] I.R. 312; *Central Dublin Development Assoc.* v. *Att.-Gen.* (1975) 109 I.L.T.R. 69; *Kiely* v. *Minister for Social Welfare* [1971] I.R. 21 and *East Donegal Co-Operatives Ltd.* v. *Att.-Gen.* [1970] I.R. 317.

by the Supreme Court case of *The State (Lynch)* v. *Cooney*.[81] The concrete question in this case was the validity of an order, made by the Minister for Posts and Telegraphs, at the time of the February 1982 General Election, directing RTE not to broadcast any programme, including a party political broadcast, inviting support for Provisional Sinn Fein. This order purported to be made under the Broadcasting Authority Act 1960, s.31, inserted by the Broadcasting Authority (Amendment) Act 1976. Under this section:

> "Where the Minister is of the opinion that the broadcasting of... any matter of a particular class would be likely to promote or incite to crime or would tend to undermine the authority of the State, he may by order direct the authority to refrain from broadcasting... any matter of the particular class, and the authority shall comply with the order."

The principal question was whether this section was unconstitutional for contravention of Article 40.6.1 which creates a right to free expression which is subject to the exception that the State must "endeavour to ensure that organs of public opinion... shall not be used to undermine public order or morality...."

On a literal reading, section 31 is extremely wide: absent bad faith, it would indeed give the Minister the power to determine his own *vires*. Following this interpretation, which had been applied in earlier Supreme Court authorities, the High Court held that it was unconstitutional because, in contrast with the exemption to Article 40.6.1, the test for the existence of the power created by the section was subjective. It is striking that the Supreme Court not only reversed the High Court but also disavowed two of its own previous decisions.[82] O'Higgins C.J.'s judgment was based on

---

[81] [1982] I.R. 337. See Gearty, (1982) 4 D.U.L.J.(n.s.) 95. In the High Court O'Hanlon J. had ruled that the section was unconstitutional as in his opinion it purported to confer an unreviewable discretionary power on the Minister which might be used to override the rights to free speech protected by Article 40.6.1. This reasoning is similar to that employed by Kenny J. in *Macauley* v. *Minister for Posts and Telegraphs* [1966] I.R. 345. Section 2(1) of the Ministers and Secretaries Act 1924 required that the Attorney-General grant his *fiat* before an action could be commenced against a Minister of State. Kenny J. ruled that the power conferred by s.21(1) was not reviewable by the courts, and he proceeded to invalidate the subsection as it impeded the citizen's right of access to the courts protected by Art. 40.3.

[82] O'Higgins C.J. said ([1982] I.R. at 360): "While the opinion of the former Supreme Court expressed in 1940 (*Re Article 26 and the Offences against the State (Amendment) Bill, 1940* [1940] I.R. 470) and 1957 (*Re*

a particularly strong application of the well-established presumption of constitutionality doctrine. Adopting this approach, the judge was able to read the wording of section 31 in an objective sense and hence to uphold the section's constitutionality. It is appropriate to re-emphasise, at this point, that the principal focus of the present Chapter is not judicial review which is founded upon some specific right established by the Constitution (a form of control which was briefly mentioned *supra*).[83] Rather we are concerned here with the comprehensive, common law power to review for reasonableness, taking irrelevant considerations into account, etc. And, as stated already, O'Higgins C.J.'s judgment in *Lynch* was grounded on Article 40.6.1 (right to free speech). Accordingly, of greater interest for present purposes is Henchy J.'s separate, assenting judgment which contains the following seminal passage:

> "I conceive the present state of evolution of administrative law in the courts on this topic to be that when a statute confers a decision-making power affecting personal rights on a non-judicial person or body, conditional on that person or body reaching a prescribed opinion or conclusion based on a subjective assessment, a person who shows that a personal right of his has been breached or is liable to be breached by a decision purporting to be made in exercise of that power has standing to seek, and the High Court jurisdiction to give, a ruling as to whether the precondition for the valid exercise of the power has been complied with in a way that brings the decision within the express or necessarily implied range of the power conferred by the statute. It is to be presumed that when Parliament conferred the power it intended it to be exercised only in a manner that would be in conformity with the Constitution and within the limitations of the power as it is to be gathered from the statutory scheme or design. This means, amongst other things, not only that the power must be exercised in good faith, but that the opinion or other subjective conclusion set as a precondition for the valid exercise of the power must be reached by a route that does not make the exercise unlawful—such as by misinterpreting the law, or by misapplying it through taking into consideration irrelevant matters of fact, or through ignoring relevant

O'Laighleis [1960] I.R. 93) reflected what was then current judicial orthodoxy, judicial thinking has since undergone a change."

[83] See p. 313. See also *The State (M.)* v. *Att.-Gen.* [1979] I.R. 73.

matters. Otherwise, the exercise of the power will be held to be invalid for being *ultra vires*."[84]

It emerges from the first sentence of the passage that for Henchy J. the *ratio* of *Lynch* is broad and is not restricted to a situation, as in the case itself, where some specific constitutional right is under attack. The passage proceeds to give a constitutional foundation to the re-statement of the general common law which is contained in the final sentence. Although the decision in the case may be taken as involving a rejection of the plain words of a statute, it is certainly in line with developments, even in Britain, where the judges do not have the aid and comfort of a written constitution.[85]

The second and final stage in the Supreme Court's reasoning was to examine whether the order, made by the Minister, banning Provisional Sinn Fein from the air-waves was *intra vires* the reduced power created by the Court's reading of section 31. Having examined evidence of the organisation's policy— "to disestablish both States, North and South"—the Court held that the Minister was fully justified—indeed Henchy J. stated that it would have been "perverse" not to hold the opinion prescribed by section 31. Accordingly the order was held to be *intra vires*.

There are a number of other instances (some of them, admittedly, only *obiter dicta*) of judicial intervention in situations which might previously have been thought to present non-justiciable issues. In *Re Haughey*[86] it is striking that the Supreme Court was prepared to consider whether the Dail Public Accounts Committee had transgressed the boundaries fixed for it by the Dail Standing Orders (though without explicitly considering the question of whether the Court was empowered to intervene in the internal proceedings of the Oireachtas).[87] In *Re Article 26 and the*

---

[84] [1982] I.R. at pp. 380–381.

[85] Henchy J. quoted De Smith's *Judicial Review of Administrative Action*, 4th ed. (1980) at p. 326 with approval: "[T]he courts will not readily be deterred by subjectively worded statutory formulae from determining whether acts done avowedly in pursuant of statutory powers bear an adequate relationship to the purposes prescribed by the statute" ([1982] I.R. at p. 380). The law has come a long way since decisions such as *Liversidge* v. *Anderson* [1942] A.C. 206 where an objectively worded statutory provision was read in a subjective fashion by the majority.

[86] [1971] I.R. 217.

[87] See *O'Crowley* v. *Minister for Finance* [1935] I.R. 536 for an affirmation of the traditional rule that the courts will not scrutinise the internal workings of Parliament.

Emergency Powers Bill 1976,[88] the Supreme Court expressly reserved for consideration the question of whether it had jurisdiction to review a declaration of emergency passed by both Houses of the Oireachtas, despite the fact that, to judge by the clear words and purpose of Article 28.3.3, it was intended that the Oireachtas should have the final say on this question. Again, in *Inspector of Taxes* v. *Minister for the Public Service*[89] the Supreme Court stated that a decision of the Minister in regard to grading, which affects the salary and career prospects of certain civil servants, is, like any other administrative action, open to review. Other decisions indicate that the exercise of certain prosecutorial discretions may be subject to review. In *The State (O'Callaghan)* v. *O'hUadaigh*[90] Finlay P. accepted that the power of the Director of Public Prosecutions to enter a *nolle prosequi* was reviewable and in *Norris* v. *Attorney-General*[91] McCarthy J. suggested that a positive decision not to prosecute in respect of all crimes of a particular nature would be unlawful, and, by implication, subject to review. Another relevant issue concerns the Civil Liability Act 1961, s.60 which makes a road authority liable even for non-feasance. The section goes on to provide that it is not to come into force until such date (after April 1, 1967) as may be fixed by Government order. By 1986, no such order had been made and in *The State (Sheehan)* v. *An Taoiseach*,[92] Costello J. granted an order of mandamus directing the Government to implement s.60 on the ground that the delay in bringing the provision into force was 'unreasonable'.

A Northern Irish example of this judicial trend is provided by *R.* v. *Governor of Maze Prison, ex p. McKiernan*.[93] In a similar case, *R.* v. *Deputy Governor of Camphill Prison ex p. King*,[94] the English Court of Appeal had ruled that considerations of public policy and

---

[88] [1977] I.R. 129. See Gwynn Morgan, "The Emergency Powers Bill Reference—II" (1979) 14 Ir.Jur.(n.s.) 252 at pp. 256–262.

[89] Supreme Court, November 7, 1985, p. 11. *A contra* High Court March 24, 1983 p. 31.

[90] [1977] I.R. 42. In *Raymond* v. *Att.-Gen.* [1982] Q.B. 839 at p. 847 Shaw L.J. observed that "Unless [the D.P.P.'s decision] is manifestly such that it could not be honestly and reasonably arrived at, it cannot . . . be impugned." *Cf.* also *Flynn* v. *D.P.P.* [1986] I.L.R.M. 290. Note that in *The State (Killian)* v. *Att.-Gen.* (1958) 92 I.L.T.R. 182 the former Supreme Court ruled that the entry of a *nolle prosequi* by the Attorney-General could not be subject to judicial review. The exact precedential status of this decision in the light of *O'Callaghan* and *Flynn* is unclear. *Cf. The State (McCormack)* v. *D.P.P.*, Supreme Court, July 30, 1986 and see Addendum.

[91] [1984] I.R. 36 at p. 81.

[92] High Court, July 29, 1986.

administrative convenience dictated that decisions of prison governors should be immune from judicial review. The Northern Ireland Court of Appeal declined to follow this decision in *McKiernan's* case. Both Lowry L.C.J. and O'Donnell L.J. were unimpressed by arguments that the availability of judicial review in these circumstances would undermine prison discipline and would be contrary to the public interest. As Lowry L.C.J. eloquently put it:

> "[It would be] quite unreasonable and contrary to the public interest in a civilised society that a [prison governor] should, in his judicial capacity, exercise an autocratic power and enjoy a freedom from High Court supervision which are denied both to the Board of Visitors and to all inferior courts."[95]

These arguments would seem to apply *a fortiori* to this jurisdiction where the dominant judicial view would appear to be that all discretionary powers are reviewable unless the Constitution itself grants an exemption.[96]

One such exemption is expressly provided for by Article 13.8.1 which states that the President shall not be answerable to "any court for the exercise and performance of the powers and functions of his office." In *Draper* v. *Ireland*,[97] the Supreme Court struck out the President from proceedings in which it was sought to prevent him from dissolving the Dail on the advice of the Taoiseach. O'Higgins C.J. described the attempt to join the President as defendant as being in "open defiance" of Article 13.8.1. A different view was taken in *The State (Walshe)* v. *Murphy*[98] where an order of certiorari was granted on the grounds that the District Justice who convicted the applicant had been invalidly appointed. It had been argued that, as the President had appointed the District Justice, to review the validity of the appointment was tantamount to impugning an official act of the President. This potentially far-reaching argument was rejected by

---

[93] (1985) 6 N.I.J.B. 6.

[94] [1985] Q.B. 735. For the rather unclear Irish position, on this question, see pp. 279–280.

[95] (1985) 6 N.I.J.B. at p. 10.

[96] It is said that one of the practical consequences of the constitutional guarantee of fair procedures is that discretionary powers cannot be exercised "unjustly or unfairly": see *per* O'Higgins C.J. in *Garvey* v. *Ireland* [1981] I.R. 75. But *quaere* does this not confuse substance and procedure?

[97] *The Irish Times*, May 14, 1981.

[98] [1981] I.R. 275.

a Divisional High Court. Finlay P. suggested that the constitutional immunity does not exist in the case of judicial examination of a function which requires the President's intervention for its effectiveness in law, but which in fact is "the decision and act of the Executive." The need to choose between *Draper* and *Walshe* would arise, for instance, if some person sought to challenge the exercise by the President (on the advice of the Government) of his "prerogative of mercy" so as to commute capital punishment to 40 years' imprisonment in all cases of capital murder since 1954, on the ground that it involves the application of an inflexible policy rule.

In some cases an immunity from judicial review may be regarded as having been implicitly conferred by the Constitution. This seems to be the only satisfactory explanation of the cases which hold that the power of the Director of Public Prosecutions to order the transfer of trials to the Special Criminal Court is unreviewable. Article 38.3.1 expressly permits the creation of such courts, and vests the Oireachtas with a plenary legislative power to regulate their "constitution, powers, jurisdiction and procedure." The Offences against the State Act 1939 now vests the Director of Public Prosecutions with power to order the trial of accused persons before the Special Criminal Court once he is satisfied that in his opinion the ordinary courts are inadequate "to secure the effective administration of justice and the preservation of public peace and order."[99] The High Court has ruled successively in *Savage* v. *D.P.P.*[1] and *Judge* v. *D.P.P.*[2] that once the D.P.P. *bona fide* holds that opinion, then the matter is not subject to any further review.

Both cases stress the security difficulties which made it impractical for the Director of Public Prosecutions to disclose the reasons for his decision. In *Judge* Carroll J. was unimpressed by the argument that such an investigation might be held *in camera*, presumably because she considered that even an *in camera* investigation would involve the danger of a "leak" of highly sensitive information. Yet in *The State (Lynch)* v. *Cooney*[3]—another "security" case—the Supreme Court was willing to review a banning order issued by the Minister for Posts and Telegraphs

---

[99] For an account of the relevant provisions, see Casey, *The Office of the Attorney-General in Ireland* (Dublin, 1980) at pp. 128–133.

[1] [1982] I.L.R.M. 385. See also *Re McCurtain* [1941] I.R. 83.

[2] [1984] I.L.R.M. 224. The Supreme Court had earlier reserved this question: see *Re Article 26 and the Criminal Law (Jurisdiction) Bill 1975* [1977] I.R. 129; *The State (Littlejohn)* v. *Governor of Mountjoy Prison*, Supreme Court, March 18, 1976.

[3] [1982] I.R. 337.

under the Broadcasting Authority Acts. This discrepancy between *Judge* and *Lynch* is probably explicable only by reference to the differing nature of the decision under review and of the range of information on which it would probably turn. In regard to the prosecution of terrorist offenders, much of this information is likely to be confidential, whereas the decision in *Lynch*, involving the public impact of *Sinn Fein* policies upon the Irish television audience, would be less likely to involve such sensitive material. But in any event, the utilitarian basis of *Savage* and *Judge*, coupled with a desire not to discommode the prosecuting authorities in such a sensitive matter, is out of line with the general judicial trend in favour of review.[4]

Carroll J. advanced another argument to bolster her conclusions in *Judge*. She felt that "no analogy could be drawn" between the opinion of the Director of Public Prosecutions under legislation authorised under Article 38.3, and the exercise of a power by a Minister under an ordinary Act of the Oireachtas. The inference, perhaps, to be drawn here is that Carroll J. felt that this matter had been entirely committed to the Oireachtas by Article 38.3.1, and that judicial scrutiny of the exercise of the Director of Public Prosecution's powers would be a breach of the separation of powers. In this instance, the conclusion hardly follows from the stated premise, for if Article 38.3.1 is one of the permitted exceptions to jury trial guaranteed in Article 38.5, must there not be "some protections implicit in the Constitution itself which requires that it cannot be avoided by the exercise of an unreviewable power?"[5] However, in principle Carroll J. may well be correct in that there may be a residual category of issues (known, collectively, in the United States, as "political questions")—some, but not all, having a strongly political flavour—which the courts have decided, for various historical or policy reasons, to treat as non-justiciable.[6] This question, and its

---

[4] The decisions in *Savage* and *Judge* have both come in for considerable criticism: see Byrne, (1981) 16 Ir.Jur.(n.s.) 86; (1984) 6 D.U.L.J.(n.s.) 177 and Pye, (1985) 3 I.L.T.(n.s.) 65.

[5] Byrne, (1984) 6 D.U.L.J.(n.s.) 177 at p. 183.

[6] Where there is a "textually demonstrable constitutional commitment" of an issue to a co-ordinate political department, or where there are no "judicially discoverable and manageable standards for resolving it" then the U.S. courts will regard the issue raised as non-justiciable in nature: see *Baker* v. *Carr*, 369 U.S. 1986 (1962). Judged by these standards, the reviewability of a declaration of emergency passed by both Houses of the Oireachtas would probably be held to be non-justiciable.

relationship to the separation of powers[7] as prescribed by the
Constitution, awaits judicial clarification.[7] This debate may be of
more importance on the conceptual than the practical plane. For
it seems likely that even were the courts to assume a power of
review in cases involving fundamental state interests (*e.g.* review of
a declaration of emergency under Article 28.3.3), the courts
would only intervene in the most extreme cases.[8]

---

[7] On broad Separation of Powers principles the courts will refrain from
interfering with the process of legislation: *O'Crowley* v. *Minister for
Finance* [1935] I.R. 536; *Halpin* v. *Att.-Gen.* [1936] I.R. 226; *Wireless
Dealers Assoc.* v. *Fair Trade Commission,* Supreme Court, March 7, 1956;
Roche v. *Ireland,* High Court, June 16, 1983 and *Finn* v. *Att.-Gen.* [1983]
I.R. 154. Yet judicial intervention will be forthcoming if the constitu-
tionally required stages of law-making have not been carried out: *R.
(O'Brien)* v. *Governor of the North Dublin Military Barracks* [1924] 1 I.R.
32; *Victoria* v. *Commonwealth* (1975) 7 A.L.R. 1; *Western Australia* v.
Commonwealth (1975) 7 A.L.R. 159.

[8] See, for example, the graduated scale of review applied in the prison
transfer cases: *The State (Smith and Fox)* v. *Governor of the Curragh
Military Barracks* [1980] I.L.R.M. 208; *The State (Boyle)* v. *Governor of the
Curragh Military Barracks* [1980] I.L.R.M. 242.

11 Remedies

1. Introduction

Prior to October 1986 a person aggrieved by a decision of an administrative body or lower court had a wide variety of remedies open to him. In addition to the principal State side orders of certiorari, prohibition and mandamus,[1] the private law remedies of the declaration and injunction could also have been invoked. These two sets of remedies differed in the scope of their application, depending on the nature of the decision, defect or public body involved. Writing in 1966, Griffith and Street commented as follows:

> "The remedies, for no practical reason are plural; some of them cannot be used if another remedy is available; the lines between them are imprecise and shifting [and] the judges employ vague concepts (which they do not define) in marking the boundaries of each remedy."[2]

Prior to the coming into force of the new Rules of the Superior

---

[1] The other State side orders are habeas corpus and quo warrato (or an application for an inquiry under Art. 40.4.2, as it is more properly described). The remedy of *habeas corpus* falls outside the scope of this book, but see Kelly, *The Irish Constitution* (Dublin, 1984). Quo warranto proceedings are now virtually obsolete, and there has been only one reported case involving quo warranto since 1922: *The State (Lycester)* v. *Hegarty* (1941) 75 I.L.T.R. 121, where the powers of the Master of the High Court in such proceedings are discussed. The modern practice is to seek a declaration that an office-holder has been invalidly appointed rather than to proceed by way of quo warranto: see *Glynn* v. *Roscommon C.C.* (1959) 93 I.L.T.R. 149. Proceedings by way of quo warranto must now be brought as an application for judicial review: see Ord. 84, r. 18(1) of the new Rules of the Superior Courts.

[2] Griffith and Street, *Principles of Administrative Law* (London, 1966) at p. 236.

Courts in October 1986[3] if an applicant sought the wrong
remedy—which happened surprisingly seldom in practice—no
relief could be granted to him because he had not asked for the
proper order.[4] The principal innovatory feature of the new
Ord. 84 is the creation of a single comprehensive procedure
(known as an "application for judicial review") which enables an
aggrieved party to test the legality of administrative action in the
High Court. The major objective behind the creation of this new
procedure is to reduce the chance of a good case being lost as a
result of the choice of the wrong remedy.[5] It would, however, be
wrong to over-estimate the significance of these changes. The
individual remedies have all been retained, and it is still necessary
to choose among them (*i.e.*, certiorari in preference to mandamus), although the court is now empowered to grant the
appropriate relief in such cases. For this reason, the previous
practice is still relevant, as the applicant still needs to ask for an
individual remedy (and he will presumably try to pick the right
remedy) and the court needs a body of law to guide it as to which
remedy is the most appropriate in the circumstances. The new
Rules also make provision for such matters as time limits[6]; *locus
standi*[7], discovery and interrogatories[8] and interim relief.[9] It must
be a matter of doubt as to whether some of these more far-
reaching changes can be said to be *intra vires* the Superior Court
Rules Committee.[10]

---

[3] S.I. 1986 No. 15. These Rules are expected to come into force on
October 1, 1986. For an account of the previous State side practice, see
Law Reform Commission Working Paper No. 8, *Judicial Review of
Administrative Action: The Problem of Remedies* (1979) and Graham,
"Judicial Review: Where to Reform" (1984) 6 D.U.L.J.(n.s.) 25. The
new Rules very largely follow the scheme of reform as proposed by the
Law Reform Commission in their working paper.

[4] As, for example, happened in cases such as *The State (Colquhoun)* v.
D'Arcy [1936] I.R. 641 and *O'Doherty* v. *Att.-Gen.* [1941] I.R. 569.

[5] Because the effect of Ord. 84, r. 19 is that the various remedies are now
interchangeable.

[6] Ord. 84, r. 21(1) imposes a general time limit of three months (six
months where the relief claimed is certiorari) from the date "when
grounds for the application first arose." The court has a discretion to
extend these time-limits. See pp. 336, 351.

[7] Ord. 84, r. 20(4) provides that the High Court shall not grant leave
unless it considers that the applicant has a "sufficient interest" in the
matter to which the application relates. See pp. 359–361.

[8] Ord. 84, r. 25. See p. 335.

[9] Ord. 84, r. 20(7). See p. 335.

[10] s.36 of the Courts of Justice Act 1924 (and as applied by ss.14 and 48 of
the Courts (Supplemental Provisions) Act 1961) empowers the Superior Court Rules Committee to make rules governing the "practice and

The new Rules distinguish between the traditional public law remedies (or "State side orders"; certiorari, prohibition and mandamus) on the one hand and the declaration and injunction on the other. In the case of the State side orders, Ord. 84, r. 18(1) requires that an application for relief "shall be made by way of an application for judicial review." By contrast, an application for a declaration or injunction *may* be made by way of an application for judicial review, and the court may grant the relief claimed if, having regard to all the circumstances of the case, it would be "just and convenient" for the declaration and injunction to be granted on an application for judicial review. These differing arrangements are in recognition of the fact that the declaration and injunction are not purely public law remedies.[11]

2. Certiorari, prohibition and mandamus

Certiorari lies to quash a decision of a public body which has been arrived at in excess of jurisdiction, whereas prohibition is sought to restrain that body from doing something which would be in excess of its jurisdiction. There is no real difference in principle between the two remedies, save that prohibition may be invoked at an earlier stage. The difference is thus almost exclusively one of tense. The principal function of mandamus is to secure the performance of a duty imposed on a public body either by statute of by common law. We must now consider (i) the procedure for an application for judicial review introduced by the new Rules of the Superior Courts and (ii) the scope of these remedies.

(i) *Applications for judicial review: practice and procedure*
The procedure in relation to applications for certiorari, prohibition and mandamus is governed by Ord. 84, r. 18(1) which provides that such applications shall be by way of an

---

procedure" of the superior courts. The Rules Committee would be acting *ultra vires* if they attempted to alter the existing substantive law: *The State (O'Flaherty)* v. *O'Floinn* [1954] I.R. 295. When similar changes were introduced in England and Northern Ireland, the precaution was taken of having these changes placed on a statutory footing: see Supreme Court Act 1981, s.31 and Judicature (N.I.) Act 1978, ss.18–21.

[11] Both the declaration and the injunction are, of course, remedies of general application in the field of both private and public law.

application for judicial review. Ord. 84, r. 20(1) requires that no application for judicial review shall be made unless the prior leave of the court has been obtained.[12] An application for leave must be made by motion *ex parte* by a notice containing, *inter alia*, details of the relief sought and the grounds on which it is sought, and an affidavit verifying the facts relied on.[13] The court may permit an application for leave to be amended on such terms (if any) as it thinks fit.[14] Leave will not be granted unless the applicant has a "sufficient interest in the matter" to which the application relates.[15] If the court grants leave, it may impose such terms as to costs as it thinks fit, and may require an undertaking as to damages.[16]

The requirement as to leave is one of the most important changes introduced by the new Rules. It serves as a "filtering device" and guards against unmeritorious claims that a particular decision is invalid.[17] This two-stage procedure also means that the High Court no longer has power to grant an absolute order of

[12] Ord. 84, r. 20(1). The requirement for leave corresponds to the former practice on the State side whereby the applicant was required to seek a conditional order. If a conditional order was granted, an application was brought by motion to make the order absolute and the respondent was required to show cause why it should not be: see Ord. 84, rr. 9, 25 and 37 of the R.S.C. 1962. Under this procedure, the applicant, if refused a conditional order, had the right to go around all the High Court judges in pursuit of his remedy: *The State (Richardson)* v. *Governor of Mountjoy Prison* [1980] I.L.R.M. 82. It would seem that an applicant may still move from judge to judge if he is refused leave to apply for judicial review. An appeal against the *refusal* of leave to apply will, presumably, lie to the Supreme Court by virtue of the general provisions of Art. 34.4.3. It is more doubtful as to whether the *respondents* could appeal a decision *to grant leave to the applicant: cf.* the comments of McCarthy J. in *The State (Hughes)* v. *O'Hanrahan* [1986] I.L.R.M. 218, 221 doubting whether anyone (other than the applicants) can appeal against an order granted *ex parte*.

[13] Ord. 84, r. 20(2). The court is entitled to refuse relief on discretionary grounds if material facts are suppressed in the affidavit: *R. (Bryson)* v. *Lisnaskea Guardians* [1918] 2 I.R. 258; *The State (Nicolaou)* v. *An Bord Uchtala* [1966] I.R. 567 and *Cork Corporation* v. *O'Connell* [1982] I.L.R.M. 505.

[14] Ord. 84, r. 20(3).

[15] Ord. 84, r. 20(4). This matter is now considered at pp. 359–361.

[16] Ord. 84, r. 20(6).

[17] This was one of the principal reasons given by the House of Lords in *O'Reilly* v. *Mackman* [1983] 2 A.C. 237 as to why challenges to administrative action brought by plenary summons (as in the case of a declaration or injunction), and which thus circumvented the requirement for leave, should be struck out as an abuse of process.

certiorari, prohibition or mandamus following an *ex parte* application.[18]

It has been said of the State side orders that they afford a:

> "[S]peedy and effective remedy to a person aggrieved by a clear excess of jurisdiction by an inferior tribunal. But they are not designed to raise issues of fact for the High Court to determine *de novo. . . .* "[19]

Thus, where a case turned on disputed facts, this used to pose difficulties for an applicant for State side relief. One way around these difficulties was to apply to cross-examine deponents on their affidavits, and this practice received the approval of the Supreme Court.[20] But while discovery was available,[21] there was no procedure for serving interrogatories, or for obtaining interlocutory relief pending the determination of the application. It was for these reasons that where issues of fact were raised in a challenge to the validity of administrative action litigants tended to proceed by way of plenary hearings and seek an injunction or a declaration.[22] These procedural restrictions have now been removed. One may now apply for discovery or interrogatories,[23] and granting of leave to apply for judicial review will generally[24] operate as a stay of the proceedings to which the application relates. The court may also direct that the application for judicial review shall be made by

---

[18] See Ord. 84, rr. 9, 28 and 38 of the R.S.C. 1962. This power was exercised in unusual cases where no proper defence to the granting of an absolute order *ex parte* could be made out: see *The State (Att.-Gen.)* v. *Coghlan*, High Court, May 10, 1974 and *Re Zwann's Application* [1981] I.R. 395.

[19] *R.* v. *Fulham Rent Tribunal, ex p. Zerek* [1951] 2 K.B. 1 at p. 11 *per* Devlin J.

[20] *The State (Furey)* v. *Minister for Defence*, Supreme Court, March 2, 1984.

[21] Ord. 31 of the R.S.C. 1962 gave the court power to order discovery "in any cause or matter," and there was no objection to the use of this power in State side applications: *The State (McGarrity)* v. *Deputy Garda Commissioner* (1978) 112 I.L.T.R. 25.

[22] See the comments of Henchy J. in *M.* v. *An Bord Uchtala* [1977] I.R. 287 at p. 297. The use of this plenary procedure in the wake of the new Rules may now amount to an abuse of process: see *O'Reilly* v. *Mackman* [1983] 2 A.C. 237 and pp. 345–347.

[23] Ord. 84, r. 25.

[24] Ord. 84, r. 20(7)(*a*) provides that upon an application for judicial review by way of certiorari or prohibition, the grant of leave will, if the court so directs, operate as a stay of the proceedings until the determination of the application or until further order. If other relief is sought, Ord. 84, r. 20(7)(*b*) empowers the court to grant such interim relief "as could be granted in an action begun by plenary summons."

plenary summons, instead of by originating notice of motion.[25] Any such notice of motion must be served on all persons directly affected within 14 days after the grant of leave, or within "such other period as the Court may direct."[26] In default of service, the stay of proceedings shall lapse.[27] The effect of a similar provision contained in the former Rules of Court was considered by Finlay P. in *The State (Fitzsimons)* v. *Kearney*.[28] In this case a conditional order of certiorari had not been served within the prescribed time limit owing to an oversight. The applicant then sought, pursuant to Ord. 108, r. 7[29] an extension of time for service of the conditional order.

Finlay P. concluded that he had no jurisdiction to grant the extension of time sought. The purpose of the Ord. 84 procedure was to ensure a rapid determination of the validity of the impugned order, and, accordingly, the High Court had no jurisdiction to extend the period of time for service once the time had elapsed. The period for service could be extended by the court when making the conditional order, or *before* the expiry of the prescribed period. If, however, the conditional order (or, under the new Rules, a grant of leave) is not served within the prescribed period, or such period as fixed by the court, then the order stands discharged, and the provision of Ord. 108, r. 7 may not be invoked to extend the period of time for service of that order.

Any respondent who intends to oppose the application for judicial review by way of motion or notice[30] must file in the Central Office a statement setting out concisely the grounds for such

[25] Ord. 84, r. 22(1). The court also has a power, upon an application for prohibition or quo warranto, to direct a plenary hearing with directions as to pleadings, discovery etc.: see Ord. 84, r. 26(7).

[26] Ord. 84, r. 22(3). In the case of a motion on notice, it shall be returnable for the first available motion day after the expiry of 10 days from the date of service, unless the court otherwise directs. An affidavit of service must be filed prior to the hearing of the motion or summons: see Ord. 84, r. 22(5).

[27] Ord. 84, r. 22(3).

[28] [1981] I.R. 406. See also *The State (Flynn & O'Flaherty Ltd.)* v. *Dublin Corporation* [1983] I.L.R.M. 125.

[29] Ord. 108, r. 7 of the 1962 Rules gave the court a special power to enlarge or abridge time. A similar power is contained in Ord. 122, r. 7 of the new Rules.

[30] If the court has directed that the application for judicial review be made by way of plenary summons under Ord. 84, r. 22(1), the respondent will presumably conduct his defence as if in a plenary action. There is, however, no specific provision for this in the Rules (save in the case of applications for prohibition or quo warranto, for which see Ord. 84, r. 26(7)).

opposition and, if any facts are relied on, an affidavit verifying such facts.[31] A copy of such statement of affidavit must be served on all parties within seven days from the date of service of the notice of motion or such other period as the court may direct.[32]

(ii) *Scope of the remedies*

Recent litigation has shown that certiorari, prohibition and mandamus are remedies of great scope and flexibility. Nevertheless, these remedies are not universal in their scope, as the following discussion will show. It is convenient to begin our discussion with the oft-quoted dictum of Atkin L.J. in *R. v. Electricity Commissioners, ex p. London Electricity Joint Committee Co. (1920) Ltd.*:

> "Whenever any body of persons having legal authority to determine questions affecting the rights of subjects, and having the duty to act judicially, act in excess of legal authority, they are subject to the controlling jurisdiction [of the High Court]."[33]

However, as we shall see, the law has not stood still since 1924 when these words were first uttered.

"Any body of persons having legal authority." These public law remedies will issue in respect of any individual or body of persons exercising statutory authority.[34] This means that persons or bodies drawing their authority from contract or from the consent of their members fall outside the scope of these remedies, and the declaration and injunction are the most suitable remedies in such a situation.[35] For example, in *The State (Colquhoun) v.*

---

[31] Ord. 84, r. 22(4).

[32] *Ibid.*

[33] [1924] 1 K.B. 171 at p. 205.

[34] Thus, prohibition will not lie to a tribunal usurping legal authority (*R. (Kelly) v. Maguire and Sheil* [1923] 2 I.R. 58) or whose authority is derived from contract or consent (*The State (Colquhoun) v. D'Arcy* [1936] I.R. 641). As for whether the State side orders will issue to extra statutory tribunals, see pp. 133, 339.

[35] It would also appear that the application for a declaration and injunction must be commenced by way of plenary summons (and not by way of an application for judicial review under Ord. 84, r. 18(2)) in this situation: see *R. v. B.B.C., ex p. Lavelle* [1983] 1 W.L.R. 23; *Law v. National Greyhound Racing Club Ltd.* [1983] 1 W.L.R. 1302. Both *Lavelle* and *Law* deal with s.31(2) of the English Supreme Court Act 1981, and the language of our Ord. 84, r. 18(2) corresponds almost exactly with that of s.31(2) of the English Act.

D'Arcy[36] it was held that the General Synod of the Church of Ireland could not be restrained by prohibition as the Synod derived its authority, not from the common law or statute, but from contract and the consent of its members. It would also seem that public law remedies may not be used to challenge decisions of public bodies which do not relate to the exercise of public law functions. In other words, the public law remedies will not lie where the circumstances of the case are governed by private law. Thus, in *R. (Butler)* v. *Navan U.D.C.*[37] the Supreme Court refused to grant mandamus to compel the respondents to carry out their statutory duty to repair a graveyard wall. Fitzgibbon J. observed that the application was misconceived because it was an attempt to secure the "performance of an alleged private right" and not the performance of any public duty. This procedural point might have been—but was not—raised in recent cases where public employees have been permitted to use public law remedies as a means of challenging the validity of their dismissal. It is at least arguable that the dismissal of public employees is governed by ordinary contract law, and that an application for certiorari or similar relief in such cases is misconceived.[38]

"Determining questions affecting the rights of subjects..."

It was traditionally understood that the public law remedies would only lie to review something in the nature of a determination or decision. The determination does not have to be absolutely final, but there are cases which hold that a requirement that the decision be approved by another person or body prevents the orders from issuing.[39] Allied to this is the notion that the public law remedies

---

[36] [1936] I.R. 641. But see *The State (Smullen)* v. *Duffy* [1980] I.L.R.M. 46, where it was assumed that certiorari would lie to quash the expulsion of a student from a community school. However, the respondent does not appear to have argued that the application for certiorari was misconceived.

[37] [1926] I.R. 466. See also *R. (Lynham)* v. *Cork C.C.* (1901) 35 I.L.T.R. 167.

[38] But, as against that, the decision to dismiss in the Garda and Defence Force cases (*e.g. The State (Gleeson)* v. *Minister for Defence* [1976] I.R. 280) has been taken pursuant to a statutory power, and this gives the cases a sufficient public dimension to bring them within the reach of certiorari: see Hogan, "Public Law Remedies and Judicial Review in the Context of Employment Law" (1985) 4 J.I.S.L.L. 9 and *R.* v. *East Berkshire Health Authority, ex p. Walsh* [1985] Q.B. 152 and *R.* v. *Home Secretary, ex p. Benwell* [1985] Q.B. 554.

[39] *Re Local Government Board, ex p. Kingstown Commissioners* (1886) 18 L.R.Ir. 509 (no prohibition to body issuing provisional orders which

will not lie to a body whose sole function is to make a recommendation, and that the impugned determination must affect rights or impose liabilities.[40] The modern tendency, however, is to eschew a rigid classification of whether a determination is "binding," "conclusive" or whether the "legal rights" of the citizen have been affected. The courts are apt to examine whether the applicant has suffered a real or possible prejudice and to see whether he has a sufficient interest in the matter.

In *The State (Shannon Atlantic Fisheries Ltd.)* v. *McPolin*[41] Finlay P. quashed a report which followed a statutory inquiry. The report was sent to the Minister for Transport and Power, who was obliged to decide whether a prosecution was called for. The investigating officer had not observed the precepts of natural justice when compiling his report concerning the wrecking of the prosecutor's fishing vessel, and Finlay P. held that the prosecutors were entitled to have the report quashed on this account. It was irrelevant that the prosecutors could no longer be charged with offences arising out of this incident[42]; they were rightly concerned with the findings of fact made in the report which affected their reputation as ship owners. Cases such as *McPolin* show that the concept of the "determination of rights" is loosely construed. It cannot be said that a preliminary report in and of itself affects legal rights or imposes liabilities. But the critical factor is often whether the prosecutors were prejudiced in the contested determination, and whether they would obtain a real benefit were the determination to be quashed.[43]

---

require confirmation by Act of Parliament before they take effect) and *R.* v. *St. Lawrence's Hospital Visitors, ex p. Pritchard* [1953] 1 W.L.R. 1158.

[40] *The State (St. Stephen's Green Club)* v. *Labour Court* [1961] I.R. 85; and the comments of Murnaghan J. in *The State (Pharmaceutical Society)* v. *Fair Trade Commission* (1965) 99 I.L.T.R. 24 at pp. 31–32 (no prohibition to respondent body as it could not affect individual rights or liabilities).

[41] [1976] I.R. 93.

[42] The six-month time limit for summary prosecutions imposed by s.10(4) of the Petty Sessions (Ireland) Act 1851 had expired.

[43] This has been the attitude taken in cases such as *The State (Hayes)* v. *Criminal Injuries Compensation Board* [1982] I.L.R.M. 210 (certiorari lies to review decisions of extra-statutory body) and *The State (Melbarien Enterprises Ltd.)* v. *Revenue Commissioners*, High Court, April 19, 1985 (certiorari lies to review refusal to grant tax clearance certificate, *i.e.* a purely administrative decision not taken pursuant to statutory power).

"Having the duty to act judicially." In *The State (Crowley)* v. *Irish Land Commission*[44] the Supreme Court accepted that not all administrative decisions were subject to review by way of prohibition or certiorari. The administrative body concerned had to be under a duty to act judicially before such remedies could issue. An administrative body acted judicially when it was required to consider the facts and circumstances of the case before it could reach a decision imposing liability or affecting the rights of others.

But this requirement does not in practice greatly restrict the scope of certiorari or prohibition. First, the duty to act judicially is implied where there is a power to affect rights or impose liabilities.[45] Secondly, mandamus will issue in cases even where there is no duty to act judicially, and this reflects the fact that until nearly the end of the nineteenth century mandamus was used to enforce administrative and ministerial duties of every description.[46] One of the effects of the new Ord. 84, r. 19 is that certiorari, prohibition and mandamus are now interchangeable remedies for all practical purposes. There is now nothing to prevent a court granting an order of certiorari *in lieu* of mandamus in a case where the decision-maker was under no duty to act judicially.[47]

"Act in excess of legal authority." Notwithstanding this qualification, traditionally, certiorari enjoyed one distinct procedural advantage over and above the other remedies. It would lie to review not only *ultra vires* decisions, but it would also quash for

---

[44] [1951] I.R. 250.

[45] *Ridge* v. *Baldwin* [1964] A.C. 40; *R.* v. *Hillingdon B.C., ex p. Royco Homes Ltd.* [1974] Q.B. 720. *The State (Conlan)* v. *Military Service Pensions Referee* [1947] I.R. 264 (certiorari does not lie to review ministerial decision to request respondent referee to review the grant of a military service pension, as Minister under no duty to act judicially) is one of the very few cases in which the applicant has failed to satisfy this requirement. It also appears that certiorari cannot be used to mount a direct challenge to the validity of a statute or delegated legislation, as no duty to act judicially arises in the case of the exercise of a legislative function: *Re Local Government Board, ex p. Kingstown Commissioners* (1886) 18 L.R.Ir. 509. Of course, certiorari can be used to mount an indirect or collateral challenge to the validity of such legislation: see Hogan, "Challenging the Validity of an Act of the Oireachtas by way of Certiorari" (1982) 4 D.U.L.J.(n.s.) 130.

[46] Wade, *Administrative Law* (Oxford, 1982) at p. 635.

[47] Note that in *O'Reilly* v. *Mackman* [1983] 2 A.C. 237, the House of Lords ruled that the duty to act judicially was no longer to be required in the case of applications for certiorari or prohibition.

error on the face of the record.[48] The effect of the new Ord. 84, r. 19 is to empower the court to quash for error on the face of the record in all applications for judicial review.

Special features of mandamus

Mandamus is, technically, a statutory remedy in that section 28(8) of the Supreme Court of Judicature (Ireland) Act 1877 permits an interlocutory order of mandamus to be granted in all cases "where it is just and convenient to do so." Thus, unlike certiorari and prohibition, it was theoretically possible to obtain interim relief in mandamus cases even prior to the new Rules of Court, although the facility does not seem to have been ever availed of in practice. Curiously enough, the Rules of Court have always assimilated the practice and procedure of mandamus applications to that of interpleader actions, and this feature of mandamus is retained in the new Ord. 84, r. 25(2). Consequently, discovery, and interrogatories have always been available in applications for mandamus, and, in a suitable case, the applicant is entitled to a jury trial.[49] Any applicant for mandamus must first call on the administrative body concerned to do its duty, and this must have been refused.[50] The requirement that there be "a demand and refusal" has much to commend it: it makes sense that the administrative body concerned is given the chance to mend its hand before the aggrieved citizen resorts to litigation. But the courts do not insist upon this requirement where it is unsuitable.[51] In some cases where the impugned order could be classified as

---

[48] Thus, a declaration could not be awarded to quash for error on the face of the record: *Punton* v. *Ministry for Pensions (No. 2)* [1964] 1 W.L.R. 226.

[49] Ord. 36, r. 7 (which applies to interpleader and, consequently, to mandamus proceedings) allows the court to order a jury trial where there is a contested issue of fact. A jury trial on an issue of fact was ordered in *The State (Modern Homes (Ire.) Ltd.)* v. *Dublin Corporation* [1953] I.R. 202.

[50] "It is an established rule that the prosecutor must make a specific demand for the performance of the public duty in question, and it must be shown that this demand has been refused, or has been followed by conduct which the Court considers as tantamount to a refusal" *per* Fitzgibbon J. in *R. (Butler)* v. *Navan U.D.C.* [1926] I.R. 466 at pp. 470–471. See also *The State (Modern Homes (Ire.) Ltd.)* v. *Dublin Corporation* [1953] I.R. 202 (refusal of applicant's demand inferred where respondents made positive decision to continue with existing law").

[51] *R.* v. *Hanley Revising Barrister* [1912] 3 K.B. 518.

being administrative (as opposed to judicial)[52] in character
mandamus was granted in place of certiorari. This practice was
known as "certiorarified mandamus," and it was developed at a
time when it was thought that certiorari would not lie in respect of
purely administrative decisions. It was implicit in the grant of
mandamus—that is, an order to the deciding official to determine
the matter according to law—that the impugned decision was a
nullity. In *The State (Keller)* v. *Galway C.C.*,[53] for example, Davitt P.
held that mandamus should issue to a medical officer who had
taken irrelevant considerations into account when rejecting an
application for a disability allowance, saying that:

> "[W]here an inferior tribunal whose duty it is to hear and
> determine certain questions according to law takes into
> consideration, and allows its determination to be affected by,
> matters which it has no right to take into account, it can be
> held to have declined jurisdiction; and may be required on
> mandamus to hear and determine the issue properly accord-
> ing to law."[54]

Despite the procedural improvements effected by the new Rules,
this form of certiorarified mandamus may still be used as a means
of review in the rare cases where mandamus is still the exclusive
remedy (*e.g.*, administrative decisions where there is no duty to act
judicially).

3. Declaration and injunction

Although it is not a purely public law remedy, the declaratory
action has come to occupy a special place in our public law, chiefly
because of the restrictions which hitherto restricted the scope of
certiorari. A declaratory judgment declares the right or legal
position of the parties to an action. Such a judgment is not of itself
coercive, although the litigant may safely assume that public
bodies will respect and obey such judgments. The declaratory
action is of comparatively modern vintage, for the common law
viewed non-coercive remedies with disfavour. As far as Ireland is
concerned, the declaratory action has its origins in the Chancery
(Ireland) Act 1867, s.155 of which stated that no action should be
open to the objection that a merely declaratory decree or order

---

[52] But this form of mandamus will not lie where the decision-making
authority is exercising judicial (or quasi-judicial) functions: see *R.
(Spain)* v. *Income Tax Commissioners* [1934] I.R. 27.
[53] [1958] I.R. 142. See also *R. (Clonmel Lunatic Asylum)* v. *Considine* [1917]
2 I.R. 1.
[54] [1958] I.R. 142 at p. 150.

was sought thereby, and that it should be possible for the court to make binding declarations of right whether any consequential relief is or could be claimed, or not.[55] The wording of section 155 is substantially reproduced in Ord. 19, r. 29 of the Rules of the Superior Court.

The power of the High Court to grant an injunction derives from section 28(8) of the Supreme Court of Judicature (Ireland) Act 1877,[56] which enabled the court to grant this remedy in all cases where it appeared just and convenient to do so. Despite the generality of the language used, this subsection did not extend the reach of the injunction to claims for which no remedy had previously existed either at law or in equity, nor were the principles governing the grant of an injunction substantially altered.

We must now consider (i) the new judicial review procedure in so far as it relates to the declaration and injunction and (ii) the scope of these remedies.

(i) *The Judicial review procedure*

A litigant seeking declaratory or injunctive relief may commence his action by plenary summons in the ordinary fashion. But if the respondent is a public body, a declaration or an injunction may now be sought through an application for judicial review. Ord. 84, r. 18(2) of the new Rules of the Superior Courts provides:

> "An application for a declaration or an injunction may be made by way of an application for judicial review, and on such an application the Court may grant the declaration or application claimed if it considers that, having regard to—
>
> (*a*) the nature of the matters in respect of which relief may be granted by way of an order of mandamus, prohibition, certiorari or quo warranto
>
> (*b*) the nature of the persons and bodies against whom relief may be granted by way of such order, and

---

[55] But note that in *Guaranty Trust Co. of N.Y.* v. *Hannay & Co.* [1915] 2 K.B. 536 at p. 568, Bankes L.J. asserted that the courts had always possessed a residual jurisdiction to grant declaratory judgments. This statement was made, however, in the context of an action to have Rules of Court permitting the granting of declarations declared *ultra vires*. Naturally the Rules would have been *ultra vires* if they did not amount to procedural improvements of a jurisdiction which already existed.

[56] As applied to the present High Court by s.8(2) of the Courts (Supplemental Provisions) Act 1961. S.28(8) of the 1877 Act only refers in terms to the granting of an interlocutory order, but this subsection encompasses the grant of a final order: *Beddow* v. *Beddow* (1878) 9 Ch.D. 89 at p. 93 *per* Jessel M.R.

(c) all the circumstances of the case,

it would be just and convenient for the declaration or injunction to be granted on an application for judicial review."

It is to be noted that unlike Ord. 84, r. 18(1) (which, of course, relates to the purely public law remedies of certiorari, prohibition and mandamus), Ord. 84, r. 18(2) is discretionary in nature. The litigant is *apparently* given a choice: he may apply for a declaration or an injunction by way of an application for judicial review or he may commence the proceedings by way of plenary summons. But the litigant's choice is not an unrestricted one: it would seem that he can apply for a declaration or an injunction by way of an application for judicial review *only* if the proceedings relate to the exercise of public law powers by a public body, *i.e.* the matter must be one coming within the traditional scope of the purely public law remedies of certiorari, prohibition and mandamus. Two examples should illustrate this point:

(1) A local authority fails to honour its contractual obligation to purchase certain products from X Company Ltd. X Company Ltd. seeks a declaration that the local authority are in breach of contract. X Company Ltd. *cannot* proceed by way of an application for judicial review, for although the respondent is a public body, the matter does not relate to the exercise of the authority's public law functions, but is governed by ordinary principles of contract. X Company Ltd. must commence declaratory proceedings by way of plenary summons. If the company proceeds by way of an application for judicial review, the court may, instead of refusing the application, order the proceedings to continue as if they had been begun by plenary summons.[57]

(2) A local authority refuses to grant planning permission to Y for a proposed development. Y seeks a declaration that this refusal is invalid. Since Y's claim relates to the exercise of public law powers by a public body, the declaratory proceedings must proceed by way of an application for judicial review. If Y commences the proceedings by way of plenary summons, the action will probably be struck out as an abuse of process. The court does not have power to "convert" an action begun by plenary summons into an application for judicial review.

---

[57] Ord. 84, r. 26(5). There is, however, no converse power allowing proceedings begun by plenary summons to proceed as if on an application for judicial review.

Example 2 raises another issue which has given rise to controversy in England. Is a litigant in a public law case obliged to proceed by way of an application for judicial review, or is it open to him to commence proceedings for a declaration and injunction by way of plenary summons? In *O'Reilly* v. *Mackman*[58] certain prisoners commenced declaratory proceedings by plenary summons against a prison board of visitors. They sought declarations to the effect that the board of visitors had acted contrary to natural justice and that disciplinary punishments imposed by them were invalid. As this complaint was likely to raise many disputed issues of fact, it was decided to proceed by way of plenary action rather than by way of an application for judicial review. The House of Lords held that the actions should be struck out as an abuse of process.

Lord Diplock pointed out that whereas formerly the courts had, by concession, encouraged the use of the declaration and injunction in public law cases in order to permit litigants to avoid the procedural defects which then attached to the purely public law remedies of certiorari, prohibition and mandamus, this concession should now be withdrawn in view of the removal of those procedural defects by the new Rules of Court. More importantly, the new judicial review procedures contained certain safeguards designed to protect public bodies from vexatious and unmeritorious claims. An applicant for judicial review must obtain leave from the High Court, and conditions may be attached to the grant of leave. There is a short time limit, and the applicant must, from the outset, put his case on affidavit, and cannot rely on merely unsworn allegations in the pleadings. Furthermore, the judicial review procedure provides for a speedy and expeditious determination of the validity of administrative action, in contrast to the delays that may be caused in the case of an action commenced by plenary summons. As Lord Diplock explained:

> "So to delay the judge's decision [as to whether to grant leave] would defeat the public policy that underlies the grant of those protections: *viz.* the need, in the interest of good administration and of third parties who may be indirectly affected by the decision, for speedy certainty as to whether it has the effect of a decision which is valid in public law. An action for a declaration and an injunction need not be commenced until the very end of the limitation period . . . and the plaintiffs are not required to support their allegations by evidence on oath until the actual trial. The period of uncertainty as to the validity of a decision that has been

[58] [1983] 2 A.C. 237. See Wade, "Procedure and Prerogative in Public Law" (1985) 101 L.Q.R. 180.

challenged or allegations that may eventually turn out to be
baseless and unsupported by evidence on oath, may thus be
strung out for a very lengthy period ... Unless such an action
can be struck out summarily at the outset as an abuse of
process of the court the whole purpose of the public policy to
which the change [in the Rules] was directed would be
defeated."[59]

It is not easy to predict whether Lord Diplock's view will be
accepted in Ireland. On the one hand, given the similarities
between the two systems of judicial review, there is much to be said
in favour of the reasoning in *O'Reilly*, especially in view of the fact
that any other result would mean that the safeguards inserted in
the new Rules which are designed to protect the interests of public
authorities could be circumvented by the use of an alternative
procedure. On the other hand, there are many British commenta-
tors who are unhappy with the *O'Reilly* v. *Mackman*, and Professor
Wade has observed that that the object of the new reforms was
"not to give new privileges to public authorities but to improve the
legal remedies available to the citizen."[60] Moreover, it does not
appear that, under the pre-1986 Rules, public authorities were
unduly troubled by the prospect of having to defend actions for
declarations or injunctions commenced by plenary summons, and,
indeed, there are still cases in England where a public law decision
can be challenged otherwise than by way of judicial review.[61] Most
striking of all, operating the *O'Reilly* gloss on the new system
would entail drawing a demarcation line between public and
private law and thus to admit by the back door the curse of
characterisation which had just been ceremoniously expelled at
the front door.

One way to avoid this dilemma would have been to establish a
single comprehensive form of action for all cases whether
involving public or private law. The speed and other advantages
attaching to the present system of judicial review could have been
preserved if the Rules of Court had provided for a special
summary procedure (with affidavit evidence and expedited hearings) in cases involving public authorities. Where the court was of

[59] [1983] 2 A.C. 237 at p. 284.
[60] Wade, "Procedure and Prerogative in Public Law" (1985) 101 L.Q.R.
180 at p. 189.
[61] The House of Lords has made it clear that there are exceptions to this
general principle, particularly where the invalidity of a decision arises
by way of defence, or as a collateral issue in a claim for the infringement
of a right of the plaintiff arising under private law: see *Davy* v. *Spelthorne
B.C.* [1984] A.C. 264; *Wandsworth L.B.C.* v. *Winder* [1985] A.C. 461 and
pp. 364–365.

opinion that actions against public authorities commenced by plenary summons should have been disposed of summarily, it could order that the case be heard as if commenced by the special summary procedure instead of striking out the action as an abuse of process. Conversely, there could have been an exceptional provision allowing the unusual cases raising complicated issues of fact to be put back for plenary hearing.[62]

(iii) *The scope of declaration and injunction*

While the power of the courts to grant declaratory relief has been stated "to be almost unlimited," it has always been understood to be confined to the context of defining the "rights of the two parties" to the action.[63] Thus, the court will not make declarations in respect of non-justiciable matters or in respect of matters of "morality and the like which fall short of being rights in law."[64] It is well settled that the court may refuse relief not only on grounds such as delay, acquiescence and the like,[65] but also on the grounds that the action is speculative, premature and raises hypothetical questions.[66] *Blythe* v. *Att.-Gen. (No. 2)*[67] is a good example of where a claim was dismissed as premature. The plaintiffs had formed an organisation known as "The League of Youth," and, fearing a possible executive ban, immediately commenced proceedings seeking a declaration that the organisation was a lawful one. Johnston J. dismissed the action, as the right of the plaintiffs to form the association had not been impugned, and no proceedings had been taken or threatened against them.

Two possible technical restrictions on the scope of the declaration have been removed by the new Rules of Court. Given that a declaration is, technically speaking, a final order, the courts were not prepared to make an interlocutory declaration.[68] Ord. 84, r. 25(1) now empowers the court to grant interlocutory relief on an application for judicial review. It was also formerly the case that the courts would not grant a declaration to quash for error of law

---

[62] See Wade, "Procedure and Prerogative in Public Law" (1985) 101 L.Q.R. 180 at pp. 189–190.

[63] *Hanson* v. *Radcliffe U.D.C.* [1922] 2 Ch. 490 at p. 507, *per* Lord Sterndale M.R.

[64] *Malone* v. *Commissioner of Police (No. 2)* [1979] Ch. 344 at p. 352, *per* Megarry V.C.

[65] See pp. 349–351.

[66] *Halligan* v. *Davis* [1930] I.R. 237; *Re Bernato* [1949] Ch. 258.

[67] [1936] I.R. 549. See also *Dyson* v. *Att-Gen.* [1910] 1 K.B. 410.

[68] *Hill* v. *C. A. Parsons Ltd.* [1972] Ch. 305 at p. 324, *per* Stamp L.J.

on the face of the record.[69] This restriction on the scope of the declaration is no longer of any practical significance, for Ord. 84, r. 19 enables the High Court upon an application for judicial review to grant an order of certiorari for this purpose *in lieu* of a declaration, notwithstanding that such relief has not been specifically claimed.

While the injunction is a remedy of wide scope, it will only be granted in support of an independent cause of action cognisable at law or equity.[70]

An injunction may be prohibitory[71] (*i.e.* restraining the commission of a wrongful act) or mandatory[72] (*i.e.* commanding the performance of a legal duty) in nature. The use of the injunction as a public law remedy has been somewhat curtailed by the alternative remedies of prohibition and mandamus. Such procedural advantages as the injunction enjoyed over the purely public law remedies have now been removed by the new Rules of Court.[73]

4. The discretionary nature of the remedies

The public law remedies, the declaration and injunction are all discretionary remedies. It is clear that this discretion is to be exercised according to settled principles, and the court will act on the same principles, regardless of the form of the proceedings.[74] The court is not entitled to deny relief to the Attorney-General on

---

[69] *Punton* v. *Ministry of Pensions (No. 2)* [1964] 1 W.L.R. 226. But the Supreme Court has already granted one such declaration: see *King* v. *Att.-Gen.* [1981] I.R. 233.

[70] *The Siskina* [1979] A.C. 210; *Caudron* v. *Air Zaire* [1986] I.L.R.M. 10. An injunction cannot be granted where the case does not raise justiciable issues: see, *e.g. Finn* v. *Att.-Gen.* [1983] I.R. 154.

[71] A special form of prohibitory injunction, known as a *quia timet* injunction, may also be granted in unusual cases to restrain anticipated future wrongful acts: see *Att.-Gen. (Boswell)* v. *Rathmines and Pembroke Joint Hospital Board* [1904] 1 I.R. 161; *McGrane* v. *Louth C.C.*, High Court, December 9, 1983.

[72] For a recent example, see *Campus Oil Ltd.* v. *Minister for Industry and Commerce (No. 2)* [1983] I.R. 88.

[73] These procedural advantages included: the availability of interim relief, discovery and interrogatories (not all of which were available upon an application for certiorari, prohibition or mandamus); and the fact that an application for declaratory and injunctive relief, together with a claim for damages, could be combined in the one set of proceedings.

[74] See the comments of Henchy J. in *The State (Nicolaou)* v. *An Bord Uchtala* [1966] I.R. 567 at p. 618 and *M.* v. *An Bord Uchtala* [1977] I.R. 287 at p. 297.

discretionary grounds.[75] Although the grounds on which relief may be denied are not closed, we must now consider the discretionary bars to relief which are most frequently encountered.

Lack of good faith. All applications for judicial review require the utmost good faith and full disclosure of all material facts on the part of the applicant.[76] Relief may be withheld where the applicant has been guilty of gross exaggeration in his affidavits or where relevant evidence has been suppressed.[77] The court will also have regard to the general conduct of the applicant[78] and the reasons for the application.[79]

Delay. Ord. 84, r. 21(1) provides that all applications for judicial review "shall be made promptly" and in any event within three months from the date when the grounds for the application first arose, or six months when the relief sought is certiorari. The court has a discretion to extend these time limits where "there is a good reason" for doing so. The decision of the Superior Court Rules Committee to impose such relatively short time limits was somewhat surprising given that the Law Reform Commission had recommended that the issue of delay should be left entirely to the discretion of the court.

Prior to the adoption of the new Rules, the general attitude of the courts had been to ask whether the delay had been such as to affect prejudicially the rights of third parties. Periods of as short as four months have been held to disentitle the applicant to relief "to

---

[75] *The State (Kerry C.C.)* v. *Minister for Local Government* [1933] I.R. 517 at p. 546 *per* Murnaghan J. It appears that the new Rules of Court do not bind the State. If such is the case, it means that the Attorney-General is not bound to seek leave to apply for judicial review nor is he bound by the time limits contained in Ord. 84, r. 21(1). *Cf. Re an Application for Certiorari* [1965] N.I. 67. See further at pp. 397–401.

[76] *Cork Corporation* v. *O'Connell* [1982] I.L.R.M. 505.

[77] *R.* v. *Kensington I.T.C.* [1917] 1 K.B. 486; *R. (Bryson)* v. *Lisnaskea Guardians* [1918] 2 I.R. 258; *The State (Vozza)* v. *O'Floinn* [1957] I.R. 227; *The State (Nicolaou)* v. *An Bord Uchtala* [1966] I.R. 567 at p. 610 (Henchy J.) and *Cork Corporation* v. *O'Connell* [1982] I.L.R.M. 505 at p. 508 *per* Griffin J.

[78] *Ex p. Fry* [1954] 1 W.L.R. 730; *Fulbrook* v. *Berkshire Magistrates Court* (1970) 69 L.G.R. 75.

[79] *The State (Abenglen Properties Ltd.)* v. *Dublin Corporation* [1984] I.R. 384 (attempt to obtain benefit "not contemplated" by the planning code); *The State (Conlon Construction Ltd.)* v. *Cork C.C.*, High Court, July 31, 1975; *R. (Burns)* v. *Tyrone JJ.* [1961] N.I. 167 (impugned order procured by perjury).

which he was otherwise entitled *ex debito justitiae*,"[80] yet in *M.* v. *An Bord Uchtala*[81] the Supreme Court declared invalid an adoption order for want of jurisdiction, despite a delay of over three years and the fact that the child had spent all of its sentient life with its adoptive parents.

Delay of itself could not be a ground for refusing relief where the applicant had suffered a "public wrong" at the hands of the State or its agents. This emerged from *The State (Furey)* v. *Minister for Defence*[82] where the Supreme Court quashed the applicant's dismissal from the Defence Forces. Although the proceedings had not been commenced more than four years after the dismissal, the court found that the applicant was unaware of his right to challenge the validity of the dismissal as being contrary to the rules of natural justice.[83] McCarthy J. commented that he could see no reason:

> "[W]hy delay, however long, should, of itself, disentitle to certiorari any applicant for that remedy who can demonstrate that a public wrong has been done to him—that, for instance, a conviction has been obtained without jurisdiction, or that, otherwise, the State has wronged him and that wrong continues to mark or mar his life."[84]

As far as criminal cases are concerned, the general principle appears to be that the applicant cannot be precluded by his delay from challenging a conviction made in excess of jurisdiction or which is bad on its face,[85] but this principle applies to convictions only and not to orders of return for trial.[86] However, it has been

---

[80] *The State (Cussen)* v. *Brennan* [1981] I.R. 181; *R. (Rainey)* v. *Belfast Recorder* (1937) 71 I.L.T.R. 272. See Hogan, "Discretion and Judicial Review of Administrative Action" (1980) 15 Ir.Jur.(n.s.) 118.

[81] [1977] I.R. 287. See also *The State (D.P.P.)* v. *O'hUuadaigh*, High Court, January 30, 1984; *The State (Murphy)* v. *Kielt* [1984] I.R. 458 (delay on the part of applicant for certiorari not such as to prejudice respondent or other third party); *The State (Gleeson)* v. *Martin* [1985] I.L.R.M. 578.

[82] Supreme Court, March 2, 1984. See Hogan "Natural and Constitutional Justice: Adieu to Laissez-Faire" (1984) 19 Ir.Jur.(n.s.) 309.

[83] Furey was actually involved in the same incident as applicant in *The State (Gleeson)* v. *Minister for Defence* [1976] I.R. 286.

[84] At p. 11 of the judgment. McCarthy J. distinguished *The State (Cussen)* v. *Brennan* [1981] I.R. 181 on the basis that in *Furey* (unlike Cussen) the granting of certiorari would not prejudice third party rights.

[85] *The State (Kelly)* v. *District Justice for Bandon* [1947] I.R. 258; *The State (Furey)* v. *Minister for Defence*, Supreme Court, March 2, 1984. But *cf.* the comments of Henchy J. to the contrary in *The State (Abenglen Properties Ltd.)* v. *Dublin Corporation* [1984] I.R. 384.

[86] *The State (Walsh)* v. *Maguire* [1979] I.R. 372; *The State (Coveney)* v. *Special Criminal Court* [1982] I.L.R.M. 284.

doubted whether even gross laches would prevent an order of prohibition issuing to restrain an inferior court from proceeding with a criminal trial where it had no jurisdiction.[87] Thus, presumably the fact that the applicant had suffered a "public wrong"—*e.g.* invalid dismissal from State employment, or conviction imposed without jurisdiction—would of itself be a "good reason" for the High Court to extend the time limits contained in Ord. 84, r. 21(1).

5. Acquiescence and waiver

The courts will not allow the creation of a wholly new jurisdiction through acquiescence or waiver.[88] Nevertheless, acquiescence and waiver may disentitle the applicant to relief. In *R. (Kildare C.C.)* v. *Commissioner of Valuation*[89] the applicant appealed to the county court against a valuation revision. It was only when the decision of the county court proved not to be as favourable as expected that the applicant claimed that the county court had no jurisdiction in the matter. The Court of Appeal ruled that, even assuming that the county court had acted without jurisdiction, relief should be refused on discretionary grounds. Holmes L.J. said that he found it difficult to conceive of a "stronger case of estoppel by conduct." Similarly in *The State (Byrne)* v. *Frawley*[90] the applicant's failure to raise certain alleged irregularities in his trial when appealing to the Court of Criminal Appeal was found to be prima facie evidence of acquiescence. Participation (or continued participation) in proceedings may constitute acquiescence where the party seeking to challenge the decision was aware of the full facts and failed to take objection to the composition or procedure of the tribunal.[91] The right to object to an irregularity of procedure or breach of natural justice may also be lost by waiver.[92]

---

[87] *The State (Coveney)* v. *Special Criminal Court* [1982] I.L.R.M. 284 at p. 289 *per* Finlay P.

[88] *Corrigan* v. *Irish Land Commission* [1977] I.R. 317 at p. 325 *per* Henchy J.; *The State (Byrne)* v. *Frawley* [1978] I.R. 326 at p. 342 *per* O'Higgins C.J. See pp. 216–221.

[89] [1901] 2 I.R. 215. See also *R. (Mathews)* v. *Petticrew* (1886) 18 L.R.Ir. 342; *The State (McKay)* v. *Cork Circuit Judge* [1937] I.R. 650 and *R. (Doris)* v. *Ministry for Health* [1954] N.I. 79.

[90] [1978] I.R. 326.

[91] *The State (Cronin)* v. *Circuit Judge for Western Circuit* [1937] I.R. 44; *The State (Redmond)* v. *Wexford Corporation* [1946] I.R. 409. But the principle does not apply where the applicant is unaware of the full facts, or has been taken by surprise *R. (Harrington)* v. *Clare JJ.* (1918) 2 I.R. 116; *The State (McDonagh)* v. *Sheerin* [1981] I.L.R.M. 149; *The State (Cole)* v. *Labour Court* (1984) 3 J.I.S.L.L. 128.

6. Where no useful purpose would be served

The court will not make an order which cannot now be implemented or which would be illegal.[93] Nor will relief be granted where this would simply cause further delay[94] or would confer no practical benefit on the applicant.[95] But the courts recognise that an applicant may have a sufficient interest in clearing his name. Thus, in *The State (Furey)* v. *Minister for Defence*[96] certiorari was granted to quash an ignominious dismissal from the Defence Forces. Even though the applicant's probationary period had long since expired, McCarthy J., rejecting the argument that a quashing order would serve no useful purpose, pointed out that an order of certiorari would allow him to vindicate his reputation. In some cases the court will withhold relief in discretion in order to give the administrative body concerned time to comply with its judgment. In *The State (Richardson)* v. *Governor of Mountjoy Prison*[97] Barrington J. concluded that the hygiene facilities provided in the womens' prison in Mountjoy were so inadequate that the State had failed in its constitutional duty to vindicate the applicant prisoner's constitutional right to bodily integrity. Nevertheless, the judge granted a short adjournment to allow the recommendations for the improvement of facilities to be implemented.

7. General attitudes to the exercise of discretion

Up to quite recently it was considered to be settled law that a person aggrieved by *ultra vires* administrative action had a prima

---

[92] *Whelan* v. *R.* [1921] 2 I.R. 310; *The State (Redmond)* v. *Wexford Corporation* [1946] I.R. 409; *Corrigan* v. *Irish Land Commission* [1977] I.R. 317; *The State (Grahame)* v. *Racing Board*, High Court, November 22, 1983.

[93] *The State (Modern Homes (Ire.) Ltd.)* v. *Dublin Corporation* [1953] I.R. 202; *The State (Foxrock Development Co. Ltd.)* v. *Dublin C.C.*, High Court, February 5, 1980; *The State (Pine Valley Developments Ltd.)* v. *Dublin C.C.* [1984] I.R. 417.

[94] *The State (Walsh)* v. *Maguire* [1979] I.R. 372; *Fulbrook* v. *Berkshire Magistrates Court* (1970) 69 L.G.R. 75.

[95] *The State (Doyle)* v. *Carr* [1970] I.R. 87; *R. (Campbell College)* v. *Department of Education* [1982] N.I. 123; *The State (Abenglen Properties Ltd.)* v. *Dublin Corporation* [1984] I.R. 384.

[96] Supreme Court, March 2, 1984. See also *The State (Shannon Atlantic Fisheries Ltd.)* v. *McPolin* [1976] I.R. 93.

[97] [1980] I.L.R.M. 82. See also *R.* v. *Greater London Council, ex p. Blackburn* [1976] 1 W.L.R. 550.

facie entitlement to relief.[98] It was true that the applicant's right to relief might be lost on account of his delay, bad conduct, etc. But generally speaking, the applicant could only be denied relief where this would prejudice the rights or interests of the administrative body concerned or third parties, *i.e.* relief would issue *ex debito justitiae*.[99]

A slightly different test appears to have been formulated by a majority of the Supreme Court in *The State (Abenglen Properties Ltd.)* v. *Dublin Corporation*.[1] This case presented a challenge to the validity of certain conditions attached to the grant of planning permission. Relief was refused on the grounds that the applicants had failed to exhaust alternative remedies and that an order of certiorari would serve no useful purpose in the circumstances of the case. But Henchy J. for the majority appeared to go further when he stated that the grant of certiorari in civil cases was purely discretionary. However, in *The State (Furey)* v. *Minister for Defence*,[2] a majority of the Supreme Court reverted to the more orthodox position by stating that a person aggrieved by *ultra vires* administrative action was entitled to relief *ex debito justitiae*. It was not enough to show, for example, that there had been undue delay on the part of the applicant. McCarthy J.'s judgment implies that the respondents would have to establish that it would now be unfair to them or third parties or that there were other exceptional circumstances present in the case before the court

---

[98] *R. (Bridgeman)* v. *Drury* [1894] 2 I.R. 489; *R. (Kildare C.C.)* v. *Commissioner for Valuation* [1901] 2 I.R. 215; *The State (Kerry C.C.)* v. *Minister for Local Government* [1933] I.R. 517; *The State (Doyle)* v. *Carr* [1970] I.R. 87 and *M.* v. *An Bord Uchtala* [1977] I.R. 287 (judgment of Henchy J.). A "person aggrieved" was defined as someone whose legal rights or interests were affected by the impugned order; *R.* v. *Thames Magistrates' Court, ex p. Greenbaum* (1957) 55 L.G.R. 129; *The State (Toft)* v. *Galway Corporation* [1981] I.L.R.M. 439.

[99] As happened in cases such as *The State (Cussen)* v. *Brennan* [1981] I.R. 181 (applicant's delay caused third parties to change position in the belief that he would not challenge *ultra vires* appointment; held, it would now be unfair to third parties to grant applicant the relief sought).

[1] [1984] I.R. 384. See Hogan, "Remoulding Certiorari: A Critique of *The State (Abenglen Properties Ltd.)* v. *Dublin Corporation*" (1982) 17 Ir.Jur.(n.s.) 32 and Jackson, "Certiorari, Alternative Remedies and Judicial Discretion" (1983) 5 D.U.L.J.(n.s.) 100.

[2] Supreme Court, March 2, 1984. Note that in *The State (R. F. Gallagher, Shatter & Co.)* v. *DeValera*, High Court, December 9, 1983, Costello J. stated that the test laid down by Henchy J. in *Abenglen Properties* was that while "aggrieved persons are entitled to certiorari only on a discretionary basis... if the requirements of justice and fairness justified the making of the order then it should be made."

would be justified in refusing relief. Although the difference between *Abenglen* and *Furey* is largely one of emphasis, the *Furey* decision does indicate a return to traditional principles on the part of the Supreme Court.

8. Availability of alternate remedies

The existence of an alternate remedy does not of itself debar an application for judicial review. Relief will not, however, be granted where an alternate remedy has been invoked and is pending,[3] or where an applicant has deliberately pursued an alternate remedy in the belief that this course of action was in his best interests.[4] At the end of the day, the question is one for the discretion of the court, and regard will be had to the adequacy of the alternate remedy,[5] the conduct of the applicant and to all the circumstances of the case.[6] But recent cases—most notably *The State (Abenglen Properties Ltd.)* v. *Dublin Corporation*[7]—definitely lean in favour of an "exhaustion of alternate remedies" requirement. In the view of

---

[3] *The State (Roche)* v. *Delap* [1980] I.R. 170; *The State (Wilson)* v. *Neilan*, [1985] I.R. 89. But *cf. The State (Cunningham)* v. *O'Floinn* [1960] I.R. 198. Note that Ord. 84, r. 20(5) provides that where certiorari is sought to quash an order which may be the subject of an appeal, the court may adjourn the application for leave until the "appeal is determined or the time for appealing has expired."

[4] *The State (Conlon Construction Co. Ltd.)* v. *Cork C.C.*, High Court, July 31, 1975. But the mere fact that alternative remedies have been invoked does not of itself preclude an application for judicial review when the pursuit of these alternative remedies proves to be unsuccessful: *The State (Ryan)* v. *Revenue Commissioners* [1934] I.R. 1; *The State (Vozza)* v. *O'Floinn* [1957] I.R. 227; *The State (N.C.E. Ltd.)* v. *Dublin C.C.*, High Court, December 4, 1979.

[5] *The State (Stanbridge)* v. *Mahon* [1979] I.R. 214; *The State (Glover)* v. *McCarthy* [1981] I.L.R.M. 47; *The State (Pheasantry Ltd.)* v. *Donnelly* [1982] I.L.R.M. 512; *Aprile* v. *Naas U.D.C.*, High Court, November 22, 1983; *The State (Redmond)* v. *Delap*, High Court, July 31, 1984; *The State (Abenglen Properties Ltd.)* v. *Dublin Corporation* [1984] I.R. 384; *The State (McInerney Properties Ltd.)* v. *Dublin C.C.* [1985] I.L.R.M. 513; *Creedon* v. *Dublin Corporation* [1984] I.R. 427 and *The State (Wilson)* v. *Neilan* [1985] I.R. 89.

[6] *The State (Litzouw)* v. *Johnson* [1981] I.L.R.M. 273; *The State (Abenglen Properties Ltd.)* v. *Dublin Corporation* [1984] I.R. 384.

[7] [1984] I.R. 384. For a similar approach, see *Creedon* v. *Dublin Corporation* [1984] I.R. 427; *The State (Collins)* v. *Ruane* [1984] I.R. 151 (Henchy J.) and *The State (Redmond)* v. *Delap*, High Court, July 31, 1984.

Henchy J., where the Oireachtas has provided a self-contained administrative scheme, the courts should not intervene by way of judicial review where—as in the instant case—the statutory appellate procedure was adequate to meet the complaint on which the application was grounded. While this principle has been applied in a number of similar cases, it remains to be seen whether the courts will insist on the "exhaustion of remedies" requirement in cases involving a breach of natural justice. It was formerly considered that non-exhaustion of remedies was immaterial in such cases[8], partly perhaps because of the particuarly grevious nature of such an error and partly because the statutory appellate bodies could only deal with the merits of each case, and could not rule on the issue of vires. But this latter reason holds true for all major errors of law, and the courts may eventually come down in favour of an exhaustion of remedies rule in all types of case, because it serves as a "filtering device," thus cutting down the number of applications for judicial review.[9]

9. Locus standi

The current law on *locus standi* is currently in a state of flux. The modern tendency of the Irish courts is to move away from a technical approach to *locus standi* towards a rationalisation of standing requirements based on considerations relating to the general administration of justice, and the separation of powers.[10] Further proof that the current trend is away from the technical approach to standing is supplied by recent dicta to the effect that the standing rules are merely rules of practice (which may be relaxed if there are "weighty countervailing considerations" justifying a departure from the ordinary rules), and that these requirements are the same regardless of the form of the proceedings.[11] It is as yet unclear what changes (if any) will be

[8] *Leary* v. *National Union of Vehicle Builders* [1971] Ch. 34; *Ingle* v. *O'Brien* (1975) 109 I.L.T.R. 6; *Moran* v. *Att.-Gen.* [1976] I.R. 400; *Irish Family Planning Assoc. Ltd.* v. *Ryan* [1979] I.R. 295 (judgment of Hamilton J.); *The State (Grahame)* v. *Racing Board*, High Court, November 22, 1983.

[9] For example Henchy J. indicated in *The State (Collins)* v. *Ruane* [1984] I.R. 151, that a person convicted in the District Court should normally appeal to the Circuit Court before applying for judicial review, even where (as here) the complaint was that natural justice had been breached at the first instance. See further pp. 293–296.

[10] See the judgment of Henchy J. in *Cahill* v. *Sutton* [1980] I.R. 269.

[11] *Cahill* v. *Sutton* [1980] I.R. 269 at p. 285 *per* Henchy J.; *The State (Lynch)* v. *Cooney* [1982] I.R. 337 at p. 369 *per* Walsh J.

brought about by the provisions of the new Ord. 84, r. 20(4) which states that leave to apply for judicial review shall not be granted unless the applicant "has a sufficient interest in the matter to which the application relates." The effect of a similar change in the English Rules of Court has been stated to permit an *actio populares* (or "citizen's action") in suitable cases.[12] As we shall see presently, it must be doubtful whether the change in the Irish rules will have a similar effect.

10. The traditional standing rules

At common law, the standing rules varied depending on the character of the remedies. The public law remedies of certiorari and prohibition always contained an element of the *actio populares*, as the purpose of these remedies was not merely to avoid injustice *inter partes*, but also to maintain order in the legal system.[13] It was thus open to anyone—even a stranger to the proceedings—to apply for certiorari or prohibition. In practice, however, relief was hardly ever given to anyone other than a "person aggrieved."[14]

A stricter approach was taken in the case of the declaration and the injunction, and here standing rules reflected the fact that these remedies were derived from private law. An applicant was required to show the existence of a legal right or other cognisable interest which was affected or threatened.[15] A recent example of this restrictive approach is provided by *Irish Permanent Building*

---

[12] Wade, *Administrative Law* (Oxford, 1982) at p. 540.

[13] Yardley, "Certiorari and the Problem of *Locus Standi*" (1955) 71 L.Q.R. 388; "Prohibition and Mandamus and the Problem of *Locus Standi*" (1957) 73 L.Q.R. 534. The *locus standi* requirements for mandamus have always been somewhat stricter than in the case of the other public law remedies: *R.* v. *Lewisham Guardians* [1897] 1 Q.B. 498 (existence of specific legal right); *R. (I.U.D.W.C.)* v. *Rathmines U.D.C.* [1928] I.R. 260 ("legal right" (Hanna J.), "specific interest in performance of duty" (O'Byrne J.)). But for a less restrictive approach, see *The State (Modern Homes (Ire.) Ltd.)* v. *Dublin Corporation* [1953] I.R. 202; *The State (A.C.C. Ltd.)* v. *Navan U.D.C.*, High Court, February 22, 1980.

[14] In cases such as *The State (Kerry C.C.)* v. *Minister for Local Government* [1933] I.R. 517; *The State (Doyle)* v. *Carr* [1970] I.R. 87 and *The State (Toft)* v. *Galway Corporation* [1981] I.L.R.M. 439, certiorari was refused to applicants who were not "persons aggrieved."

[15] *Weir* v. *Fermanagh C.C.* [1913] 1 I.R. 193; *Gregory* v. *Camden L.B.C.* [1966] 1 W.L.R. 899; *Gouriet* v. *U.P.O.W.* [1978] A.C. 435.

Society Ltd. v. *Caldwell (No. 1),*[16] where the plaintiffs had challenged the decision of the Registrar of Building Societies to register a new building society. The defendants brought a motion seeking to have the plaintiffs' claim struck out on the grounds that they had not alleged that they suffered or would suffer damage as a result of this allegedly invalid decision. Although Keane J. refused to strike out the claim on the grounds that the matter deserved "full and unhurried consideration," he did hint strongly that the infringement, or threatened infringement, of some legal right or interest was a prerequisite in declaratory proceedings of this nature.[17]

11. The law in transition

As already indicated, the Supreme Court in two major decisions, *Cahill* v. *Sutton*[18] and *The State (Lynch)* v. *Cooney*[19] has shown a willingness to move away from a technical approach to the issue of *locus standi.* In *Cahill's* case, Henchy J. adverted to the practical considerations which justified the adoption of standing rules. It would not be conducive to the general administration of justice to allow one litigant to present and argue "what is essentially another person's case." Furthermore, without concrete personal circumstances pointing to a wrong suffered or threatened, a case tended to lack "the force and urgency of reality." There was also the danger that unrestricted access to the courts might lead to a possible abuse of the power of judicial review. Bearing these considerations in mind, Henchy J. stated that the primary rule in constitutional proceedings was that the litigant must show:

> "[T]hat the impact of the impugned law on his personal situation discloses an injury or prejudice which he has either suffered or is in imminent danger of suffering."[20]

[16] High Court, December 21, 1979. But *cf. Martin* v. *Dublin Corporation,* High Court, November 14, 1977.

[17] He stated that it was "at least arguable" that the "limitations recognised by the common law on the right of a private citizen to assert a right public in its nature without the intervention of the Attorney-General were not affected by the enactment of the Constitution." The plaintiffs subsequently amended their pleadings to include a claim that they had suffered loss and damage: see *Irish Permanent Building Society* v. *Caldwell (No. 2)* [1981] I.L.R.M. 242.

[18] [1980] I.R. 269.

[19] [1982] I.R. 337. See Gearty, "Judicial Review of Ministerial Opinion" (1982) 4 D.U.L.J.(n.s.) 95.

[20] [1980] I.R. at p. 284.

This rule, however, was but a rule of practice which might be relaxed when the justice of the case so required.[21]

The question of *locus standi* arose in *The State (Lynch)* v. *Cooney* in the context of a ministerial ban made under the provisions of section 31 of the Broadcasting (Authority) Act 1960. The ministerial order purported to prevent Radio Telefis Eireann from broadcasting a party political broadcast on behalf of an organisation known as "Sinn Fein." The Supreme Court were unanimously of the view that the organisation's representatives had sufficient interest to challenge the validity of the ban in certiorari proceedings. As Walsh J. put it, irrespective of whether the applicants had a "right" or a mere "privilege," they had suffered a loss and had been affected in a material way.

The decisions in *Cahill* and *Lynch* may be said to stand for five general propositions:

(i) The rules of standing are merely rules of practice, which may be relaxed if there are "sufficient countervailing considerations" to justify this.[22]

(ii) The standing requirements should be the same irrespective of the form of the proceedings.[23]

(iii) The standing requirements should not be altered by reason of the fact that the application for judicial review involves a challenge to the validity of a law.[24]

(iv) An aggrieved party can, generally speaking, only present such arguments as are relevant to his own personal circumstances, *i.e.* he cannot plead a *jus tertii*.[25]

(v) The issue of standing is distinct from that of the relative merits or strength of an applicant's case.[26]

Because the Supreme Court did not make clear in either *Cahill* or *Lynch* the extent to which it was discarding the technical common law standing rules, the above propositions must be

---

[21] For example, where "those prejudicially affected by the impugned statute were not in a position to assert adequately, or in time, their constitutional rights."

[22] *Cahill* v. *Sutton* [1980] I.R. 269.

[23] *The State (Lynch)* v. *Cooney* [1982] I.R. 337 at p. 369 *per* Walsh J. See also *Irish Permanent Building Society* v. *Caldwell (No. 2)* [1981] I.L.R.M. 242.

[24] *The State (Lynch)* v. *Cooney* [1982] I.R. 337, 370 *per* Walsh J. See also *Cooke* v. *Walsh* [1984] I.R. 710, 729 *per* O'Higgins C.J.

[25] *Norris* v. *Att.-Gen.* [1984] I.R. 36; *Madigan* v. *Att.-Gen.*, [1986] I.L.R.M. 136. For a generous interpretation of what constitutes "imminent danger" to individual rights in the context of a constitutional challenge, see *Curtis* v. *Att.-Gen.* [1986] I.L.R.M. 358.

[26] *Cahill* v. *Sutton* [1980] I.R. 269; *The State (Lynch)* v. *Cooney* [1982] I.R. 337; *Norris* v. *Att.-Gen.* [1984] I.R. 36.

asserted somewhat tentatively given the current uncertainty. For example, if an applicant is not to be allowed to plead a *jus tertii*, this will supplant the common law rule that the courts had a discretion to grant certiorari to a stranger to the proceedings.[27] But it is not at all clear that the no *jus tertii* rule will be strictly enforced, at least where an applicant is not relying on constitutional grounds to challenge the validity of an administrative decision. In *E.S.B.* v. *Gormley*[28] the defendant was allowed to challenge the validity of a planning permission on the grounds that the advertisement indicating an intention to apply for permission (and which is required by section 26(1) of the Local Government (Planning and Development) Act 1963) was defective. It had been argued that as the defendant had acquired the lands *after* the planning permission was granted, she was not prejudiced or affected by this irregularity. Given these facts, the *Cahill* v. *Sutton* principles clearly rule out any arguments based on this ground of invalidity. Finlay C.J. thought otherwise:

> "[A] challenge to the validity of a planning permission granted by a planning authority which is based on non-compliance with the permission regulations does not depend upon the person making such challenge being able to demonstrate that the non-compliance directly affected him or her."[29]

In other words, a person prejudiced by an administrative decision is entitled to advance any argument—irrespective of whether such an argument bears on their personal circumstances or otherwise —to challenge its validity. Given that there was no suggestion that there were special reasons justifying a relaxation of the standing rules, the *ratio* of *Gormley* would appear to be directly at variance with the earlier reasoning in *Cahill* v. *Sutton*. Such is the unsettled state of the present law that an authoritative decision is necessary in order to resolve these difficult issues.

The possible impact of Ord. 84, r. 20(4)

As we have seen, Ord. 84, r. 20(4) provides that leave to apply for judicial review shall not be granted unless the court is satisfied that the applicant "has a sufficient interest in the matter to which the application relates." This rule would appear to lay down a uniform test for all applications for judicial review (including cases presenting constitutional challenges) irrespective of the form of the proceedings (*i.e.* the *locus standi* requirements would not

---

[27] See p. 356.
[28] [1985] I.R. 129.
[29] *Ibid.* at pp. 156–157.

change depending on the choice of remedy). To that extent, Ord. 84, r. 20(4) would appear to be declaratory of the present law.

A similar change in the English Rules of Court in 1977 was seized upon by the House of Lords in *I.R.C.* v. *National Association of Self-Employed and Small Businesses Ltd.*[30] to justify the abandoning of the technical rules as to standing in favour of a uniform test for *locus standi*. But the House of Lords also rejected the argument that standing should be considered independently of the merits of the case. That case concerned an application by the Federation for judicial review of the respondents' decision to grant an amnesty to a group of printing workers who for many years had defrauded the Inland Revenue and evaded income tax. The House of Lords ruled that it had not been shown that the Inland Revenue had acted *ultra vires* in granting such an amnesty, and, accordingly, it could not be said that the Federation had a "sufficient interest" in the application. If, however, there were grounds for thinking that the Revenue had acted improperly, then the Federation would have had standing to complain. This case appears to merge the hitherto distinct concepts of standing and merits. The corollary of the decision is that if an applicant can show that an administrative body is acting improperly, then he will be deemed to have "sufficient interest" to maintain the application, however remote his personal interest. This is, in effect, to permit an *actio popularis* in a suitable case.[31]

It would be surprising if the Irish courts were to take a similar view of Ord. 84, r. 20(4). For one thing, the Irish courts have always maintained that standing and merits are distinct concepts, and issues of standing have generally been regarded as preliminary issues to be decided in advance of the merits of the case.[32] Secondly, in this jurisdiction, standing rules have been seen as safeguarding the proper administration of justice, and as a feature of the separation of powers. Absent "weighty countervailing circumstances," it would seem to be inconsistent with the principles enunciated by Henchy J. in *Cahill* v. *Sutton* to permit a person with no direct interest to challenge the validity of an

[30] [1982] A.C. 617.
[31] "It would . . . be a grave lacuna in our system of public law if a pressure group, like the federation, or even a single public-spirited taxpayer were prevented by outdated technical rules of *locus standi* from bringing the matter to the attention of the court to vindicate the rule of law and getting the unlawful conduct stopped": [1982] A.C. 617 at p. 644 *per* Lord Diplock.
[32] See, *e.g.* the separate treatment of the issue of standing in cases such as *Cahill* v. *Sutton* [1980] I.R. 269; *The State (Lynch)* v. *Cooney* [1982] I.R. 337 and *Norris* v. *Att.-Gen.* [1984] I.R. 36.

administrative decision, simply because he has a good case on the merits. Irrespective of the strength of his case, a case brought by a litigant with no direct interest would tend to lack, in Henchy J.'s words, "the force and urgency of reality." It would also permit one litigant to present and argue "what is essentially another person's case." In sum, as *Cahill* v. *Sutton* amounts to a judicial recognition that unrestricted standing is not conducive to the proper administration of justice, one must doubt whether the Irish courts will permit the disinterested citizen to have access to the courts merely because he has a good case on the merits.

12. Relator actions

The Attorney-General may sue *ex officio* to enforce the law, and no special injury need be shown in such proceedings.[33] The Attorney-General may also sue at the relation (*i.e.* at the instance) of some member of the public in order to stop a breach of the law. The use of the relator action enables a private individual to sue where he might otherwise not have the necessary *locus standi*. In effect, the relator action is a form of *actio popularis*, which is subject to the control of the Attorney-General. However, the Attorney-General is at all times the plaintiff in a relator action:

> "It has been settled beyond the possibility of question that the Attorney-General alone is plaintiff. It is true that he generally permits the relator to select a solicitor to conduct the case; but such person is not the solicitor of the relator, but of the Attorney-General, who remains *dominus litis* throughout the proceedings."[34]

Nevertheless, where an undertaking as to damages has been given by the relator, the relator alone will be liable on foot of that undertaking.[35] The grant of the Attorney-General's consent (or "*fiat*") to the relator action simply means that the relator has been conferred with the necessary standing in order to permit him to litigate an arguable case, and does not necessarily imply approval of the proceedings.

In the United Kingdom it has been held that the courts cannot compel the Attorney-General to give his consent to a relator

---

[33] *Att.-Gen. (O'Duffy)* v. *Appleton* [1907] 1 I.R. 252; *Att.-Gen.* v. *Paperlink Ltd.* [1984] I.L.R.M. 373.

[34] *Att.-Gen. (Humphreys)* v. *Governors of Erasmus Smith's Schools* [1910] 1 I.R. 325 at p. 331 *per* Cherry L.J. (as Attorney-General alone is plaintiff, relator (who was not a barrister) not entitled to appear personally to argue case).

[35] *Att.-Gen. (Martin)* v. *Dublin Corporation* [1983] I.L.R.M. 254.

action: *Gouriet* v. *Union of Post Office Workers.*[36] In *Gouriet*, the
Attorney-General had refused to lend his name to proceedings
seeking an injunction restraining a breach of the criminal law. The
House of Lords held that there was no power to review the
decision of the Attorney-General in this matter, and the following
statement of Lord Halsbury L.C. in *London County Council* v.
Attorney-General was quoted with approval:

"[T]he initiation of litigation, and the determination of
whether it is a proper matter for the Attorney-General to
proceed in, is entirely a matter beyond the jurisdiction of this
or any other court. It is a question which the law of this
country has made to reside exclusively in the Attorney-
General."[37]

Professor Casey has argued that it is open to the Irish courts to
hold that the Attorney-General's consent is no more unfettered
than that of a minister, and that if the Attorney-General's consent
is unreviewable, this will be "a situation unique in Irish law." He
suggests that the Attorney-General:

"[M]ay be compelled by mandamus to grant his consent in
any case where he is found to have withheld it unreasonably.
No doubt any such jurisdiction would be exercised sparingly,
with the courts conceding the Attorney a large margin of
appreciation, but the assertion of such a jurisdiction might be
salutary."[38]

At the same time it must be noted that the above was written in
1980, before a number of more recent decisions which demonstrate that it is not every exercise of administrative discretion
which is subject to review by the courts.[39] As things stand, it is not
possible to predict with confidence what attitude Irish courts will
take to the question of the reviewability (or otherwise) of the
Attorney-General's decision: this is a matter which must await
judicial resolution).

[36] [1978] A.C. 435.
[37] [1902] A.C. 165 at p. 169.
[38] *The Office of the Attorney General in Ireland* (Dublin, 1980) at p. 156.
Professor Casey rests his argument on cases such as *East Donegal Co-
Operatives Ltd.* v. *Att.-Gen.* [1970] I.R. 317 which stress that all exercises
of administrative discretion should, in principle, be open to review.
[39] *Savage & McOwen* v. *D.P.P.* [1982] I.L.R.M. 385; *Judge* v. *D.P.P.* [1984]
I.L.R.M. 224.

12 Damages

1. Liability of the State and public authorities

Prior to the introduction of the new Rules of Court in 1986 it was not possible to combine a claim for damages with an application for a State side order, although such a claim could be combined with an application for a declaration or injunction. If damages were sought, it was necessary to commence separate proceedings.[1] It may be surmised that prior to the procedural changes effected by the new Rules in 1986 many litigants were content to secure the invalidation of the impugned administrative act, and were not prepared to commence separate proceedings in order to press their claim for damages. The new Rules of Court seek to rectify this procedural anomaly by providing for a new unified judicial review procedure. The new Ord. 84, r. 24 empowers the court to grant damages in addition to, or in lieu of, a State side order, or a declaration or an injunction. Ord. 84, r. 24 provides as follows:

"(1) On an application for judicial review the Court may, subject to paragraph (2), award damages to an applicant if

   (a) he has included in the statement in support of his application for leave under [Ord. 84, r. 20(3)] a claim for damages arising for any matter to which the application relates, and

   (b) the Court is satisfied that, if the claim had been made in a civil action against any respondent or respondents begun by the applicant at the time of making this application, he would have been awarded damages.

[1] Law Reform Commission, *Judicial Review of Administrative Action*, Working Paper No. 8, 1979 at pp. 4–5.

(2) Order 19, rules 5 and 7[2] shall apply to a statement
relating to a claim for damages as it applies to a
pleading."

The effect of these new Rules should be to make it easier for
applicants to recover damages in respect of wrongful administrative action.

One practical problem which is likely to arise is whether
Ord. 84, r. 24 provides an exclusive procedure where damages are
the *only* remedy claimed against a public authority in respect of an
allegedly wrongful exercise of its public law powers and/or duties.
The answer would appear to be that it does not, and that the
reasoning of *O'Reilly* v. *Mackman*[3] is inapplicable in this context. In
the first place, an isolated claim for damages does not directly
challenge the *validity* of an administrative decision (unlike *e.g.* a
claim for certiorari or a declaration). The same consideration
pertaining to the need to obtain a speedy decision on the validity
of an administrative decision—and which had so influenced Lord
Diplock's speech in *O'Reilly*—are generally not present where the
plaintiff's sole claim is for damages. Secondly, the wording of
Ord. 84, r. 24 is such that it seems to imply that the court's
jurisdiction to award damages in the context of an application for
judicial review is only *ancillary* to the principal remedies of
certiorari, prohibition, declaration, etc. But the judicial review
procedure would not be appropriate in cases where the sole claim
is for damages arising from the wrongful exercise of a public
power and where no specific relief (such as certiorari) is sought.
Finally, if Ord. 84, r. 24 were to prescribe an exclusive procedure
it would have the effect of withdrawing jurisdiction in certain cases
from the District and Circuit Courts, and would probably be *ultra
vires* the Courts (Supplemental Provisions) Acts 1961–1986. It
would seem, for example, that where a plaintiff claimed £15,000
damages (or less) against Ireland in an action for false imprisonment arising out of an invalid arrest under section 30 of the
Offences against the State Act 1939 by a member of the Gardai, he
would have no choice but to commence his action in the High
Court by way of an application for judicial review. This would be a
surprising development, not least because the Circuit Court

---

[2] Ord. 19, r. 5 deals with the requirement of particulars in the pleading
where fraud, misrepresentation, undue influence etc. are pleaded.
Ord. 19, r. 7 deals with the length of time available for pleading after
the delivery of particulars.
[3] [1983] 2 A.C. 237. See pp. 345–347.

currently enjoys a statutory jurisdiction to hear such cases.[4]

For the foregoing reasons, therefore, it would seem that Ord. 84, r. 24 does *not* prescribe an exclusive procedure where the plaintiff's *sole* claim is for damages against a public authority in respect of the wrongful exercise of its public law powers and/or duties.

2. Actions in tort

As a general proposition—subject to important qualifications presently to be considered—it is true to say that neither the State nor any other public authority enjoys any special position in the law of torts. The general basis of liability on the part of the State or any other public authority is fault, although liability is strict in cases of nuisance, breach of statutory duty and under the rule in *Rylands* v. *Fletcher*. This is an important aspect of the Rule of Law, and it may truly be said that an action in tort claiming damages is an effective means of securing judicial review of administrative action.

However, there are still special rules of liability for particular areas of administrative action. For example, section 28(2)(*c*) of the Fire Services Act 1981 provides that no action will lie in respect of the wrongful exercise of the fire-fighting powers conferred by that section of the Act. An even more striking contemporary example is provided by section 64 of the Postal and Telecommunications Services Act 1983 which provides that An Post shall be immune from all liability in respect of any loss or damage suffered by a person in the use of a postal service by reason of (a) failure or delay in providing, operating or maintaining, or (b) failure, interruption, suspension or restriction of a postal service. Similarly, members of staff are immune from civil liability except at the suit of the company in respect of any such loss or damage.[5] It must be questionable whether the Oireachtas may constitutionally confer such an immunity on a public authority (such as a sanitary authority) or a state-sponsored body (such as An Post). In *Byrne*

---

[4] *i.e.* by way of an action for false imprisonment: see Courts (Supplemental Provisions) Act 1961, as amended by Courts Act 1981, s.2(1)(*b*). The House of Lords appear to have reached a similar conclusion in the context of the English Ord. 53 procedure: see *Davy* v. *Spelthorne B.C.* [1984] A.C. 262.

[5] A similar immunity is provided by s.88 of the 1983 Act for Bord Telecom Eireann in respect of loss or damage suffered by reason of the failure of a telecommunications service or any error or omission in a directory published by the company or any telegrams or telexes transmitted by the company.

v. *Ireland*,[6] one of the reasons given by Budd J. as to why the
State's immunity from suit had not survived the enactment of the
Constitution was that such an immunity was inconsistent with
Article 40.3 whereby the State guarantees in its laws to defend and
vindicate the personal rights of the citizen. Although Budd J. did
not elaborate on this point, he appears to suggest that the
existence of such an immunity would infringe the citizen's right of
access to the courts and to litigate a justiciable controversy.[7]
Judged by these standards, the immunities conferred by both the
1981 and 1983 Acts would appear to be highly suspect. If, say, a
parcel is lost through the negligence of An Post there can be but
little doubt that the sender would be able to sue the company in
respect of any foreseeable loss suffered, were it not for this
statutory immunity. The net effect of the immunity in these
circumstances is to prevent the aggrieved party from litigating a
justiciable controversy.[8]

Apart from these statutory provisions, the major exception to
the proposition that the liability of public authorities is co-
extensive with that imposed by the general law on private persons
is the immunity enjoyed by local authorities in respect of damage
caused by non-repair of the highway. The principle that a local
authority is not liable for an injury to a user of the highway caused
by a hole in the road resulting from its failure can be traced back
to *Russell* v. *The Men Dwelling in the County of Devon*.[9] The basis of
this immunity is that at common law the duty of repairing
highways fell on the community. By virtue of a statute of 1612[10]
this duty was imposed on the parish. Because the inhabitants were
not a corporation they could not be sued collectively and
therefore no action lay against them in respect of their failure to
carry out their duty. But an action in damages lay against an
individual who created a danger to the highway, and as a result the
non-feasance/misfeasance dichotomy is still a feature of our law.
Despite the changes wrought by the Local Government (Ireland)
Act 1898—most notably the imposition by section 82, on every

[6] [1972] I.R. 241. See pp. 391–392.
[7] *Macauley* v. *Minister for Posts and Telegraphs* [1966] I.R. 345; *O'Brien* v.
  Manufacturing Engineering Co. [1973] I.R. 334
[8] However, special limitation periods stand on a different footing, and
  cannot of themselves be seen as unconstitutional. See *e.g.* Defence Act
  1954, s.111 (six months time limit).
[9] (1788) 2 T.R. 667.
[10] 11, 12 & 13 Jac. 1, c. 7, Irl.

county and district council of the duty of keeping the road in good condition and repair—the position remained the same.[11]

The distinction between non-feasance and misfeasance has been judicially described as both "unsatisfactory"[12] and "anomalous",[13] but it was regarded as sufficiently well established to require its abrogation by statute. Section 60 of the Civil Liability Act 1961 provides in subsection (1) that: "A local authority shall be liable for damages caused as a result of their failure to maintain adequately a public road." Subsection (7), however, provides that the section is to come into operation on a day, not earlier than April 1, 1967, as might be fixed by order of the Government. No such order has yet been made.[14]

It is possible, given recent developments in the general law of civil liability, that the Supreme Court would react favourably to arguments that road authorities are not immune from liability in respect of non-feasance. Since *Purtill* v. *Athlone U.D.C.*[15] the Irish courts have steadily recognised the existence of a duty of care in situations where formerly it had been held that the defendant was exempt from responsibility (*e.g.* liability of occupier to trespasser, liability of builder to second purchaser, liability of animal owners). Moreover, the immunity is constitutionally suspect. Might not a citizen injured in an accident due to a hole in the road and unable to recover compensation because of the non-feasance principle claim that the state had failed in its constitutional duty to vindicate his right to bodily integrity?[16] In sum, such qualifications as exist to the general principles of civil liability are merely in recognition of the reality that public authorities are not private citizens but are discharging functions under statute.

At common law, where a statute authorises the doing of a particular act, then no action will lie at the suit of any person if the inevitable consequence of the act is to cause damage, provided, of

---

[11] *Harbinson* v. *Armagh C.C.* [1902] 2 I.R. 538. The position is otherwise where the local authority repairs the highway in a negligent manner: see *Clements* v. *Tyrone C.C.* [1905] 2 I.R. 415.

[12] *Kelly* v. *Mayo C.C.* [1964] I.R. 315 at p. 324 *per* Kingsmill Moore J.

[13] *O'Brien* v. *Waterford C.C.* [1926] I.R. 1 at p. 8 *per* Murnaghan J.

[14] As for whether the Government's failure to implement s.60(1) could be subjected to judicial review, see p. 326. See now *The State (Sheehan)* v. *An Taoiseach*, High Court, July 29, 1986 where Costello J. granted an order of mandamus compelling the Government to implement s.60(1) within six months. See also Addendum.

[15] [1968] I.R. 205.

[16] The non-feasance immunity might also be vulnerable on the grounds that it amounts to an infringment of the citizen's right to litigate a justiciable controversy.

course, that it is done without negligence.[17] Conversely, where the damage is caused, not by acting in pursuance of statutory functions, but by going beyond them, then the remedy and the calculation of damages has to be dealt with by the general law. So, for example, in *Red Cow Service Staion Ltd.* v. *Murphy International Ltd. and Bord Gais Eireann*[18] it was held that, while under section 27(1)(d) of the Gas Act 1976 Bord Gais Eireann has the power to dig or break or interfere with any road, if they acted negligently, *e.g.* broke a telephone cable and caused damage to the plaintiff beyond what was essential and necessary, they could not claim the protection of the Act. The 1976 Act provides a particular remedy and method of computation for any loss caused by the operation of the Act.

The principle that *intra vires* administrative decisions are not actionable has its most important application in cases where public bodies are authorised to commit what might otherwise be a nuisance. In *Allen* v. *Gulf Oil Refining Ltd.*[19] a private Act of Parliament had authorised the defendant to construct a refinery but it did not specifically authorise the operation of the refinery, and some neighbours who complained of excessive smell, vibration and noise sued in nuisance. The House of Lords ruled that the operation of the refinery was authorised at least by necessary implication—and as a result the plaintiffs had no remedy in so far as the nuisance complained of was the inevitable result of the authorised operation.

It is difficult to believe that an Irish court would reach the same conclusion were it faced with a case with similar facts. If the Act plainly extinguished the landowner's right to sue in respect of such a nuisance, an Irish court would probably rule that such provisions amounted to an unconstitutional attack on his right to sue in court or to recover compensation in respect of this state interference with their property rights.[20] If the statute were silent in the matter,

---

[17] *Geddis* v. *Proprietors of the Bann Reservoir* (1873) 3 App. Cas. 430; *Allen* v. *Gulf Oil Refining Ltd.* [1981] A.C. 1001.

[18] (1985) 3 I.L.T.(n.s.) 15. See also *Collins* v. *Gypsum Industries Ltd.* [1975] I.R. 321. The Minerals Development Act 1940 provides for a scheme of compensation in respect of damage to land caused by mining operations. The Supreme Court held that the applicant could not recover compensation under the terms of the 1940 Act, as the special scheme of compensation did not cover physical injuries. The proper form for pursuing such a claim for personal injuries was that provided by the ordinary courts.

[19] [1981] A.C. 1001.

[20] Unless, of course, this was a case where the requirements of social justice and the exigencies of the common good did not require the

the court would probably apply the presumption of constitutionality in order to rule that there was no overt legislative intention to act in an unconstitutional fashion, and that the Oireachtas did not intend to deprive the plaintiff of his right to sue in nuisance.

Actions in tort against the State and administrative bodies can roughly be divided into four headings: actions for breach of statutory duty, negligent exercise of discretionary statutory powers, the tort of misfeasance of public office and for infringement of constitutional rights. We will consider each of the individual topics in turn.

3. Actions for breach of statutory duty[21]

No comprehensive answer can be given to the question of whether a breach of statute by a public authority gives rise to civil liability.[22] While occasionally a statute may state explicitly that a civil action may[23] or may not[24] be taken for breach of individual provisions, this is generally not the case and thus the question is usually left to the courts to decide as a matter of statutory construction.

The general rule was stated by Lord Fraser in *Gouriet* v. *Union of Post Office Workers*[25] to be as follows:

"[A] private person is only entitled to sue in respect of an interference with a public right if either there is also an interference with a private right of his or the interference with the public right will inflict special damage on him."[26]

This is essentially the test used when an action for breach of

payment of compensation: see *O'Callaghan* v. *Commissioners of Public Works* [1985] I.L.R.M. 364.
[21] For a fuller analysis of this issue, see McMahon and Binchy, *The Irish Law of Torts* (Abingdon, 1981) at pp. 278–293; Kerr and Whyte, *Irish Trade Union Law* (Abingdon, 1985) at pp. 220–223.
[22] See Buckley, "Liability in Tort for Breach of Statutory Duty" (1984) 100 L.Q.R. 204.
[23] See *e.g.* ss.21 and 55 of the Air Navigation and Transport Act 1936.
[24] See *e.g.* Fire Brigades Act 1940, s.5(2) (no action will lie for failure to comply with statutory duty to provide adequate fire service); Transport Act 1958, s.7(3) (no action will lie for failure by C.I.E. to comply with its own statutory duty to provide "reasonable, efficient and economical transport service.")
[25] [1978] A.C. 435. See also *Meade* v. *Haringey L.B.C.* [1979] 1 W.L.R. 637.
[26] [1978] A.C. 435 at p. 518.

statutory duty is brought against private bodies, but it seems clear
that the courts are reluctant to allow an action in tort "where
public bodies have violated their general statutory duties."[27] An
example of this is provided by *Siney* v. *Dublin Corporation*.[28] In this
case the plaintiff had claimed damages by reason of the defendant's failure to comply with section 11 of the Housing Act 1966
which imposes an obligation on local authorities to provide
adequate housing. O'Higgins C.J. described this section as one
creating a general duty which had been enacted for the benefit of
the public at large. Mere breach of that duty by the defendant did
not give rise to an action for damages, even at the suit of an
aggrieved party.

A good discussion of general principles is to be found in
Gannon J.'s judgment in *Walsh* v. *Kilkenny C.C.*[29] The plaintiff's
cattle had been destroyed when they strayed through a gap in the
boundary wall of a cemetery and ate the leaves of the yew trees
growing in the cemetery. By virtue of the regulations made
pursuant to section 181 of the Public Health (Ireland) Act 1878
the defendant local authority was obliged to keep the cemetery
"sufficiently fenced," and the plaintiff claimed damages for
breach of statutory duty. Gannon J. was satisfied that these
statutory duties existed only for the benefit of the public at large,
and "not for the benefit of any class of persons, nor of
individuals." Once regard was had to the provisions of the Act it
was clear that "the declared and primary purpose of the duties"
imposed on the defendants was the protection of public health,
and the "prevention of the violation of the respect due to the
remains of deceased persons." Gannon J. concluded by noting
that the duty to fence imposed by the regulations was a duty:

> "[T]o protect the property vested in the Burial Board from
> desecration or other interference by trespassers. The plain-
> tiff, who is admittedly a trespasser, cannot claim that he is a
> person for whose benefit this duty is laid upon the defen-
> dants."

At issue in *Waterford Harbour Commissioners* v. *British Railways*

---

[27] Street, *The Law of Torts* (7th ed., London, 1983) at p. 278. It is
sometimes said that where there is a public duty of a ministerial
character (*i.e.* one involving no discretion or choice), then an action will
lie, and questions of statutory construction are left aside: see Wade,
Administrative Law (Oxford, 1982) at p. 666. However, this principle
does not appear to be currently in favour: see Craig, "Compensation in
Public Law" (1980) 96 L.Q.R. 413 at pp. 422–423.

[28] [1980] I.R. 400.

[29] High Court, January 23, 1978.

Board[30] was whether a breach of section 70 of the Fishguard and Rosslare Railways and Harbours Act 1898 gave rise to an action for damages. This section imposed an obligation on the respondent Board to maintain a daily shipping service between Waterford and Fishguard in Wales. It was argued that because the provision was enacted for the public at large, no action would lie. O'Higgins C.J. rejected this contention as, in his view, the plaintiffs were among the class of persons the Act was designed to protect. He pointed out that, in any event, the plaintiffs would suffer special damage as a result of the breach, and they would lose the significant revenue which they earned from harbour fees. However, a majority of the court held that in the special circumstances of the case the plaintiffs were estopped from claiming damages for breach of statutory duty. The defendants had been in default of their statutory obligations since 1939, and the plaintiffs had since then entered into a contractual arrangement which relieved the defendants of their strict statutory obligations. However, the plaintiffs could sue in respect of the defendant's breach of contract.

These common law techniques of statutory interpretation may have to be re-evaluated in the light of constitutional provisions. If the legislature creates a justiciable controversy by imposing a statutory duty, then the courts are required by the terms of Article 40.3 to vindicate the citizen's rights in the case of injustice done. Barrington J. has pointed out that the common law methods of statutory interpretation owe their origin to the fact that:

> "The British Parliament is a sovereign legislature, and the rights of individual plaintiffs are to be ascertained by finding out what was the intention of Parliament in the particular case. If it did not intend to provide a remedy, then he has not. But in our jurisdiction the citizen would appear to have a remedy, by virtue of the provisions of Article 40.3, if he has or may suffer damage as a result of a breach of the law in circumstances which amount to an injustice."[31]

Something like this principle appears to have been applied in *Cosgrave* v. *Ireland*,[32] where the plaintiff was awarded damages in the following circumstances: the Department of Foreign Affairs had

[30] Supreme Court, February 18, 1981.

[31] *Irish Permanent Building Society* v. *Caldwell* [1981] I.L.R.M. 242 at p. 254.

[32] [1982] I.L.R.M. 48. See Cooney and Kerr, "Constitutional Aspects of Irish Tort Law" (1981) 3 D.U.L.J.(n.s.) 1. See also *O'Neill* v. *Clare C.C.* [1983] I.L.R.M. 141 (planning authority liable in damages in respect of wilful refusal to grant planning permission in circumstances where they were statutorily obliged to do so).

issued passports to the plaintiff's wife and children. McWilliam J. held that in so doing the Department infringed the plaintiff's statutory rights[33] under the Guardianship of Infants Act 1964, and awarded him damages in respect of such losses "as have been proved to be sustained by him" and also general damages for "foreseeable mental distress, anxiety and inconvenience." It is, perhaps, significant that McWilliam J. made no reference to the common law techniques of ascertaining whether a breach of statutory provisions gave rise to civil liability. While the judge was not completely explicit about this matter, it seems fair to infer that he considered that the courts would have been in default of their constitutional obligations under Article 40.3 if they failed to provide an adequate remedy for the infringment of these statutory rights.

4. Liability for the negligent exercise of discretionary public powers

To what extent should public bodies be liable for the negligent exercise (or non-exercise) of their discretionary public powers?[34] A court faced with this vexed question has a choice of three options which may be summarised thus:

i.   Require a showing of *ultra vires* as a pre-condition to any liability on the part of the public body, or
ii.   Apply a test which is similar to that employed in cases of breaches of statutory duty, *i.e.* have regard to the purpose for which the statutory powers were conferred and whether or not the plaintiff is in the class of persons which the statute was designed to assist, or
iii. Ignore the public law nature of the discretionary powers conferred on the public authority and, instead, treat the authority as if it were just a private corporate entity, *i.e.* simply apply ordinary principles of negligence without qualification.

(A) **Anns v. Merton L.B.C.** The leading case in the common law

---

[33] McWilliam J. did not find it necessary to decide whether the Department's actions had infringed the plaintiff's *constitutional* rights. As for liability in damages for infringement of constitutional rights, see pp. 382–384 and Addendum.

[34] Of course, where the action in negligence does not relate to the exercise of the authority's *statutory functions*, then the ordinary principles of liability will apply: see *e.g. O'Donovan* v. *Cork C.C.* [1967] I.R. 173 (local authority vicariously liable for employee's negligence).

world is still the majority decision of the House of Lords in *Anns* v. *Merton L.B.C.*[35] In this case a block of flats developed cracks because it had been built on inadequate foundations, and the question of whether the local authority could be liable for the failure to exercise their statutory power to inspect the foundations was among the preliminary issues raised. Lord Wilberforce drew a sharp distinction between the test for liability in the case of breach of statutory duty on the one hand, and negligent exercise of discretionary public powers on the other. In the latter case liability could not exist "unless the act complained of lies outside the ambit of the power," *i.e.* a showing of *ultra vires* was a prerequisite to liability in tort.[36] Once *ultra vires* was established then, in principle, a plaintiff could sue. But Lord Wilberforce also distinguished between what he termed "the area of policy or discretion" (where an authority has a choice of options available) and an "operational decision" (where a particular course of action is being carried out). The more "operational" a power may be, the easier it is to superimpose a common law duty of care.[37]

[35] [1978] A.C. 728. *Anns* represented the culmination of judicial thinking contained in cases such as *Dorset Yacht Co.* v. *Home Office* [1970] A.C. 1004 and *Dutton* v. *Bognor Regis U.D.C.* [1972] 1 Q.B. 373. The *Anns* analysis has been accepted by the New Zealand Court of Appeal (*Takaro Properties Ltd.* v. *Rawltng* [1978] 2 N.Z.L.R. 314) and the Canadian Supreme Court (*City of Kamloops* v. *Nielsen* (1984) 10 D.L.R. (4th.) 641), but has been rejected by the High Court of Australia (*Sutherland Shire Council* v. *Heyman* (1985) 59 A.L.J.R. 564). *Anns* has spawned a vast body of literature: see *e.g.* Craig, "Negligence in the Exercise of a Statutory Power" (1978) 94 L.Q.R. 428; Oliver, "*Anns* v. *London Borough of Merton* Reconsidered" (1980) 33 C.L.P. 269; Bowman and Bailey, "Negligence in the Realms of Public Law—A Positive Obligation to Rescue?" [1984] *Public Law* 227 and Weir, "The Answer to *Anns*" (1985) 44 C.L.J. 26.

[36] The Council inspector had acted *ultra vires* the discretion vested in him by not ensuring that the plans and foundation were in accordance with the building by-laws. The assumed facts (*Anns* was tried on a preliminary point of law) were consistent with his having been negligent either in not inspecting, or in the manner in which he inspected the foundations.

[37] Lord Wilberforce referred to *Indian Towing Co.* v. *U.S.* 350 U.S. 61 (1955), where a decision to *build* a lighthouse was classified as a "policy" decision, but the failure to keep the lighthouse in working order was described as "operational negligence." But *cf.* the comments of Costello J. in *Ward* v. *McMaster* [1985] I.R. 29 at p. 47 where he described the policy/operational distinction as one of "degree" and "certainly one which may be difficult to make with precision in many cases." See also pp. 378–379.

Anns has been applied in a series of Northern Irish decisions.[38] In *McKernan* v. *McGeown and the Department of the Environment*[39] the plaintiff sustained personal injuries in two separate road accidents. It was contended that the Department was negligent in the exercise of its discretionary powers to grit, sand and de-ice a public highway. Gibson L.J. stated that *Anns* had made clear that if an act done pursuant to a public general statute is to be actionable that act must be *ultra vires* and must also be one which would be tortious in common law. He observed that the most recent English cases had all required "this dual proof."[40] It was common case that the statutory powers in question were general in nature and could be exercised "in respect either of the whole or any part of a road as the [Department thought]." Gibson L.J. noted that so broad were the powers entrusted to the local authority that it was almost impossible to argue that the failure to grit or de-ice any part of a public highway could be *ultra vires*. Because the authority's failure to act was therefore *intra vires* no action for the negligent exercise of that discretionary power would lie:

> "[T]he decision whether to do or to refrain from doing any of the acts alleged to have been omitted would have been a decision within the ambit of the wide discretion. So, as no question of *ultra vires* could be raised, any neglect to perform any act within that general range of activity is not actionable."[41]

In *Chambers* v. *Department of the Environment*[42] the plaintiff was injured in an accident which she claimed was the result of the defendant's failure to provide adequate street lighting. The Department enjoyed a discretionary power to provide such lighting, and the lights had been out of action for four days. The Northern Ireland Court of Appeal found that it had insufficient facts before it to enable it to come to a conclusion, and the case was remitted to the county court. Lord Lowry observed that the

---

[38] See also *e.g. Fellowes* v. *Rother D.C.* [1983] 1 All E.R. 513; *Rigby* v. *Chief Constable of Northamptonshire* [1985] 1 W.L.R. 1242 (police failure to buy advanced fire-fighting equipment bona fide exercise of discretion on matter of policy in pursuance of statutory powers).

[39] [1983] N.I. 167. See also *Farrell* v. *Northern Ireland Electricity Service* [1977] N.I. 39 (pre-*Anns*); *Forsythe* v. *Evans* [1980] N.I. 230.

[40] Thus, for example, in *Dorset Yacht Co.* v. *Home Office* [1970] A.C. 1004 not only were the Borstal officers negligent in the supervision of the boys (who escaped, and damaged the plaintiff's property), but they were also acting outside any discretion delegated to them in that they disregarded the Home Office instructions.

[41] [1983] N.I. at p. 178.

[42] (1985) 3 N.I.J.B. 85.

Department's failure to provide adequate lighting might be due to a policy decision to conserve resources, etc. If this was the case, then the action would fail unless it could be shown that this policy decision amounted to a "totally unreasonable exercise of discretion" (*i.e.* was *ultra vires*). On the other hand, the plaintiff's task would be a lot easier if it could be shown that failure to provide adequate lighting resulted from negligence at the operational level.[43] Lord Lowry put it thus:

> "When one looks at policy, you must find *ultra vires* before you can consider negligence; but when looking at the purely operational sphere negligence (whether act or omission) *constitutes ultra vires* conduct."

This is tantamount to saying that for all practical purposes an action will not lie in respect of negligent policy decisions taken by public bodies—unless, of course, such policy decisions are manifestly unreasonable. On the other hand, Lord Lowry's test means that there is no special tort régime for negligent public authority decisions taken at the operational level. There is much to be said—from a strictly practical point of view—for this sort of result.

(B) Peabody Donation Fund v. Parkinson & Co. Ltd. The departure of the House of Lords from the *Anns* "dual proof test" in *Peabody Donation Fund* v. *Parkinson & Co. Ltd.*[44] has complicated an already difficult area of the law. The plaintiffs in this case were engaged on a large-scale building project, and they were obliged by statute to deposit drainage plans with the defendant local authority. The local authority approved the original plans, but in the course of the construction one of the authority's drainage inspectors approved different plans which had been drawn up by the plaintiffs' architects. Later it transpired that the drains were defective, and the plaintiffs incurred substantial loss as a result. It was claimed that the local authority should have activated their enforcement powers under the terms of the Local Government Act 1963, and that they were negligent in failing to ensure that the plaintiffs adhered to their original drainage plans.

The House of Lords rejected their claim. Lord Keith accepted that the plaintiffs' loss was a reasonably foreseeable consequence of the local authority's inaction. Nevertheless, he held that in the light of the purpose of the statutory powers, no duty of care was owed to the plaintiffs by the local authority. The purpose of the

---

[43] *e.g.* an employee's negligence in failing to repair the street lamps.
[44] [1985] A.C. 210, overruling the earlier Court of Appeal decision in *Acrecrest Ltd.* v. *Hattrell & Partners* [1983] Q.B. 260.

enforcement powers was to safeguard the occupiers of houses within the local authority's functional area, and to protect the public interest: they were not designed to protect developers such as the plaintiffs from the economic loss which they might suffer as a result of their own failure to comply with the relevant building regulations.

While the result in *Peabody* is unexceptional, it must be said that Lord Keith's reasoning is not altogether satisfactory. In particular, it is difficult to reconcile *Peabody* with *Anns*, given that Lord Keith made no mention of the *ultra vires* requirement. Furthermore, the *Peabody* test—whether the plaintiff was within the category of persons intended to be benefited by the Act—seems suspiciously like the test to determine liability in cases of breach of statutory duty. Is it correct in principle to assimilate the tests as far as powers and duties are concerned or is there more than a difference of degree between these two concepts?[45] In any event, it seems that, for the moment at any rate, the English courts are regarding *Anns* as having been overtaken by *Peabody*.[46]

(C) Siney, Weir and Ward. The courts in this jurisdiction do not appear to pay all that much attention to the public law nature of a public authority's discretionary powers. As far as liability for negligence is concerned, public authorities are treated almost as if they were private corporate entities. This is certainly the impression given by the two Supreme Court decisions on this question, *Siney* v. *Dublin Corporation*[47] and *Weir* v. *Dun Laoghaire Corporation*.[48]

In *Siney*, the plaintiff had been allocated a flat by Dublin Corporation. It transpired that it was unfit for human habitation during the currency of the tenancy owing to a design fault. The plaintiff claimed damages for negligence and breach of statutory duty against the local authority. Once the flat had been completed, and before a letting was made, an inspection had been carried out by the local authority. The Supreme Court found that this had been done negligently, since this inspection did not ensure that the accommodation provided matched up to the statutory

---

[45] Lord Denning had attempted to do so in *Dutton* v. *Bognor Regis U.D.C.* [1972] 1 Q.B. 373, but this did not meet with approval of the House of Lords in *Anns*: see [1978] A.C. at 754, *per* Lord Wilberforce.

[46] See *Industry Commercial Properties Ltd.* v. *S. Bedfordshire C.C.* [1986] 1 All E.R. 787.

[47] [1980] I.R. 400. See also *Coleman* v. *Dundalk U.D.C.*, Supreme Court, July 17 1985, and Clark and Kerr, "Council Housing, Implied Terms and Negligence—A Critique of *Siney* v. *Dublin Corporation*" (1980) 15 Ir.Jur.(n.s.) 32.

[48] [1983] I.R. 242.

requirement of fitness for human habitation. However, it is not clear whether the inspection was taken pursuant to the authority's statutory powers or statutory duties. If, as seems likely, the inspection was taken pursuant to a statutory power, then according to the *Anns* test, it would have been necessary to show that the authority's inspectors acted "outside any delegated discretion either as to the making of an inspection or as to the manner in which the inspection was made."[49] But although *Anns* was referred to with approval, no mention was made of the *ultra vires* requirement. Nevertheless, in finding that the local authority was negligent, the Supreme Court appears to have applied the standard common law principles of liability—the neighbourhood principle enunciated in *Donoghue* v. *Stevenson*.[50]

The reasoning of the Supreme Court majority in *Weir* v. *Dun Laoghaire Corporation* is even more curious. Here the plaintiff had tripped and fallen on a public road as a result of a difference in road levels caused by the construction of a bus lay-by. No warning of this difference in level had been given, the entire tarmacadam roadway had appeared level, and there was clear evidence of negligence on the part of those engaged in constructing the lay-by. The local authority had granted planning permission to a development company to build a shopping centre nearby, but it was a condition of this permission that the bus lay-by be built. The lay-by was constructed with the "knowledge and approval" of the defendant local authority.

A majority of the Supreme Court ruled that the local authority was liable in negligence. O'Higgins C.J. appeared to emphasise the fact that the local authority had insisted on the construction of the lay-by, and that the work was carried on with the knowledge and approval of the local authority in their capacity both as planning authority and highway authority. The tenor of this judgment suggests that because the local authority insisted on the condition, it must have in a sense "authorised" the work with the result that the construction company came to be regarded as the local authority's servants or agents.

Griffin J. delivered a trenchant dissent:

"[S]o to extend the liability of a highway authority for the acts

---

[49] Kerr & Clarke, *loc. cit.*, at p. 51. If one were to apply Lord Lowry's test in *Chambers*, this would be operational negligence and hence *ultra vires*.
[50] [1932] A.C. 652. According to Lord Wilberforce in *Anns*, if liability for the negligent exercise of a discretionary power is based solely on the neighbour principle this is to neglect an essential factor: "[T]hat the local authority is a public body discharging duties under statute; its powers and duties are definable in terms of public not private law" ([1978] A.C. at 754).

of a contractor engaged by a developer in doing work for which the latter had obtained planning permission, and equating this liability with that of the authority for acts of a contractor engaged by them, is warranted neither by principle nor authority."[51]

Weir is not an entirely satisfactory decision because it ignores, *inter alia*, the public law nature of a local authority's powers and functions. Just as in *Siney*, no mention was made of the *ultra vires* requirement, and no authorities were referred to in the judgments of the Supreme Court. It is also interesting to note that the result in *Weir* is the exact opposite to that arrived at by the House of Lords in *Peabody*. In both cases building developers sought to escape the consequences of their own negligence (or that of their agents) by claiming that a local authority was negligent in not activating its statutory powers. In direct contrast to the result in *Peabody*, the Supreme Court in *Weir* appears to have held that a local authority owes a duty of care in the discharge of its statutory functions to the grantee of a planning permission to protect him from the consequences of his own negligence. This is a remarkable proposition and one which—the decision in *Weir* notwithstanding—a future Supreme Court is unlikely to endorse.

The judgment of Costello J. in *Ward* v. *McMaster*[52] represents a more considered approach to this problem. In this case the plaintiff had purchased a new house which turned out to be grossly sub-standard structurally and a health risk. Proceedings were then instituted against the builder and the local authority. There were two aspects of the claim against the local authority. The plaintiff had applied to the council for a loan of £12,000 under the provisions of the Housing Act 1966 to enable him to purchase the house.[53] The council sent a valuer who reported that it was in good repair and that its market value was £25,000. The plaintiff alleged that this valuation was negligently carried out and that the council was vicariously liable.

Costello J. found that the valuer had no professional qualification relating to building construction and was employed simply to place a market value on the property. The standard of care required of him was merely that of an ordinary skilled auctioneer, and he had not been negligent. The plaintiff successfully alleged, however, that the council was directly liable in that it had broken the common law duty of care owed to him in carrying out its

[51] [1983] I.R. at p. 248.
[52] [1985] I.R. 29.
[53] Section 39 of the Housing Act 1966 provides that a local authority may lend money to a person for the purpose of acquiring or constructing a house.

statutory functions. The council had a statutory power under the 1966 Act to grant a loan to the plaintiff and a statutory duty by virtue of the relevant regulations[54] to inspect the property before granting a loan. In carrying out the inspection a duty to act with care arose, a duty which was broken by authorising an inspection by someone who lacked the necessary qualification to ascertain reasonably discoverable defects. Costello J. had no doubt, on the authority of cases such as *Anns* and *Siney* that a common law duty of care based on the principle established in *Donoghue* v. *Stevenson* might exist when statutory functions were being performed. Following a review of the relevant authorities, including *Peabody*, Costello J. concluded that the relevant principles in cases of this kind were as follows:

> "(a) When deciding whether a local authority exercising statutory functions is under a common law duty of care the court must firstly ascertain whether a relationship of proximity existed between the parties such that in the reasonable contemplation of the authority carelessness on their part might cause loss. But all the circumstances of the case must in addition be considered, including the statutory provisions under which the authority is acting. Of particular significance in this connection is the purpose for which the statutory powers were conferred and whether or not the plaintiff is in the class of persons which the statute was designed to assist.
>
> (b) It is material in all cases for the court in reaching its decision on the existence and scope of the alleged duty to consider whether it is just and reasonable that a common law duty of care as alleged should in all the circumstances exist."[55]

Applying these principles to the facts as found, Costello J. concluded that, although the plaintiff did not expressly inform any member of the council's staff that he was relying on their valuation and although the council carried it out for its own purposes and to comply with its statutory obligations, the council ought to have been aware that it was probable that the plaintiff, a person of limited means, would not have gone to the expense of having the house examined by a professionally qualified person and would have relied on the inspection which he knew would be carried out for the purpose of the loan application. There was therefore a sufficient relationship of proximity and there was

---

[54] Housing Authorities (Loans for Acquisition or Construction of Houses) Regulations 1972 (S.I. 1972 No. 29).
[55] [1985] I.R. 29 at pp. 49–50.

nothing in the dealings between the parties which restricted or limited the duties in any way. In particular no warning against relying on the proposed valuation was given. As to the scope of the duty, Costello J. concluded that the council should have ensured that the person carrying out the valuation would be competent to discover reasonably ascertainable defects which would materially affect its market value. Costello J. also held that the duty of care only extended to the person to whom they were lending the money and who had relied on the council. It did not extend to the plaintiff's wife.[56]

It should be noted that Costello J. did not attempt to draw a sharp distinction between "powers" and "duties" for the purposes of liability. He also declined to pay too much regard to the distinction drawn by Lord Wilberforce in *Anns* between "policy" and "operation," and he concluded that at bottom it was all a question of whether it was just and reasonable in all the circumstances that a common law duty of care as alleged should exist. However, it may be questioned whether Costello J. was wise to place such emphasis on *Peabody*. For all its faults, the *Anns* test gives a degree of certainty and structure to the law.

5. The tort of misfeasance of public office

At common law, an *ultra vires* act is not *of itself* tortious unless malice is established.[57] Of course, there are some *ultra vires* acts which also happen to rank as recognised torts,[58] but absent malice, there is no direct relationship between *ultra vires* acts and liability in tort. There is, however, a tort of misfeasance of public office which includes "malicious abuse of power, deliberate maladministration and perhaps other unlawful acts causing injury."[59] The rule has been stated in the following terms:

> "[I]f a public officer does an act which, to his knowledge, amounts to an abuse of his office, and he thereby causes damage to another person, then an action in tort for

---

[56] This aspect of Costello J.'s decision is criticised by Murray, "Public Authority Torts" (1985) 7 D.U.L.J.(n.s.).

[57] *Johnston* v. *Meldon* (1891) 30 L.R.Ir. 15; *O'Conghaile* v. *Wallace* [1938] I.R. 536. See generally McBride, "Damages as a Remedy for Unlawful Administrative Action" (1979) Camb.L.J. 323.

[58] Thus, *e.g.* an unlawful deprivation of liberty constitutes the tort of false imprisonment. Liability for false imprisonment is strict, *i.e.* there is no need to show malice or that the detainer knew that the detention was invalid.

[59] Wade, *Administrative Law* (Oxford, 1982) at p. 669.

misfeasance in a public office will lie against him at the suit of that other person."[60]

There are a number of recent authorities which deal with this point. The plaintiffs' in *Pine Valley Developments Ltd.* v. *Ireland*[61] claimed damages in respect of an alleged misfeasance of public office. The plaintiffs predecessors in title had been granted outline planning permission for an industrial warehouse and office development project by the Minister for Local Government. The plaintiffs then purchased the lands with the benefit of the outline planning permission in order to develop the lands for commercial purposes. However, the granting of that permission was subsequently found to be *ultra vires* by the Supreme Court.[62] The plaintiffs then commenced proceedings against Ireland and the Minister for the Environment in order to recoup the financial losses which they had incurred.

McMahon J. found that the tort of misfeasance of public office had not been established. The Minister had acted on the basis of competent legal advice, and in the circumstances he could not be made liable as no malice had been alleged and the judge found that the "Minister did not know, and had not the means of knowing that he had no power to make the order." McMahon J. quoted the following passage from Lord Diplock's speech in *Dunlop* v. *Woolahra M.C.*[63] with approval:

> "[I]n the absence of malice, passing without knowledge of its invalidity a resolution which is devoid of any legal effect is not conduct that of itself is capable of amounting to such 'misfeasance' as is a necessary element of this tort."[64]

A similar question was raised before the English Court of

---

[60] *Farrington* v. *Thompson* (1959) V.R. 286 at 293, *per* Smith J. See *Roncarelli* v. *Duplessis* (1959) 16 D.L.R. (2d) 689; *David* v. *Abdul Cader* [1963] 1 W.L.R. 834.

[61] High Court, June 28, 1985. A similar claim failed on the facts in *O'Conghaile* v. *Wallace* [1938] I.R. 536.

[62] The Court held that the Minister had no power to grant a permission which contravened the terms of the development plan: *The State (Pine Valley Developments Ltd).* v. *Dublin C.C.* [1984] I.R. 407. Retrospective legislation was passed in order to reverse this decision: see s.6(1) of the Local Government (Planning and Development) Act 1982. The Minister's powers have now devolved on to An Bord Pleanala, which has been given express power to grant a permission which contravenes materially the development plan: see s.14(8) of the Local Government (Planning and Development) Act 1976.

[63] [1982] A.C. 158.

[64] *Ibid.* at p. 172. See also Addendum.

Appeal in *Bourgoin S.A.* v. *Ministry of Agriculture.*[65] The plaintiff French companies were concerned in the production of frozen turkeys and their importation into the United Kingdom. The defendant Ministry revoked their importation licences and banned the importation of turkey meat from France. This order was subsequently declared to be invalid by the European Court of Justice,[66] and the plaintiffs claimed damages in respect of the financial loss which they suffered as a result of this *ultra vires* action. A majority of the Court of Appeal held that mere illegality of itself did not confer a right of action. Parker L.J. gave the example of an invalid ministerial ban on the importation of certain feeding stuffs. While *ultra vires* of itself would not confer a right to obtain damages, different considerations would apply if the power had been abused:

> "If the minister knew perfectly well that there was nothing wrong with the feeding stuffs and he had made the order in fact not to protect animal life but to further the interests of a company making feeding stuffs in which he held shares, the position would . . . be different. There would then be an abuse of power, for which damages would lie."[67]

Policy considerations, of course, are not very far from the surface in cases such as *Pine Valley* and *Bourgoin*. The modern formulation of the tort of misfeasance of public office ensures, by requiring an abuse of power (as distinct from a mere illegality), that public officials can discharge the duties of their office "expeditiously and fearlessly." As Parker L.J. observed in *Bourgoin*, such a state of affairs could hardly be achieved if acts done in good faith, but *ultra vires*, were actionable in damages.

6. Damages for infringement of constitutional rights

In *Meskell* v. *C.I.E.*[68] Walsh J. declared that:

> "[I]f a person has suffered damage by virtue of a breach of a constitutional right . . . that person is entitled to seek redress against the person or persons infringing that right."[69]

[65] [1985] 3 W.L.R. 1027.
[66] *Commission* v. *U.K.* (Case 40/82) [1982] E.C.R. 2793. The order was found to be in breach of Art. 30 (which guarantees free movement of goods) of the Treaty of Rome.
[67] [1985] 3 W.L.R. 1027 at pp. 1084–1085. However, the absence of just cause may prove malice: *Corliss* v. *Ireland*, High Court, July 23, 1984.
[68] [1973] I.R. 121. See also *Cotter* v. *Aherne*, High Court, February 25, 1977, and Cooney and Kerr, "Constitutional Aspects of Irish Tort Law" (1981) 3 D.U.L.J.(n.s.) 1.
[69] [1973] I.R. at 132–3.

The judge went on to observe that the infringement of a constitutional right could be vindicated by means of a civil action for damages
even though such an action might not fit into any of the ordinary
forms of action at common law or in equity. *Meskell* raises the
question of whether much of ordinary tort law has been subsumed by
constitutional principles. If such were the case, nominate torts such
as false imprisonment might disappear to be replaced by an "innomi-
nate claim for infringement of constitutional rights" based on the
guarantee of personal liberty contained in Article 40.4.1.[70]

A limited version of this trend is that the State may be regarded
as having "adequately defended and vindicated" the citizen's
personal rights by:

> "[P]roviding the law of tort as a forum for the vindication of
> damage actions, and that it is only when the common law
> remedies are inadequate or non-existent that an action based
> on the provisions of the Constitution would arise."[71]

It is this latter view of the *Meskell* doctrine which appears to have
commended itself to Costello J. in *Kearney* v. *Ireland.*[72] In this case
certain prison officials wrongly refused to pass on to the plaintiff
prisoner a number of letters addressed to him. The judge found
that these unauthorised actions amounted to an infringement of
the plaintiff's right to communicate.[73] Costello J. continued:

> "The wrong that was committed in this case was an unjustified
> infringement of a constitutional right, not a tort; and it was
> committed by a servant of the State, and accordingly Ireland
> can be sued in respect of it. . . . The wrongful act in this case
> was obviously connected with the functions for which the
> prison officer or officers who committed it are employed, and
> even though the act was unauthorised I cannot hold that it
> was performed outside the scope of his or their employment.
> The plaintiff is therefore entitled to be awarded damages
> against the State."[74]

Costello J. thereby seems to suggest that the *Meskell* principle
may be invoked only where ordinary tort law does not adequately

[70] Heuston, "Personal Rights in the Irish Constitution" (1976) 11
Ir.Jur.(n.s.) 205.
[71] Cooney and Kerr, *loc. cit.*, at p. 2.
[72] High Court, March 13, 1986.
[73] This right is a personal right protected by the terms of Article 40.3: see
Att.-Gen. v. *Paperlink Ltd.* [1984] I.L.R.M. 373.
[74] Costello J. reserved the question of whether the State could be held
liable for the acts of a servant of the State which amounts to the
infringement of a constitutional right even though done outside the
scope of the State's servant's employment.

defend or vindicate the constitutional rights of the citizen. *Kearney*
is nevertheless a decision which could have profound implications
for the use of damages as a remedy in the public law sphere. For
example, while a breach of natural justice is not of itself tortious at
common law,[75] there seems to be no reason why a plaintiff could
not sue for wrongful infringement of his constitutional right to
fair procedures. Equally, the trader who has been put out of
business by reason of an *ultra vires* decision of a local authority
might come to be entitled to recover damages for a wrongful
interference with his constitutional right to earn a livelihood.
Another possibility is that the victim of illegal telephone tapping
should be able to sue for invasion of a constitutional right to
privacy, even though illegal telephone tapping is not a tort at
common law.[76]

A more cautious approach had been taken some months earlier
by McMahon J. in *Pine Valley Developments Ltd.* v. *Ireland*, where he
held that an invalid order which caused financial loss was not an
"unjust attack" on the plaintiff company's property rights (or,
perhaps, more accurately, those of its shareholders) within the
meaning of Article 40.3 as it could always have sought judicial
review of that order. This reasoning is not especially convincing as it
ignores the fact that an admnistrative decision which emanates
from a person or body with ostensible legal authority enjoys a
presumption of validity. As a result, such a decision—which might
have irreversible consequences for a particular plaintiff—will have
full force and effect pending judicial review by the courts. McMahon J. could scarcely contend that, for example, a person who had
been wrongfully detained as a result of an invalid arrest by a
member of the Gardai could not sue for damages for infringement
of his constitutional right to liberty, if it would have been open to
him to seek judicial review of the legality of his arrest.

7. Liability in contract

Neither the State nor public authorities enjoy any immunity in
respect of the ordinary law of contract. While it is true that certain
principles of administrative law operate to restrict the power of
public bodies to enter into legally binding contracts—thus, public
bodies may not contract so as to fetter their discretionary

---

[75] *Dunlop* v. *Woollahra M.C.* [1982] A.C. 158. But *cf. Garvey* v. *Ireland
(No. 2)*, High Court, December 19, 1979 where a plaintiff who had been
dismissed from his post as Garda Commissioner in breach of natural
justice recovered arrears of salary and exemplary damages.
[76] *Malone* v. *Metropolitan Police Commissioner* [1979] Ch. 344.

powers,[77] or, in some cases, so as to create an estoppel[78]—there are no special rules applicable to contracts entered into by public bodies. These matters are considered elsewhere.

8. Liability in quasi-contract[79]

The general rule here is that money paid voluntarily under a mistake of law—as opposed to mistake of fact—is not recoverable. The rigour of this rule is tempered by the fact that a mistake of law is sometimes represented to be a mistake of fact. Furthermore, the courts will often hold that the payment is not a voluntary one, and is thus recoverable, if the parties were not on equal terms, and the defendants were responsible for the mistake. It is this latter principle which enables the courts to hold public bodies liable to make restitution where the money is had and received by such a body *colore officii*.[80]

Thus in *Rogers* v. *Louth C.C.*[81] the Supreme Court held that the plaintiff was entitled to recover an excessive sum demanded *colore officii* by the defendants as the price of the redemption of an annuity due to them under the provisions of the Housing Act 1966.[82] The court held that the payment was not a "voluntary" one, for as Griffin J. explained:

> "The parties were not on equal terms. The defendants had the power, if they thought fit, to withold payment for the redemption of the annuity; they were prepared to allow the plaintiff to redeem it but only on the conditions imposed by them, which included exacting a payment in excess of that permitted by statute. The plaintiff [had no] reason to think that she was not liable to pay the sum demanded by the defendants for the redemption of the annuity. In my view, the defendants were primarily responsible for the mistake. . . . "[83]

The same principle holds true in the case of payments unlawfully

---

[77] See pp. 225–227.
[78] See pp. 216–218.
[79] See further, Goff and Jones, *The Law of Restitution*, (1980), Chaps. 3 and 9.
[80] *i.e.* where a public official demands payment of moneys by virtue of his office for a charge which the law enables him to demand and enforce.
[81] [1981] I.R. 265.
[82] The plaintiff was the personal representative of the deceased. A cottage had previously been vested in the deceased in fee simple free from incumbrances, but subject to annual annuity due to the defendants.
[83] [1981] I.R. at p. 271. See also *Dolan* v. *Neligan* [1967] I.R. 247.

demanded, *colore officii*, by a public body. Payments of this nature, such as taxes[84] or licence fees[85] are regarded as having been demanded under duress, so that whether the action is framed at common law or in equity, such payments are recoverable *in the absence of countervailing circumstances*. In *Murphy* v. *Attorney-General*[86] the Supreme Court permitted only limited recoupment of tax collected under a statute that had subsequently been declared to be unconstitutional on the grounds that it would now be inequitable to compel the State to make restitution. The State had been led to believe, by the protracted absence of a claim to the contrary, that it was legally and constitutionally entitled to spend the taxes thus collected. In the view of Henchy J.:

> "[T]he position had become so altered, the logistics of reparation so weighted and distorted by factors such as inflation and interest, the prima facie right of the taxpayers to be recouped so devalued by the fact that, as members of the community . . . they had benefited from the taxes thus collected, that it would be inequitable, unjust and unreal to expect the State to make full restitution."[87]

Thus, the court held that laches on the part of the general body of taxpayers, and altered circumstances, made it inequitable to compel restitution save to those taxpayers who had instituted proceedings challenging the constitutionality of the collection system. The court held that the right to recover taxes which were illegally collected could be quickly extinguished by laches. *Murphy* shows that, generally speaking, only limited recoupment of the moneys collected will be possible where taxes or levies have been illegally exacted.

---

[84] *Murphy* v. *Att.-Gen.* [1982] I.R. 241 at p. 317 *per* Henchy J.
[85] *Mason* v. *New South Wales* (1959) 102 C.L.R. 108; *Bell Bros. Property Ltd.* v. *Shire of Serpentine-Jarrahdale* (1969) 121 C.L.R. 137. But *cf. William Whitley Ltd.* v. *The King* (1909) 101 L.T. 741.
[86] [1982] I.R. 241. See also pp. 203–205.
[87] [1982] I.R. at p. 320.

13 The State in Litigation

1. Prerogative rights

Prerogative rights may be taken to mean "those rights and capacities which the King alone enjoys in contradistinction to others."[1] In Britain, the prerogative still covers a large and diverse bundle of rights, powers, privileges etc., most of which are exercised by the Crown on the advice of the responsible ministers.[2] In Ireland, much of the ground which the prerogative covers in Britain is regulated by the Constitution or by statute. However, a brief summary of the present status of what was historically an important source of public law is nonetheless of relevance.

It is very doubtful whether the prerogative survived the enactment of the Constitution of the Irish Free State in 1922. Prior to the decision of the Supreme Court in *Byrne* v. *Ireland*,[3] it had been generally assumed—although without much discussion—that at least some of the prerogative rights persisted in Ireland.[4] This view was based, in the first instance, upon Article 49.1 of the Constitution which provides that:

> "All powers, functions, rights and prerogatives whatsoever exercisable in or in respect of Saorstat Eireann immediately before the 11th. day of December 1936, whether in virtue of the Constitution then in force or otherwise, by the authority in which the executive power of Saorstat Eireann was then vested are hereby declared to belong to the people."

This provision makes the inquiry turn on the antecedent question of whether the prerogative existed in Saorstat Eireann before

[1] Blackstone, *Commentaries*, i, 239. See also Wade, "Procedure and Prerogative in Public Law" (1985) 101 L.Q.R. 180.
[2] Wade, *Administrative Law* (Oxford, 1982) at p. 49.
[3] [1972] I.R. 241. See also *Webb* v. *Ireland*, High Court, July 29, 1986.
[4] See *e.g. Re Maloney, a bankrupt* [1926] I.R. 202; *Galway County Council* v. *Minister for Finance* [1931] I.R. 215; *Re Irish Mutual Employers Association Ltd.* [1955] I.R. 176.

December 11, 1936. The significance of this date lies in the fact
that it was the day when the Irish Free State Constitution was
amended to extirpate the King (formerly the head of state, in
whom all executive authority was vested.[5]) Prior to *Byrne*, it had
been assumed that the presence of the King drew with it the
prerogative. This argument was rejected by the majority in *Byrne*,
principally on the grounds that, first, the King's powers were
confined to those specified in the Constitution of 1922, and were
not the same as those which he enjoyed under the constitution of
the United Kingdom, and, secondly, that Article 2 of the
Constitution (which stated that all powers of government were
derived from the people) negated the idea that any power could
derive from the Crown.

It is unnecessary to pursue this issue, since it is very largely of
academic interest only, in view of the alternative *ratio* put forward
in *Byrne's* case, namely, that irrespective of the legal status of the
prerogative as such, a particular prerogative right could not have
survived if it was in conflict with the Constitution, a proposition
which, in any event, was beyond controversy. In *Byrne*[6], it was held
that state immunity from tort was an example of such an
"unconstitutional prerogative." It has also been established that
since the Central Fund of the Irish Exchequer does not have the
character of a royal fund it cannot attract the prerogative of
priority of debts due to the State in the case of an insolvency.[7] As
against this, certain other prerogatives have been given an
impeccable republican pedigree. Thus, in *Byrne*, Walsh J. rationalised the State's exemption from statute as a rule which although
"sometimes called a prerogative right" it is in fact "nothing more
than a reservation, or exception, introduced for the public
benefit, and equally applicable to all governments."[8] These
remarks were anticipated, in the case of public interest immunity
(or "executive privilege") from disclosure of documents, as early
as 1925. Dealing with the suggestion that only the Crown could
claim executive privilege, Meredith J. remarked:

> "This privilege has roots in the general conception of State
> interests and the functions of the Courts of Justice, which
> make it independent of the particular type of constitution

---

[5] See Arts. 41, 51, 55, 60 and 68 of the Irish Free State Constitution.
[6] See now *Webb* v. *Ireland*, High Court, July 29, 1986 and Addendum.
[7] *Re P.C., an Arranging Debtor* [1939] I.R. 306; *Re Irish Employers Mutual
Insurance Association Ltd.* [1955] I.R. 176.
[8] [1972] I.R. at p. 287, quoting from *United States* v. *Hoar* (1821) 6 Mason
311.

under the body of law which recognises that principle is administered."[9]

The net result of these decisions is that even if, as is doubtful, the prerogative does exist, it is unlikely to have much practical effect. The exercise of prerogative rights by the Government is almost certainly subject to judicial review,[10] and, in any event, it is only the very rare case where such an issue will be raised[11].

2. Liability of the State and Ministers

The purpose of this part is first to outline the relationship between the State, ministers and the civil service as these have been created (the word is used advisedly as some artificiality is involved here) by the courts in the context of tort and contract litigation.

There are two bases to the central executive organ's capacity to sue and capacity to be sued, and the relationship between these two bases has not yet been clarified. The first basis is the Ministers and Secretaries Act 1924, s.2(1) of which provides:

> "Each of the Ministers, heads of the respective departments of State . . . shall be a corporation sole under his style or name aforesaid . . . and shall have perpetual succession and an official seal . . . and may sue . . . and be sued."

The purposes of making each of the Ministers a corporation sole have been explained as follows by Sullivan P. in *Carolan* v. *Minister for Defence*[12]:

---

[9] *Leen* v. *President of the Executive Council* [1926] I.R. 456 at p. 463.

[10] This is now the position in Britain: *Council of Civil Service Unions* v. *Minister for Civil Service* [1985] A.C. 374.

[11] The constitutionality of many individual prerogatives must be doubtful. For example, the prerogative to declare war may be taken to be inconsistent with Art. 28.3.1 (which reserves this power to the Dail); the prerogative of mercy has been overtaken by the right of pardon and remission of punishment vested in the President by Art. 13.6 and the prerogative of interning enemy aliens is probably at odds with the guarantee of personal liberty enshrined in Art. 40.4.1. Some statutory provisions envisage the survival of certain prerogatives, *e.g.* Companies Act 1963, s.377(4) (survival of prerogative power to grant letters patent).

[12] [1927] I.R. 62. A distinct point should be noted: it seems that the Government, as such, is not a legal person. This, it is suggested, is the reason for the practice of suing all individual Ministers of the Government in cases involving a Government action: see *e.g. Boland* v. *An Taoiseach* [1974] I.R. 338 at p. 339; *Doyle* v. *An Taoiseach*, Supreme Court, March 29, 1985.

"1. to secure continuity of title, and obviate the need for the
transfer of State property, rights and obligations from a
Minister to his successor; 2. to secure that persons contract-
ing with the Government through any of its Departments
should have the ordinary remedy of action available in case of
breach of contract. . . . "[13]

Comment is unnecessary on the first of these functions. The
second of these functions enables the Minister to be sued in
contract in the ordinary way, rather than, as formerly, having to
proceed by way of a petition of right under the Petition of Right
(Ireland) Act 1873. It is, of course, as in private law, a
precondition of liability, that the contract was made by a person
(usually a civil servant) who can be regarded as having acted as
agent of the minister. The question of agency featured in *Grenham*
v. *Minister of Defence*[14] in which Hanna J. held that army officers,
who hired motor cars for military purposes, were not agents of the
Minister so as to make him liable on the contract. This raises the
more general question of whether—given that a civil servant's
contract of employment is with the State rather than the individual
Minister—an action arising out of a contract made by a civil
servant should be brought against the State or against the Minister
for the Department in which the civil servant worked. The passage
quoted from *Carolan* suggests that it is the Minister; but the
reasoning of *Grenham* and the tenor of *Byrne* v. *Ireland* points in
the opposite direction. The difference is not of great significance,
but it does mean that until the question is resolved the prudent
plaintiff will join both the State and the relevant Minister as
defendants.[14]

Byrne v. *Ireland* is the basis of liability in tort. Until *Byrne* the
general rule was that neither the State nor any of its organs could
be liable for an action in tort. Historically, the British Crown was
immune from actions in tort (whether directly, or vicariously,
through the behaviour of Crown servants)[15] both because of the
principle that the King could do no wrong and because of the
continued application in the area of tort of the King's disability to
command himself to appear before his own courts. In *Carolan* v.
Minister for Defence, the High Court stated that section 2 of the
Ministers and Secretaries Act 1924 (quoted above) was intended
not to alter this position because its objective was only to vest

---

[13] [1927] I.R. at p. 69.
[14] For the position in tort, see p. 394.
[15] See, *e.g. Murphy* v. *Soady* [1903] 2 I.R. 213, where the Commissioners of
Public Works were permitted to invoke the Crown immunity in an
action for negligence.

existing liabilities in the Ministers, and not to create any new responsibilities.[16]

The evident injustice of this situation was ameliorated in particular areas by statute. For instance, section 59 of the Civil Liability Act 1961 provides that where a wrong is committed through the use of a motor vehicle belonging to the State, and driven by a person acting in the course of his employment, then the Minister for Finance is liable.[17]

Although the Minister for Justice had announced in 1962 that the general principle of state immunity from actions in tort was to be uprooted by statute[18] (as has happened elsewhere), it was left to the Supreme Court in *Byrne* v. *Ireland* to introduce this change. Walsh and Budd JJ. (who delivered the two majority judgments) agreed that even if the State had been internally sovereign, this did not necessarily mean that it was immune from actions before its courts, and in fact, such a result was explicitly excluded by certain provisions of the Constitution. For instance, Article 42.4 declares that the State was to provide for free primary education. This sub-article carried the necessary implication that if the State failed in this obligation, it could be sued in respect of such continued default. Article 40.3 guaranteed the citizen the right of access to the courts and the right to sue in respect of a justiciable controversy.[19] Moreover, it was emphasised that there was a

---

[16] In fact a perusal of the *Dail Debates* reveals that the intention was to abolish the State's immunity. See the comments of the Attorney-General (Hugh Kennedy, subsequently Chief Justice) at *Dail Debates*, Vol. 5, col. 1498 (December 16, 1923), cited in Kelly, *The Irish Constitution* (Dublin, 1984) at p. 699.

[17] Originally Road Traffic Act 1933, s.116. The Minister for Finance is not liable under this provision where the state employee is not acting within the scope of his employment: *Murray* v. *Minister for Finance*, Supreme Court, April 22, 1982 (off-duty policeman). Other examples of legislative abrogation of the immunity in particular areas of the law are to be found in s.64 of the Workman's Compensation Act 1934; the Garda Siochana Acts 1941–1945, and ss.3, 100 and 118 of the Factories Act 1955.

[18] Programme of Law Reform 1962, p. 7. See also *Dail Debates*, Vol. 215, col. 1858 (May 20, 1965).

[19] *Macauley* v. *Minister for Posts and Telegraphs* [1966] I.R. 345; *O'Brien* v. *Keogh* [1972] I.R. 144. It would seem possible to enact legislation which would in some way modify the effects of *Byrne*. Such legislation might provide, for example, that injured parties could only sue the Minister for Finance and not the State, or that a special limitation period would apply to the State. Such alternative arrangements would not impinge on the citizen's right to litigate a justiciable controversy, or to sue and recover compensation in respect of injury to person or property. But it is doubtful whether legislation which sought to tamper with the

critical difference between the State in Ireland and the Crown in the United Kingdom which sufficed to explain why the former was liable in tort while at common law the Crown was set above the law. The difference is that whereas in the United Kingdom, the Crown personifies the State and is the sovereign authority, in Ireland it is the people, and not the State, who are sovereign.

The particular importance of *Byrne* arose from the well-established rule that a Minister was not vicariously liable for the acts of civil servants in his Department, as both were employees of the State.[20] Although this may be regarded as carrying constitutional nicety too far, it was a doctrine which meant that the plaintiff in *Byrne* (who had suffered injury by falling into a trench left in an unsafe condition by the negligence of employees of the Department of Posts and Telegraphs) was barred from suing the Minister for Posts and Telegraphs. Whilst opening up State liability, *Byrne* confirmed the traditional rule that civil servants and their Minister are fellow employees of the State:

> "All . . . persons employed in the various Departments of the Government and the other Departments of State, whether they be Civil Servants or not, are in the service of the State and . . . the State is liable for damages done by such person in carrying out the affairs of the State so long as that person is acting within the terms of his employment."[21]

Two procedural points which apply when the State is involved in litigation (whether as plaintiff or defendant) should be noted. The first is that the Attorney-General should be joined with the State. As Walsh J. said in *Byrne* (dealing with the case of the State as defendant):

> "[The] power or right to defend itself is one which can be exercised by the State only by or on the authority of the Government by virtue of the provisions of Article 49, s.2, of

principles enunciated in *Byrne*—such as legislation placing an upper limit on the quantum of damages recoverable in an action against the State—would survive constitutional challenge. Walsh J. had reserved these questions in *Byrne*. See further Osborough, "The Demise of the State's Immunity in Tort" (1973) 8 Ir.Jur.(n.s.) 275; "The State's Tortious Liability: Further Reflections on *Byrne* v. *Ireland*" (1976) 11 Ir.Jur.(n.s.) 11, 279.

[20] *Carolan* v. *Minister for Defence* [1927] I.R. 62.

[21] [1972] I.R. at pp. 287–289. Budd J. made similar observations.

the Constitution. If in such a case it is the Attorney-General's opinion that the Government should authorise the defence by the State of the claim brought against it, the defence is a matter of public interest and is properly financed out of public monies. If the Government does not wish to authorise the defence by the State, then the Attorney-General would not defend the case either. In all such cases it is my opinion that the correct procedure would be to sue the State and to join the Attorney-General in order to effect service upon the Attorney-General for both parties. In effect the Attorney-General would be joined in a representative capacity as the law officer of State designated by the Constitution. If the claim should succeed, judgment would be against the State and not against the Attorney-General."[22]

The second point is that where a claim is brought against the State *as such*, it does not suffice merely to join the Attorney-General. In *Murphy* v. *Attorney-General*[23] the plaintiffs had sought the recovery of monies collected by the State under the provisions of the Income Tax Act 1967 which had been earlier found to be unconstitutional. Henchy J. said of the plaintiffs' contention that the State was a constructive trustee of such monies:

"For such a claim to be valid in form and enforceable in effect, the State should have been joined as defendant. Yet the only defendant is the Attorney-General. He was made defendant merely in compliance with Order 60 of the Rules of the Superior Courts, 1962, which ensures that the Attorney-General must either be a party, or be given an opportunity of appearing, whenever the proceedings raise a question as to the validity of a law having regard to the provisions of the Constitution. But even when the Attorney-General is made a party in such proceedings, the jurisdiction of his office is such that an order may not be made against him which would necessarily bind the State. In the present case, the plaintiffs' case for the recovery of income tax collected under the constitutionally invalid sections required the State to be made a defendant."[24]

---

[22] *Ibid.* at p. 289. See also *Sheil* v. *Att.-Gen.* (1928) 62 I.L.T.S.J. 199.
[23] [1982] I.R. 241.
[24] *Ibid.* at pp. 315–316. The Attorney-General did not take this point.

Relationship between Byrne and the Ministers and Secretaries Act 1924

Unfortunately, *Byrne* v. *Ireland*, like many other epoch-making decisions, leaves many questions unanswered, in particular, its relationship with the existing basis for suing the central state authority (*i.e.* the right to sue Ministers of State created by section 2 of the 1924 Act) is unclear. Reference has already been made to one question raised by *Byrne*, namely, whether breach of contract actions should be brought against the State or the responsible Minister. A similar question arises in relation to tort actions. In the first place it is quite clear that where the tort was actually committed by a civil servant, the Minister cannot usually be held to be responsible. It was probably this rule which rendered *Byrne* necessary in the first place. As was said by Sullivan P. in *Carolan* v. *Minister for Defence*:

> "A public officer having the management of some branch of Government business is not responsible for the wrongful acts of a subordinate in the same employment as himself . . . [The Oireachtas did not intend to] create by [s.2(1)] a liability in each Minister for all the wrongful acts or defaults of all the persons employed in his Department."[25]

Yet the judge acknowledged that one of the functions of section 2 was to enable the Minister to be sued "in his corporate capacity for a wrongful act done by him as Minister, or by his orders or directions." What this probably means is that the Minister cannot be held *vicariously* liable for the torts of his civil servants, but this does not affect his *direct* liability in tort. There is an important distinction between the liability of a Minister for the acts of his civil servants and vicarious liability for the torts committed by them. If a plaintiff contends that the Minister *ordered or authorised* the civil servant to commit the action complained of, or that the Minister was careless in selecting or supervising the employee, then this is an allegation of direct or personal liability on the part of the Minister and the action can proceed under section 2(1) of the 1924 Act.[26] On the other hand, vicarious liability arises when the law attaches liability to the employer for the employee's torts even where the employer is not personally at fault. But as Sullivan P. explained in *Carolan*, Ministers and civil servants are fellow employees of the State, and the Minister cannot be made

---

[25] [1927] I.R. at pp. 68–69.

[26] In cases of direct liability, it is the Minister's negligence which is the basis of the action, and it is not crucial that the employee in question was negligent. On this general question see *Carmarthenshire County Council* v. *Lewis* [1955] A.C. 549; *Curley* v. *Mannion* [1965] I.R. 543.

vicariously liable for the torts of his civil servants. Such actions, therefore proceed against the State under the *Byrne* v. *Ireland* doctrine and not against the Minister.

However, the historical constitutional principle that, if the plaintiff prefers, the responsible public servant or ministerial incumbent may be sued personally, in place of the State or the Minister as corporation sole, remains correct. Thus, in *Lynch* v. *Fitzgerald*[27] the detectives who had unlawfully killed the son of the plaintiff during the course of suppressing a riot were found to be personally liable in an action taken under the Fatal Accidents Act 1846.

It is worth emphasising that the Minister, *qua* corporation sole is a separate legal entity from the incumbent at any particular time. *Sheil* v. *Attorney-General*[28] is a good illustration of this principle. The plaintiff had been a train-bearer to the former Master of the Rolls, and upon the abolition of that judicial office in 1924, he was granted a declaration against the Attorney-General to the effect that he was entitled to compensation under Article 10 of the Anglo-Irish Treaty 1921, to be paid out of moneys voted by the Oireachtas. Costs of the action were awarded against the Attorney-General, and the plaintiff sought to enforce this part of the judgment against Mr. John Costello, the then holder of the office. The original judgment was then rectified to make it clear that the costs were also entitled to come from funds appropriated by the Oireachtas.

The distinction between the office and the office-holder is also significant in contract actions. In *Kenny* v. *Cosgrave*[29] the President of the Executive Council had told an employer whose workers were on strike that it was essential that the strikers' demands be resisted. The President promised that the Executive Council would also indemnify him against any financial loss which resulted from this resistance. The action failed before the Supreme Court on a number of grounds,[30] which included the

---

[27] [1938] I.R. 382. This case was, of course, decided in the pre-*Byrne* era. And, for the reasons outlined in *Carolan's* case, the plaintiff could not the Minister for Justice, as the Minister and the detectives were both fellow servants of the State and thus the doctrine of *respondeat superior* could not apply. See also *Liversidge* v. *Anderson* [1942] A.C. 206 at pp. 210–211 (action for false imprisonment against British Home Secretary).

[28] (1928) 62 I.L.T.S.J. 199 (referred to in Casey, *The Office of the Attorney-General in Ireland* (Dublin, 1980) at pp. 161–162).

[29] [1927] I.R. 517.

[30] The other main ground was that a member of the Executive could not by contract fetter his discretion to act in the public interest. See further pp. 225–227 and pp. 407–408.

fact that Mr Cosgrave had been sued personally and neither a minister nor a civil servant can be held *personally* liable on a State contract.

Liability of Judges, Gardai and members of the Defence Forces

(i) Judges. At common law judges enjoyed immunity from suit in respect of judicial acts.[31] It may be asked whether this common law immunity is compatible with constitutional principles and has survived the decision in *Byrne*. The immunity is founded on public policy. As Lord Salmon explained in *Sutcliffe* v. *Thackrah*:

> "It is well settled that judges, barristers, solicitors, jurors and witnesses enjoy an absolute immunity in respect of any civil action being brought against them in respect of anything they say or do in court during the course of a trial. . . . The law recognises that, on balance of convenience, public policy demands that they shall have such an immunity. It is of great public importance that they shall all perform their functions free from fear that disgruntled and possibly impecunious persons who have lost their cause or been convicted may subsequently harrass them with litigation."[32]

But given that the State is required by Article 40.3 of the Constitution and by its laws to defend and vindicate the personal rights of the citizen, in so far as it is practicable to do so—and in view of the fact that the right to litigate a justiciable controversy is such a personal right[33]—it would not seem that considerations of public policy or administrative convenience could prevail as against this constitutional right to litigate or to recover damages.

As against this, it is well settled that the most fundamental rule of constitutional interpretation is that the Constitution must be read as a whole. And immunity from suit in respect of judicial acts would appear to be latent in Articles 34 and 35, which guarantee the administration of justice by judges and judicial independence.[34] It is probable that the constitutional right to litigate a justiciable controversy will have to give way to this judicial immunity from suit. However, it must be said that this matter awaits a definitive judicial resolution.

---

[31] *Tugham* v. *Craig* [1918] 1 I.R. 245; *Macauley* v. *Wyse-Power* (1943) 77 I.L.T.R. 61.

[32] [1974] A.C. 727 at p. 757.

[33] *O'Brien* v. *Keogh* [1972] I.R. 144.

[34] *Cf.* The discussion of this question in the context of summary trial in contempt cases in *The State (D.P.P.)* v. *Walsh* [1981] I.R. 412.

(ii) The Gardai. Such authority as exists suggests that Gardai are servants of the State. It would appear to follow that the State is responsible under the doctrine of *respondeat superior* for the wrongful acts of Gardai in accordance with the principles enunciated in *Byrne*.[35]

(iii) Members of the Defence Forces. Members of the Defence Forces are regarded as servants of the State for the purposes of the *Byrne* decision, and in the series of cases which followed this decision, the State did not attempt to dispute this point.[36]

3. State exemption from statute

As usually stated, this exemption means that the State is not "bound" (*i.e.* affected to its disadvantage) by a statute unless it is referred to either expressly or by necessary implication. An early example is provided by *Galway County Council* v. *Minister for Finance*[37] where one of the issues was whether the defendant Minister was free to set off as against the plaintiff's claim, an overpayment which he had made to them eight years earlier. The County Council submitted in reply that the Minister's claim was not statute-barred. Johnson J. was unimpressed by this argument:

> "[T]he Minister relies on prerogative rights and contends that the sub-section has no applicability to a claim such as the present, there being no indication in the subsection that it was the intention of the Legislature to bind the Crown or the State. There has been no doubt and it has not been argued in the present case to the contrary, that the prerogative and prerogative right can be relied upon by the Irish Free State, and is part of the law of the land, . . . I can see nothing in [the subsection] that suggests that it was intended to have any

---

[35] *Dowman* v. *Ireland* [1986] I.L.R.M. 111 and *McKevitt* v. *Ireland*, Supreme Court, April 18, 1986.

[36] Osborough, "Further Reflections on *Byrne* v. *Ireland* II (1976)" Ir.Jur.(n.s.) 279 at pp. 292–297. See also *Kearney* v. *Ireland*, High Court, March 13, 1986 (State vicariously responsible for unconstitutional acts of prison officers).

[37] [1931] I.R. 215.

[38] *Ibid.* at p. 232. See now s.3(1) of the Statute of Limitations 1957, which provides that the Statute shall apply to "proceedings by or against a State authority in the same manner as if that State authority were a private individual." See also, *Dail Debates*, Vol. 318, cols. 240–247 (February 20, 1980) (restriction on application to State of Landlord and Tenant (Amendment) Act 1980).

applicability to the Crown or the State and, I think, therefore, that the defendant is entitled to rely on this set-off...."[38]

In *Irish Land Commission* v. *Ruane*[39] the High Court applied the rule that the exemption may be excluded by necessary implication. The statutory provision in question in that case, the Increase of Rent and Mortgage Interest (Restriction) Act 1923, restricted the right of the landlord to recover possession unless "the dwelling house is reasonably required for the purpose of the execution of the duties... of any Government Department or... any local authority or statutory undertaking." Both Johnston and Gavin Duffy JJ. appear to have assumed[40] that this provision only applied where the Department, local authority or statutory undertaking was the landlord, and, accordingly, that the provision would be redundant if it were excluded in the case of State property. However, in *Fitzsimons* v. *Menkin*,[41] a majority of the Supreme Court ruled that the provision was of general application, and would apply even in the case of a private landlord. Although such a situation would seem likely to be rare, the Supreme Court ruled in the later case of *Cork County Council* v. *Commissioners of Public Works*[42] that this change of interpretation destroyed the premise on which the judgment in *Ruane* was founded, and this in turn meant that the State was exempt from the application of the 1923 Act in the usual way. The question of whether the State was bound by a rating enactment, the Local Government (Rates on Small Dwellings) Act 1928 had also arisen in the *Cork County Council* case. A majority of the Supreme Court rejected the argument that it was a necessary implication in the construction of the Act that it should be held to bind the State merely because, in the words of O'Byrne J., "the opposite construction would have the effect of leaving houses free from liability." The court accordingly ruled the houses owned by the defendant Commissioners were exempt from rates.

All three members of the Supreme Court accepted that the exemption of the State from the application of statutes had survived the enactment of the Constitution. However, there are clear hints in the judgments of O'Byrne and Black JJ. that this exemption could be rationalised in terms of a principle of statutory construction rather than a privilege derived from

---

[39] [1938] I.R. 148.

[40] Certainly this was the view taken of their judgments by the Supreme Court in *Cork County Council* v. *Commissioners of Public Works* [1945] I.R. 561.

[41] [1938] I.R. 805.

[42] [1945] I.R. 561.

concepts of a regal personality.[43] Walsh J. was to fasten on to this approach in *Byrne* v. *Ireland*,[44] and he quoted with approval from the judgment of Story J. in *United States* v. *Hoar*:

> "*But independently of any doctrine founded on the notion of prerogative, the same construction of statutes of this sort ought to prevail, founded upon the legislative intention.* Where the government is not expressly or by necessary implication included, it ought to be clear from the nature of the mischiefs to be redressed, or the language used, that the government itself was in contemplation of the legislature, before a court of law would be authorised to put such an interpretation before any statute. In general, acts of the legislature are meant to regulate and direct the acts and rights of citizens; and in most cases the reasoning applicable to them applies with very different, and often contrary force to the government itself. It appears to me, therefore, to be a safe rule founded in the principles of the common law, that the general words of a statute ought not to include the government, or affect its rights, unless that construction be clear and undisputable upon the text of the act."[45]

Leaving aside the question of the prerogative, this passage also throws light on an important issue of substance. In the first place, *United States* v. *Hoar* was decided in 1821, at a time when statute law was rarer than today and when governmental actions were exceptional and in an entirely different category from those of individuals. This latter point is reflected in Story J.'s remark that "the reasoning applicable to the acts and rights of citizens applies "with very different and often contrary force to the government itself." Should it not follow that, in modern times when governmental actions are commonplace, that the state exemption should

---

[43] Thus, Black J. observed: "Much time was devoted to discussing the true nature of this right and to combating the supposition that so far as it still exists, it is inseperable from the institution of kingship. If that were so, one would not expect to find such a right recognised for over a century by the Courts of the United States of America where the institution of kingship has no existence" ([1945] I.R. at p. 587).

[44] [1972] I.R. 241.

[45] The sentence in italics had been omitted by O'Byrne J. when he was quoting from the judgment of Story J. in *Hoar*. Walsh J. described this sentence as "vital," because it rationalised the principle expressed by Story J.

only apply if the statutory provision is appropriate to attract it?[46] This argument draws some support from the earlier part of the quoted passage where Story J. said that the State should be bound, not only where it is expressly or implicitly included, but also if it is clear from the purposes of the Act or its language that the Legislature intended the State to be included. In other words, the question of the applicability of statutes to the State should be determined *solely* by reference to standard principles of statutory construction. This is a slightly different test from the contemporary "necessary implication" standard, because the latter is rooted in a common law presumption *against* the application of statutes to the State.[47] Were this presumption to be dispensed with, the State's exemption from the application of statutes would be thereby narrowed as a result. Such a consequence would be more consistent with the rule of law, and the courts' general approach to constitutional issues with their emphasis on individual rights and justice.[48] However the authorities such as *Ruane* and the *Cork County Council* case have tended to adopt the wider view of the State's exemption from the application of statutes, usually[49] without considering the narrower approach advocated here. To adopt the narrower approach would involve a departure, although one which finds support in the judgment of Story J. in *United States* v. *Hoar* as approved by Walsh J. in *Byrne*.

The final question relates to what is meant by "the State" in the present context. In view of its origin in the prerogative, it includes the State and Ministers, but excludes local authorities and formally independent bodies such as state sponsored bodies. However, administrative bodies such as the Commissioners of Public Works

---

[46] Professor Street has demonstrated that in the 16th century, where the statute touched upon the rights of subjects generally then the Crown would normally be bound unless it affected the prerogative rights of the King. See H. A. Street, *Government Liability; a Comparative Study* (Cambridge, 1953) Chap. vi; P. W. Hogg, *Liability of the Crown in Australia, New Zealand and the United Kingdom* (Melbourne, 1971).

[47] See *e.g. per* Jessel M.R. in *Postmaster General* v. *Bonham* (1878) 10 Ch.D. 595 at p. 601 where he said that one must find "clear and strong words" to alter the prerogative exemption.

[48] Keane J. has suggested extra-judicially that this exemption may violate the constitutional guarantee of equality contained in Article 40.1. See Keane, "The 1963 Planning Act—Twenty Years On" (1983) 5 D.U.L.J.(n.s.) 92.

[49] But *cf.* Johnston J. in *Galway County Council* v. *Minister for Finance* [1931] I.R. 215.

have been permitted to rely on the exemption where such bodies are dealing with State property.[50]

4. Privilege against the disclosure of official documents

Traditionally it was the law that Ministers could not be compelled by court order to produce documents for inspection or even to disclose the existence of a document. This applied in all litigation, irrespective of whether the Minister or the State was a party to it. All that was necessary for the exercise of this privilege was an affadavit claiming it, signed by the responsible Minister or one of his senior civil servants. Plainly there were two elements to this privilege:

(i) There was a public interest in maintaining the confidentiality of certain official documents;
(ii) It was for the responsible Minister, and not the court, to decide whether this interest outweighed the public interest in the fair administration of justice.

As has been remarked, " . . . the newly independent State, having shaken off the yolk of the Crown, embraced with enthusiasm many of its privileges."[51] The privilege was invoked to protect communications between the Executive Council and the Shaw Commission which investigated the destruction of Ballyheigue Castle[52]; advices and minutes given to the Minister for Local Government in regard to the Electoral (Amendment) Act 1959[53] and, in a prosecution for "showing for gain an indecent and profane performance" the instructions given by their superiors to the detectives who watched the play.[54]

The law was authoritatively changed in *Murphy* v. *Dublin*

---

[50] *Irish Land Commission* v. *Ruane* [1938] I.R. 148; *Cork County Council* v. *Commissioners of Public Works* [1945] I.R. 561.
[51] Russell, "A Privilege of the State" (1967) 2 Ir.Jur.(n.s.) 88. This prescient article reviewed the former law and predicted its demise.
[52] *Leen* v. *President of the Executive Council* [1926] I.R. 456.
[53] *O'Donovan* v. *Minister for Local Government* [1961] I.R. 114.
[54] *Att.-Gen.* v. *Simpson* [1959] I.R. 335. In *Kenny* v. *Minister for Defence* (1942) Ir.Jur.Rep. 81 (an action in contract concerning the construction of army huts), Maguire P. observed that the Minister was entitled to claim privilege in respect of "documents of a confidential nature." In more recent times a prison governor was allowed to claim privilege in respect of confidential information concerning a planned prison escape: see *The State (Comerford)* v. *Governor of Mountjoy Prison* [1981] I.L.R.M. 86.

Corporation,[55] a case which arose in the wake of the objections
raised by the plaintiff to a proposed compulsory purchase order in
respect of his lands. A public inquiry was held in accordance with
the usual procedure, and the planning inspector sent a report of
the proceedings to the Minister. In dealing with the Minister's
claim for privilege in respect of the report, Walsh J. stated:

"Under the Constitution the administration of justice is
committed solely to the judiciary in the exercise of their
powers . . . Power to compel the attendance of witnesses and
the production of evidence is an inherent part of the judicial
power of government of the State and is the ultimate
safeguard of justice in the State. If . . . conflict arises during
the exercise of judicial power then, in my view, it is the
judicial power which will decide which public interest shall
prevail. This does not mean that the court will always decide
that the interest of the litigant shall prevail. It is for the court
to decide which is the superior interest in the circumstances
of the particular case and to determine the matter accordingly."[56]

Thus the courts still retain a discretion to preserve the confidential
nature of official documents in the public interest, but this matter
may not be constitutionally remitted to a non-judicial personage.[57]
That, of course, is not to say that the courts will not be reluctant to
overrule official claims for privilege, especially in sensitive areas
concerning the security or safety of the State[58]. But as Walsh J.
remarked:

"It may well be that it would be rare or infrequent for a court
after its own examination, to arrive at a different conclusion
from that expressed by the Minister, but that is a far remove
from accepting without question the judgment of the
Minister."[59]

---

[55] [1972] I.R. 215. See too *O'Leary* v. *Minister for Industry and Commerce*
[1966] I.R. 676 and *Dolan* v. *Neligan* [1967] I.R. 247.
[56] [1972] I.R. at pp. 233–234.
[57] In contrast, note the late S. A. de Smith's view that judges are poorly
equipped to hold the balance between these two aspects of the public
interest; de Smith, *op. cit.*, p. 40, n. 57.
[58] See, *e.g. Comerford's* case, n. 47 *supra* and *People* v. *Ferguson*, Court of
Criminal Appeal, October 27, 1975.
[59] [1972] I.R. at 236. See also *Geraghty* v. Minister for Local Government
[1975] I.R. 300, *Folens and Co.* v. *Minister for Education* [1981] I.L.R.M.
121 and *Incorporated Law Society of Ireland* v. *Minister for Justice*, High
Court, December 13, 1985.

McWilliam J. made a similar point in *Hunt* v. *Roscommon Vocational Education Committee*,[60] where the substantive action involved a claim for wrongful dismissal by a former headmaster of a vocational school. The Minister for Education claimed privilege in respect of documents containing the opinions expressed by individual civil servants on the case. The judge observed that the claim for privilege depended on whether there was "a likelihood of injury to the State or the public service by the production of the documents". This interest had to be balanced against that of the fair administration of justice, and the task of the court was to decide as between the merits of these competing interests. As far as the instant case was concerned, the claim of privilege failed, as it had not even been alleged that disclosure of the documents would be detrimental to the public interest. Nor was it any answer to say that the civil service administration might be adversely affected if there was an appreciation by officers of the Department that their memoranda might subsequently be read out in court.

The procedure to be followed in adjudicating upon a claim for privilege is a most important matter. In the first place, where a document is relevant, the burden of proving that it is privileged rests on the State. It may be possible for the court to decide the claim without an inspection.[61] However, before any inspection is ordered, the affidavit must be clear and must sustain at least a prima facie case that the documents are privileges. In a recent case McWilliam J. complained that to ask the court "to examine all these documents under the circumstances of the present case seems to me to be getting very close to asking the Court to prepare ... the affidavit of discovery."[62] In most cases it will be necessary for the court to inspect the documents in order to decide whether to order discovery.

There are four further points which require elaboration.

---

[60] High Court, May 1, 1981.

[61] See generally *Murphy* at pp. 234–235. It has been said that any interested person and not just the State may assert a claim for immunity; the point could even be taken by a court of its own motion. See *Rodgers* v. *Secretary of State for Home Department* [1973] A.C. 388 at pp. 400, 406, 408, 412.

[62] *Hunt* v. *Roscommon V.E.C.*, High Court, May 1, 1981. See also *Murphy* at p. 237.

(A) No "class" grounds. There is one significant point on which modern Irish law differs from that prevailing in Britain. In Britain, the courts are still prepared, in certain circumstances, to allow privilege in respect of a document not only on the grounds of its own particular content, but also on the grounds that it belongs to a class of documents, some or most of whose members will have a confidential content. The thinking underlying "class privilege" is that official documents of certain categories are so sensitive that they would not be fearlessly and candidly written if there was any possibility that they might be made public.[63] However, the concept of privilege on class grounds was rejected by the Supreme Court in Murphy as inconsistent with the principle of judicial independence enshrined in Article 34.1.

(B) Criminal proceedings. In *Murphy* v. *Dublin Corporation*, Walsh J. had been careful to refrain from expressing any opinion as to the scope of executive privilege in criminal proceedings. But it was this very point which was at issue in *D.P.P. (Hanley)* v. *Holly*.[64] At a hearing in the District Court of a charge of unlawful assault, the defence called upon the investigating Garda to produce his report of the incident. Privilege was claimed by the State, and this claim was upheld by the District Justice.

Keane J. held that this conclusion was incorrect. In the light of the principles enunciated by Walsh J. in *Murphy*, he was satisfied that a general claim of privilege in the case of police communications failed "because as a class their admission would be against the public interest is no longer sustainable." To succeed it would have been necessary for the Garda authorities to advance a specific ground of possible damage to the public interest which might result from the disclosure of such documents, although Keane J. remarked that in the circumstances of the case it seemed "highly unlikely that any such ground exists."[65]

In *People* v. *Eccles*[66] the Court of Criminal Appeal was on the other side of the line from *Holly* in that it ruled that, in the exceptional circumstances of the case, the disclosure of confidential Garda information would have been contrary to the public interest. The defendants were charged with capital murder (and

[63] *e.g. Burmah Oil* v. *Bank of England* [1980] A.C. 1090.
[64] [1984] I.L.R.M. 149. This result had been anticipated by an academic commentator: O'Connor, "The Privilege of Non-Disclosure and Informers" (1980) 15 Ir.Jur.(n.s.) 111. See also *People* v. *Ferguson*, Court of Criminal Appeal, October 27, 1975.
[65] Keane J. regarded *Att.-Gen.* v. *Simpson* [1959] I.R. 105 as having been impliedly overruled by *Murphy* v. *Dublin Corporation*.
[66] Court of Criminal Appeal, February 10, 1986.

other serious offences). They had been arrested under section 30 of the Offences against the State Act 1939, and an extension order had been served on them permitting their detention for up to forty-eight hours. The Chief Superintendent who had caused the extension order to be served on the defendants claimed that he had received information which suggested that one of the defendants should be detained for a further twenty-four hour period. The Chief Superintendent claimed privilege when asked to reveal the source of this information. Hederman J. ruled that the Special Criminal Court was correct to uphold the claim of privilege: "The Chief Superintendent was entitled to claim privilege in respect of both the source, and the nature of the source, of the sensitive, confidential information he received in respect of the applicant. Normally a member of the Garda Siochane cannot claim privilege in respect of information received from a fellow member of the force simply by virtue of its being such a communication. The circumstances in this case, however, were exceptional. [Privilege was claimed] on the ground that ... 'it would be dangerous to identify whether the source was civilian or police.' This he was clearly entitled to do."

(C) Is the privilege confined to the State? In *Murphy's* case, Walsh J. emphasised the point that "executive privilege only applied to a Minister who was exercising "the executive powers of government of the State." If this observation is taken at its face value, it would appear to restrict the immunity to Ministers exercising their executive function.[67] But if the immunity has now (in fact, since *Leen's* case in 1926) been severed from the prerogative, and put on the basis of public interest, it seems arbitrary and unnecessary to confine the immunity in this narrow fashion. And there is evidence that the immunity is not so confined. For example, in *The State (Williams)* v. *Army Pensions Board*,[68] Henchy J. assumed that privilege could be claimed, in a suitable case, in respect of the Board's documents. Again, in *Geraghty* v. *Dublin Corporation*,[69] the immunity was allowed to protect some of the documents for which it was claimed, although that case involved a Minister hearing a planning appeal, and thus taking a quasi-judicial—as opposed to executive—function. There is also a line of British authority to like effect. In *D.* v. *National*

[67] As opposed to when the Minister has merely acted as a *persona designata*, as in *Murphy* v. *Dublin Corporation*.
[68] [1983] I.R. 308.
[69] [1975] I.R. 300.

Society for the Prevention of Cruelty to Children,[70] the House of
Lords held that the defendant body (which enjoyed official status
to the extent of being an "authorised person" for the purpose of
bringing child care proceedings under the relevant English
legislation) was entitled to claim immunity on the grounds of
public interest in respect of members of the public who had given
information to them concerning child abuse.

(D) **Does the right to a fair hearing require the disclosure of
documents?** The dictates of natural justice will often require the
disclosure of relevant evidence, and this is especially so where the
decision-maker is exercising quasi-judicial—as opposed to executive—functions. In *O'Leary* v. *Minister for Industry and Commerce*[71] a
bridge in the neighbourhood of the plaintiff's farm had been
submerged by the Electricity Supply Board in the course of the
construction of a hydro-electric scheme. The Board was required
by the relevant legislation to build a new bridge unless the
defendant Minister determined that in the circumstances this was
not necessary. Privilege was claimed in respect of memoranda and
other communications exchanged between the Board and the
Minister. O'Dalaigh C.J. observed that the Minister had been cast
in a quasi-judicial role and that he was required to make "an
objective finding in effect as between the parties." The communications of the Board to the Minister were not those of an adviser in
relation to the discharge of a statutory duty, but were rather "the
representations of a party with an interest." The *audi alteram
partem* principle therefore required that such circumstances be
disclosed.[72] However, the rule will not always require that such
disclosure of relevant documents be made, and there will be
situations where the constitutional guarantee of fair procedures,
which, of course, is not absolute, may have to yield to the need to
preserve confidential information.[73]

---

[70] [1978] A.C. 171.
[71] [1966] I.R. 676.
[72] Non-disclosure of documents was also found to breach the *audi alteram
partem* rule in *Geraghty* v. *Minister for Local Government* [1975] I.R. 300
and *The State (Williams)* v. *Army Pensions Board* [1983] I.R. 308.
[73] Thus, in *The State (Williams)* v. *Army Pensions Board* [1983] I.R. 308 the
respondent Board's failure to disclose certain medical evidence in their
possession was found to be a breach of natural justice. Henchy J.
observed that there might well be other cases where for reasons such as
"State security or other considerations of public policy," the Board
might be privileged from disclosing, or making full disclosure of, the
evidence before them.

5. Obligations conditional on the Dail's approval

It used to be thought that the voting of funds by Parliament was a condition precedent to the validity of contracts to which the State is a party. This view, which is founded on the high constitutional principle that the consent of Parliament is necessary for the expenditure of public moneys, derives principally from the old case of *Churchward* v. *R.* and, in particular, from an unnecessarily wide statement in that case from Shea J.[74] The wide propositions suggested in *Churchward's* case was rejected in *New South Wales* v. *Bardolph.*[75] It has now been accepted that the result in *Churchward* depended on the peculiar fact of the case, namely that the contract in the case expressly provided that payment, for the carriage of mails between Dover and the Continent were to be made out of moneys voted by Parliament and no such moneys were voted. Thus, in foreign jurisdictions, *Churchward* is now regarded as an authority only for the unexceptionable proposition that a contract[76] may be expressly made subject to parliamentary appropriation, whether by statute, constitutional provision or, as in *Churchward*, by express words.[77]

In Ireland, the *Churchward* doctrine was explicitly relied upon just after independence in the case of *Kenny* v. *Cosgrave.*[78] Here the President of the Executive Council had told an employer whose workers were on strike that it was essential that the employer resist the demands and had promised that the Executive Council would indemnify him against any financial loss which

[74] (1865) L.R. 1 Q.B. 173
[75] (1934) 52 C.L.R. 455.
[76] And not just, of course, contracts. For example, in *Conroy* v. *Minister for Defence* [1934] I.R. 679, the Supreme Court granted a declaration that the Minister was bound to take steps for the payment of a pension to the plaintiff, and that under the terms of the Military Service (Pensions) Act 1924, he had no authority to question the plaintiff's entitlement. The Act had stipulated that no person could receive a military service pension unless money for this purpose had been voted by the Oireachtas. This meant, of according to Kennedy C.J., that it was the duty of the Minister for Defence to submit the particulars of the pensions granted by him to the Oireachtas "so that the moneys [could] be voted accordingly *if the Oireachtas so please[d]*" (emphasis supplied). It should be noted that the existence of this proviso did not relieve the Minister of his obligation to execute his part of the process.
[77] See generally, Hogg, *Liability of the Crown in Australia, New Zealand and the United Kingdom* (Melbourne, 1971), Chap. 5; Turpin, *Government Contracts* (London, 1972), Chap. 1 and Street, *Governmental Liability* (Cambridge, 1953) Chap. 3.
[78] [1926] I.R. 517.

ensued from this resistance. The promise was not honoured and the plaintiff sued for damages. Even on the assumption that there was a contract between the plaintiff and the Executive Council, his claim was rejected on the grounds that the Executive Council could not "make a binding contract to pay public money without the authority of the Oireachtas [*sc.* given in advance]."

The authority of the decision is, however, weakened by the fact that Fitzgibbon J. speaking for the Supreme Court, also rested his decision on the doctrine that the Executive may not make a contract which fetters its discretionary power[79] and apparently failed to perceive that he was dealing with separate rules.[80] It is sub-mitted, however, that the principal reason why *Kenny* does not represent present day law is the wealth of authority against it. *Bardolph's* case has already been briefly noted. The Irish authorities commence with *Leyden* v. *Attorney-General*[81] which was decided just before *Kenny*. The plaintiff, in *Leyden*, sought certain declarations in respect of his salary under a contract employing him as a teacher. His claim was resisted by the defendants on the grounds that a contract with a government department was involved, for the payment of which no grant had been made by the Oireachtas. Here the Supreme Court distinguished *Churchward* on the ground that the remedy sought was only a declaration of the plaintiff's rights. However, Murnaghan J. also observed that [*Churchward's*] doctrine will require a careful scrutiny before it is given such a wide application as was here contended for."[82] *Maunsell* v. *Minister for Education*[83] was a similar case to *Leyden* (save that no contract was involved) in that a teacher was suing for a declaration of his right to salary based on the Rules and Regulations of the Commissioners of National Education in Ireland. In *Maunsell* Gavin Duffy J. rejected an argument based on the *Churchward* doctrine with some *hauteur* founding himself, in part, on Article 34.3.1, which gives the High Court full original jurisdiction:

[79] See further at pp. 225–227.

[80] See [1926] I.R. at p. 528, where Fitzgibbon J. cited *Rederiaktiebolaqet Amphitritie* v. *The King* [1921] 3 K.B. 500 in support of the proposition that the Government could not by contract fetter its discretion to act in the public interest as it saw fit.

[81] [1926] I.R. 334.

[82] *Ibid.* at p. 367. See also *Att.-Gen.* v. *Great Southern Ry. Co.* [1925] A.C. 754, a case with an Irish connection, discussed by Street, *op. cit.* at pp. 88–89.

[83] [1940] I.R. 213. Certain other cases: such as *Kildare County Council* v. *Minister for Finance* [1931] I.R. 215 and *Latchford* v. *Minister for Industry and Commerce* [1950] I.R. 33, involved (it was claimed) a statutory debt in respect of which funds had already been approved by the Oireachtas (by an Appropriation Act or in some other way) and thus did not raise the problem examined in the text.

"Finally, I am solemnly assured that I can give no relief to the plaintiff... because the Executive cannot bind itself in law by a promise to pay... I cannot entertain any suggestion that a public servant, the conditions of whose remuneration are in dispute is precluded from invoking the jurisdiction of the High Court to declare his rights until an Appropriation Act has been enacted providing his Department with money to pay him, however necessary it may be to prove that such an Act has been passed before an order for payment is made."[84]

The final qualifying clause in this passage[85] recalls the doctrine which is now generally accepted in Britain and elsewhere in the Commonwealth: whilst parliamentary appropriation is not necessary to the validity of a contract, before the moneys can actually be paid, there must be properly authorised funds available. This point is not peculiar to contract, for there are many cases (such as actions in tort) where the problem of enforcing an action against the State could also theoretically arise. The question is, of course, most unlikely ever to arise in practice since it may be assumed that the State will fulfil its legal obligations. Where a monetary judgment against the State is concerned, a specific parliamentary vote will not usually be necessary to meet the judgment, as there will usually be an appropriate existing vote from which the money can be taken (provided, of course, that the Dail has not expressly forbidden this). And even if there is no such vote, it may be assumed that the Government would bring the necessary supplementary estimate before the Dail, and that the Dail would pass it.

However, in view of the question's inherent constitutional interest, we may briefly examine what would happen if the Dail failed to vote the necessary funds to meet the State's obligations. In Britain, the common law rule that no form of execution was available against the Crown was an aspect of the prerogative, and founded on the fiction that the King could do no wrong.[86] It is plain from *Byrne* that this doctrine did not survive in Ireland.

---

[84] [1940] I.R. at pp. 236–237.

[85] See also, to like effect, *Leyden* v. *Att.-Gen.* [1926] I.R. 334.

[86] See Wade, *op. cit.* at pp. 697–702. In *Crowley* v. *Ireland* [1980] I.R. 102, Kenny J. (at p. 129) expressly refrained from giving an opinion on "the difficult question as to whether damages may be awarded against a Minister of State or against Ireland for failure to perform a duty imposed by the Constitution." But see now *Kearney* v. *Ireland*, High Court, March 13, 1986 (State vicariously liable for damages arising from employees' wrongful breach of prisoner's constitutional rights).

However, there is another fundamental constitutional principle
which may be a barrier in the case of damages: Articles 11 and 21
make it clear that all State expenditure must be authorised by the
Dail.[87] There is, accordingly, some authority for the proposition
that any form of enforcement which required a monetary payment
would constitute an interference with this principle.[88] However,
this orthodoxy may no longer prevail, in view of both the
contemporary judicial concern for individual rights, and of the
modern recognition that the independence of the Dail from the
Government is largely formal. Such considerations probably
underlay Budd J.'s observations in *Byrne* v. *Ireland*:

> "The case [of *Comyn* v. *Attorney-General*[89]] certainly shows that
> a decree can be made against the State and that no point was
> raised as to the ultimate recovery from the State of the
> amount assessed. The event of the amount of the decree not
> being provided for in this case by the State where the rule of
> law prevails seems so remote that I feel it safe to say that no
> real difficulty of the kind envisaged has been shown to exist.
> Therefore, it is unnecessary to come to a final decision on the
> ways and means of enforcing such a decree beyond remarking
> that prima facie the ordinary procedure of execution by way
> of levy or enforcement by mandamus would both seem to be
> appropriate."[90]

As against this Finlay C.J. has stated[91] (without further discussion
or any reference to *Byrne*) that "it does not appear appropriate
that any injunction should ever be given against Ireland"[92]
(although there is, of course, no difficulty against awarding an
injunction against a Minister).

---

[87] See also the comments of Gannon J. in *K. Security Ltd.* v. *Ireland*, High
Court, July 15, 1977.

[88] It is also just possible that any enforcement involving monetary payment
would be held to constitute an interference with the business of the
Oireachtas, and would run up against Art. 15 (parliamentary privilege).
However as parliamentary privilege is so much less extensive in Ireland
than in Britain, this seems unlikely.

[89] [1950] I.R. 142.

[90] [1972] I.R. at p. 307.

[91] *Pesca Valentia Ltd.* v. *Ireland* [1985] I.R. 193. But it is difficult to think of
any reason why the State should be placed in this privileged position.
Cf. The State (King) v. *Minister for Justice* [1984] I.R. 148 (common law
rule that orders of mandamus could not be granted against Ministers of
State found to be unconstitutional).

[92] *Pesca Valentia Ltd.*, *supra*; *Yeates* v. *Minister for Posts and Telegraphs*, High
Court, February 21, 1978 and *Campus Oil Ltd.* v. *Minister for Industry
and Energy (No. 2)* [1983] I.R. 88.

Index